Microsoft Office Professional 2013

Step by Step

Beth Melton

Mark Dodge

Echo Swinford

Andrew Couch

Eric Legault

Ben M. Schorr

Ciprian Adrian Rusen

ISBN: 978-0-7356-6941-3

Sixth Printing, September 2015

Printed and bound in the United States of America.

Microsoft Press books are available through booksellers and distributors worldwide. If you need support related to this book, email Microsoft Press Book Support at mspinput@microsoft.com. Please tell us what you think of this book at *http://www.microsoft.com/learning/booksurvey*.

Microsoft and the trademarks listed at *http://www.microsoft.com/about/legal/en/us/IntellectualProperty/Trademarks/EN-US.aspx* are trademarks of the Microsoft group of companies. All other marks are property of their respective owners.

The example companies, organizations, products, domain names, email addresses, logos, people, places, and events depicted herein are fictitious. No association with any real company, organization, product, domain name, email address, logo, person, place, or event is intended or should be inferred.

Acquisitions and Developmental Editor: Kenyon Brown

Production Editor: Kara Ebrahim

Editorial Production: Online Training Solutions, Inc. (OTSI)

Technical Reviewer: Ciprian Adrian Rusen

Indexer: Bob Pfahler

Cover Design: Girvin

Cover Composition: Karen Montgomery

Illustrator: Online Training Solutions, Inc. (OTSI)

For dad. And mom.

—Eric Legault

I would like to dedicate my contribution to this book to my Aunty Hazel and my late Uncle Victor. My memories of late evening suppers, warm fires, and great conversations have served as a great inspiration. Thank you.

—Andy Couch

For Shauna, an amazing and inspiring woman who dedicated her life to helping others and lived life to its fullest. You're greatly missed, my friend.

—Beth Melton

Contents

PART 1

Office Professional 2013 fundamentals

1 Getting comfortable in Office Professional 2013 3

PART 2

Word 2013

PART 3

PowerPoint 2013

PART 4

Excel 2013

20   Analyzing data   497

21   Formatting worksheets   539

22   Manipulating workbooks and worksheets   585

23   Creating charts and graphics   625

PART 5

Outlook 2013

27   Working with tasks   731

28   Managing contacts and people   747

29 Saving time with Outlook 761

PART 6

OneNote 2013

30 Getting comfortable in OneNote 2013 783

31 Working with notebooks, sections, and pages 795

32   Using organizational tools   813

33   Sharing notes with others   839

34   Using OneNote everywhere   861

35   Saving time with OneNote   877

PART 7

Access 2013

39   Designing forms and reports   993

40 Creating and sharing a Web App 1031

PART 8

Publisher 2013

41 Getting comfortable in Publisher 2013 1067

42 Creating publications 1079

43 Saving, sharing, and exporting publications 1121

Introduction

The Microsoft Office Professional 2013 suite of programs provides the tools you need for easy and efficient word processing, presentation planning, spreadsheet creation, database building, and desktop publishing, as well as programs to help you plan, organize your ideas, schedule, and communicate with your contacts. *Microsoft Office Professional 2013 Step by Step* offers a comprehensive look at the features of Office that most people will use most frequently, particularly those new to Office Professional 2013.

Who this book is for

Microsoft Office Professional 2013 Step by Step and other books in the *Step by Step* series are designed for beginning to intermediate level computer users. Examples shown in the book generally pertain to small and medium-sized businesses but teach skills that can be used in organizations of any size. Whether you are already comfortable working in Microsoft Office and want to learn about new features in Office Professional 2013 or are new to Office, this book provides invaluable hands-on experience so that you can work with Microsoft Word, PowerPoint, Excel, Outlook, Access, OneNote, and Publisher.

How this book is organized

This book is divided into 43 chapters. The first four chapters provide information about Office fundamentals, including how to work in the Office environment, how to avail yourself of shared Office features across applications, and how to share and collaborate with Office 365 services. Chapters 5–10 show you how to create, read, and navigate, format, organize, and share Word documents. Chapters 11–16 cover how to design and create impactful presentations in PowerPoint, including working with themes, masters, and layouts, incorporating multimedia, creating customized graphics, and finalizing and making your presentation. Chapters 17–23 take you through the steps of creating, editing, and formatting database worksheets and workbooks, manipulating and analyzing data in spreadsheets, and creating charts and graphics. Chapters 24–29 show you how to work with Outlook to create and send messages, add and manage contacts, and work with and manage tasks and schedule entries. Chapters 30–35 cover all the features of OneNote, and show you how to work with notebooks, sections, and pages, and how to organize and share your notes. Chapters 36–40 walk you through creating and working with databases, including adding, manipulating, importing, and exporting data; creating basic tables and queries; and designing and generating forms reports. Finally, Chapters 41–43 show how to work with Publisher to create professional desktop designs and produce brochures, newsletters, and other publications.

The first chapter of each of the eight parts of the book contains introductory information that will primarily be of interest to readers who are new to a particular Office application or are upgrading from an earlier version. If you have worked with a more recent version of Office, you might want to skip past that material.

This book has been designed to lead you step by step through all the tasks you're most likely to want to perform with Office Professional 2013. If you start at the beginning and work your way through all the exercises, you will gain enough proficiency to be able to work with all the Office Professional applications. However, each topic is self-contained, so you can jump in anywhere to acquire exactly the skills you need.

Download the practice files

Before you can complete the exercises in this book, you need to download the book's practice files to your computer. These practice files can be downloaded from the following page:

http://aka.ms/OfficePro2013SbS/files

IMPORTANT

The following table lists the practice files for this book.

Chapter	File
Chapter 2: Using shared Office features	Fabrikam Management Team.pptx
	Sample Picture.jpg
	Simple to-do list.xlsx
Chapter 6: Navigating and reading documents	Fabrikam Rebrand Campaign.docx
	Newsletter_A.docx
	Newsletter_B.docx

Chapter	File
Chapter 7: Editing and composing documents	List Example.docx
	Newsletter_C.docx
	Sample Logo and Address.docx
Chapter 8: Formatting documents	Fabrikam Rebrand Campaign_A.docx
	Fabrikam Rebrand Campaign_B.docx
	Fabrikam Rebrand Campaign_C.docx
	Fabrikam Rebrand Campaign_D.docx
	Fabrikam Rebrand Campaign_final.docx
Chapter 9: Presenting information	Example Newsletter.docx
	List Example.docx
	List Example_B.docx
	List Example_C.docx
Chapter 10: Finalizing documents	Fabrikam Newsletter.pdf
	Newsletter_B.docx
Chapter 12: Designing and creating presentations	Fabrikam.potyx
	Fabrikam_Logo_Large.png
	Fabrikam_White_Small
	SampleContentA_Start.pptx
	SampleContentB_Start.pptx
	SampleContentC_Start.pptx
	SampleContentD_Start.pptx
	SampleContentE_start.pptx
	SampleContentF_start.pptx
Chapter 13: Creating on-slide content	SampleContentA_start.pptx
	SampleContentB_start.pptx
	SampleContentC_start.pptx
	SampleContentD_start.pptx
	SampleContentE_start.pptx
	SampleContentF_start.pptx
	SampleContentG_start.pptx
Chapter 14: Creating Office graphics	SampleContentA_Start.pptx
	SampleContentB_Start.pptx
	SamplePictureB.JPG

Chapter	File
Chapter 15: Adding animation and multimedia	Fabrikam Employee Excursion.wmv
	SampleContentA_start.pptx
	SampleContentA_end.pptx
	SampleContentB_start.pptx
	SampleContentC_start.pptx
	SampleContentD_start.pptx
Chapter 16: Finalizing and presenting	SampleContentA_Start.pptx
	SampleContentB_Start.pptx
	SampleContentC_Start.pptx
	SampleContentD_Start.pptx
	SampleContentE_Start.pptx
Chapter 18: Creating and editing worksheets	Fabrikam-Employees_start.xlsx
	Fabrikam-Management_start.xlsx
Chapter 19: Manipulating numbers and text	Fabrikam-Management2_start.xlsx
	Fabrikam-Seven-Year-Summary_start.xlsx
	Fabrikam-Seven-Year-Summary2_start.xlsx
	Loan_start.xlsx
	Real-Estate-Transition_start.xlsx
Chapter 20: Analyzing data	2015Projections_start.xlsx
	Fabrikam-Jan-2013-Sales_start.xlsx
	FabrikamJanSales2013.txt
	FabrikamQ1SalesDetail_start.xlsx
	JanSales2_start.xlsx
	RealEstateTransition_start.xlsx
Chapter 21: Formatting worksheets	Custom Formats 2_start.xlsx
	Custom Formats 3_start.xlsx
	Custom Formats_start.xlsx
	FabrikamSummary_start.xlsx
	FabrikamSummary2_start.xlsx
	FabrikamSummaryTheme.xlsx
	FabrikamSummaryTheme_start.xlsx
	Real-Estate-Transition_start.xlsx

Chapter	File
Chapter 22: Manipulating workbooks and worksheets	FabrikamQ1_start.xlsx
	FabrikamQ1-B_start.xlsx
	Q1-Summary_start.xlsx
	Q1-Transactions_start.xlsx
	Q1-Transactions2_start.xlsx
	UnitSales_start.xlsx
	UnitSales2_start.xlsx
Chapter 23: Creating charts and graphics	FabrikamLogo_start.xlsx
	FabrikamSalesTable_start.xlsx
	FabrikamSalesTable2_start.xlsx
	FabrikamSalesTable3_start.xlsx
	FabrikamSalesTable4_start.xlsx
	FabrikamSalesTable5_start.xlsx
	Logo_start.xlsx
	Report_start.xlsx
Chapter 25: Using mail	Business flyer.docx
	Cornelius Ang.jpg
Chapter 35: Saving time with OneNote	35 Practice Image 1.jpg
	35 Practice Spreadsheet 1.xlsx
Chapter 37: Understanding Access 2013 databases	CompanyNames.xlsx
	MSOfficeProBlankCompletedChapter37.accdb
	MSOfficeProData.accdb
	ReadMeChapter37.txt
Chapter 38: Creating basic tables and queries	MSOfficeProBlank.accdb
	MSOfficeProBlankCompletedChapter38.accdb
	ReadMeChapter38.txt
Chapter 39: Designing forms and reports	MSOfficeProBlank.accdb
	MSOfficeProBlankCompletedChapter39.accdb
	ReadMeChapter39.txt
Chapter 40: Creating and sharing a Web App	CompanyNames.xlsx
	MSOfficeProData.accdb
	ReadMeChapter40.txt

Chapter	File
Chapter 42: Creating publications	Fabrikam Employee Newsletter A.pub
	Fabrikam Employee Newsletter_no video.docx
	fabrikam_logo.png
	FabrikamA.pub
	FabrikamAEnd.pub
	NewsletterEnd.pub
	NewsletterStart.pub
	PictureA.JPG
	PictureB.JPG
	PictureC.JPG
	PictureD.JPG
	PictureE.JPG
	Thumbs.db
	Travel.pub
	TravelA.pub
	TravelB.pub
Chapter 43: Saving, sharing, and exporting publications	FabrikamAEnd.pub
	Newsletter.pub

Your companion ebook

With the ebook edition of this book, you can do the following:

- Search the full text
- Print
- Copy and paste

To download your ebook, please see the instruction page at the back of the book.

Getting support and giving feedback

The following sections provide information about getting help with Office Professional 2013 or the contents of this book and contacting us to provide feedback or report errors.

Errata

We've made every effort to ensure the accuracy of this book and its companion content. Any errors that have been reported since this book was published are listed on our Microsoft Press site:

http://aka.ms/OfficePro2013SbS/errata

If you find an error that is not already listed, you can report it to us through the same page.

If you need additional support, email Microsoft Press Book Support at *mspinput@microsoft.com*.

Please note that product support for Microsoft software is not offered through the preceding addresses.

We want to hear from you

At Microsoft Press, your satisfaction is our top priority, and your feedback our most valuable asset. Please tell us what you think of this book at:

http://www.microsoft.com/learning/booksurvey

The survey is short, and we read every one of your comments and ideas. Thanks in advance for your input!

Stay in touch

Let's keep the conversation going! We're on Twitter at: *http://twitter.com/MicrosoftPress/.*

Chapter at a glance

Explore

Explore the Office environment,
page 4

Work

Work with Office files,
page 16

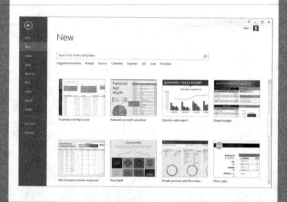

Recover

Recover unsaved files and versions,
page 23

Customize

Customize the ribbon,
page 32

Getting comfortable in Office Professional 2013

1

IN THIS CHAPTER, YOU WILL LEARN HOW TO

- Explore the Office environment.

- Work with Office files.

- Recover unsaved files and versions.

- Customize the user interface.

- Customize the ribbon.

- Choose the right application for the task at hand.

One of the biggest advantages of using Microsoft Office Professional 2013 is the similarities across the applications. The most obvious is the user interface, which is the overall look and feel of the application and how you interact with it. If you've used previous versions of Office, you may notice that many commands and features are nearly identical to those in past releases of Office, if not exactly the same, such as the commands for copying and pasting information, formatting text, creating charts, or inserting pictures. All of these similarities greatly reduce the learning curve, which allows you to apply the functionality in one application across the entire Office suite.

As you apply that knowledge and learn more about each application, you'll likely discover similar functionality that may not be initially obvious. For example, you can create a company newsletter by using Microsoft Word, Publisher, or PowerPoint. You can document company meeting notes in Microsoft OneNote or Word. And you can store lists of data in both Microsoft Access and Excel.

In this chapter, you'll learn about the Office environment, which includes the user interface, application options, and Office settings, plus you'll learn about Office terminology, Help options, and other functionality available in Office. This chapter also covers basic instructions for starting an Office application and working with Office files. At the end of this chapter, you'll get an overview of each application and tips for choosing the right application for various tasks.

PRACTICE FILES You don't need any practice files to complete the exercises in this chapter.

Exploring the Office environment

The first step in getting comfortable with Office Professional 2013 is to become familiar with your Office surroundings. In this section, you'll explore the user interface along with application options and settings that are shared across the Office applications.

TIP Even if you're already comfortable with this information from working with a previous version of Office, please read this section for tips that you may have not previously discovered.

You typically start an Office application from the Windows Start screen in Windows 8 or the Start menu in Windows 7. You can also start an application and open a file at the same time by opening a file sent to you as an email attachment or by double-clicking a file from somewhere in your computer environment, such as your Windows desktop.

With the exception of OneNote and Outlook, when you start an application without opening a file, the new application Start screen appears.

TIP OneNote and Outlook do not have an application Start screen. When you start the application, the main window is displayed.

From the application Start screen, you can open a recently used file, open an existing file, or create a new file from a template. After you create a new file or open an existing one, the main window will be displayed.

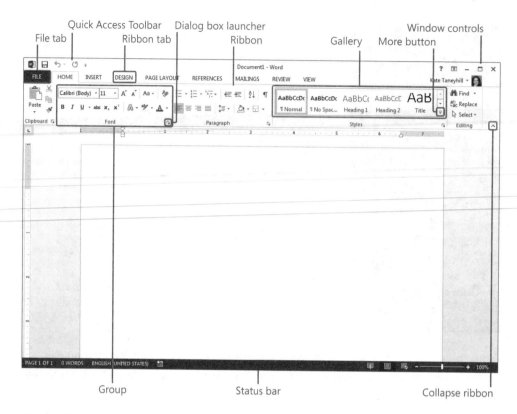

The application window has the following elements:

- **Ribbon** The main component of the Office user interface and where you'll find the primary commands for working with the content of your Office files. The ribbon includes tabs that have commands associated with a specific task. For example, objects that you insert in an Office document; like a picture, chart, or shape; are located on the **Insert** tab. This task-oriented organization also extends to the commands themselves, which are placed in related groups. For example, frequently used commands for formatting text are all located in a group named *Font* in most applications.

  TIP Some commands on the ribbon have what's known as a split control, which is a combination of a button and an arrow. An example is the Bullets command, found in Word on the Home tab in the Paragraph group. If you click the button, the default option, or the last option you selected during your editing session, will automatically be applied. When you click the arrow next to the button, a list of options will display, such as a list of available bullets.

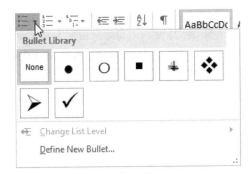

Note that for larger split controls, like the Paste button, the arrow will appear below the button instead of to the right. An easy way to determine if you're using a split control is to point to the button. If only the button or the arrow is highlighted rather than the entire button, then it's a split control.

- **Title bar** Appears at the top of the application window and displays the name of the active file and application name. In most standard Windows applications, including the Office applications, the title bar also has the program icon on the far left.

- **Window controls** Located on the far right of the title bar. Along with the standard **Minimize**, **Restore Down/Maximize**, and **Close** buttons, there are two additional buttons:

  - **Help** Clicking this button displays help for the application.

  - **Ribbon Display Options** Clicking this button gives you a list of choices for viewing the ribbon.

The Auto-hide Ribbon option gives you nearly a full screen view because it also hides the status bar along with the ribbon. Show Tabs and Show Tabs And Commands toggle the ribbon between a collapsed or expanded state, displaying only the ribbon tabs or displaying both the ribbon tabs and commands.

SEE ALSO For more information about how to hide, collapse, and expand the ribbon, see the "Customizing the user interface" section later in this chapter.

- **Quick Access Toolbar** Appears on the left end of the title bar by default. Each application has its own set of frequently used commands that are specific to the application. The most common commands are **Save**, **Undo**, and **Redo**.

- **Status bar** Located at the bottom of the application window; displays information about the application or current file. In most applications, view controls and the zoom slider are located on the right end of the status bar.

- **Dialog box launcher** Appears in the lower-right corner of a group when additional options for the related set of commands are available. Clicking the dialog box launcher opens a dialog box or pane.

- **Tool tabs** Appear in the ribbon when additional commands are available for a selected object, such as a table, picture, chart, or drawing object.

TIP You can quickly activate a tool tab for most objects by double-clicking the object.

- **Gallery** A visual list of choices, such as a collection of formats that offer multiple options. A gallery also refers to a set of related tools.

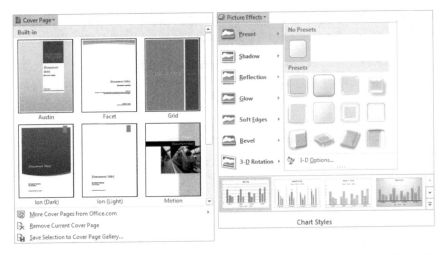

TIP Many galleries have additional options that may not appear in the ribbon. To view gallery options, right-click a gallery item. For example, to lock a shape for multiple uses, right-click a shape in the Shapes gallery and then click Lock Drawing Mode. To dismiss this mode, press the Esc key.

- **Live Preview** Enables you to view changes like pasted text or picture formatting prior to making a modification.

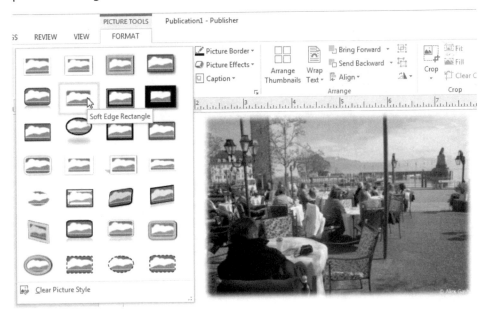

TIP Live Preview is available in all applications except OneNote.

- **Mini Toolbar** Appears on the screen in most applications when you have text or an object selected; provides quick access to the most-used formatting commands.

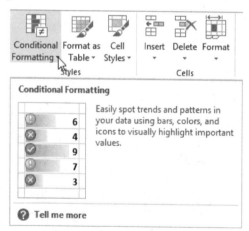

TIP The Mini Toolbar may also appear when you right-click selected text or objects.

- **ScreenTips** ScreenTips provide descriptions of commands and are displayed when you point to a ribbon command. If the command has an associated keyboard shortcut, that shortcut will appear in parentheses next to the name of the command. Several ScreenTips also include detailed help or a feature preview. For instance, in Excel, the ScreenTip for the **Conditional Formatting** command on the **Home** tab in the **Styles** group includes a detailed explanation for how to use conditional formatting. It also includes a preview of how data bars and an icon set are displayed for a range of values.

TIP If a command has an associated Help topic, Tell Me More is displayed at the bottom of the ScreenTip. Clicking the link displays the Help topic.

- **KeyTips** Enable you to navigate the ribbon by using the keyboard. To display KeyTips, press and release the **Alt** key. The KeyTips are the letters, numbers, or combinations of letters and numbers that appear on the ribbon. When you press only the **Alt** key, KeyTips for the ribbon tabs and **Quick Access Toolbar** are displayed. To view KeyTips for a specific ribbon tab, after you press the **Alt** key, press the corresponding KeyTip on the keyboard. For example, to navigate to the **Home** tab and view the KeyTips for that tab, press **Alt+H**. Or to view the KeyTips for the **Backstage** view, press **Alt+F**.

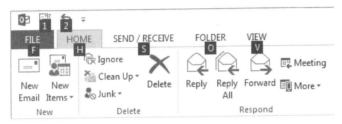

TIP Commands on the Quick Access Toolbar have sequential KeyTips associated with the position of the command. For example, your first command is automatically assigned Alt+1.

The Office environment also extends to an area called the Backstage view, which is displayed by clicking the File tab on the ribbon.

Whereas the ribbon and Quick Access Toolbar are used for working with the content inside a file, the Backstage view is used for working with the entire file and for changing application settings.

The commands in the Backstage view are separated into two groups. The first set is for file-related commands, such as Info, Open, Save As, and Print. These commands are covered in the next section of this chapter.

The last set, specifically the Account and Options commands, are related to the application and are considered part of the Office environment.

- **Account** This is where you manage a new feature in Office Professional 2013 called an Office cloud account and get information about your Office installation.

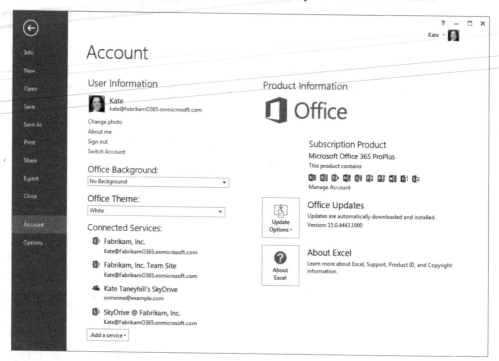

The User Information area has information about your Office cloud account, like your user name and your photo if you've elected to add one. This location is also where you can set a preferred Office background, with designs such as clouds or circles that appear in title bar of your Office applications, or where you can change the Office Theme.

SEE ALSO For more information about Office cloud accounts and connected services, see Chapter 3, "Sharing and collaborating."

The Product Information area is where you find information about your Office installation such as the Office suite you have installed and the applications that are included. This is also where you can choose how your Office installation is updated and view your update history.

- **Options** This is where you can change a variety of application preferences and customize certain behaviors that are specific to the application. In some applications, such as Excel and Access, there are also options specific to the active file.

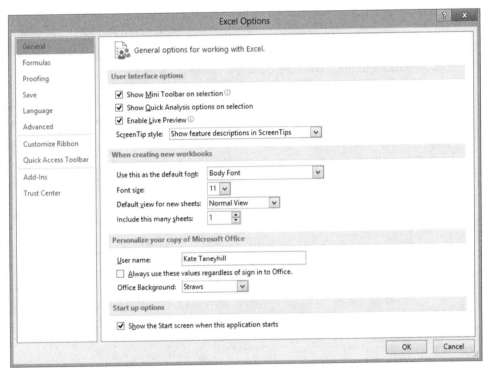

To close the Backstage view and return to the application window, click the arrow in the upper-left corner or press the Esc key.

Adjusting your ribbon display

The ribbon is dynamic and adjusts to the size of the application window, your screen resolution, and your screen magnification. If you're using a low resolution, one that makes everything appear larger, a small application window, or a screen magnification of more than 100 percent, the appearance of groups and buttons may be affected. For example, a gallery or an entire group of commands may collapse to a single group button, or button images may appear without labels, or buttons may appear stacked vertically instead of horizontally. And when you are resizing an application window, if there isn't enough room to display the ribbon, it could disappear completely. You may want to take a few minutes to resize an application window to become more familiar with the dynamic ribbon changes.

To modify your screen resolution in both Windows 8 and Windows 7, right-click an empty area of your desktop and then click Screen Resolution. In the Screen Resolution dialog box, click Resolution and drag the slider to adjust your resolution.

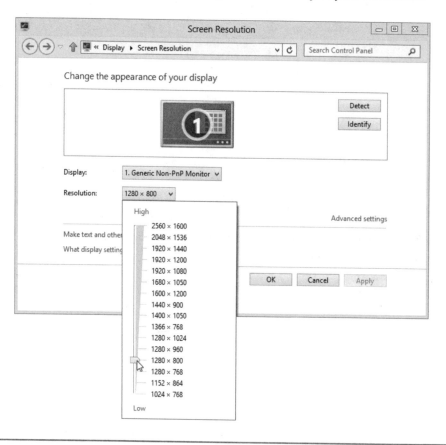

TIP Screen resolution is expressed as pixels wide × pixels high, such as 1024 × 768. The greater the screen resolution, or the higher the numbers, the greater the amount of information that will fit on your screen. The greater the number of pixels wide (the first number), the greater the number of buttons that can be shown on the ribbon. Note that screen resolution options are dependent on your monitor, but they typically range from 800 × 600 to 2048 × 1152.

As previously noted, the ribbon also adjusts to your screen magnification. To modify your screen magnification in both Windows 8 and Windows 7, right-click an empty area of your desktop and then click Personalize. In the lower-left corner, click Display and then select your preferred screen magnification.

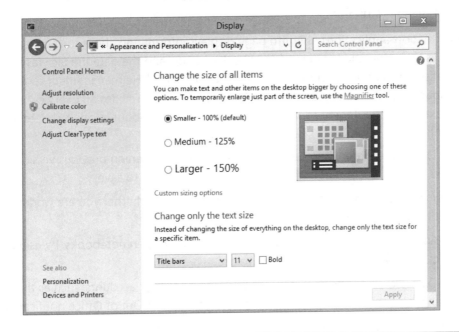

Working with Office files

In the previous section you learned about the Backstage view and how this area of the application is used for file-oriented tasks. In this section, you'll explore the primary file options that are available across the Office applications.

The pages in the Backstage view that contain commands for working with files are described in the following list:

- **Info** In most applications, the **Info** page displays information about the active file, such as the name and location of the file, the author, and the date the file was last modified. In all of the applications, you'll find specialized file management tools that are specific to the file and application. The following list provides an overview of some of the management tools and features you'll learn about in other chapters and sections of this book.

  - In Excel, PowerPoint, and Word, you'll find tools for opening previous versions of your current document and recovering files you forgot to save.

  - In Access, the management tools vary depending on whether you are working with a desktop database or a Web App.

  - In OneNote you use the **Info** page to manage your open notebooks, by using tools such as syncing and sharing options.

  - In Outlook, you'll find tools for managing your mailbox accounts, such as those with which you can archive your Outlook data and set Out of Office notifications.

  - In Publisher, there are tools for checking your publication design and embedding fonts.

SEE ALSO For more information about versions and recovering unsaved documents, see the "Recovering unsaved files and versions" section later in this chapter.

- **New** The New page is available in most applications and provides access to templates that enable you to create new files in the application. You can choose to start from scratch and select a blank template, or you can select one that already has content to help you get started on a specific type of task. For example, across the applications you'll find templates that range from newsletters, budgets, and sales reports, to contact information and asset tracking.

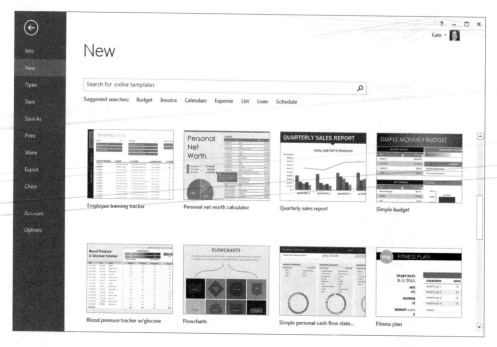

NOTE The templates shown in this book may not be the same as those that appear on your screen. New templates are added regularly, which may alter the results.

To create a new file in the applications that offer templates, simply double-click the template you want. Depending on the application and template, you may need to provide additional information before a new file is displayed in the application window. For example, in Access and OneNote, you need to provide a location and file name and then save the file before it's created. This is because both Access and OneNote automatically save certain changes.

TIP Outlook does not have a New page in the Backstage view. You can create new Outlook items from the Home tab of the main application window. You can also find email, business card, and signature templates in the Templates gallery on Office.com. In OneNote, there are page templates available in the application, and you can find entire notebook templates on Office.com. PowerPoint templates include designs and layout templates along with task-oriented templates.

- **Open** In all of the applications except Outlook, the **Open** page lists the recent files you previously opened and displays a list of available places from which you can open files.

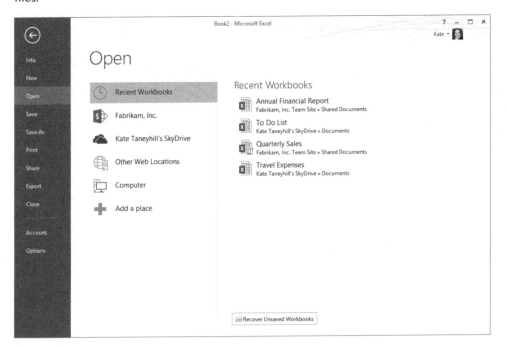

Pinning the files you use the most

To pin the files you use the most to the recent file list, point to the file and then click the pushpin to the right of the file name. Pinned files are placed at the top of the list.

To unpin the file, click the pushpin a second time. You can pin and unpin frequently used folders to the Recent Folders list on the Open and Save As pages as well. You can also right-click a recently used file for additional options such as the ability to remove a file from the list and clear all pinned files.

TIP Your recent files list can also be accessed from the main list of tabs in the Backstage view. To make this change, click Options, and then click Advanced. Locate the Display options and then click Quickly Access This Number Of Recent Workbooks. Note that in other applications the option text reflects the type of Office document you use for that application. Also in the Display area are options to change the number of recent files and unpinned folders that appear on the Open and Save As pages.

SEE ALSO For more information about opening files from Microsoft SkyDrive, Microsoft SharePoint Online, or other web locations, see Chapter 3, "Sharing and collaborating."

To view your recent files, click the Recent option near the top of the view, such as Recent Workbooks in Excel.

To open a file, if it's in the recent file list, you can click the file to open it in the application. If the file you need isn't in the list, first click the location where the file is stored, such as Computer, and then to the right of the location, click a recent folder. Or, if the folder you need isn't in the recent list, click the Browse button at the bottom. Either action displays the Open dialog box. After you select a file to open, click the Open button to open the file in the application.

TIP You can also double-click a location, like Computer, to quickly display the Open dialog box.

- **Save** When you save a file for the first time and click **Save**, the **Save As** page is displayed. After a file has been saved, clicking **Save** in the Backstage view will update the file and return you to the application window.

- **Save As** Except in Access and Outlook, the options on the **Save As** page are similar to those on the **Open** page. The main difference is that there isn't a recent file list.

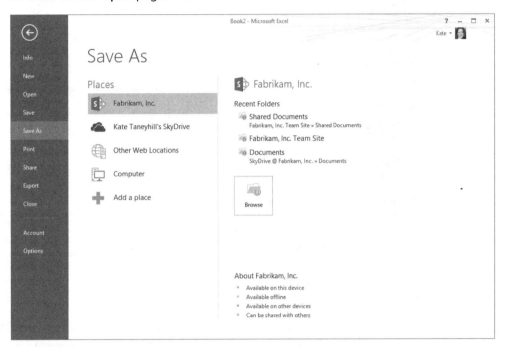

To save a file, select the location you want, and if the folder you want isn't in the recent folders list, click the Browse button. Either action displays the Save As dialog box. After you provide a file name, and if necessary, a different location in the Save As dialog box, click the Save button to save the file.

TIP In Outlook, clicking Save As displays the Save As dialog box. In Access, the Save As page has options for saving the current database or selected object. In addition, as with the Open page, you can double-click a location to quickly display the Save As dialog box.

- **Print** In all Office applications except Access and OneNote, the **Print** page provides printing and page layout options along with a preview of your file. In the **Printer** area, you can choose a different printer and set printer options. In the **Settings** section, you can specify various print and page settings prior to printing your file.

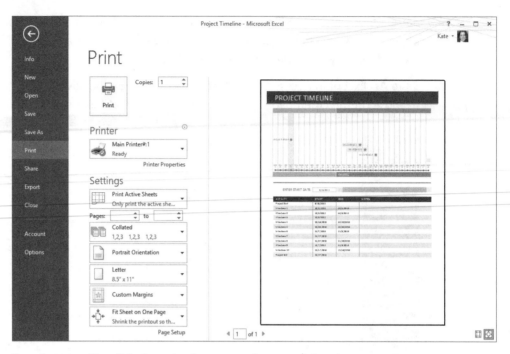

To print your file, click the **Print** button at the top of the view.

TIP Access and OneNote have similar print and preview options, but they aren't combined in the same view.

There are also additional file options available on the Share and Export pages. The Share page gives you ways to share your file with others, such as sending your file as an email attachment or sharing it with others online in a web location or through a web browser.

On the Export page, you'll find the ability to save your file in a Portable Document Format (PDF) or XML Paper Specification (XPS) format. And in PowerPoint and Publisher, you have options for converting your presentation to a video or packaging your publication for photo printing or commercial printing.

Because the majority of these options vary across Office applications or depend on additional components, you'll learn more about them and get step-by-step instructions in other chapters.

Recovering unsaved files and versions

There's a very good chance you will accidentally close a file without saving it, if you haven't already made such a mistake. The good news is that in Excel, PowerPoint, and Word, you may be able to recover your unsaved changes. And if you've spent some time working on an Office document and discover you'd like to return to a previous version of it, you may be able to do that too. File management tools for both of these situations are located in the Backstage view, on the Info page.

In the Versions area, a list of autosave files of your current document might be displayed.

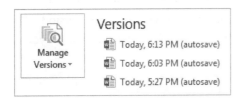

These versions are automatically created while you're working and are deleted when you save and close your Office document. There are a couple of requirements that need to be met before an autosave version is created.

- You must choose to save AutoRecover information, which is turned on on the **Save** page of the **Options** dialog box by default.

- An AutoRecover save must be made. This save is based on the time interval next to the AutoRecover information option and depends on whether you've made changes that need to be saved.

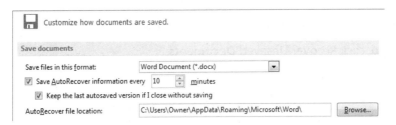

When these conditions are met, you can recover up to your last five autosave versions of your current file.

To open a previous version, click the file you want to open in the list and the autosave version will open in a separate window. You can then choose to restore your file, save the version as a new file, or close it without saving changes.

TIP If you only need to recover a portion of an autosave version, you don't need to restore your file to the earlier version. Simply copy the information you need and paste it in your main document.

The Versions area is also where you can recover a file you closed without saving. There are two types of unsaved files: those you never saved and unsaved autosave versions. The latter applies to files that were previously saved. It's the last autosave version of a file you closed without saving current changes.

IMPORTANT

As with the autosave version requirements, in order to recover an unsaved file, you must elect to save AutoRecover information. And to recover an unsaved autosave version, you must also elect to keep the last autosaved version when you close without saving. The latter option is also found in the Options dialog box near the top of the Save options.

To recover unsaved files, click Manage Versions and then do one of the following.

- In Excel, click **Recover Unsaved Workbooks**.
- In PowerPoint, click **Recover Unsaved Presentations**.
- In Word, click **Recover Unsaved Documents**.

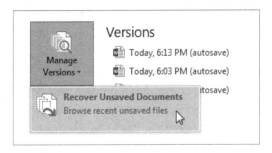

The Open dialog box appears and lists the files you can recover for the application you are using. Select the file you want and then click Open to open it in the application. And if you to want to keep that file, make sure you save your changes.

Customizing the user interface

In the first section of this chapter, you explored the user interface and became familiar with terminology and product-specific functionality. The next step is to personalize your Office surroundings to help you settle in and begin making yourself at home.

Here are some of the ways you can customize your user interface:

- To free up space on your screen, you can set the ribbon to auto-hide or you can toggle the ribbon between a collapsed and expanded state. A ribbon set to auto-hide is hidden from view. A collapsed state shows only the tabs, and the expanded state shows both the tabs and the commands.

- Set the Quick Access Toolbar to appear above or below the ribbon.

- Add additional commands to the Quick Access Toolbar or remove commands you don't need.

- Choose the information you prefer to display in the status bar, if applicable to the application.

Adapting exercise steps

The screen shots of the ribbon were captured with the author's preferred settings for screen resolution and magnification. If your display settings are different, the ribbon will appear differently on your screen due to its dynamic capabilities. For example, buttons may appear stacked vertically instead of horizontally. If you notice these differences, you can either adapt the exercise instructions to your screen or modify your display settings so that your screens match ours. Our instructions use this format:

- On the **Insert** tab, in the **Illustrations** group, click the **Chart** button.

If the command is in a list, our instructions use this format:

- On the **Home** tab, in the **Editing** group, click the **Find** arrow and then, in the **Find** list, click **Go To**.

If differences between your display settings and ours cause a button to appear differently on your screen than it does in this book, you can easily adapt the steps to locate the command. First click the specified tab, and then locate the specified group. If a group has been collapsed into a group list or under a group button, click the list or button to display the group's commands. If you can't immediately identify the button you want, point to likely candidates to display their names in ScreenTips.

In this book, we provide instructions based on traditional keyboard and mouse input methods. If you're using Office on a touch-enabled device, you might be giving commands by tapping with your finger or with a stylus. If so, substitute a tapping action any time we instruct you to click a user interface element. Also note that when we tell you to enter information in Office, you can do so by typing on a keyboard, tapping in the entry field under discussion to display and use the onscreen keyboard, or even speaking aloud, depending on your computer setup and your personal preferences.

Customizing the Office environment

In this exercise, you'll customize your Office environment by collapsing and expanding the ribbon, setting it to an auto-hide state, and moving the Quick Access Toolbar below the ribbon.

 SET UP You don't need any practice files to complete this exercise. Start Word and follow the steps.

> **IMPORTANT**

1   On the Word Start screen, click **Blank document**.

2   Double-click the active ribbon tab to collapse it.

KEYBOARD SHORTCUT Press Ctrl+F1 to toggle the ribbon between a collapsed and expanded state.

3   Click the **Home** tab to expand the ribbon, and in the **Font** group, click the **Bold** button.

4   Click in the document to return the ribbon to a collapsed state.

5   In the window controls at the right end of the title bar, click the **Ribbon Display Options** button and then from the list, click **Auto-hide Ribbon**.

6   Click the top of the application window to display the ribbon.

7   On the **Home** tab, in the **Font** group, click the **Bold** button.

8   Click in the document to return the ribbon to an auto-hide state.

9   Click the arrow at the end of the **Quick Access Toolbar** and then near the bottom of the list, click **Show Below the Ribbon**.

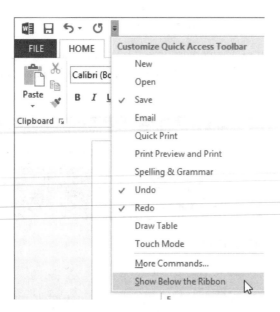

CLEAN UP Set the ribbon to your preferred auto-hide, expanded, or collapsed state. Set the position of the Quick Access Toolbar to your preference, either shown above or below the ribbon. If you're continuing to the next exercise, leave Word and your document open. Otherwise, exit Word without saving changes to the document you created.

Customizing the Quick Access toolbar

As noted in the introduction of this section, you can also customize the Quick Access Toolbar by adding frequently used commands, such as New or Open, or by adding commands directly from the ribbon. Here are two ways you can add additional commands:

- Click the arrow at the end of the **Quick Access Toolbar** and then select a command from the **Customize Quick Access Toolbar** list.

- Right-click a command on the ribbon and then click **Add to Quick Access Toolbar**.

To remove a command from the Quick Access Toolbar, right-click the command and then click Remove From Quick Access Toolbar.

In this exercise, you'll customize the Quick Access Toolbar by adding and removing commands.

You don't need any practice files to complete this exercise. If Word and your blank document are still open from the previous exercise, follow the steps. Otherwise, start Word, create a new document, and follow the steps.

1   Click the arrow at the end of the **Quick Access Toolbar** and then in the list, click **Open**.

2   On the **Home** tab, in the **Font** group, right-click the **Bold** button, and then click **Add to Quick Access Toolbar**.

> **TIP** You can also add dialog boxes or a group on the ribbon, such as the Font group, to your Quick Access Toolbar for faster access. To do so, right-click a dialog box launcher or right-click a group name and then click Add To Quick Access Toolbar.

3   On the **Quick Access Toolbar**, right-click the **Open** button and then click **Remove from Quick Access Toolbar**.

4   Remove the **Bold** button from the **Quick Access Toolbar**.

If you're continuing to the next exercise, leave Word and your document open. Otherwise, exit Word without saving changes to the document you created.

> **TIP** For more information about how to rearrange the commands on your Quick Access Toolbar or to add commands that don't appear on the ribbon, see "Customizing the ribbon" later in this chapter.

Customizing the status bar

You can also customize the status bar by choosing what you prefer to display. Similar to how you customize the Quick Access Toolbar, you can right-click the status bar to customize it. The Customize Status Bar list shows the available status bar items, and a check mark will appear next to those that are currently displayed. You then select or deselect items in the list to add or remove them. Note that some items only appear in the status bar when a feature is turned on, to help reduce status bar clutter. For example, if you choose to show Caps Lock, it will only display in the status bar if you've turned caps lock on and are typing in all caps.

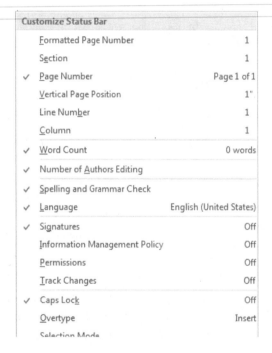

In this exercise, you'll customize the status bar in Word.

SET UP You don't need any practice files to complete this exercise. If Word and your blank document are still open from the previous exercise, follow the steps. Otherwise, start Word, create a new document, and follow the steps.

1   At the bottom of the Word window, note **Page 1 of 1** on the left end of the status bar.

2   Right-click the status bar and then in the **Customize Status Bar** list, click **Page Number** to turn it off.

3   In the **Customize Status Bar** list, click **Page Number** again to turn it back on.

4   Click in the application window to close the **Customize Status Bar** options.

✖ CLEAN UP Exit Word without saving changes in the document you created.

TIP You can also customize the behavior of the Mini Toolbar, Live Preview, or ScreenTips. To access these settings, display the Backstage view and then click Options. These user interface options are located at the top of the General section. Note that the user interface options vary across the applications. For example, Access does not have a Mini Toolbar and OneNote does not support Live Preview.

Customizing the ribbon

As noted at the beginning of this chapter, one of the biggest advantages of Office is the similarities across the applications. In this section, you'll start applying what you learn about one feature to other components that are similar, like the Quick Access Toolbar and ribbon.

In comparison, both the Quick Access Toolbar and ribbon contain the primary commands for an application and can be customized. The main difference between them, other than appearance, is that the Quick Access Toolbar holds your most frequently used commands, whereas the ribbon provides a more standardized set of commands. However, there may be times when you want to make modifications to the ribbon. For instance, there are more advanced commands that aren't in the ribbon by default that you may find beneficial. Or you might find you can work more efficiently by moving a command or group to another location or tab.

To customize the ribbon, you display the Backstage view, click Options, and then click Customize Ribbon.

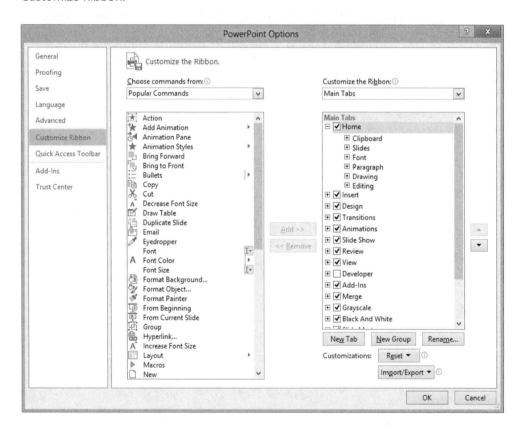

The left side of the ribbon customization settings area lists commands that can be added to the ribbon, and the right side lists the ribbon tabs. You can add commands from the list of available commands to any existing group on the ribbon, or you can create a new group and add commands to it.

You can also create a new ribbon tab and add new groups and commands or modify the tool tabs that appear when a specific object is selected, like a picture. To access all available ribbon tabs, in the Customize The Ribbon area, click the arrow next to Main Tabs and then click All Tabs.

Additionally, you can reorder built-in tabs, groups, and commands using the Move Up and Move Down arrows on the right side of the dialog box.

In this exercise, you'll customize the ribbon by adding a new tab, group, and command to the ribbon in PowerPoint. You'll then delete your customizations. At the end of this exercise, you'll apply what you learned about ribbon customization to the Quick Access Toolbar.

 SET UP You don't need any practice files to complete this exercise. Start PowerPoint, create a blank presentation, and follow the steps.

1   In the **Backstage** view, click **Options**, and then click **Customize Ribbon**. Below the ribbon tab list, click **New Tab**.

2   Click **New Tab (Custom)** to select it, and then click the **Rename** button near the bottom.

3   Enter MY CUSTOM TAB and then click **OK**.

4   Click **New Group (Custom)** and rename it to My custom group.

1

5   From the **Popular Commands** list, select any command. For instance, select **Email**.
    Click **My custom group** and then click the **Add** button near the middle of the
    Options dialog box.

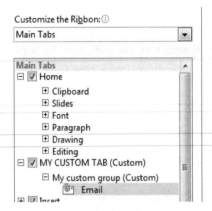

IMPORTANT

6   To review your customizations, click **OK** at the bottom of the **Options** dialog box.

7   On the ribbon, click **MY CUSTOM TAB** and note your custom group and newly added
    command.

8   Reopen the **Options** dialog box and display the ribbon customization options.

9   If necessary, select **MY CUSTOM TAB**.

10 Near the middle of the **Options** dialog box, click the **Remove** button to delete your
    custom tab and custom group.

11 Experiment with other ribbon customizations. For example, to reorder tabs, groups, or individual commands, make a selection, and then on the right side of the dialog box, click the **Move Up** and **Move Down** buttons.

12 After you're comfortable customizing the ribbon, in the **Options** dialog box, click **Customize Quick Access Toolbar** and apply what you learned in the previous steps. For example, reorder the commands or add new ones.

13 To reset all of your ribbon and **Quick Access Toolbar** customizations, click the **Reset** button near the bottom of the **Options** dialog box, and then click **Reset all customizations**.

14 Click **Yes** to confirm the deletion of your customizations.

> **TIP** To back up your ribbon and Quick Access Toolbar customizations or to share them with others, use the Import/Export options at the bottom of the dialog box.

❌ CLEAN UP Close the Options dialog box and exit PowerPoint without saving the presentation.

Choosing the right application for the task at hand

Out of all of the Office suites, Microsoft Office Professional Plus 2013 includes the widest range of applications. As noted at the beginning of this chapter, many of the applications have similar functionality. In the next chapter, you'll learn about shared features that are available to most of the Office applications. With so many overlapping capabilities, you may be wondering how to determine the application you need to use for your various work projects.

In this section, you'll get an overview of various tasks you can perform in each application that's available in the Office Professional Plus 2013 suite. This overview also extends to applications that aren't covered in this book. For the applications that have similar functionalities, you'll receive more information at the end of this section on how to choose an application to perform a specific task.

Application	Tasks
Access	■ Store, organize, and manage simple data or complex relational data.
	■ Make your data available on your company network or in a web browser by using Access Services, a component of SharePoint.
	■ Create forms for data entry and reports to present your information.
	■ Export data to other applications, such as Excel or Word, as well as other database formats.
Excel	■ Calculate and analyze numeric information such as budgets, income, expenses, loans, and scientific or statistical data.
	■ Organize and track information, such as inventory, work schedules, projects, invoices, and address lists.
	■ Summarize numeric and other data and display results in charts and PivotTables.
	■ Create forms that include controls, such as check boxes, drop-down lists, and option groups, to be filled in by other users.
OneNote	■ Organize and keep track of your notes and other information in searchable notebooks.
	■ Collect information from other Office applications or Windows Internet Explorer.
	■ Capture your notes in text, ink, drawings, images, audio, and video.
	■ Insert pictures, tables, files, spreadsheets, or diagrams.
	■ Collaborate in real time with members of your team.
Outlook	■ Send, receive, and store email messages and meeting requests.
	■ Use a calendar and tasks to keep track of your schedule and set reminders.
	■ Store contact information for your business connections.
	■ Share your Outlook information, such as your calendar, inbox, or contacts, with members of your team.
PowerPoint	■ Create presentations for a sales pitch, conference, meeting, class, or demonstration.
	■ Create photo albums to share with friends and family or for personal use.
	■ Add multimedia such as graphics, video, and audio along with animations.
	■ Present your presentation to a live audience or in an online meeting, or transform it into a video.

Application	Tasks
Publisher	▪ Create flyers, cards, calendars, brochures, certificates, catalogs, advertisements, and photo albums.
	▪ Include graphics, tables, and other visual elements.
	▪ Use built-in tools to save your publication for commercial or photo printing.
	▪ Create personalized publications for mass mailings for print and email distribution.
Word	▪ Create general documents such as letters, memos, reports, manuals, contracts, and proposals.
	▪ Create documents that contain graphics, such as newsletters, cards, flyers, invitations, and photo calendars.
	▪ Create advanced documents, such as mass mailings that can be printed and mailed or sent by email. Create a book or report with a table of contents, indexes, and cross references.
	▪ Create forms that include controls such as check boxes, drop-down lists, and date pickers, to be filled in by other users.
	▪ Generate other documents, such as envelopes, labels, blog posts, and webpages.
Microsoft InfoPath	▪ Create structured fill-in-the-blank forms that can be connected to a data source, such as an Access or SharePoint database.
	▪ Store forms on your company network or in a SharePoint library, or distribute them by email.
	▪ Add calculations, rules, data validation, and conditional formatting.
Microsoft Lync	▪ Quickly communicate with other people in your company by instant message, audio, or video.
	▪ View presence information, such as Available, Busy, Away, Off Work, and Do Not Disturb for members of your team in Lync and across the applications.
	▪ Share your desktop or an application with people both inside and outside your company.

As previously discussed, several of the Office applications provide similar functionality. For instance, you can use Word, Publisher, or PowerPoint to create Office documents that include graphics, such as newsletters, flyers, or photo albums. You can create forms in Access, Excel, InfoPath, and Word. And you can use both Access and Excel to manage lists of information.

More often than not, you'll likely choose the application you're most comfortable with and forgo learning something new. Before you do, keep in mind that each application specializes in specific capabilities and can produce better results when selected for certain tasks. Think of it as going to a restaurant—if you go to one that specializes in seafood, you might find steak on the menu, but it may not be as good as a steak you get from a steak house.

Also keep in mind that what you learn in one application can be applied to another, so the learning curve may be easier than you think. Here are a few tips to help you determine the right application for specific tasks.

- For files that include graphics, consider the type of content you want to include, the amount of text, and the complexity of the layout. If you don't need to use cross-references, fields, or other advanced text features, then use Publisher. In Publisher, it's easier to move your content and visually align objects. Plus, you can add vertical and horizontal guides for precision placement.

- For photo albums, think about the end result you want. If you want to display the album electronically on a computer or projection screen, use PowerPoint. It also enables you to add transitions and animations for a professional-looking result. Plus, you can convert your presentation to a video that can be published on websites like YouTube. If you want to print the album, use Publisher. It has a variety of photo borders to add a professional flair and tools to assist you with photo and commercial printing.

- For simple lists of data, such as an inventory or mailing list, consider using Excel. It has tools for sorting, filtering, and managing your lists. Plus, if you find you need more database management tools, you can easily import your list in Access.

- For lists of related data, such as those for tracking employees, projects, or department inventory, use Access. It has tools for working with information that's related and enables you to display and report information in various views. For example, you can create an employee directory sorted alphabetically and another grouped and sorted by department.

- For forms, if you want the data entered in a form to be automatically collected, use InfoPath or Access. There are several deciding factors in choosing which application to use. The primary factor is whether the people using the form will have access to the tools they need to fill it out. For InfoPath forms, either the users must have Microsoft InfoPath Filler, or you must have InfoPath Form Services technology so that your intended audience can use a web browser to fill out the form. For Access, either the users must have the Access application, or you must have Access Services for web browser-based forms, which is a component of SharePoint.

- Other form considerations are whether the form contains calculations. If you don't need to automatically collect your data, then use Excel. Although Word supports calculations, creating formulas in Excel is easier and more reliable. However, if your form needs to contain advanced text features or needs the page flexibility of a word processor, then create your form in Word.

This list is certainly not an exhaustive list of all of the different types of files you can create or tasks you'll perform in your work projects. This is a vast topic that could easily warrant its own book. But the information provided here should be enough to give you a good start in choosing the right application.

Key points

- The ribbon and Quick Access Toolbar have commands for working with the content of a file.

- The Backstage view has commands for working with the entire file or the application.

- You can create new documents, workbooks, presentations, publications, notebooks, and databases on the New page in the Backstage view.

- You can open, save, print, share, and export documents in the Backstage view.

- You can customize the Office user interface and modify application settings to fit your workflow.

- Choosing the right application for specific tasks can help you be more productive and get better results.

Chapter at a glance

Identify

Identify new shared features in Office
Professional 2013, page 42

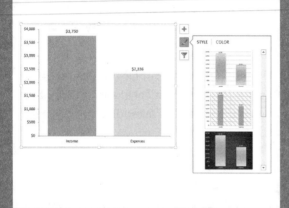

Apply

Apply Office themes,
page 47

Insert

Insert graphics, videos, charts, and diagrams,
page 50

Search

Search for online templates,
page 58

Using shared Office features

2

IN THIS CHAPTER, YOU WILL LEARN HOW TO

- Identify new shared features in Office Professional 2013.

- Apply Office themes.

- Insert graphics, videos, charts, and diagrams.

- Search for online templates.

- Present Office documents online.

As noted in Chapter 1, "Getting comfortable in Office Professional 2013," the biggest advantage of Office Professional 2013 is the similarities across the applications, which help greatly reduce the learning curve. Along with a common user interface, there are also features that work nearly the same regardless of the application you're using. For example, after you learn how to insert and work with SmartArt graphics, you can apply that knowledge to all of the applications that support SmartArt.

In this chapter, you'll get a look at the new shared Office features and learn how to get started with the primary features that are shared across the applications. You'll learn how to apply Office themes; insert graphics, videos, charts, and diagrams; search for online templates; and present Office documents online.

PRACTICE FILES To complete the exercises in this chapter, you need the practice files contained in the Chapter02 practice file folder. For more information, see "Download the practice files" in this book's Introduction.

Identifying new shared features in Office Professional 2013

Each Office release brings new features to help you make short work of otherwise cumbersome tasks, and Office Professional 2013 is no different from the rest. Along with new and improved productivity tools, this version of Office also gives you more Internet integration so you can use and access content stored in online locations, referred to as *cloud services*. Plus, with the addition of Touch Mode, you can work with your files on almost any device that supports touch.

In this section, you'll learn about new and improved features that are shared across the Office applications.

TIP The first chapter of each part of this book contains a list of key features that are specific to that Office application. Some of the new features discussed in this section may have previously been included in the Office applications but have been improved or are significantly different.

- **Microsoft SharePoint Online and Microsoft SkyDrive integration** Now you can open and save files stored in online locations from your Office applications. When your files are stored in the cloud, you can access them from other computers and devices, share them with people outside your corporate network, or work with others on the same file at the same time.

  TIP Cloud locations such as SharePoint Online and SkyDrive require a Microsoft Office 365 account or a Microsoft account. Other online locations, such as a hosted SharePoint site, can also be accessed from the Office applications.

  SEE ALSO For more information on an Office 365 or Microsoft account, see Chapter 3, "Sharing and collaborating."

- **Online templates** New templates offer a wide variety of content for business, school, and home. They range from letters, flyers, brochures, reports, and newsletters, to industry-specific presentations, sales reports, inventory tracking, and project management, to coordinating sets of templates across the applications and more. There are thousands of templates available to help you get started.

TIP New online templates are applicable to Microsoft Access, Excel, PowerPoint, Publisher, and Word.

- **Chart formatting controls** Modify your chart formatting, such as color and style, and add chart elements like titles, legends, and data labels by using new controls that are displayed when a chart is selected. The new chart filter enables you to select which data series or categories you want on your chart.

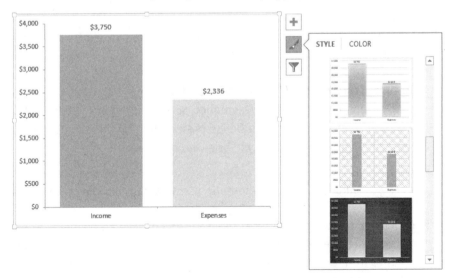

TIP New chart formatting tools are applicable to Excel, Microsoft Outlook, Power-Point, and Word.

- **Rich data labels** You can now format and size chart labels like shapes and you can clone your modifications and apply them to other data labels. Information from other cells can also be included in your labels, and leader lines can be added for almost all chart types.

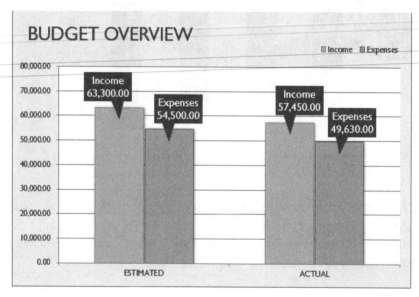

TIP New chart formatting tools are applicable to Excel, Outlook, PowerPoint, and Word.

- **Online presentation** Share your Office documents with others through Microsoft Lync or the new free Office Presentation Service from your Office application. Meeting participants can view your online presentation on their computers, tablets, or most smartphones through Lync or a web browser.

TIP Presenting through Lync is applicable to Excel, PowerPoint, and Word. Presenting online through the Office Presentation Service is applicable to PowerPoint and Word.

- **Online pictures** You no longer need to copy or save an online picture to your local or network drive in order to insert it in your Office documents. You can now embed pictures from online locations directly into an Office document. And when you're signed in to Office with a Microsoft account, you can access other places such as social networks like Facebook and Flickr.

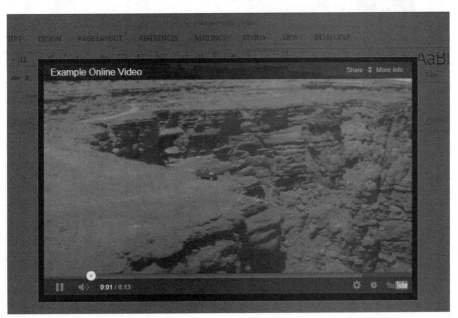

TIP The online pictures feature is applicable to Excel, Outlook, PowerPoint, Publisher, and Word.

- **Online video**   Add a link to a video from an online location, like your SkyDrive or YouTube, in an Office document and play it without leaving the application.

TIP Online video is available in PowerPoint and Word. An Internet connection is required for video playback.

■ **Posting to social networks** You can share your Office documents with your social networks, like Facebook and Twitter, directly from the application. When you set your edit or view permissions, a sharing link will be created and posted on the social networks you select. When others click the link, your shared file will open in the associated Office Web App.

TIP The Get A Sharing Link option is similar to the Post To Social Networks option. You can generate a link for—viewing only or for editing—that you can share with others through email, a website, or whichever method you choose. Posting to social networks and getting a sharing link is available in Excel, PowerPoint, and Word. You must be signed in to Office with a Microsoft account and have previously connected your social networks to your Office account, and your Office document must be saved in a shared location, such as SkyDrive, in order for the additional sharing options to be available.

SEE ALSO For more information on Microsoft accounts and connecting services, see Chapter 3, "Sharing and collaborating:"

- **Apps for Office** Insert apps in your Office documents to extend application functionality. Apps range from online dictionaries and application add-ins, such as templates for mailing labels, to interactive apps like Bing Maps, which enables you to map and visualize your geographic data.

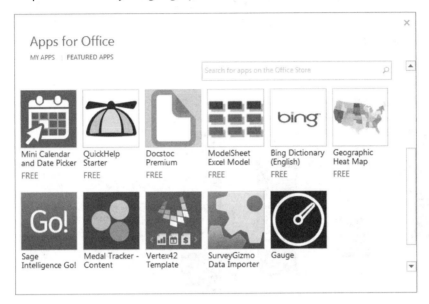

- **Touch Mode** All of the Office applications now support touch. When touch is enabled, the Office user interface is optimized for touch commands. The user interface increases in size, and more space is added between the buttons on the ribbon and Quick Access Toolbar.

Applying Office themes

Files you create in Access, Excel, PowerPoint, and Word all include a base set of formats called a *theme*. The theme is what controls the theme colors in the color palettes and the choices in numerous formatting galleries. It also controls the headings and body theme fonts at the top of the font list in most applications. Some applications also support theme effects, which apply to formatting for illustrations, such as pictures, shapes, SmartArt, and charts. Examples of these formats are border style and shadow. And in PowerPoint, formatting for slide masters and slide layouts are also part of the theme.

Files can be formatted by using theme elements, such as theme colors and theme fonts. Then if you choose a different theme from the themes gallery, the formatting will automatically update to match the formatting stored in your selected theme.

You can also start with a theme and then select different theme elements to create a custom theme. For example, you might like the colors of a theme but prefer different theme fonts or theme effects. Along with the themes gallery, which modifies all theme elements, you can modify individual theme elements by using the colors, fonts, and effects galleries.

In PowerPoint, Access, and Word, theme commands are located on the Design tab. In Excel, they're found on the Page Layout tab. In Access, a theme can be applied to the entire database or to a specific object.

TIP Microsoft Publisher has a similar functionality, called *schemes*, found on the Page Design tab. Though this section doesn't refer to Publisher specifically, you can apply theme concepts you read about here to schemes in Publisher.

In this exercise, you'll explore themes and individual theme elements.

 SET UP You need the Simple to-do list workbook located in the Chapter02 practice file folder to complete this exercise. Start Excel, open the Simple to-do list workbook, and follow the steps.

1   Examine the **Simple to-do list** workbook and take note of the colors and font appearance.

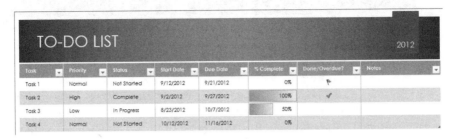

TIP The Simple to-do list workbook is based on one of the new online Excel templates that are available on the New page in the Backstage view.

2   On the **Page Layout** tab, in the **Themes** group, click the **Themes** button.

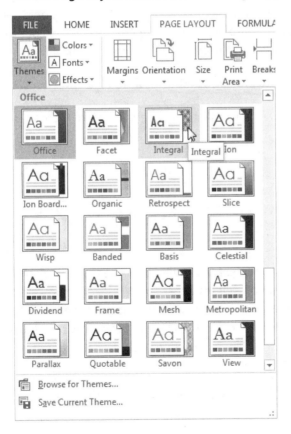

3   In the **Themes** gallery, click **Integral**. The fonts and colors automatically update to the **Integral** theme colors and theme fonts.

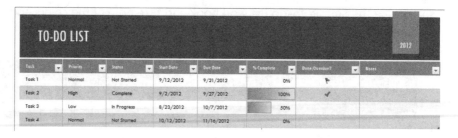

Task	Priority	Status	Start Date	Due Date	% Complete	Done/Overdue?	Notes
Task 1	Normal	Not Started	9/12/2012	9/21/2012	0%		
Task 2	High	Complete	9/2/2012	9/27/2012	100%	✓	
Task 3	Low	In Progress	8/23/2012	10/7/2012	50%		
Task 4	Normal	Not Started	10/12/2012	11/16/2012	0%		

TIP The formatting of the title shape also changed from a gradient fill to a textured fill. This may appear to be a theme effect, but it's actually a theme fill. You can access theme fills for shapes at the bottom of the Shape Style gallery on the Drawing Tools Format tool tab.

4   Experiment with other themes by applying them to the workbook.

5   After you're comfortable with themes, experiment with changing only the theme colors or theme fonts, which are also available in the **Themes** group. For example, you may like the colors of a theme but prefer to use a different set of fonts.

✖ CLEAN UP Close the Simple to-do list workbook without saving your changes.

SEE ALSO For more on themes and to learn how to create a custom theme, see Chapter 12, "Designing and creating presentations."

Inserting graphics, videos, charts, and diagrams

Documents have evolved from simple text-based files to those that contain rich images that help convey and illustrate information. For instance, graphics, like pictures or shapes, can be added for visual organization and to help break up large blocks of text. And for a combination of text and graphics, you can use SmartArt to help convey a concept. You can also use it for diagrams, lists of information, or for a collection of captioned pictures.

You don't need to hire a professional to add these visual elements. After an illustration is inserted, a variety of tools are available to help you create polished graphics and diagrams. And using those tools is much easier than you might think.

In this exercise, you'll insert a picture, shape, and SmartArt graphic by using features shared across Excel, Outlook, PowerPoint, and Word. You will also explore basic formatting options that are available to these features.

TIP Shared picture and shape features are also available in Publisher.

 SET UP You need the Sample Picture image located in the Chapter02 practice file folder to complete this exercise. Start Word, create a blank document, and follow the steps.

1   To insert an illustration, click the **Insert** tab and then locate the **Illustrations** group.

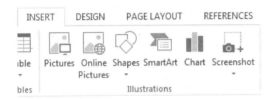

TIP In Outlook, you need to create a new Outlook item, such as an email or appointment, to access the Insert tab and Illustrations group.

2   You are going to insert a picture, so click the **Pictures** button.

TIP In PowerPoint, the Pictures button is located in the Images group. You can use the Online Pictures button to insert pictures stored on the Internet, including in places like your SkyDrive or social networks like Facebook and Flicker. Or, if the picture you want to insert is on your screen rather than a stored in a file, use Insert Screenshot to add a picture of an entire window or a screen clipping.

3   Navigate to the **Chapter02** practice file folder and select **Sample Picture**.

4   Near the bottom of the **Insert Picture** dialog box, click the **Insert** button.

5   Note the **Picture Tools Format** tool tab that appears in the ribbon when the picture is selected.

6   Click in the document away from the picture to deselect the picture and to remove the display of the picture tools.

7   Click the picture to redisplay the picture tools. Explore the commands on the **Picture Tools Format** tool tab. For example, in the **Picture Styles** gallery, click a picture style or use Live Preview to explore them. Or, in the **Adjust** group, click **Color** and apply a color wash to the picture.

> **TIP** You can swap a picture with another one and retain the size and formatting options. To do so, right-click the picture and then click Change Picture.

8   When you're finished checking out the various formatting options, select the picture and press the **Delete** key to remove the picture from the document.

9   Next you're going to insert a shape. On the **Insert** tab, in the **Illustrations** group, click the **Shapes** button, and then click the rectangle shape.

10 Point to an area in the document, and then click and drag to draw a rectangle.

11 Explore the **Drawing Tools Format** tool tab. For example, in the **Shape Styles** group, use the **Shape Styles** gallery to apply different styles, or click **Shape Effects** and explore preset shadows, reflections, glows, or 3-D effects.

12 When you're finished exploring, delete the rectangle.

13 To insert a SmartArt graphic, on the **Insert** tab, click the **SmartArt** button.

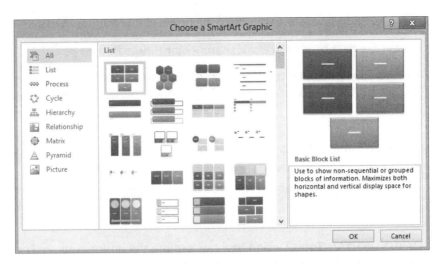

14   In the **Choose a SmartArt Graphic** dialog box, select the different SmartArt catego-
      ries and review the types of graphics that are available for the selected category.

15   To get more information on a specific graphic, click once on the preview and view the
      additional details on the right side of the dialog box.

16   Select the **List** category and then select **Basic Block List**.

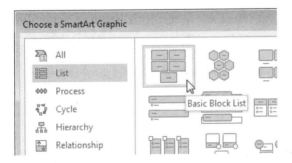

17   Click **OK** to insert your SmartArt graphic in the document.

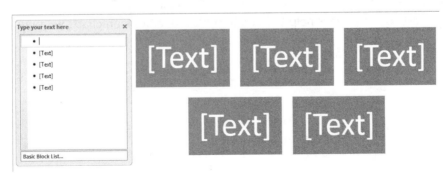

18 In the text pane, click to the right of the first bullet and enter **Word**.

19 Click in the next bullet placeholder and enter **PowerPoint**.

> **TIP** Did you notice that the text font size decreased after you entered the word *PowerPoint*? SmartArt will reduce the size of the font to help maintain uniform formatting.

20 In the text pane, enter additional text or delete the remaining bullet placeholders to remove the empty shapes.

> **TIP** To add additional shapes, click at the end of the last text entry and then press Enter.

21 On the **SmartArt Tools Design** tool tab, explore the design options. For example, use the **Layouts** gallery to switch to a different SmartArt layout, or in the **SmartArt Styles** gallery, select a different style to change the format of the graphic.

22 When you're comfortable with the basic SmartArt formatting options, click the edge of the graphic in your document to select it, and then press **Delete**.

❌ CLEAN UP Close the document without saving changes, and Exit Word.

Inserting charts

A chart is often included alongside a list of values to convey how those values relate to each other. Charts help give your information visual meaning and context, and can be comprehended faster than raw data. And as with inserting illustrations, after your chart is inserted, the Chart Tools tool tabs help you create professional-looking charts without a lot of effort.

When you insert a chart, you start with a default chart, such as a column, line, bar, or pie chart, and then customize the style, layout, and formatting to fit your needs. In Outlook, PowerPoint, and Word, after you insert a chart, a small Excel window, called a *chart sheet*, is displayed. You use the chart sheet to replace the placeholder data with your own by entering your data in place of the sample information provided. The chart will update automatically.

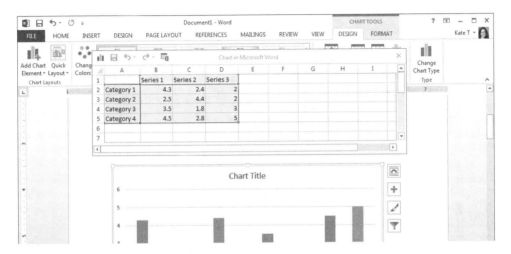

In Excel, you first add your chart sheet information to a workbook. Then you select that information and insert your chart. Although the steps to insert a chart may vary between the applications, the tools for working with a chart, such as those for applying formatting and layout features, are shared across the applications.

SEE ALSO For more information on inserting charts in Excel, see Chapter 23, "Creating charts and graphics."

In this exercise, you'll insert a default column chart in Word and explore basic formatting options.

TIP The steps for inserting a chart in this exercise are applicable to Outlook, PowerPoint, and Word.

SET UP You don't need any practice files to complete this exercise. Start Word, create a blank document, and follow the steps.

1. To insert a chart, on the **Insert** tab, in the **Illustrations** group, click the **Chart** button to display the **Insert Chart** dialog box.

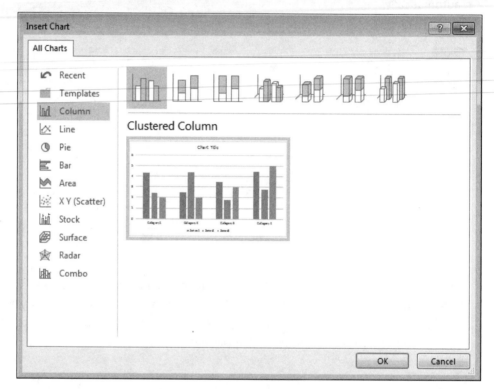

2. In the **Insert Chart** dialog box, click the various chart categories and explore the available chart types.

   TIP If you're not sure which type of chart best represents your data, try the new Recommended Charts feature in Excel. It analyzes your information by looking for patterns in your data arrangement and suggests the most relevant chart types.

SEE ALSO For more information on the Recommended Charts feature, see Chapter 23, "Creating charts and graphics."

3   From the **Column** category, select **Clustered Column**, and then click **OK**.

4   In the chart sheet, click a cell that contains a value, enter another number, and then press **Enter** to update the chart.

TIP To add an additional series or category, enter your information to the right of the last series name or below the last category name. You can delete a series or category by right-clicking the row or column heading and then clicking Delete.

5   On the chart sheet, click the **Close** button to remove the chart sheet from the screen.

TIP To redisplay the chart sheet, on the Chart Tools Design tool tab, in the Data group, click the Edit Data button. Note that this is a split control, so make sure you click the button and not the arrow.

6   On the **Chart Tools Design** tool tab, experiment with the various design options. For example, in the **Chart Layouts** group, click **Quick Layout** and select a different layout to add or remove multiple chart elements, such as the legend, titles, or gridlines. Or, in the **Chart Styles** group, click the **Chart Styles** gallery and select a different style to modify multiple formats at the same time.

SEE ALSO For more information on formatting charts, see Chapter 23, "Creating charts and graphics."

✖ CLEAN UP **Close the document without saving changes, and exit Word.**

Searching for online templates

For some tasks, you may know exactly how to begin, including the types of features you need to convey your information. For the times when you're unsure, don't stare at a blank file hoping something will magically appear. Turn to the online templates for inspiration. The online templates that appear when you first start almost all Office Professional 2013 applications, as well as those available on the New page in the Backstage view, may provide a starting point or give you ideas for how to get started.

The templates that appear first on the application Start screen are featured templates. Typically these templates are new or are those you recently used. You can choose from these templates or search the online templates to find one that is more specific to your needs.

TIP All of the online templates created for Office Professional 2013 are theme enabled. As you learned in the "Applying Office themes" section earlier in this chapter, this means that the fonts and colors can be modified to match your company's brand.

SEE ALSO For more information on creating your own theme, see Chapter 12, "Designing and creating presentations."

TIP To use online templates, you must be connected to the Internet. Online templates can be accessed from the New page in the Backstage view in Access, Excel, PowerPoint, Publisher, and Word. For Outlook, you can find email, business card, and signature templates in the Templates gallery on Office.com. The Templates gallery also has a variety of notebook templates for OneNote, such as planners, meeting notes, and appointment trackers.

In this exercise, you'll search for online templates by using Word.

 SET UP You don't need any practice files to complete this exercise. Make sure you're connected to the Internet, start Word, and follow the steps.

1   Let's start by searching for a specific type of template. Next to the list of suggested searches, click **Labels**.

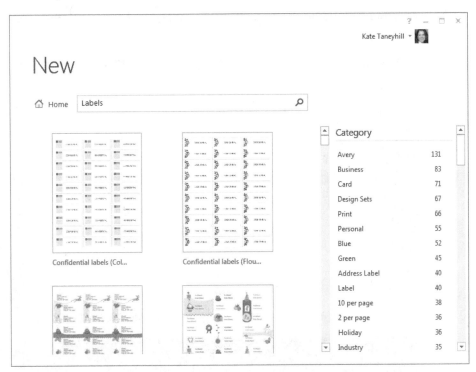

TIP The number to the right of each category is the number of templates currently available for your specified search. Note that some templates may be assigned to more than one category.

IMPORTANT

2   Point to a template thumbnail to view a ScreenTip, which displays additional details about a template, such as label vendor and product number.

3   Click once on any template to view more information and a larger preview of the template.

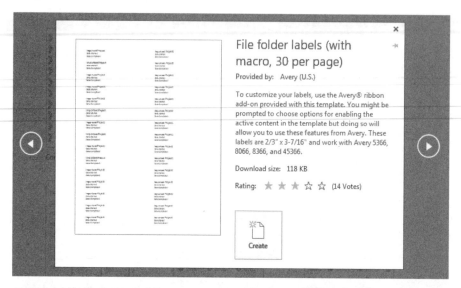

TIP You can use the arrows that appear to the left and right of the preview to browse the available templates. If the template has multiple views, More Images will display below the preview, along with navigation arrows. And in PowerPoint, if there are additional theme color variations included in the template, they are shown to the right of the template.

4   Click the **Close** button in the upper-right corner to close the preview.

5   In the category pane on the right, click **Business** to narrow your search results.

6   To narrow your search results even further, click **Industry**. Both categories will be highlighted at the top of the pane.

7   To remove the filtered category and return to a broader set of search results, point to the **Business** category and click the X that appears to the right.

8   To return to the featured templates, to the left of the **Search** text box, click **Home**.

> **TIP** You can also use the Search For Online Templates text box to find specific templates. You can use single words or phrases, but single words will return the most results. After you enter your search string, press Enter to perform the search. For applications with similar functionality, when you search for a template, you may get results for other applications below the template thumbnails. For example, if you search for *Calendar*, you'll find results for almost every application.

Search results from your other Office applications

> **X** Excel: 45
> **P** PowerPoint: 27
> **P** Publisher: 11
> **V** Visio :   1
> **P** Project: 1
> **A** Access: 3

To view the other templates, click the arrow to the left of the application name to expand the list. When you double-click a template, the application will start, and then a new file is created based on the template.

⊗ CLEAN UP Exit Word without saving changes to your document.

The templates across the applications include examples of many of the features you'll learn about in this book. Though some of them may include more advanced capabilities, such as macros used to automate tasks, we'll introduce you to the tools you'll need to utilize them so they can be modified to fit your needs.

Presenting Office documents online

Office Professional 2013 provides two ways to share your documents in real time with a live audience. If you use Microsoft Lync, you can schedule an online meeting or host an impromptu one from within your Office application. If you don't use Lync, you can use the free Office Presentation Service to share your file. With either method, participants don't need the application to view your PowerPoint presentation or Word document. They can view it in a web browser on their computer, tablet, or most smartphones.

TIP If you have meeting notes stored in a OneNote notebook, you can share that notebook with participants during your presentation. Even if you don't have specific notes, you can use a shared notebook for taking notes, capturing a brainstorming session, or as a whiteboard during your presentation. For more information about sharing OneNote notebooks, see Chapter 33, "Sharing notes with others."

TIP Presenting online through Microsoft Lync requires Lync to be installed and is applicable to Excel, PowerPoint, and Word. Presenting online through the Office Presentation Service requires an Office account and is applicable to PowerPoint and Word. Both methods require that the presenter and participants have an Internet connection. Saving the presentation in a shared location isn't required for presenting online. For more information about Office accounts, see Chapter 3, "Sharing and collaborating."

In this exercise, you'll present a PowerPoint presentation through Microsoft Lync.

 SET UP You need the Fabrikam Management Team presentation located in the Chapter02 practice file folder, and you must have Microsoft Lync installed, to complete this exercise. Make sure you're signed in to your Office account and Lync, start PowerPoint, open the Fabrikam Management Team presentation, and follow the steps.

1   Click the **File** tab to open the **Backstage** view, and then click **Share**.

2   On the **Share** page, in the **Present Online** options area to the right, make sure **Microsoft Lync** is selected.

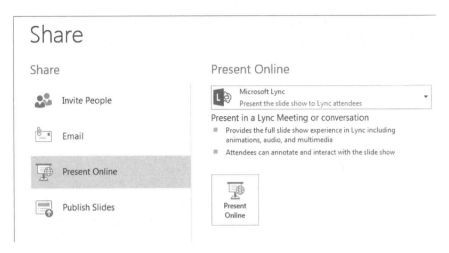

3   Click the **Present Online** button to view additional meeting options.

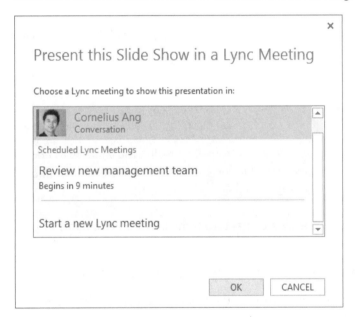

TIP In PowerPoint, the Present Online button is also available on the Slide Show tab in the Start Slide Show group.

4   From the **Present this Slide Show in a Lync Meeting** options, which shows current Lync conversations and upcoming online meetings, click **Start a new Lync meeting.**

5   Click **OK** to view a Lync conversation window with your shared presentation displayed.

6   To invite attendees, near the bottom of the conversation window, point to the **Participants** button and then click **Invite More People**.

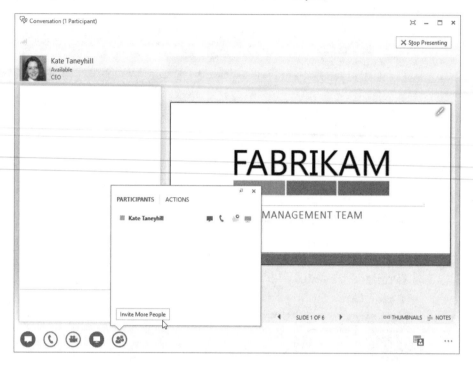

TIP You can also drag attendees from your main Lync window to add them to your online meeting. Additionally, if you select an upcoming Lync meeting rather than a new meeting, participants have already been invited.

7   To invite a contact, select a contact from the list or enter a name or phone number, and then click the **Add** button.

8   Repeat the previous step for each contact you want to add.

9   To advance to the next slide, click the **Next** button below the slides.

10   To stop presenting, click **Stop Presenting** and close the Lync conversation window.

❌ CLEAN UP Exit PowerPoint without saving changes to the practice file.

If you don't have Lync, you can use the free Office Presentation Service to present online. When you use this service, you present your slide show in PowerPoint and the participants view it in PowerPoint Web App.

Other than how the presentation is displayed, the primary difference between Lync and the Office Presentation Service is that Lync also provides audio and video capabilities. When you are using the Office Presentation Service, you'll need to use a conference line or an on-line service, such as Skype, to include audio or video.

TIP If you have Lync installed, you can also use the Office Presentation Service.

In this exercise, you'll present a PowerPoint presentation through the Office Presentation Service.

SET UP You need the Fabrikam Management Team presentation located in the Chapter02 practice file folder to complete this exercise. Make sure you are signed in to Office, start PowerPoint, open the Fabrikam Management Team presentation, and follow the steps.

1 Click the **File** tab to open the **Backstage** view, and then click **Share**.

2 On the **Share** page, in the **Present Online** options to the right, make sure **Office Presentation Service** is selected.

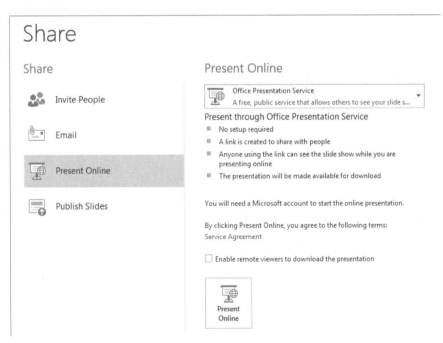

TIP In PowerPoint, the Present Online button is also available on the Slide Show tab, in the Start Slide Show group.

3   Above the **Present Online** button, note the **Enable remote viewers to download the presentation** check box. You can select this option if you want participants to be able to save a copy of your presentation.

4   Click the **Present Online** button to view additional sharing options.

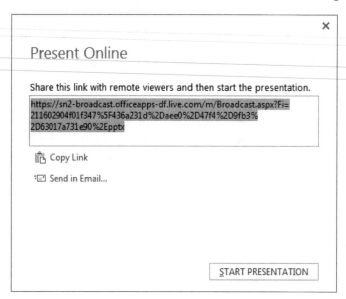

5   In the **Present Online** dialog box, click either the **Copy Link** or **Send in Email** option to share your presentation.

TIP You can copy the link and paste it in your web browser to view what the participants view when the presentation begins.

6   Click **Start Presentation**.

TIP After you start your presentation, participants will view your presentation in PowerPoint Web App.

7   To advance to the next slide, press the **Enter** key.

8   To end the presentation, press **Esc** to suspend it, and then on the **Present Online** tab, click **End Online Presentation**.

9   In the message box that confirms ending your presentation, click **End Online Presentation**.

TIP After you end your presentation, participants will view a black screen in PowerPoint Web App.

❌ CLEAN UP **Exit PowerPoint without saving changes to the practice file.**

When using the Office Presentation Service, you may want to explore the participant's view and options. As noted in a tip in this exercise, you can copy the presentation link and paste it in your web browser to view what the participants view while you're presenting. For instance, they can scroll through the presentation or document on their own, or they can use the Follow Presenter option so their screen changes as the presenter's screen changes.

Inserting online video

In both PowerPoint and Word, you can insert a linked video that's stored in an online location, like your SkyDrive, Facebook, YouTube, or another website. Note that because online videos are linked, in order to play an online video during a PowerPoint presentation or from a Word document, you must have an Internet connection, and your computer must have access to the website where the video is stored.

To insert an online video, use the Insert tab. In Word, you can then play the video from the document. In PowerPoint, you need to be in Slide Show view to play your video.

In this exercise, you'll add a link to a video into a Word document and play it after it's inserted.

SET UP You don't need any practice files to complete this exercise. Start Word, create a blank document, and follow the steps.

1   On the **Insert** tab, in the **Media** group, click the **Online Video** button.

     TIP In PowerPoint, on the Insert tab, in the Media group, click Video, and then from the list, click the Online Video button.

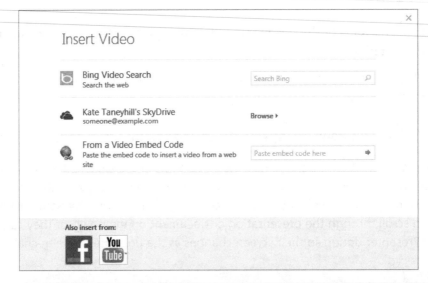

IMPORTANT

2   In the **Insert Video** dialog box, click in the **Search Bing** text box, enter Office 2013 microsoft.com and then press the **Enter** key to view your search results.

3   Click once on any video to select it and display more information about the selected video at the bottom of the dialog box.

4   To preview the video, click the **View Larger** button in the lower-right corner of the video.

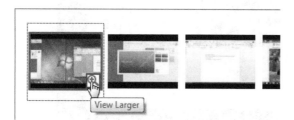

5   In the video preview, click the **Play** button in the center to play the video.

6   Click the **Close** button in the upper-right corner to close the preview.

7   Next let's insert a video in the document. Click a video to select it, and in the lower-right corner of the **Insert Video** dialog box, click **Insert**.

8   Click the **Play** button in the center of the video preview picture to play the inserted video from the Word document. If the video doesn't begin to automatically play, click the **Play** button at the bottom of the video.

TIP When the video is playing, controls to pause, adjust the volume, and show the video in a full screen are available.

TIP In PowerPoint, you need to be in Slide Show view to play a video.

9   Click anywhere in the Word document that is outside of the video screen to end the video.

> **TIP** In PowerPoint, clicking a slide away from the video will advance to the next slide. In either application, you can also press the Esc key to end a video.

✕ CLEAN UP **Exit Word without saving changes to your document.**

> **SEE ALSO** For more information on working with video in PowerPoint, see Chapter 15, "Adding animation and multimedia."

Key points

- The Office applications have features that are shared across Office, which means they work almost the same regardless of the application you're using.

- You use the Insert tab to add illustrations, such as pictures, shapes, SmartArt graphics, and charts.

- To format illustrations and charts, click the object to select it, and then use the tools that automatically appear in the ribbon for the selected object.

- You can share your Office documents with others in real time through Microsoft Lync or the free Office Presentation Service.

- When you insert an online video in an Office document, only a link to where the video is stored online and a preview picture are inserted. You need to be connected to the Internet to play the video.

Chapter at a glance

Explore

Explore the Office account,
page 76

Connect

Connect cloud services,
page 80

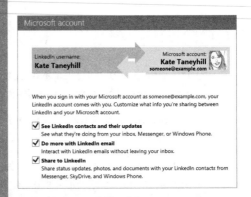

Open

Open files from the cloud,
page 92

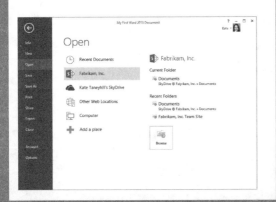

Sync

Sync your files with the cloud,
page 94

Sharing and collaborating

3

IN THIS CHAPTER, YOU'LL LEARN HOW TO

- Define the term *cloud service.*

- Sign in and manage your Office account.

- Connect cloud services to your Office account.

- Sync files with SkyDrive for offline use.

- Get started with co-authoring.

A cloud service typically refers to online file storage, resources, or applications that are accessed through the Internet. These can range from apps for your smartphone, Internet games, social networks, and web-based email to secure private networks.

These services are becoming part of our everyday lives. You may have documents and other files like pictures or videos stored on Microsoft SharePoint, Microsoft SkyDrive, Flickr, or YouTube. And you may have contact information stored on various social networks like Facebook, Twitter, or LinkedIn.

In this chapter, you'll learn about how Microsoft Office Professional 2013 connects you to your various cloud services through your Office account. You'll also learn how you can use cloud services to share and collaborate with others, whether they're sitting in the next cubicle or in an office thousands of miles away from your corporate network.

PRACTICE FILES You don't need any practice files to complete the exercises in this chapter.

Defining the term These days you may work across numerous computers and devices. You may use a desktop computer while at your desk and use a laptop, Microsoft Surface, or other tablet, or smartphone when you're on the go. And there may be times when you use a public computer, such as one in a hotel business center or Internet café. Or, you may work at a co-worker's desk or from home on your personal computer.

Imagine switching to another computer or device and picking up exactly where you left off, right down to the last paragraph in a document you were editing in Microsoft Word or the last slide you were working on in Microsoft PowerPoint.

You could have almost achieved this capability in past versions of Office, but it may not have been as seamless as you'd have liked it to be. Prior to Office Professional 2013, personal settings, such as recently used document and folder lists, were associated with the account you used to log in to Windows. That account may be limited to a specific computer, or you may have a roaming profile that lets you access your information when you're connected to your company network.

Office Professional 2013 takes the concept of the roaming profile a step further. Instead of a profile that can be accessed only by a specific computer or while you are connected to your company network, personal settings can now be stored online in your Office account. This lets you access your information from almost anywhere. And not just from another computer, but also from devices such as Surface or a Windows Phone.

Plus, you can connect other cloud services that store contact information, documents, photos, and videos and access them right from your Office applications.

TIP To access your Office account on another computer, it must be running Windows 7 or Windows 8 and be connected to the Internet. It also needs to either have Office Professional 2013 installed, or you need a Microsoft Office 365 subscription that includes Microsoft Office on Demand.

SEE ALSO For more on connecting cloud services, see "Connecting cloud services to your Office account" later in this chapter; for more on Office 365 or Office on Demand, see the sidebar "What is Office 365?" later in this chapter.

In order to store your information in the cloud, you need an Office account. This account is associated with an email address that you use for various Microsoft services, such as those in the following account types:

- **Microsoft account** This account type, previously called Windows Live ID, is typically associated with a personal email address. For example, if you use Windows Live Messenger, Windows Live Hotmail, or Microsoft Xbox LIVE, you have a Microsoft account.

  TIP Even though a Microsoft account is typically associated with a personal email address, you can use almost any email address to create a Microsoft account.

- **Organizational account** This account type is provided to you by an administrator for Microsoft SharePoint Online services. If your company or educational organization uses Office 365, then you have an organizational account.

IMPORTANT

If your email account lets you use Microsoft services, then you already have an Office account. All you need to do to start using it is sign in to Office, and you'll learn how to do that in the next section.

Need a Microsoft account for Office?

Outlook.com, an upgrade to Hotmail, is a new email service from Microsoft. It has a better Office integration experience than its predecessor, along with features that are more like the desktop version, Microsoft Outlook. And as with Hotmail, SkyDrive is included for online file storage along with Microsoft Office Web Apps.

SEE ALSO For more information on SkyDrive, see the sidebar "What is SkyDrive?" later in this chapter.

To get your new email account, go to *www.outlook.com* and sign up. Or, if you already have a Hotmail account, you can upgrade it to an Outlook.com account in your Hotmail account options.

Signing in and managing your Office account

As previously mentioned, in order to take advantage of the cloud integration features, you need to sign in to your Office account with an email address that gives you access to various Microsoft services.

Although the option to sign in occurs during the Office Professional 2013 installation or appears the first time you start Office Professional 2013, you may have skipped that step, or Office may have already been started on your computer.

TIP If you're using Windows 8 and are logged in with an account that's connected to Microsoft services, the Office installation signs you in to your Office account.

In this exercise, you'll sign in to your Office account.

 SET UP You don't need an email address that lets you use Microsoft services to complete this exercise. Start Word, create a blank document, and follow the steps.

1   Click the **File** tab to display the **Backstage** view, and then click **Account**.

2   Below the **User Information** section, click **Sign in**.

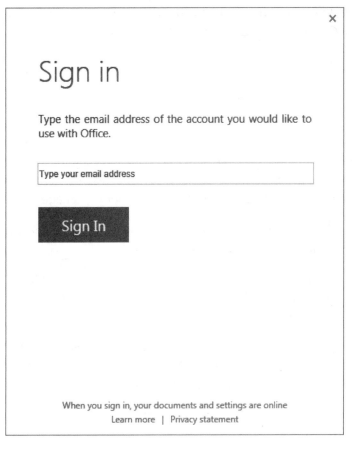

3   On the **Sign in** screen, enter your email address and then click the **Sign In** button.

4   Complete one of the following actions:

- If you already have email address that lets you use Microsoft services, enter your Microsoft account password and then click **Sign In**.

- If you don't have an email address that lets you use Microsoft services, click **Sign Up Now**, and then complete the sign up form.

TIP If you're signing up for a Microsoft account, you can use an email address you already have for the account name. For security purposes, you may want to create a password that's different from your email account password for your Microsoft account.

✖ CLEAN UP Close the document without saving changes.

When you sign in to Office, you sign in across the Office applications. And in any application, your sign in name will appear in the upper-right corner above the ribbon.

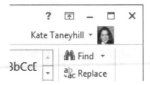

Additionally, you're not limited to a single Office account and can have more than one. Some people have accounts for both business and personal use. This lets them keep their recently used files and other preferences separate and easier to manage.

If you have multiple Office accounts, one for business and one for personal use, you can easily switch between them from any Office application.

To switch accounts, use the Account page in the Backstage view and the Switch Account option, or click your name in the right corner above the ribbon and then click Switch account, and complete the sign in process.

Note that after you sign in to Office, you stay logged in even if you have switched to another Office account. This way, after you have added at least two Office accounts, you can switch between them without the need to repeat the sign in process.

In this exercise, you'll switch to another Office account.

 SET UP You need a second Office account to complete this exercise. Start Word if necessary, create a blank document, and follow the steps.

1   In the **Backstage** view, click **Account**.

2   Click **Switch Account**.

   TIP You can also click your name in the upper-right corner above the ribbon and click Switch Account.

3   On the **Sign in** screen, enter your email address and then click the **Sign In** button.

4   Enter your account password, and then click **Sign In** to log in to your other Office account.

5   To view your available accounts, display the **Switch Account** screen again.

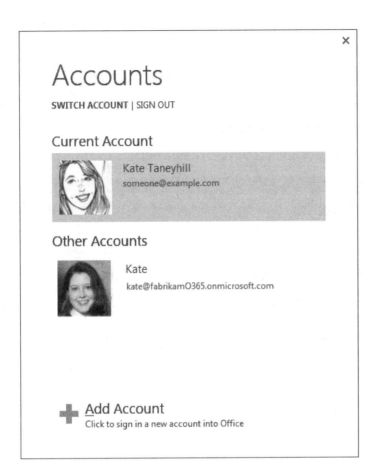

6   To switch between accounts, click an account name below **Other Accounts**.

   ✖ CLEAN UP Close the document without saving changes.

As noted, after you sign in to Office, you stay signed in on that computer. This isn't an issue if it's your work or personal computer, but if you're using a public computer, it's important that you sign out of Office.

When you sign out of your Office account, you're removing the account from the computer you are using. Part of the sign out process is to delete any personal data that an Office application may have created while you were using the computer. However, it won't remove documents or other information you may have created. So, if you don't want that information on the computer, you'll need to manually delete those items. For example, if you saved a file to the computer's local drive, then it will still be there after you sign out of your account. And even though you removed your account from the computer, you can sign back in at any time and all of your personal settings that are stored in your Office account will be redisplayed.

In this exercise, you'll sign out of your Office account.

SET UP You need to be signed in to Office to complete this exercise. Start Word if it's not already running, create a blank document, and follow the steps.

1   In the **Backstage** view, click **Account**.

2   Below the **User Information** section, click **Sign out**.

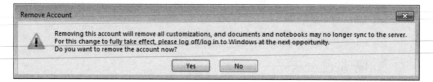

3   In the **Remove Account** confirmation message box, click **Yes** to remove the account.

4   Exit Word and restart Windows to complete the sign out process.

CLEAN UP If you exited Word and restarted Windows, there are no additional clean up steps.

Connecting cloud services to your Office account

Cloud services help us stay connected to our information and other people. However, these services can result in information that's scattered in several different locations, depending on the number of cloud services you have. For example, you could have an Organizational account, a Microsoft account, as well as business and personal accounts on social networks. You might often need to sign in to various websites to locate a document or recall which social network you need to access to find contact information for someone.

As noted in the section titled "Defining the term *cloud service*" earlier in this chapter, you can connect these various online services to your Office account. Doing so gives you the ability to open and save files to your cloud locations. In addition, you can search for contact information across your services. You can also insert your online pictures or videos in an Office document and even get social updates from within your Office applications like Outlook.

SEE ALSO For more information on Office 365, see the sidebar "What is Office 365?" later in this section. For more information on SkyDrive, see the sidebar "What is SkyDrive?" also later in this section.

You can connect to cloud services on the Account page in the Backstage view. The available connected service options for your Office account depend on the type of account you're using for Microsoft services. For example, with either a Microsoft account or Organizational account, both SharePoint Online and SkyDrive connections are available. But if you have a Microsoft account type, you'll have sharing options for personal cloud services like Facebook, LinkedIn, Twitter, and Flickr. These may not be shown if you have an Organizational account, because this account type is more school oriented or business oriented.

TIP If you have an Office 365 account, your file storage locations on SharePoint Online may be connected and available when you sign in.

In this exercise, you'll first connect a SharePoint Online or SkyDrive cloud storage service to your Office account. Then you'll have the option to connect a personal cloud service like LinkedIn.

 SET UP You need to be signed in to Office and be connected to the Internet. To complete the optional steps for connecting a personal cloud service, you must be signed in with a Microsoft account and have a Facebook, LinkedIn, or Twitter account. Start Word if necessary, create a blank document, and follow the steps.

1   In the **Backstage** view, click **Account**.

2   In the account options, click **Add a service**, point to **Storage**, and then click either **Office 365 SharePoint** or **SkyDrive**.

IMPORTANT

3   On the **Sign in** screen, enter the email address for your cloud storage account and complete the sign in process. Your connected service will be listed under the account settings in the **Backstage** view.

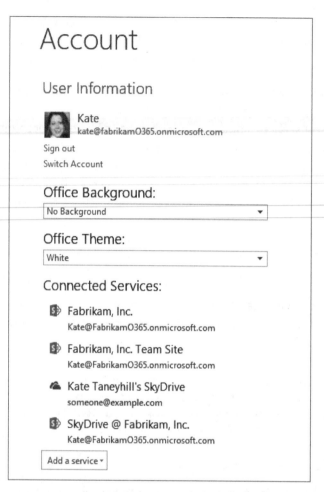

If you have a Microsoft account type and want to connect a personal cloud service like Facebook, LinkedIn, or Twitter, then follow these optional steps.

IMPORTANT

4   In the **Backstage** view, click **Account**.

5   Click **Add a service**, point to **Sharing**, and then click the cloud service you want to
     add to display the options for connecting your Office account. For example, if you
     have a LinkedIn account, click **LinkedIn**.

6   Complete the sign in steps as directed by the service you selected.

IMPORTANT

CLEAN UP Close the document without saving changes.

TIP Some personal cloud services have additional options that let you choose the type of information you share between the service and your Microsoft account. In the Backstage view, on the Account page, if a Manage link appears next to the service, click the link to view the options. For example, if you click the Manage link for LinkedIn, you'll find options for viewing LinkedIn contacts, their status updates, and using LinkedIn email in Outlook. You'll also find an option for sharing status updates and files with your LinkedIn contacts through other social services like Microsoft Messenger, SkyDrive, or your Windows phone.

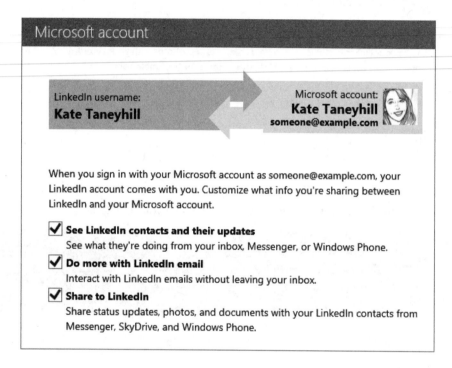

Your Microsoft account options are also where you'll find the ability to remove the personal cloud service. Other services, such as SkyDrive, can be removed from the Backstage view.

What is Office 365?

Office 365 is a subscription-based cloud service for hosted Microsoft server products, such as Microsoft Exchange Server, SharePoint Online, and Microsoft Lync Server. These services give you email and shared calendars, online file storage and sharing, along with instant messaging and web conferencing. Office 365 can also include Office on Demand along with the desktop version of Office Professional 2013.

TIP Office on Demand is a service that lets you take Office Professional 2013 with you to other locations. You can temporarily use, or stream, an Office Professional 2013 application on computers in which Office Professional 2013 isn't installed, such as those in a hotel business center or Internet café. In order to stream Office Professional 2013 on another computer, it must be running Windows 7 or Windows 8 and be connected to the Internet.

What you get with your subscription depends on the plan you choose. You can select home and family plans, small business plans, or a large enterprise plan.

SEE ALSO For more information on Office 365, along with plans and pricing, visit *www.Office365.com*.

One of the biggest advantages of using Office 365 is you don't need to make a large investment in hardware or software. Nor do you need expert knowledge of server installation or even administration. And, with your subscription, you'll always get the most current Office technologies.

If you already have an Office 365 account, to access it from a web browser, go to *www.Office365.com* and sign in.

3

What is SkyDrive?

SkyDrive is a cloud storage service hosted by Microsoft for storing documents, photos, and other files and is included with your Microsoft account. If you have an Office 365 subscription that includes SharePoint Online, you'll get a version of SkyDrive called SkyDrive Pro for your work-related files. To access your SkyDrive account from a web browser, go to *www.SkyDrive.com* and sign in. To access SkyDrive Pro, go to *www.Office365.com* and sign in.

IMPORTANT

With your SkyDrive, you can access your files on almost any device with an Internet connection. It gives you the ability to share files with others too. For example, if a file attachment is too large to be sent through email, you can save it on your SkyDrive. Then in the email message, you can send a link to the file.

SkyDrive also includes Office Web Apps, which are browser-based companions to your Office applications. As an added bonus for those with a Microsoft account, you can access various SkyDrive applications from both Microsoft and third parties. For example, there are SkyDrive apps that let you manage your SkyDrive files on most smartphones.

Most importantly, SkyDrive now has more integration across Office applications, and you'll learn more about those features throughout this book.

Saving files on SharePoint Online and SkyDrive

In the previous sections, you learned how your Office cloud account lets you take your Office settings with you. You also learned how to sign in to your Office account and connect to cloud services. But, if you want to access your recently used files or other files across various computers and devices, those files need to be saved in a cloud service like SharePoint Online or SkyDrive. Now that Office has integrated cloud services for opening and saving documents, you'll find that using these locations is just as easy as using a local or network drive.

In this exercise, you'll create a new document in Word and save it to either SharePoint Online or SkyDrive.

3

 SET UP You need either a SharePoint Online location or SkyDrive added to your connected services to complete this exercise. Start Word if necessary, and follow the steps.

TIP The steps for saving files to the cloud also apply to Excel, PowerPoint, and Microsoft Publisher. For Microsoft Access and OneNote, saving a file is part of the creation process, and the steps you use are slightly different than the following procedure.

SEE ALSO For information about creating and saving a new Access Web App to a cloud location, see Chapter 40, "Creating and sharing a Web App." For information about creating and saving a new OneNote notebook to a cloud location, see Chapter 31, "Working with notebooks, sections, and pages."

1   From the Word **Start** screen, click **Blank Document**.

KEYBOARD SHORTCUT Press Ctrl+N to create a new blank document.

TIP If Word is already running and the Start screen doesn't appear, click the File tab and then click New to display the Start screen.

2   In the blank Word document, enter some sample text.

TIP To quickly add sample text, you can enter *=rand* or *=lorem* followed by an open and close parenthesis, such as *=rand()*, and then press Enter.

3   Click the **File** tab, and then click **Save As**.

KEYBOARD SHORTCUT Press Ctrl+S to save the document.

TIP In the Backstage view, you can click Save instead of Save As. However, since the document hasn't been previously saved, the Save As option will be displayed.

4   In the **Backstage** view, click your SharePoint Online or SkyDrive location.

IMPORTANT

5   To the right of your selected location, either click a recent folder or click **Browse** to select an alternate folder.

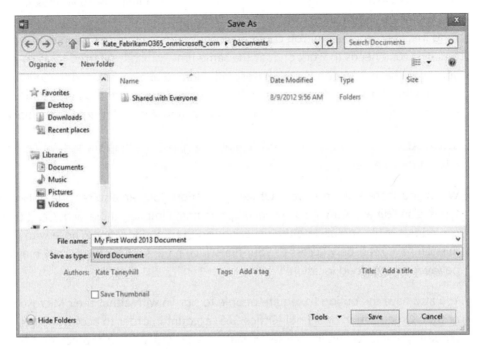

6   In the **Save As** dialog box, in the **File name** text box, enter My First Word 2013 Document and then click **Save**.

7   To close the document, click the **File** tab, and then click **Close**.

⊗ CLEAN UP Close the document without saving changes.

Sharing files with others from SharePoint Online or SkyDrive

After you save a document or notebook to SharePoint Online or to your SkyDrive location, you can share the file with others. For example, you might have a file that's too large to send in an email message. You could be collaborating with other people on a document and everyone needs to work on it at the same time, which is referred to as *co-authoring*. Or, you might have a notebook with notes that meeting attendees need to view for an upcoming meeting. Office Professional 2013 has made sharing easier than ever before by adding sharing options for Excel, OneNote, PowerPoint, and Word files right in the Backstage view.

SEE ALSO For more information on co-authoring, see "Getting started with co-authoring" later in this chapter.

When you share a file from your Office application, you can also set one of two permission types, Can Edit and Can View. As each option name implies, those with Can Edit permission can edit your file and update their changes on the cloud location. Those with Can View permission have read-only access to your file, which means any changes they may make cannot be saved to the cloud location.

You also have the option to require people to sign in with either their Microsoft account or their Organization or School (Office 365) account in order to access the file. Although requiring others to sign in may seem like an extra step, it helps protect your file. When you share a file, you send a sharing link, which can potentially be sent to other people. If you require sign in, only those you've explicitly shared your file with will be able to access it.

In this exercise, you'll share the document that you created in the "Saving files on SharePoint Online and SkyDrive" section with others.

 SET UP All of the steps in the previous exercise need to be completed. Start Word if it's not already running, and follow the steps.

TIP The steps for sharing files also apply to Excel, OneNote, and PowerPoint.

1   Click the **File** tab to display the **Backstage** view, and then click **Open.**

2   From the **Recent Documents** list, click **My First Word 2013 Document** to open the document in Word.

3   In the **Backstage** view, on the **Share** page, click **Invite People.**

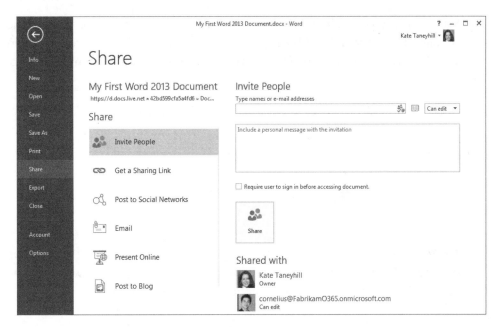

TIP After you send your sharing invitations, the people you shared your file with will be displayed in the Shared With section, along with the type of permission you assigned to them.

4   In the **Invite People** section, enter the names or email addresses of the people with whom you want to share the document.

   TIP To select people from your address book instead of typing, click the Address Book button to the right of the names and email addresses text box.

5   Note the **Permissions** drop-down box on the far right of the names and email addresses text box. You can change the permissions from **Can Edit** to **Can View,** if you want.

6   Enter a message in the **Include a personal message** text box, if you want.

7   Select the **Require user to sign in before accessing the document** option, if you want.

8   Click **Share** to share the document and send the sharing invitation.

❌ CLEAN UP Close My First Word 2013 document without saving changes.

After you send your sharing invitation, each person will also receive an email message that contains a link to your file. Clicking the link will open the file in the corresponding Office Web App. For example, if the file is a Word document, it will open in Word Web App.

Kate has a document to share with you on SkyDrive. To view it, click the link below.

My First Word 2013 Document.docx

Share your files with SkyDrive.

TIP You can change or remove sharing permissions for a user after the invitations have been sent. To do so, open your shared file and in the Backstage view, on the Share page, right-click the person to view the change and remove options.

Opening files from the cloud

After you have saved files on SharePoint Online or on SkyDrive, you essentially use the same steps for opening a file from the cloud as you would for saving files to the cloud.

In the previous exercise, you opened My First Word 2013 Document from your Recent Documents list. In this exercise, you'll open the document by using the Open dialog box.

➡ SET UP **All of the steps in the exercise from the "Saving files on SharePoint Online and SkyDrive" section earlier in this chapter need to be completed. Start Word if necessary, and follow the steps.**

TIP The steps for opening files from the cloud also apply to Access, Excel, OneNote, PowerPoint, and Publisher.

1   Click the **File** tab and then click **Open**.

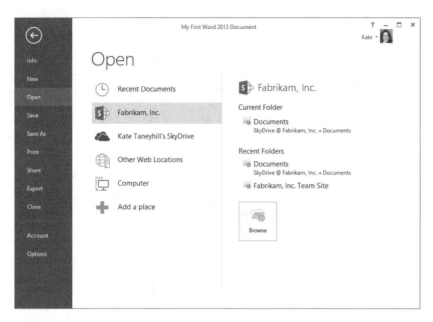

2   In the **Open** options, click the same location in which you saved **My First Word 2013 Document**, such as your SkyDrive.

3   On the right side, below **Recent Folders**, click the folder where you saved **My First Word 2013 Document** to display the **Open** dialog box.

4   Select **My First Word 2013 Document** and then click **Open** to view your document in Word.

5   On the **Quick Access Toolbar**, note the green arrows in the lower-right corner of the **Save** button, which indicate that your changes will be synced with your cloud location when you save the document.

⊗ CLEAN UP Close My First Word 2013 Document without saving changes.

Can I access my files through SharePoint locations hosted by my company?

Although connected services for your Office account are designed to be used with Office 365 and SkyDrive, you can still open and save files stored on a hosted, on-premises SharePoint Server from Office applications. In the Backstage view, from either the Open or Save As option, click Other Web Locations and then enter the URL for the server. After you've used another web location, it will be added to your Recent Folders list for quick reference. These locations are also saved in your Office account so you'll be able to access them whenever you sign in to Office.

Syncing files with SkyDrive for offline use

In the previous exercises, you learned how to open and save files in the cloud. You may be wondering at this point about what happens if you don't have an Internet connection, or if you're limited to using a web browser to manage your files. The good news is SkyDrive has an answer for both. You can create a sync location for files stored in the cloud to a network or local drive so they can be used even when an Internet connection isn't available. The sync folder also provides the ability to access and manage your files directly from Windows 8 File Explorer or Windows Explorer on Windows 7. Best of all, after you create the location, your files will sync when you're connected to the Internet.

TIP In Windows 8, File Explorer has replaced Windows Explorer. Throughout this book, we refer to this browsing utility by its Windows 8 name. If your computer is running Windows 7, use Windows Explorer instead.

If you're wondering how this works exactly, when you create a sync location, you're essentially creating a shortcut to your cloud service that can be accessed from your computer. But unlike a shortcut that needs the location to be available in order to access it, in a sync location offline copies of your files are created in the folder. Then when an Internet connection is available, your online files are updated.

In this exercise, you'll create a sync location for SkyDrive Pro, and then you'll get the SkyDrive app for a Microsoft account to sync your files. If you don't have both SkyDrive Pro and a Microsoft account, choose the set of instructions in this exercise that fits the type of SkyDrive you're using.

SEE ALSO For more information on determining the type of SkyDrive you have, see the sidebar "What is SkyDrive?" earlier in this chapter.

Syncing with SkyDrive Pro

If you have an Office 365 account with SharePoint Online and want to sync your files with SkyDrive Pro, follow these steps.

SET UP You need an Office 365 account that includes SharePoint Online for this exercise. Open a web browser and follow the steps.

1   In the address bar of your web browser, enter www.Office365.com and press the **Enter** key.

2   If necessary, sign in to Office 365 with your email address and password.

3   In the navigation options near the top of the page, click **SkyDrive**.

4   In the upper-right corner, below your sign in name, click **SYNC**.

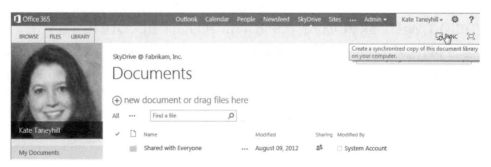

5 In the **Microsoft SkyDrive Pro** dialog box, click **Sync Now** to create a folder with a name similar to **SkyDrive @ Fabrikam, Inc.** in the location you specified.

TIP If you want to use a location other than the default sync folder, click Change and select an alternate location or folder.

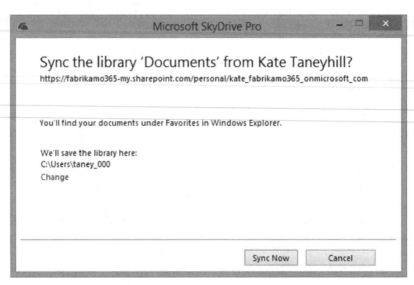

CLEAN UP Close your web browser.

Syncing with SkyDrive for a Microsoft account

If you have a Microsoft account and want to sync your files with SkyDrive, follow these steps.

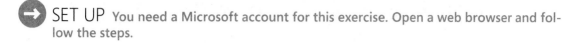 SET UP You need a Microsoft account for this exercise. Open a web browser and follow the steps.

1   In the address bar of your web browser, enter www.SkyDrive.com and press the **Enter** key.

2   If necessary, sign in to SkyDrive with your email address and password.

3   In the navigation options on the left, near the bottom of the screen, click **Get SkyDrive apps**.

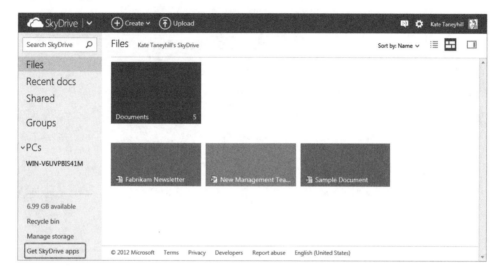

4   Locate the SkyDrive app for Windows Desktop, then download and install the application.

   TIP You may need to log in to your Microsoft account during the installation.

5   When the **Introducing your SkyDrive Folder** message box displays, click **Next** and complete the installation.

   TIP If you want to use a location other than the default sync folder, click Change and select an alternate location or folder.

Introducing your SkyDrive folder

Look for your SkyDrive folder in File Explorer. Files in here are on your other devices and SkyDrive.com.

Your SkyDrive folder is here: C:\Users\taney_000\SkyDrive

Change

Next

CLEAN UP Close your web browser.

After you follow either set of steps, a shortcut to your SkyDrive folder is created and added to your Favorites list in File Explorer. Additionally, because your Favorites list appears in most Windows dialog boxes for opening and saving files or inserting file attachments in an email message, you can access your SkyDrive from almost every application.

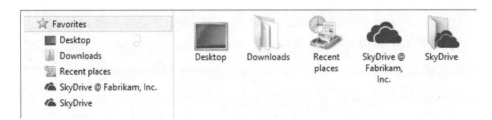

TIP You can use also use the SkyDrive Pro 2013 or Microsoft SkyDrive apps on your Windows 8 Start screen to quickly access your SkyDrive sync location.

Getting started with co-authoring

When you collaborate with others on Office documents, you may encounter a situation in which more than one person needs to work on a file at the same time. Consider the following scenarios:

- Multiple people need to contribute to a company newsletter, and the deadline is in a few hours.

- Several people are taking part in a last-minute presentation, and they all need to add speaker notes to their slides.

- Your team's project notes are stored in a OneNote notebook, and you need to collaborate on them during a meeting.

- Each region of your company is responsible for adding their sales data to a workbook for an upcoming financial review.

- You need to edit a document, but another person left it open and is at lunch or has left the office for the day.

If you've ever encountered any of these scenarios, you've likely waited for the original file to be available. With the co-authoring feature, you don't need to wait. Multiple people can edit an Office document or a notebook at the same time.

TIP In OneNote, co-authoring is typically referred to as *sharing* rather than *co-authoring*.

Here's a list of the Office applications that support co-authoring:

- Excel Web App

- OneNote and OneNote Web App

- PowerPoint and PowerPoint Web App

- Word and Word Web App

To start a co-authoring session, the following requirements must be met:

- The file must be opened in a supported application.

- The Office document or notebook must be stored on SharePoint, SharePoint Online, or SkyDrive.

- The file needs to be shared with other co-authors.

Ideally, co-authoring is seamless, and it's not something you necessarily plan. If the require-ments are met and more than one person edits a document or notebook at the same time, co-authoring is automatic. With the exception of Excel files, one person can even be using the desktop application and another can be using the associated Office Web App.

For Excel, if multiple people need to edit a workbook at the same time, all they need to do is open it in Excel Web App. For this scenario, some coordination with others may be necessary.

When more than one person opens the same shared file, a notification appears in the status bar and reflects the total author count. When you click the count in the status bar, you'll get a list of the people currently using the file.

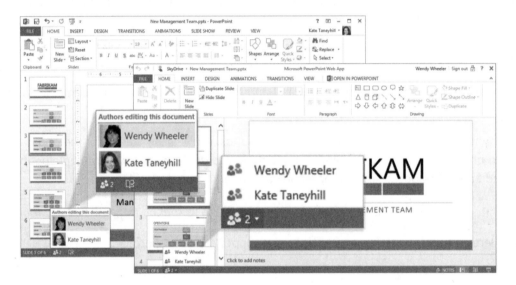

Key points

- A cloud service is an online file storage service, resource, or application that is accessed through the Internet.

- To store your Office settings, such as recently used files and folders, in the Office cloud, you need an email account that gives you access to Microsoft services.

- Examples of Microsoft services are SharePoint Online, SkyDrive, Hotmail, and Windows Live Messenger.

- You can connect cloud services like SkyDrive, Facebook, Twitter, LinkedIn, and Flickr to your Office account to share information between the service and Office.

- To access your Office documents from almost any computer or device, the files need to be stored in a cloud service such as SharePoint Online or SkyDrive.

- Co-authoring is supported in Excel Web App, OneNote, OneNote Web App, PowerPoint, PowerPoint Web App, Word, and Word Web App.

- To start a co-authoring session, the Office document or notebook must be stored in a cloud service such as SharePoint Online or SkyDrive and shared with your co-authors.

3

Chapter at a glance

Get

Get comfortable with Office on a tablet,
page 103

Use

Use touch mode,
page 105

Select

Select content with touch,
page 108

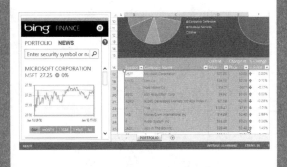

Work

Work with ink in Office,
page 110

Using touch in Office 4

IN THIS CHAPTER, YOU WILL LEARN HOW TO

- Get comfortable with Office on a tablet.
- Use touch mode.
- Select content with touch.
- Work with ink in Office.

One of the biggest enhancements made to Microsoft Office Professional 2013 is the addition of touch mode. Though you can use previous versions of Office on a touch-enabled device, the previous Office applications didn't include features that optimized touch input and focused more on using inking features, such as annotating files in your own handwriting. The new touch mode and better gesture support makes using touch in Office as easy as using a mouse and a keyboard.

In this chapter, you'll get an overview of using Office Professional 2013 on a tablet, such as Microsoft Surface. You'll learn how to adapt the exercises in this book to touch gestures, and how to select text and multiple objects. At the end of this chapter, you'll use inking tools.

PRACTICE FILES You don't need any practice files to complete the exercise in this chapter.

Getting comfortable with Office on a tablet

For using Office on a tablet, two editions of Windows 8 are available. The tablet edition of Windows 8, called *Windows RT*, comes with Microsoft Office Home & Student 2013 RT, which includes Microsoft Word 2013 RT, PowerPoint 2013 RT, Excel 2013 RT, and OneNote 2013 RT. Tablets that support the full edition of Windows 8, such as Surface with Windows 8 Pro, also support the installation of a full edition of Office, such as Microsoft Office Professional 2013.

Regardless of the edition you're using, using Office on a tablet isn't too different from using Office on your desktop or laptop computer. In fact, the user interface and your Office files look almost identical when viewed on a tablet device.

Looking at unsupported features

If you're using a tablet that has the Office Home & Student 2013 RT edition preinstalled, it's important to note that it doesn't have all of the same features as the full editions of Office. This is primarily due to security and mobility requirements. The following is a list of the primary unsupported features, along with any available workarounds.

- **Macros and add-ins** Programs created in Microsoft Visual Basic for Applications (VBA) to automate various tasks or to add additional functionality to an application are not supported. Developers are creating apps for Office, available from the Microsoft Office Store, as an alternative.

  TIP You can find available apps for Office on the Insert tab, in the Apps group. Additionally, some of the templates created for Office Professional 2013 also include apps, such as the Bing Finance app, which is included in the Financial Portfolio online template for Microsoft Excel.

- **Email features** Emailing from inside an application isn't supported, because Microsoft Outlook and other desktop email applications aren't supported on Windows RT. These commands include the **Email** options on the **Share** page in the **Backstage** view and email-related commands on the ribbon. The commands are still present in the user interface, but they are either unavailable or result in an error message when you try to use them. An alternative is to create a new email message by using the Windows RT email app, or another email app from the Windows Store, and manually attach your documents or links.

- **Flash video and recording narrations in PowerPoint** Inserting or playing back Flash videos isn't supported, and you can't record audio narrations. However, presentations that already include audio narrations will still play correctly.

- **Audio and video recordings and inserting from a scanner in OneNote** Recording and scanning through OneNote isn't supported, but you can use other third-party software for these types of content and then insert the file into a OneNote page.

4

TIP Tablets that support the full version of Windows 8 and Office, such as Surface with Windows 8 Pro, will support the items in this list.

Using touch mode

The primary difference with using touch mode in Office is that the user interface is optimized for touch commands. When touch is enabled, the user interface increases in size, and more space is added between the buttons on the ribbon and Quick Access Toolbar.

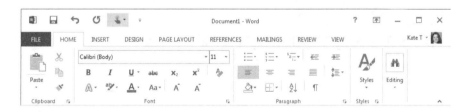

TIP To enable or disable touch mode, tap the Touch Mode button on the Quick Access Toolbar. When you enable or disable touch mode, it takes effect across the Office applications. If the Touch Mode button isn't visible, tap the arrow at the end of the Quick Access Toolbar, and then in the Customize Quick Access Toolbar list, tap Touch Mode.

You can work through the majority of the exercises provided in this book by using touch input and gestures, if you opt to use them instead of keyboard and mouse input. The following list provides the primary methods you can use to adapt the exercises to touch, along with additional touch tips.

- Substitute tap or double-tap for click and double-click.

- To right-click, press and hold until the shortcut menu is displayed. One exception to this is for spelling errors that appear in most applications that check your spelling as you type. When you tap a word to correct a spelling error, the list of spelling suggestions is displayed at the same time.

TIP To correct grammar errors as you type, or in OneNote, to correct spelling errors, press and hold to right-click and then tap the arrow at the end of the Mini Toolbar to display a list of suggestions.

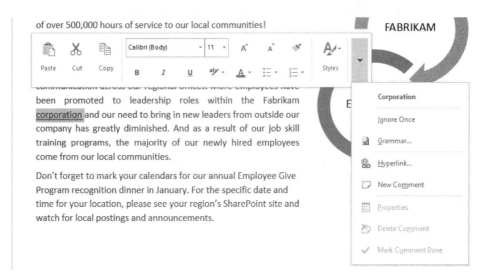

- To enter information, you can type on a keyboard or tap the on-screen keyboard. You can also use voice or handwriting recognition if your device supports these capabilities. Additionally, many of the applications, such as Word and PowerPoint, offer word completion when you enter text by using the on-screen keyboard. When the correct suggested word is displayed, tap the suggestion to insert it.

  TIP The word completion feature may not be supported, depending on the device you are using.

- To move the cursor or in Excel, the cell pointer, tap the desired location on the screen. Depending on your device, after you tap to move the cursor, the on-screen keyboard may appear. If you're not entering text, you can tap the **X** in the upper-right corner of the on-screen keyboard to dismiss it. If the on-screen keyboard doesn't appear, tap the keyboard icon located in the Windows Taskbar.

- To scroll, swipe your finger up, down, left, or right, in the direction you want to navigate.

- To zoom in by using pinch gestures, use two fingers and stretch them apart. To zoom out, pinch your fingers together. You can use more than two fingers to pinch and stretch, but using only two fingers typically produces the best results.

- To move or resize an object, such as a shape, tap it once to select it and then drag it to another location, or drag a sizing handle to change its size.

Additionally, some features may work a little differently when you are using touch. For example, when you insert a shape, the shape you tap is inserted directly into your file in a predetermined size, rather than drawn with the mouse. The majority of the differences are minor and you may need to modify your steps slightly, but they shouldn't prevent you from completing a task by using touch.

If you're having difficulty adapting an exercise, you can use a mouse instead. For example, if you use your mouse to select a shape instead of tapping it, you can draw it the same way you would do it on a non-touch enabled device.

Selecting content with touch

Selecting content by using touch is similar to using the mouse. The main difference is that your finger or stylus is your mouse pointer, and you drag it on the screen. First, you tap to start your selection, and then you drag the selection handle below the cursor, called a *gripper*, through the area you want to select. In Excel, the active cell has grippers in the upper-left and lower-right corners, and you can drag either of them to select a range. When text or a cell range in Excel is selected, grippers are displayed at the beginning and end of the selection, and you can use them to adjust your selection at any time.

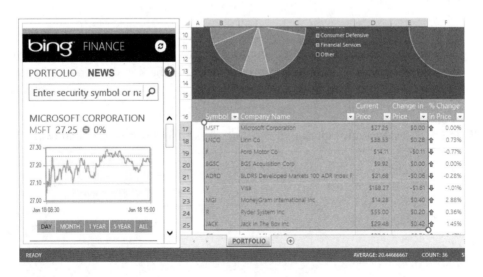

To remove a selection, tap in an area that's not part of your selection.

To select multiple objects by using touch, such as shapes or pictures, keep your finger on one object and then use another finger to tap each object you want to include in your selection. Note that not all applications support this selection method, and that you can also hold the Shift key on the keyboard and tap each object you want to select.

TIP In PowerPoint, you can select multiple slides in the Slides pane or in the Slide Sorter view by dragging them slightly to the right.

When you are working with dialog boxes, such as the Insert Picture dialog box, to select multiple files, tap the check boxes that appear in the upper-left corner for each file you want to select.

Working with ink in Office

When Office is installed on a device that supports ink, tools for inking are enabled. In Word, Excel, and PowerPoint, the Start Inking button is located at the end of the Review tab, in the Ink group.

TIP Using ink isn't the same as using handwriting recognition, which converts your handwriting to digital text characters as you write.

After you tap the Start Inking button, the Ink Tools Pens tool tab is displayed on the ribbon. Prior to inking, you can choose a different pen style, color, or pen thickness. Then, use your finger or stylus on the screen to add inked handwriting or drawings in your file.

TIP In OneNote, the inking tools are located on the Drawing tab, and you don't need to use a Start Inking command in order to use them. You start inking by selecting a pen style. Additionally, the ink tools in OneNote are also enabled on devices that don't support touch, because you can also use a mouse to add ink.

The following list provides a few ways you can incorporate ink in your Office files:

- Add drawings and handwritten annotations.
- If your touch device supports the full version of Office, you can send handwritten email messages in Outlook.
- Add handwritten comments in Word while reviewing a document.

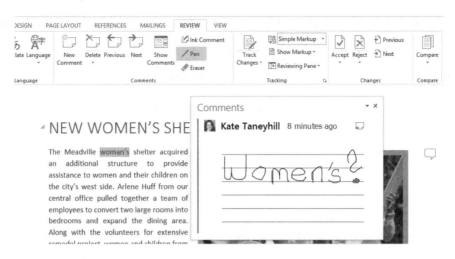

TIP To add a handwritten comment, on the Review tab, in the Comments group, tap the Ink Comment button.

- In PowerPoint, notate slides while creating your presentation or while presenting it on-screen.

- In OneNote, use handwriting to capture your notes during a meeting or sketch your ideas to capture them.

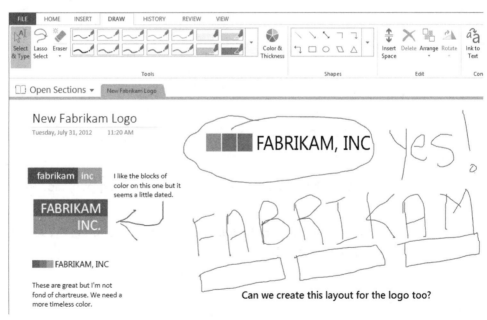

The available ink tools also include commands to select your inked handwriting or drawings as well as an eraser to remove them. Additional inking tools vary across the Office applications. For example, in PowerPoint, you can convert your drawings to shapes as you draw them in ink. In OneNote, you can convert your handwriting to text.

In this exercise, you'll convert an inked drawing to a shape in PowerPoint, move the converted shape, and resize it by using touch.

 SET UP You don't need any practice files to complete this exercise. Start PowerPoint, create a blank presentation, and then follow the steps.

1. To change the layout to a blank slide, on the **Home** tab, in the **Slides** group, tap **Layout**, and then tap **Blank** in the gallery.

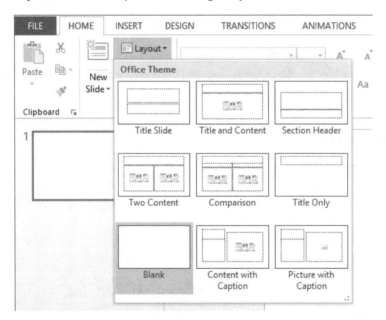

2. To activate the ink tools, on the **Review** tab, in the **Ink** group, tap the **Start Inking** button.

3. Before drawing a shape, on the **Ink Tools Pen** tool tab, in the **Ink Art** group, tap the **Convert to Shapes** button.

4   Using your finger or stylus, draw a rectangle on the slide.

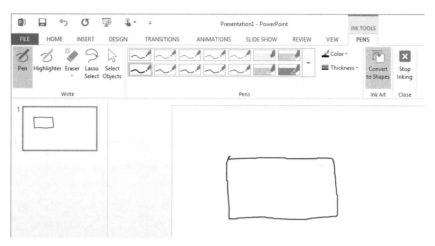

5   Lift your finger off the screen after the drawing is complete. The inked rectangle is converted to a shape.

6   To move the converted shape, on the **Ink Tools Pens** tool tab, in the **Write** group, tap the **Select Objects** button.

7   Tap the border of the converted rectangle to select it.

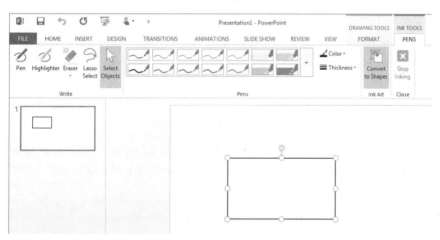

8   Place your finger or stylus on the border of the rectangle between the sizing handles and drag to move it.

9   To change the size, place your finger or stylus on the sizing handle in the lower-right corner and drag to resize the rectangle.

> **TIP** To format the shape, use the commands on the Drawing Tools Format tool tab, which is displayed when a shape is selected.

 CLEAN UP **Close the presentation without saving changes, and exit PowerPoint.**

Key points

- The tablet edition of Windows 8, called *Windows RT*, includes Microsoft Office Home & Student 2013 RT.

- The Office Home & Student 2013 RT edition doesn't support all features available in the full edition of Office.

- Tablets that support the full edition of Windows 8, such as Surface with Windows 8 Pro, also support the installation of a full edition of Office, such as Microsoft Office Professional 2013.

- To adapt the exercises in this book to touch gestures, substitute tap for click and double-tap for double-click. To right-click, press and hold, and to scroll, swipe the screen in the direction you wish to navigate.

- You can add handwritten comments in Word, convert handwriting to text in OneNote, and convert ink drawings to shapes in PowerPoint.

- Using ink in Office applications isn't the same as using handwriting recognition, which converts your handwriting to digital text characters as you write.

Chapter at a glance

Modify

Modify your document view,
page 121

Change

Change other view options,
page 124

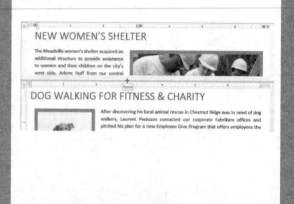

Discover

Discover what's new in Word 2013,
page 125

Getting comfortable in Word 2013

5

IN THIS CHAPTER, YOU WILL LEARN HOW TO

- Explore the Word 2013 user interface.

- Modify your document view.

- Change other view options.

- Discover what's new in Word 2013.

Microsoft Word 2013 is a word processing application that you can use for a wide range of tasks. You can create basic documents, such as letters, memos, reports, forms, newsletters, envelopes, labels, contracts, and more. And you can use Word for more complex documents, like a book or report that includes a table of contents, figures, indexes, footnotes, endnotes, and cross-references.

Whether your document is simple or complex, this part of the book provides you with the foundation for all of your document needs—from creating, formatting, layout, and pagination essentials to preparing your document for print, sharing, or exporting.

In this chapter, you'll get familiar with the Word 2013 user interface and learn how to modify your document view options so they're more suited to your specific work flow. And at the end of this chapter, you'll get an overview of the key new and improved features for Word 2013.

Exploring the Word 2013 user interface

You typically start Microsoft Word 2013 from the Start screen in Windows 8 or the Start menu in Windows 7. You can also start Word 2013 and open a file at the same time by opening a document from an email attachment or by double-clicking a document from a place like your desktop.

TIP If you have Windows set to view file extensions, the primary file extension for Word documents is .docx. Windows associates a file extension with an application, which enables you to open a document and start Word at the same time.

When you start Word without opening a file, the new Word Start screen appears.

From the Start screen, you can open a recent document, open an existing document, or create a new one from a template.

TIP If you haven't previously used Word 2013, the Recent documents list on the Start screen may appear empty.

After you create or open a document, the main window is displayed with a blank document along with the tools for working with the content of a document, such as the ribbon and Quick Access Toolbar.

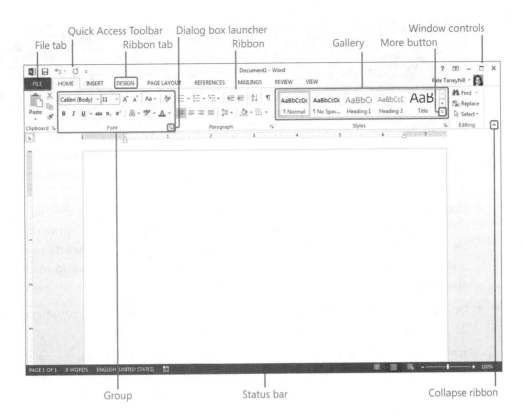

Quick Access Toolbar | Dialog box launcher | Window controls
File tab | Ribbon tab | Ribbon | Gallery | More button
Group | Status bar | Collapse ribbon

- **Ribbon** The ribbon is the main component of the Word interface and where you'll find the primary commands for working with the content of your documents. The ribbon is comprised of task-oriented tabs and each tab has groups of related commands. For example, on the **Home** tab, the **Clipboard** group contains commands for copying and pasting information in your Word documents. Groups that have additional commands that aren't shown on the ribbon have a dialog box launcher. Clicking the dialog box launcher will display a task pane or dialog box with options that are related to the group. For example, if you click the dialog box launcher for the **Font** group, the **Font** dialog box will be displayed, giving you more formatting choices such as **Strikethrough**, **Superscript**, and **Subscript**.

SEE ALSO For instructions on how to modify your display settings and adapt exercise instructions, see Chapter 1, "Getting comfortable in Office Professional 2013."

- **File tab** This is the first tab on the ribbon. Unlike other ribbon tabs, the **File** tab displays the **Backstage** view where commands for working with the entire document, such as **Save As**, **Print**, **Share**, and **Export**, are located. The **Backstage** view is also where application options are located and where you can find information about your user account and your version of Office.

- **Quick Access Toolbar** This toolbar holds your most frequently used commands. By default, **Save**, **Undo**, and **Redo** have already been added.

  TIP To add other commands to your Quick Access Toolbar, right-click the command you want and then click Add To Quick Access Toolbar. To remove a command from the Quick Access Toolbar, similar to adding a command, just right-click the command you wish to remove and then click Remove From Quick Access Toolbar.

- **Title bar** This bar is located at the top of the window, and it displays the name of the active document along with the application name. If you're working with a document that hasn't been saved, a name such as *Document1—Word* is displayed. After the document has been saved, the title bar will reflect the name of the saved document.

- **Window controls** These controls are displayed at the right end of the title bar. Along with the standard **Minimize**, **Restore Down/Maximize**, and **Close** buttons, there are two additional buttons—**Help** and **Ribbon Display Options**.

  TIP To minimize the ribbon, you can use the Ribbon Display Options, click the Collapse Ribbon button located on the far right end of the ribbon, or press Shift+F1.

- **Status bar** The status bar is located at the bottom of the window and displays information about the current document, such as the page and word count. On the far right end of the status bar are the viewing options for switching your document to a different view, along with a zoom slider to change the magnification of your active document.

SEE ALSO For a more comprehensive list of ribbon and user interface elements, along with detailed instructions on how to customize your user interface, including the ribbon and Quick Access Toolbar, see Chapter 1, "Getting comfortable in Office Professional 2013."

Modifying your document view

You can modify how Word displays a document on your screen by changing the document view and zoom level on the View tab.

Word 2013 has five main document views:

- **Read Mode** The new **Read Mode** is optimized for reading and hides the ribbon and other elements that aren't specific to reading a document. Unlike the **Full Screen Reading** view in earlier versions of Word, **Read Mode** allows you to zoom in on objects, like pictures and charts, and adjust the column layout. This view is also the default view when you open a document from an Internet source, such as an email attachment.

    SEE ALSO For more information on using Read Mode, see Chapter 6, "Navigating and reading documents."

- **Print Layout** This is the default view for Word 2013. In this view, your document looks almost identical to how it will look when it's printed. All page margins and other elements of your document are displayed, such as multiple columns, tables, graphics, headers, and footers.

TIP To toggle the view of the top and bottom page margins along with any headers and footers in Print Layout view, place your mouse pointer between two pages and double-click to suppress the white space. To redisplay the white space, double-click the line that divides the pages.

- **Web Layout** This view is used when creating a webpage or a blog post. Similar to viewing a webpage, text will wrap to the size of your window and zoom setting, rather than page margins. Objects like pictures and charts will align differently than in other views and will appear as they will be displayed when viewed in a web browser.

- **Outline view** The **Outline** view shows the document's organization according to paragraphs that have been formatted with a heading style, such as **Heading 1**, **Heading 2**, and **Heading 3**. In **Outline** view, you can choose to show only specific heading levels and quickly rearrange entire sections of your document by dragging a collapsed section to another location.

- **Draft view** Formerly known as **Normal** view in earlier versions of Word, **Draft** view is similar to the old **Normal** view, because it displays the page margins and headers; the footers are suppressed. However, **Draft** view also suppresses the view of objects, such as pictures and charts, and multi-column layouts are displayed as a single column.

In the Zoom group, the majority of the options are fairly self-explanatory, such as setting your zoom to 100% or choosing whether you want to view a single page or multiple pages. Of the zoom options, the Page Width command is one that may need a little more explanation. When you click Page Width, your document is scaled to fit the width of the available document space. The available space for your document is determined by the size of your application window and any task panes you have displayed. For example, if you're using a wide screen monitor and do not have any task panes open, your zoom level may increase to 154%. But if your application window is restored and the Clipboard task pane is open, your zoom level may decrease to 80%.

You can also switch to Read Mode, Print Layout, or Web Layout and set your zoom level in the lower-right corner of the status bar.

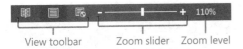

View toolbar   Zoom slider   Zoom level

To increase or decrease your zoom level, drag the slider or click the plus and minus icons. You can also click the Zoom Level button to display the Zoom dialog box, which lets you set several zoom options at the same time.

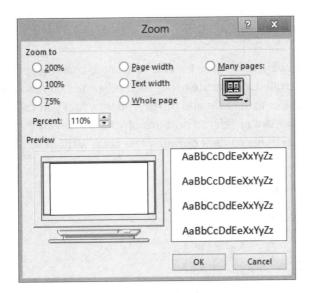

With the exception of the Draft and Outline views, your last view and zoom level will be saved with your document. If you save and close a document in Draft or Outline view, the document will reopen in Print Layout view. Additionally, new documents you create will inherit your last zoom setting.

TIP To enable documents to be opened in Draft view, click the File tab to display the Backstage view, and then click Options. On the Advanced page, scroll to the bottom of the options to the General section, and then select Allow Opening A Document In Draft View. Note that this is an application option, which means it isn't saved with the document. If you send your document to someone else, whether it opens in Draft view depends on their settings.

IMPORTANT

Changing other view options

You can modify your document's view by turning on the ruler display or splitting your screen into two panes that can be scrolled independently of each other. You can use the ruler to view or modify page margins or to set tabs and modify indents. And you can split a document window if you want to compare or refer to portions of your document that aren't located beside each other, or you can move content between two areas without scrolling back and forth.

Both of these options are also on the View tab.

To toggle the ruler view, on the View tab, in the Show group, select the check box for Ruler.

To split your document window, on the View tab, click Split. After you click Split, the name of the command changes to Remove Split. Your document window will be split into two equal panes. Initially, the split will appear on your current page. Scroll the contents in either pane to view different areas of your document. If you prefer a larger top or bottom pane, you can drag the splitter to resize them.

To remove the split view, click Remove Split, drag the splitter to the top or bottom of your document window, or double-click the splitter.

TIP In earlier versions of Word, a toggle for showing and hiding the ruler and the ability to split the window were located above the horizontal scrollbar. These options are no longer available in Word 2013. If you frequently use these commands, you can add them to your Quick Access Toolbar. To do so, right-click the command in the ribbon and then click Add To Quick Access Toolbar.

SEE ALSO For more information on how to customize your Quick Access Toolbar, see Chapter 1, "Getting comfortable in Office Professional 2013."

Discovering what's new in Word 2013

This section introduces you to key new and improved features for Word 2013 along with screenshots where applicable. The majority of the features included are discussed in detail along with step-by-step instructions throughout this part of the book.

- **Read Mode** In **Read Mode**, commands that aren't essential for reading are hidden from view and text is reflowed in columns to fit the available screen. While in **Read Mode**, you can right-click or double-click objects, like tables, charts, and images, to zoom in and view the details.

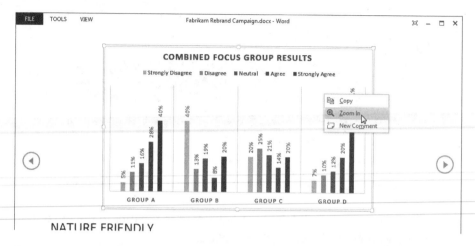

- **Resume reading** When you close a document, Word creates a bookmark of the last location where you were working inside the document. When you reopen a document, click the resume reading notification to pick up right where you left off.

- **PDF Reflow** Now you can open and convert PDF files in Word for editing. With PDF Reflow, tables, headers, footers, footnotes, and lists are all converted into editable content.

- **One-click table row/column insertion** Insert new rows and columns without the need to visit the ribbon or use a shortcut menu. Point to the left of the table between two rows or above the table between two columns. Watch for the on-screen insertion indicator to appear, and then click the indicator to insert a new row or column.

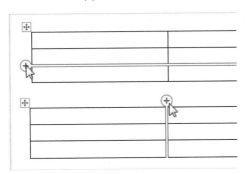

- **Table Border tools** The new **Border Styles** gallery provides you with a variety of border formatting choices that are coordinated to match the current theme. After you make a selection from the gallery, you use the new **Border Painter** to apply, or "paint" the border formatting on your tables. With the new **Border Sampler**, you can transfer existing border formatting to the **Border Painter** for reuse.

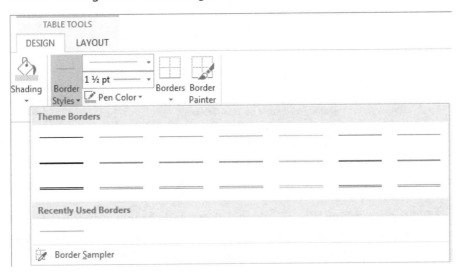

5

- **Collapsible headings** While editing or reading a document, you can expand or collapse paragraphs that are formatted with a **Heading** style. When a heading is collapsed, all of the content that's associated with it is hidden from view. Large documents can be collapsed to a summary view for faster navigation.

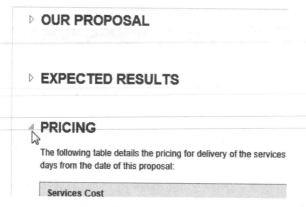

- **Threaded comments** When multiple people review a document, they can reply to each other's comments and check them off as they're completed. With the new comment indicator, you can click to show or hide a specific set of comments.

- **Simple markup** When working with tracked changes, simple markup reduces the view of revisions in your documents. Clicking a revision mark will toggle the display of all changes, making it easier to switch between a clean and marked-up view.

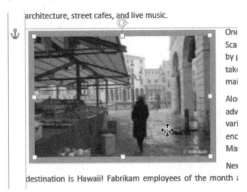

- **Alignment guides and Live Layout** New alignment guides help you visually align objects, like pictures, shapes, and diagrams, to paragraphs and page margins. With **Live Layout**, now you can view the exact placement of a photo, video, or shape as you drag it into position in a document.

- **Layout Options** When you select an image, shape, or SmartArt graphic, the **Layout Options** button will appear. Clicking the button displays layout options, such as text-wrapping choices, along with a link to view more advanced layout options.

- **Design tab** The new **Design** tab contains commands for setting default formatting for your documents. Now you can change a document's theme, colors, fonts, paragraph spacing, and more from a single place. And the new **Style Sets** gallery enables you to quickly change the collection of styles that are displayed on the **Home** tab in the **Styles** gallery.

- **Building Blocks** New cover page, header, and footer building blocks have been added to help you create coordinating documents across the applications. For example, find new cover pages along with headers and footers that match the **Ion** slide design in Microsoft PowerPoint.

- **File Format** The Word file format has been updated to accommodate page layout improvements. Along with improvements for graphics, text wrapping, and pagination, the most noticeable change is to table layout. In earlier versions of Word, the text in a table aligned to text outside of the table. In Word 2013, the table borders, rather than the text in the table, now align to the surrounding text.

Nature Friendly Products

All new buildings will be constructed with nature such as those in the following list:

Sustainable products
• Bamboo
• Rattan
• FSC certified wood

Other materials
• Recycled

Past versions of Word

Nature Friendly Products

All new buildings will be constructed with nature such as those in the following list:

Sustainable products
• Bamboo
• Rattan
• FSC certified wood

Other materials
• Recycled

Word 2013

SEE ALSO For more information on the layout changes in Word 2013, see *www.support. microsoft.com/kb/2740483.*

When should I use Microsoft Publisher instead of Word?

Microsoft Publisher is an application designed for creating documents that require a specific layout like brochures, greeting cards, and newsletters. Word also has publishing capabilities, and online templates are available to help you create these types of documents. With the improved layout engine and new graphic features, you'll get more predictable layout results in this version of Word.

However, if your document has an intricate layout, like a multi-column newsletter with graphics, pull quotes, and continuation text, you might discover that Publisher can produce better results with less effort. This doesn't mean that Word can't be used for this type of task, but it will be much easier if you can simplify the layout.

To help give you a better understanding of a simplified layout compared to an intricate one, we've used the same newsletter content in a practice file for both the Word and Publisher parts of this book so that you can use it for comparison.

SEE ALSO For more information on how to choose the best application for a specific task, see Chapter 1, "Getting comfortable in Office Professional 2013."

5

What happens to documents created in an earlier version of Word?

Documents created in an earlier version of Word will open in compatibility mode in Word 2013 and [Compatibility Mode] will be displayed to the right of the file name in the title bar. This mode will maintain the previous file format and layout. To convert the document to the new file format, click the File tab and then on the Info page, click the Convert button.

However, if you have a document that contains tables, graphics, multiple columns, or a more complex layout, it's recommended that you create a backup copy of your document prior to converting it, or choose to not convert the document and continue to use compatibility mode.

SEE ALSO For more information on sharing documents that you create in Word 2013 with an earlier version of Word, see Chapter 10, "Finalizing documents."

Key points

- You start Word 2013 from the Start screen in Windows 8 or the Start menu in Windows 7.

- The ribbon is made up of task-oriented tabs for working with your document's content.

- Use the View tab to change your document's view, modify your zoom settings, turn on the ruler display, or split your screen.

- With the exception of the Draft and Outline views, your last view and zoom level will be saved with your document.

- New documents will inherit your last zoom setting.

- You can also modify your zoom settings and switch to the Read Mode, Print Layout, and Web Layout views in the status bar on the View toolbar.

5

Chapter at a glance

Move

Move around in documents by using the keyboard and mouse, page 136

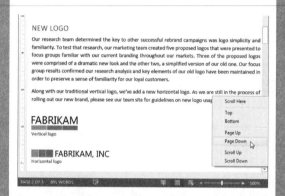

Search

Search documents by using the navigation pane, page 137

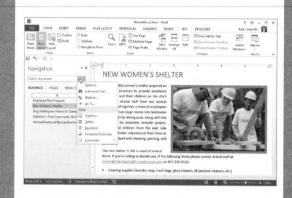

Collapse

Collapse and expand document content, page 143

Read

Read documents in Read Mode, page 146

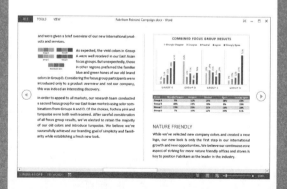

Navigating and reading documents

IN THIS CHAPTER, YOU WILL LEARN HOW TO

- Navigate a document by scrolling and using keyboard shortcuts.

- Search and navigate a document by using the Navigation pane.

- Collapse and expand document content.

- Work with documents in the new Read Mode.

- Explore research tools in Read Mode.

In the previous chapter, you were introduced to various ways of viewing a document, such as switching to Read Mode, viewing options, and turning on the ruler display. In this chapter, you'll learn more methods for navigating documents that range from scrolling to using the Navigation pane. You'll also learn about new features that have been added, such as collapsing and expanding document content for quick navigation. In addition, you'll learn how to use the new Read Mode and research tools.

PRACTICE FILES To complete the exercises in this chapter, you need the practice files contained in the Chapter06 practice file folder. For more information, see "Download the practice files" in this book's Introduction.

Navigating a document by scrolling and using keyboard shortcuts

The most common method for document navigation is scrolling, which is achieved by using the scroll bars, the mouse wheel, or the scroll area on a touchpad. You can also use keyboard shortcuts to navigate, which also moves the cursor. When using the scroll bars to navigate in a document, you need to click the mouse to position your cursor at your desired location.

TIP In Microsoft Word 2013, the scroll bars will disappear from view after a few seconds of mouse inactivity or when you begin entering text. They will reappear after you move your mouse.

The size of a scroll box is related to the size of the document—the smaller the scroll box, the larger the document. Additionally, the position of the scroll box in the scroll bar indicates where you are in a document.

Use the following methods for scrolling by using the vertical scroll bar. Keyboard shortcuts that produce the same or a similar action follow each item in the list.

- Click above or below the scroll box to scroll one screen forward or backward.

  KEYBOARD SHORTCUT Press Page Up or Page Down.

- Click the arrows on the scroll bar to scroll one line at time.

  KEYBOARD SHORTCUT Press the Up Arrow or Down Arrow key.

- Drag the scroll box to scroll a greater distance forward or backward.

  KEYBOARD SHORTCUT Press Ctrl+Home to move to the beginning of the document and press Ctrl+End to move to the end of the document.

- Right-click the scroll bar to display a list of scrolling options. For example, if you want to scroll down one page, click the **Page Down** command.

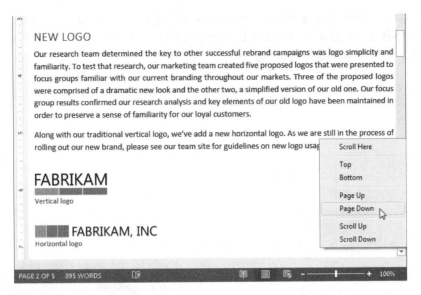

NEW LOGO

Our research team determined the key to other successful rebrand campaigns was logo simplicity and familiarity. To test that research, our marketing team created five proposed logos that were presented to focus groups familiar with our current branding throughout our markets. Three of the proposed logos were comprised of a dramatic new look and the other two, a simplified version of our old one. Our focus group results confirmed our research analysis and key elements of our old logo have been maintained in order to preserve a sense of familiarity for our loyal customers.

Along with our traditional vertical logo, we've add a new horizontal logo. As we are still in the process of rolling out our new brand, please see our team site for guidelines on new logo usag

FABRIKAM
Vertical logo

FABRIKAM, INC
Horizontal logo

PAGE 2 OF 5   895 WORDS   100%

TIP The Scroll Here command that appears when you right-click the scroll bar will scroll the document relative to the location at which you right-clicked. For example, if you right-click at the top of the scroll bar and then click Scroll Here, you'll scroll to the top of the document. Additionally, scrolling by using the horizontal scroll bar is similar to scrolling with the vertical scroll bar, but you move left and right instead of up and down.

When you are using a mouse wheel or scroll area on a touchpad, the number of lines you scroll, or whether you scroll a full screen of text, is dependent on the wheel settings for your mouse or touchpad as set in the Mouse Properties of the Control Panel.

Searching and navigating a document by using the Navigation pane

Another way to navigate a document is to use the Navigation pane. Unlike scrolling, using the Navigation pane navigates based on the content of your document, such as a search term, heading, graphic, or table, rather than by screens or lines.

The Navigation pane is accessed on the View tab, in the Show group. To view other navigation methods or search options, click the magnifying glass displayed on the right side of the Search box on the Navigation pane.

TIP You can also click the page number on the left end of the status bar to toggle the view of the Navigation pane.

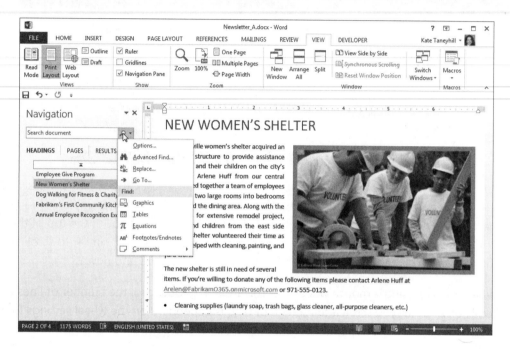

The following options are initially displayed in the Navigation pane:

- **Search document** Enter a search term in the **Search** box. Yellow highlighted results are shown in both the document and the **Navigation** pane as you enter the text. To jump between search results, click the **Next** and **Previous** buttons below the **Search** box.

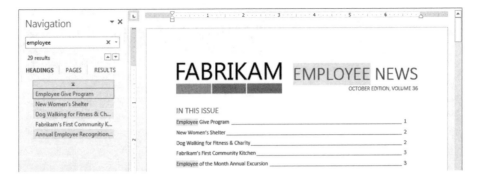

TIP The Next and Previous buttons will cycle through the entire document. For example, if you're at the beginning of the document and click Previous, you'll jump to the last search result in the document.

- **Headings** The **Headings** section provides a clickable mini table of contents. The text that appears in the **Navigation** pane corresponds to paragraphs that are formatted with heading styles that are used to outline a document. To jump to a different heading in a document, click the corresponding heading.

  When you are searching a document, the headings in the Navigation pane will also be displayed with a yellow highlight, indicating that the search term can be found below the heading. You can click a highlighted heading to jump to that location in the document and then use the Next button to find your search term below the heading.

  TIP The heading for the current cursor location in a document will have a blue highlight. When you are searching a document, if your current location heading is included in the search results, it will be displayed with an outline and blue font color.

  SEE ALSO For more information about formatting a document by using heading styles, see Chapter 8, "Formatting documents."

- **Pages** The pages feature displays a thumbnail of each page in the document. Click a thumbnail to navigate to that page.

  When you are searching for a specific term or phrase in a document, the yellow highlighted search results will also be displayed on the page thumbnails.

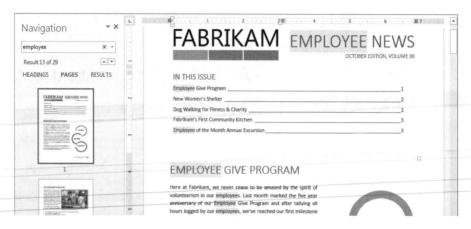

- **Results** This option displays a summary of search results with the term formatted in bold. As with the other **Navigation** pane views, you can click a search summary to jump to that location in the document.

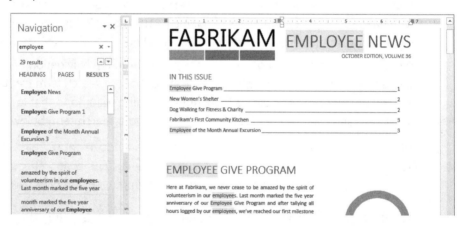

The other search options that are displayed when you click the magnifying glass to the right of the Search box, such as Advanced Find, Graphics, and Tables, work the same as searching for a term. You use the Next and Previous buttons below the Search box to jump between results or click a highlighted heading to jump to the general location. However, you won't find highlighted results or a summary of results when viewing Page or Results in the Navigation pane.

To clear the search results for both search terms and other search options, click the X that appears to the right of the Search box. The results will also be cleared when you close the Navigation pane.

In this exercise, you'll navigate a document by using the Navigation pane and then search for text and graphics.

→ SET UP You need the Newsletter_A document located in the Chapter06 practice file folder to complete this exercise. Open the Newsletter_A document and then follow the steps.

1   On the **View** tab, in the **Show** group, select the **Navigation Pane** check box.

    KEYBOARD SHORTCUT Press Ctrl+F.

2   On the **Navigation** pane, in the **Search** box, enter employee.

3   Note the total of 29 results that is displayed below the **Search** box and the first occurrence of the word **employee** in the document.

4   Below the **Search** box, click the **Next** button a few times to navigate to additional occurrences of the word **employee**.

    KEYBOARD SHORTCUT Click in the document and then press Ctrl+Page Down.

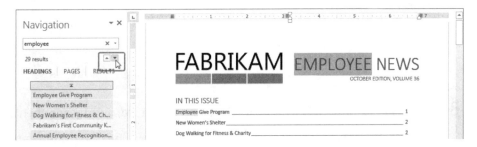

5   Click the **Previous** button to navigate to the previous occurrence of the word **employee**.

    KEYBOARD SHORTCUT Click in the document and then press Ctrl+Page Up.

6   On the **Navigation** pane, in the **Headings** section, click **Dog Walking for Fitness & Charity** to view the occurrences of the search term **employee** below that heading. Also note how only the exact letters you entered in the **Search** box are highlighted in the word **employees** rather than the entire word.

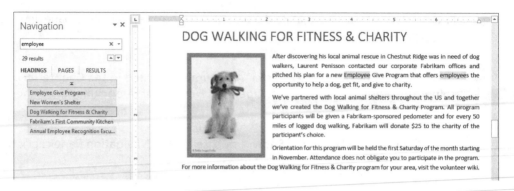

7   To specify that you want only whole words highlighted, on the **Navigation** pane, click the arrow at the end of the **Search** text box and then click **Options**.

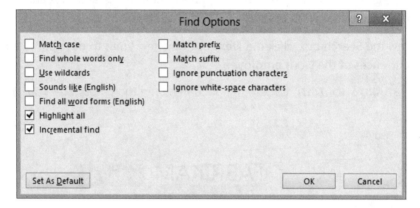

8   In the **Find Options** dialog box, select **Find whole words only** and then click **OK**.

    TIP Your changes in the Find Options dialog box will be reset to the defaults after you exit Word. To make your modifications the default settings, click the Set As Default button.

9   When you change the search settings, the results are cleared. Search for **employee** again and note there are now 14 total results instead of 29.

10   Click the **X** on the right side of the **Search** box to clear the results.

11   Press **Ctrl+Home** to navigate to the beginning of the document.

12   To navigate by graphics, on the **Navigation** pane, click the magnifying glass and then click **Graphics**.

13   Click the **Next** button to jump to the next graphic.

14   Clear the search results and move the cursor back to the beginning of the document.

15   Close the **Navigation** pane.

❌ CLEAN UP **Exit Word without saving changes to the document.**

Collapsing and expanding document content

As noted in the previous section, the headings in the Navigation pane are paragraphs that are formatted with heading styles that create outline levels in a document. For example, a paragraph formatted with Heading 1 is a first level paragraph. Heading 2 is a second level paragraph, or subheading, and so forth. Along with providing a quick way to jump to different locations from the Navigation pane, heading styles are also used to create a table of contents, to create chapter-style numbering, and more. In Word 2013, headings play an even greater role. Now you can collapse all content below a heading or quickly collapse an entire document and display only the first level headings, making it even easier to navigate within a document.

6

Expand button

FABRIKAM EMPLOYEE NEWS

OCTOBER EDITION, VOLUME 36

▷ EMPLOYEE GIVE PROGRAM

▷ NEW WOMEN'S SHELTER

▷ DOG WALKING FOR FITNESS & CHARITY

▷ FABRIKAM'S FIRST COMMUNITY KITCHEN

▷ ANNUAL EMPLOYEE RECOGNITION EXCURSION

TIP The title of the newsletter isn't included in the collapsed view, because the paragraphs formatted with heading styles begin after the title.

To collapse a heading, point to the left of a paragraph that has been formatted with a heading style, and then click the triangular collapse button that is displayed. When a heading is collapsed, the expand button will always show. Clicking the button will expand the content that appears below the heading.

If a document contains subheadings, there will be collapse and expand buttons in the Navigation pane as well. Clicking these buttons only affects the headings in the Navigation pane and not the document's contents.

In this exercise, you'll use the new collapse and expand capabilities of headings in both the document and the Navigation pane.

SET UP You need the Newsletter_B document located in the Chapter06 practice file folder to complete this exercise. Open the Newsletter_B document and then follow the steps.

1   In the document, point to the left of the heading **Employee Give Program** and click the collapse button.

▷ EMPLOYEE GIVE PROGRAM

NEW WOMEN'S SHELTER

The Meadville women's shelter acquired an additional structure to provide assistance to women and their children on the city's west side. Arlene Huff from our central office pulled together a team of employees to convert two large rooms into bedrooms

2   To expand the heading, click the expand button.

3   To quickly collapse the entire document and display only the first level headings, right-click the first heading, point to **Expand/Collapse**, and then click **Collapse All Headings**.

TIP Collapsing all headings is a quick way to display an outline view of your document for printing.

4   Expand the **Annual Employee Recognition Excursion** heading.

5   At the end of **Annual Employee Recognition Excursion**, expand the, **Next Year's Destination Is...** subheading.

6   To expand all headings, right-click a heading, point to **Expand/Collapse**, and then click **Expand All Headings**.

7   View the **Navigation** pane and, below **Annual Employee Recognition Excursion**, note the subheading **Next Year's Destination Is...**.

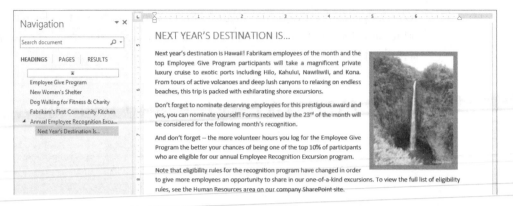

TIP Only the Annual Employee Recognition Excursion heading has the expand/collapse button in the Navigation pane, since it's the only heading that has a subheading.

8   In the **Navigation** pane, click the collapse button to the left of **Annual Employee Recognition Excursion** and note that the document content does not change.

9   Click the expand button to redisplay it.

10 Turn off the display of the **Navigation** pane.

✖ CLEAN UP **Exit Word without saving changes to the document.**

Working with documents in the new Read Mode

When you're viewing a document in Read Mode, the primary focus is placed on reading rather than how the document looks when printed. The size of text is increased and reflowed into columns that automatically adjust to fit the available space on your screen. The size of objects, such as charts, tables, and pictures, are decreased to fit the available column width. In addition, words are automatically hyphenated, the ribbon and Quick Access Toolbar are not displayed, and the available commands pertain to reading and commenting rather than editing.

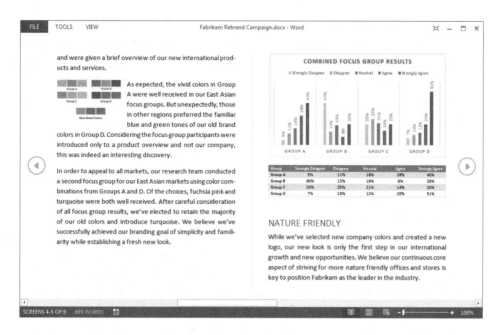

Although the focus is placed more on reading text than viewing objects, you can double-click an object to magnify it and zoom in on the details.

The following list provides the view options that are located on the View menu for Read Mode:

- **Edit Document** Closes **Read Mode** and returns to **Print Layout** view.

- **Show Comments** Displays review comments in the markup area on the right side of the screen.

- **Navigation Pane** Toggles the view of the **Navigation** pane. If you previously turned on the **Navigation** pane, it will automatically be displayed in **Read Mode**.

- **Column Width** This option changes the number of columns that will display the document's contents. If you're viewing multiple columns of text, called *screens*, a dividing line is displayed between them. To navigate to the next or previous set of screens, click the arrows on the far right and left side of the window.

There are three options for Column Width: Narrow, Default, and Wide. The narrower the column, the smaller the line of text on each screen. For both the Narrow and Default options, the number of viewable screens depends on your display settings, such as resolution, magnification, document zoom level, and the size of your document window. For example, if you select Narrow and you're using a small restored document window, the text may only appear on a single screen. Typically, when you choose Narrow, the information is displayed in three screens; Default displays two screens, and Wide displays the content in one screen.

TIP When using Read Mode on devices that automatically rotate the screen, such as Microsoft Surface, select either Narrow or Default. This will allow the columns to adjust to an optimal reading width when you rotate the device.

- **Page Color** There are three page color options: **None**, **Sepia**, and **Inverse**. Sepia uses a brown color scale instead of a black and white scale. If your page is white, the content will be displayed as a light pinkish-brown color. Inverse is similar to a photo negative. Dark colors become light and light colors are dark. If you're reading black text in a document with a white background, it will appear as a document with a black background with white text.

  TIP The inverse colors are dependent on your format settings, such as font color and paragraph or table shading rather than page color, which is located on the Design tab in the Page Background group.

- **Layout** This option toggles the document's content between **Column Layout** and **Paper Layout**. When using **Paper Layout**, the document view is similar to **Print Layout**, but the ribbon and Quick Access Toolbar are suppressed and editing is disabled. Additionally, column and page color modifications are not displayed.

In this exercise, you'll explore the available view options for Read Mode.

SET UP You need the Fabrikam Rebrand Campaign document located in the Chapter06 practice file folder to complete this exercise. Open the Fabrikam Rebrand Campaign document and then follow the steps.

1 If the practice file isn't already displayed in Read Mode, on the **View** tab, in the **Views** group, click the **Read Mode** button.

2 To advance to the next set of screens, click the arrow at the right side of the window.

   TIP The number of the current screens you're viewing and the total screen count are displayed on the left side of the status bar. Keep in mind that your status bar may not look the same as the ones in the screenshots due to your display settings.

3   To return to the previous screen, click the arrow on the left side of the window.

4   If the **Navigation** pane isn't displayed, click **View** and then click **Navigation Pane**.

5   In the **Navigation** pane, click **Brand Colors**.

6   In the document, click the collapse button to the left of **Brand Colors** to collapse the heading.

7   If the **Combined Focus Group Results** chart and table are not shown, below **Brand Colors**, use the horizontal scroll bar to scroll to the right.

8   To magnify the chart, double-click the chart.

   TIP Right-click the chart and then click Zoom In.

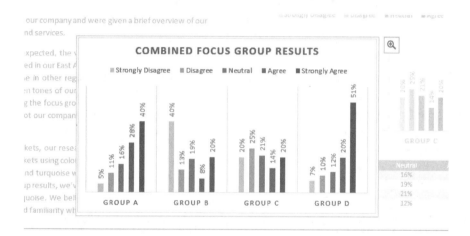

9   In the upper-right corner of the magnified chart, click the **magnifying glass** to increase the chart's magnification.

10   To close the magnified view, click away from the chart in the document window.

11   Double-click the table to increase its magnification and then close the magnified view.

12   To view a single screen of text, click the **View** menu, point to **Column Width**, and then click **Wide**.

13   To change the page color, click **View**, point to **Page Color**, and then click **Sepia**.

14   Repeat step 13 but change the page color to **Inverse**.

15   To view a layout that includes headers, footers, and page margins, click **View**, point to **Layout**, and then click **Paper Layout**.

16   Use the vertical scrollbar on the right side of the window to scroll through the document.

17   To return to a column layout, click **View**, point to **Layout**, and then click **Column Layout**.

18   Set the page color and column width to your preference.

19   Turn off the display of the **Navigation** pane.

20   To exit Read Mode, click **View** and then click **Edit Document**.

KEYBOARD SHORTCUT Press the Esc key to exit Read Mode.

❌ CLEAN UP **Exit Word without saving changes to the document.**

TIP When you open a document that originated from an Internet location, like an email attachment, it will be displayed in Read Mode by default. To bypass Read Mode for those documents, click the File tab to display the Backstage view, click Options, and then near the bottom of the General tab, clear the check box for Open Email Attachments And Other Uneditable Files In Reading View.

Exploring research tools in Read Mode

While reading a document, you may encounter words or phrases you're not familiar with or that you may want to find more information about on the Internet. Instead of reaching for a dictionary or opening a web browser, you can use the research tools available on the shortcut menu in Read Mode. To use these tools, right-click a word and then click Define, Translate, or Search With Bing.

FABRIKAM'S FIRST COMMUNITY KITCHEN

Greenville is set to launch our pilot Community Kitchen program starting in November. The first phase of the program is to offer low-cost healthy eating classes to the local community. The Eating for Health series is created to increase healthy food preparation skills and knowledge. Our goal is to involve the community in local and sustainable and start developing farm-to-table relationsl

When classes aren't in the kitchen will be av those in need of cor kitchen space certifie Health Department fi food-related business such as

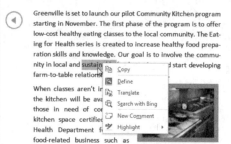

| Copy |
| Define |
| Translate |
| Search with Bing |
| New Comment |
| Highlight |

Phase two of our pilot community kitchen program is to develop a curriculum with volunteer chefs and offer culinary classes to help increase job skills within the community. The culinary program will also provide students with real-life experience working in a commercial kitchen. Students will plan and prepare meals that will be served in the community center and for organization fundraising events. Along with determining cost and nutrition analysis for each meal, students will also be responsible for cooking, expediting, and food service for each dinner. All dinner proceeds will benefit the culinary program.

IMPORTANT

Below is an overview of the research tools:

- **Define** This option searches for a word in an online dictionary and displays the results in a pop-up window. Along with a definition, most dictionaries include a list of synonyms and a verbal pronunciation of the word. To hear a verbal pronunciation of a search term in an online dictionary, click the speaker button displayed next to the word.

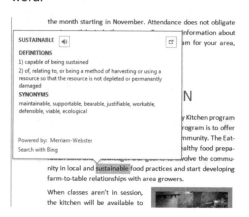

the month starting in November. Attendance does not obligate

SUSTAINABLE 🔊

DEFINITIONS
1) capable of being sustained
2) of, relating to, or being a method of harvesting or using a resource so that the resource is not depleted or permanently damaged

SYNONYMS
maintainable, supportable, bearable, justifiable, workable, defensible, viable, ecological

Powered by: Merriam-Webster
Search with Bing

nformation about am for your area,

y Kitchen program rogram is to offer mmunity. The Eat- ealthy food prepa-

nity in local and sustainable food practices and start developing farm-to-table relationships with area growers.

When classes aren't in session, the kitchen will be available to

initially provide kitchen space as a rental service but we hope this will change as we receive more donations to offset the overhead costs.

Phase two of our pilot community kitchen program is to develop a curriculum with volunteer chefs and offer culinary classes to help increase job skills within the community. The culinary program will also provide students with real-life experience working in a commercial kitchen. Students will plan and prepare meals that will be served in the community center and for organization fundraising events. Along with determining cost and nutrition analysis for each meal, students will also be responsible for cooking, expediting, and food service for each dinner. All dinner proceeds will benefit the culinary program.

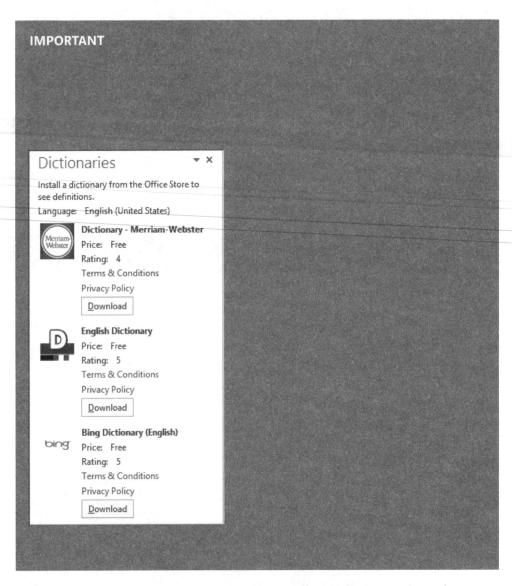

SEE ALSO For more information on signing in to Office and using a Microsoft account, see Chapter 3, "Sharing and collaborating."

- **Translate** When you want to translate a word into another language, this feature opens the **Research** pane with a translation of the word or selected sentence. While the pane is displayed, when you click another word or select another sentence, the word or phrase will be translated.

KEYBOARD SHORTCUT Press the Alt key and then click the word or selected phrase to translate it.

TIP Subsequent automatic translation may not occur on all devices. For example, when using Microsoft Surface, you may need to tap or click the Translate command each time you want to translate a word or selected sentence.

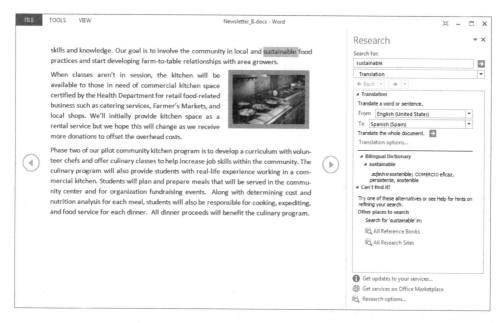

IMPORTANT

You can also obtain dictionary definitions and synonyms in the Research pane. To change from the translation option to another option, near the top of the pane, click Translation to display a list of choices.

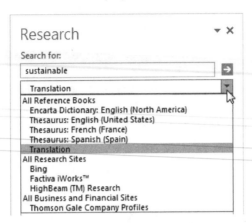

TIP A translation service provided by a computer only gives you a basic translation and does not change sentence structure or tone that might be required in order to convey meaningful information in another language. It's recommended that you use a human translation service for important or sensitive files.

- **Search with Bing** When you choose this option, a web browser opens and uses Bing as the web search engine to search and display results for the word or phrase you specified.

The research tools are also available when you right-click a word or phrase in the other document views, such as Print Layout. The Define and Translate commands are also located on the Review tab, along with Thesaurus. However, the results may be displayed differently in other views. For example, when you use the Define command, the results will be displayed in a Dictionary pane instead of a small window like you previously viewed in Read Mode.

Key points

- The most common document navigation method is scrolling.

- Heading styles are used to outline a document, to create a table of contents, and for viewing features, such as the Navigation pane.

- The Navigation pane can be used as a mini table of contents for documents that have paragraphs formatted with heading styles.

- With the Navigation pane, you can move through a document based on the content, such as a search term, heading, graphic, or table, rather than by screens or lines.

- You can click the arrow to the left of a heading paragraph to collapse and expand the content below the heading.

- The primary focus of Read Mode is to read a document rather than edit it or view how it will look when it is printed.

- Almost all editing commands are disabled when using Read Mode.

- Research tools, such as Define and Translate, are available when you right-click a word or selected phrase.

6

Chapter at a glance

Select

Select text by using the keyboard and mouse, page 158

Use

Use formatting marks during document composition, page 163

Name		Amount¶
Kim·Abercrombie	→	$11¶
Tomasz	→	$502¶
Cornelius	→	$66¶
Michiyo	→	$67¶

Insert

Insert symbols, international characters, and other special characters, page 167

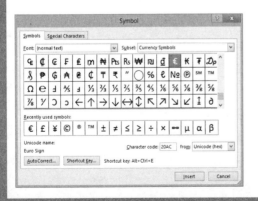

Compose

Compose documents faster by using building blocks, page 178

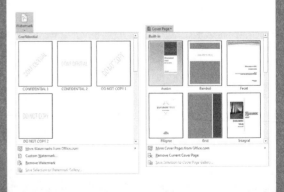

Editing and composing documents

7

IN THIS CHAPTER, YOU WILL LEARN HOW TO

- Move the cursor by using keyboard shortcuts.

- Select text by using the keyboard and mouse.

- Use formatting marks during document composition.

- Insert symbols, international characters, and other special characters.

- Use AutoCorrect.

- Compose documents faster by using building blocks.

In this chapter, you'll learn basic editing techniques, such as using the keyboard to quickly move between sentences or paragraphs, along with text selection methods. You'll also learn document composition essentials and how to insert symbols, international characters, and other special characters. At the end of this chapter, you'll learn how to compose documents by using building blocks to insert frequently used information and save valuable time.

PRACTICE FILES To complete the exercises in this chapter, you need the practice files contained in the Chapter07 practice file folder. For more information, see "Download the practice files" in this book's Introduction.

Moving the cursor by using keyboard shortcuts

The first step in editing a document is to move the cursor to the location where you want to make a change. If you're using the mouse, click the left (primary) mouse button to position the cursor.

If you're using the keyboard, use the keyboard shortcuts listed in the following table.

Navigation	Keyboard shortcut
Next or previous character	Right Arrow key or Left Arrow key
One line up or down	Up Arrow key or Down Arrow key
Word to the right	Ctrl+Right Arrow
Word to the left	Ctrl+Left Arrow
Beginning of the line	Home
End of the line	End
One paragraph up	Ctrl+Up Arrow
One paragraph down	Ctrl+Down Arrow
One screen up	Page Up
One screen down	Page Down
Top of the document	Ctrl+Home
End of the document	Ctrl+End

After you've moved the cursor, you can begin entering text or editing. To remove characters or words, use one of the keyboard shortcuts listed in the following table.

Delete	Keyboard shortcut
Character after the cursor	Delete
Character before the cursor	Backspace
Word after the cursor	Ctrl+Delete
Word before the cursor	Ctrl+Backspace

TIP To delete several characters or words, hold down the shortcut keys. If you delete too much, you can reverse your action by clicking the Undo button on the Quick Access Toolbar or by pressing Ctrl+Z.

Selecting text by using the keyboard and mouse

For larger edits, such as deleting a paragraph or making formatting changes, you highlight, or *select*, the text you want to change. When you make a selection, you're identifying *what* you want to work with. After it's selected, you then specify *how* you want to work with it by using your mouse or keyboard to issue a command.

EMPLOYEE GIVE PROGRAM

Here at Fabrikam, we never cease to be amazed by the spirit of volunteerism in our employees. Last month marked the five year anniversary of our Employee Give Program and after tallying all hours logged by our employees, we've reached our first milestone of over 500,000 hours of service to our local communities!

The Employee Give Program is mutually beneficial to our company, the employees, and our local communities. Since starting this campaign we've seen an increase in job satisfaction, morale, and communication across our regional offices. More employees have been promoted to leadership roles within the Fabrikam corporation and our need to bring in new leaders from outside our company has greatly diminished. And as a result of our job skill training programs, the majority of our newly hired employees come from our local communities.

FABRIKAM

EMPLOYEES

TIP Although this chapter talks about working with text, the selection methods can be applied to almost all of your document's content, such as pictures, SmartArt graphics, or charts.

You can use a variety of methods to select text. The most common is the click-and-drag method. That is, you move the mouse pointer to where you want to begin your selection, click and hold the left (primary) mouse button, and then drag through the text you want to select. Additional methods include using the keyboard and other mouse actions, which are discussed in the following sections.

7

IMPORTANT

Selecting text by using the keyboard

You can use the keyboard to select text by pressing the Shift key in combination with a navigation keyboard shortcut. Your selection starts from the location of the cursor. For example, if your cursor is positioned at the beginning of a paragraph, you can press Shift+Ctrl+Down Arrow to select the entire paragraph. But if your cursor is positioned in the middle of the paragraph when you press Shift+Ctrl+Down Arrow, you'll select all the text from the location of the cursor to the end of the paragraph.

The following table provides the most frequently used methods for selecting text by using the keyboard. Keep in mind that these are the navigation shortcuts combined with the Shift key, and that you can also use the Shift key in combination with any of the navigation keyboard shortcuts provided in the previous section.

To make a selection from the cursor through the...	Keyboard shortcut
Next character	Shift+Right Arrow
Previous character	Shift+Left Arrow
Word to the right	Shift+Ctrl+Right Arrow
Word to the left	Shift+Ctrl+Left Arrow
End of the paragraph	Shift+Ctrl+Down Arrow
Beginning of the paragraph	Shift+Ctrl+Up Arrow
Beginning of the document	Shift+Ctrl+Home
End of the document	Shift+Ctrl+End

IMPORTANT

Another method for selecting text by using the keyboard is to use selection mode, which is turned on by pressing the F8 key. When selection mode is activated, it's similar to holding the Shift key, and you can use any of the navigation shortcuts to select text without pressing and holding the Shift key. You can also press F8 consecutively to select specific amounts of text. For example, pressing F8 two times will select the current word; three times will select the current sentence; four times will select the current paragraph; and five times will select the entire document. To turn off selection mode, press the Esc key or perform an action on your selection, such as editing or formatting.

TIP To visually determine if selection mode is turned on, you can display an indicator in the status bar. Right-click the status bar and in the Customize Status Bar options, click Selection Mode. When section mode is turned on, the words *Extend Selection* will appear in the status bar.

Selecting text by using the mouse

When using the mouse to select text, you can place your mouse pointer in the document and use the text select arrow, also called an *I-beam pointer*. Or, you can point to the area to the left of the document margin. This area is called the *selection bar*. It isn't labeled, but you know you're in the selection bar when your mouse pointer changes from the text select arrow to an arrow that points up and to the right. Each time you click in the selection bar you select text.

EMPLOYEE GIVE PROGRAM

Here at Fabrikam, we never cease to be amazed by the spirit of volunteerism in our employees. Last month marked the five year anniversary of our Employee Give Program and after tallying all hours logged by our employees, we've reached our first milestone of over 500,000 hours of service to our local communities!

The Employee Give Program is mutually beneficial to our company, the employees, and our local communities. Since starting this campaign we've seen an increase in job satisfaction, morale, and communication across our regional offices. More employees have

FABRIKAM

The following table lists mouse actions for both the text select arrow and the selection bar.

Selection	Mouse action
One word	Double-click
One line	Click the selection bar next to the line
Multiple lines	Click next to the first line in the selection bar and then drag up or down
One sentence	Press the Ctrl key and click the sentence
One paragraph	Triple-click in the paragraph or double-click next to the paragraph in the selection bar
Entire document	Press Ctrl and click in the selection bar or triple-click in the selection bar

You can also use a combination of the mouse, keyboard, and Shift key to select text. For example, if you didn't select enough text, simply press the Shift key and then click where you want your selection to end, or use the keyboard to modify your selection.

Using other selection methods

Microsoft Word also has selection methods for selecting multiple words, phrases, sentences, and columns of text anywhere in a document.

To make text selections that are not next to each other, after you make your first text selection, press the Ctrl key and use a mouse action to select additional text.

EMPLOYEE GIVE PROGRAM

Here at Fabrikam, we never cease to be amazed by the spirit of volunteerism in our employees. Last month marked the five year anniversary of our Employee Give Program and after tallying all hours logged by our employees, we've reached our first milestone of over 500,000 hours of service to our local communities!

The Employee Give Program is mutually beneficial to our company, the employees, and our local communities. Since starting this campaign we've seen an increase in job satisfaction, morale, and communication across our regional offices. More employees have been promoted to leadership roles within the Fabrikam corporation and our need to bring in new leaders from outside our company has

FABRIKAM

EMPLOYEES

To select a vertical column of text, press and hold the Alt key and use the mouse to drag through the text you want to select.

Name	Amount
Kim Abercrombie	$11
Tomasz	$502
Cornelius	$66
Michiyo	$67

IMPORTANT

TIP You can also use the Navigation pane to select a heading and its related content. On the Navigation pane, right-click the heading you want to select, and then click Select Heading And Content. For more information about using the Navigation pane, see Chapter 6, "Navigating and reading documents."

Using formatting marks during document composition

Each time you press the Tab, Spacebar, or Enter key, characters called *formatting marks* are inserted into the document. Normally these formatting marks are not shown on the screen, but you can toggle their display by clicking the Show/Hide ¶ button, located on the Home tab in the Paragraph group.

KEYBOARD SHORTCUT Press Ctrl+Shift+8.

When you press Enter, a paragraph mark, also called a *pilcrow sign*, (¶) is inserted into your document. Each press of the Tab key adds a right-pointing arrow (→), and a dot in the middle of the line (·) indicates that the Spacebar was pressed.

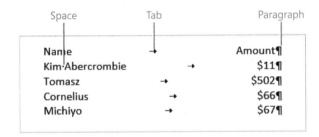

TIP To always view specific formatting marks on the screen without using the Show/Hide ¶ button, click the File tab to display the Backstage view, click Options, and then on the Display page, select the formatting marks you want to make visible.

If you use multiple spaces and tabs for horizontal alignment, or press the Enter key several times to change vertical alignment or to create blank lines, it can complicate the editing and formatting processes, because each character uses a specific amount of space.

The best practices for document composition include using formatting methods rather than pressing the Tab, Spacebar, and Enter key multiple times:

- To add space between information on the same line, add formatted spacing by setting a manual tab.

- To add space between paragraphs, add formatted spacing before or after paragraphs.

TIP The blank lines that are created by pressing the Enter key multiple times are called *empty paragraphs*.

SEE ALSO For information about setting manual tabs, see Chapter 9, "Presenting information." For information about adding paragraph spacing, see Chapter 8, "Formatting documents."

In this exercise, you'll examine how document composition can have an impact on editing. You'll edit two lists of information. One list uses tabs and spaces for alignment, and the other uses a manual tab to achieve the same result. You'll also use formatted space to change the position of a paragraph.

→ SET UP You need the List Example document located in the Chapter07 practice file folder to complete this exercise. Open the List Example document and then follow the steps.

1   Below the **List with multiple tabs and spaces** heading, move the cursor to the right of **Kim**.

    KEYBOARD SHORTCUT Press the Down Arrow key twice and then press Ctrl+Right Arrow.

2   Press the **Spacebar** key, enter Abercrombie, and note how the $11 amount for Kim moved to the right when you added her last name.

List with multiple tabs and spaces		
Name	Amount	
Kim Abercrombie		$11
Tomasz	$502	
Cornelius	$66	
Michiyo	$67	

3   To realign $11 to the other amounts, with the cursor still positioned after **Abercrombie**, press the **Delete** key two times.

4   To add a new item to the **List with multiple tabs and spaces** list, move the cursor to the end of the last line, after the $67 amount.

KEYBOARD SHORTCUT Press the Down Arrow key three times and then press the End key.

5   Press **Enter**.

6   On the newly added line, enter Kate, and then press the **Tab** key or **Spacebar** as needed to move the cursor to the **Amount** column.

7   Enter $400.

8   Add tabs or spaces if needed to align the amount you entered to the other amounts in the list.

List with multiple tabs and spaces	
Name	Amount
Kim Abercrombie	$11
Tomasz	$502
Cornelius	$66
Michiyo	$67
Kate	$400

9   Below the **List without multiple tabs and spaces** heading, move the cursor to the right of **Kim** and enter Abercrombie. The amount didn't move and additional edits aren't needed.

TIP If you want more insight into the underlying differences between the lists, on the Home tab, in the Paragraph group, click the Show/Hide ¶ button to display the formatting marks.

List·with·multiple·tabs·and·spaces¶

Name→ → → → ············Amount¶
Kim·Abercrombie → → → ·······$11¶
Tomasz⁺ → → → → ·····$502¶
Cornelius· → → → → ·······$66¶
Michiyo → → → → ·······$67¶

List·without·multiple·tabs·and·spaces¶

Name → Amount¶
Kim·Abercrombie → $11¶
Tomasz → $502¶
Cornelius → $66¶
Michiyo → $67¶

Examine the number of tabs and spaces in the first list. Because Kim's last name takes about as much space as two default tabs, you'll need to remove two tabs to correct the alignment. For the second list, a manual tab was used to add formatted space. This enables you to enter text up to the amount while maintaining the alignment.

10 Below the last list item, enter your name, press the **Tab** key, and then enter an amount, which will be aligned with the other amounts.

11 Make other edits to both lists. For example, change **$11** to $110 and notice that additional edits aren't needed to align the amounts in the second list.

12 To demonstrate the advantage of using formatted space to modify the position of a paragraph, place the cursor in the **List without multiple tabs and spaces** paragraph.

TIP The cursor doesn't need to be at the beginning of the paragraph.

13 On the **Page Layout** tab, in the **Paragraph** group, next to **Spacing Before**, click the **Up Arrow** to increase the space from **6 pts** to **18 pts**.

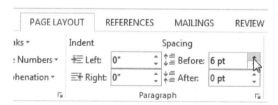

CLEAN UP Close the document without saving changes.

Inserting symbols, international characters, and other special characters

To insert symbols, such as the ohm sign (Ω), or international characters, such as the letter "a" with an acute accent (á), you can use the Symbol dialog box or a keyboard shortcut.

To display the Symbol dialog box, on the Insert tab, in the Symbols group, click the Symbol button, and then click More Symbols.

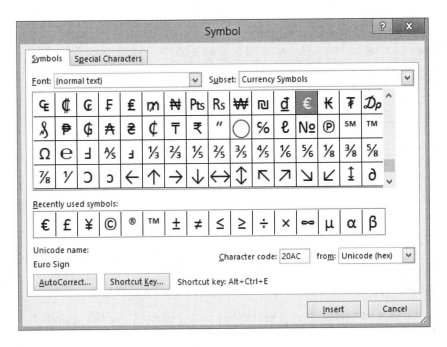

From the list of symbols, double-click the symbol you want to insert, or click the symbol once to select it and then click the Insert button.

TIP You don't need to close the Symbol dialog box to insert multiple symbols. After your first insertion, click in your document to activate it, and then move the cursor to a new location. Then, click the Symbol dialog box to activate it and insert another symbol. If the dialog box is in your way, drag its title bar to move it to another location on your screen.

Here are a few tips for using the Symbol dialog box:

- When (**normal text**) is selected in the **Font** drop-down list, symbols will be inserted by using the current font. If you select a different font, the insertion will be the same as the font you selected from the **Font** list.

- After you insert a symbol, it will be added to the **Recently used symbols** list near the bottom of the **Symbol** dialog box and on the **Symbol** drop-down list in the ribbon.

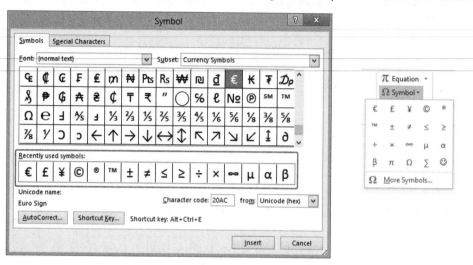

- As you scroll through the available symbols, the **Subset** area to the right of the font will change. You can jump to a specific group of symbols by selecting an item from the **Subset** drop-down list, such as **Mathematical Operators**.

- To insert glyph characters, select **Webdings** or any of the three **Wingdings** fonts from the **Font** drop-down list.

  TIP Webdings, Wingdings, Wingdings 2, and Wingdings 3 are the main Windows fonts that contain glyphs. You may have other glyph fonts installed that you can use as well.

If a selected symbol has an associated keyboard shortcut, it will be listed near the bottom of the dialog box next to the Shortcut Key button. There are four basic keyboard shortcut methods that you can use to insert symbols.

The following table provides an example of each method and a description of how to enter the keyboard shortcut.

Symbol	Keyboard shortcut	How to enter it
¿	Alt+Ctrl+?	Press the Alt, Ctrl, and ? keys simultaneously. You may also need to hold the Shift key in order to enter a question mark.
¥	Alt+0165	Make sure Num Lock is turned on, hold the Alt key, and then press the numbers on the numeric keypad. The character will be inserted after you release the Alt key. The numbers on the main keyboard can't be used for this keyboard shortcut.
Ø	Ctrl+/, Shift+O	Press Ctrl and / simultaneously and release the keys. Then press Shift and O simultaneously.
≤	2264, Alt+X	Enter 2264 and then immediately press Alt and X simultaneously. The numbers will be replaced with the character after you press Alt+X.

TIP You can also use AutoCorrect to enter frequently used symbols. Select the symbol and then click the AutoCorrect button near the bottom of the dialog box. For information about how to create a custom AutoCorrect entry, see the "Using AutoCorrect" section later in this chapter.

If you use international characters that have accents, such as á or ÿ, you don't need to memorize each individual keyboard shortcut for them. You can use the built-in keyboard shortcuts for the accent character instead, which are listed in the following table.

To insert an accent, first press the keyboard shortcut, release the keys, and then enter the character.

Accent	Keyboard Shortcut	Character	Example
acute	Ctrl+'	a, e, i, o, u, y, d	ý
cedilla	Ctrl+,	c	ç
circumflex	Ctrl+^	a, e, i, o, u	î
grave	Ctrl+`	a, e, i, o, u	ò
tilde	Ctrl+~	a, n, o	ñ
umlaut	Ctrl+:	a, e, i, o, u, y	ë

Assigning a custom keyboard shortcut to a character or symbol

If you frequently use the same character or symbol that has a complex keyboard shortcut, you can define your own custom keyboard shortcut instead of memorizing the built-in one. In the Symbol dialog box, select a character or symbol, and then click Shortcut Key. In the Customize Keyboard dialog box that appears, in the Press New Shortcut Key text box, press the keys for your preferred keyboard shortcut. For example, press Ctrl+Shift+Y.

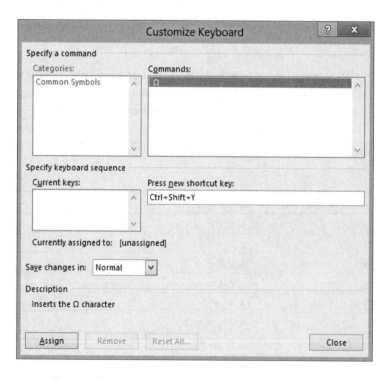

It's important to note that prior to assigning your new keyboard shortcut, you should first check whether the keyboard shortcut you want to use is assigned to another command. After you enter your keyboard shortcut, the existing keyboard shortcut assignment will be listed below the Current Keys list box.

If the shortcut is already assigned, and it's one you don't use, you can override the built-in assignment with your custom keyboard shortcut by clicking the Assign button. If you later decide you want to use the originally assigned keyboard shortcut, you can redisplay the Customize Keyboard dialog box for your symbol, select your custom keyboard shortcut from the list of current keys, and then click Remove. To reset all custom keyboard shortcuts, click Reset All.

Inserting special characters

The Special Characters page of the Symbol dialog box has a collection of special punctuation symbols, such as an em dash (—), and formatting characters, such as a nonbreaking space, that aren't available on most keyboards. You can insert them exactly like you insert symbols or international characters, by using the Symbol dialog box or the corresponding keyboard shortcut.

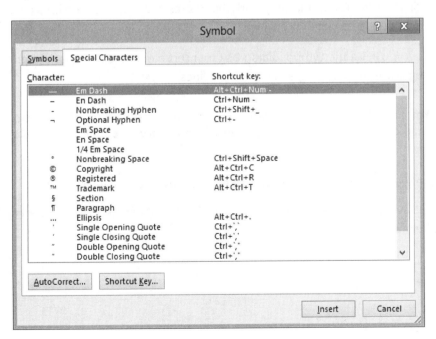

Of the available special characters, there are a few that are especially useful for specifying how words or phrases should wrap between lines of text if they fall at the end of a line. The following table describes each of these and provides a description of the formatting mark that's displayed for each when you click the Show/Hide ¶ button on the Home tab.

Character	Description	Formatting mark
Optional Hyphen	An optional hyphen is displayed only when part of the text wraps to the next line. If the text remains on the same line, the hyphen doesn't appear.	hooked hyphen (¬)
Nonbreaking Hyphen	Keeps text before and after the nonbreaking hyphen together on the same line.	long hyphen(–)
Nonbreaking Space	Keeps text before and after the nonbreaking space together on the same line.	small raised circle (°)

TIP The formatting marks for an em space and en space are also displayed as a small raised circle, but extra space is added to the left of the symbol for an en space and extra space is added to the left and right for an em space. A 1/4-em space is shown as a vertical bar (|).

A manual line break, which isn't in the Symbol dialog box, is another special formatting character for controlling line wrapping. This type of break is used to force text to start on a new line without starting a new paragraph. For example, you may have several short lines that you want to treat as a single paragraph, such as an address. To enter a manual line break, press Shift+Enter. The formatting mark that represents a manual line break is a right-angle arrow pointing to the left.

In this exercise, you'll use the Symbol dialog box to insert a nonbreaking space to prevent a telephone number from wrapping across multiple lines.

 SET UP You need the Newsletter_C document located in the Chapter07 practice file folder to complete this exercise. Open the Newsletter_C document and then follow the steps.

1   On the **View** tab, in the **Show** group, select the **Navigation Pane** check box.

2   In the **Navigation** pane, click **New Women's Shelter**. If necessary, scroll to view the text below the picture.

3   On the **Home** tab, in the **Paragraph** group, click the **Show/Hide ¶** button.

4   Select the space after **(971)**.

5   On the **Insert** tab, in the **Symbols** group, click **Symbol**, and then click **More Symbols**.

6   On the **Special Characters** page, double-click **Nonbreaking space**.

KEYBOARD SHORTCUT Press Ctrl+Shift+Spacebar.

7   Close the **Symbol** dialog box and note that the entire phone number wrapped to the next line.

8   Edit the first part of the sentence with the phone number to read To donate instead of **If you wish to donate** and note that the phone number moves to the previous line.

TIP Move the cursor to the beginning of the sentence and press Ctrl+Delete three times. Then press Delete to remove the lowercase t, and enter a capital T.

✖ CLEAN UP Close the document without saving changes.

Using AutoCorrect

As you enter text into a document, various typing mistakes and misspellings are corrected for you by a feature called *AutoCorrect*. If you're familiar with using AutoCorrect on a smartphone, the feature in Word is similar, but it does more than correct commonly misspelled words. Other corrections range from capitalizing the first letter of sentences and days of the week to toggling the case of characters if you accidently enter them with Caps Lock on. For example, if you enter the word "teh" as the first word of a sentence, AutoCorrect will both capitalize the first letter and change the word to "the" after you press the Spacebar.

You also have the ability to reverse the action if it isn't correct and remove words that you don't want corrected automatically. When a correction is made, point to the word to display the AutoCorrect Options button, and then click the button to display a menu of choices.

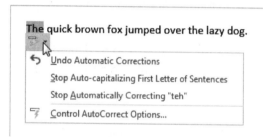

To reverse the correction, click the first option, which will start with either *Change back* or *Undo*. For the example previously provided, when the word "teh" as been entered at the beginning of a sentence, the first option is Undo Automatic Corrections, because two corrections were made. Clicking the option will reverse both the spelling of the word "the" and the capitalization.

TIP You can also press Ctrl+Z to undo a correction immediately after it's made.

If you never want the correction to be made again, click a *Stop* option, such as Stop Automatically Correcting "teh". Keep in mind that this will delete the entry and will take effect for all documents. After an entry is deleted, you'll need to manually add the entry in the AutoCorrect dialog box in order for Word to start correcting it again.

To view all of the AutoCorrect options, click Control AutoCorrect Options at the bottom of the menu to display the AutoCorrect dialog box.

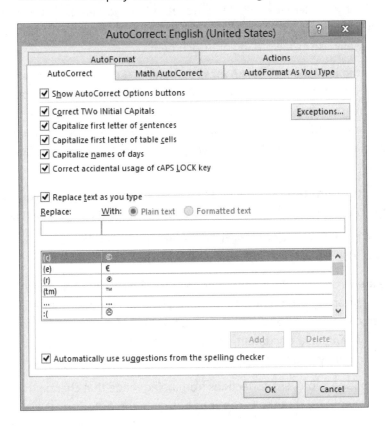

TIP To display the AutoCorrect dialog box, you can also click the File tab to display the Backstage view, and click Options. Then on the Proofing tab, click the AutoCorrect Options button. Alternatively, you can press Alt, T, A. That is, press and release the Alt key, press and release T, and then press A.

In the AutoCorrect dialog box, you can choose to turn the options on or off, delete words that are automatically corrected, or add your own entries to the AutoCorrect list.

To add custom entries, enter the characters you want to replace in the Replace text box. In the With text box, enter your replacement text, and then click the Add button.

Here are a few tips for using the AutoCorrect dialog box:

- Don't use a word for your **Replace** text. If you do, each time you enter that word in a document, it will be corrected. It's best to use abbreviations or a group of characters you wouldn't normally use as a word in your documents.

- Enter your text in the **Replace** text box in lowercase characters in order to make your entry case insensitive. That is, if you enter your **Replace** text in lowercase characters, you can use uppercase or lowercase characters in your document to trigger a correction. If you enter your **Replace** text in all uppercase or mixed case, you must enter it exactly as it's displayed in the **AutoCorrect** dialog box in order to have AutoCorrect correct your entry.

- Enter your text in the **With** text box exactly as you want it to be entered in your document, including punctuation and uppercase, lowercase, or mixed case characters.

- To quickly find an entry in the **AutoCorrect** list, enter it in the **Replace** text box. As you enter the text, the list will scroll to matching characters.

- Custom entries aren't only for words you frequently misspell. You can also use the **AutoCorrect** feature for frequently used phrases or your company name. For example, you can create an entry such as Replace: *finc* With: *Fabrikam, Inc.* Then to add your company name in a document, you would enter *finc*, and after you press the **Spacebar**, *Fabrikam, Inc.* will be inserted.

- You can add exceptions to prevent corrections from being made that change the case of words. To add exceptions, click the **Exceptions** button in the **AutoCorrect** dialog box.

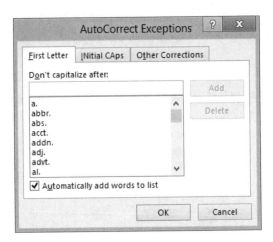

Following are the types of exceptions you can add:

- **First Letter** A list of abbreviations that end with a period. If exceptions for these aren't specified, the first letter of the word after the abbreviation will automatically be capitalized.

- **Initial Caps** A list of words that have mixed uppercase and lowercase letters that should not be corrected.

IMPORTANT

- You can also use **AutoCorrect** to insert formatted text, like a symbol. Select your formatted text in a document. When you display the **AutoCorrect** dialog box, your selection will be added in the **With** text box. Then, add your **Replace** characters and select the **Formatted Text** option before clicking the **Add** button.

TIP Several frequently used symbols, such as ©, ™, and ®, are already included in AutoCorrect. To view them, scroll to the top of the AutoCorrect list.

Composing documents faster by using building blocks

Building blocks, formerly known as AutoText in previous versions of Word, are pieces of information that you can quickly insert into your documents. You can insert built-in building blocks, such as watermarks and cover pages, or your own custom entries.

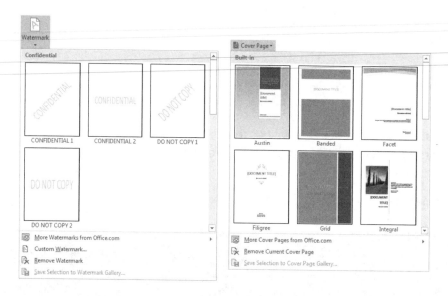

TIP The built-in building blocks are theme enabled, which means that the fonts and colors will match your document's current theme. Also, if you change the theme, the thumbnails in the galleries will reflect the theme change. For more information about using themes, see Chapter 2, "Using shared Office features."

Following is a list of the primary building block galleries and their locations on the ribbon:

- **Cover Page** On the **Insert** tab, in the **Pages** group.

- **Quick Tables** On the **Insert** tab, in the **Tables** group. (Click **Table** and then point to **Quick Tables**.)

- **Headers**, **Footers**, **and Page Numbers** On the **Insert** tab, in the **Header & Footer** group.

- **Text Box and Quick Parts** On the **Insert** tab, in the **Text** group.

- **Watermark** On the **Design** tab, in the **Page Background** group.

- **Tables of Contents** On the **References** tab, in the **Table of Contents** group.

> **TIP** The Automatic Table 1 and Automatic Table 2 built-in building blocks in the Tables Of Contents gallery use heading styles in your document to generate a table of contents. For more information on using heading styles, see Chapter 8, "Formatting documents."

To insert a building block, simply click the building block you want to insert in your document. Some of the building block galleries, like the Cover Page gallery, have additional commands for inserting building blocks. To display these commands, right-click a building block in the gallery.

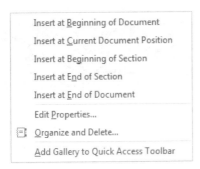

The Quick Parts gallery doesn't have built-in building blocks and can be used for your custom entries. Custom building blocks can range from frequently used text, such as a signature block or boilerplate text for a letter or other document, to pictures and other graphics. Additionally, unlike built-in building blocks, custom building blocks can be inserted by using the keyboard. Just enter the name of the building block and watch for the AutoComplete ScreenTip. When the ScreenTip is displayed, press Enter to insert the building block. Typically, you only need to enter the first few characters of the name and the AutoComplete ScreenTip will be displayed.

In this exercise, you'll create a custom building block for the Fabrikam company logo and address and then insert it by using the ribbon and keyboard.

1 Point to the left of the logo and address in the selection bar and click once to select it.

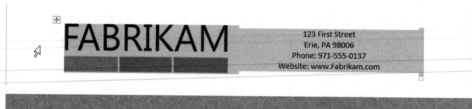

IMPORTANT

2 On the **Insert** tab, in the **Text** group, click **Quick Parts**, and then click **Save Selection to Quick Part gallery**.

KEYBOARD SHORTCUT Press Alt+F3.

3 In the **Create New Building Block** dialog box, in the **Name** text box, enter Company Logo and Address.

4 In the **Save-in** list, click **Normal**.

TIP To add custom building blocks to other galleries, such as Cover Page or Header, select the gallery you want in the Gallery list. If you create a lot of building blocks, you can use the Category option to organize them in the gallery.

5   Click **OK**.

6   To test your newly created building block, create a blank document.

   KEYBOARD SHORTCUT Press Ctrl+N.

7   On the **Insert** tab, click **Quick Parts**, and then click **Company Logo and Address**.

8   To insert the logo by using the keyboard, add a new paragraph below the previously inserted logo and begin entering Company. When the **AutoComplete** ScreenTip is displayed, press **Enter** to insert the logo.

   KEYBOARD SHORTCUT Enter the first few characters of the building block name, and then press F3.

❌ CLEAN UP Close the document without saving changes, and exit Word.

Here are some important tips to remember when you are creating custom building blocks:

- To use the keyboard to insert your building block by using the **AutoComplete** ScreenTip, you must save your entry in the **Normal** template or a custom template.

- When you are creating more than one custom building block, if the first few characters of the building block name aren't unique, you'll need to enter the first non-unique character before the **AutoComplete** ScreenTip will be displayed.

- The **AutoComplete** ScreenTip will not be displayed for building blocks containing pictures or other objects unless text is also included.

- To revise a building block, recreate the entry by using the same name and other properties, such as category, gallery, and save location. When you save the building block, you'll be prompted to redefine the entry.

- You can edit building block properties or delete a building block in the **Building Blocks Organizer**. To display it, on the **Insert** tab, in the **Text** group, click **Quick Parts**, and then click **Building Blocks Organizer**.

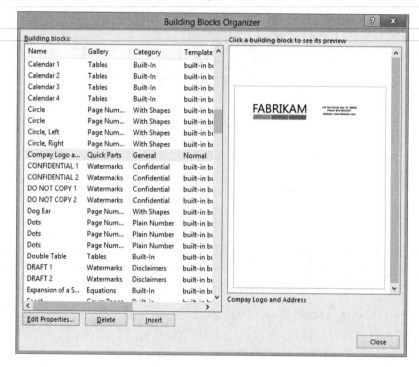

Key points

- To select text by using the keyboard, you can use navigation keyboard shortcuts combined with the Shift key.

- The selection bar is the area to the left of your document's left margin, rather than to the left of your text. If your pointer does not point up and to the right, try moving the pointer further to the left.

- To select pieces of text that are not next to each other, press the Ctrl key between selections and use a mouse action to add to your selection. If you use a keyboard action, your previous selection will be removed.

- When you are composing a document, avoid pressing the Spacebar, Tab, and Enter keys multiple times to move the cursor or add extra space.

- AutoCorrect actions are triggered when you press the Spacebar.

- You can press Ctrl+Z to undo an AutoCorrect action immediately after the correction has been made.

- To display the AutoComplete ScreenTip for a building block, you must save the entry in the Normal template, and the first few characters of the name must be unique.

7

Chapter at a glance

Set

Set default document formatting, page 190

Modify

Modify character and paragraph formats, like font color and indents, page 194

Use

Use styles for fast and flexible formatting, page 194

Manage

Manage how text flows between pages through formatting, page 205

Formatting documents   8

IN THIS CHAPTER, YOU WILL LEARN HOW TO

- Format documents more efficiently.

- Set default document formatting for your documents.

- Apply section, paragraph, and character formatting to text.

- Use styles to format documents faster and increase formatting flexibility.

- Manage document pagination through formatting.

Document formatting is one of the primary tasks in Microsoft Word and has the broadest set of features. Formatting ranges from changing a font or font size, to modifying line spacing or paragraph indents, to setting page margins and pagination options, such as specifying that all lines of a paragraph should stay together on the same page.

In this chapter, you'll learn about the four main categories of formatting and how you can format documents faster and more efficiently by using styles. At the end of this chapter, you'll learn how to manage document pagination through manual page breaks and formatting.

PRACTICE FILES To complete the exercises in this chapter, you need the practice files contained in the Chapter08 practice file folder. For more information, see "Download · the practice files" in this book's Introduction.

Formatting documents more efficiently

Formatting can be one of the most time-consuming tasks if you're not familiar with the fundamentals. Similar to how document composition can affect editing, as covered in the previous chapter, the methods you use to format a document determine the amount of time you spend formatting, and many times, reformatting.

The primary document formatting fundamental to become familiar with first is the fact that, when you begin entering text into a document, the text you're entering is already formatted. For example, when you create a new blank document, default formats are already applied. The font is Calibri and the font size is 11 points. There are other default formats as well. The space between each line of a paragraph, which is called *line spacing*, is by default 1.08 points, and the space after each paragraph, which is referred to as *paragraph spacing*, is 8 points by default.

The next fundamental to understand is that all text is associated with a named set of formatting attributes called a *style*. Styles that are frequently used in a document are on the Home tab, in the Styles gallery.

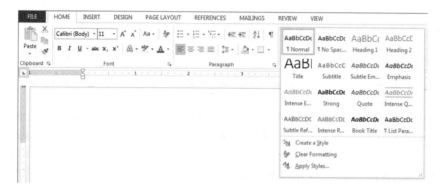

TIP To expand the Styles gallery, click the More button in the lower-right corner.

You don't have to implement styles in your documents, but they give you flexibility and consistent formatting. Best of all, you can apply multiple formats with a single click, which enables you to instantly change text formatting associated with a style throughout a document simply by modifying the style's formatting attributes. You'll learn more about styles throughout this chapter.

The last formatting fundamental is to break formatting down into separate tasks to help make it more manageable. Here are the four main formatting categories:

- **Document** Initial formatting attributes that are applied to the entire document, referred to as *document defaults*. These formats include a set of fonts for your heading and body text and the initial colors displayed in the color palettes. They also include paragraph and line spacing formats. The primary location for setting these formats is on the **Design** tab.

TIP Examples of heading text are the section titles in this book, which are formatted with the Segoe Light font. Other text is considered body text, which is formatted as Segoe.

To modify document defaults, you don't need to select any text, because these formats are applied to the entire document.

SEE ALSO For more information on text selection, see Chapter 7, "Editing and composing documents."

The Design tab also has sets of pre-built styles called *style sets* in the Document Formatting group. The formatting that appears in the preview of each style set gives you a general idea of how your document will look when it's formatted with the available styles.

TIP If you select a different theme or change individual theme elements, the fonts and colors that are displayed in the style set preview will be updated to match your selection.

When you select a style set, you're changing both the document defaults and the collection of styles that are displayed on the Home tab in the Styles group. If you're working with a document that already has styles that are named the same as those in the style set applied, such as Title and Heading 1, the formatting will be updated to match your selected style set. Keep in mind that the set you choose only provides the initial formats. You can change a style's formatting attributes at any time.

■ **Section** Formats that are applied to a division in a document such as a page or a group of pages. All pages within a section have the same section formats, such as page margins, orientation, and page size. These formats are located on the **Page Layout** tab.

To apply section formats, make sure your cursor is positioned in the section you want to modify.

SEE ALSO For more information on how to create additional sections in a document, see "Setting section formatting," later in this chapter.

- **Paragraph** Formats that are applied to a paragraph as a whole, such as alignment, indents, line spacing, and paragraph spacing. Other paragraph formats include page break options, such as specifying that all lines of a paragraph should stay together on the same page. The primary paragraph formats are located on the **Home** tab, in the **Paragraph** group.

To apply paragraph formatting for a single paragraph, text selection isn't necessary. You can place your cursor in the paragraph you want to format and then make your modifications. For multiple paragraphs, select all paragraphs you want to format.

- **Character** Formatting that can be applied to individual characters, such as font, font size, color, or bold. Primary character formatting is located on the **Home** tab, in the **Font** group.

TIP You can specify a font size as small as 1 point and as large as 1,638 points by entering it in the Size text box. You can also enter half-sizes, such as 10.5 points. When you enter a specific size, enter decimals for half-sizes and don't include a comma for large numbers.

To apply character formatting to a single word, click in the word you want to format and then make your changes. To format a single character or multiple words, select the text you want to format. Note that commands such as bold, italic, subscript, and superscript are toggle commands. This means you perform the same action when you want to apply and remove the formatting.

For setting other formats, such as the font type and font color, you can either apply a different format or remove it. For formats such as text effects, typography, and text highlight color, you remove applied formats by selecting the option that starts with the word *No*, such as No Color for Text Highlight Color.

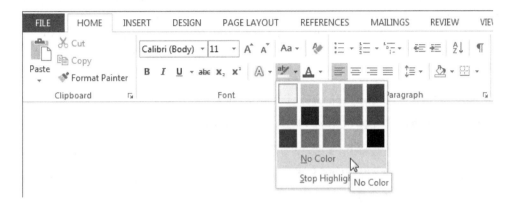

TIP Text Highlight Color is an example of a split control, and it's one that works without the need to select text. You can click the Text Highlight Color button to apply the color that's shown on the button, or you can click the arrow next to the button and select your preferred highlight color. If your text is highlighted, the color will be applied. If you don't have text selected, your mouse pointer will change to a highlighter tool that you can drag through text to highlight it. If you use the latter method, to turn off the highlighter, click the button again or press the Esc key.

You don't necessarily need to format your document in the same order that the formatting categories have just been described. However, a best formatting practice is to start with your document and section formats, because these can affect your paragraph and character formatting. The remaining sections of this chapter cover each formatting category in more detail, along with step-by-step exercises.

8

Serif and sans serif fonts

Fonts are either serif or sans serif. The way to differentiate between them is that serif fonts have "hooks," called *serifs*, at the end of each stroke of the character. Sans serif fonts, however, do not have "hooks." In French, *sans* means *without*; therefore, sans serif fonts do not have hook characters. Examples of serif fonts are Cambria and Times New Roman. Examples of sans serif fonts are Calibri and Arial.

Cambria: The quick brown fox jumps over the lazy dog.

Times New Roman: The quick brown fox jumps over the lazy dog.

Calibri: The quick brown fox jumps over the lazy dog.

Arial: The quick brown fox jumps over the lazy dog.

It's fairly common for printed content to have a sans serif font for headings and serif fonts for body text, because this combination is the easiest to read on paper. But for online documents, the combination is often reversed for easier onscreen reading; a serif font is used for headings, and a sans serif font is used for body text. The main reason for this is that serifs may appear faint or jagged on a screen due to the display itself and various display settings. When choosing fonts, you may want to keep the main output of your document in mind. If it's to be read electronically, then choose a sans serif font for your body text to help make sure it's easy to read on all devices.

Setting default document formatting for your documents

The first set of formats you should change for a document are the document defaults, because they affect your entire document and set the base formats for your paragraph and character formatting.

In this exercise, you'll change document defaults by modifying theme elements and by changing line and paragraph spacing. You'll also select a style set for initial paragraph and character formats.

SET UP You need the Fabrikam Rebrand Campaign_A document located in the Chapter08 practice file folder to complete this exercise. Open the Fabrikam Rebrand Campaign_A document. Then follow the steps.

1   Scroll through the document and take note of the current fonts, font color, line and paragraph spacing, and how the colors don't match the Fabrikam logo colors on the first page.

2   To change the document theme, on the **Design** tab, in the **Themes** group, click **Themes** and then click **Retrospect**.

3   To change only the theme colors so they match the colors in the Fabrikam logo, on the **Design** tab, in the **Document Formatting** group, click **Colors** and then click **Blue II**.

4   To select an initial style set, on the **Design** tab, in the **Document Formatting** group, in the **Style** gallery, click **Basic (Elegant)**.

   TIP The title, Rebrand Campaign, is now formatted as uppercase. It's no longer centered, but you'll correct this in another exercise.

5   To change the default paragraph and line spacing, on the **Design** tab, in the **Document Formatting** group, click **Paragraph Spacing**, and then click **Tight**.

   SEE ALSO For more information about themes, see Chapter 2, "Using shared Office features."

CLEAN UP Save Fabrikam Rebrand Campaign_A as My Rebrand Campaign_B. If you're proceeding to the next exercise, leave the My Rebrand Campaign_B document open. Otherwise, close My Rebrand Campaign_B and exit Word.

TIP To view your current document defaults along with all of the document defaults that can be changed, on the Design tab, in the Document Formatting group, click Paragraph Spacing. Then click Custom Paragraph Spacing to view the Set Defaults page of the Manage Styles dialog box.

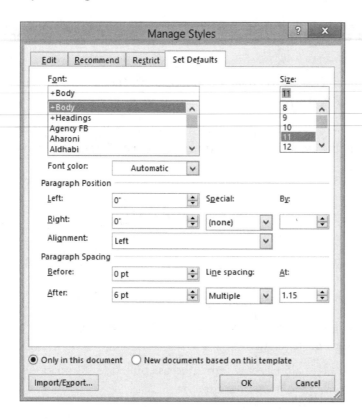

Setting section formatting

When you think of page margins and page orientation, you probably think of formats that belong to a page. Though they are essentially page formats, it would be time consuming to set page formatting for every single page in a document. Instead, you can format a document section so that all pages in the section will have the same formats applied.

Every new blank document starts with a single section. To add additional sections, you insert section breaks by using the Breaks command, located on the Page Layout tab, in the Page Setup group.

Here is a list of each type of section break, along with some examples for how they're used:

- **Next Page** If your document needs pages with both portrait and landscape orientation, different page margins, or different headers and footers, you can add a **Next Page** section break at the beginning of each change in section formats.

  TIP You don't need to use section breaks for a different first page header and footer or for different odd and even headers and footers.

- **Continuous** This is the only type of section break that doesn't result in a new page. Typically, a continuous break is used to add newspaper-style columns on the same page as text that spans the entire width of the page.

- **Even Page or Odd Page** This type of break forces a page to start on an even-numbered or odd-numbered page and is typically used in documents with multiple chapters that are printed on both sides of the paper. The most common usage is adding an odd page section break at the beginning of a chapter to make sure the first page of the chapter is an odd-numbered page.

TIP To view section information in your status bar, right-click the status bar, and in the Customize Status Bar options, click Section.

In this exercise, you'll insert a section break and set different page margins starting on page 2.

SET UP If the My Rebrand Campaign_B document you saved in the previous exercise is still open, follow the steps. If you skipped the previous exercise, open the Fabrikam Rebrand Campaign_B document located in the Chapter08 practice file folder to complete this exercise, then follow the steps.

1   To place the title and logo on its own page, place the cursor at the beginning of the first full paragraph that begins with **Our international office**.

2   On the **Page Layout** tab, in the **Page Setup** group, click **Breaks**, and then click **Next Page**.

3   To change the margins starting at the second page, on the **Page Layout** tab, in the **Page Setup** group, click **Margins**, and then click **Normal**.

CLEAN UP Save the document as My Rebrand Campaign_C. If you're proceeding to the next exercise, leave the My Rebrand Campaign_C document open. Otherwise, close My Rebrand Campaign_C and exit Word.

SEE ALSO For more information on section breaks and using headers and footers, see *Microsoft Word 2013 Step by Step* by Joan Lambert and Joyce Cox (Microsoft Press, 2013).

Using styles for paragraph and character formats

Many Word tutorials consider styles to be an advanced formatting technique. Though there are some advanced style topics, styles are such an integral part of Word that you need to know style essentials and how to use them, even if you're a beginning Word user. As noted in the "Formatting documents more efficiently" section earlier in this chapter, frequently used styles are located on the Home tab, in the Styles group.

Styles are document specific. This means that any changes you make to styles will be applied only to your current document. The two primary types of styles in Word are related to the paragraph and character formatting categories. A character style contains only character formats and is applied to individual words and even single characters. A paragraph style is applied to an entire paragraph and contains both character and paragraph formatting. Of the two, paragraph styles are used more frequently, because they enable you to apply more formats at the same time.

Another type of style to know about is a linked style, which is a combination of a paragraph style and a character style. A linked style has the same characteristics as a paragraph style, but if you apply it to a selected portion of a paragraph, only the character formats are applied. In contrast, if you're using a paragraph style, the entire paragraph is formatted, even if you have only a portion of it selected.

Of all the built-in styles, those that have other features connected to them are the heading styles, which are Heading 1 through Heading 9. For example, the headings that are displayed in the Navigation pane are paragraphs that have a heading style applied. And heading styles are also used for creating a table of contents.

SEE ALSO For more information on how to create a table of contents, see *Microsoft Word 2013 Step by Step* by Joan Lambert and Joyce Cox (Microsoft Press, 2013).

Each heading style has an outline level associated with it, which helps give your documents structure. Heading 1 is the highest outline level and Heading 9 is the lowest. This chapter is a good example of a structured document. Each main topic is formatted as Heading 1, and related content, or subtopics, are formatted as Heading 2.

TIP By default, only the Heading 1 and Heading 2 styles are displayed in the Styles gallery. After you apply Heading 2, the Heading 3 style will appear, and so on.

8

In this exercise, you'll modify paragraph and character formats, apply a style to a document, and modify style formatting.

 SET UP If the My Rebrand Campaign_C document that you saved in the previous exercise is still open, follow the steps. If you skipped the previous exercise, open the Fabrikam Rebrand Campaign_C document located in the Chapter08 practice file folder to complete this exercise, then follow the steps.

1   To make the document easier to navigate, on the **View** tab, in the **Show** group, select the **Navigation Pane** check box.

2   In the **Navigation** pane, click **Nature Friendly Products**.

3   Place your cursor in the paragraph with the text **Sustainable products**.

4   On the **Home** tab, in the **Styles** gallery, click **Heading 2**.

5   Apply the **Heading 2** style to the following paragraphs: **Other materials**, **Fixtures and appliances**, and **Miscellaneous**.

> **KEYBOARD SHORTCUT** After applying the first Heading 2 style, place your cursor in the next paragraph that needs the Heading 2 style applied and press F4 to repeat your last action of applying the Heading 2 style.

6   To change the font color and font size for all paragraphs with the **Heading 2** style applied, select **Sustainable products**.

> **TIP** You can select any paragraph that has the Heading 2 style applied.

7   On the **Home** tab, in the **Font** group, click the arrow next to **Font Color**, and from the color palette, select the last color in the top row, **Teal, Accent 6**.

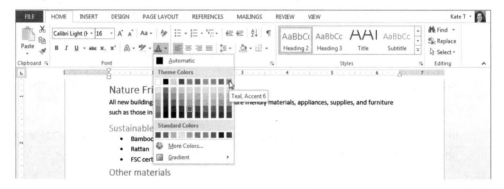

8   Change the font size from **16** points to **14** points.

9   To update all **Heading 2** paragraphs to the new font color and font size, with **Sustainable products** still selected, on the **Home** tab, in the **Styles** gallery, right-click **Heading 2**, and then click **Update Heading 2 to Match Selection**.

> **TIP** Keep in mind that the changes you are making to the styles are limited to this document.

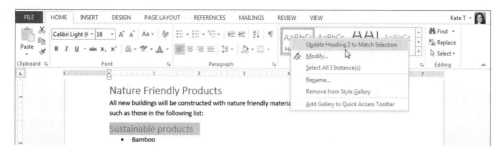

10   Move the cursor to the top of the document.

KEYBOARD SHORTCUT Press Ctrl+Home.

TIP Your cursor should be in the title paragraph, Rebrand Campaign. Because you're making a paragraph formatting change, the title doesn't need to be selected.

11   To center the title, on the **Home** tab, in the **Paragraph** group, click **Center**.

KEYBOARD SHORTCUT Press Ctrl+E.

12   To add formatted space before the first paragraph and to position it vertically on the page, on the **Page Layout** tab, in the **Paragraph** group, change the **Before** spacing to **228** points.

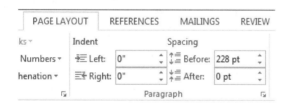

TIP You can click the up arrow to change the spacing or enter 228 in the text box, and then press the Enter key. You don't need to enter *pts*, because Word will add that for you.

13   In the **Styles** gallery, update the **Title** style to match your current selection.

TIP Repeat step 9 to update the Title style.

14   Scroll through the document and view the formatting changes.

❌ CLEAN UP Save the document as My Rebrand Campaign_D. If you're proceeding to the next exercise, leave the My Rebrand Campaign_D document open. Otherwise, close My Rebrand Campaign_D and exit Word.

You can also add additional formats to text that aren't already included in the style. However, if you have several places that use the same style and need the same format, it's best to modify the style or create a new style instead.

TIP To reset all character formats to only those formats that are included in the style, press Ctrl+Spacebar. To reset paragraph formats only to those included in the style, press Ctrl+Q. If you want to reset text to the document defaults, or the Normal style, on the Home tab, in the Font group, click Clear All Formatting.

Word has over 200 built-in styles that you can use and modify to fit your formatting needs. However, there may be times when you need to create a custom style. The easiest way to do this is to create a new style based on your existing formatting. To do so, add the formatting changes you want to include in your style to your text. Then, on the Home tab, in the Styles group, click the More button in the lower-right corner of the Styles gallery, and then click Create A Style. Then in the Create New Style From Formatting dialog box, name your style and then click OK. The style you created will appear in the Styles gallery for your current document.

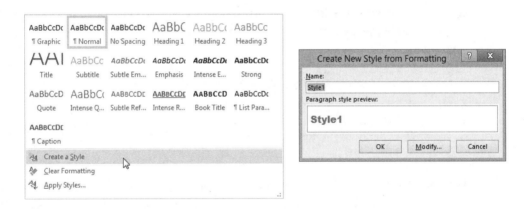

SEE ALSO For more information about styles and style management options, see *Microsoft Word 2013 Step by Step* by Joan Lambert and Joyce Cox (Microsoft Press, 2013).

Exploring other paragraph formats

In addition to the basic formatting options on the Home tab in the Paragraph group, Word provides a number of other paragraph formats, which are available in the Paragraph dialog box. To display it, click the dialog box launcher in the Paragraph group.

Here's a list of the additional formats:

- **Outline level** This format is what triggers paragraphs to be displayed in the **Navigation** pane. The heading styles already have an outline level format, but you can use this format for any paragraph.

- **Indentation** You can use the **Increase Indent** and **Decrease Indent** commands in the **Paragraph** group on the **Home** tab for left indents only. If you want to set a right indent or a special indent, such as **First Line** or **Hanging**, you can use the **Paragraph** dialog box or ruler.

  Here are the indent types:

  - **Left Indent** Indents each line of a paragraph on the left.

  - **Right Indent** Indents each line of a paragraph on the right.

  - **First Line** Indents only the first line of a paragraph on the left.

- **Hanging** Indents every line of a paragraph on the left with the exception of the first line. This indent type is typically used for paragraphs with bullets or numbering.

- **Space Before and Space After** Adds formatted space before or after each paragraph. As a general rule, 12 points is around the same size as a line of text formatted with a 12-point font size for most fonts. The default setting for new blank documents is 8 points of space after each paragraph.

  The Don't Add Space Between Paragraphs Of The Same Style option will suppress formatted space both before and after paragraphs that are next to each other and have the same style applied. This option is typically used for lists of information, such as a bulleted or numbered list.

- **Line Spacing** Changes the space between the lines of a paragraph. The default setting for a new blank document is **Multiple**, **1.08** lines.

TIP You can also set left and right indents and change before and after paragraph spacing on the Page Layout tab in the Paragraph group.

Setting indents by using the ruler

To use the ruler to modify text indents, drag the indent markers on the ruler. The indent marker on the left, which looks like an hourglass, has three indents. The top triangle sets a first line indent, the bottom triangle sets a hanging indent, and the box at the bottom sets a left indent. The indent marker on the right changes the right indent only.

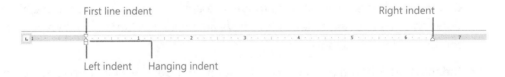

First line indent   Right indent

Left indent   Hanging indent

TIP When dragging indent marks on the ruler, you can display your preferred unit of measure, such as inches or centimeters, instead of tick marks. To do so, hold down the Alt key and then drag an indent marker.

When a paragraph is indented, the indent markers on the ruler will reflect the indent type and size of the indent for the current paragraph.

Additional paragraph formats on the Line And Page Breaks page of the Paragraph dialog box are covered later in this chapter, in the section titled, "Managing pagination through formatting."

Exploring other character formats

Like paragraph formats, additional character formats can be accessed in the Font dialog box, which can be displayed by clicking the dialog box launcher in the Font group.

KEYBOARD SHORTCUT Press Ctrl+D.

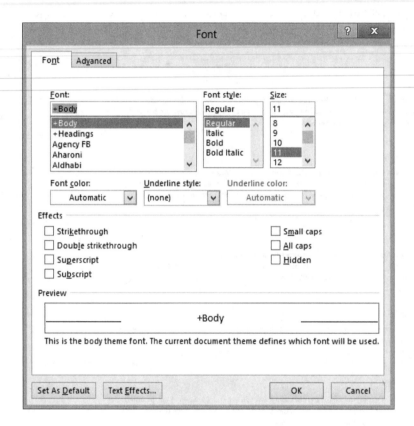

Here is a list of those additional formats:

- **Double Strikethrough** Similar to **Strikethrough**, but an additional horizontal line is added in the middle of the text.

- **Small Caps** Displays lowercase characters as uppercase but maintains the lowercase character height.

  KEYBOARD SHORTCUT Press Ctrl+Shift+K.

- **All Caps** All characters appear in uppercase.

  KEYBOARD SHORTCUT Press Ctrl+Shift+A.

- **Hidden** Used to exclude text from printing or appearing on the screen. Additionally, several advanced features use hidden text formatting, such as table of contents and index fields. To display hidden text, click the **Show/Hide ¶** command on the **Home** tab in the **Paragraph** group. The formatting mark for hidden text is a dotted underline.

  KEYBOARD SHORTCUT Press Ctrl+Shift+H.

  This·is·text·with·the·Hidden·format·applied.¶

TIP To print hidden text, click the File tab to display the Backstage view, and then click Options. On the Display tab, under the Printing options section, select Print Hidden Text.

8

Changing case

You might encounter a situation in which you want to change lowercase text to all caps, all caps to lowercase, mixed-case text to title case, and so on. Instead of making a lot of edits, you can change the case of text in Word as easily as changing the font, by using the Change Case command, located on the Home tab, in the Font group.

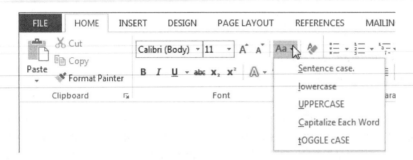

TIP Even though it's placed among other formatting commands, the Change Case feature isn't considered formatting, because it actually converts text characters. Keep in mind that formatting only changes the appearance of your text in a document, which may not be preserved if you make other changes, or if your text is pasted into a different application. The All Caps format in the Font dialog box, however, is a format. You may have noticed that the case of the title for the practice file used in this chapter changed to uppercase in the exercise for the section titled, "Setting default document formatting for your documents." This is because the All Caps format is included in the Title style, and the actual case of the text isn't changed.

You can change the case to one of the following options:

- **Sentence case** Capitalizes the first letter of each sentence

- **Lowercase** Converts all characters to lowercase

- **Uppercase** Converts all characters to uppercase

- **Capitalize each word** Capitalizes the first letter of each word, including words that aren't typically capitalized, such as *and*, *the*, and *or*

- **Toggle case** Converts each uppercase letter to lowercase and each lowercase letter to uppercase

KEYBOARD SHORTCUT You can also use Shift+F3 to change the case of text. Unlike with most keyboard shortcuts, each time you press Shift+F3, it will cycle through the Change Case options, which are determined by your text selection. If you select a paragraph or sentence, provided the period or full stop is selected, Shift+F3 will cycle through uppercase, lowercase, and sentence case. If your selection doesn't include a period or full stop, it will cycle through uppercase, lowercase, and capitalizing each word.

Managing pagination through formatting

Pagination is how your document is divided into pages and how your content flows from one page to the next. Word sets page breaks, called *automatic page breaks*, based on the amount of text and other elements, like pictures and charts, that can fit on a page. If you want to change where Word ends a page, you have two options:

- **Manual Page Break** Sets a point where the following content will begin on a new page, similar to a **Next Page** section break. The best practice for using manual page breaks is to add them where you want to always start a new page. For example, you might add a manual page break after a cover page to force content that doesn't belong on the cover page to start on a new page. If you use a manual page break to keep content together on the same page, then this can result in pages with large amounts of white space when your document is opened on another computer. The reason for this is that every printer has a different printable area. For example, some ink jet printers don't print below 0.7 inches on a page, compared to most laser jet printers, which can print to the edge of a page. Because Word takes the printer you're using into account when it paginates a document, where it places an automatic page break may not always be the same.

  To insert a manual page break, on the Insert tab, in the Pages group, click Page Break.

  KEYBOARD SHORTCUT Press Alt+Enter.

8

- **Paragraph pagination options** These pagination options give you the most control over how text flows from one page to the next and are located on the **Line and Page Breaks** page of the **Paragraph** dialog box.

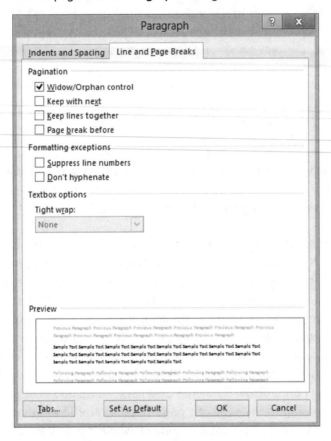

- **Widow/Orphan Control** This option is set by default for all text. It keeps at least two lines of a paragraph on a page. It prevents the last line of a paragraph from being printed by itself at the top of a page or the first line of a paragraph from being displayed by itself at the bottom of a page.

- **Keep with next** Keeps text on the same page as the next paragraph. The built-in **Heading** styles include this option, because you typically don't want a heading to print at the bottom of a page without accompanying text. Another example is if you have text that refers to a picture and you want to keep the picture with the descriptive text.

  You can also use this option to keep table rows together. If you want to keep all rows of a table together on the same page, add this format to every row except the last one.

  SEE ALSO For more information on tables, see Chapter 9, "Presenting information."

- **Page break before** This format is similar to a manual page break. It's added as a paragraph option so it can be included in a style. For example, if each chapter of a book needs to start on a new page, you can add the page break before to the style you're using for the chapter title. This way, each time you use the style, you're also starting a new page.

- **Keep lines together** Keep all lines in a paragraph on the same page. Set this option if you don't want a paragraph to break across two pages.

The formatting mark for all paragraph pagination options is a tiny black square to the left of the first line of the paragraph; it looks similar to a square bullet character.

▪ Along·with·our·traditional·vertical·logo,·we've·add·a·new·horizontal·logo.·As·we·are·still·in·the·process·of·rolling·out·our·

new·brand,·please·see·our·team·site·for·guidelines·on·new·logo·usage.·¶

Vertical·logo¶

In this exercise, you'll add a pagination format to keep a paragraph on the same page as a picture.

➔ SET UP If the My Rebrand Campaign_D document you saved in the previous exercise is still open, follow the steps. If you skipped the previous exercise, open the Fabrikam Rebrand Campaign_D document located in the Chapter08 practice file folder to complete this exercise, and then follow the steps.

1   On page **3**, notice how the top of the page displays a picture and text, and the previous page has the heading, **Brand Colors** and a short introduction paragraph.

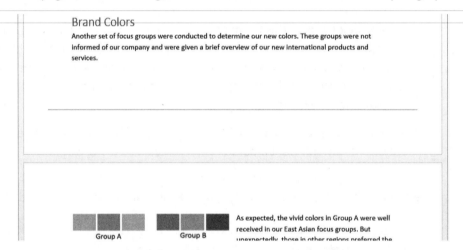

2   To move the **Brand Colors** introduction text to the next page, place your cursor in the paragraph below the **Brand Colors** heading.

3   On the **Home** tab, in the **Paragraph** group, click the dialog box launcher to display the **Paragraph** dialog box.

4   On the **Line and Page Breaks** page, select the check box for **Keep with next,** and then click **OK**.

5   Notice how both the **Brand Colors** heading and introduction paragraph were moved to the next page.

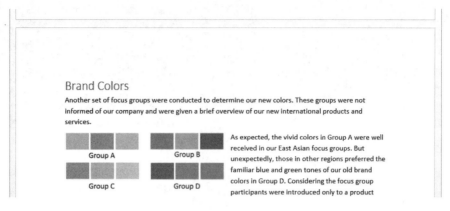

Brand Colors

Another set of focus groups were conducted to determine our new colors. These groups were not informed of our company and were given a brief overview of our new international products and services.

Group A Group B

Group C Group D

As expected, the vivid colors in Group A were well received in our East Asian focus groups. But unexpectedly, those in other regions preferred the familiar blue and green tones of our old brand colors in Group D. Considering the focus group participants were introduced only to a product

TIP Because the Brand Colors paragraph is formatted with the Heading 1 style, the Keep With Next format has already been applied, and it moves to the next page as well.

⊗ CLEAN UP Save the document as My Rebrand Campaign_final, close it, and exit Word.

TIP The Chapter08 practice file folder also has a Fabrikam Rebrand Campaign_final document, if you want to compare yours to the completed result.

Key points

- The first set of formats you should change in a document is the document defaults, located on the Design tab.

- Use section breaks to change page formats such as page margins, page orientation, and paper size, in a portion of a document.

- Utilize styles in your documents to help save time when formatting a document, and to help maintain consistent formatting.

- The Change Case command, on the Home tab, in the Font group, converts your text characters.

- The All Caps format in the Font dialog box doesn't convert your text and only makes text characters appear uppercase.

- Use a manual page break only when you always want to start a new page.

- Use paragraph pagination options to control how text flows from one page to the next.

8

Chapter at a glance

Format

Format simple lists by using bullets or numbering, page 212

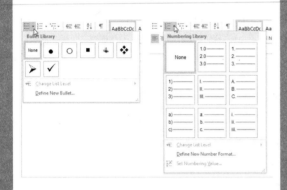

Create

Create tabbed lists by using manual tabs, page 215

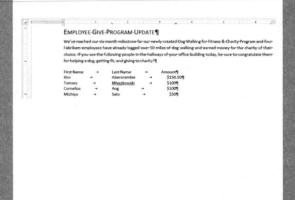

Convert

Convert tabbed lists to tables and insert new tables, page 219

Enhance

Enhance tables by using built-in table styles, page 225

First Name	Last Name	Amount
Kim	Abercrombie	$150
Tomasz	Mieszkowski	$100
Cornelius	Ang	$100
Michiyo	Sato	$50

Presenting information

9

IN THIS CHAPTER, YOU WILL LEARN HOW TO

- Format simple lists by using bullets and numbering.
- Create tabbed lists.
- Insert and convert tables.
- Enhance tables.

Most of the time you can use paragraphs of text to convey your information. Other times you may need to present your information in a more structured format, such as in a list or in multiple columns. Or you may use structured elements to make your document easier to follow. For example, if you have a long list of information separated by commas, you can use bullets or numbering to break it down into smaller paragraphs. Or if you have several pieces of related information that you want to keep next to each other on the same line, you can use a tabbed list or a table.

The following provides a description of various ways to present information in a structured format in Microsoft Word.

- **Numbered list** This is a series of paragraphs that begin with a number and are usually formatted with a hanging indent so wrapped lines of the paragraph align to the text and not the number. This type of list is typically used for sequential steps when the order is important, such as a set of step-by-step instructions.
- **Bulleted list** This is similar to a numbered list, but each item begins with a symbol instead of a number. Like a numbered list, it's usually formatted with a hanging indent so wrapped lines of the paragraph align to the text and not the bullet. You use a bulleted list when the order of the paragraphs isn't important, such as a list of inventory items or a summary of information.

- **Tabbed list** This is simply columns that are separated by tabs, such as a list of names and addresses.

- **Table** A table is an arrangement of rows and columns typically used for more complex information. Unlike the other list types, tables have more formatting options, such as the ability to add shading to alternating rows or columns. You can also add table column headings that can be set to repeat at the top of a page for long lists of information.

In this chapter, you'll create a simple numbered and bulleted list, and a tabbed list that uses manual tabs. At the end of the chapter, you'll create tables and convert existing text into a table. You'll also enhance tables by using built-in table styles and new border formatting features.

PRACTICE FILES To complete the exercises in this chapter, you need the practice files contained in the Chapter09 practice file folder. For more information, see "Download the practice files" in this book's Introduction.

Formatting simple lists by using bullets and numbering

There are two methods you can use to create a simple list formatted with bullets or numbers:

- **Automatic** Word has an **AutoFormat As You Type** feature that converts characters you enter into a bulleted or numbered list. For a bulleted list, precede your paragraph text with an asterisk and then press the **Spacebar**. After the space is added, the asterisk is converted to a bullet character, and then a bulleted list is created. For a numbered list, precede your paragraph text with the number 1 followed by a period or closing parenthesis. As with a bulleted list, a numbered list is created when you press the **Spacebar**. You can also press **Tab** after the number and the numbered list will be created when you press **Enter**.

  TIP To turn off the automatic bullets and numbering feature, or to explore other AutoFormat As You Type options, click the File tab to display the Backstage view, and then click Options. On the Proofing page, click the AutoCorrect Options button and then click the AutoFormat As You Type tab. In the Apply As You Type section, clear the check boxes for Automatic Bulleted Lists and Automatic Numbered Lists.

- **Bullets and Numbering galleries** The **Bullets** and **Numbering** galleries are located on the **Home** tab, in the **Paragraph** group.

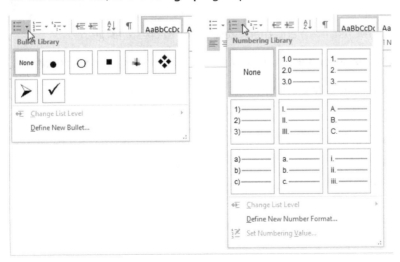

You can use these galleries to format existing selected paragraphs as a bulleted or numbered list, or you can select a bullet or numbering format before you begin creating the list.

When you use either method, Word also formats your text with the built-in List Paragraph style, which adds an indent and suppresses the space between the paragraphs.

SEE ALSO For more information on styles, see Chapter 8, "Formatting documents."

In this exercise, you'll create an automatic numbered list, modify the number format, and then change the numbered list to a bulleted list.

 SET UP You don't need any practice files to complete this exercise. Start Word, create a blank document, and then follow the steps.

1   On the first line of your document, enter 1) and press the **Spacebar**.

> **TIP** If you click the AutoCorrect Options button that's displayed to the left of your numbered list, you can undo the automatic numbering, turn the feature off, or display the AutoFormat As You Type dialog box.

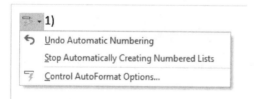

2   Enter First list item and then press **Enter** to create list item 2.

3   Next to the second list item, enter Second list item and press **Enter**.

4   Create a total of five list items.

> 1) First list item
> 2) Second list item
> 3) Third list item
> 4) Fourth list item
> 5) Fifth list item

5   After you enter the fifth list item, press **Enter** two times to end the numbered list and return to normal text.

> **TIP** Pressing Enter twice is built-in functionality for ending a numbered or bulleted list, and you're not adding an empty paragraph. Within a list, if you place your cursor at the beginning of the paragraph, you can press Backspace to remove the number or bullet and keep the indent. Pressing Backspace twice will format the paragraph as normal text.

6   Select all of your list items, and on the **Home** tab, in the **Paragraph** group, click the arrow next to the **Numbering** button, and in the **Numbering Library**, select another numbering format, such as one that uses Roman numerals or alpha characters.

7   To change your numbered list to a bulleted list, on the **Home** tab, in the **Paragraph** group, click the arrow next to the **Bullets** button, and in the **Bullets Library**, select another bullet style, such as a square bullet.

- First list item
- Second list item
- Third list item
- Fourth list item
- Fifth list item

❌ CLEAN UP Close your document without saving changes.

> **SEE ALSO** For more advanced information on formatting bulleted and numbered lists and using multilevel lists, see *Microsoft Word 2013 Step by Step* by Joan Lambert and Joyce Cox (Microsoft Press, 2013).

9

Creating tabbed lists

A tabbed list can be used for a small amount of information that will stay together on the same page and within a small number of columns. To easily control the position of each column and align the data in the columns, you set your own tabs, called *manual tab stops*. When you press the Tab key without first setting a manual tab stop, you move between default tab stops that are left aligned and occur every 0.5 inches, or 1.27 centimeters.

As demonstrated in the exercise for composing documents in Chapter 7, "Editing and composing documents," you only want to press the Tab key once to align information horizontally. A manual tab stop overrides the default tab stop, enabling you to press the Tab key once to position your data. This functionality also enables you to reposition a column after your data is entered, by moving the tab stop.

There are three tabs for aligning text: left, center, and right. Similar to the text alignment commands, the tabs align text within the columns to the specified type. For example, a center tab will align each item in a column at the center of the tab stop. The manual tab used specifically for numbers is a decimal tab. This tab type aligns numbers to the decimal point position, and the numbers in a table will align to a decimal tab without being preceded by a tab character.

TIP Decimal tabs are preferred over right tabs when aligning numbers, because this setting aligns numbers according to the position of the decimal, or period, even if you're not using decimals. You can also use a decimal tab to align any type of data that contains a period or full stop.

To select a manual tab type, click the tab selector, located at the intersection of the vertical and horizontal ruler. Each time you click the tab selector, you cycle through the different types of tabs. Then, to set a tab, click the ruler at the location where you want the tab to be set. To remove a tab, drag it up or down off the ruler.

Tab selector

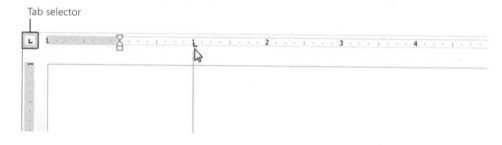

TIP The first line and hanging indent markers are also available when you cycle through the tab selector, and you can set those like you do manual tabs. Another tab type is the vertical bar. This tab doesn't position data. Instead, it inserts a vertical bar at the manual tab stop position. To determine the type of tab or indent that's displayed in the tab selector or on the ruler, point to the tab and view the ScreenTip.

In this exercise, you'll set a manual tab stop for existing data and change the position of the tab after it's been set. You'll also set a manual tab to create a memo heading.

SET UP You need the List Example document located in the Chapter09 practice file folder to complete this exercise. Open the List Example document, and then follow the steps.

1   If your ruler isn't displayed, on the **View** tab, in the **Show** group, select the check box for **Ruler**.

2   On the **Home** tab, in the **Paragraph** group, click the **Show/Hide ¶** button to view the formatting marks.

3   Note the single tab between all of the list items and how the amounts don't align correctly. Place your cursor in one of the lines in the list and note the left manual tab stop in the ruler.

   TIP The list doesn't have additional formatted space between the list items. This is because the built-in No Spacing style has been applied to all paragraphs in the list.

4   To set a decimal tab and align the amounts, select the list headings and all employee information.

   TIP To select the list data, place your mouse to the left of the list items, point at the list headings, and then click and drag down through Michiyo Sato's data.

5   At the intersection of the vertical and horizontal ruler, click the tab selector until a **Decimal Tab** is displayed.

6   On the ruler, click the 5-inch or 13-centimeter mark to set the decimal tab and note how the amounts correctly align.

IMPORTANT

7   To reduce the amount of space between the last names and amounts, with the list selected, drag the decimal tab to the 3.5-inch or 9-centimeter mark.

> **TIP** For precision, hold the Alt key while dragging to view measurements on the ruler instead of the tick marks.

8   To demonstrate how numbers align to the decimal point position, change the first amount in the list to $150.50.

9   Press **Ctrl+End** to move your cursor to the end of the document and remove the text selection.

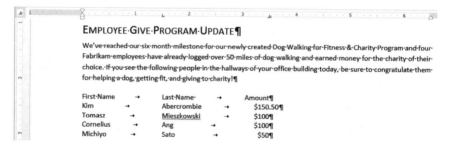

10   To set a manual tab for the memo heading, move the cursor after the word **TO:** near the top of the document.

11   Click the tab selector until a left tab is displayed, and set a left tab at the 1-inch or 2.5-centimeter mark.

12   Press the **Tab** key, enter All Employees, and then press **Enter**.

13   Enter FROM:, press the **Tab** key, and then enter Human Resources.

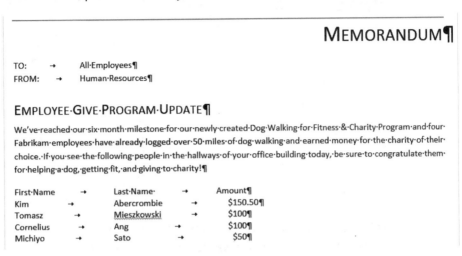

✖ CLEAN UP Turn off the display of formatting marks, save the List Example document as My List Example, and then close the document.

Inserting tables

A table is a grid-like structure with columns and rows. The intersection of each column and row forms a cell, and the data you enter is entered in the cell. You can put almost anything in a cell that you can put in normal document text, and you can format table text the same way you format a paragraph of text. There are several methods you can use to create a table, which are located on the Insert tab, in the Tables group.

- **Table gallery** Creates an empty table using the dimensions you select by clicking the table grid at the intersection of the number of columns and rows you want to use in your table. The inserted table spans the width of the text area with evenly distributed columns and rows.

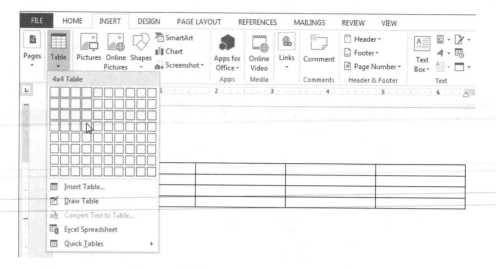

- **Insert Table** For adding additional options to a table before it's created, the **Insert Table** dialog box enables you to select the number of rows and columns, similar to the **Table** gallery. But unlike the **Table** gallery, the **Insert Table** dialog box allows you to select an **AutoFit** behavior.

The following provides descriptions for each of the AutoFit options:

- **Fixed Column Width** You can set a default size for each column or use the **Auto** setting to insert a table that spans the width of the text area with evenly distributed columns and rows.

- **AutoFit to contents** Inserts a table with small columns that resize as you enter your information.

First Name	Last Name	Amount		

- **AutoFit to window** The inserted table initially spans the width of the text area with evenly distributed columns and rows. But unlike in the fixed column width option, column sizes and the table size are based on percentages rather than fixed measurements. If you change the paper size or page orientation, the table will be resized to fit the new text area.

- **Draw Table** For a less structured table that doesn't have uniform columns and rows, you can use the **Draw Table** command to draw your table in a document. This type of table is good for creating a fill-in-the-blank type of form or for a complex page layout.

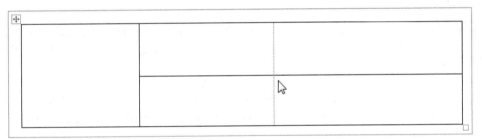

SEE ALSO For more information on using a table for a complex page layout, see the sidebar titled "Using tables to lay out information on a page" at the end of this section.

- **Convert Text to Table** Converts list data that is separated by a divider, such as a tab or comma, to a table. The **Convert Text to Table** dialog box has the same **AutoFit** behavior options as the **Insert Table** dialog box, and it also includes options to identify the character to replace with a table column.

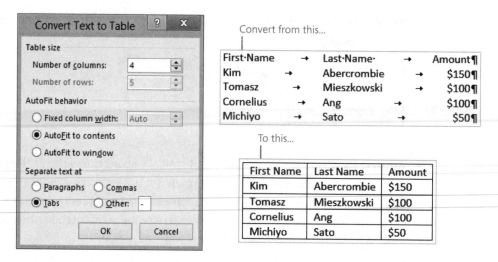

In this exercise, you'll convert the tabbed list you created in a previous exercise to a table that will always maintain the same width of the text area, and you'll change the page orientation to gain a better understanding of the AutoFit To Window option. You'll then insert a new table by using the Table gallery.

SET UP You need the List Example_B document located in the Chapter09 practice file folder to complete this exercise. Open the List Example_B document, and then follow the steps.

1 Select the list of names, including the headings, and on the ruler, at the 3.5-inch mark, drag the decimal tab off the ruler to delete it. (You'll add it back in another exercise.)

   TIP If you have difficulty deleting the decimal tab, point to the tab and watch for the ScreenTip. After it appears, click the tab and drag it up or down off of the ruler.

2 On the **Insert** tab, in the **Tables** group, click the **Table** button, and then click **Convert Text to Table**.

3 In the **Convert Text to Table** dialog box, note that the number of rows and columns match the tabbed selection, and near the bottom, under **Separate text at**, the **Tabs** option is selected.

4 Click **OK** to convert the tabbed list to a table.

5 To view how the table will be resized to fit your text area, on the **Page Layout** tab, in the **Page Setup** group, click the **Orientation** button, and then click **Landscape**.

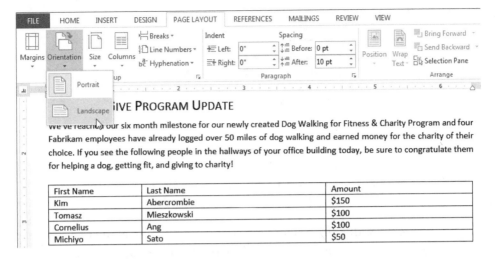

...IVE PROGRAM UPDATE

We've reached our six month milestone for our newly created Dog Walking for Fitness & Charity Program and four Fabrikam employees have already logged over 50 miles of dog walking and earned money for the charity of their choice. If you see the following people in the hallways of your office building today, be sure to congratulate them for helping a dog, getting fit, and giving to charity!

First Name	Last Name	Amount
Kim	Abercrombie	$150
Tomasz	Mieszkowski	$100
Cornelius	Ang	$100
Michiyo	Sato	$50

6   Change the page orientation back to portrait.

7   To insert a table by using the **Table** gallery, press **Ctrl+End** to move the cursor to the end of the document and press **Enter** twice.

TIP A paragraph must be added between two separate tables.

8   On the **Insert** tab, in the **Tables** group, click **Table** and then, in the grid, select a 3-column-by-5-row table.

TIP In the Table gallery, above the grid, a 3 × 5 Table label will appear, and the table will be shown being created in the document as you make your grid selection.

✖ CLEAN UP Save the document as My List Example. If you're proceeding to the next exercise, leave Word and My List Example open. Otherwise, close the document and exit Word.

When you create a table, you're not limited to the number of rows and columns you initially selected, and you can resize both the columns and the rows. To add new rows or columns, point to the left of the table between two rows or above the table between two columns. Watch for the on-screen insertion indicator to appear, and then click the indicator to insert a new row or column. When you are inserting new columns, if the width of the table is the same size as the text area, the width of the table columns will be reduced to accommodate the newly added column.

9

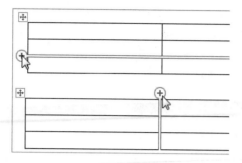

TIP You can also use the Table Tools Layout tools tab and the Rows & Columns group to insert new rows and columns.

To change the width of a column or height of a row, point at the right border of the column you want to resize or point to the bottom border of the row you want to resize. Watch for the mouse pointer to change to a sizing pointer, and then drag.

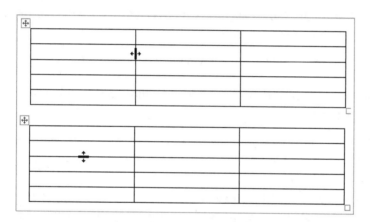

To delete cells, rows, columns, or the entire table, place your cursor in the table element you want to delete. On the Table Tools Layout tool tab, in the Rows & Columns group, click Delete, and then click the command that corresponds with what you want to delete, such as Delete Rows.

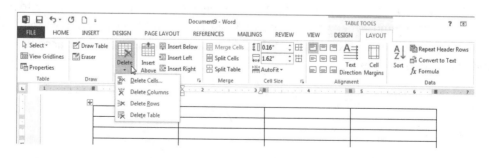

TIP To delete multiple cells, rows, or columns, select what you want to delete before clicking your desired delete command.

SEE ALSO For more information on creating tables, such as drawing tables, see *Microsoft Word 2013 Step by Step,* by Joan Lambert and Joyce Cox (Microsoft Press, 2013).

Enhancing tables

When you insert a table, all of the columns and rows are formatted with a 1/2 point border by default. After your table is created, you can modify the border formatting or shade rows and columns. To format a table, place your cursor in the table, and then click the Table Tools Design tool tab.

The following list provides descriptions of the primary tools that are located on the Table Tools Design tool tab:

- **Table Styles gallery** The **Table Styles** gallery contains preformatted table styles that match your current document theme. To apply a table style, click a style in the gallery.

- **Table Style Options group** The options in the **Table Style Options** group enable you to turn on or off special formats that are included in most of the table styles. For example, if the first row of your table has text that identifies each column, you can use the **Header Row** option to format it differently than other rows. The **Total Row**, **First Column**, and **Last Column** options will also add different formatting to the corresponding table element. The **Banded Rows** and **Banded Columns** options will format odd and even rows or columns differently. The exact formats that are added by these options will vary depending on the table style you choose. You can select options in this group before you apply a table style, and the gallery will be updated to reflect the formats. You can also turn the table style options on or off after a table style has been applied to modify the table formatting.

    TIP The Total Row is the last row of a table. You typically use Total Row formatting for tables with values. However, if you're not working with values and need to format the last row of a table differently, you can still add Total Row formats.

9

- **Border Styles gallery** The **Border Styles** gallery provides a collection of border styles that match the current document theme.

Theme Borders

Recently Used Borders

✎ Border Sampler

When you select a style from the gallery, it turns on the Border Painter, located at the end of the Table Tools Design tool tab, in the Border group. Using the Border Painter is similar to drawing a table, because you *paint* borders by dragging through the borders you want to format.

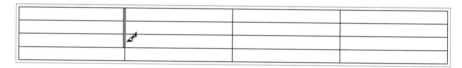

TIP The Border Sampler command at the bottom of the Border Styles gallery can be used to pick up existing table border formats for the Border Painter, which makes it easy to ensure that you have consistent formatting.

After your table is formatted, you can add additional formats to the contents of a table just like you would do for text and paragraphs, using the Home tab and either the Font or Paragraph group.

In this exercise, you'll format names and amounts in a table that you created in the previous exercise, using the Table Styles gallery, the Table Style options, and the Border Painter.

➡ SET UP If the My List Example document and Word are still open from the previous exercise, then follow the steps. Otherwise, you need the List Example_C document located in the Chapter09 practice file folder to complete this exercise. Open the List Example_C document, and then follow the steps.

1   Place your cursor in the table of names and amounts.

2   On the **Table Tools Design** tool tab, in the **Table Styles** gallery, click the third table style, **Plain Table 1**.

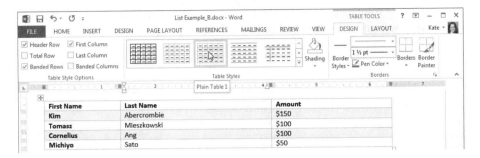

3   To remove the bold formatting from the first column, in the **Table Style Options** group, clear the check box for **First Column**.

4   To gain a better understanding of alternating row formatting, in the **Table Style Options** group, clear the check box for **Banded Rows**.

5   Turn the banded row formatting back on.

6   To resize the **Last Name** column, place your mouse pointer on the right border of the column, watch for the sizing pointer, and then drag to the left until it's about 1.27 inches or 3.23 centimeters wide.

TIP Hold the Alt key while you're dragging to display measurements instead of tick marks on the ruler.

7   Resize the **Amount** column so it's about 0.8 inches or 2 centimeters wide.

8   To add the decimal tab back and align the values in the **Amount** column, point to the top edge of the **Amount** column, watch for the column select arrow, and then click to select the entire column.

Amount
$150
$100
$100
$50

TIP To select a row, place your mouse in the selection bar, point at the row you want to select, and then click to select the entire row. To select the entire table, click the icon with the multidirectional arrows in the upper-left corner of the table. You can also use the icon to drag a table to another location, so make sure you click, rather than click and drag, when using it to select a table.

9   On the ruler, click the tab selector until a **Decimal Tab** is displayed, and then set a decimal tab near the right end of the **Amount** column.

10   Click anywhere in the document to remove the column selection.

First Name	Last Name	Amount
Kim	Abercrombie	$150
Tomasz	Mieszkowski	$100
Cornelius	Ang	$100
Michiyo	Sato	$50

TIP You don't need to delete the decimal tab prior to converting your text to a table. This step is added to demonstrate how numbers in a table are aligned to a decimal tab without a preceding tab character. To enter a tab in a table, press Ctrl+Tab.

 CLEAN UP Save the document as My List Example_B, and exit Word.

Using tables to lay out information on a page

Though tables can be used for lists of data, they can also be used for complex layouts, to position information, or to flow paragraphs in parallel side-by-side columns. When tables are used in this manner, columns and rows don't appear in a printed document; all you get is the information. In the document, you can turn the table gridlines on or off while you're working by using the Gridlines button in the Tables group on the Table Tools Layout tool tab. This type of table is called a *borderless table*.

An example of a borderless table is located in the Example Newsletter document included in the Chapter09 practice file folder. The top of the newsletter has a two-column table. It is used to place the newsletter title along with the edition and volume to the right of the company logo. The second column is divided into two rows in order to create a taller cell for the newsletter title, *Employee News*, so more space can be added above and below the title.

FABRIKAM EMPLOYEE NEWS

OCTOBER EDITION, VOLUME 36

To remove border formatting from a table, select the table and on the Table Tools Design tool tab, in the Borders group, click the arrow below Borders, and then in the Borders gallery, click No Border.

Key points

- You can present your information in a more structured format, such as in a list or in multiple columns.

- To create a bulleted list while entering text, enter an asterisk and then press the Spacebar.

- To create a numbered list while entering text, enter the number 1 followed by a period or closing parenthesis and then press the Spacebar.

- You can change a bulleted list to a numbered list by choosing a number format from the Numbering Library, and vice-versa.

- A tabbed list is best for small amounts of information that will stay together on the same page and for a small number of columns.

- For lists that may not stay together on the same page or have several columns, use a table instead of a tabbed list.

- You can convert a tabbed list to table.

- The AutoFit To Window option in the Insert Table dialog box will create a table that automatically resizes to the text area if the page orientation or page margins change.

- When you are formatting tables by using built-in table styles, the Table Style Options group on the Table Tools Design tool tab enables you to turn special table formats, such as a header row, on or off.

9

Chapter at a glance

Correct

Correct proofing errors,
page 232

Inspect

Inspect documents before publishing,
page 235

Create

Create PDF files in Word,
page 241

Print

Print documents,
page 247

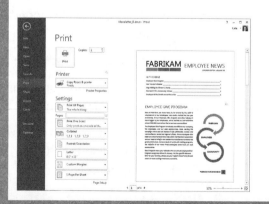

Finalizing documents

10

IN THIS CHAPTER, YOU WILL LEARN HOW TO

- Correct proofing errors.

- Inspect documents before publishing.

- Mark documents as final.

- Create PDF files in Word.

- Print documents.

There are two different ways to distribute a final Microsoft Word document: You can print a hard copy of your document or publish it electronically through email, your company network, or on a website. Prior to its delivery, there are a few things you should consider.

First, regardless of how your document will be distributed, you want to ensure there are no proofing errors you haven't already addressed. Second, if you'll deliver your document electronically, you may want to remove personal data and make sure there isn't other information in your document that you don't know about, such as hidden text. Then for an electronic file, you can mark it as a final copy to let others know additional edits shouldn't be made, or deliver it as a PDF file rather than as a Word document. Finally, it's also a good idea to review it in its final format to make sure there are no errors you may have previously missed. Keep in mind that the proofing tools won't catch everything, and you are the best proofreader.

In this chapter, you'll learn how to perform a final proofing check, use the Document Inspector to inspect a document, and remove personal information. You'll also learn how to mark your document as a final copy and create a PDF file that contains navigation bookmarks. At the end of this chapter, you'll learn how to print your entire document, along with how to print a portion of it if you find that certain pages need to be reprinted after your final review.

PRACTICE FILES To complete the exercises in this chapter, you need the practice file contained in the Chapter10 practice file folder. For more information, see "Download the practice files" in this book's Introduction.

Correcting proofing errors

By default, the following types of proofing errors are flagged as you enter text in Word 2013:

- **Spelling errors** A red wavy line is displayed below words that might be misspelled. The red wavy line doesn't necessarily mean that a word is misspelled; it means that the word isn't in a built-in or custom dictionary.

- **Grammar errors** A blue wavy line is displayed below a word, phrase, or sentence that breaks a grammar rule or a frequently confused word, such as *affect* or *effect*. The blue wavy line doesn't always mean that there's an error; as with misspelled words, it's up to you to determine if it's correct.

    TIP In previous versions of Word, grammatical errors are identified with a green wavy line. Additionally, grammar errors may not be identified until you correct spelling errors or complete a sentence by entering a period, or full stop, and pressing the Space-bar key. A blue wavy line under a frequently confused word might also appear as you're typing a sentence and then disappear as you provide more context. Because of this, it's best to correct grammar errors after you've entered the full sentence.

To correct a proofing error as you enter text, you can right-click the word or phrase that has a wavy line underneath it and select an option from the list of available corrections.

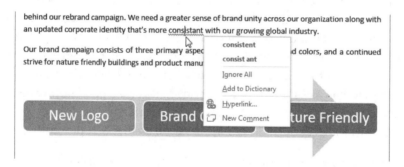

If you're like most users, you likely correct spelling and grammar errors as you're composing a document. Even if you may have made corrections while working, as noted at the beginning of this chapter, it's a good idea to perform a final proofing check prior to distribution. A quick way to determine if your document has proofing errors is to view your status bar.

If the Spelling And Grammar Check icon, which looks like a book, displays an X, there are errors in your document. If the icon shows a check mark, then there are no proofing errors.

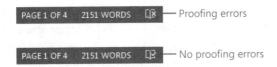 — Proofing errors

PAGE 1 OF 4   2151 WORDS — No proofing errors

If your document has proofing errors, you can perform a final proofing check by using one of the following methods:

- On the **Review** tab, in the **Proofing** group, click the **Spelling & Grammar** button.

- Click the **Spelling and Grammar Check** icon in the status bar.

Either method will display the new proofing pane, which identifies the type of error and the error itself at the top of the pane. It also provides suggestions and more information to help you make the right correction.

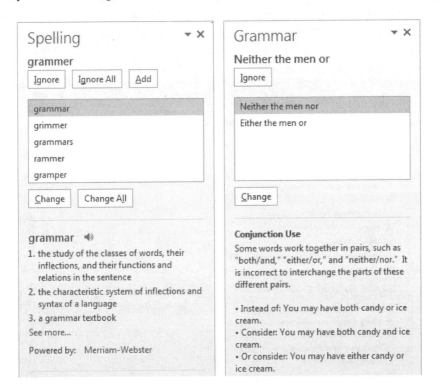

TIP If the listed suggestions for a spelling error aren't correct or if you don't get any suggestions, edit the word in the document and try to get closer to the correct spelling.

If the error is a spelling error, you can click each suggested alternate word and obtain a definition to help you make the right selection. For grammar errors, suggestions are provided along with details about the error. Most have additional examples for rewording the sentence or phrase to make it grammatically correct. As you correct or ignore the various errors, Word will find the next error and display it in the proofing pane. You can also click a spelling or grammar error in a document and the proofing pane results will reflect your current selection.

TIP If you choose to add a correctly spelled word to your dictionary, note that it's added to your custom dictionary only and may appear as a spelling error if the document is opened on someone else's computer.

Additionally, if you often enter words in all caps, a default setting in Word ignores words in uppercase. You may want to change this setting to ensure a more accurate spell check. Another default setting ignores words that contain numbers. If you don't work with a lot of numbers, you may want to change this setting as well. Otherwise, words that may have a number one instead of an *L*, or a zero instead of an *O*, could be missed. To view the available proofing options, click the File tab to display the Backstage view, click Options, and then click Proofing.

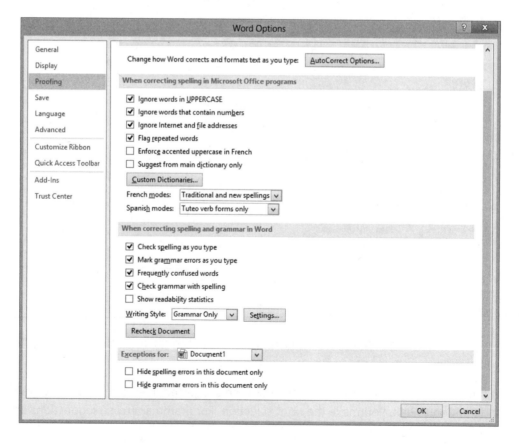

Inspecting documents before publishing

If you're publishing your document electronically outside your company—for example, sending it by email, or publishing it on a webpage or as a PDF file—it's a good idea to remove information that's stored with your document in the document properties. The properties of a document can contain personal information, such as the name of the author and other data that may have been added to the document, including document tags. It's also a good idea to make sure your document doesn't contain information that is not visible, such as hidden text or collapsed headings that may be suppressed from view, even if you don't intend to distribute it externally. To view both document properties and a list of items that you may not be aware of, click the File tab to display the Backstage view, and then click Info.

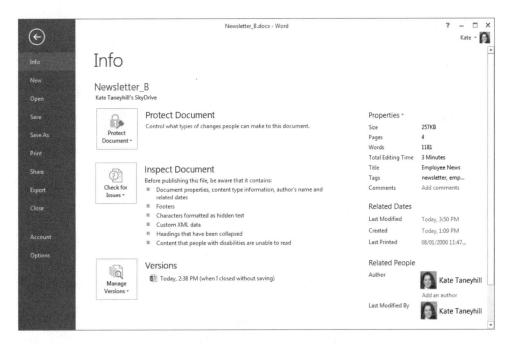

Document properties are listed on the right side of the Info page. A list of items to review before publishing is located under the Inspect Document heading.

TIP To view all document properties, on the right side of the Info page, click Properties and then click Advanced Properties.

Instead of manually scrutinizing your document and deleting information you may not want to share, you can use the Document Inspector to check your document and remove that information for you. To view the Document Inspector, on the Info page, click the Check For Issues button, and then click Inspect Document.

When you inspect a document, the Document Inspector doesn't automatically remove document properties or other data. It checks whether the document contains the type of content listed and presents you with the inspection results for each type of check it preforms. You can then choose to remove the data, make corrections in your document, or not change the information after you've determined it's okay to keep.

In this exercise, you'll run the Document Inspector and correct the issues it discovers.

SET UP You need the Newsletter_B document located in the Chapter10 practice file folder to complete this exercise. Open the Newsletter_B document, and then follow the steps.

1   On page **1**, to the left of the **Employee Give Program** heading, click the **Collapse** button.

> **TIP** You can also right-click the Employee Give Program heading, point to Expand/ Collapse, and then click Collapse Heading.

2   Scroll through the document and note the footer, **Fabrikam Employee News** along with the page number, at the bottom of each page.

3   Click the **File** tab to display the **Backstage** view. If the **Info** page is not displayed, click **Info**.

4   Review the document properties on the right side of the **Info** page, such as the title, tags, and author names. Review the list of items to be aware of prior to publishing, below the **Inspect Document** heading.

5   To the left of the **Inspect Document** heading, click the **Check for Issues** button and then click **Inspect Document**.

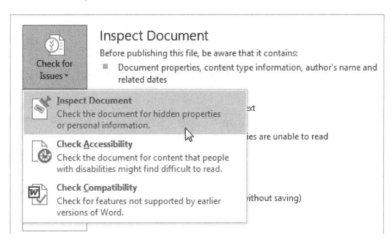

6   In the **Document Inspector** dialog box, click the **Inspect** button to run it and review the inspection results.

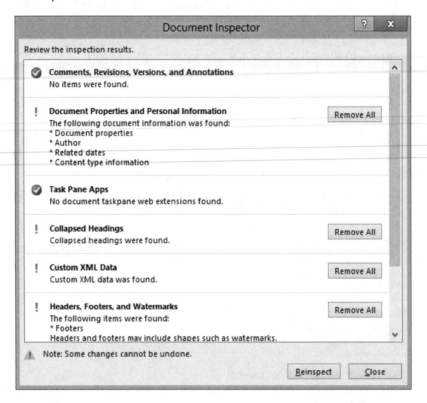

7   To the right of **Document Properties and Personal Information**, click the **Remove All** button.

8   To the right of **Collapsed Headings**, click the **Remove All** button.

9   Close the **Document Inspector** dialog box without removing additional data.

TIP Because there is a visible footer at the bottom of each page, you don't want to remove it. Additionally, the table of contents in the newsletter creates both custom XML data and hidden table of contents fields. The custom XML data can't be removed, and even though hidden text is reported in the list of items on the Info page, because it's associated with the table of contents, it passed the test and the Document Inspector doesn't offer to remove it.

10   On the **Info** page, note that the title, tags, and author names were removed.

11   Click the **Back** arrow to close the **Backstage** view and return to the document.

KEYBOARD SHORTCUT Press the Esc key to close the Backstage view.

12   View page **1** and note that the **Employee Give Program** heading is now expanded.

 CLEAN UP Save the document as My Newsletter_B. If you're proceeding to the next exercise, leave the document and Word open. Otherwise, close the document and exit Word.

The Document Inspector will continue to remove document properties each time you save your document. Other elements, such as headers, footers, or comments, aren't automatically removed, and you'll need to run the Document Inspector again if you make additional editing changes.

To allow Word to start saving document properties after they're removed, on the Info page, below the list of items to be aware of, click the link titled Allow This Information To Be Saved In Your File.

Inspect Document

Before publishing this file, be aware that it contains:

Check for Issues ▾

- ■ Footers
- ■ Characters formatted as hidden text
- ■ Custom XML data
- ■ Content that people with disabilities are unable to read
- ■ A setting that automatically removes properties and personal information when the file is saved
  Allow this information to be saved in your file

TIP To review and correct content that people with disabilities are unable to read, such as missing alt text for graphics, you can run the Accessibility Checker. To run it, click the Check For Issues button and then click Check Accessibility.

Marking documents as final

If you're publishing a final version of your document and want to make sure additional edits aren't made, you can mark your document as final to let others know they're viewing the final version. To do so, on the Info page, click the Protect Document button, and then click Mark As Final.

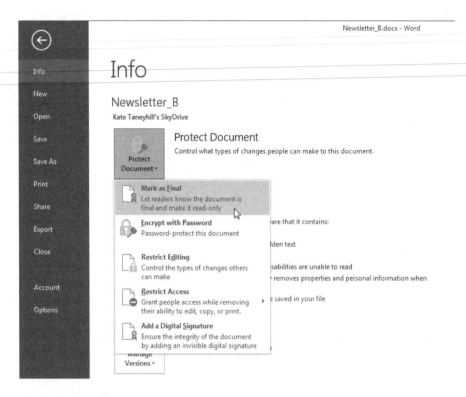

Keep in mind that marking a document as final isn't a security option, and other users can still edit the document. After a document has been finalized, an Info bar is displayed at the top of the document. Although it discourages editing, it also includes an Edit Anyway button. If this button is clicked, the Mark As Final option is removed.

Creating PDF files in Word

If you're sharing a final document with others, your document may not look the same as it does on your computer. The recipient may be using a different printer, which can change document pagination, or he or she may be viewing it in Word Web App, or on another device, such as a Microsoft Surface or smartphone. If exact layout and pagination is a concern, you can save your document as a PDF file, which helps prevent layout changes and can be viewed using a number of PDF viewers, such as the new Windows 8 Reader.

IMPORTANT

To create a PDF file, click the File tab to display the Backstage view, click Export, and then click the Create PDF/XPS button.

When you publish a document as a PDF file, rather than using a PDF printer to create it, you also have the ability to include additional options. For example, you can use heading styles in the document to create navigation bookmarks when it's viewed in readers such as the Windows 8 Reader or Adobe Reader.

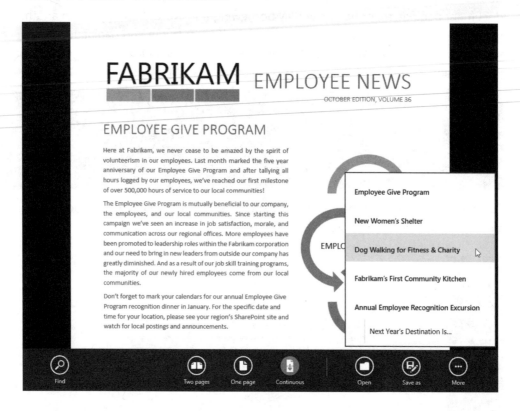

SEE ALSO For more information on heading styles, see Chapter 8, "Formatting documents."

In this exercise, you'll create a PDF document and add navigation bookmarks by using the heading styles.

SET UP If Word and My Newsletter_B are still open from the previous exercise, then follow the steps. Otherwise, you need the Newsletter_B document located in the Chapter10 practice file folder to complete this exercise. Open the Newsletter_B document, and then follow the steps.

1 Click the **File** tab to display the **Backstage** view, and then click **Export**.

2 Verify that the **Create PDF/XPS Document** page is selected, and then click the **Create PDF/XPS** button to display the **Publish as PDF or XPS** dialog box.

   TIP You can also double-click Create PDF/XPS Document below the Export heading to display the Publish As PDF Or XPS dialog box.

3 If you prefer to save the PDF in a location other than your Chapter10 practice files folder, navigate to that location. For example, choose your Microsoft SkyDrive, if desired.

4 In the **File Name** text box, enter My Newsletter_PDF.

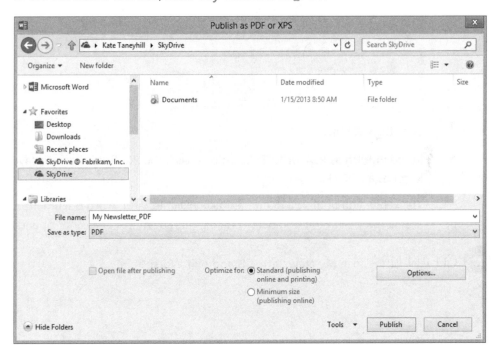

5   Click the **Options** button.

6   In the **Options** dialog box, below **Include non-printing information**, select the check box for **Create bookmarks using** and verify that the **Headings** option is selected.

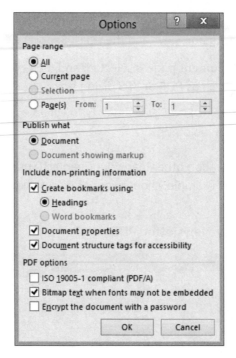

7   Click the **OK** button.

8   In the **Publish as PDF or XPS** dialog box, click the **Publish** button to save the newsletter as a PDF file.

> **TIP** When you publish a document as a PDF file, your Word document remains open and is saved with the original file name. The saved PDF file is not opened in Word.

❌ CLEAN UP   Close My Newsletter_B and exit Word.

TIP The Export page in the Backstage view also has a Change File Type option for saving your Word documents in other formats files, such as OpenDocument or HTML.

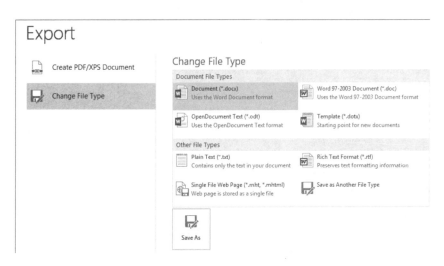

Converting PDF files for editing

A new feature in Word 2013 is PDF Reflow, which converts tables, headers, footers, footnotes, and lists into editable content in Word. You open a PDF file just like you do other Word documents. However, Word doesn't open the original PDF file for editing. Instead, it converts the contents of the PDF file to a Word document. After you make your modifications, you'll need to create the PDF file again by using the steps provided in the "Creating PDF files in Word" section earlier in this chapter.

10

TIP If you want to try this feature, open the My Newsletter_PDF document you created in the previous exercise in Word. If the PDF files are not displayed in the Open dialog box, to the right of the file name near the bottom, click the File Type list and select All Word Documents or PDF files.

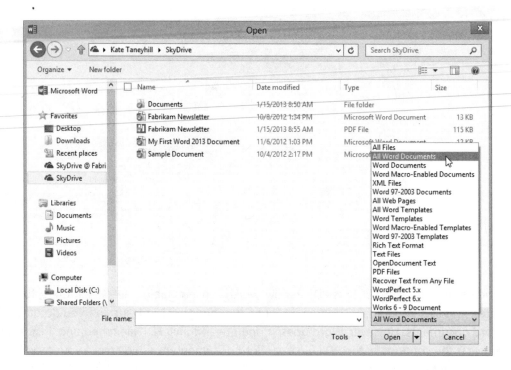

Printing documents

To print a document in Word, you click the File tab to display the Backstage view, and then click Print. The Print page displays a full-page print preview along with printing and page layout options.

TIP If you want to send your document directly to your default printer without previewing it first, you can use the Quick Print command. To add the command to your Quick Access Toolbar, click the arrow at the end of your Quick Access Toolbar and then click Quick Print.

SEE ALSO For more information on customizing your Quick Access Toolbar, see Chapter 1, "Getting comfortable in Office Professional 2013."

In the Printer section, if the printer shown isn't the printer you want to use, click the printer to display a list of additional printers. In the Settings section, there are several options that change your document settings and those that change only how the document will print. The options that will modify your document are page orientation, paper size, and page margins.

The options that will effect only how the document is printed are:

- **Print One-Sided** If your printer can automatically print on both sides of the paper, which is called *duplexing*, then you'll have an option to print on both sides. Otherwise, you'll have a manual option that requires you to reload the paper to print on the other side of the page when prompted.

- **Collated** If you are printing multiple copies of your document, the **Collated** option will print each copy of your document in sequential order. If you want to group each copy of a page together when it prints, select **Uncollated**.

- **1 Page per Sheet** You can change this option to print multiple pages of your document on a single sheet. For example, you may want to print two pages per sheet to proof a draft copy of your document to save paper.

  TIP The 1 Page per Sheet list also has a Scaling option that will print your document on a different paper size. This option only affects how the document prints and doesn't change the page settings in your document.

Word also allows you to print only a portion of your document; for example, if you want to only print the current page. To choose what part of the document to print, click Print All Pages, directly below the Settings heading, and select another option, such as Print Selection, Print Current Page, or Custom Print.

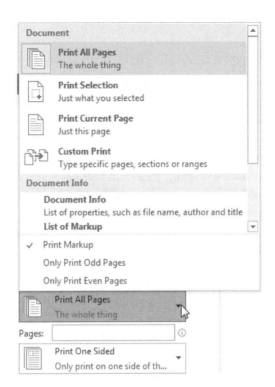

Most of the options are self-explanatory, such as printing only your selected content in the document or the current page. When you select the Custom Print option, you enter a print range in the Pages text box. To print multiple pages that aren't next to each other, enter each page number separated by a comma, as in *3, 6, 8*. To enter a range of pages, separate the starting page number and ending page number with a hyphen, as in *2-5*.

TIP When you choose an option other than Print All Pages, the document preview to the right will not update to reflect your selection and will still show all pages in your document.

After you've made any needed adjustments, click the Print button at the top of the page to send your document to the printer.

10

Printing documents with sections

If your document has section breaks, and you want to print a portion of your document, you use the Custom Print option and enter the section and page information. If you want to print an entire section, enter an *s* followed by the section number. For example, if you want to print only section 1, you enter *s1*. To enter a specific page in a section, you enter a *p* followed by the page number and then an *s* followed by the section number. For example, to print page 4 in section 3, you enter *p4s3*. If you want additional examples of how to enter pages and sections, point to the information icon to the right of the Page text box to display the ScreenTip.

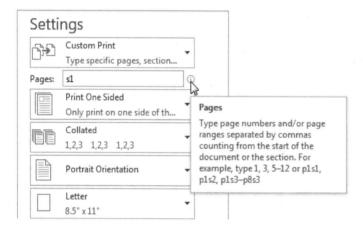

TIP To determine section numbers for your pages, click in the part of the document you want to print and view the section information in the status bar. If this information is not displayed, right-click the status bar and in the Customize Status Bar options, click Section. The page number information should be displayed in the status bar, by default. If it is not displayed, right-click the status bar and then click Page Number.

SEE ALSO For more information on working with sections, see Chapter 8, "Formatting documents."

TIP If your document has heading styles, and you want to print a specific heading and its related content, you can use the Navigation pane to select that portion of your document and set the print options on the Print page in the Backstage view. To do so, in the Navigation Pane, right-click the heading you want to print and then click Print Heading and Content.

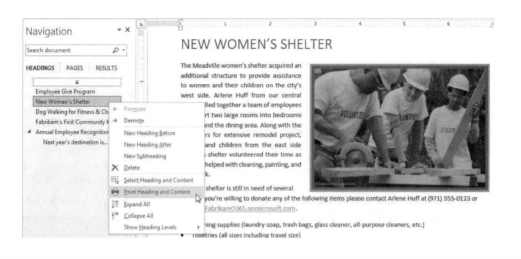

10

Key points

- Even if you correct spelling and grammar errors while you're composing your document, you should include a final proofing check prior to finalizing a document.

- To quickly check for proofing errors, view the Spelling And Grammar icon on your status bar. If the icon displays an X, there are still proofing errors in your document.

- You can use the Document Inspector to remove personal information, such as document properties, and check for items you may not be aware of, such as collapsed headings, hidden text, or other data that may not be visible in a document.

- You don't have to remove all items identified by the Document Inspector. Some information may need to be kept, such as headers and footers. Other information can't be removed, such as the custom XML data that is created by the table of contents feature.

- A document that's been marked as final can still be edited.

- If you're creating a PDF file and your document contains headings, you can add navigation bookmarks that can be used in the PDF viewer.

- Creating a PDF file doesn't prevent it from being edited.

- PDF files can be converted into editable content in Word 2013.

- You can print an entire document or print only a portion of it.

Chapter at a glance

Familiarize

Familiarize yourself with new features,
page 261

Resume

Resume where you left off,
page 261

Welcome back!

Pick up where you left off:

Slide 5
10/08/2012 - 1:36 PM

Add

Add guides to slide masters,
page 261

Getting comfortable in PowerPoint 2013

11

IN THIS CHAPTER, YOU WILL LEARN HOW TO

- Get started working with PowerPoint 2013.

- Explore the PowerPoint 2013 tools.

- Discover the new features in PowerPoint 2013.

Microsoft PowerPoint is arguably the world's most common presentation tool, and PowerPoint 2013 makes it even easier to create and deliver presentations than ever before. Better integration with the cloud and Internet means that accessing online content is more streamlined, and online storing, sharing, and collaboration tools are front-and-center features.

In this chapter, you'll explore the PowerPoint 2013 interface and work with new and improved features.

Getting started working with PowerPoint 2013

As with Microsoft Word and Excel, you typically start PowerPoint 2013 from the Start screen in Windows 8 (not the Start screen in PowerPoint) or the Start menu in Windows 7. You can also start PowerPoint 2013 and open a file at the same time by opening a presentation from an email attachment or by double-clicking one from a place like your Windows Desktop.

Regardless of how you open or start a presentation, before too long, you will more than likely create and edit slides in the PowerPoint workspace interface, which is also known as Normal view.

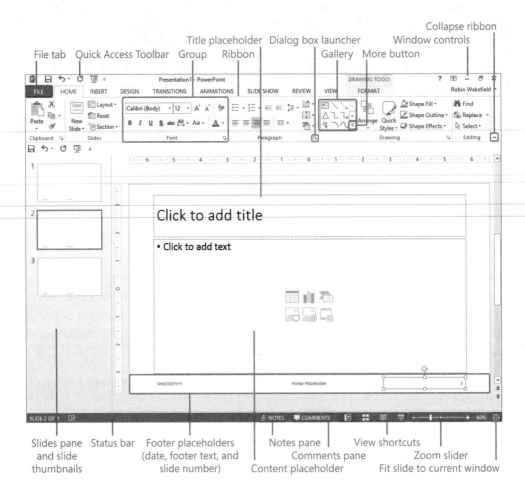

Collapse ribbon
Window controls
Title placeholder   Dialog box launcher
File tab   Quick Access Toolbar   Group   Ribbon   Gallery   More button

Click to add title

• Click to add text

Slides pane   Status bar   Footer placeholders   Notes pane   View shortcuts
and slide   (date, footer text, and   Comments pane   Zoom slider
thumbnails   slide number)   Content placeholder   Fit slide to current window

- **Ribbon** The ribbon is the main component of the PowerPoint interface. It's where you'll find most of the tools for working with your presentations. The ribbon contains task-oriented tabs, and each tab has groups of related commands. For example, on the **Home** tab, the **Clipboard** group contains commands for copying and pasting information in your files. Groups that have additional commands that aren't shown on the ribbon have a dialog box launcher. Clicking the dialog box launcher will display a task pane or dialog box with options that are related to the group. For example, if you click the dialog box launcher for the **Font** group, the **Font** dialog box will be displayed, giving you more formatting choices, such as **Small Caps**, **Superscript**, and **Subscript**.

- Also note the **More** button, which is found on most galleries. Clicking the **More** button expands a gallery and displays all of its options at once. (Alternatively, you can use the up and down arrows immediately above the **More** button to scroll through the gallery line by line.)

IMPORTANT

SEE ALSO For instructions on how to modify your display settings and adapt exercise instructions, see Chapter 1, "Getting comfortable in Office Professional 2013."

- **File tab** This is the first tab on the ribbon. Unlike other ribbon tabs, the **File** tab displays the **Backstage** view where commands for working with the entire contents of a document, such as **Save As**, **Print**, **Share**, and **Export**, are located. The **Backstage** view is also where application options are located and where you can find information about your user account and your version of Microsoft Office.

- **Quick Access Toolbar** This toolbar holds your most frequently used commands. By default, **Save**, **Undo**, **Redo**, and **Start Slide Show** have already been added.

  TIP To quickly add other commands to your Quick Access Toolbar, right-click a command on the ribbon, and then click Add To Quick Access Toolbar. To remove a command from the Quick Access Toolbar, right-click the command you wish to remove and then click Remove from Quick Access Toolbar. Opting to show the Quick Access Toolbar below the ribbon gives you more room for tools and puts them closer to your workspace.

- **Title bar** The title bar appears at the top of the window and displays the name of the active document, along with the application name. If you're working with a presentation that hasn't been saved, the title bar will display a name such as *Presentation3 - PowerPoint*. After the file has been saved, the title bar will reflect the name of the saved file.

11

- **Window Controls** These display at the right end of the title bar. Along with the name of the account you signed into Office with, there are standard **Minimize**, **Restore Down/Maximize**, and **Close** buttons, in addition to the **Help** and **Ribbon Display Options**.

- **Collapse ribbon** To collapse the ribbon, click the button on the right end of the ribbon. Double-click any tab (except the **File** tab) to restore the ribbon.

- **Status bar** This appears at the bottom of the window and displays information about the current presentation, such as the number of slides. You can also open the **Notes** and **Comments** panes from here. The right end of the status bar has view options for switching your presentation to a different view, along with a zoom slider to change the magnification of your active document and a button that resizes your slide to fit the available workspace.

- **Slides pane** This pane appears at the left of the window and lets you access any slides in the presentation. Click a thumbnail to select a slide, and it will appear in the main workspace so you can edit it.

- **Notes pane** Click this button to open a pane where you can enter notes. These notes will be available to you in **Presenter** view, but will not be displayed for the audience to see.

- **Placeholders** Placeholders are preformatted content holders. PowerPoint has placeholders for slide titles, for subtitles, and for content such as text, pictures, tables, charts, SmartArt graphics, and video.

Exploring the PowerPoint 2013 tools

The Home tab in PowerPoint contains most of the tools you'd use to create a quick, basic presentation. You'll find the same Clipboard tools here that you'll find in Word, Excel, and Publisher, along with font and paragraph formatting tools.

In addition, the Home tab has drawing tools that include the Shapes gallery, Arrange tools (for alignment, ordering, and so on), and object formatting tools. Find, Replace, and Selection tools are at the end of this tab. When in doubt, head to the Home tab.

If a button is unavailable and appears to be grayed out, then try selecting an object that can use that command. For example, in order for the buttons in the Font group on the Home tab to be available, you need to select a text box or shape on a slide.

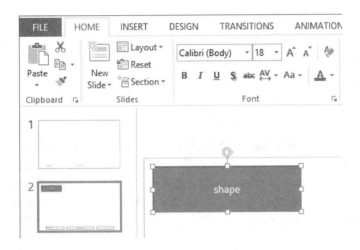

Don't forget about the ability to right-click. You might find tools you didn't even know existed. For example, on the Design tab, right-click one of the themes in the gallery, and you'll notice that an option will appear that allows you to set that theme as your default theme.

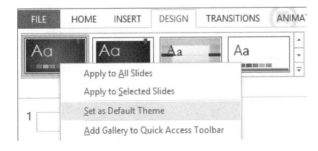

11

Access the formatting panes quickly and easily by right-clicking an object. For example, right-click a shape and choose Format Shape to open the Format Shape pane.

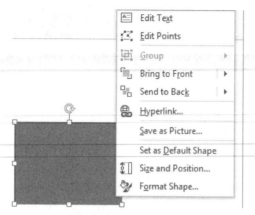

The best thing you can do to become quicker and more proficient with PowerPoint 2013 is to set up your Quick Access Toolbar. You can right-click any command on the ribbon and add it to the Quick Access Toolbar. You can also right-click the Quick Access Toolbar itself and choose Customize Quick Access Toolbar to add tools that are not available on the ribbon and to apply other customizations.

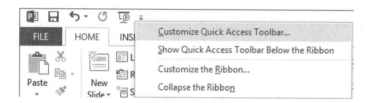

SEE ALSO For more step-by-step instructions on customizing your Quick Access Toolbar, see Chapter 1, "Getting comfortable in Office Professional 2013."

Discovering the new features in PowerPoint 2013

This section introduces you to key application features for PowerPoint 2013, offering screen shots where applicable. Many of the features included are discussed in detail along with step-by-step instructions throughout this part of the book.

- **16:9 slide size default** New presentations are automatically created with a 16:9 aspect ratio for widescreen monitors and displays. And the new scaling options help you convert a widescreen slide size (16:9) to a standard slide size (4:3).

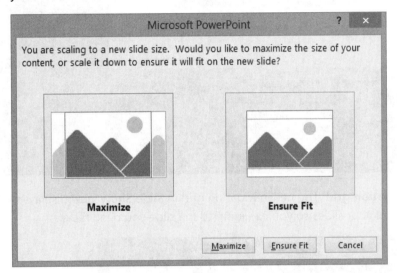

11

- **Presenter view** The redesigned look of **Presenter** view makes it easier to determine exactly what the audience sees. And you can now rehearse your presentation in **Presenter** view without the need for two monitors.

- **Navigation grid** The new navigation grid in **Slide Show** view displays thumbnail views of your slides so you can jump to the slide you need faster.

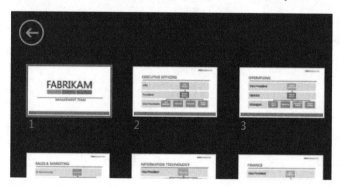

- **Slide Show zoom** Now you can call attention to specific details during your presentation by zooming in on a portion of your slide.

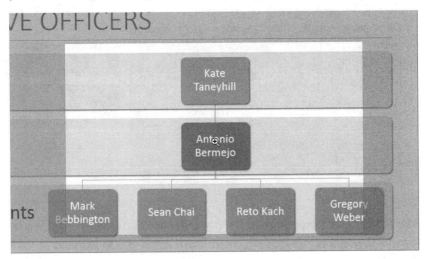

- **Slide Show Popup Toolbar** The new Popup Toolbar in **Slide Show** view gives you more tools for presenting.

- **New Transitions** New transitions include **Page Curl** and **Peel Off**.

- **Resume Reading** When you close a presentation, PowerPoint automatically creates a bookmark for your last position. When you reopen the presentation, you can pick up right where you left off.

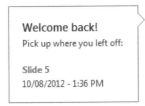

- **Theme variants** New themes for PowerPoint now include variants to give you more color choices for a specified theme.

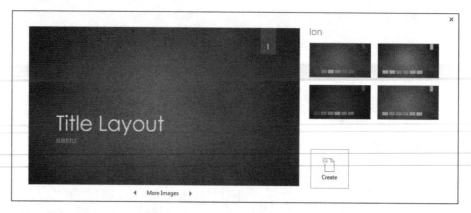

- **Master and slide layout guides** Now you can set guides on slide masters and layouts so you won't accidently move them when you're working on slides. For the guides you want to move, you can still add those to individual slides.

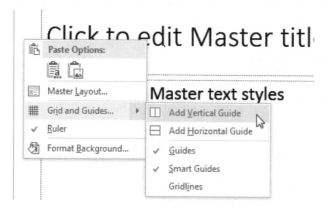

- **Eyedroppers** Select fill, outline, and glow colors for text and shapes and apply them to others. Use colors from within your presentation or from any color that appears on your screen. You can also use the **Eyedropper** to add a color wash to pictures.

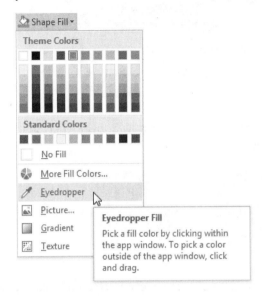

- **Improved motion paths** When you add or edit a motion path, a subdued view of your object will appear at the endpoint so you can visually see where the object will begin and end.

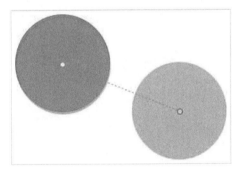

11

- **Fragment shapes** Use the new **Fragment** tool to break up overlapping shapes into new separate shapes.

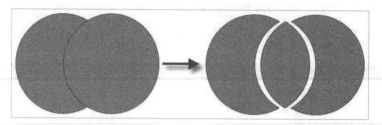

- **Smart Guides for equal distance** Smart Guides now appear when shapes are placed an equal distance from each other.

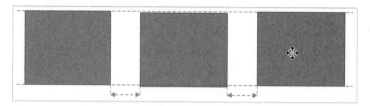

- **Threaded comments** When multiple people review a presentation, they can now reply to each other's comments. And the new **Comments** pane makes it easier to keep track of those conversations.

Key points

- Setting up your Quick Access Toolbar helps you work more quickly.

- The PowerPoint interface will change depending on your log-in status and your screen resolution.

- PowerPoint 2013 introduces a number of new tools for presenters: enhanced Presenter view, a navigation grid, a newly designed Popup Toolbar, and slide show zoom.

11

Chapter at a glance

Create

Create a new presentation,
page 270

Customize

Change theme colors,
page 279

Add

Add graphics to the slide master,
page 290

Create

Create a custom layout,
page 293

Designing and creating presentations

12

IN THIS CHAPTER, YOU WILL LEARN HOW TO

- Create a new presentation based on a theme or template.

- Apply a theme to an existing presentation.

- Customize your file with colors, fonts, and effects.

- Apply theme effects to your presentation.

- Add graphics to the slide master and layouts.

- Create a custom slide layout.

- Change your presentation from a 16:9 to a 4:3 format.

Microsoft PowerPoint is such a popular tool because it is practically synonymous with presentations. Used thoughtfully, it is a great program for producing clear, professional presentations to share ideas and concepts with an audience.

Creating an effective PowerPoint presentation is mostly a matter of form following function. You don't want the available features to overwhelm the content of your presentation. For that reason, when you are planning a presentation, it's best to work on the content before you bring PowerPoint and all its bells and whistles into the mix.

There are a number of recommendations for ways of doing this—jot ideas on sticky notes and rearrange them into blocks of content, create an outline in Microsoft Word, or even scribble thoughts on the back of a napkin. Regardless of how you do it, the goal is to concentrate on the content before you worry about how things look.

With that said, Microsoft Office themes and PowerPoint templates give you a lot of power and flexibility so you don't have to worry so much about how things look as you're creating your content. A good theme or template can help make that happen, because nearly everything in a presentation is affected by one or more theme elements.

In this chapter, you'll start creating a presentation based on a variant of an existing theme, and then you'll tweak the layout to better suit your needs. You'll learn how to change colors and font themes as well as create your own customized layout. You'll also learn how to add graphics to a slide master.

PRACTICE FILES To complete the exercises in this chapter, you need the practice files contained in the Chapter12 practice file folder. For more information, see "Download the practice files" in this book's Introduction.

Creating a new presentation based on a theme or template

Like all the other Office Professional 2013 applications, PowerPoint uses the new Start user interface, complete with a thumbnail gallery and dynamic previews of available themes. The themes that appear might vary a bit depending upon whether you're signed into Office. Either way, PowerPoint 2013 takes the theme preview concept a step further—each theme now has variations where the fonts or colors have been changed. These are called variants, and they're displayed in the preview windows. You can select a variant to quickly change the look and feel of a theme or template.

In this exercise, you'll start a new presentation based on a theme variant.

 **SET UP** You don't need any practice files to complete this exercise. Just start PowerPoint and follow the steps.

1   On the PowerPoint **Start** screen, click the **Retrospect** theme thumbnail to open the **Preview** window.

   TIP If you've already moved past PowerPoint's Start screen, you can click the File tab and then click New to return to the Start screen.

2   In the **Preview** window, click the blue variant.

3   Click the arrows next to **More Images** to view how the blue variant looks on some sample content.

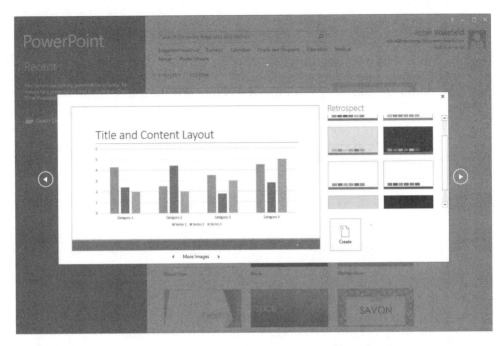

4   Click **Create** to create a new presentation based on the blue variant of the **Retrospect** theme.

❌ CLEAN UP Save the presentation if you want, and then close it.

SEE ALSO For more information about the Start screen, see Chapter 1, "Getting comfortable in Office Professional 2013." For more information about themes and templates, see Chapter 2, "Using shared Office features." For more information about signing into Office, see Chapter 3, "Sharing and collaborating."

Applying a theme to an existing presentation

You won't always start from scratch when creating a presentation. In fact, you'll often begin with a presentation you've already done. That's not a problem, because you can apply a theme and its variants to your slides from the Design tab in PowerPoint. You can even right-click the thumbnails in the Themes and Variants galleries to apply them to specific slides in the presentation.

In this exercise, you'll apply a theme and a variant to an existing presentation.

SET UP You need the SampleContentA_start presentation located in the Chapter12 practice file folder to complete this exercise. Open the SampleContentA_start presentation, and save it as SampleContentA. Then follow the steps.

1   In the slide thumbnails pane on the left side of the PowerPoint workspace, click slide **2** so you can view how changing the theme affects the sample content.

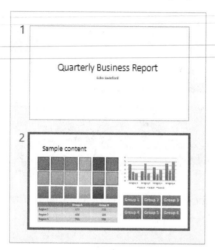

2   Click the **Design** tab, and then in the **Themes** gallery, click the **Retrospect** theme to apply it to the presentation.

TIP You can scroll through the Themes and Variants galleries by using the arrows on the right, or you can click the More button to expand the gallery.

TIP The theme name will appear in a ScreenTip when you point to a thumbnail in the gallery.

3   In the **Variants** gallery, click the blue variant to apply it to all slides in the presentation.

4   Select the title slide (slide **1**) in the slide thumbnails pane.

5   In the **Variants** gallery, right-click the gray variant and choose **Apply to Selected Slides** to apply this variant to the title slide only.

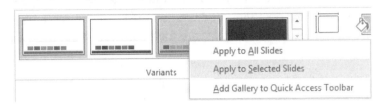

TIP If you want to apply a theme to multiple slides (but not to the entire presentation), select those slides in the thumbnails pane first.

6   Click the blue variant again to reapply the color change to the title slide.

KEYBOARD SHORTCUT Press Ctrl+Z to undo the previous action.

❌ CLEAN UP **Save the SampleContentA presentation and then close it.**

TIP If you don't find the theme or template you want to apply, click the More button to expand the Themes gallery and then choose Browse For Themes. Even though it specifies "themes" there, both themes and templates are displayed in the folders.

Customizing your file with colors, fonts, and effects

Every theme, even the blank Office theme, has a set of colors, fonts, and effects built in. And since every template is based on a theme, the colors, fonts, and effects are also built into every template. Of course, because every PowerPoint file is based on a template or a theme, the colors, fonts, and effects sets are built into every presentation as well.

As shown in the two previous exercises, applying a theme to a presentation can completely change its appearance. This is because the slide master and layouts are part of the theme, and they affect how the content is positioned on the slides. You'll learn more about this in upcoming exercises.

For now, it's most important for you to know that you don't have to apply an entire theme (the full set of colors, fonts, effects, and slide layouts) to a presentation. You can change the look and feel of a presentation at any time by simply applying different theme colors, fonts, or effects.

12

Theme fonts

You'll find the theme fonts that are used in a presentation listed on the Home tab in the Font gallery. Click into any text on a slide, and then on the Home tab, click the arrow to open the Fonts list. At the top of the Fonts list are the theme fonts that are used in the presentation.

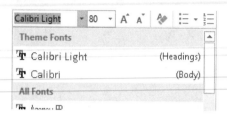

Heading fonts are generally applied to titles and subtitles, whereas the Body font is used for most other text.

You can choose a different theme font set from the Theme Font gallery by expanding the Variants gallery on the Design tab of the ribbon. If you don't find a font set you like, you can create your own there as well.

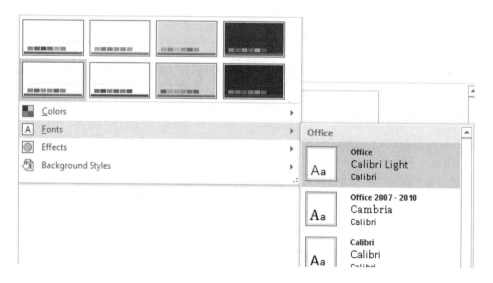

TIP You can also access theme colors, fonts, effects, and background styles from Slide Master view, but it's usually faster to access these galleries by expanding the theme Variants gallery on the Design tab. To access Slide Master view, click the View tab, and then the Slide Master button.

TIP Click the More button on the Variants gallery to expand it.

Theme colors

You'll find theme colors in almost every option that has anything to do with color. They show up in all formatting galleries—Shape Styles, Tables, Charts, SmartArt, and Pictures—as well as in the fill and outline colors for shapes, lines, and fonts.

Theme color sets consist of 12 colors: two light/dark combinations, six accent colors, and a hyperlink and a followed hyperlink, although the hyperlink and followed hyperlink colors don't actually show in any of the galleries. The full palette is derived from tints and shades of the theme colors.

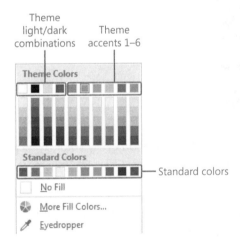

12

The two light and dark combinations are generally used for text and slide background colors. They're designed to work together. If you change your slide background style from white to black, for example, any text that was black will turn white so it will be visible on the black background. SmartArt, tables, and charts all rely on dark/light combinations for their font colors as well.

Text color changes to
contrast with background

Text color changes to
contrast with background

The accent colors are used for everything else. You'll find these on every color gallery throughout the PowerPoint interface—Shape Styles, Table Styles, Chart Styles, SmartArt Styles, fill, line, and font colors, and more.

When you are applying a theme color to an object (or when PowerPoint applies it for you), that color is really just referencing a position in the theme color gallery. For example, if you fill a square shape with Accent 2 (which happens to be orange in the default Office theme), and you change themes, your orange shape will become whatever color the new theme uses for Accent 2. Think about how the colors changed in the SampleContentA file when you changed from Retrospect with its brown and yellow colors to the blue variant; that is a color theme in action.

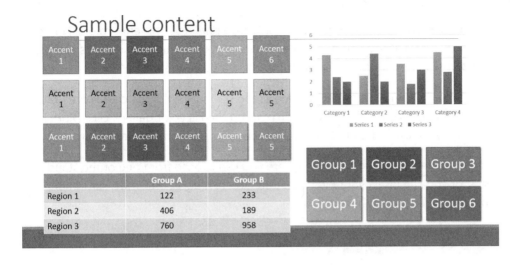

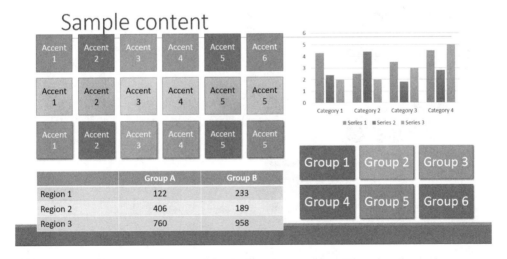

You can choose a new theme color set from the Colors gallery that's accessed by expanding the Variants gallery. If you don't find a color set that you like, you can create your own set of theme colors.

Using absolute colors

Sometimes a red is just a red, and you don't have one in your theme colors. No problem! You can always use colors that aren't part of your theme. These colors are known as *absolute colors*, and they won't change when you change theme colors.

To access non-theme colors, choose one of the standard colors or click More Colors on any color gallery. For example, if you're using the Fill color gallery, click More Fill Colors. If you're using the Outline color gallery, choose More Outline Colors.

This opens the familiar honeycomb where you can choose from one of the standard colors, or you can insert your own RGB (red, green, blue) or HSL (hue, saturation, luminosity) values on the Custom tab.

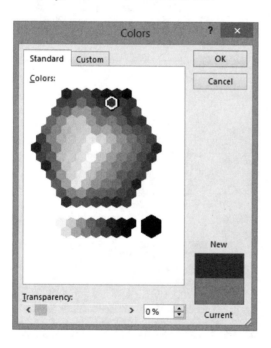

Applying theme effects to your presentation

Theme effects are things like default shadows and gradients or other fill styles that are built into a theme. You can view different theme effects in action by expanding the Variants gallery and pointing to the various sets of effects to view how they affect and change your slides. Some of the theme effects, like the default Office theme, will be fairly subtle. Others, like Grunge or Milk Glass, will have textured fills or extreme gradients and shadows.

SEE ALSO For an overview of how themes work, see Chapter 1, "Getting comfortable in Office Professional 2013."

In this exercise, you'll apply new theme fonts and effects to an existing presentation. You'll also customize and apply a new theme color set to the presentation.

→ SET UP You need the SampleContentB_start presentation located in the Chapter12 practice file folder to complete this exercise. Open the SampleContentB_start presentation, and save it as SampleContentB. Then follow the steps.

1   With slide **2** selected (to demonstrate how changing theme effects, colors, and fonts affects the sample content), expand the **Variants** gallery on the **Design** tab and click **Fonts** to open the **Theme Fonts** gallery. Scroll through the theme font sets to display a live preview of their effect on the fonts in the presentation.

2   Click the **Franklin Gothic** theme font set. This applies the **Heading font**, **Franklin Gothic Medium**, to slide titles and subtitles, and the **Body font**, **Franklin Gothic**, to all other text.

   TIP To create your own theme font set, click Customize Fonts at the bottom of the Theme Fonts gallery.

3   Expand the **Variants** gallery again and click **Colors**. Scroll through the **Theme Colors** gallery to view how the different theme color sets would affect your presentation.

12

4   Click **Customize Colors** at the bottom of the **Theme Colors** gallery.

5   Click **Accent 6**, and then click the **More Colors** option.

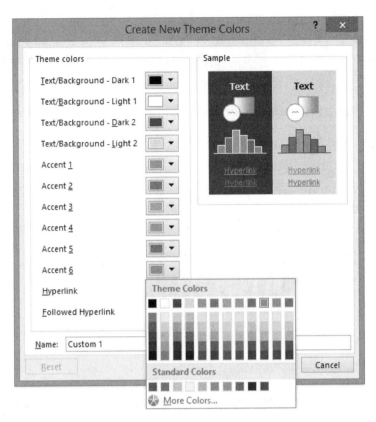

6   On the **Custom** tab, enter **122** for **Red**, **188** for **Green**, and **50** for **Blue**, and then click **OK** to close the **Colors** dialog box.

7   Click the **Hyperlink** color swatch, and then click **Turquoise, Accent 3** in the **Theme Colors** palette.

TIP When you point to each color swatch in the Theme Colors palette, the name of the color will appear in a ScreenTip.

12

TIP The Hyperlink color is automatically applied to hyperlinked text. The Followed Hyperlink color will only be displayed in the Slide Show view after a hyperlink has been clicked. These colors will not be shown in the color galleries, so you won't be able to choose them for other objects.

8   Click the **Followed Hyperlink** color swatch and change it to a shade of gray by selecting a tint or shade of black or white in the **Theme Colors** palette.

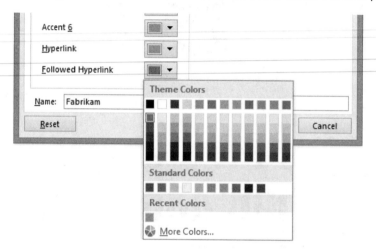

9   Name your new **Theme Colors** set by entering Fabrikam in the **Name** box.

10   Click **Save** to save and apply the new theme colors.

    TIP If you want to edit or delete a custom color theme, you can expand the Variants gallery and right-click the color set in the Theme Colors gallery.

11   Expand the **Variants** gallery and click **Effects**. Point to the different theme effects sets to see how they will affect your content.

12   Click **Office** to apply the **Office Professional 2013** theme effects to your file.

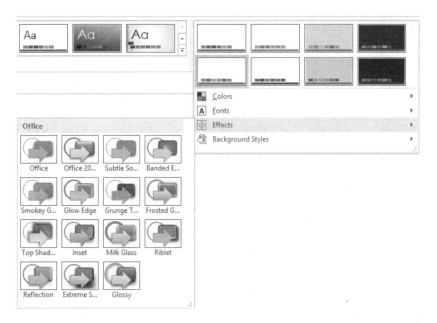

TIP Although you can customize theme fonts and colors, you cannot customize Theme Effects sets from within PowerPoint.

✖ CLEAN UP Save the SampleContentB presentation, and then close it.

Applying background styles to your presentation

Every theme includes a set of background styles, which are also accessed by expanding the Variants gallery on the Design tab.

These background styles work with the text and background color combinations (the first four color swatches) in your color theme to ensure that text is always visible. That's why it's important to make sure those dark and light text and background colors have enough contrast when you're creating a custom color theme. It's also generally a good idea to choose your text colors from those background and text colors, because then the text color will be updated when you change the slide background style or paste the slide into a new presentation.

12

TIP In the Create New Theme Colors dialog box, the first four theme colors are called Text/Background Dark 1, Text/Background Light 1, Text/Background Dark 2 and Text/Background Light 2. In the ScreenTips that appear when you point to a color in the various color galleries in PowerPoint, they're called Background 1, Text 1, Background 2, and Text 2.

In this exercise, you'll apply new theme background styles to view how they affect font colors and visibility.

SET UP You need the SampleContentC_start presentation located in the Chapter12 practice file folder to complete this exercise. Open the SampleContentC_start presentation, and save it as SampleContentC. Then follow the steps.

1   Expand the **Variants** gallery on the **Design** tab and click **Background Styles**. Notice that the slide uses the white background style.

2   Point to the lower-right thumbnail in the **Background Styles** gallery. (The ScreenTip will say **Style 12**). Click to apply this dark background to all slides. Black text that wouldn't be visible on the dark background changes to white.

3   Open the **Background Styles** gallery again and click **Style 5** (first column, second row) to apply a subtle light gradient to all slides.

4   With slide **1** selected, open the **Background Styles** gallery again, right-click **Style 12**, and choose **Apply to Selected Slides** to give the title slide a more dramatic look.

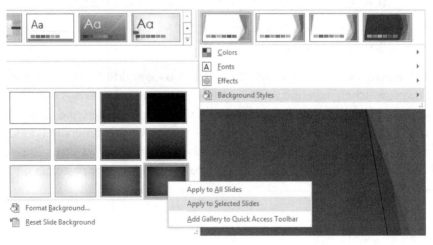

CLEAN UP Save the SampleContentC presentation, and then close it.

TROUBLESHOOTING If your text disappears when you copy a slide from a dark presentation to a light one or vice-versa, make sure the slide background style is selected, and make sure the text uses a contrasting text or background color.

Formatting placeholders on the slide master

Many people don't realize that the PowerPoint slide master and layout features give you a lot of control over the look of your slides. You can add graphics and images to the master, and you can format the placeholders on the master as well. These settings trickle down to the individual layouts, which provide combinations of placeholders to help you create content for your slides.

Placeholders are preformatted content containers. When you apply formatting to them on the slide masters and layouts, then any content that's created in a placeholder on a regular slide will inherit those settings.

Although PowerPoint provides you with a set of layouts built into each theme, template, and presentation, you can still create your own custom layout that has exactly the placeholders and graphics you need.

Most formatting that can be applied to shapes can be applied to placeholders as well, but the most common way to format a placeholder is to format the settings that are specific to the text; for example, the font color and size, paragraph settings, and bullet points.

TIP Text formatting can be applied to any text in your presentation, but it's best to apply these settings to the placeholders on the slide master and layouts to create consistency throughout your slides. You can always apply manual formatting to override the placeholder, if necessary.

Text formatting, such as bold, italics, and underlines, is probably obvious to most PowerPoint users, but you might not think of PowerPoint as having "paragraphs," and you'd be right! A PowerPoint paragraph is the text that's included in a bullet point. You can have up to nine levels of text in a presentation (although this is definitely not recommended), but PowerPoint shows only five by default in Slide Master view. You'll want to specify common paragraph settings, such as line spacing and the indentation size for each paragraph level of text.

SEE ALSO For more about formatting text, see Chapter 13, "Creating on-slide content."

12

In this exercise, you'll format placeholders on the slide master and layouts.

SET UP You need the SampleContentD_start presentation located in the Chapter12 practice file folder to complete this exercise. Open the SampleContentD_start presentation, and save it as SampleContentD. Then follow the steps.

1 Click the **View** tab, then **Slide Master** to open Slide Master view. Scroll to the top of the **Slides** pane and click the large **Slide Master** thumbnail.

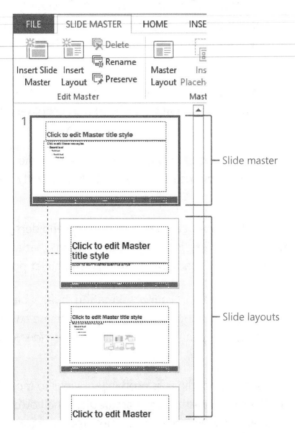

2 Select the **Title** placeholder (the one that says, **Click to edit Master title style**) by clicking its edge.

TIP If you're having trouble selecting a placeholder, click inside the text area, and then press the Esc key on your keyboard.

Body placeholder   Title placeholder

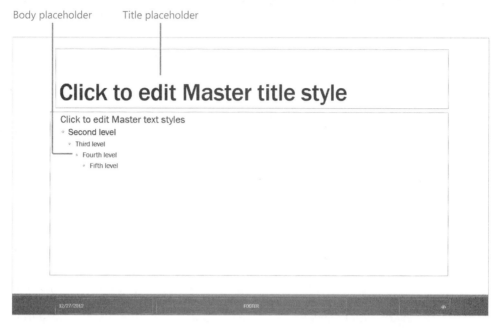

3   Click the **Home** tab and then click the **Font Size** drop-down list. Click the **Decrease Font Size** button twice to apply a smaller font size to the title placeholder.

KEYBOARD SHORTCUT Press Ctrl+Shift+< to decrease font size.

TIP You can apply a different font size by clicking the arrow next to the Font Size box on the Home tab and selecting from the list. Or you can enter a number directly into the Font Size box. To apply your new font size, press the Enter key after you enter the number.

4   Select the **Body** placeholder (the one with five levels of bulleted text). On the **Home** tab, click the **Increase Font Size** button once to increase the size for all levels of text in the placeholder.

KEYBOARD SHORTCUT Press Ctrl+Shift+> to increase font size.

12

5   Click in the top level of text in the **Body** placeholder. On the **Home** tab, expand the **Bullets** gallery by clicking the arrow next to the **Bullets** button. Choose **Filled Round Bullets** to add a bullet to the top level of text.

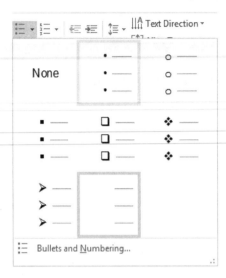

TIP If you need to change the color or size of the bullet symbol, expand the Bullets gallery, click Bullets And Numbering, and change the color and size there. You can also click Customize to choose a different symbol or even a picture.

6   To adjust the positioning of the bullet, first turn on the ruler by selecting the **Ruler** option on the **View** tab.

7   With your cursor still in the top line of text, on the ruler, click and drag the upward-pointing indent marker to adjust the space between the bullet point and the text.

TIP Press the Ctrl key for finer control over the indent markers on the ruler.

8   With your cursor still in the top level of text, click the **Paragraph** dialog box launcher on the **Home** tab to adjust the line spacing between first-level paragraphs of bulleted text.

Dialog box launcher

9   In the **Paragraph** dialog box, increase the **Before** spacing from **12 pt** to **18 pt**, and click **OK** to close the dialog box.

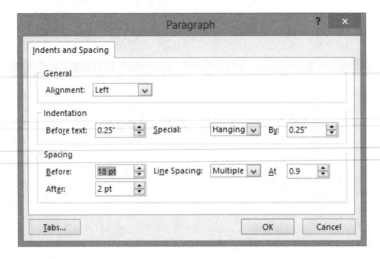

TIP Before and After spacing refers to the space before and after the paragraph levels of the bulleted text. Line spacing refers to the space within a level of text. Click the Line Spacing box and select Single for single-spaced text. Use Multiple at .9 for line spacing that is 90% as tall as single-spaced text. Going below about .7 will cut off the ascenders and descenders of letters on many fonts.

10   Click the **Title Slide** layout directly below the **Slide Master**. Select the **Title** placeholder and change the font size to **66 pt**.

11   Review the slide layouts to confirm that the bullet has been added to all top-level text and the spacing has been adjusted according to the changes you made on the master.

✖ CLEAN UP Save the SampleContentD presentation, and then close it.

Adding graphics to the slide master and layouts

In this exercise, you'll add graphics to the slide master and layouts.

You need the SampleContentE_start presentation and the Fabrikam_Logo_Large.png and Fabrikam_White_Small.png images located in the Chapter12 practice file folder to complete this exercise. Open the SampleContentE_start presentation, and save it as SampleContentE. Then follow the steps.

1 On the **View** tab, click **Slide Master** to open Slide Master view.

2 With the **Slide Master** selected, on the **Insert** tab, click **Pictures**. Navigate to the **Fabrikam_White_Small.png** file and click **Insert**.

3 Select the **Fabrikam** logo in the center of the **Slide Master** and then click the **Picture Tools Format** tab. In the **Size** group, enter **2** in the **Width** box and press **Enter**. The logo height will change proportionately.

> **TIP** You can drag a corner of a picture (or other object) to resize it. Press Shift while you drag to be sure the picture or object doesn't stretch out of proportion.

4 Drag the logo to the lower-right corner of the slide. Pay attention to the PowerPoint Smart Guides. They will help you align the logo vertically and horizontally to the footer placeholders that hold dates, page numbers, and footer text. Place the logo so its left edge is in the same position as the left edge of the slide number placeholder. It should also align vertically with the center of the slide number placeholder.

Smart guides

5 Select the slide number placeholder. Press **Shift** and drag the placeholder to the left so it's no longer behind the logo.

> **TIP** Use the tools on the status bar to zoom in while you're positioning the logo and moving the slide number placeholder. Click the Fit Slide To Current Window button to return to the normal zoom status.

12

6   Select the **Title Slide** layout (the first layout beneath the slide master). Right-click away from the slide and choose **Format Background**.

> **TIP** Point to a layout in the Layouts pane, and its name will appear in a ScreenTip.

7   In the **Format Background** pane, clear the **Hide Background Graphics** check box to unhide the graphics that the layout has inherited from the **Slide Master**. The thin grey line inherited from the **Slide Master** appears near the top of the **Title** placeholder.

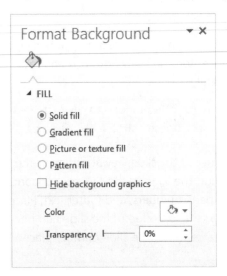

8   Select the two blue rectangles at the bottom of the slide and move them so you can view the identical graphics and small **Fabrikam** logo from the **Slide Master** beneath.

> **TIP** Selecting Hide Background Graphics on a layout hides all the graphics inherited from the Slide Master. If you need some of the graphics, copy them from the Slide Master and paste them onto the slide layout.

9   Press **Ctrl+Z** twice to undo steps 6 and 7.

10   Click the **Insert** tab and then click **Pictures**. Navigate to **Fabrikam_Logo_Large.png** and click **Insert**.

11   Select the logo, and change its width to 3". Drag the logo to the upper-right corner of the slide.

CLEAN UP Click Close Master View on the Slide Master tab to return to Normal view. Save the SampleContentE presentation, and then close it.

Creating a custom slide layout

In this exercise, you'll create a custom slide layout, rename it and the Slide Master, and save the file as a template.

SET UP You need the SampleContentF_start presentation located in the Chapter12 practice file folder to complete this exercise. Open the SampleContentF_start presentation, and save it as SampleContentF. Then follow the steps.

1   On the **View** tab, click **Slide Master** to open Slide Master view. Right-click the **Slide Master** and choose **Rename Master**.

12

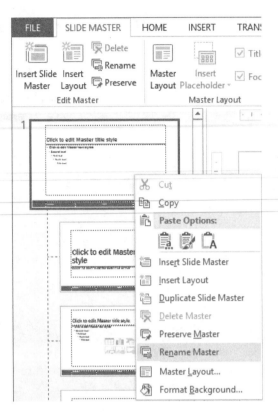

2   In the **Rename Master** dialog box, enter Fabrikam, Inc and click **Rename**.

3   Point to the layouts beneath the **Slide Master** to find the one called **Title and Content Layout**. Select that layout.

4   On the **Slide Master** tab, click **Insert Layout** to add a new layout after the **Title and Content** layout. The new layout will have title and footer placeholders.

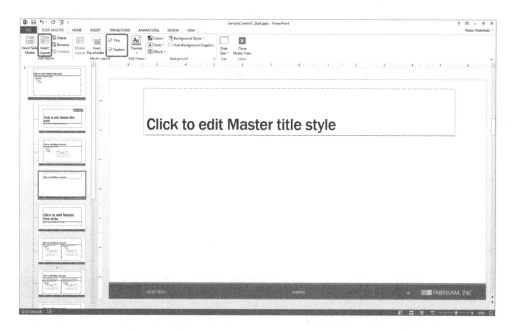

TIP You can turn off the title and footer placeholders by clearing their check boxes on the Slide Master tab.

5   Right-click the new layout and choose **Rename Layout**. Name the layout Speaker Bio.

6   With the **Speaker Bio** layout selected, on the **Slide Master** tab, click **Insert Placeholder**, then **Picture**. Drag the slide to create a rectangular picture placeholder for the speaker's headshot. It should be about as wide as the date placeholder.

7   Click inside the picture placeholder and enter Click icon to insert speaker photo.

8   On the **Slide Master** tab, click **Insert Placeholder** again, and then click **Text**.

9   Click and drag on the slide to create a text placeholder. It should start near the up-per-right corner of the picture and extend the width of the title placeholder.

10 Select the edge of the placeholder you just created, and change the font size to **16 pt** by selecting that size from the **Font Size** list on the **Home** tab. Click the bullet icon to remove the bullets from all levels of text.

11 Select the first level of text and enter Type speaker affiliations here.

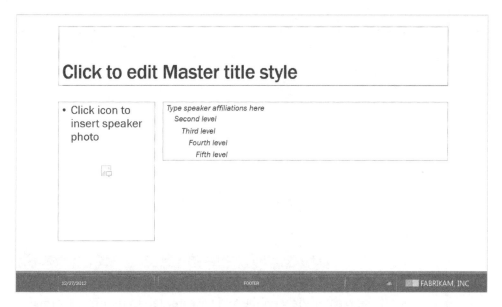

12   Copy the text placeholder (**Ctrl+C**) you added in step 8 and press **Ctrl+V** to paste it onto the layout. Drag the new placeholder into position directly beneath the original.

13   Select the edge of the placeholder and increase the font size to **20 pt**. Select the first level of text and enter Type speaker biography here.

12

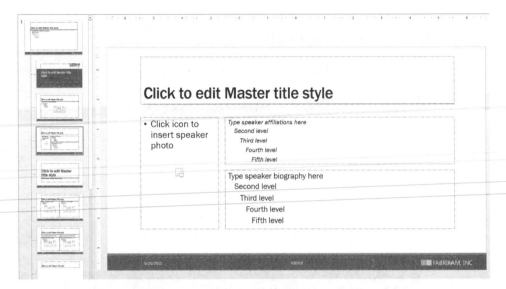

14   Click **Close Master View** on the **Slide Master** tab to return to **Normal** view.

15   Click **File**, then **Save As**. Under **Save As**, select **Computer**, then click **Browse** to open the **Save As** dialog box.

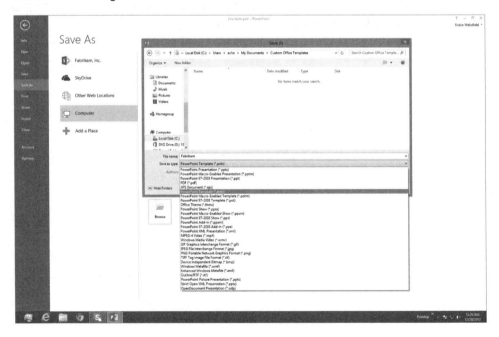

16 In the **Save As** dialog box, click the **Save As Type** drop-down list and choose **PowerPoint Template (*.potx)** to save your file as a template. Enter Fabrikam in the **File name** field, and then click **Save**.

> **TIP** When you save a PowerPoint template, PowerPoint will automatically take you to the folder where your custom templates should be saved. Templates saved here will appear in the File, New interface on the Custom tab.

> **TIP** You can change the location of your custom PowerPoint templates by going to File, Options, then Save and typing a file path in the Default personal templates location field.

❌ CLEAN UP Close the file after you save it as a template.

Changing your presentation from a 16:9 to a 4:3 format

You've probably noticed this already, but in case you haven't, the default slide size in PowerPoint 2013 is 16:9. Actually, that's the default proportion. The actual slide size is 13.33 inches wide by 7.5 inches tall. Previous versions of PowerPoint used a default slide size of 10 inches wide by 7.5 inches tall, which is a 4:3 proportion. The 4:3 format is the typical sort-of-square, old-school slide projector and screen size, whereas a 16:9 format is considered wide-screen, which is more in line with most of our computers, monitors, and television screens today.

You might be wondering why this is important. In previous versions of PowerPoint, when you would change an existing presentation from 16:9 to 4:3 (or vice-versa), your content would be distorted. Squares would become narrow rectangles, people in pictures would look skinnier, and SmartArt diagrams would get rearranged.

12

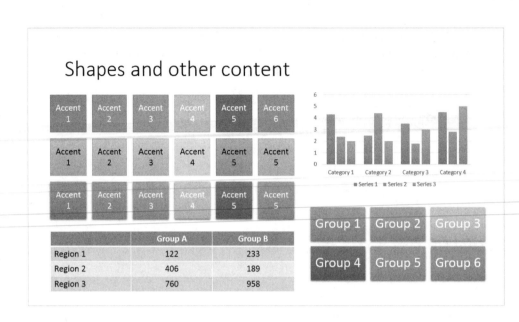

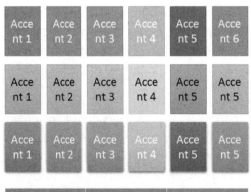

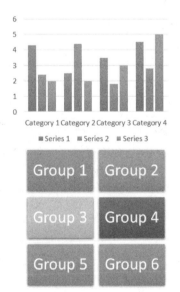

PowerPoint 2013 works a lot better than previous versions, and it actually gives you a couple of options when you're changing the proportions of a presentation or template. You'll still want to choose your proportion before developing your content whenever you can, but at least now when you change the slide size, you'll have a choice of whether to make the content as large as it can be (taking into account that it might extend beyond the edge of the slide), or scale your content so it will fit on the new slide size. Either way, your content won't be distorted!

In this exercise, you'll change a 16:9-proportioned slide to a 4:3 format, and then you'll revert to the original size.

 SET UP You need the Fabrikam.POTX template located in the Chapter12 practice file folder to complete this exercise. Double-click the Fabrikam.POTX template to open a presentation based on the Fabrikam PowerPoint template. Save the file as SampleContentG. Then follow the steps.

1   On the **Design** tab, click **Slide Size**, then click **Standard (4:3)**.

2   Choose **Maximize**, which doesn't scale your content. PowerPoint maximizes the slide content, keeping everything the same size and letting it fall off the edges of the new 4:3 slide as necessary.

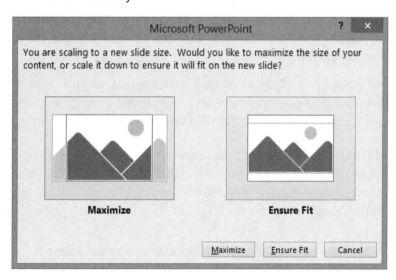

TIP You can click either the icons or the buttons in the Slide Size dialog box.

12

3   Press **Ctrl+Z** to undo the last step and return to the original slide size.

4   Click **Slide Size**, then **Standard (4:3)**, and choose **Ensure Fit**. PowerPoint scales the content so it fits on the slide without distortion.

5   On the slide, select the first blue shape labeled **Accent 1**, and look at its font size on the **Home** tab. You'll notice that PowerPoint changed it to **13.5** to help with the fit.

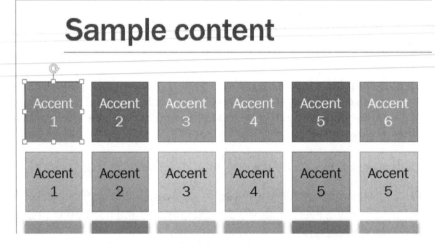

6   Click **Slide Size** again, and this time, click **Widescreen (16:9)**. PowerPoint will reposition the objects on the slide, but they will not become any larger. The font size will remain at 13.5 points.

TIP Even though PowerPoint won't distort the content on your slides, graphics on the slide backgrounds are another story. Be sure to look for logos or other content that may have become distorted on the Slide Master or any of the layouts.

TROUBLESHOOTING PowerPoint will reapply the original theme when it resizes a presentation. If you've made any customizations to your theme, template, or Slide Masters and layouts, you may need to re-save the template and reapply it to your presentation before using this feature.

❌ CLEAN UP Save the SampleContentG presentation, and then close it.

Key points

- A theme is a set of colors, fonts and effects, along with Slide Masters and layouts for PowerPoint.

- A template is a theme plus content (usually sample slides). A PowerPoint presentation can be based on either a template or a theme.

- The theme elements are built into all template and presentation files.

- You aren't required to apply the whole theme. You can apply theme colors, fonts, and effects separately. Mix and match 'em! Have fun!

- Slide layouts inherit their settings from the Slide Master.

- Graphics added to the Slide Master appear on all slide layouts unless you choose to hide background graphics.

- Placeholders are preformatted content holders that can help you create consistency and cohesion throughout your presentation.

- Right-click a theme or variant to apply it only to selected slides as opposed to the entire presentation.

12

Chapter at a glance

Add

Add and format tables,
page 315

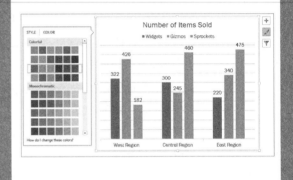

Insert

Insert and format charts,
page 318

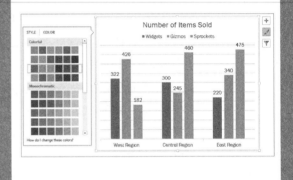

Create

Create SmartArt diagrams,
page 322

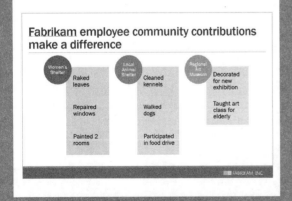

Reuse

Reuse existing slides,
page 328

Creating on-slide content

13

IN THIS CHAPTER, YOU WILL LEARN HOW TO

- Choose a slide layout and add text in placeholders.

- Add manual check boxes.

- Add and format tables.

- Insert and format charts using chart styles and layouts.

- Create and format SmartArt diagrams.

- Reuse slides and keep their source formatting.

You can add many different types of content to a presentation. Some of it, like text and SmartArt graphics, is created directly within Microsoft PowerPoint. Other types, such as pictures or video, are developed elsewhere and simply added to PowerPoint. Either way, there are multiple methods of adding or constructing content and then modifying it once it's on the slide.

In this chapter, you'll learn to leverage slide layouts to quickly create and position content. You'll also learn more about formatting text as well as creating SmartArt, charts, and tables.

PRACTICE FILES To complete the exercises in this chapter, you need the practice files contained in the Chapter13 practice file folder. For more information, see "Download the practice files" in this book's Introduction.

Choosing a slide layout and adding text in placeholders

When you begin a new presentation, PowerPoint provides you with a title slide to help you get started. The title slide has two text placeholders: one for the title of the presentation, and the other for a subtitle. If you insert another slide, you'll typically get a title and content layout. This layout also provides you with two placeholders: one for the slide title and another that can hold a variety of content, such as text, tables, charts, SmartArt diagrams, video, or pictures from either your computer or online sources.

These placeholders are preformatted containers just waiting for your content. They provide consistency throughout your presentation and eliminate repetitive formatting tasks. Remember how we formatted the graphic and placeholders on the slide master in the previous chapter? As you know, that formatting (including colors, fonts, effects, and graphics from the theme or template) trickles down to all the slide layouts. Taking it a step further, the actual slides inherit their formatting from the layout they're based on.

To experience this in action, click the bottom of the New Slide button on the Home tab. Choosing the layout that most closely matches your intended content can save you a lot of time.

TIP If you don't find a layout that works with your content, you may want to create your own custom layout, which might save you time in the long run.

SEE ALSO For more about placeholders and creating custom layouts, see Chapter 12, "Designing and creating presentations."

In this exercise, you'll insert a slide and add text in a placeholder. You'll also change text from first-level bulleted text to second-level and vice versa.

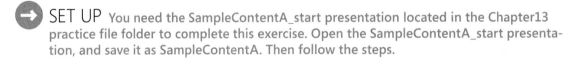 **SET UP** You need the SampleContentA_start presentation located in the Chapter13 practice file folder to complete this exercise. Open the SampleContentA_start presentation, and save it as SampleContentA. Then follow the steps.

1   On the first slide, click in the title placeholder, which prompts you with **Click to add title**, and enter Quarterly Report.

2 Click in the subtitle placeholder, which reads **Click to add subtitle**, and enter Robin Wakefield.

3 On the **Home** tab, in the **Slides** group, click the top of the **New Slide** button to add a new slide based on the title and content layout.

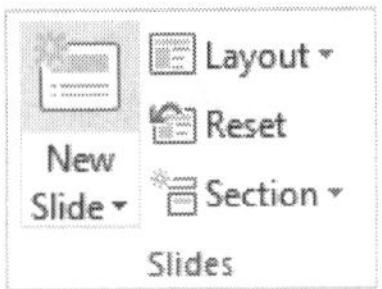

TIP When you click the top of the New Slide button, PowerPoint inserts a new slide based on the layout of the selected slide. The exception is when you've selected a slide that uses the title slide layout. In such a case, PowerPoint always inserts a slide based on the title and content layout. If you want to choose a different type of layout, click the bottom of the New Slide button.

TIP Clicking the bottom of the New Slide button lets you choose the layout you want to use when you create a slide. If you want to change the layout of an existing slide, just click the Layout button and choose a different layout.

4   Click in the title placeholder of the slide you just created and enter Fabrikam employee community contributions make a difference. (Don't enter the period. Punctuation at the end of bullet points can add a lot of clutter to a slide, so it's a common practice to omit it.)

5   Click in the content placeholder and enter Women's shelter. Press the **Enter** key and then press **Tab** to create a second-level bullet point, then enter Raked leaves. Press **Enter** to create another second-level bullet and enter Repaired windows. Press **Enter** and enter Painted 2 rooms.

6   Press **Enter** to create the next line, then press **Shift+Tab** to change the text to first-level bulleted text. Enter Local animal shelter.

KEYBOARD SHORTCUT Press Tab or Alt+Shift+Right Arrow to demote text. Press Shift+Tab or Alt+Shift+Left Arrow to promote text.

TIP You can also use the Decrease List Level and Increase List Level buttons to promote or demote the text to different levels.

TROUBLESHOOTING Many templates don't have a bullet point on the first level of text. This looks great, but it can cause problems if you're used to using the Tab key to create lower levels of bulleted text. If your first-level text doesn't have a bullet point and you press Tab to create second-level bulleted text, the bullet character won't appear as expected on the second level. Instead, enter the first-level text, then press Enter and use the Increase List Level button on the ribbon or the keyboard shortcut Alt+Shift+Right Arrow to create second-level text with a bullet character. Alternatively, click View, then Outline, and enter your text in the Outline pane, where Tab and Shift+Tab create levels of text as expected.

7   Press **Enter** and enter Cleaned kennels. Press **Enter** and enter Walked dogs. Press **Enter** and enter Participated in food drive. Press **Enter** and enter Regional art museum.

8   Click anywhere in the **Cleaned kennels** text. Press and hold the left mouse button and drag until you've selected at least part of the **Participated in food drive** text.

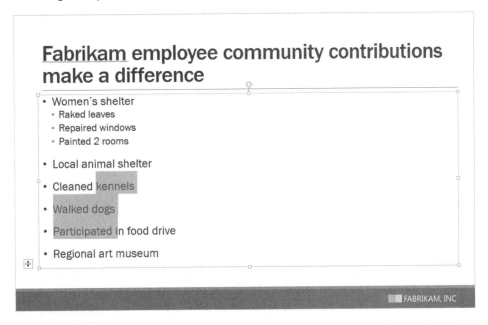

9   Click the **Increase List Level** button on the ribbon to change the three primary bullet points into second-level bulleted text.

13

10   Place the cursor at the end of the word **museum** and press **Enter**, then press **Shift+Alt+Right Arrow** on the keyboard to create second-level bulleted text. Enter Decorated for new exhibition. Press **Enter**, then enter Taught art class for elderly.

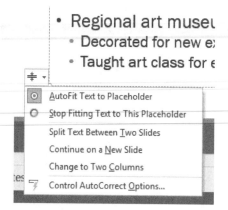

11   Click the **Autofit Options** button that appears near the bottom of the placeholder and select **Stop Fitting Text to This Placeholder** to prevent PowerPoint from shrinking the text and line spacing to force it to fit within the placeholder.

TIP Experiment with the various selections in the Autofit Options menu. For example, if you want to move some of the text to a new slide, choose Split Text Between Two Slides.

✖ CLEAN UP Save the presentation if you want, and then close it.

Adding manual text boxes

PowerPoint automatically formats and positions any text you add to placeholders. This saves a tremendous amount of time, but it's not always what you want. For example, sometimes you might need to label a diagram or graphic, or maybe you want to add a reference to the slide. For this, you'll use a manual text box.

In this exercise, you'll create and format text in manual text boxes.

TIP These ad hoc, manual text boxes are designed for small bits of text, so they're not very robust when it comes to things like multiple levels of bullets.

1   On either the **Home** tab or the **Insert** tab, click the **Shapes gallery**.

     TROUBLESHOOTING Depending on the size of your screen and your PowerPoint window, the Shapes gallery may appear as a lot of shapes or it may appear as a big icon. (See Chapter 1, "Getting comfortable in Office Professional 2013," for more information about how screen resolution and window size affect your display.) In the gallery with a lot of shapes, click the arrows or the More button (see Chapter 11, "Getting comfortable in PowerPoint 2013") to display all the shapes. If your Shapes gallery is a large icon, just click it to display the entire set of shapes.

2   Click the **Text Box** shape. It will be in **Basic Shapes** if it's not already at the top in the **Recently Used Shapes** section.

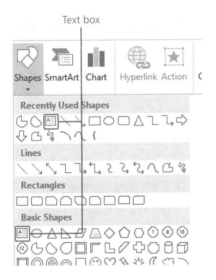

Text box

3   Click anywhere on the slide and begin entering text to create a text box that expands as you enter the text. Enter the words Conference Area.

     TIP If you click and drag to create the text box on the slide, it will remain that width as you enter information, but its height will expand to accommodate your text.

4   Click the edge of the text box to select it.

13

TIP When your cursor is inside the text box, the text box edge will display a dotted line, which indicates that you're working with the text and not the entire text box. Press Esc or the F2 key on your keyboard or click the edge of the text box to select the text box itself. Then format all of the text in it at once. You'll know you've selected the text box when its edge is a solid line.

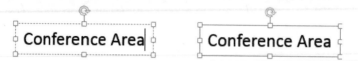

5   On the **Home** tab, in the **Font** group, click **Bold** to make the text bold.

KEYBOARD SHORTCUT Ctrl+B applies bold formatting to selected text. Ctrl+I applies italics, and Ctrl+U applies underlining.

6   Click the **Decrease Font Size** button twice to change the font size to 14 points like the rest of the labels in the diagram.

7   Click the dialog box launcher in the **Font** group to open the **Font** dialog box.

Dialog box launcher

8   Select the **All Caps** check box to change the text to uppercase, and then click **OK** to close the dialog box.

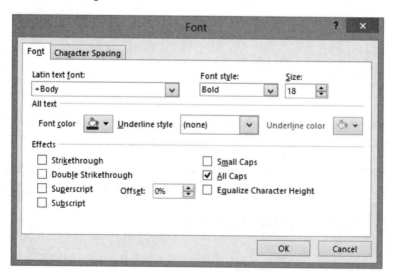

9   Select the text box by clicking its edge, and then drag it into place in the upper-left corner of the diagram. Smart Guides will appear to help you align the label with the others in the diagram.

New Seattle office floor plan

	60'	

CONFERENCE AREA | WOMEN'S BATH | MEN'S BATH | OFFICE 1 | OFFICE 2

26'

RECEPTION | ENTRY | OFFICE 3 | OFFICE 2 | OFFICE 1

SEE ALSO For more information about SmartGuides, see Chapter 14, "Creating Office graphics."

10   With the **Conference Area** text box selected, click the arrow next to the **Copy** button on the **Home** tab and select **Duplicate** to create a duplicate text box. Drag the duplicate away from the original text box so it's easier to work with.

KEYBOARD SHORTCUT Use Ctrl+C to copy the selected text or object. Use Ctrl+V to paste it. Ctrl+D will duplicate an object; it's like a combined copy-paste. Pressing Ctrl while you drag an object will also create a copy!

11   Click in front of the **C** and drag until you've selected all the text. Enter the words Break Area. The selected text will be replaced with the new text as you enter it.

TIP You don't have to worry about pressing the Caps Lock key, because you changed the formatting to All Caps.

TIP You can select a single word by double-clicking it. Triple-clicking selects all text in the paragraph. Try it for yourself!

12   Select the **Break Area** text box and click the rotation arrow at the top. When the pointer turns into a circular arrow, click and drag to the right to rotate the text box 90 degrees.

TIP Press Shift while you rotate to constrain the rotation to 15-degree increments.

TIP There are additional rotation tools available on the Home tab, in the Drawing group under Arrange tools, and on the Drawing Tools Format tab, in the Arrange group. These let you flip objects and rotate them 90 degrees with just one click.

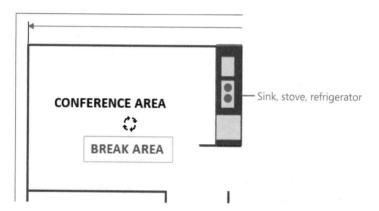

13   Drag the **Break Area** label into place next to the icons for the sink, stove, and refrigerator at the right end of the **Conference Area** text.

14   Change the color of the **Break Area** text by selecting the text box (the edge will display a solid line) and, on the **Home** tab, in the **Font** group, clicking the arrow next to the font color icon. In the **Theme Colors** gallery, click the **Accent 2 (orange)** color swatch.

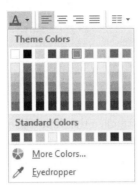

TIP All the formatting you're doing with manual text can be done to text in place-holders as well. If you need to apply a lot of manual formatting (for example, making all top-level text a different color or size), you should probably make that change on the slide master or on one of the slide layouts.

15 Create another duplicate of the **Conference Area** text box, replace the text with the word Storage, and place it in the small square at the upper-right of the diagram.

✖ CLEAN UP Save the presentation if you want, and then close it.

Adding and formatting a table

There are a number of ways to add a table to a slide. You can click the table icon in the content placeholder, or you can use the Table tool on the Insert tab, which gives you three additional options! If you use the icon in the placeholder, the inserted table will fill the width of the placeholder. If you use the table tool on the Insert tab, the table will be inserted into the center of the slide.

Regardless of how you add the table, after it's on the slide, you can easily format the table by using the Table tools.

13

In this exercise, you'll add and quickly format a table.

SET UP You need the SampleContentC_start presentation located in the Chapter13 practice file folder to complete this exercise. Open the SampleContentC_start presentation, and save it as SampleContentC. Then follow the steps.

1   Select slide **2**. In the content placeholder on the left, click the **Table** icon to open the **Insert Table** dialog box. Enter 3 in the **Number of Columns** field and 4 for the number of rows. Then click **OK** to close the dialog box and insert the table.

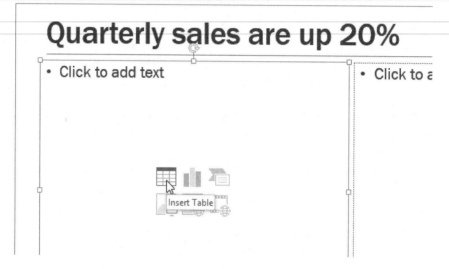

2   Place your cursor in the first cell of the table, then press the **Tab** key to move to the second cell of the top row. Enter Q1. Press **Tab** again and enter Q2 in the last cell of the top row.

3   In the first cell of the second row, enter Widgets. Press **Tab** to move to the next cell and enter $129. Press **Tab** to move to the third cell and enter $254. Press **Tab** again to move to the first cell in the third row.

4   Enter Sprockets in the first cell of the third row. Press **Tab** and enter $653. Press **Tab** again and enter $997. Press **Tab** again to move to the first cell in the fourth row.

5   Enter **Gizmos** and press **Tab** to move to the next cell. Enter $278, press **Tab** again, and enter $690.

6   Press **Tab** to create another row. Enter **Total** in the first cell. Press **Tab** and enter $1060. Press **Tab** again and enter $1941.

7   On the **Table Tools Design** tab, in the **Table Style Options** group, click **Total Row** to apply special formatting to the last row in the table.

	Q1	Q2
Widgets	129	254
Sprockets	653	997
Gizmos	278	690
Total	1060	1941

8   With the cursor in the table, on the **Table Tools Design** tab, in the **Table Styles** gallery, click the style labeled **Medium Style 3 - Accent 2**.

TIP As with all the other galleries, you can click the single arrows to scroll through the gallery line by line, or you can click the More button to expand the gallery completely.

IMPORTANT

| FILE | HOME | INSERT | DESIGN | TRANSITIONS | ANIMATIONS | SLIDE SHOW | REVIEW | VIEW | DESIGN | LAYOUT |

Header Row   First Column
Total Row   Last Column
Banded Rows   Banded Columns

Table Style Options   Table Styles   Quick Styles   WordArt Sty...   1 pt   Pen Color   Draw I

13

9   Select the table and drag the bottom edge to increase the height of the table and give the text a bit of breathing room.

10   With the table still selected, click the **Table Tools Layout** tab, then in the **Alignment** group, click the **Center Vertically** button to center the text vertically within the cells. (This small task makes your table look 100 percent better!)

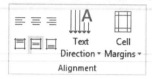

11   Move your mouse pointer above the middle column until the pointer changes to a downward-pointing arrow. Click and drag to the right to select the **Q1** and **Q2** columns.

	Q1	Q2
Widgets	129	254
Sprockets	653	997
Gizmos	278	690
Total	**1060**	**1941**

12   On the **Table Tools Layout** tab, in the **Alignment** group, click the **Center** alignment button to horizontally center the text in those two columns.

KEYBOARD SHORTCUT Ctrl+E centers text. Ctrl+L left-aligns text, and Ctrl+R right-aligns it.

✖ CLEAN UP Save the presentation if you want, and then close it.

Inserting and formatting charts

As with tables, there are multiple ways to add a chart to a slide. The most straightforward ways are to click the chart icon in a content placeholder or to use the Chart tool on the Insert tab. Either way, the Insert Chart dialog box will appear; in it you can choose the type of chart you want to add. You can format charts with just a few clicks.

In this exercise, you'll insert a chart, add your own data, and apply formatting with just a few clicks.

SEE ALSO For more about creating and formatting charts, see Chapter 23, "Creating charts and graphics".

SET UP You need the SampleContentD_start presentation located in the Chapter13 practice file folder to complete this exercise. Open the SampleContentD_start presentation, and save it as SampleContentD. Then follow the steps.

1   Click the chart icon in the empty placeholder on slide **3**.

2   Click **OK** to insert the default **Clustered Column** chart.

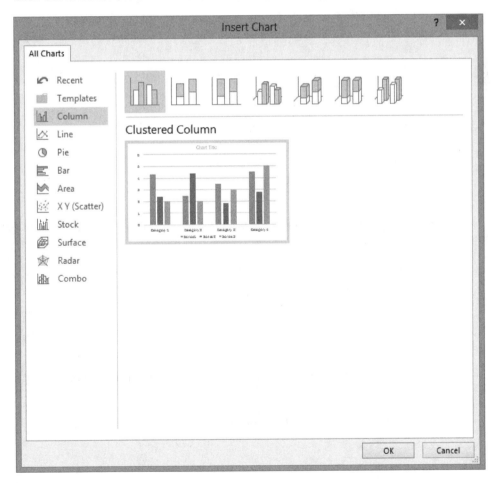

TIP Select the type of chart (such as column, line, or pie) from the list on the left of the Insert Chart dialog box. Select the subtype from the options across the top (such as clustered column or stacked column).

TIP Three-dimensional charts can make data very difficult to discern, and in fact, they can be quite misleading. It's really best to stick with two-dimensional charts.

3   In the chart sheet that appears above the chart on your slide, replace the sample data with your own. As you enter your own data over the sample data, the chart will update.

4   Click and drag the lower-right corner of the blue line that indicates the data range to eliminate any cells that shouldn't be included in the chart. Again, the chart's information will update.

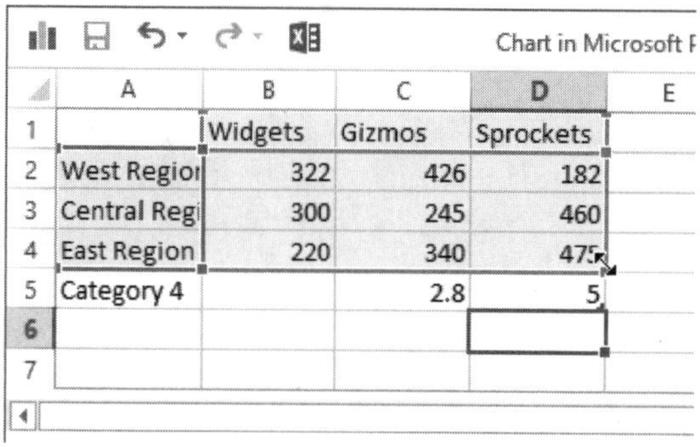

5   When you've finished entering your data, click the **X** in the upper-right corner of the chart sheet to close it.

TROUBLESHOOTING You must close the chart sheet before inserting another chart. If you don't, you'll get this message: The Chart Data Grid Is Open ... To Insert A New Chart You Need To Close It First.

TIP Reopen the chart sheet by right-clicking the chart and selecting Edit Data.

6   Select the **Chart Title** text and change it by entering these words: Number of Items Sold.

7   Click the + icon next to the chart to open the **Chart Elements** list.

8   Click the arrow next to **Axes** and uncheck **Primary Vertical** to turn off the vertical axis.

9   Select the check box next to **Data Labels** to add those to the chart.

10 Click the arrow to the right of **Legend** and then click **Top** to reposition the legend.

TIP Click the More Options button on any element to access the formatting pane, where you'll find many more options.

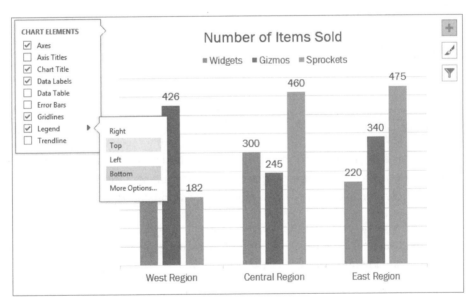

11 Click the paintbrush icon next to the chart and then click **Color**. Select the third color set so the data is easier to discern.

13

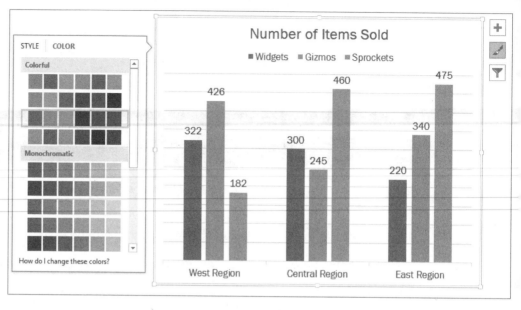

TIP Use the Chart Filters tool (the funnel icon) to highlight specific series or categories of data on the chart.

⊗ CLEAN UP Save the presentation if you want, and then close it.

Creating and formatting SmartArt diagrams

SmartArt is a diagramming tool that helps you create visual representations of information. SmartArt graphics match the look and feel of your presentation and can be used to create process flows, cycle diagrams, pyramids, organization charts, and more.

There are several ways to add SmartArt diagrams to your presentation. As you might guess, you can always click the icon in a content placeholder to open a dialog box where you can choose from any number of SmartArt graphics.

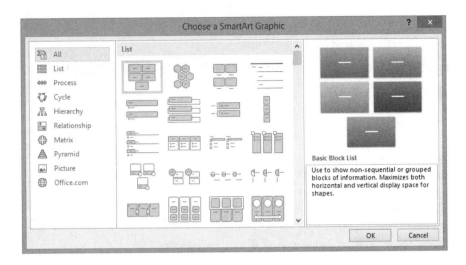

You can, of course, use the SmartArt icon on the Insert tab as well, and it will open the same dialog box. But PowerPoint also lets you turn bulleted text into SmartArt graphics with just a few clicks! It's a quick and easy way to make a boring bulleted slide into a more visual presentation.

In this exercise, you'll change bulleted list text into a SmartArt graphic and format it.

SET UP You need the SampleContentE_start presentation located in the Chapter13 practice file folder to complete this exercise. Open the SampleContentE_start presentation, and save it as SampleContentE. Then follow the steps.

1 Select slide **2** in the thumbnail pane on the left of the workspace. Right-click and choose **Duplicate Slide** to create a copy of the slide.

   TIP Always create a copy of your slide before drastically changing the formatting. In case you don't like the new slide, you can go back to the original!

2 With your cursor inside the body text on slide **2**, right-click and select **Convert to SmartArt**. Point to the **SmartArt graphic** options in the gallery to determine if any are appropriate for your text. Click the one labeled **Horizontal Bullet List** to apply it.

13

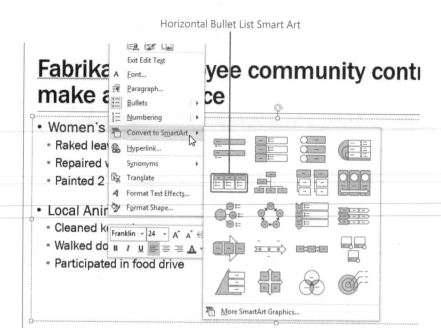

Horizontal Bullet List Smart Art

TIP If you don't like any of the diagrams in the gallery, click More SmartArt Graphics to open the Choose A SmartArt Graphic dialog box, where you can select from the entire set of diagrams.

3 Click at the end of the text in the text pane, then press **Enter** and type Regional Art Museum, which adds the text both in the pane and in the diagram. Press **Enter** again and type Decorated for new exhibition. Press **Enter** again and type Taught art class for elderly.

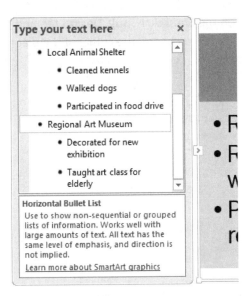

TIP You can add or edit text in the text pane or in the diagram itself, whichever is easier for you. If you add or delete bullet points in the pane, shapes will be added or removed from the diagram and vice-versa.

TIP Click the X in the upper-right corner of the text pane to close it. Use the small arrow on the left side of the diagram to reopen the pane. Or turn it on and off by toggling the Text Pane button on the SmartArt Tools Design tab, in the Create Graphic group.

4   Click the **Up Arrow** key on your keyboard until your cursor is in the line of text reading **Regional Art Museum**, and then press **Shift+Tab** to promote that text in the pane and create a new shape in the diagram at the same time.

13

5   Click the **Change Colors** button on the **SmartArt Tools Design** tab and select
    Colorful Range - Accent Colors 2 to 3 to change the colors of the diagram.

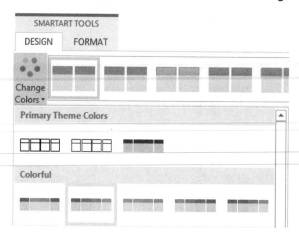

TIP You can use the SmartArt Styles gallery on the SmartArt Tools Design tab to apply various looks to your diagram. Use the tools in the Create Graphic group of the SmartArt Tools Design tab to rearrange and add shapes to your diagram.

6   Click the **More** button in the **SmartArt Layouts** gallery to expand the gallery. Click
    More Layouts to display the entire dialog box.

7   Click **List** on the left and choose **Stacked List**

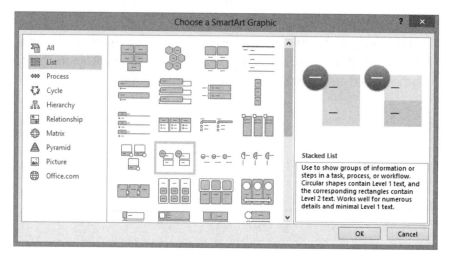

8   Click **OK** to change the diagram.

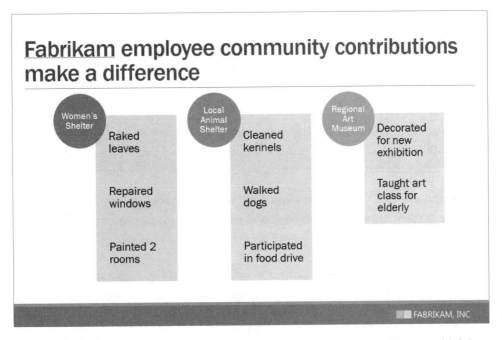

TROUBLESHOOTING Sometimes the text in a diagram doesn't size like you think it should. You can use any of the text tools on the Home tab to change the text size, but then your diagram won't resize the font if you later add or remove text.

TIP Because SmartArt diagrams are essentially Office graphics, you can apply manual formatting to any elements in tables, charts or SmartArt diagrams just like you can with any shape. See Chapter 14, "Creating Office graphics," for more information.

✖ CLEAN UP   Save the presentation if you want, and then close it.

Reusing slides and keeping their source formatting

Creating content directly in your presentation is great, but often that content will already exist in another presentation. Those are the times you just need to reuse the slide, not reinvent the wheel!

By default, slides automatically take on the formatting attributes of any presentation you paste them into. Sometimes this is a good thing, but other times you might want the slides to retain their original look. It's okay either way, because PowerPoint lets you do both!

In this exercise, you'll insert slides from the Reuse Slides gallery and move them around in the presentation. You'll also copy and paste slides into a presentation and keep the original formatting.

 **SET UP** You need the SampleContentF_start and SampleContentG_Start presentations located in the Chapter13 practice file folder to complete this exercise. Open the SampleContentF_start presentation, and save it as SampleContentF. You will open SampleContentG_Start as part of the exercise.

1   Select slide **3**. On the **Home** tab, click the bottom of the **New Slide** button and select **Reuse Slides** to open the **Reuse Slides** pane.

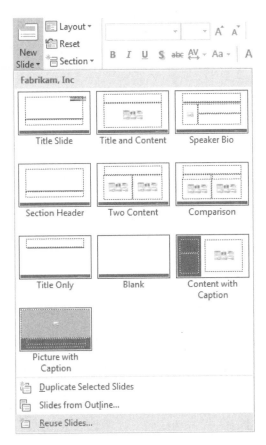

2   In the **Reuse Slides** pane, click the **Browse** button and then **Browse File** to insert
slides from a file on your hard drive. Alternatively, click the **Open a PowerPoint File**
link just below the **Browse** button. The link will take you to the same **Browse** dialog
box so you can find the file on your computer.

13

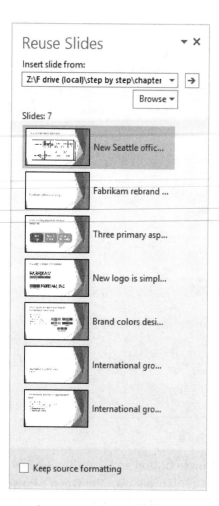

TIP If your company uses the Slide Library feature on Microsoft SharePoint, choose Browse Slide Library to access files from that location.

TIP When you've accessed a file from the Reuse Slides pane, you can select it from the drop-down list at the top of the pane, which provides handy access to files you frequently use to copy slides.

3　In the **Browse** dialog box, navigate to the **SampleContentG_Start** file and click **Open**.

4   In the **Reuse Slides** pane, click the sixth thumbnail, titled **International growth plan**, to add it to the presentation. Then click the last thumbnail to add it. Note that the formatting of the inserted slides is updated to match the template used in the SampleContentF file.

    TIP If you want to insert all slides in the Reuse Slides pane, right-click one of the thumbnails and choose Insert All Slides.

5   Select the **Keep Source Formatting** check box at the bottom of the **Reuse Slides** pane, and then click the first thumbnail (**New Seattle office floor plan**) to insert it into the presentation.

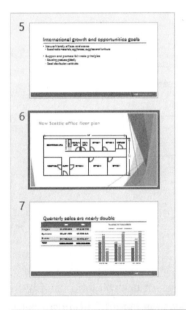

IMPORTANT

13

6   Because **Keep Source Formatting** was selected, this slide doesn't pick up the formatting of the SampleContentF presentation when it's inserted. To change this slide to the blue Fabrikam template so it matches the rest of the presentation, select it and on the **Home** tab, click the **Layout** button. Select the **Title Only** layout from the Fabrikam, Inc. set of layouts.

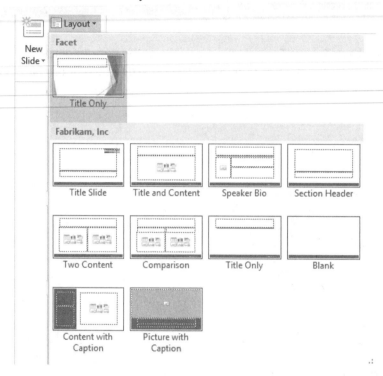

TIP When your slide has a title, but your content doesn't lend itself to including it in a placeholder, at least choose the Title Only slide layout. This ensures that your slide titles are all located in the same place and won't jump around as you move from slide to slide in your presentation. Jumping titles, logos, and other repeated graphics are telltale signs of an amateur-designed presentation.

7   Click the **X** in the upper-right corner of the **Reuse Slides** pane to close it.

8   Click the **File** tab, then **Open**, **Computer**, and then **Browse**. Navigate to the SampleContentG_Start file and click **Open** to open it.

9   Click the **View** tab, and in the **Window** group, click **Arrange All** to position the presentations side by side.

10   In the **SampleContentG_Start** file, click slide **2**, press and hold the **Shift** key, and click slide **5** to select slides **2**, **3**, **4**, and **5**.

     TIP Press and hold the Shift key, then click the first and last slides to select a set of contiguous slides. Press and hold the Ctrl key to select noncontiguous slides.

11   Right-click and choose **Copy**, or press **Ctrl+C** to copy the four slides.

12   In the **SampleContentF** file, right-click slide **6** and choose the **Use Destination Theme** paste option (the first paste icon).

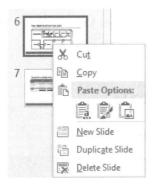

     KEYBOARD SHORTCUT You can use Ctrl+C to copy and Ctrl+V to perform the default paste action, which is to use the destination theme.

     TIP Click the second paste icon to paste the slides and keep the source formatting.

13   Slides **7** through **10** should still be selected following the paste procedure. If they are not, then select them by pressing **Shift** and clicking slide **7** and then slide **10**. Drag them into position immediately following the first slide.

13

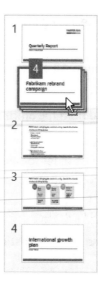

14   Click the **Slide Sorter** button on the status bar to switch to **Slide Sorter View**.

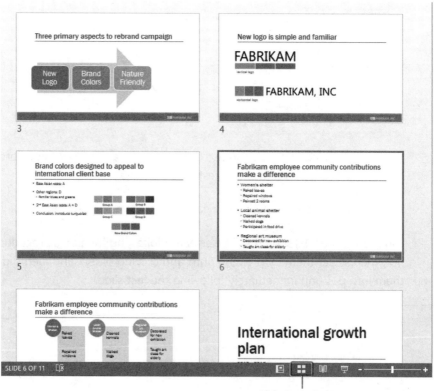

Slide Sorter button

15   Select slide **6**, the text version of the Fabrikam employee community contributions, and press **Delete** on your keyboard to delete it.

16   After you delete slide **6**, the **Employee Contributions** SmartArt graphic slide will become the new slide **6**. Select it and drag it to the end of the slides.

17   Click the **Normal** button on the status bar to return to **Normal** (editing) view.

❌ CLEAN UP **Save the presentation if you want, and then close both presentations.**

TIP PowerPoint 2013 remembers the view you're in, the slide you're on, and the zoom percentage you're at when you save a presentation.

Key points

- Slide layouts can save you time and effort by providing consistency throughout your presentation.

- Placeholders can also save you time and effort by providing formatting for your text and positioning for your other content.

- Quickly format charts, tables and SmartArt graphics by choosing styles and color combinations from the galleries on the Chart, Table and SmartArt tool tabs.

- Chart, Table, and SmartArt styles are all based on the colors in the Color Theme.

- You can reuse slides by copying and pasting them into your presentation or by inserting them through the Reuse Slides pane.

- By default, old slides inserted into your new presentation will use the new formatting.

- If you want inserted slides to maintain their original formatting, select Keep Source Formatting in Paste Options or in the Reuse Slides pane.

13

Chapter at a glance

Add

Add and format shapes,
page 338

Apply

Apply enhanced fills and effects,
page 344

Create

Create your own shapes,
page 351

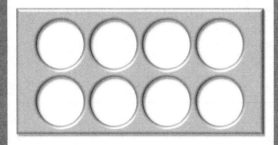

Insert

Insert, crop, and format pictures,
page 356

Creating Office graphics 14

IN THIS CHAPTER, YOU WILL LEARN HOW TO

- Add and format shapes.

- Apply enhanced fills and effects.

- Create your own shapes.

- Insert, crop, and format pictures.

Many people don't realize it, but Microsoft PowerPoint is actually an extremely powerful drawing application. Not only can you format shapes as you'd expect by applying solid and gradient fills and outlines, but you can also add 3-D effects and other enhancements, such as shadows and reflections. PowerPoint even gives you some new tools to create your own shapes.

You can apply most of this formatting to pictures as well, all of which helps you create an attractive, cohesive presentation. Picture features in PowerPoint 2013 include a background removal tool, a picture cropping tool, recoloring options, and artistic filters to go along with the more common shadows, reflections, and 3-D settings.

After you've gotten your shapes and pictures looking beautiful, you need to position them on the slide. PowerPoint 2013 has a number of enhanced features to help with alignment and distribution, including enhanced Smart Guides and new colorable guides that can be locked to the slide master.

In this chapter, you'll learn all about creating and formatting shapes and pictures. You'll also learn about using the alignment tools and the new guides and Smart Guides to position objects after you've created them.

PRACTICE FILES To complete the exercises in this chapter, you need the practice files contained in the Chapter14 practice file folder. For more information, see "Download the practice files" in this book's Introduction.

Adding and formatting shapes

You may already be familiar with the Shapes gallery in PowerPoint. It gives you common shapes like lines, rectangles, arrows, and other frequently used shapes. What you may not realize is that there are a number of different ways to add and format these shapes.

In this exercise, you'll insert a shape. You'll also position shapes by using the Smart Guides, and format them by using the Shape Styles gallery, the Theme Color palette, and the new Eyedroppers.

 SET UP You don't need any practice files to complete this exercise. Open PowerPoint to a new, blank presentation, and then follow the steps.

1   Select the first (and only) slide. On the **Home** tab, click the **Layout** button and choose the **Blank** layout so the content placeholders don't get in your way while you're drawing.

2   On either the **Home** or the **Insert** tab of the ribbon, click the **Shapes** button to expand the **Shapes** gallery.

   SEE ALSO For more information about how screen resolution and window size affect your display, see Chapter 1, "Getting comfortable in Office Professional 2013."

3   Click the **Rectangle** tool, (accessed from **Rectangles** or **Recently Used Shapes**), then click and drag on the slide to create a rectangle.

   TIP To create a perfect square, circle, or other shape, select the shape from the Shapes gallery and press the Shift key while you click and drag on the slide. Or just click once on the slide to create a 1" × 1" square, circle, triangle, or similar.

4   Select the **rectangle** and enter Rectangle 1. The text is added to the rectangle.

5   Select the rectangle and press **Ctrl+D** to duplicate it.

6   Drag the duplicated rectangle alongside the original rectangle. **Smart Guides** appear to help you align the two shapes.

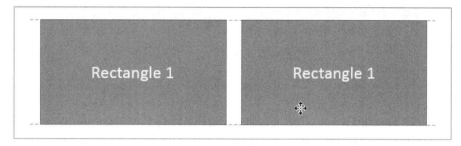

7 Press **Ctrl+D** again. PowerPoint creates a duplicate rectangle perfectly aligned and distributed with the other two! Press **Ctrl+D** again to create a fourth aligned and distributed rectangle.

8 Select the number **1** in the second rectangle. Enter **2** so the text reads **Rectangle 2**. Change the text in the third and fourth shapes to **Rectangle 3** and **Rectangle 4**.

   TIP Shapes with text behave like manual text boxes. Look for a solid outline to indicate that the shape itself is selected. If your cursor is inside the text, the shape's outline will be dotted.

9 Right-click **Rectangle 1**. Click the **Style** button to expand the **Shape Styles** gallery.

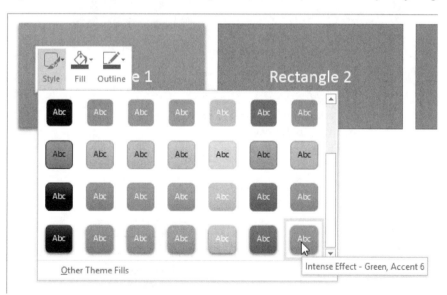

   TIP You can also access the Shape Styles, fill color, and outline color galleries from the Drawing Tools Format tool tab, which appears when you select a shape.

14

TROUBLESHOOTING If a menu displaying options to Move Here, Copy Here, or Cancel appears when you right-click an object on a slide, you've moved your mouse (probably very slightly) when you right-clicked. Just click away from the object and try again.

10　Point to the different formatting chips in the gallery to view how each would affect the selected shape. (This is called Live Preview.) Scroll to the bottom of the gallery and click the green chip in the bottom row to apply it. (It's labeled **Intense Effect - Green - Accent 6**.)

11　Right-click **Rectangle 2**. Click the **Fill** button, then select the chip that represents Orange, Accent 2 on the top row of the **Theme Colors** palette.

12　Click the **Outline** button and select the last chip in the **Accent 2 Orange** column to change the outline color of the rectangle to dark orange.

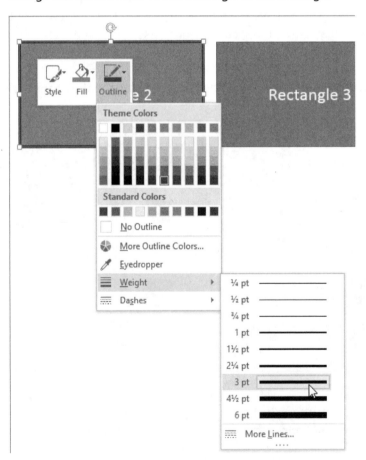

13 Click **Outline** again, then **Weight**, then **3 pt** to add a thicker border to the rectangle.

14 Right-click **Rectangle 3**. Click the **Fill** button to expand the **Fill Colors** gallery, and choose **Eyedropper** from the list.

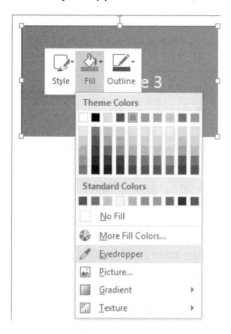

15 Move the **Eyedropper** to **Rectangle 2** and click when the color swatch turns orange to apply the orange color to **Rectangle 3**.

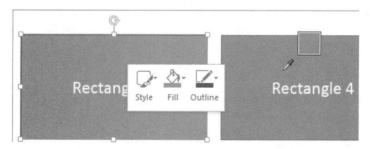

16 Right-click **Rectangle 3** and click **Outline**, then **Eyedropper**. Move the **Eyedropper** over **Rectangle 4** until it turns blue, then click to apply a blue outline to **Rectangle 3**. Click **Outline** again, then **Weight**, then **3 pt** to apply a 3-point border to **Rectangle 3**.

14

TIP The Eyedropper Text Fill tool works on text, too. Select the text and click the Font button on the Home tab so you can access the Eyedropper. You can also access this tool from the Drawing Tools Format tool tab, in the WordArt Styles group, by clicking the Text Fill button.

 CLEAN UP **Save the presentation if you want, and then close it.**

Alignment tools

The enhanced Smart Guides in PowerPoint 2013 are extremely helpful. They assist not only with alignment, but also with spacing (also known as *distributing*) objects on the slides. But sometimes they can get in the way. If that happens, you can always turn them off by right-clicking the slide and choosing Grid And Guides. Clear the Smart Guides option to turn them off. Of course, select the Smart Guides option if you want to turn them on again.

In addition to the powerful Smart Guides, PowerPoint 2013 also has enhanced guides. Guides are dotted lines that show up on the sides. They're very useful for indicating text-safe zones and margins, for example. To turn them on, right-click the slide, choose Grid And Guides, and then either Add Horizontal Guide or Add Vertical Guide. Turn the guides on and off by selecting Guides in that same dialog box. To change the color of any guide, right-click it, and then select Color. Drag to position guides on your slide.

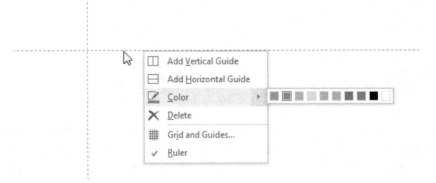

KEYBOARD SHORTCUT Use Alt+F9 (the function key) to toggle guides on and off. Press Ctrl and drag a guide to create more guides.

New in PowerPoint 2013 is the ability to add guides to the slide master and layouts! Users have asked for lockable guides for a long time, and this is the next best thing. Put guides that you don't want to grab and move by mistake onto the slide masters and layouts. You can still create guides directly on the slides when you need them quickly, and these guides will be selectable and moveable on the slides.

Finally, the conventional Alignment And Distribution tools are still available from the Arrange group on either the Home tab or tool tabs, but with the new guides and Smart Guides, you may never need to use them!

Theme colors vs. direct colors

It can be really confusing when you copy objects or slides from one presentation to another and all the colors change. It might seem like PowerPoint is doing something wrong, but it's actually just PowerPoint trying to be helpful.

The colors at the top of any of the Color galleries are called Theme Colors, and as you learned in Chapter 12, "Designing and creating presentations," all templates and presentations have a set of theme colors built in. If you think about the theme colors as being positional, that might help. For example, if you apply the Accent 2 color—whatever it might be—to a rectangle, when you apply a different template (which often happens if you copy a slide into a new presentation), then the rectangle updates its color to the new template's Accent 2 color.

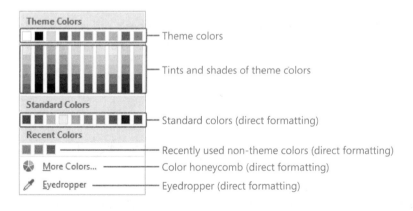

Theme Colors
— Theme colors
— Tints and shades of theme colors

Standard Colors
— Standard colors (direct formatting)

Recent Colors
— Recently used non-theme colors (direct formatting)
More Colors... — Color honeycomb (direct formatting)
Eyedropper — Eyedropper (direct formatting)

14

Not all colors are theme colors, though. If you click More Colors, the familiar honey-comb will appear. You can select colors from it, or you can click the Custom tab and input your own RGB (red, green, and blue) values.

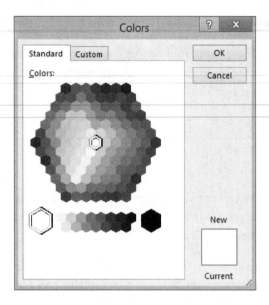

The colors you select in this dialog box show up in the Color Gallery as Recent Colors, and they are all considered direct or absolute formatting. This means that they are not theme colors, so they will not change when you apply a new template or color theme. Any colors you apply with the Eyedropper tools are also direct colors, not theme colors.

Finally, the Standard Colors are also direct colors. Hey, sometimes a red is just a red and you need it even though there's not a red in your template color theme. That's the purpose of the standard colors.

Applying enhanced fills and effects

Although the Shape Styles gallery often includes at least one gradient style, there are times when you need to create your own. In addition to enhanced fills, PowerPoint also offers a wide variety of effects; for example, soft shadows, reflections, and bevels.

In this exercise, you'll apply and edit a gradient fill. You'll also apply a shadow and 3-D effects to a shape.

SET UP You don't need any practice files to complete this exercise. Open PowerPoint to a new, blank presentation, and then follow the steps.

1   Select the first (and only) slide. On the **Home** tab, click the **Layout** button and choose the **Blank** layout so the content placeholders don't get in your way while you're drawing.

2   Draw a rectangle on the slide.

3   Double-click the rectangle to activate the **Drawing Tools Format** tool tab, and then click the **Shape Fill** button to open the **Shape Fill** list.

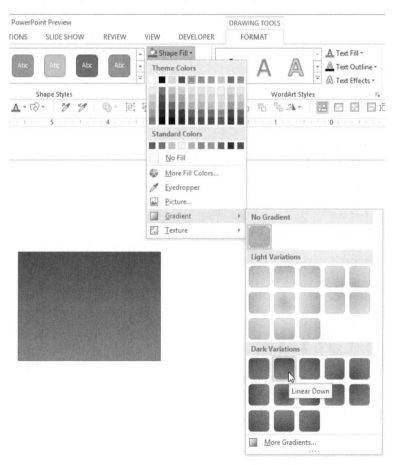

4   Click **Gradient** and then select the **Linear Down** option from the gallery.

5   Right-click the rectangle and choose **Format Shape** to open the **Format Shape** pane.

   TIP You can also access the Format Shape pane by selecting More Gradients at the bottom of the Gradient gallery.

6   On the **Shape Options Fill and Line** (paint bucket) pane, click **Fill** to expand the fill options part of the pane.

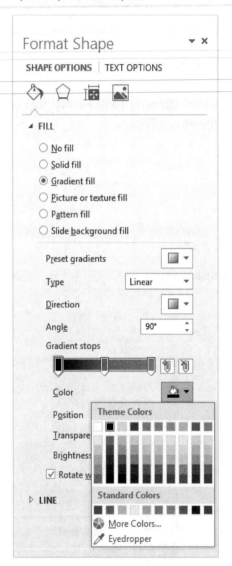

7   Look for the **Gradient stops** slider. Click the first gradient stop on the left, then click the **Color** button and select the black swatch in the **Theme Colors** gallery to change the first gradient stop to black.

8   Select the second gradient stop (in the middle), and then click the **Remove Gradient Stop** button to delete it.

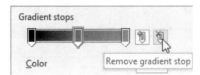

9   In the **Format Shape** pane, with the **Fill** and **Line** pane still active, click **Line** to expand that section of the pane, and then click **No Line** to remove the border from the rectangle.

> **TIP** You can use the tools that appear on the Drawing Tools Format tool tab, on the Format Shape pane, or on the shortcut menu to format shapes.

10 In the **Format Shape** pane, click **Shape Options**, then click **Shadow** to access the shadow options. Click **Presets** and choose **Offset Diagonal Bottom Right** to apply a soft drop shadow.

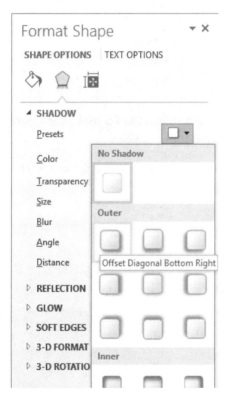

14

11 In the **Distance** field, enter **10**. In the **Blur** field, enter **12** to soften the shadow.

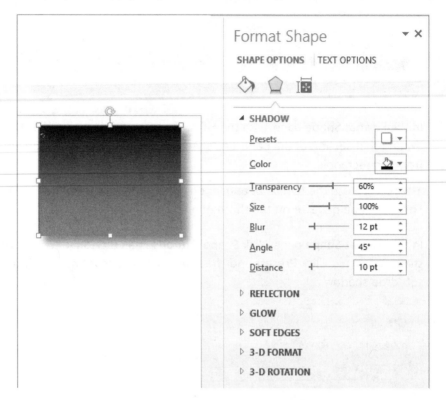

12 With the rectangle still selected, click **Shadow** in the **Format Shape** pane to collapse those tools. Click **3-D Format** to expand those options.

13 In the **Format Shape** pane, in **3-D Format** tools, click **Top Bevel** and choose the **Circle** option. In the **Depth** field, enter **75**.

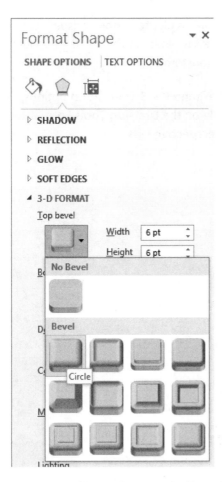

TIP All the fills, outlines, and effects that you can apply to shapes can also be applied to text, because PowerPoint 2013 considers text to be just another type of shape. Look for the text formatting tools on the Drawing Tools Format tool tab in the Word-Art Styles group. Or click Text Options in the Format Shape pane.

TIP If you're looking for a way to make circular text, don't despair! Select your text, then head to the Drawing Tools Format tool tab. In the WordArt Styles group, click the Text Effects button and choose Transform.

14   Collapse the **3-D Format** tools and expand the **3-D Rotation** options. Click the **Presets** button (which is also available on the **Drawing Tools Format** tool tab in the **Shape Effects** list) and choose **Perspective Left**.

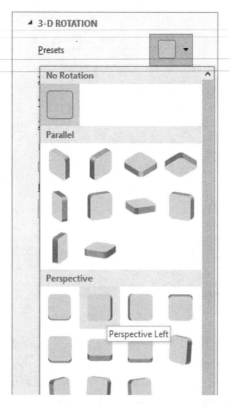

15   Enter 40 in the **X Rotation** field, 5 in the **Y rotation** field, and 50 in the **Perspective** field.

16   Expand the **Shadow** tools in the **Format Shape** pane and change the **Angle** to 0.

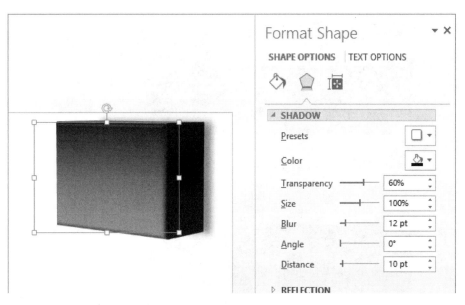

CLEAN UP Save the presentation if you want, and then close it.

Creating your own shapes

In addition to allowing you to format shapes with a huge variety of options, PowerPoint gives you the ability to manipulate shapes as well as create your own. These are wonderful things to know about so you can create exactly the shape you need.

In this exercise, you will use the adjustment handles and edit points to modify shapes. You'll also use the new Merge Shapes tools to create your own.

SET UP You need the SampleContentA_start presentation located in the Chapter14 practice file folder to complete this exercise. Open the SampleContentA_start presentation, and save it as SampleContentA. Then follow the steps.

1   Select the arrow on the first slide.

2   Click the yellow adjustment handle on the head of the arrow and drag it to the left. Release the mouse button to apply the change to the arrow.

14

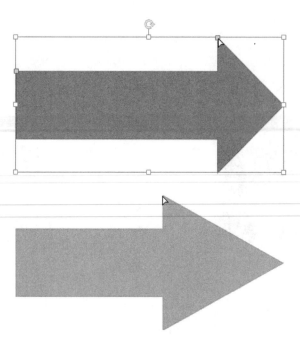

3   Click the yellow adjustment handle on the shaft of the arrow and use it to make the
     arrow slightly narrower.

4   Select the rounded rectangle. Drag the adjustment handle to the left to make the
     round corner less round.

5   On either the **Home** or **Insert** tab, in the **Shapes Gallery**, in the **Lines** area, choose **Freeform**.

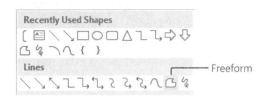

6   Click the slide to begin your freeform. Click again a few inches away. Click again as though you were creating a rough rectangle. Click a fourth time near the first point to close the rectangle.

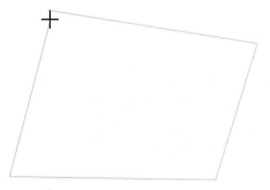

7   Right-click the shape and choose **Edit Points**, the PowerPoint equivalent of Bezier Curves.

8   Click one of the points and move it to change the shape of the freeform.

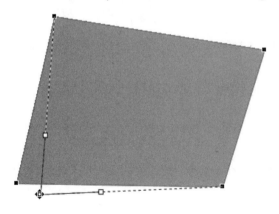

14

TIP You can also right-click the points in Edit Points mode to change them to Corner, Straight, or Smooth points. Grab the white square on the adjustment handles to modify the curve of the segments adjacent to these points. Right-clicking also lets you add and delete points and segments.

TIP You can use Edit Points on all shapes (except lines), not only on freeform shapes you've created yourself.

9 Click away to deselect the shape and exit **Edit Points**.

10 On **Slide 2**, select the red circle on the right and drag it toward the two circles above. Let go when the arrows appear on the **Smart Guides** to indicate that the distance between the circles is equal.

11 Duplicate one of the circles and drag it into place at the end of the row.

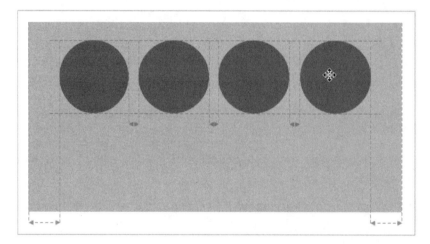

12 Press **Shift** and click each circle to select all four. Press **Ctrl+C** to copy them and **Ctrl+V** to paste.

13 With all four circles still selected, drag them into place below the top row. The **Smart Guides** will appear again to assist.

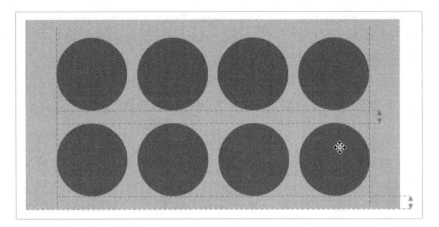

14   Press the **Esc** key to ensure you have nothing selected. Click the grey rectangle to select it. Press **Shift** and click each red circle in turn to select them all.

15   On the **Drawing Tools Format** tool tab, click **Merge Shapes**, then click **Combine** to cut out the circles from the rectangle.

IMPORTANT

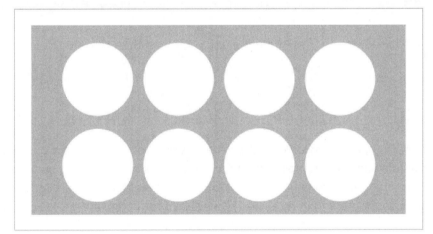

14

16   Right-click the shape and choose **Format Shape** to open the **Format Shape** pane. Use the techniques you learned in the previous exercise to apply a bevel and shadow to the shape.

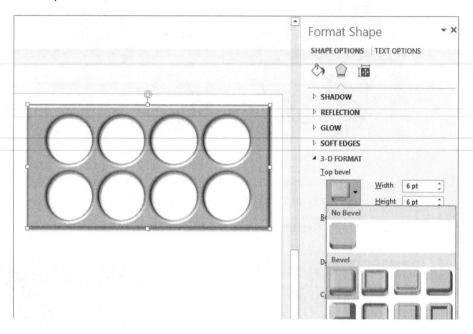

TIP You can format your new custom shape just as you would any other shape.

❌ CLEAN UP **Save the presentation if you want, and then close it.**

Inserting, cropping, and formatting pictures

As with most things in PowerPoint, there are a number of ways to insert pictures into your presentation. And, as with most other types of graphics in PowerPoint, pictures have a huge set of formatting tools to enhance their look and feel. Applying these effects to pictures throughout your presentation can also make a set of disparate images look like they go together.

In this exercise, you'll insert a screen shot as well as a picture from your computer. You'll use the crop tool and the picture formatting tools to enhance it.

SET UP You need the SampleContentB_start presentation and the SamplePictureB image file located in the Chapter14 practice file folder to complete this exercise. Open the SampleContentB_start presentation, and save it as SampleContentB. Then follow the steps.

1   Select the last slide, and then on the **Insert** tab of the ribbon, click **Screenshot**.

2   Thumbnails of your open windows appear. This includes other PowerPoint files, but not the current file. (If only PowerPoint is open, there will be only one thumbnail.) Click a thumbnail to add it to your presentation.

3   Press **Ctrl+Z** to undo the action and remove the screen shot.

4   On the **Insert** tab, click **Pictures** to insert a picture from your computer or network drives. Navigate to the **SamplePictureB.png** file and click **Insert** to add it to the slide.

14

SEE ALSO For more information about inserting online pictures, see Chapter 2, "Using shared Office features."

5 Press and hold **Ctrl+Shift** and drag a corner of the picture toward the center. (**Shift** keeps the image aspect ratio intact, and **Ctrl** sizes it from the center.)

6 On the **Picture Tools Format** tool tab, click the top of the **Crop** button. Move your pointer toward the crop handle on the right edge of the picture until it turns into a black T-bar. Click the right edge of the picture and drag it left to crop. Click away from the picture to apply the crop.

7 On the **Picture Tools Format** tool tab, click **Color** to open the **Recolor** gallery. Select **Turquoise, Accent color 1 Light** to apply a duotone look to the image.

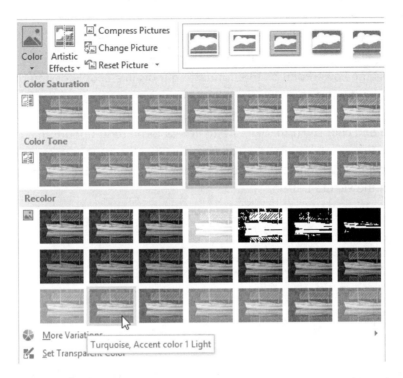

8   To give the image a more abstract look, click the **Artistic Effects** button. Select **Pencil Grayscale**.

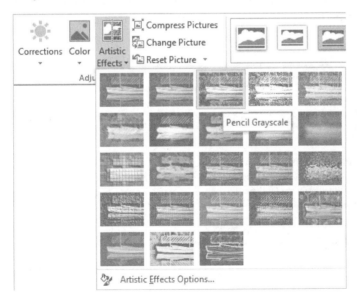

14

Picture tools are right at your fingertips

You can access the PowerPoint picture formatting tools in a couple of different places. Throughout this picture exercise, we've been using the tools on the Picture Tools Format tool tab that appears when you select a picture. You can also right-click a picture and choose Format Picture to access formatting options in a task pane. Artistic Effects settings are accessed from the Effects button, and settings for Picture Corrections (sharpen/soften, brightness/contrast), Picture Color, and Crop are accessed from the Picture button.

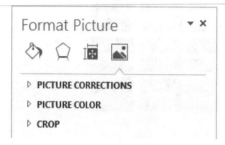

If your pictures are very large, you may want to use Compress Pictures to help keep your PowerPoint file size manageable. Select this tool from the Picture Tools Format tool tab that appears when you select a picture. It gives you options to permanently delete the cropped parts of pictures, and you can choose from four compression options.

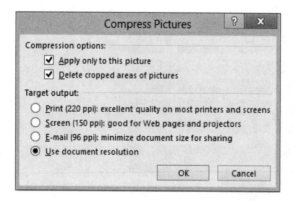

9   To add a frame to the image and make it look like a snapshot, click the **Picture Tools Format** tool tab, then click the **More** button to expand the **Picture Styles** gallery. In the gallery, select **Rotated, White**.

TIP If you mess up your picture while you're playing with the picture formatting tools (after all, they're pretty darned fun!), click the Reset Picture button on the Picture Tools Format tool tab.

10   Move and size the picture so it overlaps the title a bit.

14

11 Click inside the **Title** placeholder. On the **Home** tab, click **Arrange** and then **Bring to Front** so the text is in front of the image.

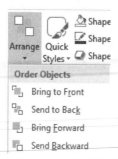

TIP The Order Objects tools (Bring to Front, Send to Back, and so on) can be used on all images and objects, including shapes, SmartArt graphics, tables, charts, videos, placeholders, and text boxes. They are located on the Home tab in the Drawing Group, from the Arrange button. They can also be accessed from the formatting tabs. The Selection pane is an extension of these tools. It can be accessed from the Editing group on the Home tab. Click the arrow next to the Select button, and then choose Selection Pane from the list.

❌ CLEAN UP Save the presentation if you want, and then close it.

Removing the background from a picture

PowerPoint has a couple of tools you can use to remove backgrounds from pictures. These can be especially handy, for example, when you are working on a dark slide and your logo or other image has a white background.

To use the Remove Background tool, insert a picture, then click the Remove Background button on the Picture Tools Format tool tab.

PowerPoint will add a selection area to the part of the picture it thinks you want to keep.

Expand or contract the selected area by dragging the selection handles, and use the tools on the Background Removal tool tab to mark additional areas to keep or remove.

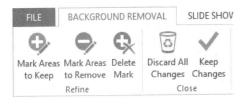

When you apply the changes, PowerPoint will remove parts of the image that are colored magenta. Click Keep Changes (or simply click away from the picture to deselect it) to apply the changes.

14

The other tool you can use to remove some backgrounds is the Transparent Wand tool. It's located on the Picture Tools Format tool tab, under the Color button, as the Set Transparent Color tool.

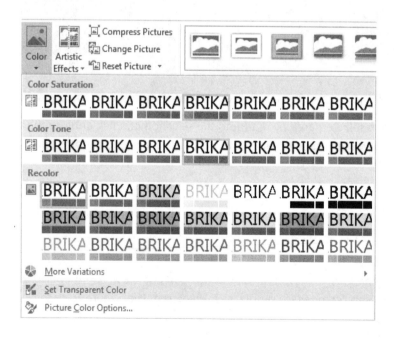

Click it, then click the color you want to remove on your image. The transparent wand tool removes pixels of color with the exact RGB values as the pixel you click.

Key points

- Using the styles galleries can save you time and provide consistency for your presentation.

- PowerPoint lets you apply and tweak settings for special effects such as shadows, reflections, glows, soft edges, and 3-D.

- Formatting tools can be found on the tabs that appear when you select an object.

- Most of the same formatting tools can be found by right-clicking an object and selecting Format Shape, Format Picture, or Format Text.

- You can create your own shapes by using the Merge Shapes tools.

14

Chapter at a glance

Animate

Animate by using the Animation Painter,
page 368

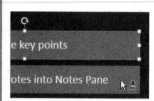

Edit

Edit video and apply transitions,
page 373

Save

Save your presentation as a video,
page 377

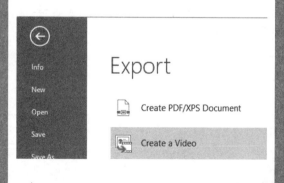

Adding animation and multimedia

15

IN THIS CHAPTER, YOU WILL LEARN HOW TO

- Add animation to text and shapes.

- Edit video and apply transitions.

- Insert and play online video.

- Save your presentation as a video.

Microsoft PowerPoint 2013 makes it easy to include audio and video in presentations, along with more common animation and transition effects. In fact, you can even perform some basic multimedia editing tasks right inside PowerPoint. Have you ever needed to snip just a couple of seconds off the end of a video in your presentation? Well, now you can.

As we become increasingly more dependent on the cloud, PowerPoint follows suit, offering a number of options for inserting online media content. In addition, PowerPoint 2013 takes it a step farther and gives you the ability to save your own presentations as videos, in either MPEG-4 or Windows Media Video format.

In this chapter, you'll learn how to apply basic animations to text and shapes, how to add video to your slides, how to edit videos, how to insert an online video, and how to save your presentation as a video.

PRACTICE FILES To complete the exercises in this chapter, you need the practice files contained in the Chapter15 practice file folder. For more information, see "Download the practice files" in this book's Introduction.

Adding animation to text and shapes

Animation can add splash to your presentation, but it's important to use it effectively. Animation should have a purpose—to demonstrate a process, to emphasize a point, to control the flow of text, and so on. It should not be added "just because." Keeping it simple is a good rule of thumb when working with animation effects in PowerPoint.

In this exercise, you'll apply entrance and exit animation effects to placeholder text and shapes.'

➡ SET UP You need the SampleContentA_start presentation located in the Chapter15 practice file folder to complete this exercise. Open the SampleContentA_start presentation, and save it as SampleContentA. Then follow the steps. The SampleContentA_end. PPTX file has also been included in the practice file folder to help you monitor your success with this exercise.

1 Click the edge of the text placeholder on slide **3** to select it.

   TROUBLESHOOTING If you're having trouble selecting a placeholder by clicking its edge, click the text inside, and then press the Esc key on your keyboard.

2 On the **Animations** tab, click **Fade** in the **Animation** gallery. The animation will be displayed on the slide.

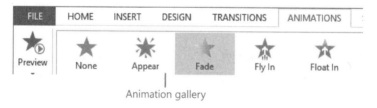

Animation gallery

3 Notice the numbers next to the text on the slide. These will be displayed when the **Animations** tab is active on the ribbon. This shows you the sequential order of the animated objects.

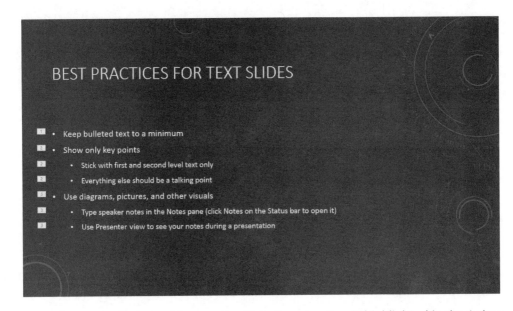

TIP When you select an object on the slide, its animation is highlighted in the Animation pane. Likewise, if you select an animation in the Animation pane, the sequence number will be highlighted next to it on the slide.

4   Press **Shift+F5** to start a presentation on this slide and review how the animation works in Slide Show view. Click once to reveal the first bullet point, and then click a second time to reveal the second point and its sub-bullets. Click again to reveal the third point and its sub-bullets. Keep clicking or press **Esc** to end the slide show.

5   Go to slide **2** and select the top rectangle. In the **Animation** gallery, click **Wipe**, which will bring the object onto the slide with a wiping motion from bottom to top.

6   With the top rectangle still selected, click **Effect Options** on the **Animations** tab, then click **From Top** to change the direction of the wipe animation you just added.

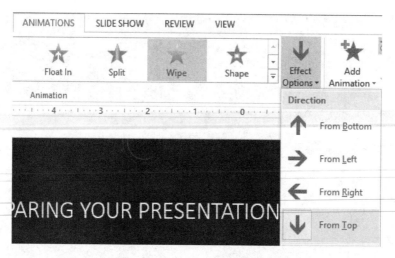

7   With the top rectangle still selected, click **Add Animation**. Scroll down to the **Exit** animations and click **Fade**. A **Fade** exit animation will be added to the top rectangle.

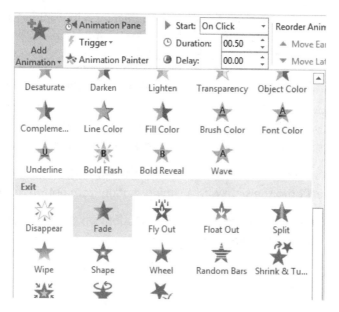

8   Click the **Animation** pane button on the ribbon to open the **Animation** pane.

     TIP Entrance animations are indicated with a green icon, exit animations with red, and emphasis animations with yellow.

9   Select the second animation in the **Animation** pane. This is the exit animation you applied to the rectangle in step 7. On the ribbon, change **Start (On Click)** to **Start**

With Previous so that the rectangle disappears at the same time the previous animation occurs.

TIP If there is a number next to the animation in the Animation pane, then that animation starts when you click the mouse. If there is no number alongside the animation, then it is set to Start With Previous (which means it starts at the same time as the prior animation), or After Previous (which means the animation starts at the completion of the prior animation).

10   Select the top rectangle on the slide, and then double-click the **Animation Painter** to activate it.

TIP Click the Animation Painter once to paint animation settings from one object to another. Double-click the Animation Painter to make it "sticky" so you can apply animations to more than one object. Press Esc to deactivate it when you're finished.

11   Click each of the remaining rectangles on the slide to apply the same animation settings as you did with the top rectangle. Press **Esc** to exit the **Animation Painter**.

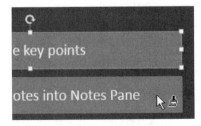

12   In the **Animation** pane, select the **Rectangle 6** exit animation. Drag it into position after the **Rectangle 9** entrance animation. This causes **Rectangle 6** to fade away at the same time **Rectangle 9** wipes in.

> **TIP** PowerPoint 2013 lets you drag animations into the Animation pane. Or, you can use the up and down arrow buttons to reorder animations.

13   Select the **Rectangle 9** exit animation and drag it into place immediately following the **Rectangle 12** entrance animation. This causes **Rectangle 9** to fade away at the same time **Rectangle 12** wipes in. Rearrange the remaining exit animations so that one rectangle exits when the next rectangle enters.

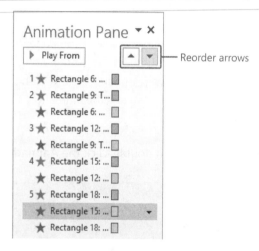

14   Select the **Rectangle 18** exit animation in the **Animation** pane and press **Delete** to remove the animation. This guarantees that **Rectangle 18** won't disappear as it appears!

> **TIP** If you have a long or complex animation sequence, select one of the animations in the Animation pane and then click Play From at the top of the pane. PowerPoint will begin playing the animation from that point, temporarily hiding the previous animations, so you don't have to watch them.

15   Press **F5** to begin the presentation from the first slide and click through it to review the animations. The **SampleContentA_end.PPTX** file has been included in your practice files to help you monitor your success with this exercise.

✖ CLEAN UP Save the presentation if you want, and then close it.

Editing video and applying transitions

Animation lets you add movement to an object on a slide. Transitions let you add movement between one slide and the next slide. And video adds another dimension of movement altogether. You can easily add all these to your presentations.

15

In this exercise, you'll add and edit a video and apply transitions to your presentation.

➡ **SET UP** You need the SampleContentB_start presentation and the Fabrikam Employee Excursion.wmv video located in the Chapter15 practice file folder to complete this exercise. Open the SampleContentB_start presentation, and save it as SampleContentB. Then follow the steps.

1   With slide **3** selected, click the bottom of the **New Slide** button on the **Home** tab, then click **Blank** to add a new slide based on the **Blank** layout.

2   With the new slide (slide **4**) selected, on the **Insert** tab, click **Video**, and then click **Video on My PC**.

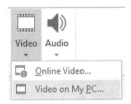

3   Navigate to the **Fabrikam Employee Excursion.wmv** file, select it, and then click **Insert** to add the video to slide **4**. The video will be inserted in the middle of the slide.

TIP Audio and video files are embedded by default when you insert them into PowerPoint 2013. If you prefer to link a multimedia file, in the Insert dialog box, click the arrow next to the Insert button and choose Link To File.

4   With the video selected, click the **Video Tools Playback** tab and change the **Start On Click** setting to **Start Automatically** so the video begins playing as soon as you transition to slide **4**.

TROUBLESHOOTING When an animation is set to Start On Click, the animation begins when you click the mouse. You don't have to click anything special or have your mouse pointer in a specific location. With video, however, Start On Click indicates that the video will start when you click the multimedia controls, which appear when you move your mouse pointer near the video. This means you must move your pointer to the video in order to play it; a random mouse click won't do.

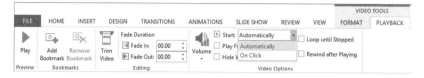

5 With the video still selected, click the **Trim Video** button to open the **Trim Video** dialog box.

6 Slide the green **Start Time** indicator to the right until it is at timepoint **00:10.669**. Use the arrows in the **Start Time** field, if necessary, or enter 10.669 directly into the **Start Time** field and press **Tab** to set the **Start** time.

7 Slide the red **End Time** indicator to the left until it is at timepoint **00:33.213**. As with the **Start Time** field, you can manually input time into the **End Time** field as necessary.

8 Click **OK** to apply the trims.

9   On the **Transitions** tab, scroll through the transitions until you can click **Peel Off**, which is located in the **Exciting** group of transitions. Click **Apply To All** to add a page turn transition to all of your slides.

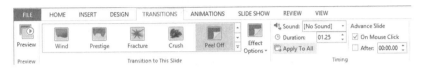

TIP Use simple transitions for the bulk of your slides. Nobody wants to sit through a whole presentation of Vortex or Glitter transitions! When in doubt, a modest fade is always a good bet. Save the more dramatic transitions to add extra impact to your title slides and section dividers.

✖ CLEAN UP Save the presentation if you want, and then close it.

Playing sound across slides

Inserting an audio file is basically like inserting anything else. Click the Insert tab, click Audio, and then choose whether you want to add a sound file from your computer or insert a sound file that will download from Office.com.

After the audio file has been inserted into your presentation, you can trim it and fade it just as you can with video. In addition, you can insert a sound file on the first slide and then click the Play In Background button on the Audio Tools Playback tab to have PowerPoint treat your sound as a background track. (The buttons to Start Automatically, Play Across Slides, Loop Until Stopped, and Hide During Show are all activated when you click Play In Background.)

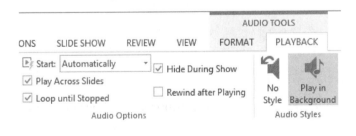

Inserting and playing online video

It's not unusual to want to put a short video clip from an online source (such as YouTube) into your presentation. PowerPoint 2013 makes it easy to do that by using the video's embed code. Be aware that even though you're using an embed code to control the video, it's still online, and it's still linked to your presentation. That means you'll need a good solid Internet connection in order to play the online video during your presentation.

In this exercise, you'll insert an online video into your presentation.

→ SET UP You need the SampleContentC_start presentation located in the Chapter15 practice file folder to complete this exercise. You will also need an Internet connection in order to insert an online video. Open the SampleContentC_start presentation, and save it as SampleContentC. Then follow the steps.

1 Select slide **5**, choose **Insert**, then **Video**, and then **Online Video**.

2 If necessary, click the **Also Insert From YouTube** icon to enable adding video from YouTube.

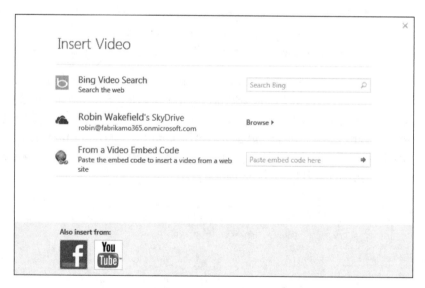

3 Enter Fabrikam Employee Excursion in the YouTube search box and press **Enter**.

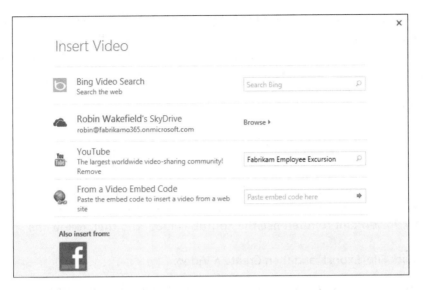

4   There will be only one search result. Select the video, and then click **Insert**.

5   Press **Shift+F5** to play the presentation and test the video. Click the **Play** button on the YouTube video to start it.

TIP Your video must be public in order to search for it. If the video is not public, paste the embed code into the From A Video Embed Code field.

TROUBLESHOOTING If you need to get an embed code from YouTube, on the You-Tube video page, click Share, then Embed, and then Use Old Embed Code. Copy and paste that embed code into the From A Video Embed Code field.

❌ CLEAN UP Save the presentation if you want, and then close it.

Saving your presentation as a video

PowerPoint 2013 gives you the option to save your presentation as either a .wmv or an .mp4 formatted video. It does a very good job of keeping animations and transitions intact, but they are all converted to automatic animations. After all, you can't click to animate an object in a video. PowerPoint also includes most audio and video you've added to the presentation, so you can create a video of a video! However, some files, such as online videos, will not be included when you save your presentation as a video.

If you've added automatic transition timings (Advance After __ Seconds), then PowerPoint will use those as it creates the video. Otherwise, you will have the option of specifying how long PowerPoint will remain on each slide. You also have options to choose different sizes of video, which comes in handy when you're creating videos for various purposes.

In this exercise, you'll save your presentation as a video.

SET UP You need the SampleContentD_start presentation located in the Chapter15 practice file folder to complete this exercise. Open the SampleContentD_start presentation, and save it as SampleContentD. Because the Fabrikam Employee Excursion video from YouTube has been inserted into this file, you may receive a security warning, "References to external media objects have been blocked." Click the Enable Content button to allow PowerPoint to reference the YouTube video, and then follow the steps.

1   Click **File**, **Export**, and then **Create a Video**.

2   In the **Create a Video** settings on the right, change **Seconds Spent on Each Slide** from **5.00** to **7.00**.

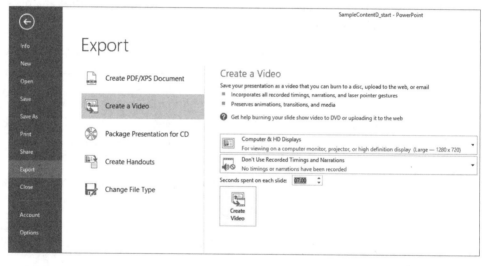

3   Leave the **Computer & HD Displays** option set at **Computer & HD Displays** (Large size).

4   Click the **Create Video** button, enter a name for the video, and click **Save**.

TIP To save the video in a .wmv format instead of the default .mp4 video format, click the Create Video button. Then in the Save As dialog box, change the Save as Type from MPEG-4 Video to Windows Media Video.

5   A message box appears to explain that some of the media in the presentation can't be included in the video. Click **Continue without media**.

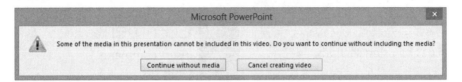

TIP While PowerPoint is saving your video, a progress bar appears on the status bar at the bottom of the PowerPoint window. If you need to cancel the video creation for any reason, click the X to the right of the progress bar.

6   Play the video in your favorite video application. You'll find that the animations and transitions have all become automatic, the YouTube video is missing from the last slide, and just a static picture of the first frame is displayed.

✖ CLEAN UP Save the presentation if you want, and then close it.

Key points

- Animations add movement to objects on a slide, whereas transitions move the presentation from one slide to the next.

- When it comes to animations and transitions, "less is more" is a good rule of thumb.

- Audio and video files are embedded into PowerPoint 2013 by default.

- Even if you use an embed code to insert an online video into your presentation, that video is *not* embedded in your presentation.

- You can save your presentation as a video, and PowerPoint will leave animations, transitions, and most multimedia intact.

- Online video is not included when you save your presentation as a video.

Chapter at a glance

Organize

Organize slides by using sections,
page 382

Comment

Insert comments,
page 386

Finalize

Finalize your presentation,
page 393

Present

Practice with Presenter view,
page 403

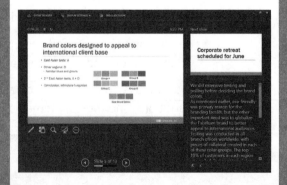

Finalizing and presenting

16

IN THIS CHAPTER, YOU WILL LEARN HOW TO

- Add and rename sections.

- Insert comments.

- Print a presentation.

- Finalize a presentation.

- Deliver a presentation.

- Practice with Presenter view.

You may need to collaborate with others as you develop your presentation. Microsoft PowerPoint 2013 makes this process easy, with features that support commenting, sharing, and broadcasting online. You may also need to use these tools and others as you finalize and deliver your presentation.

In this chapter, you'll work with sections, comments, and tools such as the Document Inspector and the Accessibility Checker.

PRACTICE FILES To complete the exercises in this chapter, you need the practice files contained in the Chapter16 practice file folder. For more information, see "Download the practice files" in this book's Introduction.

Adding and renaming sections

Sections are a useful administrative tool for grouping slides. For example, you might divide a presentation by subject to make it easier to navigate when you're giving the presentation. Or you might divide it among a number of colleagues, each of whom takes responsibility for developing the slides in one section of the presentation. Whatever the reason, sections can be tremendously helpful for managing content within a PowerPoint file.

In this exercise, you'll add and manipulate sections.

➡ SET UP You need the SampleContentA_start presentation located in the Chapter16 practice file folder to complete this exercise. Open the SampleContentA_start presentation and click Enable Content if you're prompted to do so. Save the presentation as SampleContentA. Then follow the steps.

1   With slide **6** selected, on the **Home** tab, in the **Slides** group, click **Section**, then **Add Section**. A section called **Untitled Section** will be added, and the slides in it (slides **6** through **10**) will be selected. (Another existing section begins with slide **11**.)

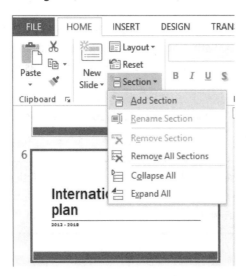

2   With the **Untitled Section** still selected, click the **Section** button on the **Home** tab again and choose **Rename Section**.

TROUBLESHOOTING Click the name of a section to select it. When a section is selected, its name will be bold and orange, and all slides in the section will be selected.

TIP You can add, edit, and manipulate sections by right-clicking a slide thumbnail or section name in the Slides pane.

3   In the **Rename Section** dialog box, enter Future Growth (Taneyhill) and click **Rename**. **Untitled Section** changes to **Future Growth (Taneyhill)** in the **Slides** pane.

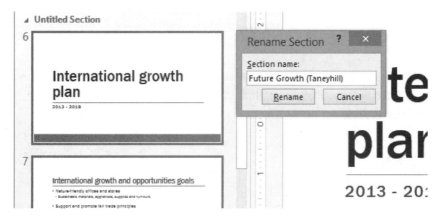

4   On the **View** tab, click **Slide Sorter** to switch to **Slide Sorter** view.

TIP You can access Slide Sorter view from either the View tab or the status bar.

5   On the **Home** tab, click **Section**, then **Collapse All** to collapse all sections.

6   Click the last section, **HR info (Wakefield)**, to select it. Drag the section ahead of the previous **Future Growth** section. When you release the mouse button, the section will be repositioned.

7 Click the arrows next to the **Introduction** and the **New Branding** sections to expand them.

8 Click slide **1** to select it. Drag it into the **New Branding** section just before slide **2**, the Fabrikam rebrand campaign slide. Release the mouse button to place the slide in the **New Branding** section.

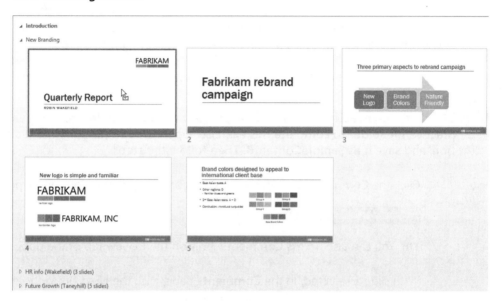

9 Click the **Introduction** section, and on the **Home** tab, click **Section**, then **Remove Section** to delete the empty **Introduction** section.

> **TIP** Remove Section removes a section designation, but it doesn't remove any slides. If you want to delete all the slides in a section, right-click the section name in the Slides pane or in Slide Sorter view and choose Remove Section & Slides.

> **TIP** You can double-click a slide thumbnail in Slide Sorter view to return to Normal view.

✖ CLEAN UP Save the presentation if you want, and then close it.

Inserting comments

Like sections, comments are also very helpful when developing a presentation. When you add a comment to a slide or an object, anyone reviewing the file in Normal view will be able to view and respond to it, but the comments will not be displayed in Slide Show view. This makes comments a handy way to communicate with colleagues as you're developing a presentation. The introduction of the new threaded Comments pane improves this feature in PowerPoint 2013, especially to enhance collaboration via the cloud.

In this exercise, you'll add comments to your PowerPoint file.

SET UP You need the SampleContentB_Start presentation located in the Chapter16 practice file folder to complete this exercise. Open the SampleContentB_Start presentation, and save it as SampleContentB. Then follow the steps.

1   Click the **Comments** button on the status bar to open the **Comments** pane.

TIP You can also access Comments tools on the Review tab of the ribbon.

2   With slide **1** selected, in the **Comments** pane, click the **Next** button to move to the next comment in the file. You'll be taken to slide **3**.

3   Click **Next** again, and you'll be taken to slide **8**. In the **Comments** pane, click inside the **Reply** box and enter No, it's an embedded video. Then press **Enter** to create the comment.

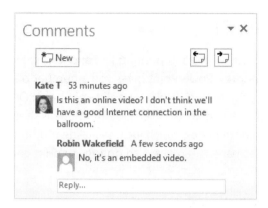

4   Select slide **5** and in the **Comments** pane, click **New** to add a new comment. Enter **Kate, be sure to review notes**, and then press **Enter** to create the comment.

Comments icon

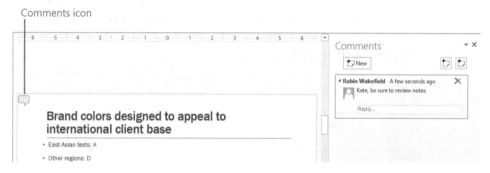

TIP You can click a Comments icon on the slide to open the Comments pane to that comment.

TIP You can move Comments icons on a slide. Just drag them.

5   Click the **Next** button four times, until Kate's comment on slide **13** is selected.

6   Click the **X** in the upper-right corner of Kate's comment to delete it.

TIP To quickly delete all comments in a file, click the bottom of the Delete button on the Review tab and choose Delete All Comments And Ink In This Presentation.

✖ CLEAN UP **Save the presentation if you want, and then close it.**

Printing slides and notes

Although we're moving to a more digital world and printing less and less, sometimes you still need to print your slides or your notes. PowerPoint gives you a number of options for this. You can print full page slides if you need to display one slide per page. Or you can print handouts, which lets you choose how many smaller slide thumbnails should appear on each page. You can also print the note pages, which include a slide thumbnail plus any speaker notes you added in the Notes pane. There are also options to print comments or print only a specific section.

In this exercise, you'll print your PowerPoint file.

 SET UP You need the SampleContentC_Start presentation located in the Chapter16 practice file folder to complete this exercise. Open the SampleContentC_Start presentation, and save it as SampleContentC. Then follow the steps.

1   Choose **File**, then **Print**.

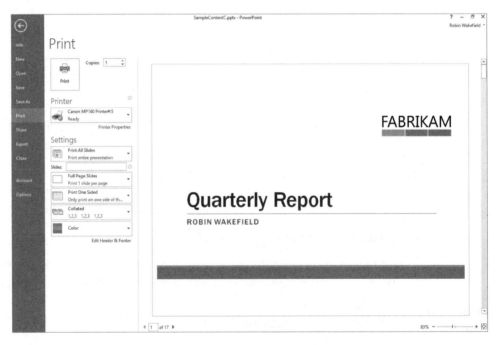

   TIP If there are comments in the file, PowerPoint will print them by default. If you do not want to print comments, deselect them by going to File, Print. In the Print Layout options (where you can choose to print full page slides or multiple slides per page), clear the option to Print Comments And Ink.

2   In the **Print** dialog box, click **Print All Slides** to access options for which slides to print. Choose **HR info (Wakefield)** in the **Sections** options to print only slides included in that section.

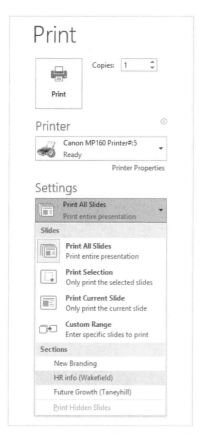

3   Click **Full Page Slides** to access the **Print Layout** settings.

4   Select **Notes Pages** to print your slides with their speaker notes. Also make sure that **Print Comments and Ink Markup** remains checked so the comments included in the file will print.

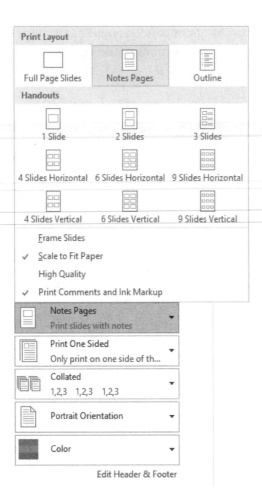

5   Below the preview of the slides, use the next and previous arrows to move through the pages to see how your notes pages will look when printed.

6   When you get to page **4**, Use the **Zoom** slider at the lower-right of the **Print** page
to help you view the comments more clearly, then click the **Zoom to Page** button
to view the entire page again.

Print Preview navigation   Zoom to Page button

TIP To create a PDF of your presentation, choose File, Export, Create PDF/XPS Document, then click the Create PDF/XPS Document button to open the Publish As PDF Or XPS dialog box. Click Options in that dialog box if you want to print notes pages or multiple slides per page.

7   Click the **Print Preview** nagivation arrow to show the print preview of page **5**. Click it
     again to view a preview of page **6**, which displays the leftover notes from slide **5**.

⊗ CLEAN UP If you have a printer connected to your computer, click Print to print the
six notes pages. Otherwise, save the presentation if you want, and then close it.

Finalizing your presentation

PowerPoint has a number of tools you might want to use as you finalize your presentation. Although you can check spelling from the Review tab, most of the other finalization tools are located in the Backstage view. To access them, click the File tab, then Info.

If there are any multimedia files in your presentation, you may find options to Optimize Compatibility and Compress Media. Clicking Optimize Compatibility converts older .wmv files as well as video file types such as QuickTime .mov files to newer Windows Media Video format so they're more likely to play on other PCs. It also prompts you to embed any linked multimedia files so they're not lost if you transfer your presentation to another computer. Use Compress Media to make the media files smaller, which in turn makes your PowerPoint file size smaller. Be sure to run the presentation in Slide Show view after you compress it to ensure that the media quality hasn't suffered.

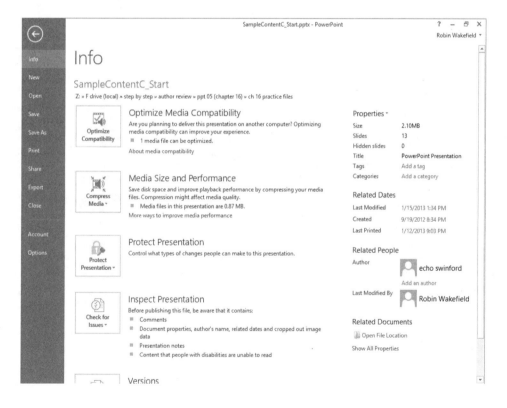

Protect Presentation includes an option to Mark As Final, which prevents users from making changes to the file. Note that this is only an administrative tool. Its sole purpose is to prevent users from making inadvertent changes to the presentation. Anyone can simply click Mark As Final again to unmark the presentation and allow changes again, or someone can click the Edit Anyway button that appears when a presentation that's been marked as final is opened.

Inspect Presentation includes tools to Inspect Document, Check Accessibility, and Check Compatibility.

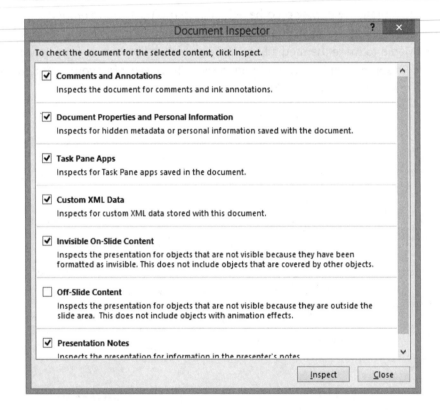

The Document Inspector is a great way to remove unwanted or personal content from your presentation all at once. For example, if you want to remove your speaker notes before sending your presentation to a client, click Inspect Document and choose the Presentation Notes option. Be sure to do this on a copy of your presentation, so you don't lose the only copy of your notes! You can also remove all comments and ink annotations in the file by using the Document Inspector.

Check Accessibility helps you make your presentation easier for people with disabilities to read. Select an object in the Accessibility Checker pane and then scroll through the Additional Information to get tips for fixing the associated accessibility problems.

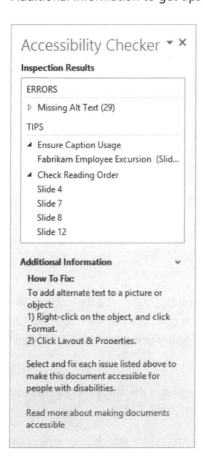

The Compatibility Checker tells you what issues you may experience when you save your file in a format for a previous version of PowerPoint (with a .ppt file extension). It runs by default when you save in that earlier file format, but you can access it at any time. For example, running the Compatibility Checker is helpful if you're wondering what types of issues people using previous versions of PowerPoint might encounter when trying to edit or view your .pptx file.

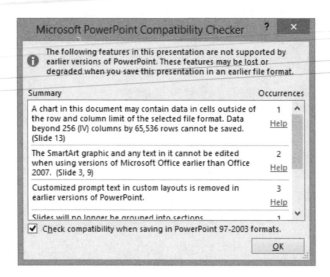

Delivering a presentation

To deliver a presentation to an audience, you must first put the presentation into Slide Show view. There are a number of ways to do this. You can click the shortcut icon on the status bar, click one of the options in the Start Slide Show group on the Slide Show tab, or press F5 on your keyboard.

KEYBOARD SHORTCUT Press F5 to start a presentation from the beginning. Press Shift+F5 to begin the presentation from the slide that's currently selected.

If your computer doesn't have another monitor (or a projector) attached to it, any of those actions will open the Slide Show view of your presentation. This is the full-screen presentation that your audience sees.

Fabrikam rebrand campaign

Popup Toolbar

If you have a second monitor or a projector attached to your computer, PowerPoint will also open Presenter view by default when you begin a slide show. Presenter view displays thumbnails of your current slide and the next slide, your speaker notes, a timer, and various navigation and inking tools. Your audience will see everything that happens in Slide Show view, but only you will see Presenter view.

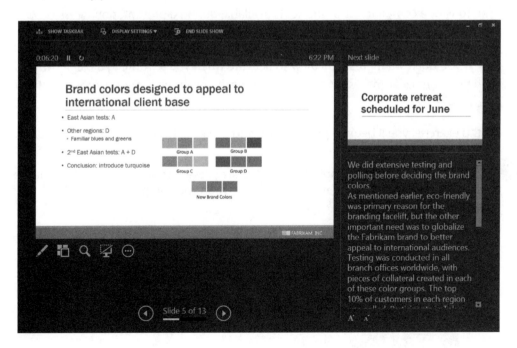

TROUBLESHOOTING If you start a slide show and don't see the full-screen Slide Show view on the correct monitor, choose a different monitor in the Monitors group on the Slide Show tab.

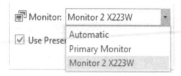

When you're in Slide Show view, there are a number of ways to navigate. Press the mouse button to move forward. On a touch device, you can swipe backward and forward. If you have a keyboard available, you can also press the spacebar, the Right Arrow key, the Down Arrow key, or the N key to move to the next slide. The Left Arrow key, the Up Arrow Key, or the P key will take you to the previous slide. Pressing the B key will black out the screen, which is a great way to bring focus back to you during a question and answer session, for example. If you know your content well, you can also enter the slide number and press the Enter key to jump to that slide. If you don't want to remember all those slide numbers (and who does?), PowerPoint 2013 also has a new See All Slides feature that shows thumbnails of all your slides, which allows you to quickly jump to any slide in the presentation.

TIP To view a complete list of shortcuts available during a presentation, press F1 while you're in Slide Show view.

TIP If you don't want Presenter view to activate when you're running Slide Show view with two monitors, clear the Use Presenter View check box in the Monitors group of the Slide Show tab.

In this exercise, you'll begin a presentation and navigate through some of the slides.

 **SET UP** You need the SampleContentD_Start presentation located in the Chapter16 practice file folder to complete this exercise. Open the SampleContentD_Start presentation, and follow the steps.

1   Select slide **2** in the **Slides** pane.

2   With slide **2** selected, click the **Slide Show** button on the status bar to begin your slide show from the selected slide.

Slide Show

TIP You can also begin your presentation by using the From Beginning or From Current Slide buttons in the Start Slide Show group on the Slide Show tab.

3   While in **Slide Show** view, press the **Down Arrow** key to advance one slide.

4   Press the **Up Arrow** key to move back to slide **2**.

5   Press the **Spacebar** to advance to slide **3**.

6   Press the **9** key and then press **Enter** to jump to slide **9**, which is titled *Fabrikam employee community contributions make a difference.*

7   Move your mouse pointer to the lower-left corner of the screen to activate the **Popup Toolbar**.

8   Click the **See All Slides** button to open the **Navigation Grid** that displays thumbnails of all the slides in the presentation.

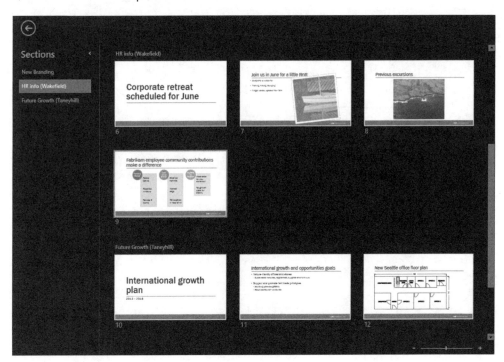

TIP While you're in the Navigation Grid, click a section to go to the first slide of that section.

9   Click the slide **12** thumbnail to see slide **12** in full-screen **Slide Show** view.

10   In **Slide Show** view, right-click anywhere on the screen and choose **Pointer Options**, then **Highlighter**.

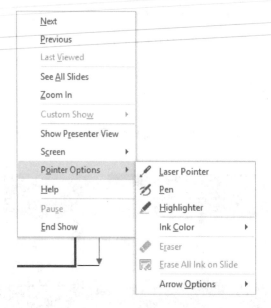

TIP All of the tools on the right-click shortcut menu can also be accessed from the Popup Toolbar.

11   Drag the yellow highlighter cursor over the words **Conference Area** to highlight them on the slide.

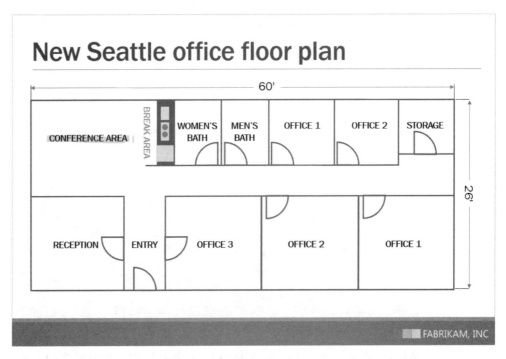

12   Press **Esc** to turn off the highlighter and return to the arrow pointer.

13   Click the **Zoom** tool on the **Popup Toolbar**.

14   When the pointer becomes a magnifying glass icon, click near the highlight you just
      added to zoom in on the conference area of the slide.

15   When the pointer turns into a hand icon, drag to pan around the slide.

16   Press **Esc** to exit pan and zoom mode.

      TIP When you're using a touch-enabled device, you can stretch your fingers apart to
      zoom in on a slide. Pinch them together to zoom out. When you're not zoomed in on
      a slide, pinching will take you to See All Slides view.

17   Press **Esc** again to end your slide show and return to **Normal** view.

18   Click **Keep** if prompted to keep or discard your ink annotations.

✖ CLEAN UP Save the presentation if you want, and then close it.

TIP If you want your presentation to open in Slide Show view when you double-click it in a window, save the presentation as a PowerPoint Show (*.ppsx).

TIP To edit a presentation that's been saved as a slide show (with a .ppsx extension), open PowerPoint and choose File, then Open, and navigate to the file. When you open it from PowerPoint this way, it opens in Normal view so you can edit as you wish.

Practicing with Presenter view

Presenter view has been included in PowerPoint for many versions. It's an option that lets you see your slide thumbnails and speaker notes on your computer, while your audience sees only your full-screen slides on the projected screen.

PowerPoint 2013 takes Presenter view to a whole new level. Not only is it easier to find on the Slide Show tab of the ribbon, but it's also already turned on by default. Probably the most important enhancement is that you can now use Alt+F5 to open Presenter view without having a projector attached to the computer! This makes it simple and convenient to practice your delivery with Presenter view so you're fully prepared once you do get in front of an audience.

In this exercise, you'll open a presentation in Presenter view and navigate through it.

SET UP You need the SampleContentE_Start document located in your Chapter16 practice file folder to complete this exercise. Open the SampleContentE_Start document, and then follow the steps.

1 Press **Alt+F5** to open the presentation on slide **1** and access **Presenter** view.

IMPORTANT

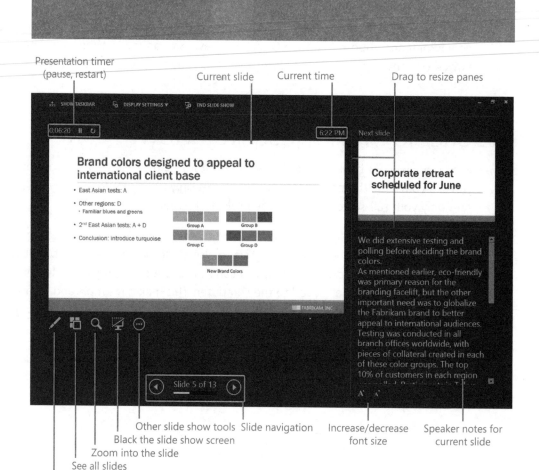

Presentation timer (pause, restart)
Current slide
Current time
Drag to resize panes

Other slide show tools   Slide navigation   Increase/decrease font size   Speaker notes for current slide
Black the slide show screen
Zoom into the slide
See all slides
Pen and laser pointer tools

TROUBLESHOOTING If you do not see Presenter view on the correct monitor, try selecting a different monitor in the Monitor options on the Slide Show tab.

2   Click the right arrow at the bottom of the **Presenter** view screen until you get to slide **5**.

3   Move your mouse pointer over the vertical line separating the current slide from the notes and the next slide. When the mouse pointer turns into a double-headed arrow, drag to the left to increase the width of the **Next Slide** and **Notes** panes.

4   Move your mouse pointer over the horizontal line separating the next slide from the notes. When the mouse pointer turns into a double-headed arrow, drag up to increase the height of the **Notes** pane and decrease the height of the **Next Slide** pane.

5   Click the **Increase Font Size** button at the bottom of the screen to increase the size of your notes.

6   Click the **See All Slides** button to open the **Navigation Grid**. You will see thumbnails of all your slides, but your audience won't.

7   Click slide **8** in the **Presenter** view **Navigation Grid** to advance the presentation to that slide.

8   In the current slide thumbnail in **Presenter** view, click the video to start it. Your audience won't see this happen. They will only see the video begin to play in **Slide Show** view.

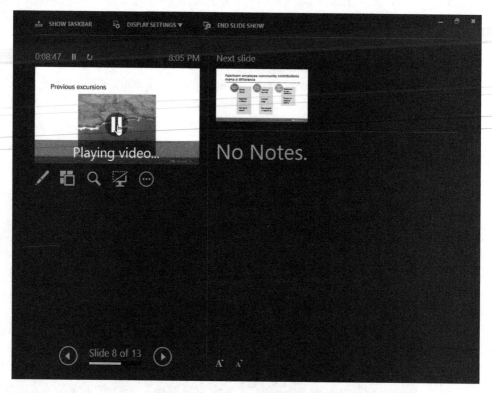

9   Navigate to slide **9** by using the arrows at the bottom of **Presenter** view.

10   Click the **Pen and Laser Pointer Tools** icon and select **Highlighter**. Your mouser pointer changes to a yellow rectangle.

11   On the slide thumbnail in **Presenter** view, drag over the words **Raked Leaves** to highlight them. When you let go of the left mouse button, the highlight will appear in **Slide Show** view also.

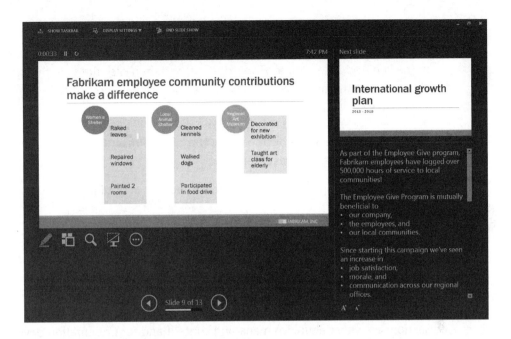

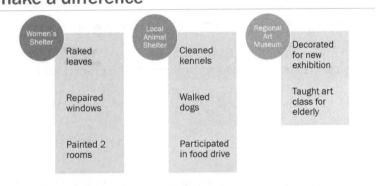

16

12   Press **Esc** to return to the arrow pointer.

> **TIP** To point to an object on the slide while in Presenter view, select the Laser Pointer in the Pen And Laser Pointer Tools options, and then click the slide thumbnail. If you click the slide thumbnail with the typical arrow pointer, the audience won't see it in Slide Show view.

13   Click the **End Slide Show** button at the top of the **Presenter** view window to end the presentation and leave **Presenter** view.

14   Click **Keep** if prompted to keep or discard your ink annotations.

✖ CLEAN UP Save the presentation if you want, and then close it.

Key points

- Sections are very helpful for managing content and for presentation development.
- Mark As Final doesn't keep people from making edits to your presentation.
- PowerPoint 2013 uses a friendly threaded comments pane.
- The redesigned Popup Toolbar makes slide show tools easier to access using touch-enabled devices.
- You can click the Zoom tool in Slide Show view or Presenter view to pan and zoom on your slide.
- You don't have to have a second monitor to practice with Presenter view.

Chapter at a glance

Flash Fill

Quickly extract text from adjacent data to fill a column, page 415

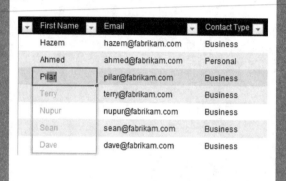

Analyze

Use Quick Analysis tools to apply formats, add totals, and more, page 416

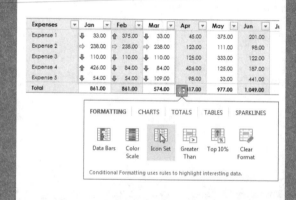

Chart

Let Excel provide recommendations based on selected data, page 417

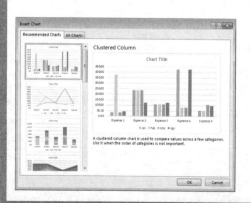

Filter

Use the Timeline feature to display data from a specific timeframe, page 418

Getting comfortable in Excel 2013   17

IN THIS CHAPTER, YOU WILL LEARN HOW TO

- Start Excel 2013.

- Identify what's new in Excel.

- Use the new features in Excel 2013.

Microsoft Excel 2013 is a spreadsheet application that allows you to organize, sort, calculate, and otherwise manipulate data by using formulas. Excel spreadsheets are organized into columns and rows but can also include other features, such as graphs and charts.

It doesn't matter if your spreadsheet is simple or complex, because this part of the book provides you with the foundation for all of your needs. In this chapter, you'll get familiar with the Excel 2013 user interface and using the ribbon. You will also get a glance at features that are new to this latest version of Excel.

Starting Excel 2013

You typically start Excel 2013 from the Windows Start screen in Windows 8 or the Start menu in Windows 7. You can also start Excel 2013 and open a file at the same time by opening a workbook from an email attachment, or by double-clicking a file on the desktop or in the File Explorer.

When you start Excel without opening an existing file, the new Start screen is displayed.

From the Start screen, you can open a recently used workbook, open an existing workbook, create a new workbook from a template, or just start with a fresh, blank workbook.

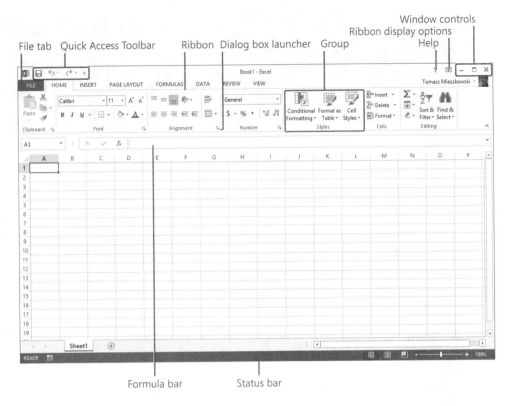

File tab Quick Access Toolbar Ribbon Dialog box launcher Group Window controls
Ribbon display options Help

Formula bar   Status bar

The following list describes some of the most important interface elements; places you'll visit almost every time you employ Excel.

- **Ribbon** The main component of the Excel interface is where you'll find the primary commands for working with the content of your workbooks. The ribbon contains task-oriented tabs; each tab contains groups of related commands. For example, on the **Home** tab, the **Clipboard** group contains commands for copying and pasting information in your workbooks. Command groups with additional commands not shown on the ribbon include a dialog box launcher button. Clicking the dialog box launcher displays a dialog box or a pane that contains related options. For example, if you click the dialog box launcher for the **Font** group, the **Font** dialog box appears, providing more formatting choices such as **Strikethrough**, **Superscript**, and **Subscript**.

IMPORTANT

SEE ALSO For instructions on how to modify your display settings and adapt exercise instructions, see Chapter 1, "Getting comfortable in Office Professional 2013."

- **File tab** The first tab on the ribbon is unlike other ribbon tabs. Clicking the **File** tab does not display a ribbon tab; it instead displays the **Backstage** view, a place where you can find commands that apply to the entire workbook, such as **Save As**, **Print**, **Share**, and **Export**. The **Backstage** view is also where application options are located and where you can find information about your user account and your version of Office.

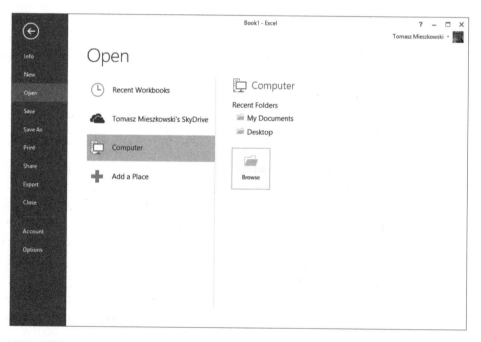

- **Quick Access Toolbar** Holds your most frequently used commands. By default, **Save**, **Undo**, and **Redo** have already been added.

TIP To add commands that you use the most to your Quick Access Toolbar, right-click the command you want and then click Add To Quick Access Toolbar. To remove a command from the Quick Access Toolbar, right-click it and then click Remove From Quick Access Toolbar.

- **Title bar** Appears at the top of the window and displays the name of the active workbook along with the application name. If your workbook hasn't yet been saved, the title bar displays a name such as *Book1 – Excel*. After the workbook has been saved, the title bar will reflect the name of the saved workbook.

- **Window controls** Along with the standard **Minimize, Restore Down/Maximize**, and **Close** buttons available on the right side of the title bar, there are two additional buttons, the **Help** button and the **Ribbon Display Options** button, which is new in Excel 2013.

- **Status bar** Appears at the bottom of the window and displays information about the current workbook, such as the total and average of the values in the currently selected cells. On the right side of the status bar are view options for switching your workbook to a different view, along with a zoom slider to change the magnification of your active workbook.

SEE ALSO For a more comprehensive list of ribbon and user-interface elements, along with detailed instructions on how to customize your user interface, including the ribbon and Quick Access Toolbar, see Chapter 1, "Getting comfortable in Office Professional 2013."

Identifying what's new in Excel 2013

A lot of work went into the Windows 8 and Office underpinnings for this release of Excel. Microsoft also invested effort in producing some excellent, helpful new features, plus extensions and improvements of existing features.

- **Flash Fill** When you are entering data, **Flash Fill** uses predictive fills and offers to autocomplete the remaining pattern for you. Use **Flash Fill** to split a full name into first and last names, change the case of text, extract a name from an email address, and more.

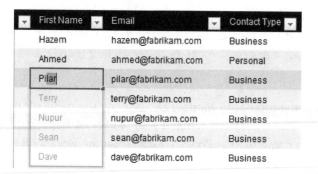

■ **Separate workbook windows** Workbook windows no longer share the same user interface. Now you can display workbook windows on separate monitors and compare formulas between workbooks. Each workbook has its own ribbon that can be used independently of other open Excel windows.

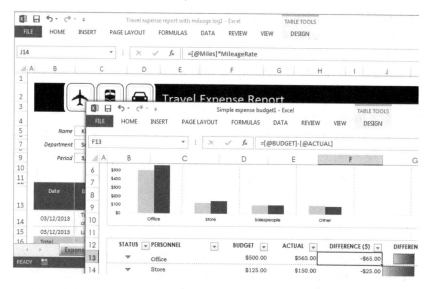

■ **Quick Analysis** Get applicable conditional formatting, charts, totals, tables, Pivot-Tables, and in-cell charts, called *sparklines*, for a selected region of data. If you're not sure about what to use, a live preview will help you visualize a suggestion prior to applying it.

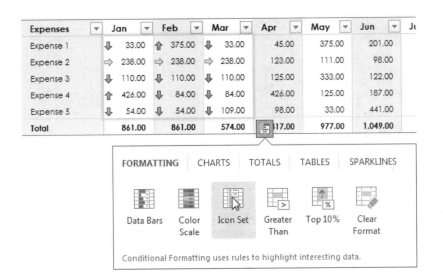

- **Table Slicers** These filter lists of information to your selected **Slicer** items. And, when your list is filtered, **Table Slicers** show you what you've selected along with other list data that's relevant to your current filter.

Bid Details

BID #	CUSTOMER	DATE RECEIVED	AMOUNT
1	Contoso, LTD	09/21/2012	$2,000.00
9	Contoso, LTD	09/21/2012	$6,949.00
13	Contoso, LTD	09/21/2012	$3,427.00
14	Contoso, LTD	09/21/2012	$6,607.00
21	Proseware, Inc.	09/21/2012	$4,423.00

DATE RECEIVED
09/03/2012
09/11/2012
09/16/2012
09/21/2012
10/14/2012
10/21/2012

CUSTOMER
Contoso, LTD
Fourth Coffee
Litware, Inc.
Proseware, Inc.

- **Recommended Charts** If you know you need a chart, but aren't sure about where to begin, the **Recommend Charts** feature will display the most relevant chart suggestions by using your selected data to help you determine which chart to use.

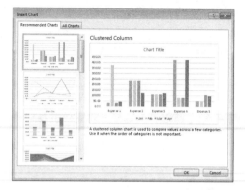

- **Recommended PivotTables** Get help summarizing and creating reports for your information. Instead of trying to determine a **PivotTable** layout prior to adding one, you can use the **Recommended PivotTables** feature, which will suggest various layouts based on your data that will assist you with creating a **PivotTable**.

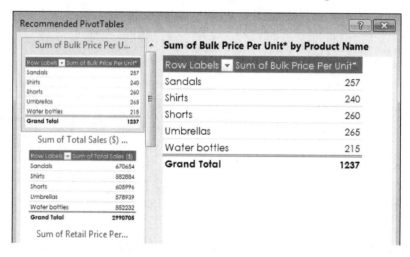

- **Timeline** When working with information that includes dates, you can add a timeline to filter your content to specific months or years.

 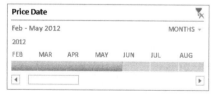

- **Multiple data sources in PivotTables** Instead of being limited to a single data table, you can relate tables with common information and add fields from those tables to your **PivotTable** report.

Using the new features in Excel

The following is a list of discussions in this book that explain how to use some of the new features in Excel 2013, with handy cross-references.

- **Flash Fill** See "Introducing Flash Fill" in Chapter 18.

- **Quick Analysis** See "Using the Quick Analysis tools" in Chapter 20.

- **Recommended PivotTables** See "Creating a PivotTable" in Chapter 20.

- **New Templates** See "Exploring a built-in template" in Chapter 20.

- **Recommended Charts and PivotCharts** See "Creating and modifying a chart" in Chapter 23.

- **Timeline** See "Adding a timeline to a chart" in Chapter 23.

Other enhancements, improvements, and feature upgrades

The following are some other changes that you'll notice in Excel 2013:

■ **One sheet in a new workbook** There is now only one sheet in a new workbook, not three, as in previous versions of Excel. You add sheets by clicking the **New Sheet** plus-sign button (+).

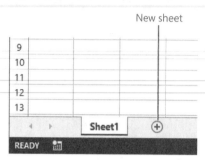

TIP Specifying the number of sheets in a new workbook is one of the many settings that you can change. For example, to construct a number of annual-summary-type workbooks, you might find it helpful to begin with 13 sheets; one for each month plus a summary sheet. To increase or decrease the default number of sheets that appear in new workbooks, change the Include This Many Sheets option on the General page of the Excel Options dialog box. You can specify up to 255 sheets.

SEE ALSO For more information about working with multiple worksheets, see "Creating a multisheet workbook" in Chapter 22, "Manipulating workbooks and worksheets."

■ **New functions** There are about 50 new functions in Excel 2013, most of which were added for increased compatibility with Open Document Format (ODF) 1.2, a universal royalty-free document format used by spreadsheet, chart, word-processing, and presentation applications, including StarOffice and OpenOffice.

■ **New chart controls** Charts now have new dynamic floating controls—**Chart Elements**, **Chart Styles**, and **Chart Filters**—to make reworking an existing chart quicker and easier.

■ **Rich chart data labels** You can now apply more formatting and graphic treatments to data labels in charts. You can even change the chart type, while preserving the label formatting.

- **Chart animation** When you change the underlying data for a chart, rather than changing immediately, the resulting change animates the chart as it changes to show the new values, which serves to emphasize the effects on the bigger picture.

- **Slicers** Slicers have a new interface in Excel 2013, which makes it easier to understand relationships. You can now use Slicers in data tables, not just in **PivotTables**.

- **PivotTable Field List** The new **Field List** includes fields from one table or multiple tables.

- **Standalone Pivot Charts** You can now detach a chart created by using **PivotTable** data, so that it can be repurposed elsewhere without its parent **PivotTable**.

- **Excel Data Model** Some of the functionality of the **PowerPivot** add-in is now built in as the Excel Data Model, allowing you to access multiple large data sources quickly and efficiently.

- **PowerView** Create presentation-quality reports by using graphics and data from multiple tables with the **PowerView** add-in, which uses data from the Excel Data Model exclusively.

- **Strict Open XML file format** For anyone who has experienced problems calculating data by using dates from 1900 or earlier, the Strict Open XML file format is compliant with the ISO8601 specification, solving leap-year and 2-digit-year problems.

17

Key points

- The major interface elements of Excel 2013 are unchanged from 2010.

- Most of the tools you need to do your work are located on the ribbon; if you need more tools, click a dialog-box launcher button to display a relevant dialog box with more options.

- There are many new features in Excel 2013, which you will learn more about in the upcoming chapters.

Chapter at a glance

Adjust

Adjust the width of columns to fit your data, page 425

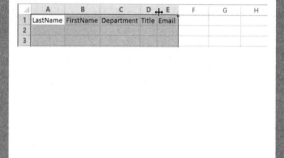

AutoFill

Quickly create a series of numbers or numbered text, page 431

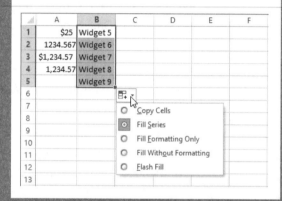

Name

Name cells and ranges for easy reference, page 436

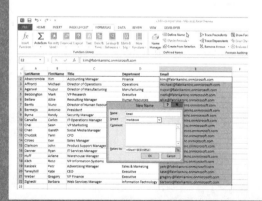

Copy

Copy a cell or range in an operation, page 449

Creating and editing worksheets

18

IN THIS CHAPTER, YOU WILL LEARN HOW TO

- Modify Excel options.

- Format as you enter text.

- Extend a numeric series.

- Extend a series based on adjacent data.

- Assign names to cells and ranges.

- Select and navigate by using the keyboard.

- Customize and move column widths and row heights.

This chapter will cover some of the basics of spreadsheet construction and maintenance, including techniques for entering and organizing data and ways to manipulate cells and move among them.

If you are familiar with Microsoft Excel 2010, you will notice very little functional difference at first glance on the Home tab, beyond the new simplified Microsoft Office look. However, if you are logged into a Windows Live, Microsoft SkyDrive, Outlook, or Hotmail account, your name and image may appear among the window controls in the upper-right corner of the Login menu, This allows you to access your account settings, switch accounts, and even change your profile photo. One more small difference is that the Full Screen button (formerly on the View tab) now lives in the upper-right corner along with the window controls. These changes were designed to facilitate performance on a range of devices and displays, from phones to desktops, tablets, and TVs.

SEE ALSO For more information, see Chapter 4, "Using touch in Office."

So, it may look like not much has changed—Excel is a "mature" application, after all—but there are some great new features, hidden in buttons and commands, some of which may just happen before you know they're there. Exploring the other tabs on the ribbon will reveal more, especially on the Insert and Data tabs.

In this chapter, you'll learn some of the most useful basic techniques for creating and organizing worksheets and workbooks, entering data, making calculations, analyzing data, and preparing for presentation. In such a short discussion, we won't be able to tell you everything there is to know about Excel, but we encourage you to explore at every juncture. When a dialog box is open for a procedure, examine its contents; click other tabs; try a procedure in a different way; use your own data after trying the practice files, and so on. Remember, you can undo up to 100 actions, with a few exceptions like saving workbooks and deleting worksheets.

PRACTICE FILES To complete the exercises in this chapter, you need the practice files contained in the Chapter18 practice file folder. For more information, see "Download the practice files" in this book's Introduction.

Entering and organizing data

The general rule of thumb is to put whatever you have the most of into rows, and try to fit all of your columns across a sheet of paper, even if it will print in landscape mode. That way, if you have more than one page of data, the bottom of a page leads naturally to the top of the next page, not the top of the next column. Your audience is more accustomed to "paging down" than "paging right."

	1990	1991	1992	1993	1994	1995	1996	1997	1998	1999	2000	2001	2002	2003	2004	2005	2006	2007	2008	2
Product 1	$ 208.00	$ 157.00	$ 180.00	$ 175.00	$ 182.00	$ 152.00	$ 116.00	$ 200.00	$ 215.00	$ 112.00	$ 160.00	$ 175.00	$ 190.00	$ 208.00	$ 189.00	$ 153.00	$ 192.00	$ 163.00	$ 125.00	$ 14
Product 2	63.00	74.00	20.00	71.00	21.00	21.00	62.00	61.00	15.00	13.00	12.00	13.00	27.00	44.00	36.00	42.00	50.00	44.00	24.00	7
Product 3	222.00	140.00	174.00	220.00	194.00	146.00	113.00	114.00	138.00	137.00	178.00	189.00	198.00	158.00	183.00	172.00	150.00	120.00	156.00	1!
Product 4	44.00	60.00	88.00	51.00	58.00	40.00	37.00	80.00	49.00	46.00	64.00	76.00	43.00	38.00	35.00	58.00	80.00	59.00	34.00	!
Product 5	91.00	95.00	96.00	95.00	99.00	91.00	91.00	93.00	91.00	91.00	96.00	93.00	95.00	98.00	95.00	95.00	89.00	92.00	97.00	!
Product 6	146.00	175.00	152.00	138.00	128.00	157.00	128.00	183.00	175.00	168.00	169.00	144.00	144.00	131.00	149.00	147.00	127.00	144.00	163.00	14
Product 7	52.00	72.00	17.00	44.00	42.00	43.00	56.00	37.00	97.00	72.00	74.00	83.00	90.00	18.00	47.00	94.00	59.00	34.00	91.00	8
Product 8	144.00	137.00	129.00	149.00	138.00	154.00	139.00	143.00	148.00	184.00	130.00	152.00	136.00	139.00	136.00	181.00	124.00	140.00	130.00	1!
Product 9	50.00	103.00	72.00	99.00	111.00	47.00	49.00	104.00	68.00	114.00	155.00	132.00	79.00	80.00	100.00	152.00	147.00	66.00	64.00	1!

	A	B	C	D	E	F	G	H	I	J	K	L	M	N
1		Product 1	Product 2	Product 3	Product 4	Product 5	Product 6	Product 7	Product 8	Product 9				
2	1990	$ 208.00	$ 63.00	$ 222.00	$ 44.00	$ 91.00	$ 146.00	$ 52.00	$ 144.00	$ 50.00				
3	1991	157.00	74.00	140.00	60.00	95.00	175.00	72.00	137.00	103.00				
4	1992	180.00	20.00	174.00	88.00	96.00	152.00	17.00	129.00	72.00				
5	1993	175.00	71.00	220.00	51.00	95.00	138.00	44.00	149.00	99.00				
6	1994	182.00	21.00	194.00	58.00	99.00	128.00	42.00	138.00	111.00				
7	1995	152.00	21.00	146.00	40.00	91.00	157.00	43.00	154.00	47.00				
8	1996	116.00	62.00	113.00	37.00	91.00	128.00	56.00	189.00	49.00				
9	1997	200.00	61.00	114.00	80.00	93.00	133.00	37.00	143.00	104.00				
10	1998	215.00	15.00	133.00	49.00	91.00	175.00	97.00	143.00	63.00				
11	1999	112.00	13.00	137.00	46.00	91.00	168.00	72.00	134.00	114.00				
12	2000	160.00	12.00	178.00	64.00	96.00	169.00	74.00	130.00	155.00				
13	2001	175.00	13.00	189.00	76.00	93.00	144.00	33.00	152.00	132.00				
14	2002	190.00	27.00	198.00	43.00	95.00	144.00	90.00	136.00	79.00				
15	2003	208.00	44.00	158.00	38.00	98.00	131.00	18.00	139.00	80.00				
16	2004	189.00	36.00	183.00	35.00	95.00	149.00	47.00	136.00	100.00				
17	2005	153.00	42.00	172.00	58.00	95.00	147.00	94.00	131.00	152.00				
18	2006	192.00	50.00	150.00	80.00	89.00	127.00	59.00	124.00	147.00				
19	2007	163.00	44.00	120.00	59.00	92.00	144.00	34.00	140.00	66.00				
20	2008	125.00	24.00	156.00	34.00	97.00	163.00	91.00	130.00	64.00				
21	2009	147.00	72.00	151.00	54.00	91.00	143.00	85.00	157.00	139.00				
22	2010	218.00	45.00	190.00	76.00	98.00	153.00	18.00	147.00	42.00				
23	2011	142.00	64.00	216.00	37.00	94.00	153.00	19.00	133.00	79.00				
24	2012	219.00	67.00	172.00	70.00	94.00	168.00	79.00	135.00	81.00				
25	2013	177.00	62.00	143.00	64.00	94.00	159.00	84.00	128.00	131.00				
26	2014	175.00	71.00	220.00	51.00	95.00	138.00	44.00	149.00	99.00				
27	2015	182.00	21.00	194.00	58.00	99.00	128.00	42.00	138.00	111.00				
28	2016	152.00	21.00	146.00	40.00	91.00	157.00	43.00	154.00	47.00				
29	2017	116.00	62.00	113.00	37.00	91.00	128.00	56.00	139.00	49.00				
30	2018	200.00	61.00	114.00	80.00	93.00	133.00	37.00	143.00	104.00				

Think about the audience and the output you plan to produce. Size matters: are you printing, emailing, or web-publishing your work? Content matters: will you share your work, or is it just for your own use? Details matter: do you need an executive summary? Appearance matters: how about presentation graphics? Documentation matters: do you need to make sure others know how to use your workbooks in the future without your personal intervention? Sometimes, it's all (or most) of the above.

Generally, the more people you plan to share with, the less data you should share. Find ways to summarize—this is what analysis is all about. It's almost impossible to comprehend the big picture when you're looking at details. Sending the VP a raw worksheet with thousands of rows of data probably won't get your point across as well as a summary table with a few rows and columns and an accompanying chart.

Luckily, you can start small and then create whatever you need later. Virtually everything else in the Excel portion of this book will help you to craft your data to address the questions posed earlier.

Changing column widths

One fundamental requirement of any Excel user is to make sure all your data is visible and readable. If it is not, column widths are probably part, if not all, of the problem. The default 64-pixel column width was chosen to accommodate a typical formatted numeric entry such as $1,234.56 without adjustment. When you enter numbers, Excel usually adjusts the width of the column to accommodate the entry. Not so with text, however. The following graphic shows a simple example of what is possibly the most common spreadsheet task of all time—a list.

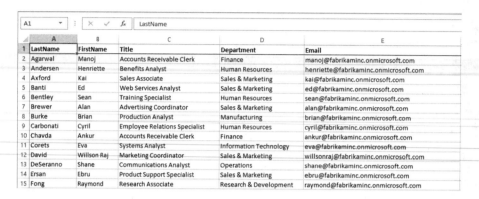

A simple list can be used for various purposes; for example, for generating mailing lists, organization charts, and departmental rosters. Most times, it is best to keep your detail data simple and easy to edit and manipulate. Then you can create additional sheets to summarize or otherwise interpret the data.

In this exercise, you begin creating a sheet like this to illustrate a few techniques.

→ SET UP You don't need any practice files to complete this exercise. Start Excel and follow the steps.

1   Click the **File** tab and click **New** to display the opening screen, if it is not already visible.

2   Click **Blank Workbook** to create a new file with a clean, new worksheet.

3   Enter LastName in cell **A1** (don't press **Enter**), then press the **Tab** key to activate the next cell to the right.

> **TIP** The simple act of moving to another cell finalizes your cell entry. Pressing Enter does it, but so does pressing Tab, any arrow key, or clicking another cell. Pressing Esc before leaving a cell discards your entry.

4   Enter FirstName in cell **B1**, then press the **Tab** key.

5   Enter Department in cell **C1**, then press the **Tab** key.

6   Enter Title in cell **D1**, then press the **Tab** key.

7   Enter **Email** in cell **E1**, and then press the **Tab** key.

8   Press the **Home** key to select cell **A1**.

9   Press and hold the **Shift** and **Ctrl** keys and then press the **Right Arrow** key to select all the headings you just entered. Notice that all the columns are the same default width.

	A	B	C	D	E	F	G	H	I	J
1	LastName	FirstName	Departme	Title	Email					
2										

10 In the **Font** group on the ribbon, click both the **Bold** button and the **Bottom Border** button. If the **Bottom Border** button is not currently visible, click the arrow next to the **Border** button and select **Bottom Border** from the list.

11 Click the column heading letter **A** to select the entire column, then, still holding the mouse button down, drag through the column letters from **A** to **E**. Notice as you drag that Excel displays a ScreenTip showing the dimensions of the selected range, which in this case is 1,048,576 rows deep (all the rows in the worksheet, because you selected the entire column) by 5 columns wide. Excel designates rows by appending an *R* to the row number, and it does the same for columns, with a *C* to the column number, as shown in the ScreenTip.

	A	B	C	D	E	1048576R x 5C	G	H	I	J
1	LastName	FirstName	Departme	Title	Email					
2										
3										

12 Point to the border line to the right of any selected column letter until it becomes a double-headed arrow pointer, and then double-click to auto-fit all selected columns to their widest entries. Notice that the columns are now different widths.

	A	B	C	D	E	F	G	H	I	J
1	LastName	FirstName	Department	Title	Email					
2										
3										

13 With the columns still selected, click the right border line of any selected column heading (don't double-click) and drag it to the right to make it wider. Notice that not only are all of the selected columns wider now, they are also all the same width.

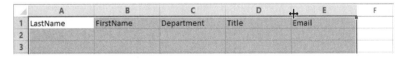

	A	B	C	D	E	F
1	LastName	FirstName	Department	Title	Email	
2						
3						

❌ CLEAN UP   Close the workbook without saving.

The great thing about this feature is that you don't have to scroll down a long worksheet to determine if a column is wide enough for everything it contains; simply double-clicking the column-letter border essentially does that for you. If a column seems too wide after auto-fitting, it may point out a problem somewhere else, such as data entered or imported incorrectly into a cell, or a label out of place.

TIP It works for rows, too. Excel increases row height automatically if you increase the font size or apply the Wrap Text format, but does not decrease it automatically if the cell contents no longer warrant it. Just like columns, you can drag to resize rows, or you can auto-fit them by double-clicking the border below the row number to fit its tallest entry.

Using formatting to alter the appearance of data

A worksheet can be a façade; what is displayed isn't necessarily all there is to it. The displayed values on the screen may not be exactly the same as the underlying values that appear if you select a cell and look in the formula bar. How numeric entries are formatted makes a huge difference in how they appear.

To Excel, everything is a value, including text. What you enter and how you enter it changes the way that Excel responds to the entry. Fractions, dates, times, currency, scientific values, and percentages are all just raw numeric values that are formatted so that they are displayed in familiar ways. This allows Excel to perform calculations on the raw numbers, while allowing you to view the more easily readable formatted values.

For example, Excel uses numeric values to calculate dates. The serial (sequential) value representing Christmas Day 2013 is 41633, which is the actual number of days that have elapsed since (and including) January 1, 1900. If a cell containing this number has the Short Date format applied, it appears in the more understandable form *12/25/2013*.

TIP Enter any date into a cell, then click the Number Format drop-down menu (located in the Number group on the Home tab), and click General to format the date so that it displays its serial value. Then you can click one of the Date formats to display the number as a date again.

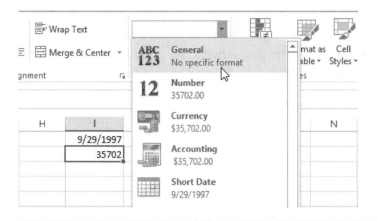

IMPORTANT

In this exercise, you'll find that although you can always apply formatting by using buttons on the ribbon, when entering numeric values, you can specify many kinds of formats "by example" as you enter data, including currency, percentages, and dates.

SET UP You don't need any practice files to complete this exercise. Start Excel, open a blank workbook, and follow the steps.

1   In cell **A1**, enter $1000 and press **Enter**.

2   Press the **Up Arrow** key to reselect the cell, and notice the difference between the entry in the cell itself and the entry as shown in the formula bar above.

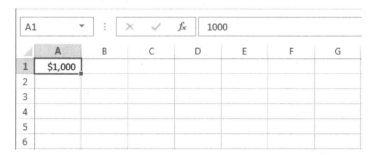

3   Now, in cell **A1**, enter 25 (no dollar sign) and notice that even though you replaced the number you first entered in dollars, the cell still displays a dollar sign, because the cell is formatted as currency. After you format a cell "by example," it stays in that format until you explicitly change it by using formatting commands.

A1	▼	⋮	✕	✓	*fx*	25		
	A	B	C	D	E	F	G	
1	$25							
2								
3								
4								
5								
6								

4   In cell **A2**, enter 1234.567 and press **Enter**, then enter $1234.567 and press **Enter**, then enter 1,234.567 and press **Enter** (making sure to add the comma). If you select each cell that contains the numbers you just entered, you'll notice that the numbers all look exactly the same in the formula bar.

A4	▼	⋮	✕	✓	*fx*	1234.567		
	A	B	C	D	E	F	G	
1	$25							
2	1234.567							
3	$1,234.57							
4	1,234.57							
5								
6								

This example illustrates the difference between the formatted values displayed on the worksheet and the underlying values displayed in the formula bar. It also shows that Excel interprets numeric entries based on the way you enter them and applies formatting accordingly. Entering a dollar sign in front of a number tells Excel to format the entry as currency, which Excel dutifully applies for you. This particular currency format (there are several) includes a dollar sign and comma separators, and rounds the decimal portion to two places. Because you entered a comma separator along with the value in cell A4, Excel applied a different currency format without dollar signs. However, as shown in the formula bar, the formatting only appears on the worksheet. The actual values you enter are not altered. The underlying values in cells A2, A3, and A4 are identical; only the formatting is different.

TIP Understand that applying formats does not alter underlying values. Even though cell A4 displays 1,234.57, calculations that refer to that cell will always use the underlying value 1234.567.

❌ CLEAN UP Close the workbook without saving.

Extending a series with AutoFill

Excel provides a few tools you can use to quickly fill a cell range with a series of numbers, dates, formulas, or even text ending with serial numeric values such as Q1, Q2, and so on. For example, you could enter three numbers or dates into adjacent cells, select them, and then drag to extend a series based on the selected cells. They need not be consecutive. Excel extrapolates the numeric or date series by using the example increments.

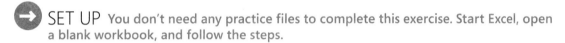

In this exercise, you'll create simple series by dragging or by using commands on the ribbon.

➡ SET UP **You don't need any practice files to complete this exercise. Start Excel, open a blank workbook, and follow the steps.**

1   In cell **B1**, enter Widget 5.

2   In cell **B2**, enter Widget 6.

3   Click cell **B1** and drag to cell **B2** to select both cells.

4   Click the tiny black dot at the lower-right corner of the selection, called the *selection handle*, and drag down to cell **B5**. You'll notice that Excel displays a ScreenTip (**Widget 9**) showing you what the value in that cell will be.

5   Release the mouse button to apply the fill and reveal a numbered series of widgets.

6   Click the **AutoFill Options** menu—the little box that appears near the lower-right corner of the selection after dragging—to display a few additional options you can apply even after you're done. The default option selected is **Fill Series**, which is what you want, so you can press **Esc** to dismiss the menu.

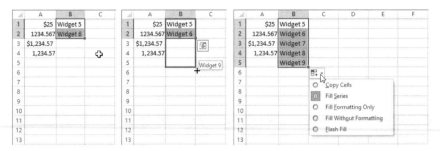

AutoFill makes it easy to extend a series of numbers, dates, or text/numeric entries, as in the Widgets example. You can also click and drag the fill handle by using the right mouse button. Then, instead of immediately extending the series, Excel presents you with a menu of options first, including trends and dates. (Commands appear grey if they are not applicable to the selected values.) You can also use the Fill menu, located in the Editing group on the Home tab, to apply different types of fills.

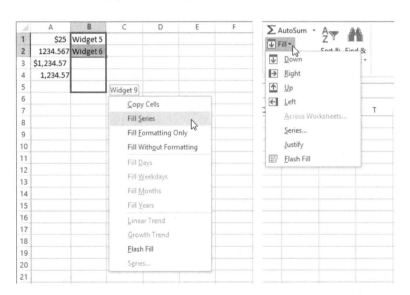

✖ CLEAN UP Close the workbook without saving.

SEE ALSO For more about using AutoFill with formulas, see Chapter 19, "Manipulating numbers and text." For more about filling across worksheets, see "Creating a multi-sheet workbook" in Chapter 22, "Manipulating workbooks and worksheets."

Another helpful feature of AutoFill is that it recognizes certain text/number combinations as special cases. For example, if you enter Q1 into a cell, and then drag the fill handle, you'll notice that Excel extends it, stops at Q4, and keeps repeating Q1, Q2, Q3, and Q4, over and over, rather than copying the cell or extending the numeric series. Excel recognizes that these are common designations used to specify annual quarters, and will perform the same trick if you start with "Quarter 1" or "1st Quarter."

TIP If you really just want to make copies, you can temporarily suppress AutoFill by holding down Ctrl while dragging the fill handle.

Introducing Flash Fill

The new Flash Fill command in the Data Tools group on the Data tab is a clever cousin of AutoFill. It evaluates example data, compares it to existing data in adjacent cells, tries to determine a pattern, and suggests entries for you. (The Flash Fill command is also available on the Fill menu that appears when you click the Fill button in the Editing group on the Home tab.)

For example, suppose your company switches to a brand new email domain, and you need to create a new set of unique email addresses for all of your employees.

In this exercise, you'll quickly create a list of email addresses and combine first and last names from separate cells into a single cell.

SET UP You need the Fabrikam-Management_start.xlsx workbook located in the Chapter18 practice file folder to complete this exercise. Open the Fabrikam-Management_start.xlsx workbook, and save it as Fabrikam-Management.xlsx.

1   Open the **Fabrikam-Management.xlsx** sample workbook and make sure cell **E5** is selected.

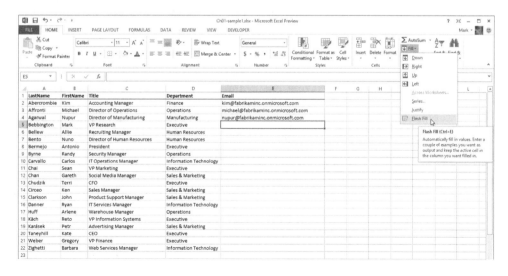

2   Click the **Fill** menu in the **Editing** group on the **Home** tab, and click **Flash Fill**.

	A	B	C	D	E	F
1	LastName	FirstName	Title	Department	Email	
2	Abercrombie	Kim	Accounting Manager	Finance	kim@fabrikaminc.onmicrosoft.com	
3	Affronti	Michael	Director of Operations	Operations	michael@fabrikaminc.onmicrosoft.com	
4	Agarwal	Nupur	Director of Manufacturing	Manufacturing	nupur@fabrikaminc.onmicrosoft.com	
5	Bebbington	Mark	VP Research	Executive	mark@fabrikaminc.onmicrosoft.com	
6	Bellew	Allie	Recruiting Manager	Human Resources	allie@fabrikaminc.onmicrosoft.com	
7	Bento	Nuno	Director of Human Resources	Human Resources	nuno@fabrikaminc.onmicrosoft.com	
8	Bermejo	Antonio	President	Executive	antonio@fabrikaminc.onmicrosoft.com	
9	Byrne	Randy	Security Manager	Operations	randy@fabrikaminc.onmicrosoft.com	
10	Carvallo	Carlos	IT Operations Manager	Information Technology	carlos@fabrikaminc.onmicrosoft.com	
11	Chai	Sean	VP Marketing	Executive	sean@fabrikaminc.onmicrosoft.com	
12	Chan	Gareth	Social Media Manager	Sales & Marketing	gareth@fabrikaminc.onmicrosoft.com	
13	Chudzik	Terri	CFO	Executive	terri@fabrikaminc.onmicrosoft.com	
14	Circeo	Ken	Sales Manager	Sales & Marketing	ken@fabrikaminc.onmicrosoft.com	
15	Clarkson	John	Product Support Manager	Sales & Marketing	john@fabrikaminc.onmicrosoft.com	
16	Danner	Ryan	IT Services Manager	Information Technology	ryan@fabrikaminc.onmicrosoft.com	
17	Huff	Arlene	Warehouse Manager	Operations	arlene@fabrikaminc.onmicrosoft.com	
18	Käch	Reto	VP Information Systems	Executive	reto@fabrikaminc.onmicrosoft.com	
19	Karásek	Petr	Advertising Manager	Sales & Marketing	petr@fabrikaminc.onmicrosoft.com	
20	Taneyhill	Kate	CEO	Executive	kate@fabrikaminc.onmicrosoft.com	
21	Weber	Gregory	VP Finance	Executive	gregory@fabrikaminc.onmicrosoft.com	
22	Zighetti	Barbara	Web Services Manager	Information Technology	barbara@fabrikaminc.onmicrosoft.com	
23						

These email addresses simply use employees' first names with a common email domain. Excel correctly determined the desired outcome, even though those first names were several columns away. (Both columns need to be part of the same table, though.) Excel analyzed the examples entered into cells E2 through E4, and then with the next cell in the table selected, Flash Fill finished the entries and stopped at the end of the table, saving a lot of time entering text. Flash Fill doesn't always get it right, but if not, add more examples.

TIP When you enter a complete email or web address into a cell, Excel formats it as a hyperlink (blue underlined text). When you click a hyperlink, it opens the target; for example, an email program, web browser, or file. Excel actually applies the hyperlink format as a second action after you press Enter. If you would rather not have active hyperlinks in your worksheet (as in this example), press Ctrl+Z immediately after you enter to undo the last action. Because there were actually two actions that took place after you pressed Enter, (you entering the value in the cell, and Excel applying the hyperlink), only the hyperlink is undone, and the unlinked text remains.

One of the most common list-management tasks is managing contact or address lists. For example, first and last names are often kept together in the same cell (or the same record in an imported database). But sometimes first and last names are kept separate; at times you need just the first or last name. Flash Fill offers options for combining (concatenating) or splitting (parsing) cell entries.

3   Select cell **F2** and enter Kim Abercrombie.

4   In cell **F3**, begin entering Michael Affronti. Even before you finish entering the word *Michael*, Excel fills in the rest of the name in cell **F3**, and simultaneously shows what **Flash Fill** thinks you're trying to do in the cells following.

	A	B	C	D	E	F	G
1	LastName	FirstName	Title	Department	Email		
2	Abercrombie	Kim	Accounting Manager	Finance	kim@fabrikaminc.onmicrosoft.com	Kim Abercrombie	
3	Affronti	Michael	Director of Operations	Operations	michael@fabrikaminc.onmicrosoft.com	Michael Affronti	
4	Agarwal	Nupur	Director of Manufacturing	Manufacturing	nupur@fabrikaminc.onmicrosoft.com	Nupur Aga	
5	Bebbington	Mark	VP Research	Executive	mark@fabrikaminc.onmicrosoft.com	Mark Bebi	
6	Bellew	Allie	Recruiting Manager	Human Resources	allie@fabrikaminc.onmicrosoft.com	Allie Belle	
7	Bento	Nuno	Director of Human Resources	Human Resources	nuno@fabrikaminc.onmicrosoft.com	Nuno Ben	
8	Bermejo	Antonio	President	Executive	antonio@fabrikaminc.onmicrosoft.com	Antonio B	
9	Byrne	Randy	Security Manager	Operations	randy@fabrikaminc.onmicrosoft.com	Randy Byr	
10	Carvallo	Carlos	IT Operations Manager	Information Technology	carlos@fabrikaminc.onmicrosoft.com	Carlos Car	
11	Chai	Sean	VP Marketing	Executive	sean@fabrikaminc.onmicrosoft.com	Sean Chai	
12	Chan	Gareth	Social Media Manager	Sales & Marketing	gareth@fabrikaminc.onmicrosoft.com	Gareth Ch	
13	Chudzik	Terri	CFO	Executive	terri@fabrikaminc.onmicrosoft.com	Terri Chud	
14	Circeo	Ken	Sales Manager	Sales & Marketing	ken@fabrikaminc.onmicrosoft.com	Ken Circe	
15	Clarkson	John	Product Support Manager	Sales & Marketing	john@fabrikaminc.onmicrosoft.com	John Clark	
16	Danner	Ryan	IT Services Manager	Information Technology	ryan@fabrikaminc.onmicrosoft.com	Ryan Dann	
17	Huff	Arlene	Warehouse Manager	Operations	arlene@fabrikaminc.onmicrosoft.com	Arlene Hu	
18	Käch	Reto	VP Information Systems	Executive	reto@fabrikaminc.onmicrosoft.com	Reto Käch	
19	Karásek	Petr	Advertising Manager	Sales & Marketing	petr@fabrikaminc.onmicrosoft.com	Petr Karás	
20	Taneyhill	Kate	CEO	Executive	kate@fabrikaminc.onmicrosoft.com	Kate Tane	
21	Weber	Gregory	VP Finance	Executive	gregory@fabrikaminc.onmicrosoft.com	Gregory W	
22	Zighetti	Barbara	Web Services Manager	Information Technology	barbara@fabrikaminc.onmicrosoft.com	Barbara Zi	
23							

5   Press **Enter** to accept the **Flash Fill** suggestions.

6   Double-click the right border of column heading **F** to auto-fit its contents.

7   Select cell **G2** and enter Kim in Finance.

8   Select cell **G3** and enter Michael in Operations.

9   Select cell **G3** and begin entering Nupur in Manufacturing.

	A	B	C	D	E	F	G	H
1	LastName	FirstName	Title	Department	Email			
2	Abercrombie	Kim	Accounting Manager	Finance	kim@fabrikaminc.onmicrosoft.com	Kim Abercrombie	Kim in Finance	
3	Affronti	Michael	Director of Operations	Operations	michael@fabrikaminc.onmicrosoft.com	Michael Affronti	Michael in Operations	
4	Agarwal	Nupur	Director of Manufacturing	Manufacturing	nupur@fabrikaminc.onmicrosoft.com	Nupur Agarwal	Nupur in Manufacturing	
5	Bebbington	Mark	VP Research	Executive	mark@fabrikaminc.onmicrosoft.com	Mark Bebbington	Mark in Ex	
6	Bellew	Allie	Recruiting Manager	Human Resources	allie@fabrikaminc.onmicrosoft.com	Allie Bellew	Allie in Hu	
7	Bento	Nuno	Director of Human Resources	Human Resources	nuno@fabrikaminc.onmicrosoft.com	Nuno Bento	Nuno in H	

10   Press **Enter** to accept the suggested entries.

❌ CLEAN UP Save the Fabrikam-Management.xlsx workbook.

This time, it took three examples before Flash Fill figured out the pattern, including an incorrect guess on the second entry. Just keep entering text if the suggestions don't work.

Similarly, you could use Flash Fill to split, or parse, the full names you entered in column F back into individual cells by simply entering *Abercrombie* into cell H2, and *Affronti* into cell H3. Flash Fill springs to life, offering correct suggestions by around the third letter of the second name. This is one very powerful feature that you'll want to experiment with.

Selecting and naming cell ranges

You know how to select a cell—just click it. You know how to select multiple cells—just click and drag to select a range. In Excel, you can also select multiple nonadjacent (also known as *noncontiguous*) ranges, a technique that comes in handy if you need to apply formatting, styles, or certain editing techniques to noncontiguous cells. You can apply most kinds of formatting to noncontiguous ranges, but many editing techniques are prohibited, including copying and pasting.

Sometimes, especially in large worksheets, it is helpful to assign names to cells and ranges. A name is simply an easy way to identify specific cells. Names can be used to quickly select ranges, or they can be used in formulas as proxies for cryptic cell addresses or to identify the results of other formulas; for example, *net_profit*. Names can also be used to identify cells containing often-used static values such as sales_tax_rate. Names can be easier to remember and work with than cell or range addresses.

In this exercise, you'll select nonadajacent cells and assign names to cells.

→ SET UP You need the Fabrikam-Management2_start.xlsx workbook located in the Chapter18 practice file folder to complete this exercise. Open the Fabrikam-Management2_start.xlsx workbook and save it as Fabrikam-Management2.xlsx.

1   Open the **Fabrikam-Management2.xlsx** workbook.

2   Click cell **A5** and drag to the right, selecting cells **A5:C5**. Note that this is how Excel identifies a cell range; the ID of the cell in the upper-left corner and the ID of the cell in the lower-right corner, separated by a colon.

3   Hold the **Ctrl** key while selecting the corresponding cells in columns **A** through **C** for each of the other members of the Executive department (the 1x3 cell ranges **A8:C8**, **A11:C11**, **A13:C13**, **A18:C18**, and a 2x3 range, **A20:C21**).

4   While still holding the **Ctrl** key, press the **B** key to apply **Bold** formatting to all the selected cells. Alternatively, you could click the **Bold** button on the **Home** tab of the ribbon.

▲	A	B	C	D
1	**LastName**	**FirstName**	**Title**	**Department**
2	Abercrombie	Kim	Accounting Manager	Finance
3	Affronti	Michael	Director of Operations	Operations
4	Agarwal	Nupur	Director of Manufacturing	Manufacturing
5	**Bebbington**	**Mark**	**VP Research**	Executive
6	Bellew	Allie	Recruiting Manager	Human Resources
7	Bento	Nuno	Director of Human Resources	Human Resources
8	**Bermejo**	**Antonio**	**President**	Executive
9	Byrne	Randy	Security Manager	Operations
10	Carvallo	Carlos	IT Operations Manager	Information Technology
11	**Chai**	**Sean**	**VP Marketing**	Executive
12	Chan	Gareth	Social Media Manager	Sales & Marketing
13	**Chudzik**	**Terri**	**CFO**	Executive
14	Circeo	Ken	Sales Manager	Sales & Marketing
15	Clarkson	John	Product Support Manager	Sales & Marketing
16	Danner	Ryan	IT Services Manager	Information Technology
17	Huff	Arlene	Warehouse Manager	Operations
18	**Käch**	**Reto**	**VP Information Systems**	Executive
19	Karásek	Petr	Advertising Manager	Sales & Marketing
20	**Taneyhill**	**Kate**	**CEO**	Executive
21	**Weber**	**Gregory**	**VP Finance**	Executive
22	Zighetti	Barbara	Web Services Manager	Information Technology
23				

IMPORTANT

5   Select all the email addresses.

TIP Be careful if your addresses are hyperlinked. If you click a link directly, it will activate to your email program. Instead, click in an empty part of the cell to avoid activating the link, then drag to select the range.

6   Click the **Formulas** tab on the ribbon.

7   Click the **Define Name** command in the **Defined Names** section to display the **Define Name** dialog box. The first email address is displayed and highlighted in the **Name** field of the dialog box.

8   Enter Email. This replaces the highlighted email address.

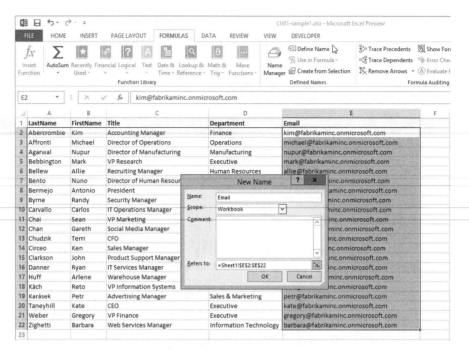

9   Press **Enter** and then look at the box on the left side of the formula bar; this is called the **Name** box, and it normally displays the address of the active cell, unless a named cell or complete named range is selected. After you click **Enter**, the **Name** box should display the name **Email**.

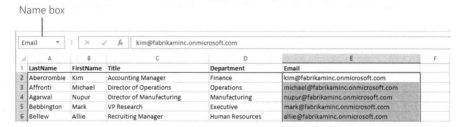

10   Click to select any cell outside the **Email** range.

11   Click the arrow next to the **Name** box and click **Email**, which re-selects the named range. You can also click the **Name** box and enter email (case-insensitive) to select the associated cell or cells.

> **SEE ALSO** For more information, see Chapter 19, "Manipulating numbers and text."

❌ CLEAN UP Save the Fabrikam-Management2.xlsx workbook and then close it.

TIP When you first create a defined name, you can use the Scope options in the New Name dialog box to limit the usage of the name to a specific sheet in the workbook (which, of course, doesn't matter if there is only one sheet). Normally, Workbook is the selected Scope, meaning that you can use the name on any sheet. If you specify a sheet in the Scope drop-down list, you will only be able to use the name on that sheet.

Using column headers to define names

You can define multiple names at once by using the Create From Selection command on the Formulas tab of the ribbon. Remember that when you defined the name Email in the previous example, you selected the data but not the column heading. When you use the Create From Selection command, you need to select the headers along with the data.

In this exercise, you'll create names by using column headings, and you'll begin by using a keyboard-selection trick to select the table.

➡ SET UP You need the Fabrikam-Management3_start.xlsx workbook located in the Chapter18 practice file folder to complete this exercise. Open the Fabrikam-Management3_start.xlsx workbook and save it as Fabrikam-Management3.xlsx.

1   Open the **Fabrikam-Management3.xlsx** workbook.

2   Click cell **A1** to select it.

3   Hold down the **Shift** and **Ctrl** keys and then press the **Right Arrow** key to select the top row of the table.

4   While still holding **Shift** and **Ctrl**, click the **Down Arrow** key to select the entire table.

5   Click the **Formulas** tab if it is not already active, and click the **Create From Selection** command in the **Defined Names** group.

6   Click the **Left Column** option in the **Create Names From Selection** dialog box to deselect it, because you want to create names just from the column headers at this time.

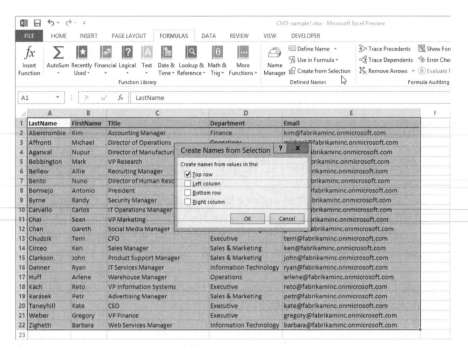

7   Click **OK** to create a set of names based on the column headers you selected.

8   Click the **Name** box in the formula bar to display the list of names you just created.

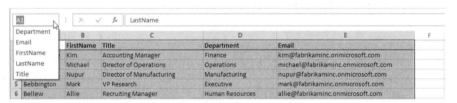

9   Click the **Name Manager** command on the **Formulas** tab of the ribbon for another way to view the names you just created, including the ranges (shown in the **Refers To** column) and values associated with the names.

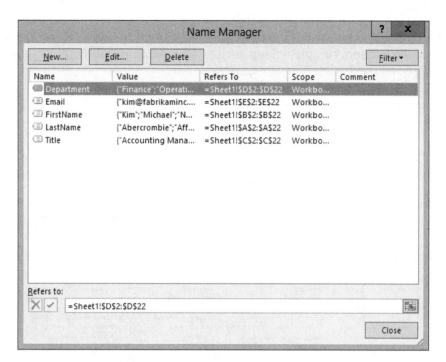

10   Click the **Close** button.

✖ CLEAN UP Save the Fabrikam-Management3.xlsx workbook, and then close it.

SEE ALSO For more information, see Chapter 19, "Manipulating numbers and text."

Moving around in the worksheet

In the previous exercise, you used a keyboard-navigation technique to select a table. Although using the pointer for selecting and navigating is okay, using keyboard short-cuts can save time, frustration, and repetitive movements, especially when working with larger worksheets.

In this exercise, you'll navigate between and among regions, which are defined as blocks of contiguous cells.

SET UP You need the Fabrikam-Employees_start.xlsx workbook located in the Chapter18 practice file folder to complete this exercise. Open the Fabrikam-Employees_start.xlsx workbook, and save it as Fabrikam-Employees.xlsx.

1 Open the **Fabrikam-Employees.xlsx** workbook. Make sure that cell **A1** is selected.

2 Hold down **Ctrl** and press the **Down Arrow** key to jump to the last entry in column **A**.

	A	B	C	D	E
1	LastName	FirstName	Title	Department	Email
2	Agarwal	Manoj	Accounts Receivable Clerk	Finance	manoj@fabrikaminc.onmicrosoft.com
3	Andersen	Henriette	Benefits Analyst	Human Resources	henriette@fabrikaminc.onmicrosoft.com
4	Axford	Kai	Sales Associate	Sales & Marketing	kai@fabrikaminc.onmicrosoft.com
5	Banti	Ed	Web Services Analyst	Sales & Marketing	ed@fabrikaminc.onmicrosoft.com
6	Bentley	Sean	Training Specialist	Human Resources	sean@fabrikaminc.onmicrosoft.com
7	Brewer	Alan	Advertising Coordinator	Sales & Marketing	alan@fabrikaminc.onmicrosoft.com
8	Burke	Brian	Production Analyst	Manufacturing	brian@fabrikaminc.onmicrosoft.com
9	Carbonati	Cyril	Employee Relations Specialist	Human Resources	cyril@fabrikaminc.onmicrosoft.com
10	Chavda	Ankur	Accounts Receivable Clerk	Finance	ankur@fabrikaminc.onmicrosoft.com

	A	B	C	D	E
60	Tupy	Richard	Recruiting Analyst	Human Resources	richard@fabrikaminc.onmicrosoft.com
61	Veronesi	Giorgio	Developer	Information Technology	giorgio@fabrikaminc.onmicrosoft.com
62	Volodin	Viktor	Payroll Analyst	Finance	viktor@fabrikaminc.onmicrosoft.com
63	Weadock	Kelly J.	Client Services Representative	Information Technology	kellyj@fabrikaminc.onmicrosoft.com
64	Wheeler	Wendy	Customer Service Representative	Sales & Marketing	wendy@fabrikaminc.onmicrosoft.com
65	Xylaras	Ioannis	Production Contracts Analyst	Manufacturing	ioannis@fabrikaminc.onmicrosoft.com
66	Yair	Shmuel	Controller	Finance	shmuel@fabrikaminc.onmicrosoft.com
67	Yuan	Joanna	Regional Manager	Sales & Marketing	joanna@fabrikaminc.onmicrosoft.com
68	Zhang	Frank	Social Media Analyst	Sales & Marketing	frank@fabrikaminc.onmicrosoft.com
69					

3 While pressing **Ctrl**, press the **Down Arrow** key again and notice that cell **A1048576** is selected—the last row in the worksheet.

4 While pressing **Ctrl**, press the **Up Arrow** key to return to the previous location (cell **A68**).

5 While pressing **Ctrl**, press the **Right Arrow** key to jump to the last active cell in the table (cell **E68**).

6 While pressing **Ctrl**, press the **Up Arrow** key to jump to the top of the table (cell **E1**).

7 While pressing **Ctrl**, press the **Left Arrow** key to jump back to cell **A1**.

8 Click the **Sheet 2** tab at the bottom of the workbook.

9 Make sure that cell **A3** is selected, then hold down **Ctrl** and press the **Right Arrow** key, pause, then repeat this three more times, pausing to notice what happens each time. Cell **H3** should be selected.

18

10 Now hold down **Ctrl** and **Shift** together, and press the **Down Arrow** key to select the data in column **H**.

11 Holding **Ctrl** and **Shift**, press the **Left Arrow** key to select the region **F3:H21**.

❌ CLEAN UP Close the Fabrikam-Employees.xlsx workbook without saving.

When you press any Ctrl+Arrow combination when an empty cell is selected, the selection moves to the first active cell in the next region. If you do this when an active cell is selected, the selection moves to the last active cell in the same region. If there are no active cells in the direction you move, Excel selects the last available cell on the worksheet.

Moving and adjusting cells

You probably, already know plenty about clicking and dragging; these are core competencies of anyone who uses a computer. Things work differently in Excel than in writing apps, considering the grid or "graph paper" model. Word-processing programs are linear; most text-based documents are essentially one long string of characters. Excel is modular; you can put strings of characters into each cell, like tiny books on a million-shelf bookcase (1,048,576, to be exact). Of course, the tiny books have skills. For now, let's drag stuff around.

SEE ALSO For more information about formulas and functions, see Chapter 19, "Manipulating numbers and text."

In this exercise, you'll select and drag cell regions to new locations on a worksheet, and you'll quickly adjust column widths and row heights afterward.

➜ SET UP You need the Fabrikam-Employees.xlsx workbook created in the previous exercise to complete this exercise. Or open the Fabrikam-Employees.xlsx workbook located in the Chapter18 practice file folder and save it as Fabrikam-Employees.xlsx.

1   Open the **Fabrikam-Employees.xlsx** workbook.

2   Click the **Sheet2** tab at the bottom of the workbook window.

3   Select the region **C3:D21**.

4   Point to one of the borders of the selection, until a 4-headed arrow pointer appears.

5   Click and drag the region one cell up and one cell to the left (cell **B2** becomes the upper-left corner).

6   Select the region **F3:H21**, then drag it one cell up and two cells to the left (adjacent to the first region). Notice that in some of the cells, single letters are wrapping within the cells, other entries are cut off, and others extend beyond the cell borders.

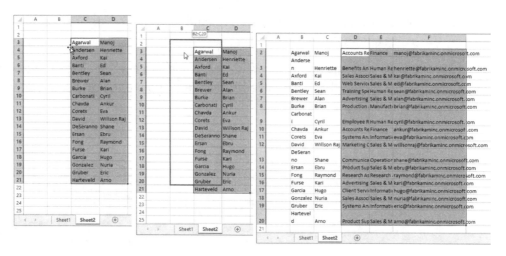

7   Drag through the column headers **B** through **F** to select them.

8   Click the border to the right of column **F** and drag the column header to the right to make all selected columns wider.

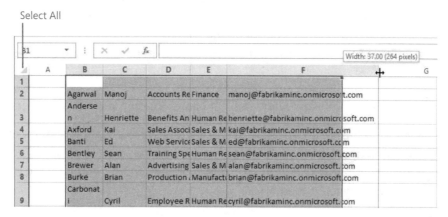

9   All the entries fit in the cells now, but some columns are too wide and some rows are too deep, so click the **Select All** button located at the intersection of the row and column headers to select all the rows and columns in the worksheet.

10   Double-click any border between column headers to auto-fit all columns to their widest entries.

11   Double-click any border between row headers to auto-fit all rows to their tallest entries (notice that the double-headed arrow pointer points up and down when manipulating row heights).

In this example, there was an intentionally introduced "issue" to illustrate one of the problems that may crop up when moving cells around. The cells containing first names were needlessly formatted with text wrapping turned on (it happens), which is why even individual letters wrapped within cells (for example, see cell B3 in the "before" graphic). Excel makes the row taller when text wraps in a cell, but it does not re-adjust the row height if you widen the column enough to avoid wrapping. To fix this, we first made the cells too wide, then we auto-fit both the rows and the columns.

If you want, you can turn off text wrapping.

12   Select the column containing the first names (column **B** in the "after" graphic earlier).

13   Click the **Wrap Text** button twice (the button is located in the **Alignment** group on the **Home** tab): once to turn wrapping on in all the selected cells, and once to turn it off. The **Wrap Text** button should turn gray when text wrapping is on, and it turns white again when turned off.

❌ CLEAN UP Close the Fabrikam-Employees.xlsx workbook without saving.

Moving and copying rows and columns

Often you just need to move things around in your workbooks, and in a grid like Excel, simple copying and pasting is a needlessly awkward way of doing it. If your worksheet is set up properly, you should be able to drag entire rows and columns around without too much trouble. You simply select and drag to move and replace, or hold down Ctrl and drag to move and insert.

In this exercise, you'll move rows and columns and copy them, too.

SET UP You need the Fabrikam-Employees.xlsx workbook created in the previous exercise to complete this exercise. Or open the Fabrikam-Employees.xlsx workbook located in the Chapter18 practice file folder and save it as Fabrikam-Employees.xlsx.

1   Open the **Fabrikam-Employees.xlsx** workbook, and make sure **Sheet1** is selected.

2   Scroll down to row **43** and click the row header to select the entire row. Notice that **Giuseppe Russo** is out of alphabetical order in this table. We'll fix that.

3   Point to any part of the selection border around row **43** until the pointer becomes a 4-headed arrow.

4   Press the **Shift** key, then click and drag row **43** down. Notice that while you are dragging, an "I-beam" type insertion cursor appears between rows, indicating the new location.

5   Release the mouse button when the insertion cursor is between rows **47** and **48**.

	A	B	C	D	E
41	Phillips	Jeff	Developer	Information Technology	jeff@fabrikaminc.onmicrosoft.com
42	Pogulsky	Grigory	Production Facilities Specialist	Manufacturing	grigory@fabrikaminc.onmicrosoft.com
43	Russo	Giuseppe	Research Associate	Research & Development	giuseppe@fabrikaminc.onmicrosoft.com
44	Railson	Stuart	Web Services Analyst	Sales & Marketing	stuart@fabrikaminc.onmicrosoft.com
45	Rao	Arvind B.	Regional Manager	Sales & Marketing	arvind@fabrikaminc.onmicrosoft.com
46	Richardson	Don	Production Logistics Analyst	Manufacturing	don@fabrikaminc.onmicrosoft.com
47	Roth	Tali	Cost Accountant	Finance	tali@fabrikaminc.onmicrosoft.com
48	Sałas-Szlejter	Karolina	Maintenance Technician	Operations	karolina@fabrikaminc.onmicrosoft.com
49	Scholl	Boris	Accounts Payable Clerk	Finance	boris@fabrikaminc.onmicrosoft.com

	A	B	C	D	E
41	Phillips	Jeff	Developer	Information Technology	jeff@fabrikaminc.onmicrosoft.com
42	Pogulsky	Grigory	Production Facilities Specialist	Manufacturing	grigory@fabrikaminc.onmicrosoft.com
43	Russo	Giuseppe	Research Associate	Research & Development	giuseppe@fabrikaminc.onmicrosoft.com
44	Railson	Stuart	Web Services Analyst	Sales & Marketing	stuart@fabrikaminc.onmicrosoft.com
45	Rao	Arvind B.	Regional Manager	Sales & Marketing	arvind@fabrikaminc.onmicrosoft.com
46	Richardson	Don	Production Logistics Analyst	Manufacturing	don@fabrikaminc.onmicrosoft.com
47	Roth	Tali	Cost Accountant	Finance	tali@fabrikaminc.onmicrosoft.com
48	Sałas-Szlejter	Karolina	Maintenance Technician	Operations	karolina@fabrikaminc.onmicrosoft.com
18:48 Scholl	Boris		Accounts Payable Clerk	Finance	boris@fabrikaminc.onmicrosoft.com

	A	B	C	D	E
41	Phillips	Jeff	Developer	Information Technology	jeff@fabrikaminc.onmicrosoft.com
42	Pogulsky	Grigory	Production Facilities Specialist	Manufacturing	grigory@fabrikaminc.onmicrosoft.com
43	Railson	Stuart	Web Services Analyst	Sales & Marketing	stuart@fabrikaminc.onmicrosoft.com
44	Rao	Arvind B.	Regional Manager	Sales & Marketing	arvind@fabrikaminc.onmicrosoft.com
45	Richardson	Don	Production Logistics Analyst	Manufacturing	don@fabrikaminc.onmicrosoft.com
46	Roth	Tali	Cost Accountant	Finance	tali@fabrikaminc.onmicrosoft.com
47	Russo	Giuseppe	Research Associate	Research & Development	giuseppe@fabrikaminc.onmicrosoft.com
48	Sałas-Szlejter	Karolina	Maintenance Technician	Operations	karolina@fabrikaminc.onmicrosoft.com
49	Scholl	Boris	Accounts Payable Clerk	Finance	boris@fabrikaminc.onmicrosoft.com

✖ CLEAN UP Save the Fabrikam-Employees.xlsx workbook and then close it.

TIP If you press Ctrl while dragging a selection, Excel makes a copy of the selected cells and pastes them in the new location rather than inserting them (and replaces the contents of the destination cells). Pressing Ctrl+Shift while dragging both makes a copy of the selected cells and inserts them at the new location.

You use the same techniques when moving and copying columns, too.

Copying one or more cells to many

In this exercise, you'll use a handy trick for making a lot of duplicate entries, rather than extending a series of entries.

→ SET UP **You don't need any practice files to complete this exercise. Open a blank workbook and follow the steps.**

1   In cell **A1**, enter One to Many.

2   Select cell **A1** and press **Ctrl+C** to copy it.

3   Click cell **C1** and drag to select cells **C1:C6**.

4   Press **Ctrl+V** to paste, and notice that Excel fills in the entire range of selected cells with the same entry.

5   Select cells **E3:J5** by dragging through the range, and click **Ctrl+V** again to paste the entry into a 2-dimensional range.

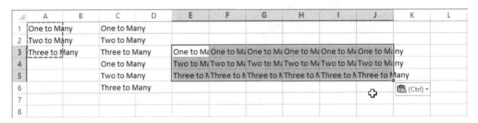

6   Select cell **A2** and enter Two to Many.

7   Select cell **A3** and enter Three to Many.

8   Select cells **A1:A3** and press **Ctrl+C** to copy.

9   Select cells **C1:C6** again and press **Ctrl+V** to paste.

10   Select cells **E3:J5** again and press **Ctrl+V** to paste.

	A	B	C	D	E	F	G	H	I	J	K	L
1	One to Many		One to Many									
2	Two to Many		Two to Many									
3	Three to Many		Three to Many		One to Ma	One to Ma	One to Ma	One to Ma	One to Ma	One to Many		
4			One to Many		Two to Ma	Two to Ma	Two to Ma	Two to Ma	Two to Ma	Two to Many		
5			Two to Many		Three to N	Three to N	Three to N	Three to N	Three to N	Three to Many		
6			Three to Many								(Ctrl) ▾	
7												
8												

Excel repeats the sequence to fill your selections. You can select as many cells as you like before you paste, and Excel will keep repeating the sequence you copied until the range is filled.

❌ CLEAN UP Close the workbook without saving.

Key points

- Number formatting changes the appearance of numbers, but not the underlying values.

- You can apply number formatting as you enter data by using currency symbols, percentage symbols, or commas, or by entering dates "in format."

- You can extend a series of numbers, dates, and even text entries with numeric values by dragging.

- Flash Fill learns by example to fill a range of cells based on entries in an adjacent column.

- You can assign names to cells to make it easier to remember values, to quickly select ranges, or to create more understandable formulas.

- Manipulate borders between column letters to change column widths: double-click to auto-fit all selected columns; drag to make all selected columns the same width.

- You can use the Select All button to select the entire worksheet, which is useful for formatting and adjusting row heights and column widths.

- Use the Ctrl key with an arrow key to navigate around in a worksheet.

- You can drag cells, ranges, or entire rows and columns to move them around. Pressing Shift while dragging allows you to insert the item into the new location. Pressing Ctrl makes a copy in the new location.

- In calculations, Excel always uses the underlying values displayed in the formula bar, even though the formatted values displayed on the worksheet may be different.

- If you paste a copied cell or range into a larger selected range, Excel repeats the copied cells as many times as necessary to fill the destination range.

18

Chapter at a glance

Deduce

Create simple formulas by typing operators and clicking cells, page 454

	E	F	G	H

'ear Summary

	2010	2011	2012	2013
	$ 151,841.00	$ 165,049.52	$ 169,605.83	$ 179,930.28
	76,773.91	79,380.61	79,805.13	81,684.44
	75,067.09	85,668.9	89,800.69	98,245.84
	4,622.18	4,668.09	4,650.72	4,675.54
	2,896.65	2,908.06	2,909.82	2,918.02
	67,548.26	=F5-F6-F7	82,240.15	90,652.28
	23,641.89	25,131.56	28,784.05	31,728.30
	$ 43,906.37	$ 46,672.90	$ 53,456.10	$ 58,923.98

Summarize

Use the AutoSum button to create quick totals and more, page 459

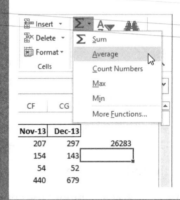

Calculate

Use built-in functions to create complex formulas, page 466

C6		:	×	✓	fx	=-PMT(B6/12,C3*12,C5)	

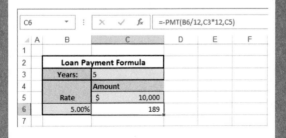

	A	B	C	D	E	F
1						
2		**Loan Payment Formula**				
3		**Years:**	5			
4			Amount			
5		Rate	$	10,000		
6		5.00%		189		
7						

Simplify

Use defined names to make formulas easier to read, page 472

D10		:	×	✓	fx	=Net_Profit-Taxes

	A	B	C	D
1				Fabrikam, Inc. Seven-Y
2	*$1 = $1,000*	2007	2008	2009
3	Income	$ 134,137.45	$ 142,728.38	$ 138,632.47
4	Expenses	70,962.31	75,924.87	74,167.20
5	Gross Profit	63,175.14	66,803.51	64,465.27
6	Depreciation	4,517.77	4,656.92	4,576.27
7	Interest Expense	2,745.82	2,893.11	2,885.24
8	Net Profit	55,911.55	59,253.48	57,003.76
9	Taxes	19,569.04	20,738.72	19,951.31
10	Aftertax Profit	$ 36,342.51	$ 38,514.76	$ 37,052.44
11				

Manipulating numbers and text

19

IN THIS CHAPTER, YOU WILL LEARN HOW TO

- Create, edit, and copy formulas.

- Use functions.

- Work with text in Excel.

- Restrict cell entries.

There are some pretty flashy features in Microsoft Excel, more with every new release. This chapter has possibly the lowest flash quotient of any in this section, because we're covering the basics of Excel—manipulating numbers. In other words, we're talking more about adding, subtracting, multiplying, dividing, rounding, truncating, converting, extrapolating, square-rooting, and otherwise manipulating raw data to create information. It's why Excel exists; it's what Excel does best, and it's all about what you need to know.

As a bonus, we'll look at how to manipulate text. If you routinely process a lot of text-based data like inventory or address lists, and you combine first and last names into full names, Excel may become your favorite tool.

In this chapter, you'll learn to use cell references and functions in formulas, give names to cells and ranges for easier referencing, and use formulas to edit text.

PRACTICE FILES To complete the exercises in this chapter, you need the practice files contained in the Chapter19 practice file folder. For more information, see "Download the practice files" in this book's Introduction.

Creating, editing, and copying formulas

Formulas are "backward" in Excel. In other words, we all learned in elementary school that 1+1=2 is how you write a formula. But in Excel, you flip the equal sign to the other side, so typing =1+1 into a cell returns the desired result. Putting the equal sign in front of the expression is the signal that tells Excel that you are entering a formula for which you want a calculated result. Anything else is just text, as far as calculations are concerned.

1+1=	This is a text entry in Excel.
=1+1	This is a formula in Excel.

TIP Though Excel also allows you to begin a formula with a plus or minus sign instead of an equal sign, after you press Enter, Excel adds a preceding equal sign anyway, and keeps the sign if it's a minus.

So, you begin entering your formula with an equal sign, and then by using the correct language, including numbers (or constants), math operators, cell references, and functions, you can calculate just about anything from a shopping list to an Excel music video.

In this exercise, you will use the most common formula-editing features in Excel to create a simple formula and copy it to other cells.

➡ SET UP You need the Fabrikam-Seven-Year-Summary_start.xlsx workbook located in the Chapter19 practice file folder to complete this exercise. Open the Fabrikam-Seven-Year-Summary_start.xlsx workbook, and save it as Fabrikam-Seven-Year-Summary.xlsx.

1 Open the **Fabrikam-Seven-Year-Summary.xlsx** workbook, and make sure that cell **B10** is selected.

2 Enter = (an equal sign), then click cell **B8** (containing the 2007 Net Profit figure), and you'll notice several things: cell **B10** remains selected, there is a dotted marquee around cell **B8**, and the cell reference =B8 appears in both cell **B10** and the formula bar.

B8	▾	:	✕	✓	*fx*	=B8		

◢	A	B	C	D	E	F	G	H
1				Fabrikam, Inc. Seven-Year Summary				
2	*$1 = $1,000*	2007	2008	2009	2010	2011	2012	2013
3	Income	$134,137.45	$142,728.38	$138,632.47	$151,841.00	$165,049.52	$169,605.83	$179,930.28
4	Expenses	70,962.31	75,924.87	74,167.20	76,773.91	79,380.61	79,805.13	81,684.44
5	Gross Profit	63,175.14	66,803.51	64,465.27	75,067.09	85,668.91	89,800.69	98,245.84
6	Depreciation	4,517.77	4,656.92	4,576.27	4,622.18	4,668.09	4,650.72	4,675.54
7	Interest Expense	2,745.82	2,893.11	2,885.24	2,896.65	2,908.06	2,909.82	2,918.02
8	Net Profit	55,911.55	59,253.48	57,003.76	67,548.26	71,804.47	82,240.15	90,652.28
9	Taxes	19,569.04	20,738.72	19,951.31	23,641.89	25,131.56	28,784.05	31,728.30
10	Aftertax Profit	=B8						
11								

3   Enter – (a minus sign), and then click cell **B9**.

4   Press the **Enter** key, then press the **Up Arrow** key to reselect cell **B10**.

| B10 | ▼ | : | × | ✓ | fx | =B8-B9 | | | |

◢	A	B	C	D	E	F	G	H
1				Fabrikam, Inc. Seven-Year Summary				
2	*$1 = $1,000*	**2007**	**2008**	**2009**	**2010**	**2011**	**2012**	**2013**
3	Income	$ 134,137.45	$ 142,728.38	$ 138,632.47	$ 151,841.00	$ 165,049.52	$ 169,605.83	$ 179,930.28
4	Expenses	70,962.31	75,924.87	74,167.20	76,773.91	79,380.61	79,805.13	81,684.44
5	Gross Profit	63,175.14	66,803.51	64,465.27	75,067.09	85,668.91	89,800.69	98,245.84
6	Depreciation	4,517.77	4,656.92	4,576.27	4,622.18	4,668.09	4,650.72	4,675.54
7	Interest Expense	2,745.82	2,893.11	2,885.24	2,896.65	2,908.06	2,909.82	2,918.02
8	Net Profit	55,911.55	59,253.48	57,003.76	67,548.26	71,804.47	82,240.15	90,652.28
9	Taxes	19,569.04	20,738.72	19,951.31	23,641.89	25,131.56	28,784.05	31,728.30
10	Aftertax Profit	$ 36,342.51						
11								

Fill handle

Although you could arrive at the same result by typing =55911.55-19569.04 into cell B10, a better way to leverage Excel's talents is to use references to cells containing values that appear on the worksheet. This example formula should always produce a correct result, even if the numbers in cells B8 and B9 change. And sometimes the referenced cells contain other formulas, which is the case in this example (cell B8).

5   Click cell **B8** and notice the formula =**B5-B6-B7**, which calculates net profit by subtracting depreciation and interest expense from gross profit.

6   Click cell **B3** (2007 Income), enter 123456, and notice that cells **B5**, **B8**, **B9**, and **B10** all change accordingly, because they are all dependent upon the value in cell **B3**, called a precedent cell.

7   Press **Ctrl+Z** to undo your last entry, and the dependent cells return to their previous values.

8   Select cell **B10** and drag the fill handle across to **column H** to fill in the rest of the formulas.

9   Press **Tab** to inspect the formula in cell **C10**; repeat until you reach cell **H10** and notice that the new formulas all reflect their relative locations. The cell references were adjusted by **AutoFill**. This is the easiest way to complete a row or column of identical formulas.

19

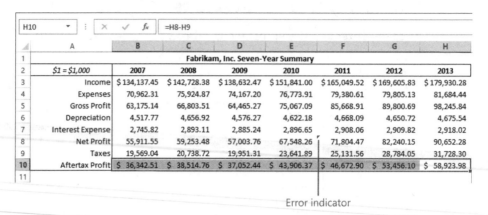

Error indicator

You'll notice that there is a small triangle in the corner of cell F8. This is an indication that there is something different about this cell; that it somehow does not match the adjacent cells. It alerts you that there might be a problem with your formula.

10   Click cell **F8** and an **alert symbol** will appear adjacent to the cell; click it to display the menu shown below.

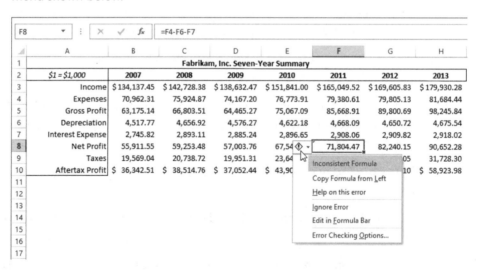

11 This menu offers possible solutions for the erring formula, and in this case, you could choose **Copy Formula from Left**, which would solve the problem. Instead, double-click cell **F8** to enter **Editing** mode. Notice that the word Edit appears in the lower-left corner of the Excel window, and that each cell referenced in the formula is highlighted.

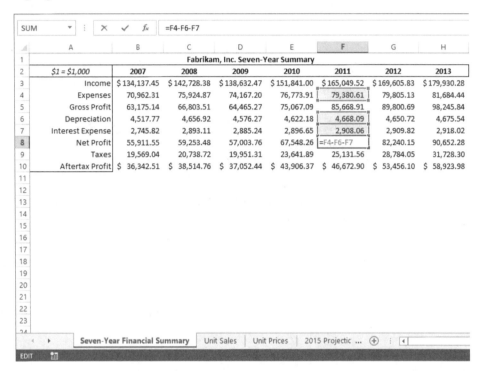

This formula was entered incorrectly; subtracting depreciation and interest from cell F4, expenses, instead of cell F5, gross profit. You could simply highlight the reference in the formula and enter the correct reference, or you can manipulate the references directly. Whenever possible, it is always advisable to use direct manipulation with cell references in formulas, in order to minimize errors. Plus, it's just easier to see the relationships among cells.

12   Point to the thick border of the box highlighting cell **F4** and notice that it thickens just a bit when you pass over it.

13   Click the border and drag the box from cell **F4** down to cell **F5**; the formula changes to reflect the newly highlighted cell.

LOOKUP ▾	:	✕	✓	*fx*	=F5-F6-F7		

◢	A	B	C	D	E	F	G	H
1				Fabrikam, Inc. Seven-Year Summary				
2	*$1 = $1,000*	2007	2008	2009	2010	2011	2012	2013
3	Income	$ 134,137.45	$ 142,728.38	$ 138,632.47	$ 151,841.00	$ 165,049.52	$ 169,605.83	$ 179,930.28
4	Expenses	70,962.31	75,924.87	74,167.20	76,773.91	79,380.61	79,805.13	81,684.44
5	Gross Profit	63,175.14	66,803.51	64,465.27	75,067.09	85,668.91	89,800.69	98,245.84
6	Depreciation	4,517.77	4,656.92	4,576.27	4,622.18	4,668.09	4,650.72	4,675.54
7	Interest Expense	2,745.82	2,893.11	2,885.24	2,896.65	2,908.06	2,909.82	2,918.02
8	Net Profit	55,911.55	59,253.48	57,003.76	67,548.26	=F5-F6-F7	82,240.15	90,652.28
9	Taxes	19,569.04	20,738.72	19,951.31	23,641.89	25,131.56	28,784.05	31,728.30
10	Aftertax Profit	$ 36,342.51	$ 38,514.76	$ 37,052.44	$ 43,906.37	$ 46,672.90	$ 53,456.10	$ 58,923.98
11								

14   Press **Enter**; the triangle indicator disappears, and the newly edited formula returns the correct net profit amount.

You can drag the formula-editing boxes anywhere on the sheet, or if you click one of the square dots in the corners, you can drag to expand the cell reference to include more rows and columns of cells.

✖ CLEAN UP Save the Fabrikam-Seven-Year-Summary.xlsx workbook, and then close it.

Using functions

You can create a lot of formulas by using math operators: addition, subtraction, multiplication (asterisk), division (forward slash), square root (caret), parentheses, and percentage symbols. But far more computational power is at your disposal with functions, which are essentially pre-packaged formulas that perform specific calculations. All functions are followed by a set of parentheses, and most require specific arguments to be entered between them.

Although you can use cell references with math operators in simple formulas, you cannot use range references. But when you use functions, range references are perfectly acceptable to use as arguments, when appropriate.

The simplest and most-often-used function is SUM, which accommodates any number of arguments up to 255. For example, the following formulas all return totals:

```
=12+334
=C6+C7+C8
=SUM(C6:C8)
=SUM(12,334)
=SUM(12,334,C6:C8)
```

With most functions, you can combine different types of arguments, including single cell references, cell ranges (C6:C8), static values (12), and even other formulas. (Formulas within formulas are said to be nested.)

TIP It is usually better to enter cell references in formulas, rather than entering static values, because you can see and change values entered into cells, but they are "hidden" in formulas; only the result of the formula is displayed. Keeping your numbers visible makes it easier to troubleshoot and audit worksheets.

19

Using the AutoSum button and built-in function

You might expect that Excel would offer a quick and easy way to apply the most-often-used function in the galaxy, and you would be correct.

In this exercise, you will use the "epsilon" button, also known as the Sum button or AutoSum, for more than just totals.

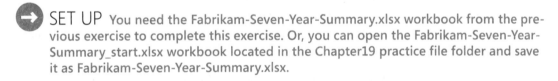 SET UP You need the Fabrikam-Seven-Year-Summary.xlsx workbook from the previous exercise to complete this exercise. Or, you can open the Fabrikam-Seven-Year-Summary_start.xlsx workbook located in the Chapter19 practice file folder and save it as Fabrikam-Seven-Year-Summary.xlsx.

1 Open the **Fabrikam-Seven-Year-Summary.xlsx** workbook, and click the **Unit Sales** worksheet tab.

2 Click cell **A3**, then hold down the **Ctrl** key and press the **Right Arrow** key to jump to the rightmost end of the table. Cell **CG3** should be selected.

3   Press the **Right Arrow** key once to select cell **CH3**.

4   Click the **AutoSum** button, located in the **Editing** group on the **Home** tab. (You can also hold down the **Alt** key and press = to enter a **SUM** function.)

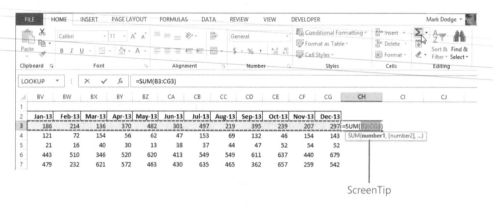

ScreenTip

Notice what just happened. After you clicked the AutoSum button, Excel inserted an equal sign, the function name, a set of parentheses, and the suggested argument, eliminating the need to type them. In this case, Excel correctly identified the range you want to sum. You can scroll back to the left to check this before you press Enter to lock in the formula. The AutoSum button sometimes gets it wrong, especially if the row or column label (for example, "FABK-0001" in cell A3) is a calculable numeric value such as a date, so you always need to check. You can also get help on the function before you press Enter.

5   Click the **SUM** function name that is displayed in the ScreenTip floating just below cell **CH3**, and the **Excel Help** window appears, displaying information about the function.

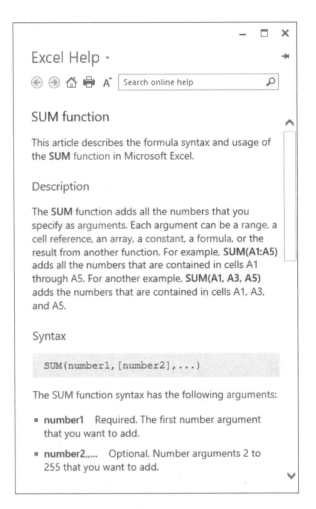

6   Close the **Help** window by clicking the **X** in the upper-right corner.

7   Press **Enter** to finish the formula in cell **CH3**.

8   Click the tiny downward-pointing arrow to the right of the **AutoSum** button to display a menu of additional functions you can apply by using this button, in addition to SUM.

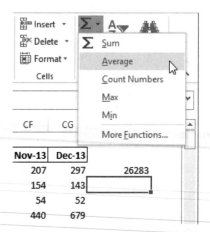

CF	CG			
Nov-13	**Dec-13**			
207	297	26283		
154	143			
54	52			
440	679			

9   Click **Average** to enter the function on the worksheet; you'll see that cell **CH3** is the suggested argument to the **AVERAGE** function, which is definitely not what you want.

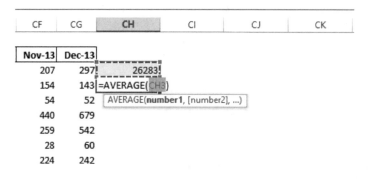

CF	CG	**CH**	CI	CJ	CK
Nov-13	**Dec-13**				
207	297	26283			
154	143	=AVERAGE(CH3)			
54	52	AVERAGE(**number1**, [number2], ...)			
440	679				
259	542				
28	60				
224	242				

10   With the **AVERAGE** function still visible and the cell still in **Edit** mode, click cell **CG4**, just to the left of the new formula.

11   Hold down **Ctrl** and press the **Left Arrow** key to jump all the way to the left end of the table (cell **A4**), then release the **Ctrl** key and press the **Right Arrow** key to select cell **B4** instead.

12   Hold down both the **Shift** and **Ctrl** keys, and then press the **Right Arrow** key to select cells **B4:CG4**.

CF	CG	CH	CI	CJ	CK

Nov-13	Dec-13		
207	297	26283	
154	143	=AVERAGE(B4:CG4)	
54	52	AVERAGE(**number1**, [number2], ...)	
440	679		
259	542		
28	60		
224	242		

13   Press **Enter**, then press the **Up Arrow** key to reselect cell **CH4** so you can see the formula, which now displays the average unit sales for this product, 100.8928571.

14   Decimal values in your averages are distracting, so to fix this, make sure that cell **CH4** is still selected and click the **Decrease Decimal** button, located in the **Number** group on the **Home** tab, and keep clicking until the decimal portion of the number is hidden from view and until the rounded integer value **101** appears. (Remember that the actual value has not changed, only the displayed value.)

TIP An integer value is, quite simply, a number without decimals.

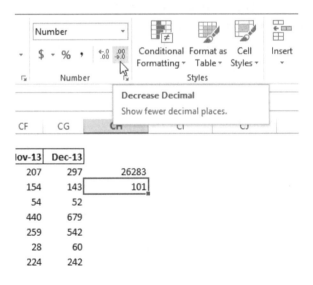

CF	CG	CH	CI	CJ

lov-13	Dec-13		
207	297	26283	
154	143	101	
54	52		
440	679		
259	542		
28	60		
224	242		

❌ CLEAN UP Close the Fabrikam-Seven-Year-Summary.xlsx workbook without saving it.

As you can see, when you click the menu arrow next to the AutoSum button, it offers other functions, including:

- **Count Numbers** Returns only the number of cells in the referenced area that contain numbers; cells containing text are ignored.

- **Max** Returns the maximum value in the referenced area.

- **Min** Returns the minimum value in the referenced area.

- **More Functions** Opens the **Insert Function** dialog box, where you can select any function. Contrary to what you might expect, this does not add the selected function to the **AutoSum** menu.

Using the status bar to check totals and more

The status bar is another handy feature you can use to quickly check the sum or average of any selected cells. Select some cells containing, well, anything, and then look at the bottom of the Excel window at the status bar. There you'll see the Average, Count, and Sum. (Note that the default status bar readout for Count is a tally of cells with contents of any kind, not just cells containing numbers.) If you don't need to create a formula, this is a real timesaver. You can modify the items displayed in the status bar by right-clicking the status bar to display the Customize Status Bar menu.

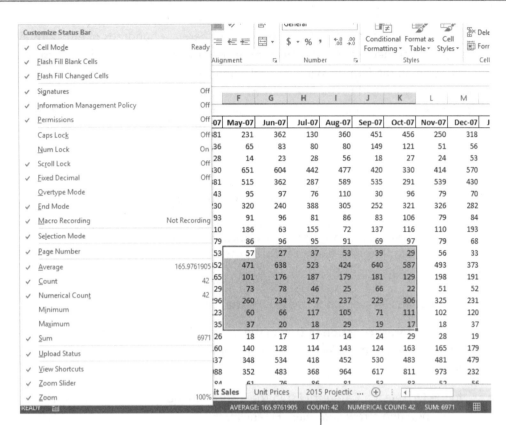

Status bar readout area

All items with check marks on the Customize Status Bar menu are currently active, even if there is no current corresponding item visible in the status bar. When, for example, you use Flash Fill, one of the two Flash Fill "mode" messages appears on the left side of the bar. Most of the menu items are mode indicators that appear only when appropriate. The last three—View Shortcuts, View Slider, and Zoom—turn the controls on the right end of the status bar on and off. You can add status bar readouts for Numerical Count, Minimum, and Maximum; to do so, click the corresponding menu item.

Inserting functions

The SUM function is pretty easy to figure out, but there are hundreds of functions available, and most of them are not nearly as intuitive. Click the Insert Function button—the little fx button on the formula bar—to display the Insert Function dialog box, which comes in handy when you need to use functions with multiple arguments. Offering assistance in context, it explains the function and its possible variations, and makes it easy to enter even the most complex nested-formula arguments correctly. If you want more information and "live examples," you can still access the Help system from the Insert Function dialog box by clicking the question mark in the title bar.

In this exercise, you'll create a formula and work with the formula bar.

 SET UP You need the Loan_start.xlsx workbook located in the Chapter19 practice file folder to complete this exercise. Open the Loan_start.xlsx workbook, and save it as Loan.xlsx.

1   In the **Loan.xlsx** workbook, make sure that cell **C6** is selected.

2   Click the **Insert Function** button in the formula bar, and notice that Excel inserts an equal sign (=) in the selected cell, in preparation for the formula that you are about to enter.

3   In the **Or Select a Category** list in the **Insert Function** dialog box, click the downward-pointing arrow and select **Financial**.

4   In the **Select a Function** box, scroll down the list and select **PMT**, which calculates the monthly payment on a simple loan; the syntax and description of the selected function appears below the function list.

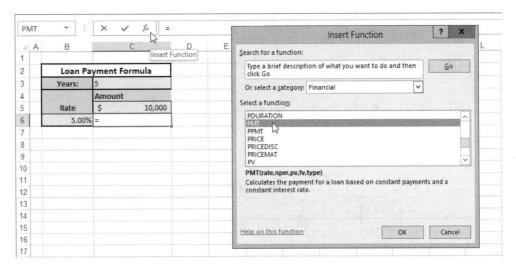

5   Click **OK** to insert the function into the cell, which dismisses the **Insert Function** dialog box and displays the **Function Arguments** dialog box.

6   The first box in the **Function Arguments** dialog box—the **Rate** box—is active; click cell **B6** (containing the percentage **5.00%**) to insert that cell's reference as the **Rate** argument. Notice that a short description of the selected argument appears in the bottom half of the dialog box. If you need more information, click the **Help on This Function** link at the bottom of the dialog box.

7   After the cell reference has been inserted, the cursor is still flashing in the **Rate** box; enter **/12** to convert the rate from annual to monthly to create a nested formula within the PMT function; you can create up to 64 levels of nesting by using parentheses.

8   Click in the **Nper** box and then click cell **C3** to insert the cell reference for the **Years** entry.

9   While the cursor is still in the **Nper** box, enter *12 to convert the time periods from years into months.

10 Click in the **Pv** box (present value), and then click cell **C5**; the loan amount is the present value.

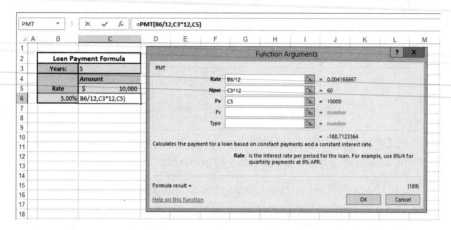

As you add arguments in the Function Arguments dialog box, you'll notice that Excel displays the actual calculated value of each argument to the right of each edit box, and shows the overall result that will be returned by the function, just below the argument values. If you watch cell C6 or the formula bar, you can keep an eye on the formula as it takes shape. Only the arguments that are displayed in bold in the dialog box are required; the Fv (future value) and Type arguments are optional.

11 Press **OK** to enter the formula.

This simple formula shows that your payments would be $189, but the result is displayed in parentheses as a negative number, because payments represent money spent rather than received. You might need to express cash outflows as negative values in a double-entry accounting worksheet, for example. However, if you don't, it is common practice to reverse the sign for display purposes.

12 Select cell **C6**.

13 In the formula bar, click between the equal sign and the PMT function and enter – (a minus sign).

14 Press **Enter**.

| C6 | ▾ | : | ✕ | ✓ | *fx* | =-PMT(B6/12,C3*12,C5) |

⊿ A	B	C	D	E	F
1					
2	**Loan Payment Formula**				
3	Years:	5			
4		Amount			
5	Rate	$ 10,000			
6	5.00%	189			
7					

✖ CLEAN UP Save the Loan.xlsx workbook, and then close it.

You can explore the Insert Function dialog box to give yourself some perspective on the array of functions available and how they are organized.

Using relative, fixed, and mixed cell references

There are three kinds of references in Excel: fixed, relative, and mixed. All of the cell references we have used thus far have been relative references, such as C4. Using relative references in formulas allows you to copy or fill the formula, and the relative references will adjust automatically. This is fine for many one-dimensional purposes like totals, as long as the data cells and the formula cells are always in the same relative positions.

For example, suppose in cell A1, you enter the formula =B1+C1. What this formula says, essentially, is "take the value in the next cell to the right, and add it to the value two cells to the right." You can copy this formula anywhere, and the relative references will adjust automatically; the formula will always add the two cells to the right of the formula, wherever it is located.

But frequently, you might want to use a single value in multiple formulas, such as a percentage rate. You could use a relative cell reference, but only if you didn't need to copy it elsewhere. Otherwise, you could use a fixed reference, such as $C$4. A dollar sign preceding the row number and column letter tells Excel to hold that position so it will not adjust when you copy it. You can use $C$4 in a formula, copying it as needed, and the cell reference will not change, because both the row and column are fixed.

You can also specify mixed references, in which one row or column is fixed and the other is relative; for example, $C4. When you copy this reference, the row adjusts automatically, but the column does not. You'll use this ability to fix and mix your references in the next exercise.

In this exercise, you'll change the reference style by using the F4 function key, which is a special unnamed reference-switching key that only works when you are editing formulas. This makes it easier and more reliable to edit formulas and requires a lot less squinting and typing the dollar signs yourself.

 SET UP You need the Loan_start.xlsx workbook from the previous exercise to complete this exercise. Or, you can open the Loan_start.xlsx workbook located in the Chapter19 practice file folder. Save the workbook as Loan.xlsx.

1   In the **Loan.xlsx** workbook, click the **Loan Table** worksheet tab.

2   Make sure cell **C6** is selected, and enter =-PMT(to begin the formula. (Make sure to include the minus sign after the equal sign.)

3   Click cell **B6**, which contains the **3.00%** rate, to add the cell reference into the formula.

4   Press the **F4** key and notice that the reference changes to the fixed form, **$B$6**.

5   Press **F4** again, and it changes to **B$6**.

6   Press **F4** a third time to change the reference to **$B6**, which is what you want; if you press **F4** again, the reference returns to normal; you can keep pressing **F4** to cycle through the sequence.

7   Following the reference **$B6**, enter /12 to convert the annual interest rate into a monthly amount.

C6	▼	:	✕	✓	ƒx	=-PMT($B6/12	
	A	B	C	D	E	F	G
1							
2		**Loan Payments Table**					
3		Years: 5					
4			Loan Amount				
5		Rate	$ 10,000	$ 20,000	$ 30,000	$ 40,000	
6		3.00%	=-PMT($B6/12				
7		3.50%	PMT(rate, nper, pv, [fv], [type])				
8		4.00%					
9		4.50%					
10		5.00%					
11							

8   Enter a comma to separate the first argument from the next, then click cell **C3**, which contains the number of years.

9   Press the **F4** key just once this time, settling on the locked-row-and-column version of the mixed reference, **$C$3**.

10   Following the reference **$C$3**, enter *12 to convert years into months.

11   Enter a comma (,) and then click cell **C5**, which contains the **$10,000** loan amount.

12   Press the **F4** key twice this time to enter the locked-row version of the mixed reference, **C$5**.

13   Enter a closed parenthesis sign ()) to finish the function arguments.

14   Press **Enter**. Now you're ready to copy the formula.

> **TIP** When you are in Edit mode and are working on a formula with multiple cell references, click the one you want to fix or mix; pressing F4 adjusts that reference only. And yes, you could just type the dollar signs yourself, but F4 actually does make it easier if you're working with more than one reference.

19

| C6 | ▼ | ⋮ | ✕ | ✓ | *fx* | =-PMT($B6/12,$C$3*12,C$5) |

⊿	A	B	C	D	E	F	G
1							
2			**Loan Payments Table**				
3		Years:	5				
4				**Loan Amount**			
5		Rate	$ 10,000	$ 20,000	$ 30,000	$ 40,000	
6		3.00%	180				
7		3.50%					
8		4.00%					
9		4.50%					
10		5.00%					
11							

15   Select cell **C6** and drag the fill handle to the right to cell **F6**.

16   Drag the fill handle from cell **F6** down to cell **F10**.

17   Press **Shift+Tab** to highlight cell **F10**. (You can press **Tab** to move the selected cell to the right or down in a selected block of cells without losing the selection; pressing **Shift+Tab** moves the selection in reverse.)

| F10 | | ⋮ | ✕ | ✓ | ƒx | =-PMT($B10/12,$C$3*12,F$5) |

Loan Payments Table

	Rate	$ 10,000	$ 20,000	$ 30,000	$ 40,000
Years: 5					
		Loan Amount			
3.00%		180	359	539	719
3.50%		182	364	546	728
4.00%		184	368	552	737
4.50%		186	373	559	746
5.00%		189	377	566	755

In all of the copied formulas, the fixed reference $C$3 stayed locked on the Years cell, and the mixed references performed as expected, adjusting to use the correct rate in column B, and the proper loan amount in row 5. Filling in formulas even in a table this small would have been an unduly tedious and error-prone endeavor, had we entered each formula manually. Spending a little time crafting the formula made the table easier to create and rendered the results more reliable.

✖ CLEAN UP Save the Loan.xlsx workbook, and then close it.

Using names in formulas and validating cell entries

Another way to construct formulas is to use named ranges instead of cell references. Applying familiar names to cells and ranges makes them easier to remember.

In this exercise, you'll create names to apply to cell references and ranges.

➔ SET UP You need the Fabrikam-Seven-Year-Summary2_start.xlsx workbook located in the Chapter19 practice file folder to complete this exercise. Open the Fabrikam-Seven-Year-Summary2_start.xlsx workbook, and save it as Fabrikam-Seven-Year-Summary2.xlsx.

1 Open the **Fabrikam-Seven-Year-Summary2.xlsx** workbook.

2 Click the tiny arrow in the **Name** box on the left end of the formula bar, and select **NamesRange** from the list to select the range **A3:H10**.

3 On the **Formulas** tab, click **Create From Selection** in the **Defined Names** group.

Name box

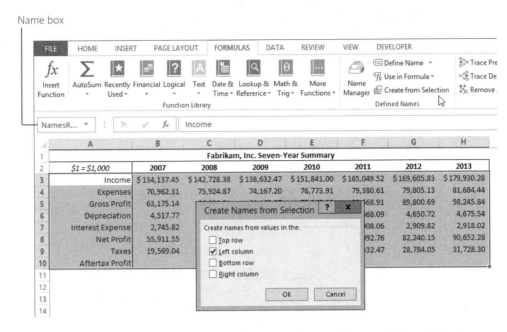

4   Select the **Left Column** check box, if it is not already selected, and then click **OK**.

5   Select cell **B10**.

6   Enter **=Net_Profit-Taxes** and press **Enter**.

7   Select cell **B10** again and drag the fill handle to cell **H10** to copy the formula.

D10		fx	=Net_Profit-Taxes				
	A	B	C	D	E	F	G	H
1				Fabrikam, Inc. Seven-Year Summary				
2	$1 = $1,000	2007	2008	2009	2010	2011	2012	2013
3	Income	$ 134,137.45	$ 142,728.38	$ 138,632.47	$ 151,841.00	$ 165,049.52	$ 169,605.83	$ 179,930.28
4	Expenses	70,962.31	75,924.87	74,167.20	76,773.91	79,380.61	79,805.13	81,684.44
5	Gross Profit	63,175.14	66,803.51	64,465.27	75,067.09	85,668.91	89,800.69	98,245.84
6	Depreciation	4,517.77	4,656.92	4,576.27	4,622.18	4,668.09	4,650.72	4,675.54
7	Interest Expense	2,745.82	2,893.11	2,885.24	2,896.65	2,908.06	2,909.82	2,918.02
8	Net Profit	55,911.55	59,253.48	57,003.76	67,548.26	78,092.76	82,240.15	90,652.28
9	Taxes	19,569.04	20,738.72	19,951.31	23,641.89	27,332.47	28,784.05	31,728.30
10	Aftertax Profit	$ 36,342.51	$ 38,514.76	$ 37,052.44	$ 43,906.37	$ 50,760.29	$ 53,456.10	$ 58,923.98
11								

These formulas all create the same totals as the ones that you created in the first exercise in this chapter, except that now all the formulas in row 10 are exactly the same. This illustrates one of Excel's hidden features, implicit intersection. The names Net_Profit and Taxes each represent a range of cells, not a single cell, but Excel correctly assumed that you wanted to use only the cell in each range that appears in the same column as the formula.

8   Select the **Net Profit** formulas in cells **B8:H8**.

9   Enter = (an equal sign), then click the **Use in Formula** menu in the **Defined Names** group.

10 Select **Gross_Profit** from the list of names, and then enter – (a minus sign).

11 Select **Depreciation** from the **Use in Formula** menu, and then enter – (a minus sign).

12 Select **Interest_Expense** from the list.

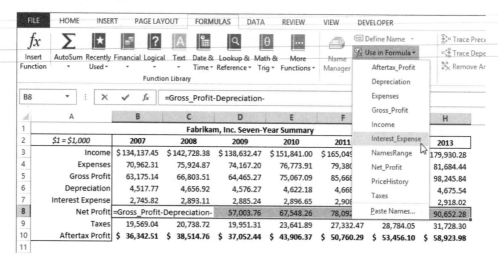

13 Press **Ctrl+Enter** to insert the formula into all the selected cells at once.

There is one more row of formulas you can edit yourself. Just perform the last four steps of this procedure on row 5 instead of row 8, and create the formula =Income-Expenses.

❌ CLEAN UP Save the Fabrikam-Seven-Year-Summary2.xlsx workbook, and then close it.

Looking at useful functions

The categories listed in the Insert Function dialog box represent all functions, including very specialized functions that are used for such things as programming, engineering, and querying databases. There are frequently used functions in every category, of course, but for most of us, some categories will never have representatives in our favorites list. Viewing the Formulas tab on the ribbon reveals the types of functions available.

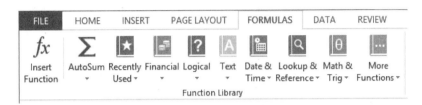

Next to giant versions of the Insert Function and AutoSum buttons (everyone's favorites), the Function Library reveals the categories that we all use most; less frequently used functions are relegated to the More Functions menu. The Recently Used menu collects your own personal favorites.

TIP When you have an idea of what you're looking for, the Formulas tab may be more beneficial to you than the available choices in the Insert Function dialog box. When you select a function from the Function Library group, you skip the Insert Function dialog box and go directly to the Function Arguments dialog box.

In this section, we'll focus on some helpful functions from the six categories represented on the Formulas tab, and you'll be provided with brief explanations of each category. We encourage you to use the Excel Help system to enhance your understanding. You can access the Help system at any time by pressing F1 on your keyboard or clicking the Help button on the ribbon. You can also directly access a specific Help topic by clicking the More Help On This Function link at the bottom of the Insert Function dialog box.

19

In the Help topics, you'll find descriptions and definitions, and most function topics will include live examples that you can download and test for yourself.

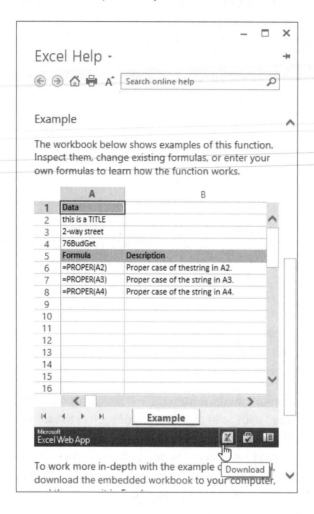

Handy math and trig functions

The following eight math and trig functions can be accessed through the AutoSum button:

- **SUMIF(range, criteria, sum_range)** This command combines the IF and SUM functions to add specific values in a range according to the criterion you supply. For example, the formula =SUMIF(G5:G12, "X", J5:J12) returns the total of all numbers in J5:J12, in which the cell in the same row in column G contains an X.

- **COUNTIF(range, criteria)** This command is similar to SUMIF, but counts cells in the specified range that match your specified criterion.

- **SUMPRODUCT(array1, [array2], [array3], …)** This function multiplies each value in array1 by the corresponding value in array2, array3, and so on, then adds the totals. All the arrays (up to 255) must consist of an identical shape and size.

- **PRODUCT(number1, [number2], …)** This function multiplies all of its arguments (up to 255). If you need to multiply a lot of numbers, using this function is easier than creating a formula such as =A1+A2+A3+A4.

- **RANDBETWEEN(bottom, top)** This function generates a random integer that falls between two provided integer values, inclusive. It is also volatile, meaning that it recalculates every time you open or edit a worksheet or press F9 (recalculate).

- **ROUND(number, num_digits)** You can round a number by using this function for a specified number of digits. When num_digits is zero, number is rounded to an integer value; if num_digits is greater than zero, number is rounded to the specified number of decimal places; if num_digits is less than zero, the number is rounded to the indicated number of places to the left of the decimal point.

- **ROUNDDOWN(number, num_digits)** Similar to ROUND, this function always rounds a number down, toward zero.

- **ROUNDUP(number, num_digits)** Also similar to ROUND, this function rounds a number up, away from zero.

19

IMPORTANT

Handy logical functions

You can use logical functions to create complex conditional formulas, such as those mentioned in the following list:

- **IF(logical_test, [value_if_true], [value_if_false])** This function applies a logical test (for example, C5>200) that results in a true or false and optionally allows you to specify different values for both True and False results.

- **Nested IF** This function creates a hierarchy of tests. For example, the formula: =IF(A1=1, "Yes", IF(AND(A1>=1, A1<10), "Maybe", IF(AND(A1>=10, A1<20), "No", "N/A"))) returns Yes if the value is 1, Maybe for values of 2 through 9, No for values between 10 and 20, and N/A if none of these conditions is true.

- **AND(logical1, logical2, ...)** This function returns FALSE if any of its arguments are false, and returns TRUE only if all of its arguments are true. Generally, this function is used as an argument to another function, such as IF, which allows you to apply multiple logical tests instead of just one. Conversely, the OR function returns FALSE only if all of its arguments are false, and returns TRUE if any of its arguments are true. Either function can accept up to 255 arguments.

- **IFERROR(value, value_if_error)** This function returns a specified value (or a message enclosed in quotation marks, such as "We have a problem!") if the value argument evaluates to FALSE. You can use this function to test the results of other formulas by nesting them within the IFERROR function as the value argument.

Handy text functions

Many functions can manipulate text. Some of them are pretty esoteric; for example, the BAHTTEXT function coverts any number into text in the Thai language.

Following are a few of the more useful text functions, shown with their arguments.

- **CLEAN(text)** Removes all nonprintable characters. This is useful when you are importing data from other sources, which sometimes includes errant code symbols, returns, or line-break characters.

- **CONCATENATE(text1, text2, ...)** See "Combining text from multiple cells into one string" later in this chapter.

- **EXACT(text1, text2)** This function compares two text strings to see if they are the same. The function returns TRUE if they are exactly the same; otherwise, it returns FALSE. It is case-sensitive, but not formatting-sensitive.

- **LEFT(text, num_characters)** This function returns the first num_characters in a text string. For example, the formula =LEFT("Step by Step",4) returns Step. Note that text entered directly into a formula must be enclosed in quotation marks. This tells Excel that you have entered a text string; the quotation marks don't count as characters. If you use references to text in other cells; no quotation marks are needed. If cell C3 contained the text Step by Step, the formula =LEFT(C3,4) would also return Step.

- **LEN(text)** Returns the number of characters in a text string. For example, the formula =LEN("Step by Step") returns a value of 12.

- **LOWER(text)** Converts text into all-lowercase characters.

- **PROPER(text)** See "Changing the case of text" later in this chapter.

- **RIGHT(text, num_characters)** Returns the last num_characters in a text string. For example, the formula =RIGHT("Step by Step",7) returns the text by Step. Yes, spaces count as characters.

- **TRIM(text)** See "Removing extra spaces" later in this chapter.

- **UPPER(text)** Converts text into all-uppercase characters.

Handy date and time functions

You can use dates in formulas and functions as you would any other value. If cell A1 contains the date 7/4/2013, the formula =A1+300 returns the date that falls exactly 300 days later: 4/30/2014 (or the serial date value 41759).

To find the elapsed number of weeks between two dates, you can enter a formula such as =(("12/13/14")-("11/12/13"))/7, which returns 56.6 weeks. If you enter dates "in format," then enclose them in quotation marks. Or you can use serial date values. But it's always better to use cell references instead of entering any values into formulas directly, simplifying the previous formula to something like =(C4-D4)/7.

19

Following are several functions that do things that formulas cannot accomplish:

- **TODAY()** Inserts the current date. This function takes no arguments, but you must include the empty parentheses anyway. You may also need to apply a date format, if the date appears as an integer. This function is said to be volatile, meaning that it recalculates every time you open or edit the worksheet.

- **NOW()** Similar to the TODAY function, but it inserts both the current date and time. This function is also volatile and takes no arguments. The result includes an integer (the date) and a decimal value (the time).

- **WEEKDAY(serial_number, return_type)** Returns the day of the week for a specific date. The serial_number can be a date value, a cell reference, or text such as "1/27/11" or "January 27, 2011" (you need to include the quotation marks). The function returns a number that represents the day of the week on which the specified date falls, where day 1 is Sunday if the optional return_type argument is 1 or omitted. If return_type is 2, then day 1 is Monday, if return_type is 3, then Monday is day 0, and Sunday is day 6.

- **WORKDAY(start_date, days, holidays)** Returns a date for a specified number of working days before or after a given date. If the days argument is negative, the function returns the number of workdays before the start date; if days is positive, then it returns the number of working days after the start date. Optionally, you can include an array or range of other dates you wish to exclude as the holidays argument.

- **NETWORKDAYS(start_date, end_date, holidays)** This function is similar to the WORKDAY function but calculates the number of working days between two given dates. This function does not count weekends.

Handy lookup and reference functions

These two lookup functions are designed to search for the largest value (either numerically or alphabetically) in a specified row or column of a table that is less than or equal to the lookup value, not for an exact match. The functions return errors if all the values in the first row or column of the table are greater than the lookup value, but if all the values are less than the lookup value, the function returns the largest value available.

- **VLOOKUP(lookup_value, table_array, col_index_num, [range_lookup])** Searches the first column of table_array and returns a value from the same row, in the column indicated by col_index_num. The values can be numbers or text, but it is essential that table_array is sorted in ascending order, top to bottom. No lookup_value should appear more than once in a table. This function returns the largest value that does not exceed lookup_value, not necessarily an exact match, unless you set the optional range_lookup argument to FALSE.

- **HLOOKUP(lookup_value, table_array, row_index_num, [range_lookup])** Searches the first row of table_array and returns a value from the same column, in the row indicated by row_index_num. Otherwise, this function performs identically to the VLOOKUP function, except that table_array must be sorted in ascending order from left to right rather than top to bottom.

- **ROW([reference])** Returns the row number of the reference; if the reference argument is omitted, returns the current row.

- **ROWS(array)** Returns the number of rows in the specified range.

- **COLUMN([reference])** Returns the column number (not the letter) of the reference; if the reference argument is omitted, returns the current column.

- **COLUMNS(array)** Returns the number of columns in the specified range.

Handy financial functions

Most of the financial functions involve various aspects of amortizing or annuitizing. There are clusters of functions that address such specifics as T-bills, mortgages, loans, and depreciation.

The following lists some of the most commonly used financial functions:

- **PMT(rate, number of periods, present value, future value, type)** Computes the payment required to amortize a loan over a specified number of periods. For an example, see "Using relative, fixed, and mixed references" earlier in this chapter.

- **IPMT(rate, period, number of periods, present value, future value, type)** Computes the interest portion of an individual loan payment, assuming a constant payment and interest rate. PPMT takes the same arguments as IPMT but returns the principal portion of the payment.

- **NPER(rate, payment, present value, future value, type)** Computes the number of periods required to amortize a loan, given a specified payment.

- **SLN(cost, salvage, life)** Calculates straight-line depreciation for an asset.

Working with text in Excel

People always think numbers when they think about Excel, but in reality, Excel is frequently used as a layout grid for text. Most of the time, this sort of thing would be better accomplished with Microsoft Word, but people use what they know and are comfortable with. However, there are some things you can do with text in Excel that you can't do in Word. After learning a few more tricks, you may think about massaging text in Excel first, before copying it into a Word document.

Combining text from multiple cells into one string

In this exercise, you'll put strings of text together any way you want by using the CONCATENATE function. Whenever you use a cell reference in the function, you use the ampersand (&) as a connector to the next item, which can be another cell reference, or text enclosed in quotation marks. Anything you enter between the quotation marks is treated as text.

SET UP You need the Fabrikam-Management2_start.xlsx workbook located in the Chapter19 practice file folder to complete this exercise. Open the Fabrikam-Management2_start.xlsx workbook, and save it as Fabrikam-Management2.xlsx.

1   In the **Fabrikam-Management2.xlsx** workbook, make sure that cell **I2** is selected.

2   Begin entering =CON. A suggested list of functions appears below the cell.

G	H	I	J	K	L
State	Zip	FullName	FullAddress	CityStZip	
PA	98006	=Con			
PA	98272		Joins several text strings into one text string		
PA	98008				
PA	98004				
PA	98201				
PA	98006				
OH	83720				

CONCATENATE
CONFIDENCE.NORM
CONFIDENCE.T
CONVERT
CONFIDENCE

3   Double-click **CONCATENATE**.

4   Click cell **B2** and then enter &" "& (a space enclosed with quotation marks and ampersands).

5   Click cell **A2** and press **Enter**.

6   Press the **Up Arrow** key, reselecting cell **I2** to view the formula.

I2		fx	=CONCATENATE(B2&" "&A2)							
	A	B	C	D	E	F	G	H	I	J
1	LastName	FirstName	Title	Department	Address	City	State	Zip	FullName	FullAddress
2	Abercrombie	Kim	Accounting Manager	Finance	1234 S 34th	Erie	PA	98006	Kim Abercrombie	
3	Affronti	Michael	Director of Operations	Operations	123 Broadway	Meadville	PA	98272		

7   Select cell **J2**.

8   Enter =CON and double-click **CONCATENATE**.

9   Click cell **E2** and enter &", "& (a comma and a space enclosed with ampersands and quotation marks).

10   Click cell **F2** and enter &", "&

11   Click cell **G2** and enter &" "&

12   Click cell **H2** and press **Enter**.

J2		fx	=CONCATENATE(E2&", "&F2&", "&G2&" "&H2)			
	E	F	G	H	I	J	K	L
1	Address	City	State	Zip	FullName	FullAddress	CityStZip	
2	1234 S 34th	Erie	PA	98006	Kim Abercrombie	1234 S 34th, Erie, PA 98006		
3	123 Broadway	Meadville	PA	98272				

13 Double-click the **border** next to the Column letter **J** to auto-fit the contents.

14 Double-click cell **J2** to activate **Edit** mode.

15 In the formula bar, drag through the entire formula you just created and press **Ctrl+C** to copy it.

16 Press **Esc** to leave **Edit** mode.

17 Click cell **K2** and press **Ctrl+V** to paste the formula. Notice that the cell references did not adjust. When you copy a formula using **Edit** mode, you can paste it into a new cell and the references are preserved.

18 Double-click cell **K2** to activate **Edit** mode.

19 Drag to select the first part of the formula in parentheses **E2&", "&** and press the **Delete** key. Notice that the formula argument selection box disappears from cell **E2**.

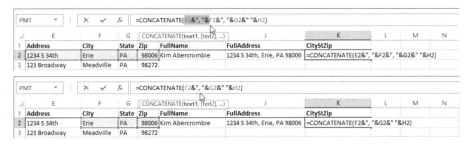

20 Press **Enter**.

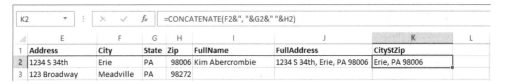

21 Select cells **I2** to **K2**, then drag the fill handle down to row **23** to copy the relative-reference formulas.

Formula bar: I2 | =CONCATENATE(B2&" "&A2)

Row	E Address	F City	G State	H Zip	I FullName	J FullAddress	K CityStZip
1	Address	City	State	Zip	FullName	FullAddress	CityStZip
2	1234 S 34th	Erie	PA	98006	Kim Abercrombie	1234 S 34th, Erie, PA 98006	Erie, PA 98006
3	123 Broadway	Meadville	PA	98272	Michael Affronti	123 Broadway, Meadville, P	Meadville, PA 98272
4	456 Center St	Erie	PA	98008	Nupur Agarwal	456 Center St, Erie, PA 9800	Erie, PA 98008
5	2345 N 56th	Erie	PA	98004	Mark Bebbington	2345 N 56th, Erie, PA 98004	Erie, PA 98004
6	123 First St	Edinboro	PA	98201	Allie Bellew	123 First St, Edinboro, PA 96	Edinboro, PA 98201
7	456 12th Ave	Erie	PA	98006	Nuno Bento	456 12th Ave, Erie, PA 9800(	Erie, PA 98006
8	3456 Main St	Ashtabula	OH	83720	Antonio Bermejo	3456 Main St, Ashtabula, OF	Ashtabula, OH 83720
9	345 Cherry St	Erie	PA	98020	Randy Byrne	345 Cherry St, Erie, PA 9802	Erie, PA 98020
10	890 1st Ave	Girard	PA	98012	Carlos Carvallo	890 1st Ave, Girard, PA 9801	Girard, PA 98012
11	12 State St	Erie	PA	98003	Sean Chai	12 State St, Erie, PA 98003	Erie, PA 98003
12	456 Second St	Conneaut	OH	83702	Gareth Chan	456 Second St, Conneaut, O	Conneaut, OH 83702
13	4567 Maple	North East	PA	98007	Lee Theng Chia	4567 Maple, North East, PA	North East, PA 98007
14	678 W 23rd	Edinboro	PA	98201	Terri Chudzik	678 W 23rd, Edinboro, PA 96	Edinboro, PA 98201
15	345 Third St	Erie	PA	98003	Ken Circeo	345 Third St, Erie, PA 98003	Erie, PA 98003
16	5678 Central Ave	Ripley	NY	97303	John Clarkson	5678 Central Ave, Ripley, N'	Ripley, NY 97303
17	3456 Fourth St	Erie	PA	98011	Ryan Danner	3456 Fourth St, Erie, PA 980	Erie, PA 98011
18	23 S 34th	Meadville	PA	98272	Arlene Huff	23 S 34th, Meadville, PA 98;	Meadville, PA 98272
19	6789 Meridian	Erie	PA	98012	Reto Käch	6789 Meridian, Erie, PA 980	Erie, PA 98012
20	367 Center St	Erie	PA	98007	Petr Karásek	367 Center St, Erie, PA 9800	Erie, PA 98007
21	2345 10th Ave	Erie	PA	98005	Kate Taneyhill	2345 10th Ave, Erie, PA 980(	Erie, PA 98005
22	34 N 56th	Sherman	NY	97322	Gregory Weber	34 N 56th, Sherman, NY 973	Sherman, NY 97322
23	345 12th Ave	Erie	PA	98002	Barbara Zighetti	345 12th Ave, Erie, PA 9800;	Erie, PA 98002

❌ CLEAN UP Save the Fabrikam-Management2.xlsx workbook, and then close it.

If you were to concatenate cell references with only ampersands, the concatenated contents of the cells may not be separated by spaces, which is why we added them. You can also concatenate cells containing formulas; only the displayed results are included, not the formulas themselves. Thus, you could use a formula like the following to create a sentence that changes depending on the formula's result:

```
=CONCATENATE("Sales for the month came in at "&E5&"!!")
```

Assuming that cell E5 contains a monthly sales formula; this would result in a displayed value such as:

```
Sales for the month came in at $67,890!!
```

Removing extra spaces

It's inevitable that extra spaces will appear, especially in a document containing a lot of text that was entered by hand at some point in its history. In the previous exercise, for example, you might create or propagate double spaces when combining the contents of other cells. Fortunately, there's a function in Excel to remove extra spaces.

In this exercise, you'll remove extra spaces using formulas, and then you'll copy and paste the results—only the displayed values from those formulas—to replace the spaced-out text.

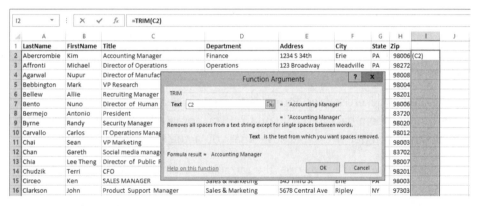

SET UP You need the Fabrikam-Management2.xlsx workbook from the previous exercise to complete this exercise. Or, you can open the Fabrikam-Management2_start. xlsx workbook, located in the Chapter19 practice file folder, and save it as Fabrikam-Management2.xlsx.

1. In the **Fabrikam-Management2.xlsx** file, make sure that **Sheet2** is selected and that the cell range **I2:I23** is selected. Some entries in column **C** have extra spaces in them; for example, **C7**.

2. Click the **Insert Function** button in the formula bar.

3. Click the **Or Select a Category** list and click **Text**.

4. Scroll down through the list of **Text** functions and double-click **Trim**.

5. Click cell **C2** to enter the cell reference into the **Text** box.

19

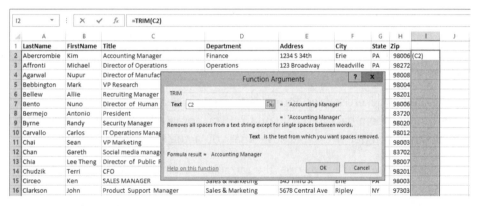

6. Press the **Ctrl** key and click the **OK** button; if you press **Ctrl** when entering any formula, Excel not only inserts the formula into the active cell, it also inserts it into all the selected cells.

   Now, the cells that previously contained extra spaces have the spaces removed due to the use of the TRIM function (specifically, rows 7, 13, 16, 19, and 23).

	C	D	E	F	G	H	I	J	K
I2		fx	=TRIM(C2)						
1	Title	Department	Address	City	State	Zip			
2	Accounting Manager	Finance	1234 S 34th	Erie	PA	98006	Accounting Manager		
3	Director of Operations	Operations	123 Broadway	Meadville	PA	98272	Director of Operations		
4	Director of Manufacturing	Manufacturing	456 Center St	Erie	PA	98008	Director of Manufacturing		
5	VP Research	Executive	2345 N 56th	Erie	PA	98004	VP Research		
6	Recruiting Manager	Human Resources	123 First St	Edinboro	PA	98201	Recruiting Manager		
7	Director of Human Resources	Human Resources	456 12th Ave	Erie	PA	98006	Director of Human Resources		
8	President	Executive	3456 Main St	Ashtabula	OH	83720	President		
9	Security Manager	Operations	345 Cherry St	Erie	PA	98020	Security Manager		
10	IT Operations Manager	Information Technology	890 1st Ave	Girard	PA	98012	IT Operations Manager		
11	VP Marketing	Executive	12 State St	Erie	PA	98003	VP Marketing		
12	Social media manager	Sales & Marketing	456 Second St	Conneaut	OH	83702	Social media manager		
13	Director of Public Relations	Sales & Marketing	4567 Maple	North East	PA	98007	Director of Public Relations		
14	CFO	Executive	678 W 23rd	Edinboro	PA	98201	CFO		
15	SALES MANAGER	Sales & Marketing	345 Third St	Erie	PA	98003	SALES MANAGER		
16	Product Support Manager	Sales & Marketing	5678 Central Ave	Ripley	NY	97303	Product Support Manager		
17	IT Services Manager	Information Technology	3456 Fourth St	Erie	PA	98011	IT Services Manager		
18	Warehouse Manager	Operations	23 S 34th	Meadville	PA	98272	Warehouse Manager		
19	VP Information Systems	Executive	6789 Meridian	Erie	PA	98012	VP Information Systems		
20	Advertising Manager	Sales & Marketing	367 Center St	Erie	PA	98007	Advertising Manager		
21	CEO	Executive	2345 10th Ave	Erie	PA	98005	CEO		
22	VP Finance	Executive	34 N 56th	Sherman	NY	97322	VP Finance		
23	Web Services Manager	Information Technology	345 12th Ave	Erie	PA	98002	Web Services Manager		

✖ CLEAN UP Save the Fabrikam-Management2.xlsx workbook, but keep it open for the next exercise.

Copying cells containing formulas and pasting only their resulting values

The previous exercise used formulas to create a clean set of titles in column I, but now how do you get them back into column C? If you copy cells I2:I23 and simply paste them into column C, you get errors, because what you actually copied were formulas.

In this exercise, you'll copy only the formulas' results into column C.

➜ SET UP You need the Fabrikam-Management2.xlsx workbook from the previous exercise to complete this exercise.

1   Make sure that **Sheet2** is selected and that the range **I2:I23** is selected, and then press **Ctrl+C** to copy it.

2   Click cell **C2**.

3　Click the menu arrow below the **Paste** button on the **Home** tab of the ribbon to display the **Paste Options** palette.

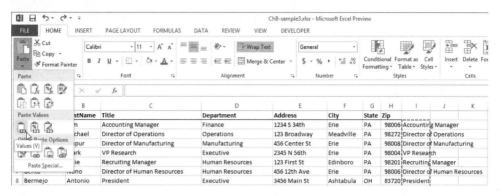

4　Click the **Values** button in the **Paste Values** group to replace the **Titles** in column **C** with the newly trimmed titles from your formulas.

TIP When you copy a range of cells, you don't need to select an equivalent range of cells before copying. You can just click the cell where you want the copy function to begin, and then paste. Just make sure you don't paste over existing data.

5　Click the heading in column **I** to select the entire column.

6　Click the **Clear** button in the **Editing** group on the **Home** tab of the ribbon, and then click **Clear Contents**.

❌ CLEAN UP Save the Fabrikam-Management2.xlsx workbook, but keep it open for the next exercise.

Changing the case of text

Case is another issue that comes up frequently when working with large amounts of text. You might have some text in caps and some in all lowercase, for example. Excel provides the tools you need to make the text formatting consistent.

In this exercise, you'll change the case of text entries.

1   In the **Fabrikam-Management2.xlsx** workbook, make sure **Sheet2** is selected.

2   Click cell **I12** and then click the **Insert Function** button in the formula bar.

3   Select the **Text** category, then scroll down through the function list, click **PROPER**, and then click **OK**.

4   Click cell **C12** to enter its reference in the **Text** box, and then press **Enter**.

5   Select cell **C12** and drag the fill handle down to cell **C15** to copy the formula.

The Proper function did its job, but at the same time, it created other issues. The four text values in column I are now in proper case, meaning that the first letter of every word is capitalized. This is what you wanted in cells I12 and I15. However, the text in cells I13 ("Of") and I14 ("Cfo") contain some incorrect capitalization, but they serve to illustrate the function's effect. We'll copy only the ones we want and paste them, but this time we'll use the right mouse button to display a shortcut menu.

6   Click cell **I12** and press **Ctrl+C** to copy.

7   Click cell **C12**, then click the right mouse button. Select **Paste Special**, and then click the **Values** button.

8   Click cell **I15** and press **Ctrl+C** to copy.

9   Click cell **C15**, then click the right mouse button, select **Paste Special**, and then click the **Values** button.

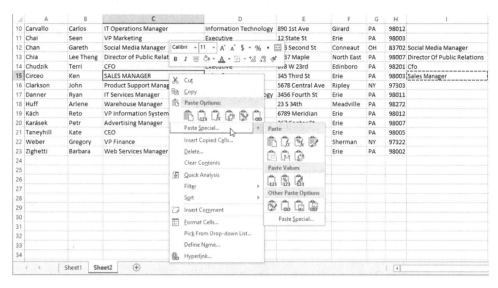

10   Select cells **I12** to **I15** and press the **Delete** key to delete the formulas.

CLEAN UP Save the Fabrikam-Management2.xlsx workbook, and then close it.

Restricting cell entries

Wouldn't it be nice if there were ways to prevent people (ourselves included) from entering the wrong type of data in critical cells? For example, let's say you have a workbook that several people use to enter collected sales data every month—sales totals, inventory, and contact information—in dollars, integers, and text. A stray text character entered into a cell used in calculations could result in error values popping up all over the workbook. Worse yet, sometimes entry errors produce no visible errors, just bogus results. Excel addresses these concerns and offers Data Validation features to enhance the integrity of your data.

In this exercise, you'll restrict cell entries to protect your data.

SET UP You need the Real-Estate-Transition_start.xlsx workbook located in the Chapter19 practice file folder to complete this exercise. Open the Real-Estate-Transition_start.xlsx workbook, and save it as Real-Estate-Transition.xlsx.

1   In the **Real-Estate-Transition.xlsx** workbook, make sure that cell **B2** is selected.

2   Enter any letter into cell **B2** and press **Enter**. Notice that many **#VALUE!** errors suddenly appear.

3   Press **Ctrl+Z** to undo the last entry.

4   With cell **B2** selected, click the **Data** tab on the ribbon and click the **Data Validation** button in the **Data Tools** group.

5   In the **Data Validation** dialog box, select **Whole number** in the **Allow** list.

6   In the **Data** box, select **greater than**.

7   Enter **0** (zero) into the **Minimum** box.

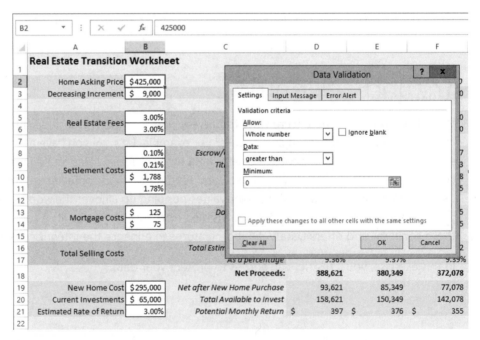

8   Click **OK**.

9   Enter any letter into cell **B3** and press **Enter**.

Notice that Excel will not allow text to be entered into this cell, and an error message is displayed when you try to enter text into the cell.

10 Click **Cancel**.

11 Click the **Data Validation** button again.

12 Click the **Input Message** tab.

13 In the **Title** box, enter Values Only.

14 In the **Input Message** box, enter this text: Enter the asking price for your existing home.

15 Click the **Error Alert** tab.

16 In the **Title** box, enter Oops!

17 In the **Error Message** box, enter Make sure you enter only numbers in this cell.

18 Click **OK**.

19 Enter any letter into cell **B3**, and press **Enter**.

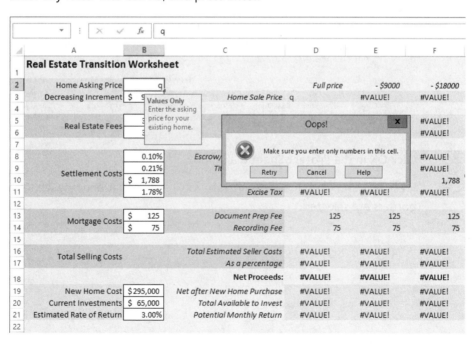

Now, any time you try to make an invalid entry into cell B3, a customized error message appears.

20   In the **Oops!** dialog box, press **Cancel**.

21   Click the **Home** tab.

22   Click the **Format** button in the **Cells** group, and then click **Protect Sheet** to display the **Protect Sheet** dialog box.

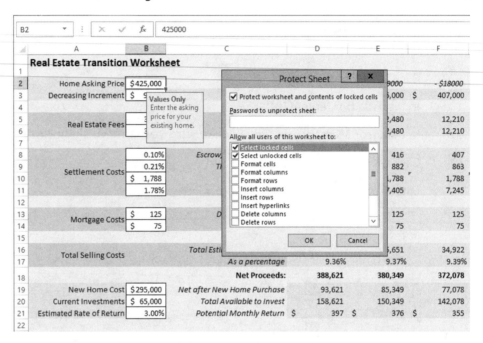

23   Click **OK** in the **Protect Sheet** dialog box.

24   Press **Tab**, and continue pressing **Tab**; you'll notice that only the white cells with borders are selected.

The last two steps show what happens when you protect a sheet with specific cells unlocked. In the original practice file for this exercise, the bordered cells were unlocked, but the sheet wasn't protected. By definition, all cells are "locked" in a new workbook, which actually means that the "locked format" has been applied. You can see this by clicking the Format button on the Home tab and looking at the Lock Cell command near the bottom of the menu. If the icon next to the Lock Cell command has a box around it, then the cell is locked; if not, it is unlocked. But this has no effect on anything until you click the Protect Sheet command (located above the Lock Cell command). When you click the Protect Sheet command, the Protect Sheet dialog box is displayed, offering editing options that allow changes to be made in unlocked cells when the sheet is protected. And, as shown in Step 24, when a sheet is locked, pressing the Tab key will always move the selection to the next unlocked cell; locked cells are ignored.

25   Click the **Home** tab on the ribbon, then click the **Format** button in the **Cells** group, and click **Unprotect Sheet**.

26   Select cell **B21** (Estimated Rate of Return).

27   Click the **Data** tab, click **Data Validation**, and in the **Allow** list on the **Settings** tab, select **List**.

28   Click in the **Source** box and enter =rates.

29   Click **OK**.

30   Click the **Home** tab, then click the **Format** button in the **Cells** group, and click **Protect Sheet**.

Now, when you re-select cell B21, a small menu arrow appears alongside it, offering a number of different interest rates. Cells A35:A39 contain this list of options (the range is named rates). We could have entered the formula =$A$35:$A$39 into the Data Validation dialog box, but the name is not only easier to enter, it also makes it easier to edit. If you move or add more items to the list, just select the new list and redefine the name.

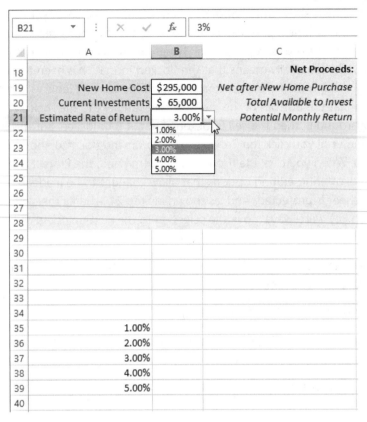

The Data Validation and Lock Cells features allow you to build bulletproof worksheets and maintain control of available options for specific data points. These features are beneficial when creating workbooks that will be used by new Excel users.

❌ CLEAN UP Save the Real-Estate-Transition.xlsx workbook, and then close it.

Key points

- All formulas in Excel begin with an equal sign.
- Double-click an existing formula to change cell references directly by dragging.
- Excel automatically adjusts relative references in formulas when you copy or fill the cells containing them.

- Adding a dollar sign before either the row number or column letter in a cell reference makes it a mixed reference, fixing that position and allowing the other to change automatically when copied.

- Adding dollar signs before both the row number and column letter in a cell reference makes it a fixed reference, allowing you to copy the formula anywhere; it will always refer to the same cell.

- If you double-click a cell containing a formula (putting it into Edit mode), you can copy the formula in the cell and paste it into another cell while preserving the references, whether they are mixed, fixed, or relative.

- Using the AutoSum button is the easiest way to enter formulas to compute totals and averages, find the maximum or minimum value, and more.

- The Insert Function dialog box provides a helpful user interface when you are using functions in formulas, and it provides information about the function, along with descriptive text and assistance for entering arguments.

19

- You can use the CONCATENATE function to combine separate strings of text into one.

- You can use the PROPER function to capitalize the first letter of every word in a text string.

- When you copy cells containing formulas, you can use the Paste Special Values button to paste only their displayed values.

- You can restrict cell entries to accept only numbers, dates, times, text, and more.

- All cells are locked by default; when you protect a worksheet, only the unlocked cells are available for editing.

Chapter at a glance

Use

Use Goal Seek to determine the optimum value needed to solve a problem, page 500

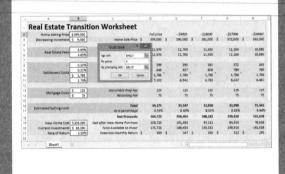

Track

Track changing values with the Scenario Manager, page 501

Apply

Apply an appropriate function to selected data using the Quick Analysis tools, page 504

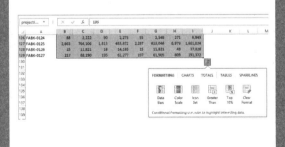

Examine

Examine your data in new ways with PivotTables, page 528

Analyzing data   20

IN THIS CHAPTER, YOU WILL LEARN HOW TO

- Perform goal-seeking operations and manage multiple scenarios.

- Use the Quick Analysis tools.

- Apply conditional formatting.

- Import data from outside sources.

- Create, edit, and manipulate Excel tables.

- Perform customized sorting procedures.

- Create a PivotTable.

After the data is entered into a workbook, your most tedious work is done. In this chapter, you'll learn to work with many of Excel's analysis features to help reveal the truths that are hidden beneath the numbers.

PRACTICE FILES To complete the exercises in this chapter, you need the practice files contained in the Chapter20 practice file folder. For more information, see "Download the practice files" in this book's Introduction.

Exploring a built-in template

Microsoft Excel 2013, like all the Microsoft Office Professional 2013 applications, comes with numerous ready-made templates you can use right out of the cloud (the old aphorism *right out of the box* no longer seems appropriate). Many of the built-in templates are sophisticated applications all by themselves; the astute spreadsheet student would do well to study them.

Many of these templates represent hundreds of hours of work and deep understanding of features, some of which will be introduced in this book. They are aspirational and provide examples of many of the features that you'll use, as building blocks to create your own mini-applications. Use these excellent template applications if you can, or modify them to fit your needs, but learn from them as well.

In this exercise, you'll create a new document based on a template.

 SET UP You don't need any practice files to complete this exercise. Start Excel, open a clean, blank workbook, and follow the steps.

1   Click the **File** tab, and then click **New**.

2   Click any of the template sample images once to view a visual preview.

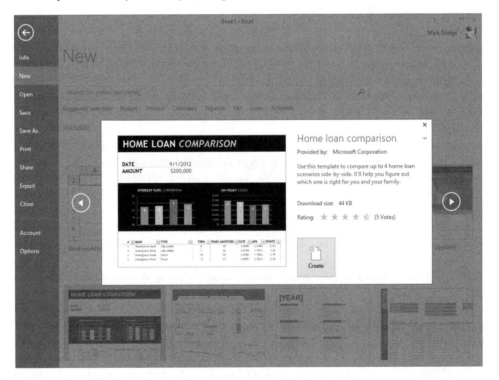

3   Click the **Create** button to open a new worksheet based on the template. (Double-clicking a template sample image is the same as clicking the **Create** button in the preview window.)

4 Click the menu arrow next to the **Name** box in the formula bar, and then click **Loans**. A selected table will be displayed below the charts.

5 Click the **View** tab.

6 Click the **Zoom** button.

7 Click the **Fit Selection** option to adjust the size of the worksheet so that it fits on the screen. (Note that depending on your screen size, this zoom option may either increase or decrease the size of the worksheet.)

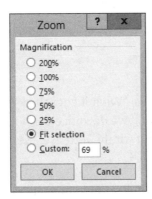

8 Click **OK**. The entire width of the worksheet should be visible on your screen.

9 Click any cell to deselect the table.

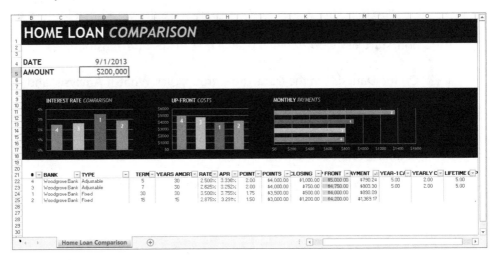

This is one of the simpler templates, but it's useful and instructive, just like all the templates that are available in Excel 2013. Before you start building a workbook for a specific task, you should take the time to look for an existing template that may perfectly suit your needs. If you enter a keyword or two into the *Search online templates* box on the New page, a vast and ever-growing catalog of cloud-based templates will be displayed. New ones are added constantly; all are updated if bugs, typos, or other issues arise, making this a preferred source for safe and useful tools.

 CLEAN UP Close the workbook without saving the file.

Performing what-if analyses

You do it every day. You probably have thoughts such as, "What if I get stuck in traffic with no gas in the tank?" or "What if I get a raise?" or "What if we downsize the house?" Excel can help you answer at least two of those questions, but for the next exercise, let's use the latter question.

In this exercise, you'll work with the workbook created in the previous chapter. It explores the costs within a range of acceptable prices when selling a home and purchasing a less expensive and less expansive home (values only, ignoring loan and equity issues).

 SET UP You need the RealEstateTransition_start.xlsx workbook located in the Chapter20 practice file folder to complete this exercise. Open the RealEstate-Transition_start.xlsx workbook, and save it as RealEstateTransition.xlsx.

1 On the **Data** tab, in the **Data Tools** group, click **What-If Analysis**, and then click **Goal Seek**.

2 With the cursor in the **Set Cell** box, click cell **H21**.

3 In the **To Value** box, enter 0 (zero).

4 Click the **By Changing Cell** box, and then click cell **B19**.

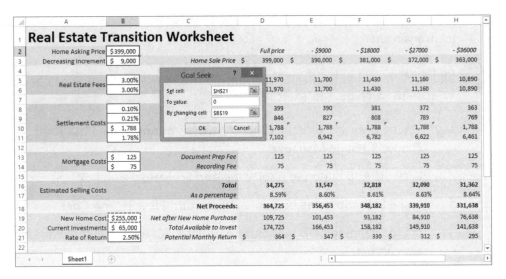

5   Click **OK** in the **Goal Seek** dialog box, and then click **OK** again to dismiss the **Goal Seek Status** dialog box.

Now when you examine the worksheet, the Goal Seek command has increased the cost of a new home until all of the money (both net proceeds from the existing home sale and current investments) is used up at the lowest acceptable sale price in column H (thus yielding a zero potential monthly return). This tells you that you can spend up to about $396,000 on a new home, if you don't mind spending some or all of your savings.

You could have used the good old trial-and-error method to do this, but by using the Goal Seek command, Excel allows you to reach a faster and more precise conclusion.

✖ CLEAN UP Save the RealEstateTransition.xlsx workbook, but keep it open for the next exercise.

Managing multiple what-if models

When you use the Goal Seek command, you can instantly view the results of one possible scenario, and then you can use the Undo command to revert to the original values on the worksheet. Usually, however, there is more than one possible scenario, and it would be helpful if you could keep track of them. Excel provides the Scenario Manager for just this purpose.

IMPORTANT

In this exercise, you'll save sets of variables in scenarios, naming them so you can display them again later.

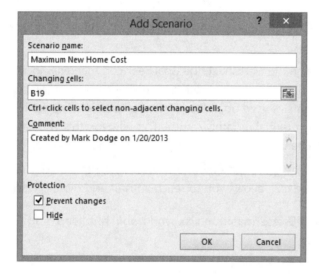 SET UP You need the RealEstateTransition.xlsx workbook you created in the previous exercise to complete this exercise.

1   On the **Data** tab, click the **What-If Analysis** button in the **Data Tools** group and choose **Scenario Manager**.

2   Click the **Add** button to display the **Add Scenario** dialog box.

3   In the **Scenario name** box, enter Maximum New Home Cost.

4   In the **Changing Cells** box, enter B19, if it is not already entered (the active cell appears here).

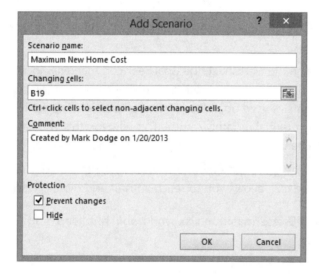

5   Click **OK**, and the **Scenario Values** dialog box appears, showing the current value in cell B19. Make sure it says **396,638** (and if not, change it).

6   Click **OK**, and the **Scenario Manager** dialog box reappears with your new scenario in the **Scenarios** list.

> **TIP** There are normally no scenarios listed in the Scenario Manager, but a scenario called *Normal* was created with the original value of $255,000 that appeared in cell B19. When creating multiple scenarios, you might want to first create one using the starting values.

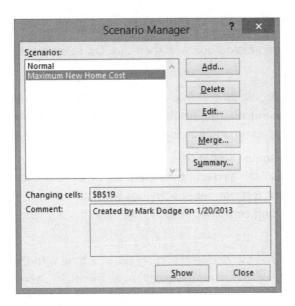

7   Close the **Scenario Manager** dialog box.

8   Click the **What-If Analysis** button and then click **Goal Seek**.

9   With the cursor in the **Set Cell** box, click cell **D21**.

10   In the **To Value** box, enter 500.

11   Click the **By Changing Cell** box, and then click cell **B19**.

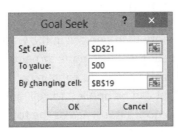

12   Click **OK** in the **Goal Seek** dialog box, and then click **OK** to dismiss the **Goal Seek Status** dialog box.

13   Click the **What-If Analysis** button, and then click **Scenario Manager**.

14   In the **Scenario Manager** dialog box, click **Add**.

15   In the **Scenario Name** box, enter Maximum monthly income.

16   Make sure that **B19** is specified as the **Changing Cell**.

17   Click **OK** in the **Add Scenario** dialog box, and then click **OK** to dismiss the **Scenario Values** dialog box.

18   With the **Scenario Manager** dialog box open, you can select each scenario on the list, click the **Show** button, and view the results on the worksheet. Otherwise, you can double-click the name of the scenario you want, which will dismiss the dialog box.

You can also build multi-variable scenarios, perform goal seeking, or just enter values you want to use in cells. You can also add a different set of scenarios for each new changing cell. Then you can test one set of scenarios with other sets of scenarios and save the most compelling combined results as yet another scenario with all the changing cells specified.

TIP Although you can only solve for one changing cell at a time with the Goal Seek command, you can specify up to 32 changing cells in a scenario. To seek goals using more than one variable, use the Solver—a sophisticated analysis tool that is beyond the scope of this book. Excellent Solver help and examples are available in the online Help system.

✖ CLEAN UP Save the RealEstateTransition.xlsx workbook.

Using the Quick Analysis tools

You may have noticed that every time you select more than one cell in the worksheet (as long as the cells are not empty), an icon appears near the lower-right corner of the selection. This is called the *Quick Analysis* button, and it offers a menu containing many of the commands and features available on the ribbon that can be applied to cell ranges. The Quick Analysis menu is like a mini-ribbon, with categories (tabs) across the top. Click a category to change the available command buttons, as illustrated in the following exercise.

In this exercise, you'll use the Quick Analysis tools to apply formatting and add totals to a selected range.

➜ SET UP You need the 2015Projections_start.xlsx workbook located in the Chapter20 practice file folder to complete this exercise. Open the 2015Projections_start.xlsx workbook, and save it as 2015Projections.xlsx.

1 Make sure that the **2015 Projections** worksheet tab is selected.

2 Click the small downward-pointing arrow in the **Name** box to the left of the formula bar, and select the name **projections** to select all the values in the table.

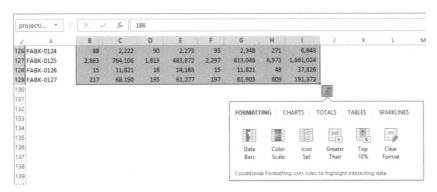

3 Scroll to the bottom of the selection and click the **Quick Analysis** button. (Point to each command icon on the menu to display an instant preview.)

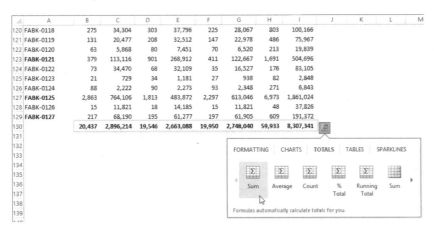

4 Click the **Totals** category, and then click the first **Sum** button to add a row of totals below the selected table. (The second **Sum** button adds totals on the right instead of at the bottom.)

	A	B	C	D	E	F	G	H	I	J	K	L	M
120	FABK-0118	275	34,304	303	37,796	225	28,067	803	100,166				
121	FABK-0119	131	20,477	208	32,512	147	22,978	486	75,967				
122	FABK-0120	63	5,868	80	7,451	70	6,520	213	19,839				
123	FABK-0121	379	113,116	901	268,912	411	122,667	1,691	504,696				
124	FABK-0122	73	34,470	68	32,109	35	16,527	176	83,105				
125	FABK-0123	21	729	34	1,181	27	938	82	2,848				
126	FABK-0124	88	2,222	90	2,273	93	2,348	271	6,843				
127	FABK-0125	2,863	764,106	1,813	483,872	2,297	613,046	6,973	1,861,024				
128	FABK-0126	15	11,821	18	14,185	15	11,821	48	37,826				
129	FABK-0127	217	68,190	195	61,277	197	61,905	609	191,372				
130		20,437	2,896,214	19,546	2,663,088	19,950	2,748,040	59,933	8,307,341				

20

5   Click the **Quick Analysis** button and then click the **Totals** category.

6   Click the **Running Total** button.

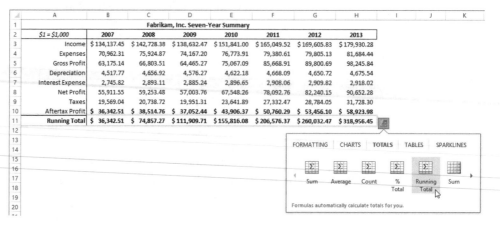

This time, because you selected the label in column A in the selection, Excel added the Running Total label in row 11. When you select an appropriate label, along with the data, Excel adds a new label for you.

An example of inappropriate labels would be the year numbers at the top of the table on the Seven-Year Summary tab in the 2015Projections.xlsx workbook; dates are numeric, so any formulas you apply using AutoSum or Quick Analysis will attempt to include them in calculations.

A running total simply combines the values in the selected cell(s) one by one, creating an incremental tally, from either left to right or top to bottom.

Take a few minutes to explore all the options on the Quick Analysis menus. More features will be explained later.

 CLEAN UP Save the 2015Projections.xlsx workbook.

Formatting conditionally

Sometimes astute analysis may consist of simply being aware when something in your worksheet reaches a limit or crosses a threshold. The conditional formatting features in Excel do that and a lot more, such as highlighting cells that contain specific text or proximate dates, and using icons or shading to give visual cues about cell contents. On the Quick Analysis menu, all of its formatting commands are actually conditional formats.

In this exercise, you'll use Conditional Formatting to highlight the important details on a worksheet.

SET UP You need the 2015Projections.xlsx workbook from the previous exercise to complete this exercise.

1   Make sure the **2015 Projections** worksheet tab is active.

2   Click the downward-pointing arrow in the **Name** box, to the left of the formula bar, and select the name **total2015sales** to select the values in column I.

3   Click the **Conditional Formatting** button on the **Home** tab, click **Top/Bottom Rules**, and click **Top 10%**.

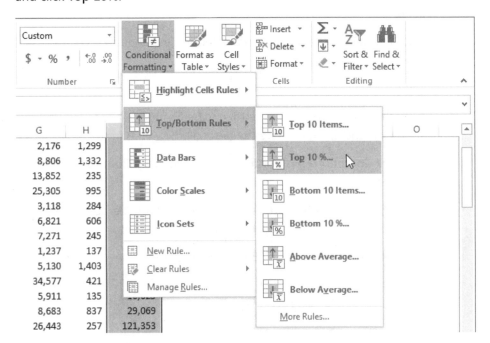

A dialog box appears that allows you to change the format and the percentage. (This does not happen when you use the equivalent command on the Quick Analysis menu. Instead, it uses the default settings.) With the dialog box open, you can choose options and view the results displayed on the worksheet before clicking OK.

	A	B	C	D	E	F	G	H	I	J	K	L	M	N
112	FABK-0110	85	15,973	86	16,161	92	17,289	263	49,423					
113	FABK-0111	117	1,659	100	1,418	121	1,716	338	4,793					
114	FABK-0112	80	11,242	52	7,308	113	15,880	245	34,430					
115	FABK-0113	113	1,066	142	1,339	186	1,754	441	4,159					
116	FABK-0114	26	245	61	575	46	434	133	1,254					
117	FABK-0115	81	381	39	183	47	221	167	785					
118	FABK-0116	84	11,673	111	15,425	135	18,760	330	45,857					
119	FABK-0117	43	8,081	37	6,953	27	5,074	107	20,107					
120	FABK-0118	275	34,304	303	37,796	225	28,067	803	100,166					
121	FABK-0119	131	20,477	208	32,512	147	22,978	486	75,967					
122	FABK-0120	63	5,868	80	7,451	70	6,520	213	19,839					
123	FABK-0121	379	113,116	901	268,912	411	122,667	1,691	504,696					
124	FABK-0122	73	34,470	68	32,109	35	16,527	176	83,105					
125	FABK-0123	21	729	34	1,181	27	938	82	2,848					
126	FABK-0124	88	2,222	90	2,273	93	2,348	271	6,843					
127	FABK-0125	2,863	764,106	1,813	483,872	2,297	613,046	6,973	1,861,024					
128	FABK-0126	15	11,821	18	14,185	15	11,821	48	37,826					
129	FABK-0127	217	68,190	195	61,277	197	61,905	609	191,372					

Top 10% [?] [x]

Format cells that rank in the TOP:

[10] % with [Light Red Fill with Dark Red Text ▾]

[OK] [Cancel]

4　In the **Top 10%** dialog box, enter or select the percentage that you want to change to **20%**.

5　Click **OK**, and all the products projected to be in the top 20 percent of sales in 2015 are highlighted.

6　Click the **Unit Sales** worksheet tab.

7　Click the downward-pointing arrow in the **Name** box to the left of the formula bar and select the name **unitsales** to select all the values in the table.

8　Click the **Conditional Formatting** button, click **Highlight Cells Rules**, and then click **Less Than**.

9　In the **Format Cells that are Less Than** box, enter 0 (zero); there should be no unit sales less than zero, so a negative entry must be a typo.

10　Click **OK**, and notice that cell **BY87** is highlighted.

	BT	BU	BV	BW	BX	BY	BZ	CA	CB	CC
85	99	95	91	101	79	96	108	82	105	102
86	93	84	62	96	83	94	73	62	63	85
87	86	76	92	72	75	-90	81	68	71	93
88	180	175	193	196	172	150	111	102	157	163
89	56	32	36	23	27	23	48	56	28	52
90	114	110	115	120	114	110	110	114	101	100

11   Select cell **BY87** and enter **90**, and notice that the highlight disappears.

Because you have applied the *less than zero* formatting parameter to this table, any time another negative value appears, the errant cell will be highlighted unless you remove the formatting. You can do so by using the Conditional Formatting button, Clear Rules command, and clicking either the Clear Rules From Selected Cells command, or the Clear Rules From Entire Sheet command.

Experiment with the other commands in the Conditional Formatting menu, but use these formats carefully; they may provide too much clutter to be helpful. The Data Bars command inserts a small one-bar chart into each cell that indicates the cell's value in relation to other selected cells. The Icon Sets offer graphic alternatives to bars, but you will probably need to widen some cells; for these; icons are actually inserted into cells, though all other conditional formats are more or less transparent. The Color Scales command tints each cell in a solid color according to its rank, and the Data Bars command puts varying sizes of bars of the same color into cells like individual columns in a horizontal column chart.

12   Click the **Seven-Year Financial Summary** tab.

13   Click the downward-pointing arrow in the **Name** box to the left of the formula bar and select the name **SummaryTotal** to select all the values in the table.

14   Click the **Conditional Formatting** button, click **Data Bars**, and position your mouse pointer to point to the **Orange Data Bar** command to preview the results on the worksheet. (Click the command if you want to apply the previewed formatting.)

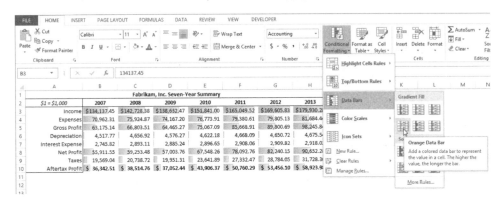

❌ CLEAN UP Save the 2015Projections.xlsx workbook.

Analyzing data from another source

Sometimes data you work with does not reside in a workbook, but in a corporate database, a document created by another program, on the web, or elsewhere. Click the Data tab and take a look at the commands in the Get External Data group. Including the commands on the From Other Sources menu, Excel provides ten different connection options, but in this next exercise, you'll focus on importing data from a text file. Even if your data is stored in a Microsoft Access database or another program, you can save it as a text-based document; this is called a *universal sharing format*.

In this exercise, you'll import data from a text file created by another program.

SET UP You need the FabrikamJan2013Sales.txt file located in the Chapter20 practice file folder to complete this exercise. Start by opening a new, blank workbook.

1   Click the **Data** tab on the ribbon.

2   In the **Get External Data** group, click the **From Text** button to display the **Import Text File** dialog box.

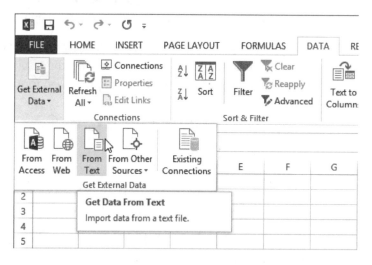

3   Select the **FabrikamJanSales2013.txt** file and click the **Import** button to display the **Text Import Wizard**.

4   Select the **My Data Has Headers** check box.

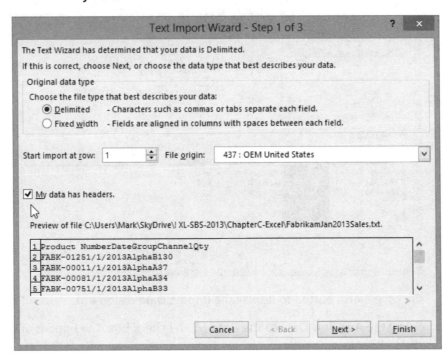

5   Make sure that the **Delimited** option is selected, and then click the **Next** button.

6   Make sure that **Tab** is the selected delimiter (a sample is available in the **Data Preview** area), and then click the **Next** button.

7   In the **Data Preview** area, click the **Date** column.

8   Click the **Column Data Format** option button labeled **Date** and make sure that **MDY** is selected.

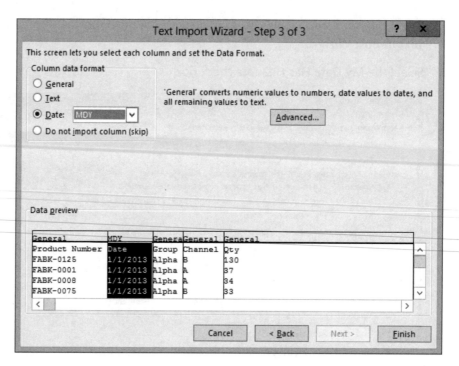

9   Click the **Finish** button to display the **Import Data** dialog box.

10   Select the **Add This Data to the Data Model** check box. The options at the top of the
     dialog box become active.

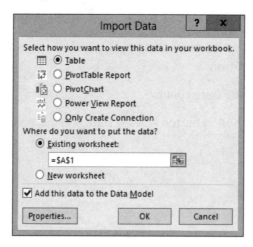

11 Click **OK** to import the data formatted as a table, which is the default selection in the **Import Data** dialog box.

	A	B	C	D	E	F	G
1	Product Number ▼	Date ▼	Group ▼	Channel ▼	Qty ▼		
2	FABK-0012	1/10/2013	Epsilon	B	100		
3	FABK-0074	1/8/2013	Alpha	E	42		
4	FABK-0115	1/22/2013	Beta	A	10		
5	FABK-0009	1/4/2013	Alpha	A	50		
6	FABK-0125	1/11/2013	Omega	A	130		
7	FABK-0115	1/1/2013	Beta	A	10		
8	FABK-0003	1/3/2013	Alpha	C	6		
9	FABK-0046	1/7/2013	Omega	E	110		
10	FABK-0088	1/3/2013	Omega	C	30		
11	FABK-0054	1/10/2013	Gamma	B	50		
12	FABK-0001	1/1/2013	Alpha	A	37		
13	FABK-0112	1/10/2013	Beta	E	20		
14	FABK-0027	1/8/2013	Kappa	E	48		
15	FABK-0012	1/24/2013	Epsilon	B	100		
16	FABK-0125	1/28/2013	Kappa	B	130		

20

12 Click the header for column **B** to select the entire column.

13 Click the **Number Format** drop-down menu on the **Home** tab of the ribbon, and click **Short Date**.

14 Click the **Save** button (located on the **Quick Access Toolbar**); because the data was imported into a new workbook, the **Save As** dialog box appears.

15 Name the file Fabrikam-Jan-2013-Sales.xlsx and click the **Save** button.

✖ CLEAN UP Keep the new workbook open for the next exercise.

The Excel Data Model

The Data Model is a new concept in Excel 2013. It allows you to analyze disparate data sources in the same workbook and allows Excel to perform relational database–style analysis using multiple tables. Although you use only one table in the Fabrikam January Sales example, activating the Data Model allows this data to be analyzed by using PivotTables and PivotCharts. You can add other tables to the Data Model, from different sources such as websites, SQL tables, Microsoft Access databases, other workbooks, and text files. Excel collects information about all the tables within a workbook that have been added to the Data Model, which allows you to build relationships among them, similar to relational database programs. You can search for more information about the Excel Data Model in the online Help system.

Filtering data with tables

Tables have evolved a lot over the years. In previous versions of Excel, tables were called lists. In the 1990s, Microsoft did a lot of usability research, and they were surprised to find that *list management* was the number one reason that people used Excel. In Excel 2013, tables not only offer prepackaged formats (like them or not), but they also contain sophisticated mechanisms you can use to sort, filter, and summarize data.

In this exercise, you'll turn a cell range into a table, and use Excel's table features to manipulate it.

1   Click anywhere in the table on **Sheet1**, then click the **Table Tools Design** tool tab that appears whenever a table is selected.

2   Click the **More** button on the **Table Styles** drop-down palette to display the full complement of available styles.

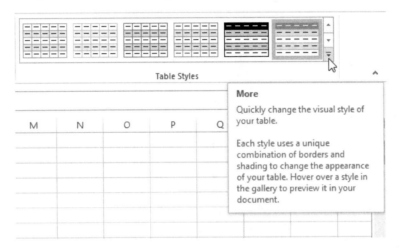

3   Select **Table Style Light 19** from the palette.

4   In the **Table Style Options** group, select the **Banded Columns** check box, and clear the **Banded Rows** check box.

20

5   Click the **Date** column's **Filter Button** (the arrow adjacent to the **Date** header) to display the **Filter** menu.

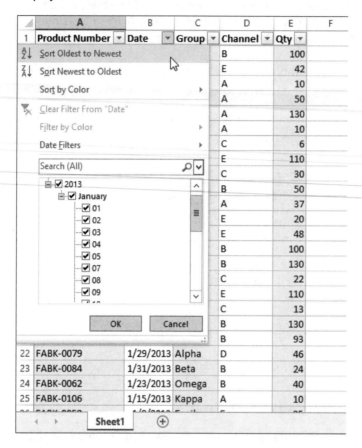

6   Click the **Sort Oldest to Newest** option in the **Date** column's **Filter** menu to put the dates in ascending order.

7   Click the **Channel** column's **Filter** button, and then select the **Select All** check box, which actually clears all the check boxes, because all of the channels were already selected.

8   Select the **A** check box, and then click **OK**.

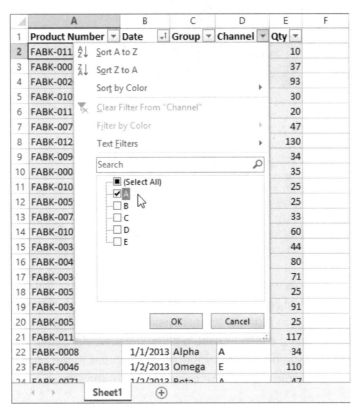

9   Click the **Group** column's **Filter** button, and then select the **Select All** check box to deselect all the groups.

10   Select the **Alpha** check box, and then click **OK**.

◢	A	B	C	D	E
1	**Product Number** ▾	**Date** ▾↓	**Group** ▾▼	**Channel** ▾▼	**Qty** ▾
3	FABK-0001	1/1/2013	Alpha	A	37
22	FABK-0008	1/1/2013	Alpha	A	34
42	FABK-0009	1/3/2013	Alpha	A	50
58	FABK-0009	1/4/2013	Alpha	A	50
97	FABK-0001	1/8/2013	Alpha	A	37
147	FABK-0001	1/11/2013	Alpha	A	93
160	FABK-0007	1/14/2013	Alpha	A	44
180	FABK-0008	1/15/2013	Alpha	A	34
182	FABK-0009	1/15/2013	Alpha	A	57
226	FABK-0007	1/18/2013	Alpha	A	44
249	FABK-0006	1/22/2013	Alpha	A	45
259	FABK-0007	1/22/2013	Alpha	A	44
306	FABK-0009	1/25/2013	Alpha	A	100
346	FABK-0009	1/29/2013	Alpha	A	50
374	FABK-0007	1/31/2013	Alpha	A	44
380	FABK-0006	1/31/2013	Alpha	A	46

The Excel table features make it easy to create quick reports like this one that shows all January 2013 sales of Fabrikam's Alpha product line through marketing channel A. The filters allowed you to instantly collapse nearly 400 rows of data into just 16 (look at the row numbers on the left). The table hides any rows eliminated by your filters. When you apply a column filter, a tiny funnel icon appears in the Filter button, so it's more evident to you which filters have been applied to the table.

TIP You may sometimes find the filter buttons annoying, especially when you want to print a table, but it's easy to hide them by clearing the check box adjacent to the Filter button in the Table Tools Design tool tab, in the Table Style Options group.

Because this table was created by importing data from a text file, Excel has established a connection to the text file that can be easily updated.

11 Click the arrow below the **Refresh** button on the **Table Tools Design** tool tab to display the **Refresh** menu.

12 Click the **Connection Properties** command to display a dialog box of the same name.

13 Select the **Refresh Data when Opening the File** check box.

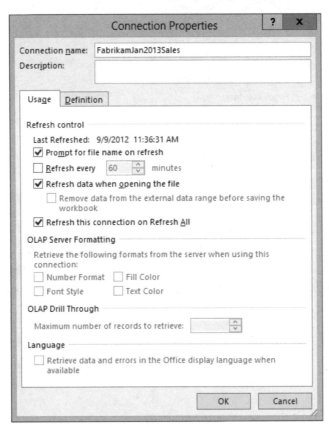

14 Click **OK**.

15 On the **Table Tools Design** tool tab, click the **Properties** button in the **External Table Data** group.

Note that there are two different Properties dialog boxes available for this table.

16 Click **Insert entire rows for new data, clear unused cells**.

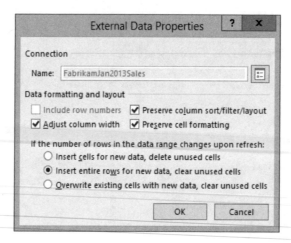

17   Click **OK**.

When the data in the text file changes, Excel automatically updates the workbook each time you open it. Because this is a database-style, row-oriented file, you will be inserting entire rows of new data to eliminate errors caused by the possible insertion of individual cells.

❌ CLEAN UP Save the Fabrikam-Jan-2013-Sales.xlsx workbook and keep it open for the next exercise.

Filter menu commands

You've already used the Filter buttons to sort a column and focus on a particular data set. The Filter menu offers the following additional features you should know about:

- **Sort** There are two **Sort** commands that may perform different functions, depending on the contents of the column. For example, for a column of text, the commands are **Sort A to Z** and **Sort Z to A**. If the column contains numbers, the commands are **Sort Smallest to Largest**, and **Sort Largest to Smallest**. If the column contains dates, the commands are **Sort Oldest to Newest** and **Sort Newest to Oldest**.

- **Clear Filter** This command removes the filter from the selected column.

- **Sort by Color/Filter by Color** This means exactly what it says, and is used when your data uses a hierarchical color scheme.

- **Date Filters** This command appears only when the column contains dates, and offers a list of options, such as **Today**, **Next Week**, and **Last Month**, as well as customizable options like **Before** and **Between** that display a dialog box that allows you to add date criteria.

- **Text Filters** This command appears only when the column contains text; it offers a list of options, such as **Begins With**, **Ends With**, **Contains**, and **Does Not Contain**.

- **Number Filters** This command appears only when the column contains numeric data, and offers a list of options such as **Greater Than**, **Between**, **Top 10**, and **Below Average**.

Adding data to tables

Adding data is actually easier with a range converted to an Excel table than it is with a regular cell table on a worksheet. One thing you can do in a table is use the Tab key to jump to the next cell in the table. When you press Tab to move to the last cell in a row, pressing Tab again jumps the selection to the first cell in the next row. But when you reach the last row of data in a table, the Tab key adds a row instead.

In this exercise, you'll insert a new row and a new column into an existing table.

 SET UP You need the Fabrikam-Jan-2013-Sales.xlsx file saved in the previous exercise to complete this exercise. In the Import Text File dialog box, click the Import button to update the data connection. (This happens because the Refresh Data When Opening File option was set in the Connection Properties dialog box.)

1   If your table still has filters applied from the previous exercise, clear them. To do so, click the **Filter** button in a filtered row (the button displays a funnel image when there is an active filter), and click the **Clear Filter** command.

2   Click the **Total Row** button in the **Table Tools Design** tool tab, in the **Table Style Options** group. This adds a row of totals to the bottom of the table and activates the new row so that it is visible on the screen. In this case, it adds only one total, to the **Qty** column, because this is the only column that contains numeric data. (The active cell must be somewhere within the table for the **Table Tools Design** tab to appear.)

3   Select cell **E387**, just above the new total.

4   Press the **Tab** key.

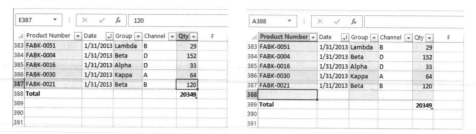

All you need to do is press the Tab key with the last cell in the table selected. Even when there is a totals row, Excel adds the new row above the total and adds any new values to the totals in the summarized columns. Also, adding a table row this way automatically propagates the table formatting and formulas (if any) to the new row.

5   Press the **Undo** button to remove the unneeded row.

6   Press **Ctrl+Home** to jump to the first cell in the worksheet.

7   Select cell **F1**, located to the right of the **Qty** column header.

8   Enter Note and press **Enter**, and notice that Excel automatically expands the table with a new formatted column, and a **Filter** button is added to the new heading.

9   Click the **AutoCorrect Options** button and notice that the menu that appears offers a command to undo the previous auto-expansion, or you can keep it from happening again by clicking the **Stop Automatically Expanding Tables** command. In addition, you can click the **Control AutoCorrect Options** command to open a dialog box that lets you choose whether you want to enable or disable these and other **AutoCorrect** options.

10   Press the **Esc** key to dismiss the **AutoCorrect** options menu.

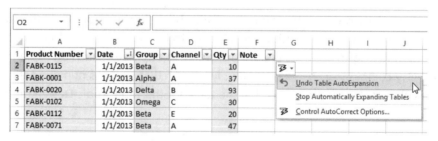

❌ CLEAN UP Save the Fabrikam-Jan-2013-Sales.xlsx workbook.

TIP Tables are great tools, but there are times when you may want to lose the strict table structure. Click the Convert To Range button in the Tools group on the Table Tools Design tool tab to remove the table architecture and return the table to plain cells, which still contain the formatting.

Sorting data

You explored one way to sort data in "Filtering data with tables" earlier in this chapter, but not all data will be in tables, and the sorting commands on the Filter menus only go so far. The Excel Sort and Filter commands offer a few more tricks you can use to get your data in order.

In this exercise, you'll use Excel's sorting tools to rearrange data on a worksheet.

 SET UP You need the JanSales2_start.xlsx workbook located in the Chapter20 practice file folder to complete this exercise. Open the JanSales2_start.xlsx workbook, and save it as JanSales2.xlsx.

1   In the **JanSales2.xlsx** workbook, select cell **B2** (the first date in the **Date** column).

2   Click the **Sort Z to A** button in the **Sort & Filter** group to sort the table by date (newest first).

3   Click the **Sort** button in the **Sort & Filter** group to display the **Sort** dialog box.

4   Clear the **My data has headers** check box, and notice what happens to the selected cells in the table (the headers are included in the sort range, which in this case would not be a good thing).

5   Select the **My data has headers** check box again.

6   In the **Sort by Area** (called a *level*), make sure that **Date** is selected in the **Column** drop-down list.

7   Make sure that the **Values** option is selected in the **Sort On** drop-down list.

8   In the **Order** drop-down list, select **Oldest to Newest**.

9   Click the **Add Level** button to add a **Then by** level after the **Sort by** level. (The **Sort** dialog box allows you to specify up to 64 levels of sorting criteria.)

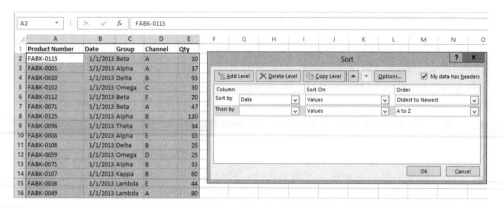

10   In the **Then by** level, click the **Column** drop-down list and select **Channel**.

11   Make sure that the default **Sort On** option is selected (**Values**).

12   In the **Order** drop-down list, make sure that **A to Z** is selected.

13   Click the **Options** button and note the possibilities here (just so you know).

14   Click **Cancel** to dismiss the **Sort Options** dialog box.

15   Click **OK**.

	A	B	C	D	E	F
1	**Product Number**	Date	Group	Channel	Qty	
2	FABK-0115	1/1/2013	Beta	A	10	
3	FABK-0001	1/1/2013	Alpha	A	37	
4	FABK-0071	1/1/2013	Beta	A	47	
5	FABK-0049	1/1/2013	Lambda	A	80	
6	FABK-0036	1/1/2013	Lambda	A	71	
7	FABK-0008	1/1/2013	Alpha	A	34	
8	FABK-0020	1/1/2013	Delta	B	93	
9	FABK-0125	1/1/2013	Alpha	B	130	
10	FABK-0108	1/1/2013	Delta	B	25	
11	FABK-0075	1/1/2013	Alpha	B	33	
12	FABK-0107	1/1/2013	Kappa	B	60	
13	FABK-0102	1/1/2013	Omega	C	30	
14	FABK-0055	1/1/2013	Gamma	C	25	
15	FABK-0059	1/1/2013	Omega	D	25	
16	FABK-0112	1/1/2013	Beta	E	20	

The result of this exercise gives you a list of sales made each day during January 2013, sorted by sales channel. If you click the Sort button again and change the *Then by* column option to Group, you get a similar result, sorted by product group.

⊗ CLEAN UP Save the JanSales2.xlsx workbook.

TIP If you get unexpected results, check the data in the cells adjacent to the apparent sorting error to check if there are any numbers formatted as text, or leading spaces in cells. If so, delete the leading spaces, or select the entire column and format it as text, because Excel will sort numbers first, followed by numbers formatted as text. If all the numbers are in the same format, Excel will sort them correctly.

Creating a custom sort list

Sometimes neither numerical sequences nor the alphabet provide the criteria you would like to use to sort data. Let's say, for example, that you want to sort your list by Product Group, but not in order of sales or names or dates, but by some other arbitrary criteria for which there are no standard ways to sort, such as strategic value.

In this exercise, you'll create your own sorting criteria.

→ SET UP You need the JanSales2.xlsx workbook created in the previous exercise to complete this exercise.

1   In the **JanSales2.xlsx** workbook, click the **Data** tab.

2   Click the **Sort** button in the **Sort & Filter** group on the **Data** tab, and notice that the sort criteria you used in the previous exercise is still there.

3   Click the **Delete Level** button twice to remove both criteria levels.

4   Click the **Add Level** button.

5   In the **Column** drop-down list, select **Group**.

6   In the **Sort On** drop-down list, make sure that **Values** is selected.

7   In the **Order** drop-down list, select **Custom List**.

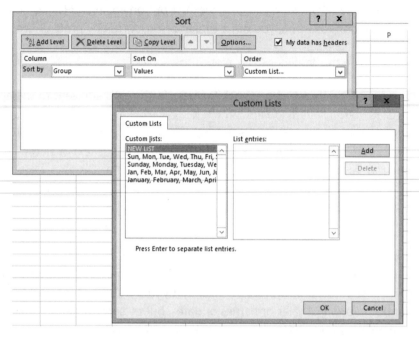

8   Make sure that **New List** is selected in the **Custom lists** box, and then click the **Add** button. (Clicking the **Add** button simply activates the **List Entries** box; a flashing cursor will appear.)

9   Enter Lambda and press **Enter**.

10   Enter Beta and press **Enter**.

11   Enter Alpha and press **Enter**.

12   Enter Gamma and press **Enter**.

13   Enter Omega and press **Enter**.

14   Enter Theta and press **Enter**.

15   Enter Epsilon and press **Enter**.

16 Enter Kappa, and then press the **Add** button to add your new list to the **Custom Lists** box.

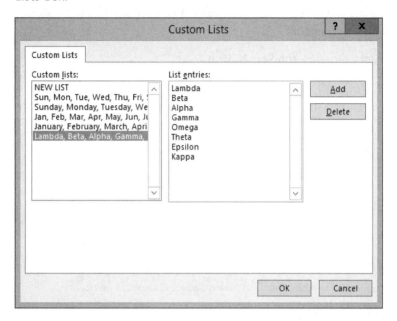

17 Click **OK** to dismiss the **Custom Lists** dialog box.

18 Click **OK** to dismiss the **Sort** dialog box and apply the sorting criteria to the sales table.

	A	B	C	D	E	F
1	**Product Number**	**Date**	**Group**	**Channel**	**Qty**	
2	FABK-0049	1/1/2013	Lambda	A	80	
3	FABK-0036	1/1/2013	Lambda	A	71	
4	FABK-0038	1/3/2013	Lambda	A	44	
5	FABK-0049	1/4/2013	Lambda	A	80	
6	FABK-0038	1/8/2013	Lambda	A	44	
7	FABK-0087	1/15/2013	Lambda	A	23	
8	FABK-0038	1/16/2013	Lambda	A	42	
9	FABK-0049	1/31/2013	Lambda	A	80	
10	FABK-0037	1/4/2013	Lambda	B	39	
11	FABK-0051	1/10/2013	Lambda	B	27	
12	FABK-0051	1/15/2013	Lambda	B	27	
13	FABK-0050	1/15/2013	Lambda	B	43	
14	FABK-0042	1/15/2013	Lambda	B	43	
15	FABK-0050	1/25/2013	Lambda	B	43	
16	FABK-0051	1/28/2013	Lambda	B	27	

You can create as many custom sorting lists as you like. Your custom lists are preserved with the workbook and will be available the next time you open it. In fact, for every custom sort list that you create, Excel automatically creates a second one for you, in reverse order.

19   On the **Data** tab, click the **Sort** button.

20   Click the arrow adjacent to the **Order** drop-down list, and notice that there are two custom lists there now; the second one is the reverse of the one you entered.

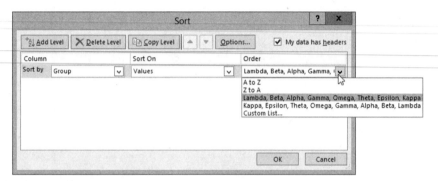

21   Click the **Cancel** button.

CLEAN UP Save the JanSales2.xlsx workbook.

Creating a PivotTable

PivotTables are powerful tools for summarizing and analyzing data that is stored in workbooks, or data collected from external sources. PivotTables do not contain data; they link to it. That disconnection from the source data allows you the freedom to rearrange PivotTable information without fear of corrupting the underlying values.

PivotTables work best on data with common relationships. For example, the Fabrikam sales data you worked with in the previous exercises comprises a lot of individual rows (records), but every record includes one of eight product groups, one of six sales channels, one of 31 dates, and one of 127 product numbers. So, by using a PivotTable, you can display the unit sales from each product group by sales channel, by date, or by product number. And, with a few clicks of the mouse, you can *pivot* your results using any other combination of these criterion.

New in Excel 2013 is the Recommended PivotTables feature, which starts with the PivotTable command and jumps ahead a step, saving you some time by making educated guesses about the kind of PivotTables you can build, based on the data you select. It offers several options in visual form, showing an example of the results before you commit.

In this exercise, you'll create a new PivotTable and manipulate it.

SET UP You need the FabrikamQ1SalesDetail_start.xlsx workbook located in the Chapter20 practice file folder to complete this exercise. Open the FabrikamQ1Sales-Detail_start.xlsx workbook, and save it as FabrikamQ1SalesDetail.xlsx.

1 In the **FabrikamQ1SalesDetail.xlsx** workbook, click the **Insert** tab.

2 Making sure that the active cell is within the table of data, click the **Recommended PivotTable** button in the **Tables** group on the **Insert** tab, which automatically selects your data and displays a dialog box of the same name. (If you were to click the **Blank PivotTable** button at the bottom of the dialog box, it would be the equivalent of clicking the **PivotTable** button on the **Insert** tab, which bypasses the recommendations.)

20

IMPORTANT

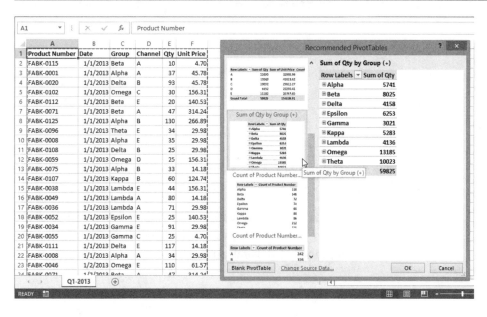

3   Scroll down the list of recommendations, click the **Sum of Qty by Group** option, and click **OK**, which inserts a PivotTable on a new worksheet and displays the **PivotTable Fields** pane.

4   Move the mouse pointer toward the top of the **PivotTable Fields** pane until the pointer turns into a four-headed arrow.

5   Drag the **PivotTable Fields** pane to the left, so that it "undocks" from the side of the window and becomes a floating pane.

6   Drag the floating pane all the way to the left side of the screen, until it docks on the left, just for fun. (Feel free to move about the window. Note that this works only when the Excel window is maximized.)

7　Select the **Channel** check box. Now **Channel** appears under **Rows** on the right side of the **PivotTable Fields** pane. This adds the data to the PivotTable, but it is buried in detail rows, as indicated by the tiny plus-sign icons adjacent to each **Product Group** name.

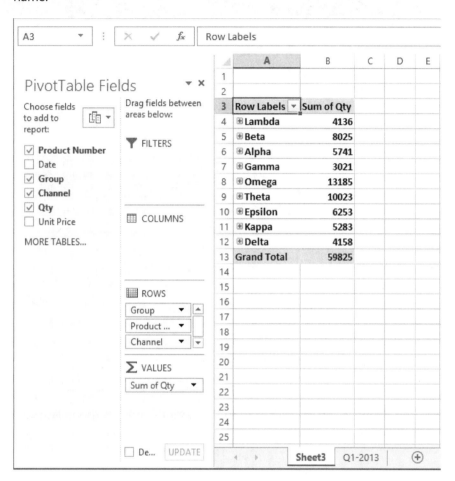

8　Under **Rows**, drag the **Channel** box up, and place it under **Columns**. The result is that each channel gets its own column, and the total quantities appear below it for each product group.

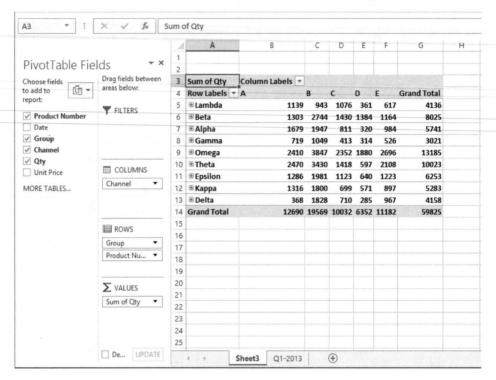

9   Click the plus-sign icon adjacent to the **Lambda** product group label to display the detail data.

Row Labels	A	B	C	D	E	Grand Total
⊟ Lambda	1139	943	1076	361	617	4136
FABK-0035				156	84	240
FABK-0036	152		73			225
FABK-0037		76			47	123
FABK-0038	217	105	47	51	128	548
FABK-0039	31	37	29			97
FABK-0040	50	167	391		102	710
FABK-0041	231	51	357	50	58	747
FABK-0042		89		51		140
FABK-0049	324	172	90			586
FABK-0050	47	86		53	97	283
FABK-0051	64	137	56		101	358
FABK-0087	23	23	33			79
⊞ Beta	1303	2744	1430	1384	1164	8025
⊞ Alpha	1679	1947	811	320	984	5741
⊞ Gamma	719	1049	413	314	526	3021
⊞ Omega	2410	3847	2352	1880	2696	13185
⊞ Theta	2470	3430	1418	597	2108	10023
⊞ Epsilon	1286	1981	1123	640	1223	6253
⊞ Kappa	1316	1800	699	571	897	5283
⊞ Delta	368	1828	710	285	967	4158

(Sum of Qty — Column Labels)

This PivotTable now shows the total unit sales for each product, by product group and by sales channel. PivotTables allow you to try different arrangements of rows and columns in the easiest way imaginable. It would be prohibitively difficult to do this manually, working with the actual raw data in cells. Plus, using the PivotTable insulates the original data for inadvertent harm.

10 Click the **Lambda** plus-sign icon again to collapse the detail rows.

11   In the **PivotTable Fields** pane, clear the **Product Number** check box. The plus-sign icons disappear, and the icons and detail rows are hidden for a cleaner presentation. The totals remain unchanged, except that they are no longer displayed with a bold font.

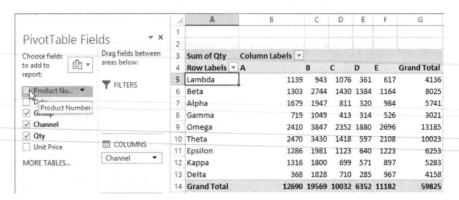

Row Labels	A	B	C	D	E	Grand Total
Lambda		1139	943	1076	361	617	4136
Beta		1303	2744	1430	1384	1164	8025
Alpha		1679	1947	811	320	984	5741
Gamma		719	1049	413	314	526	3021
Omega		2410	3847	2352	1880	2696	13185
Theta		2470	3430	1418	597	2108	10023
Epsilon		1286	1981	1123	640	1223	6253
Kappa		1316	1800	699	571	897	5283
Delta		368	1828	710	285	967	4158
Grand Total	12690	19569	10032	6352	11182	59825

12   On the right side of the **PivotTable Fields** pane, drag the **Channel** box down and put it under **Rows**, then drag the **Group** box up and put it under **Columns**; the result is that the table *pivots*.

13   On the left side of the **PivotTable Fields** pane, select the **Date** check box, and the table immediately expands to include every date in the quarter.

14   Select cell **A5**.

15   Click the **PivotTable Tools Analyze** tab.

16   Click the **Collapse Field** button in the **Active Field** group.

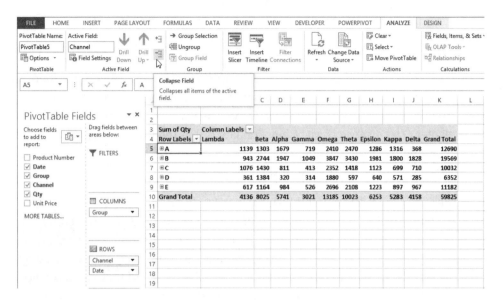

CLEAN UP Save the FabrikamQ1SalesDetail.xlsx workbook.

Clicking the Collapse Field button was a shortcut; you could have clicked each plus-sign icon individually. But consider this your formal introduction to the two PivotTable Tools tabs, Analyze and Design, brimming with buttons. The Design tab has controls similar to the table controls you learned about earlier in this chapter. Tools on the Analyze tab will be discussed in later chapters.

SEE ALSO For information about creating a PivotChart, a Slicer, or a Timeline, see Chapter 23, "Creating charts and graphics."

Pivot and Power features

PivotTables debuted as a feature in Microsoft Excel back in 1993. Since then, pivot functionality has matured and expanded into a suite of features, at the core of which is the Excel Data Model. (See the sidebar "The Excel Data Model," earlier in this chapter.) The essence of *pivot* functionality is that the PivotTable is separate from, but linked to the underlying data, which enhances the ability to instantly, and non-destructively, change the entire analysis.

The Data Model transparently adds the ability to address more than one table of data at a time (think of a cube consisting of stacked layers of tables). The combination of these concepts provides a foundation for expanded relational PivotTable functionality, and unleashes the PowerPivot and PowerView features, each of which leverages the Data Model to explore relationships among tables. Each of these features would take several chapters to explore; indeed, there is an entire book just on PowerPivot, which takes PivotTable functionality way beyond the scope of this book. You are encouraged to explore the excellent Excel Help topics available on PowerPivot and PowerView, which range from philosophical overviews to detailed tutorials.

As of this writing, the PowerPivot and PowerView features are included only with specific configurations of Office Professional 2013. The PowerPivot feature, which was available in all versions of Excel 2010, is available only in Office Professional Plus 2013, Microsoft SharePoint 2013 Enterprise Edition, SharePoint Online 2013 Plan 2, and the E3 or E4 editions of Microsoft Office 365. The PowerView feature, new in Excel 2013, is included with the same versions as PowerPivot. Happily, the Excel Data Model is supported in all configurations of Excel 2013. The variety of available configurations may change, however, so stay tuned.

Key points

- You can use the Goal Seek command to arrive at individual scenario values, and you can manage multiple goals and values by using the Scenario Manager.

- Use the Quick Analysis menu to perform many relevant operations on a selected cell range without using the ribbon.

- You can use conditional formatting to highlight important values in a worksheet when they meet or exceed predetermined thresholds.

- You can easily import data from remote sources by using the Get External Data commands on the Data tab.

- The Excel table format is a sophisticated mechanism you can use to sort, filter, and summarize data.

- You can sort data by using up to 64 criteria, including custom sort lists that you can create yourself.

- PivotTables allow you to quickly change your perspective and directly manipulate relationships among data sets by dragging.

20

Chapter at a glance

Format

Format with styles,
page 544

Create

Create custom themes,
page 548

Work

Work with custom number formats,
page 553

Set

Set view options,
page 576

Formatting worksheets 21

IN THIS CHAPTER, YOU WILL LEARN HOW TO

- Apply number formatting.

- Format with styles.

- Create custom themes.

- Create custom number and date formats.

- Protect worksheets.

- Open extra windows in the same workbook.

Most of you have used formatting controls, buttons, and commands, so you're most likely familiar with fonts and styles. In this chapter, you'll learn how to format numbers and dates in Microsoft Excel, how to use styles, and how to create custom themes. In addition, you'll open extra windows in your workbook and use worksheet protection.

It's been mentioned before, but it bears repeating: formatting does not change the underlying values in cells, even though it may appear to do so. So feel free to experiment. Ctrl+Z (Undo) is your friend.

PRACTICE FILES To complete the exercises in this chapter, you need the practice files contained in the Chapter21 practice file folder. For more information, see "Download the practice files" in this book's Introduction.

Applying number formatting

Formatting is the easiest way to turn a group of numbers into something resembling information, and it really doesn't take much work to get results.

In this exercise, you'll work with a worksheet that is devoid of formatting, which means that everything is in the *General* format. Though you may have viewed similar worksheets before, this one is much harder to decipher without formatting.

	A	B	C	D	E	F	G	H
1	Fabrikam, Inc. Seven-Year Summary							$1 = $1,000
2								
3		2007	2008	2009	2010	2011	2012	2013
4	Income	134137.45	142728.38	138632.4724	151840.9952	165049.518	169605.8256	179930.2767
5	Expenses	70962.31	75924.87	74167.2032	76773.9078	79380.6124	79805.1313	81684.44067
6	Gross Profit	63175.14	66803.51	64465.2692	75067.0874	85668.9056	89800.6943	98245.836
7	Depreciation	4517.77	4656.92	4576.2732	4622.1812	4668.0892	4650.7198	4675.535333
8	Interest Expense	2745.82	2893.11	2885.2396	2896.6476	2908.0556	2909.8244	2918.019333
9	Net Profit	55911.55	59253.48	57003.7564	67548.2586	78092.7608	82240.1501	90652.28133
10	Taxes	19569.0425	20738.718	19951.31474	23641.89051	27332.46628	28784.05254	31728.29847
11	Aftertax Profit	36342.5075	38514.762	37052.44166	43906.36809	50760.29452	53456.09757	58923.98287
12								
13								

➡ SET UP You need the FabrikamSummary_start.xlsx workbook located in the Chapter21 practice file folder to complete this exercise. Open the FabrikamSummary_start.xlsx workbook, and save it as FabrikamSummary.xlsx. Then follow the steps.

1   In the **FabrikamSummary.xlsx** workbook, select all the cells containing numbers (except the dates)—cells **B4** to **H11**.

2   Click the **Comma Style** button, located in the **Number** group, on the **Home** tab. All the decimals in the selected cells are rounded to the nearest hundredth.

3   Click the **Accounting Number Format** button, also in the **Number** group, on the **Home** tab, which adds dollar signs to the format.

4   Click the tiny downward-pointing arrow adjacent to the **Accounting Number Format** button to display a menu of the same name.

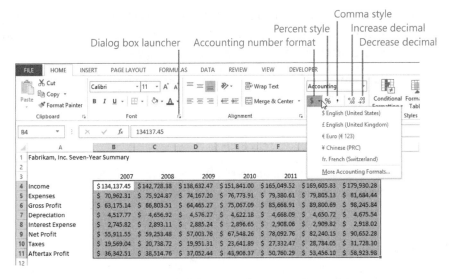

Comma style
Percent style   Increase decimal
Dialog box launcher   Accounting number format   Decrease decimal

5   Click **fr. French (Switzerland)**.

Note that changing the currency symbol does not change the values of the numbers (as with all formatting), but notice that the values in row 4 now display a series of pound signs (########), indicating that the contents of those cells are too wide to display. This is because the format adds a space and *fr.* to the right of each number, which takes up more space in a cell than any of the other currency symbols.

6   Click the **Accounting Number Format** button and then click **$ English (United States)**.

7   Select cells **B5:H10** (all the numbers except those for **Income** and **Aftertax Profit**). Standard accounting style dictates that dollar signs should only appear in the first and last rows of a table. You don't necessarily need to follow that rule, but it does make the table a lot easier to read.

8   Click the **Comma Style** button (which removes dollar signs from the selected cells).

9   Select all the cells containing numbers (not dates): **B4:H11**.

10   In the **Number** group, on the **Home** tab, click the **Decrease Decimal** button *twice*. In a summary worksheet like this, where large sums of money are being reported, pennies are a distraction and don't need to be displayed.

11   Click the **Center** button, in the **Alignment** group, on the **Home** tab, and notice that nothing happens; the numbers remain right-aligned. The alignment properties of number formatting override text alignment formatting.

12   Select the year headings: cells **B3:H3**.

13   Click the tiny dialog box launcher in the lower-right corner of the **Number** group, on the **Home** tab, to display the **Format Cells** dialog box.

TIP You can also press Ctrl+1 to open the frequently used Format Cells dialog box.

14   In the **Category** list, on the **Number** page, click **Number**.

15   In the **Decimal places** box, enter or select 0.

16   In the **Negative numbers** box, click the third option, **(1234)**.

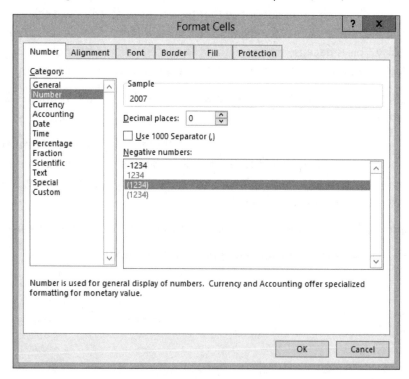

17   Click **OK**.

18 Press **Ctrl+Z** to undo your changes..

19 Press **Ctrl+Y** to redo your changes. Now the date headers line up with the columns.

> **TIP** If you press Ctrl+Z (Undo) repeatedly, Excel steps back through the last 100 actions.

	A	B	C	D	E	F	G	H
1	Fabrikam, Inc. Seven-Year Summary							$1 = $1,000
2								
3		2007	2008	2009	2010	2011	2012	2013
4	Income	$ 134,137	$ 142,728	$ 138,632	$ 151,841	$ 165,050	$ 169,606	$ 179,930
5	Expenses	70,962	75,925	74,167	76,774	79,381	79,805	81,684
6	Gross Profit	63,175	66,804	64,465	75,067	85,669	89,801	98,246
7	Depreciation	4,518	4,657	4,576	4,622	4,668	4,651	4,676
8	Interest Expense	2,746	2,893	2,885	2,897	2,908	2,910	2,918
9	Net Profit	55,912	59,253	57,004	67,548	78,093	82,240	90,652
10	Taxes	19,569	20,739	19,951	23,642	27,332	28,784	31,728
11	Aftertax Profit	$ 36,343	$ 38,515	$ 37,052	$ 43,906	$ 50,760	$ 53,456	$ 58,924

✕ CLEAN UP Save the FabrikamSummary.xlsx workbook, but keep it open for the next exercise.

Accounting formats and the phantom parentheses

21

After step 10 in the previous exercise, the date headers no longer lined up with the columns. So what happened? The rows with dollar signs were formatted by using the Accounting Format button. The Comma Style button was used on the middle rows, but it actually applied an accounting format without currency symbols. Accounting formats conform to standard accounting practices, which include the addition of parentheses around negative numbers.

To make positive and negative numbers line up in a column, Excel adds a blank space after positive numbers that is exactly as wide as one parenthesis. The accounting formats force comma separators for thousands, millions, and so on, which are not welcome in dates (such as the year headers in row 3 from the previous exercise). Instead, a number format was selected, because it uses parentheses for negatives, but allows the option of eliminating the comma separators.

Yes, it would have been much easier to use text headings, but less instructive. You can create your own custom formats by using special codes, and you can create different display options for positives, negatives, zero values, and text. We'll describe this in more detail later in this chapter, in the section titled "Working with custom number formats."

Formatting with styles

Styles are not always useful in sheets full of numbers, but they can come in handy for more presentation-oriented uses, and of course, if you like the design. Styles can be created by using the regular formatting tools, so if you don't like something about a style, you can modify it and save it for future reference. Because the numbers were formatted in the previous exercise, let's continue formatting the sheet.

In this exercise, you'll apply formatting to the FabrikamSummary worksheet and save it as a style that can be used elsewhere.

SET UP You need the FabrikamSummary.xlsx workbook you saved at the end of the previous exercise to complete this exercise. Open the FabrikamSummary.xlsx workbook (if it is not already open), and follow the steps.

1 Select cells **A1:I12** (one row deeper and one column wider than the table).

2 On the **Home** tab, click the **Cell Styles** button to display the **Styles** gallery.

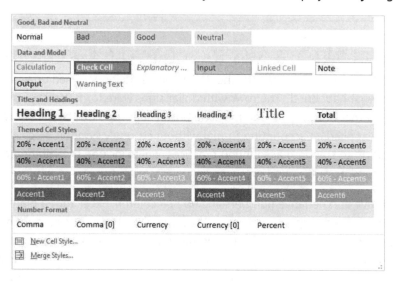

3   Click **20% - Accent 1**.

4   Select all the numbers below the year headings (cells **B4:H11**).

5   Click the **Cell Styles** button and then click **20% - Accent 6**.

6   Select cell **A1**.

7   Click the **Cell Styles** button and then click **Title**.

8   Select all the numbers in the **Gross Profit** row (cells **B6:H6**).

9   Hold down the **Ctrl** key and select all the numbers in the **Net Profit** row (cells **B9:H9**), adding them to the selection.

⊿	A	B	C	D	E	F	G	H
1	Fabrikam, Inc. Seven-Year Summary							$1 = $1,000
2								
3		2007	2008	2009	2010	2011	2012	2013
4	Income	$ 134,137	$ 142,728	$ 138,632	$ 151,841	$ 165,050	$ 169,606	$ 179,930
5	Expenses	70,962	75,925	74,167	76,774	79,381	79,805	81,684
6	Gross Profit	63,175	66,804	64,465	75,067	85,669	89,801	98,246
7	Depreciation	4,518	4,657	4,576	4,622	4,668	4,651	4,676
8	Interest Expense	2,746	2,893	2,885	2,897	2,908	2,910	2,918
9	Net Profit	55,912	59,253	57,004	67,548	78,093	82,240	90,652
10	Taxes	19,569	20,739	19,951	23,642	27,332	28,784	31,728
11	Aftertax Profit	$ 36,343	$ 38,515	$ 37,052	$ 43,906	$ 50,760	$ 53,456	$ 58,924
12								

21

10   Click the **Cell Styles** button and then click **Heading 3**.

11   Select all the numbers in the **Aftertax Profit** row (cells **B11:H11**).

12   Click the **Cell Styles** button and then click **Total**.

13   Select the year headers (cells **B3:H3**).

14   Click the **Cell Styles** button and then click **Heading 3**.

15   Select all the labels (cells **A4:A11**).

16   Click the **Cell Styles** button and then click **Heading 4**.

17   Select the blank cells between the table and the headings (cells **A2:H2**).

18   On the **Home** tab, in the **Font** group, click the arrow adjacent to the **Fill Color** button and click a slightly darker shade of blue.

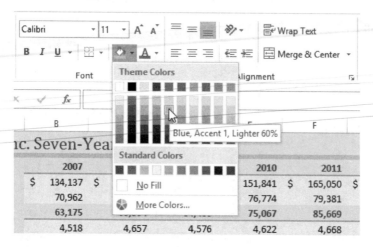

19   Click cell **I2**.

20   On the **Home** tab, in the **Cells** group, click the **Format** button, and then click **Row Height**.

21   Enter **5** and press **Enter**.

22   Click the **Format** button, and then click **Column Width**.

23   Enter **3** and press **Enter**.

24   Click anywhere outside the table and look at the results..

	A	B	C	D	E	F	G	H	I
1	Fabrikam, Inc. Seven-Year Summary							$1 = $1,000	
3		2007	2008	2009	2010	2011	2012	2013	
4	Income	$ 134,137	$ 142,728	$ 138,632	$ 151,841	$ 165,050	$ 169,606	$ 179,930	
5	Expenses	70,962	75,925	74,167	76,774	79,381	79,805	81,684	
6	Gross Profit	63,175	66,804	64,465	75,067	85,669	89,801	98,246	
7	Depreciation	4,518	4,657	4,576	4,622	4,668	4,651	4,676	
8	Interest Expense	2,746	2,893	2,885	2,897	2,908	2,910	2,918	
9	Net Profit	55,912	59,253	57,004	67,548	78,093	82,240	90,652	
10	Taxes	19,569	20,739	19,951	23,642	27,332	28,784	31,728	
11	Aftertax Profit	$ 36,343	$ 38,515	$ 37,052	$ 43,906	$ 50,760	$ 53,456	$ 58,924	
12									

Perhaps it's not the most beautiful worksheet you've ever seen, but it's certainly easy to read. You can enhance the appearance of the table by modifying fonts, colors, borders, fills, and number formats any way you like. Then you can save the new formats for easy retrieval directly from the Cell Styles menu. Try it.

25 Click cell **A2**.

26 Click the **Cell Styles** button, and then click the **New Cell Style** command at the bottom of the gallery.

27 In the **Style name** box, enter AccentColor and press **Enter**.

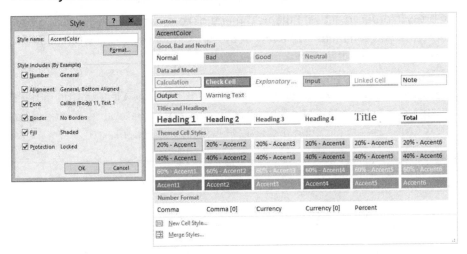

Now when you click the Cell Styles button, AccentColor appears at the top of the gallery.

Unfortunately, custom formats travel with the workbook and are not even available to other workbooks that might be open at the same time. However, you can use the Merge Styles command located in the lower-left corner of the Cell Styles gallery to propagate custom styles from one open workbook to another. You can also save collections of colors, fonts, and effects as a theme, which we'll explore next.

❌ CLEAN UP Save the FabrikamSummary.xlsx workbook.

Keyboard access to menus and commands

Pressing the Alt key activates keyboard access to the menus and commands in Microsoft Office applications, and this functionality remains active until you either complete a command or press the Alt key again. The feature turns on and off or toggles an action with each press of the Alt key; keep pressing and watch the ribbon. Letter labels appear adjacent to each available command whenever the feature is activated. The first letter you press activates a tab (menu). For example, when you press Alt, and then press H, it activates the Home tab and displays the letters you need to press in order to activate the next menu or command. If you like using keyboard shortcuts, you can memorize a few of the key sequences. Don't worry if you forget a letter—just press Alt and look at the ribbon.

TIP It's easy to fix a bad formatting experiment. Click the Clear button in the Editing group on the Home tab, and then click Clear Formats. Here's the keyboard equivalent: press Ctrl+A (select all), then press Alt, H, E, F (in succession).

Creating custom themes

When you apply a theme, you change the appearance of everything in the workbook, regardless of what is currently selected. Themes are made up of colors, fonts, and effects. They do not apply number, alignment, or protection formats. Themes are not workbook dependent. When you save a custom theme, it is available to use with other workbooks, and it's also available for use in other Office applications.

In this exercise, you'll apply a theme, then modify it, and then save it as a new theme.

 SET UP You need the FabrikamSummaryTheme_start.xlsx workbook located in the Chapter21 practice file folder to complete this exercise. Open the FabrikamSummaryTheme_start.xlsx workbook, and save it as FabrikamSummaryTheme.xlsx.

Fabrikam, Inc. Seven-Year Summary							$1 = $1,000
	2007	2008	2009	2010	2011	2012	2013
Income	$ 134,137	$ 142,728	$ 138,632	$ 151,841	$ 165,050	$ 169,606	$ 179,930
Expenses	70,962	75,925	74,167	76,774	79,381	79,805	81,684
Gross Profit	63,175	66,804	64,465	75,067	85,669	89,801	98,246
Depreciation	4,518	4,657	4,576	4,622	4,668	4,651	4,676
Interest Expense	2,746	2,893	2,885	2,897	2,908	2,910	2,918
Net Profit	55,912	59,253	57,004	67,548	78,093	82,240	90,652
Taxes	19,569	20,739	19,951	23,642	27,332	28,784	31,728
Aftertax Profit	$ 36,343	$ 38,515	$ 37,052	$ 43,906	$ 50,760	$ 53,456	$ 58,924

1   In the **FabrikamSummaryTheme.xlsx** workbook, click the **Page Layout** tab and then click the **Themes** button.

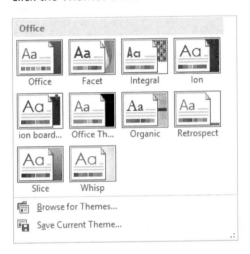

2   Point to a theme in the gallery to display a preview on the worksheet. Because this table was formatted by using cell styles, all the fonts and colors used in the table change according to the selected theme (along with effects, if any graphic objects were present).

3   Click the **Integral** theme.

Fabrikam, Inc. Seven-Year Summary							$1 = $1,000
	2007	2008	2009	2010	2011	2012	2013
Income	$ 134,137	$ 142,728	$ 138,632	$ 151,841	$ 165,050	$ 169,606	$ 179,930
Expenses	70,962	75,925	74,167	76,774	79,381	79,805	81,684
Gross Profit	63,175	66,804	64,465	75,067	85,669	89,801	98,246
Depreciation	4,518	4,657	4,576	4,622	4,668	4,651	4,676
Interest Expense	2,746	2,893	2,885	2,897	2,908	2,910	2,918
Net Profit	55,912	59,253	57,004	67,548	78,093	82,240	90,652
Taxes	19,569	20,739	19,951	23,642	27,332	28,784	31,728
Aftertax Profit	$ 36,343	$ 38,515	$ 37,052	$ 43,906	$ 50,760	$ 53,456	$ 58,924

21

4   On the **Page Layout** tab, in the **Themes** group, click the **Colors** button. (Point to various color sets to preview their effects.)

5   Click the **Blue Green** color set.

6   In the **Themes** group, click the **Fonts** button. (Point to various font sets to preview their effects.)

7   Scroll down the list and click the **Arial Black** font set (or your favorite, if **Arial Black** is not available on your system).

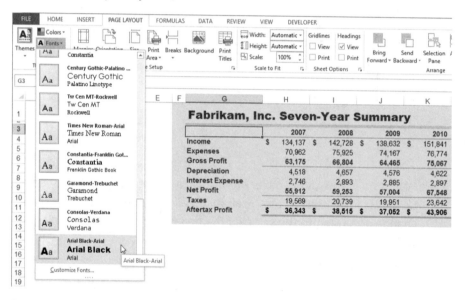

8   In the **Themes** group, on the **Page Layout** tab, click the **Themes** button and then click **Save Current Theme** at the bottom of the gallery. You'll notice that the default folder is the **Microsoft\Templates\Document Themes** folder, a global settings folder that is available to other Office applications.

9   Enter Fabrikam1 in the **File name** box.

10 Click **Save**.

11   Click the **Themes** button again, and the **Fabrikam1** theme appears at the top of the gallery, beneath the **Custom** heading.

You can create as many themes as you want, and you can add themes from other disk or network locations by using the Browse For Themes command located in the lower-left corner of the Themes gallery. If you later decide you don't want to keep it, it's easy to delete a custom theme.

12   Click the **Themes** button.

13   In the **Themes** gallery, right-click the **Fabrikam1** theme to display a shortcut menu.

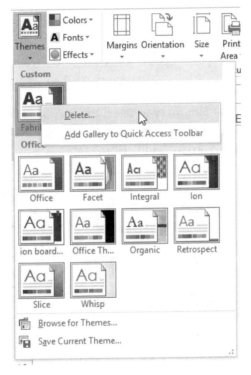

14   If you want to remove a custom theme, click **Delete** to remove it from both the **Themes** gallery and the **Document Themes** folder. But make sure this theme isn't in use in other workbooks or other Office documents.

15   Press the **Esc** key.

✖ CLEAN UP Save the FabrikamSummaryTheme.xlsx workbook, but keep it open for the next exercise.

Formatting in cells

This is a little-used feature that went largely unnoticed when it appeared in a previous version of Excel. Prior to that version, it was possible to apply formatting only to the entire contents of a cell, but today, you can format individual characters within a cell. This is a useful feature when you are organizing workbooks and trying to fit into the cell structure with linear content like headings and paragraphs of text.

In this exercise, you'll apply formatting to individual characters in a cell.

→ **SET UP** You need the FabrikamSummaryTheme.xlsx workbook you saved at the end of the previous exercise to complete this exercise. Open the FabrikamSummaryTheme.xlsx workbook (if it is not already open), and follow the steps.

1   Double-click cell **G1**. A flashing text cursor appears in the cell.

2   Drag through the words **Seven Year Summary** to select them. A small floating toolbar called the Mini Toolbar appears. You can use this toolbar to edit the selected text (or you can use the tools in the **Font** group, on the **Home** tab).

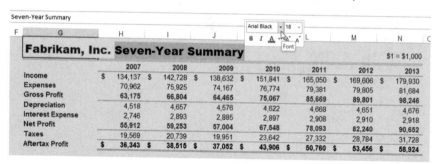

3   Select **Arial** from the **Font** list.

4   Reduce the font size to **11**.

5   Click the **Italic** button.

6   Change the font color to your favorite theme color (we chose **Aqua**).

7   Click anywhere outside the table to view the changes.

Fabrikam, Inc. *Seven-Year Summary*

	2007	2008
Income	$ 134,137	$ 142,728
Expenses	70,962	75,925
Gross Profit	63,175	66,804

❌ CLEAN UP Save the FabrikamSummaryTheme.xlsx workbook.

Individuals who have used Excel for a long time (before in-cell formatting was possible) might attempt to put *Fabrikam, Inc.* and *Seven-Year Summary* into two separate cells and then apply formats to each cell individually. That process works, too, but the cells won't line up correctly. The result will look something like the text in the following graphic.

Fabrikam, Inc.   *Seven-Year Summary*

	2007	2008	2009
Income	$ 134,137	$ 142,728	$ 138,632
Expenses	70,962	75,925	74,167
Gross Profit	63,175	66,804	64,465

Working with custom number formats

Custom number formats are like programming code; very easy programming code. Excel has its own number-formatting language. Every built-in number format can be expressed by using code, and thus can be easily modified for your own purposes.

In this exercise, you'll work with some of these formatting codes.

➡ SET UP You don't need any practice files to complete this exercise. Open a blank workbook and follow the steps.

1   Select cells **A1:A4**.

2   Click the **Accounting Number Format** button (**$**) on the **Home** tab.

3   Press **Ctrl+1** to display the **Format Cells** dialog box (or click the dialog box launcher in the **Number** group on the **Home** tab).

4   Click the **Number** tab, if it is not already active.

5   Click the **Custom** category.

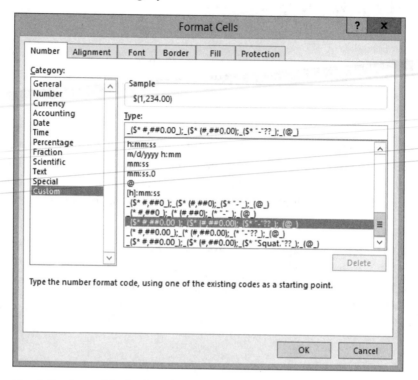

The following table further describes the code behind the format applied by using the Accounting Number Format button. You can view the code behind any format in the Format Cells dialog box, in the Category list, by first clicking the category and then selecting the format you want to use. Then click the Custom category. The code for the currently selected format is displayed in the Type box, and it is editable. You cannot overwrite a built-in code, so if you edit a code and click OK, a new code is added to the Type list and is available the next time you open the Format Cells dialog box.

We created a modified version of the Accounting Number Format code, as shown in the following table. Format codes have four components separated by semicolons:

($* #,##0.00_);_($* (#,##0.00);_($* "-"??_);_(@_)			
Values	Positive	Negative	Zero	Text
Code	_($* #,##0.00_)	_($* (#,##0.00)	_($* "-"??_)	_(@_)
Entered	1234	–1234	0	Hello!
Displayed	$ 1,234.00	$ (1,234.00)	$ -	Hello!

6   Click **OK** to exit the dialog box.

7   Click cell **A1**. Enter 1234 and press **Enter**.

8   In cell **A2**, enter -1234 and press **Enter**.

9   In Cell **A3**, enter 0 and press **Enter**.

10 In cell **A4**, enter Hello! and press **Enter**.

	A	B
1	$ 1,234.00	
2	$(1,234.00)	
3	$ -	
4	Hello!	
5		

11 Select cells **A1:A4**.

12 Press **Ctrl+1** to display the **Format Cells** dialog box (or click the dialog box launcher on the **Home** tab, in the **Number** group).

13 Click the **Custom** category.

14 In the **Type** box, replace the dash (–) in the third section of the format code with the word Zero. Be careful not to delete the quotation marks.

15 Click **OK**.

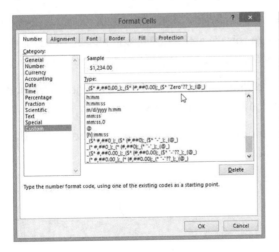

If you were wondering why they went to the trouble of specifying codes for the text section of the Accounting Number format, because text would display anyway, you'll notice that *Hello!* lines up perfectly with the dollar signs, which would not be the case without the special code. Details matter.

TIP You can create a formatting code that explicitly excludes one or more of the four value types from being displayed. For example, simply delete everything after the third semicolon (but not the semicolon itself) in the Accounting Number Format code to hide all text entries. The code 0.00;;; displays only positive numbers and hides everything else. And the handy ;;;; (four semicolons) code hides everything. You might use this trick to hide a formula on the worksheet; the result of which you need to use elsewhere, but don't need to display.

Following are the descriptions of the formatting codes that were used in the table shown previously:

- **Underscore (_)** Adds an invisible space that is exactly the same width as the character immediately following it. Each section in the previous code begins with an underscore and an opening parenthesis. (This adds a parenthesis-sized space before anything else in the cell, for visual balance. In all but the negative values section, there is a matching underscore at the end of the code section. This adds a balancing blank space on the right side of the cell. Negative values are, of course, surrounded by fully visible parentheses. Adding these spaces allows positive and negative numbers to be correctly aligned in a column.

- **Asterisk (*)** The character immediately following is to be repeated sufficiently to fill the column width. So, in this case, the dollar sign always stays on the left side of the cell, with as many spaces added between it and the number as necessary.

- **Zero (0)** This is a required digit placeholder. If there are no other digits to display in that position, Excel will always display zeros.

- **Pound sign (#)** This is an optional digit placeholder; if there is no digit in that position, it remains blank.

- **Question mark (?)** This is a required spaceholder. Even if there are no other digits to display in that position, Excel will always add a space. It is employed in the previous code to add two spaces after the dash, corresponding to two decimal places. This ensures that dashes (indicating zero values) will always line up with decimal points in a column of otherwise-nonzero numbers.

- **Quotation marks (" ")** These indicate a text component. In the code created previously, a dash is enclosed in quotation marks in the zero values position. In the accounting formats, only a dash is displayed if an entry equals zero.

- **At symbol (@)** This is a text placeholder, similar to the # that is a number placeholder. If there is text in the cell, it is displayed at this position.

- **Comma (,)** Otherwise known as a comma separator, this tells Excel to add commas to separate numbers, such as thousands, millions, and so on. It can also be used to apply gross rounding and scaling. For example, the format code #,###,### would display 4567890 as 4,567,890, but if you apply the code #,###, to the same number, the cell displays the number as 4,568. This kind of rounding/scaling can be used to make reports easier to read when they're displaying numbers in the millions and billions.

TIP For the complete inventory of custom formatting codes, click the question-mark Help button in the upper-right corner of the Excel window, and enter *custom number format* into the search box. The topic *Create or Delete a Custom Number Format* contains all the options available.

16 Select cell **D1**.

17 Press **Ctrl+1** to display the **Format Cells** dialog box (or click the dialog box launcher on the **Home** tab, in the **Number** group).

18 Click the **Special** category and click **Social Security Number**.

19 Click the **Custom** category to view the custom formatting code **000-00-0000**, which is used to format social security numbers. If you go back to the **Special** category and click either of the **Zip code** options, similar codes appear that are made up of zeros (and dashes). This indicates that each of these format codes will correctly display the exact number of digits indicated, and if no digit exists, a zero is displayed.

20   Click the **Special** category, select **Phone Number**, and click **OK** to apply the format to cell **D1**.

21   Press **Ctrl+1** and click the **Custom** category.

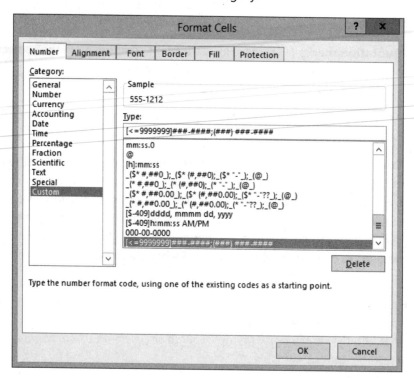

TIP When you create a custom format, it is saved with the workbook and remains available in the Format Cells dialog box's Custom category. If you want to use it elsewhere, you can copy a formatted cell from one workbook to another; the custom format travels with it.

Let's take a closer look at this formatting code in the following table. Notice that it has only two sections separated by a semicolon. This would seem to indicate that only positive and negative numbers are specified in this code, but actually, because there is a *comparison operator* (<=) involved, the semicolon is used to specify an either/or alternative. If the condition specified in the first section does not apply, then the second section is used.

SEE ALSO For information about Excel's Conditional Formatting command that allows you to easily apply selective formatting depending on the contents of the cells, see Chapter 20, "Analyzing data."

Values	Condition 1	Condition 2
	[<=9999999]###-####;(###) ###-####	
Code	[<=9999999]###-####	(###) ###-####
Entered	5551212	2065551212
Displayed	555-1212	(206) 555-1212

This is a clever code. The bracketed comparison value eliminates anything larger than 7 digits, displaying only phone numbers that do not include area codes. If the number entered is larger than 7 digits, the second section of the formatting code takes over and adds parentheses around the first three numbers. Let's modify it.

22 Edit the second section of the code in the **Type** box as follows (delete the first parenthesis and replace the second one with a dash):

[<=9999999]###-####;###-###-####

23 Click **OK**.

24 Enter 2065551212 and press **Enter**.

C	D	E
	206-555-1212	

Custom formats remain available for use in the workbook in which they were created during the current session. However, if you save the workbook without actually applying a custom format to any values, it will not be available the next time you open the workbook. These are all good reasons to keep track of the custom formats you want to keep.

✖ CLEAN UP Save the workbook as Custom Formats.xlsx, and keep it open for the next exercise.

TIP For more information about using operators in formatting codes, click the Help button in the upper-right corner of the Excel window and enter *custom number format* into the search box. In the topic *Create or Delete a Custom Number Format*, scroll down to *Guidelines for using decimal places, spaces, colors, and conditions.*

Note that the special Phone Number code will display as many numbers as you enter the digits for (unlike the social security number and ZIP code formats, which always display the same number of digits, adding leading zeros if necessary). For example, if you were to enter an incorrect numbers of digits into cells formatted with the Phone Number code, the numbers will be displayed as entered, such as in *23-4567* or *(12) 345-6789 or (1234) 567-8909.* Leading zeros are ignored in the Phone Number code, but not in the other Special codes.

TIP You can add bracketed conditions such as [<=9999999] to any formatting code, but be aware that when you use conditions, the usual four-part *positive-negative-zero-text* code structure changes to *condition1-condition2-condition3*, where the optional condition3 is essentially the *else* condition to be applied if the first two conditions are not met. If you still want to control negative values, then you can manually add the [<0] operator to the second condition.

Working with percentage formats

When you apply a percentage format to a number, Excel essentially moves the decimal point two places to the right, adds a percent sign, and rounds to a specified number of decimal places (depending on the format selected). For example, if a cell contains the number .3456 and you format it by clicking the Percent Style button (which applies a percentage format with no decimal places), Excel displays 35% in the cell.

Note this fact about percentage formats: after you apply one, Excel assumes there should be a decimal point even if you don't enter one. So, if you want to change the percentage in that same cell to 38%, you can just enter 38 (which is really 3800%) rather than .38. Microsoft learned that when changing a number displayed as a percentage, most people just enter an integer, not a decimal, so they made the format smart enough to deal with it. But, of course, if you really meant to enter 3800% when you entered 38, you'll have to go back and enter 3800.

There's not much you need to modify with percentages. You just need to decide whether or not you want to display decimals. You can display up to 30 decimal places. You can also add custom formatting. In this exercise, you'll do both.

1   In the **Custom Formats.xlsx** workbook, click the **New Sheet** button next to the **Sheet1** tab at the bottom of the workbook window to create a new worksheet. You will save the custom formats from each exercise on a separate sheet in this workbook.

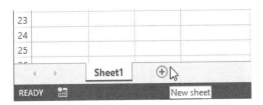

2   In cell **A1**, enter 45.67 and press **Enter**.

3   Select cells **A1:A2**.

4   On the **Home** tab, in the **Number** group, click the **Percent Style** button.

5   Select cell **A2**.

6   Enter 45.67 and press **Enter**. Notice the difference between applying the format before or after entering values. Most of the time, you'll apply percentage formats to cells containing formulas that generate actual percentages, but if not, check the values after applying a percentage format to a large range of cells containing existing values.

	A	B
1	4567%	
2	46%	
3		
4		
5		

7   Select cell **A1**, enter 45.67, and then press **Enter**.

8   Select cells **A1:A2**.

9   Press **Ctrl+1** to display the **Format Number** dialog box, and notice that **Decimal Places** is the only option you can change in the **Percentage** category.

10   Click the **Custom** category.

11   In the **Type** box, replace the existing code (**0%**) with the following:

"Profits are up "0%;[Red][<0]"Profits are down "0%

12   Press **Enter**.

13   Enter *-45.67* into cell **A2**

14   Press **Enter**.

	A	B
1	Profits are up 46%	
2	Profits are down 46%	
3		
4		
5		

✖ CLEAN UP Save the Custom Formats.xlsx workbook, and keep it open for the next exercise.

Working with fraction formats

If you want the look of fractions and do not require the precision of decimals, Excel offers formatting options that allow plenty of control over their display. However, you may need to adjust fraction formats to suit your needs. Though fraction formats often apply a rounding factor to the actual value in the cell (unless there is no remainder, or MOD value), doing so changes the display, but as always, does not alter the underlying value.

In this exercise, you'll apply fraction formatting and work around some of its idiosyncrasies.

➔ SET UP You need either the Custom Formats.xlsx workbook you saved at the end of the previous exercise or the Custom Formats 2_start.xlsx workbook located in the Chapter21 practice file folder to complete this exercise. If you are using the Custom Formats 2_start.xlsx workbook, open it and save it as Custom Formats.xlsx.

1   In the **Custom Formats.xlsx** workbook, click the **New Sheet** button next to the sheet tabs at the bottom of the workbook window to create a new worksheet. You will save the custom formats from each exercise on a separate sheet in this workbook.

2   In cell **A1**, enter 67.89 and press **Enter**.

3   Select cell **A1**.

4   On the **Home** tab, in the **Number** group, click the **Number** list and select **Fraction**. The fraction displayed in the cell uses a denominator (9) not commonly used in fractions. This may be the closest actual fractional value (67.8888...), but we need to adjust our fraction so that it uses a more conventional denominator.

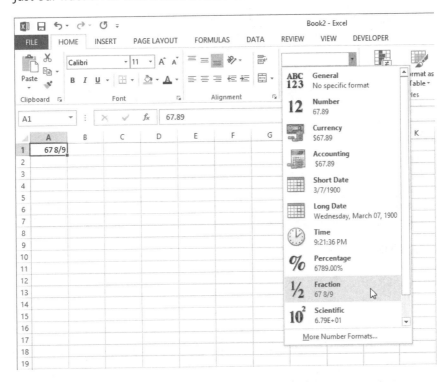

5   Press **Ctrl+1** to display the **Format Cells** dialog box.

6   In the **Type** list, scroll down to the bottom.

7   Select **As tenths (3/10)**.

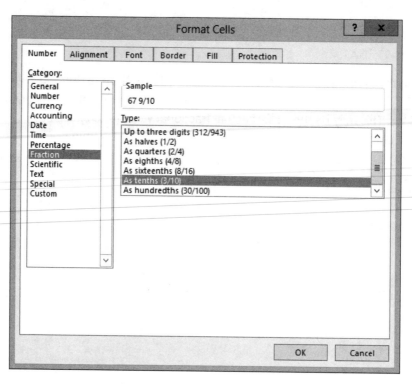

8   Click **OK**.

	A	B
1	67 9/10	
2		
3		
4		
5		

There are a number of fraction formats available, some of which seem barely usable. Consider the Up To Three Digits (312/943) format, which would actually raise precision considerably, while equally reducing intelligibility and making the use of decimals seem more prudent. But the essential options are all here: Halves, Quarters, Eighths, Sixteenths, and Hundredths. But what if you need a few more?

9   Select cell **A1**, and then press **Ctrl+1** to display the **Format Cells** dialog box.

10   Click the **Custom** category.

11   In the **Type** box, replace the existing code (**# ?/10**) with the following:

?/32

12   Click **OK**.

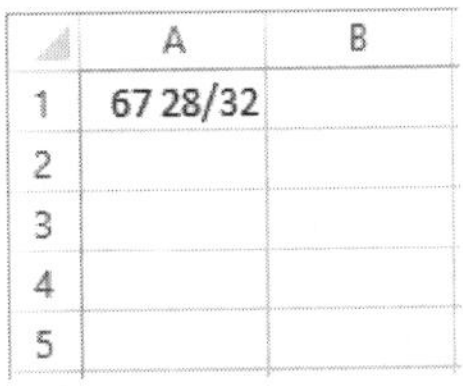

	A	B
1	67 28/32	
2		
3		
4		
5		

13   Press **Ctrl+1** to open the **Format Cells** dialog box again.

14   Click the **Custom** category.

15   In the **Type** box, replace the existing code with the following:

?/64

16   Click **OK**.

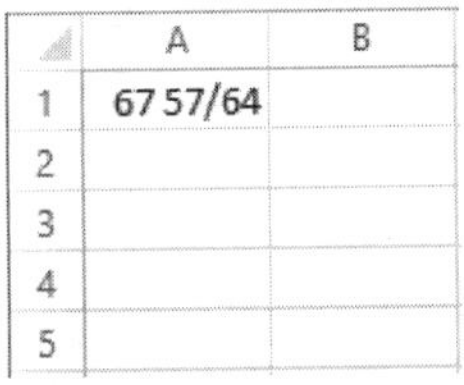

	A	B
1	67 57/64	
2		
3		
4		
5		

21

When you open the Format Cells dialog box, the two formats you just created appear somewhere in the list of Custom formats. These two happen to show up at the bottom.

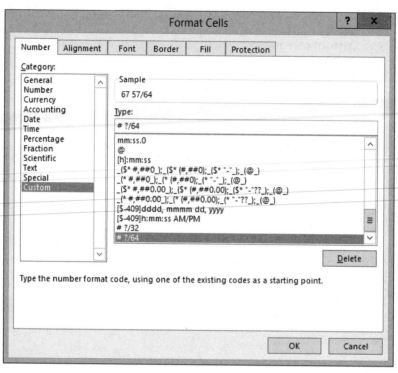

Working with date formats

Excel stores dates as serial numeric values starting from January 1, 1900; each day counts as 1. For example, this sentence was written at around 41182.66937 (decimal values, as you might guess, indicate exact time of day), otherwise known as 4:03 P.M. on September 30, 2012. This numeric date system allows you to manipulate dates and times in Excel as easily as other numbers. The time and date formatting options and their associated codes are appropriately different from any of the others.

In this exercise, you'll apply date formatting and create custom date formats.

SET UP You need either the Custom Formats.xlsx workbook you saved at the end of the previous exercise or the Custom Formats 3_start.xlsx workbook located in the Chapter21 practice file folder to complete this exercise. If you are using the Custom Formats 3_start.xlsx workbook, open it and save it as Custom Formats.xlsx.

1   In the **Custom Formats.xlsx** workbook, click the **New Sheet** button next to the sheet tabs at the bottom of the workbook window to create a new worksheet. You will save the custom formats from each exercise on a separate sheet in this workbook.

2   In cell **A1**, enter 41182.66937, and then press **Enter**.

3   Select cell **A1**, click the **Number** drop-down list on the **Home** tab, and then click **Short Date**.

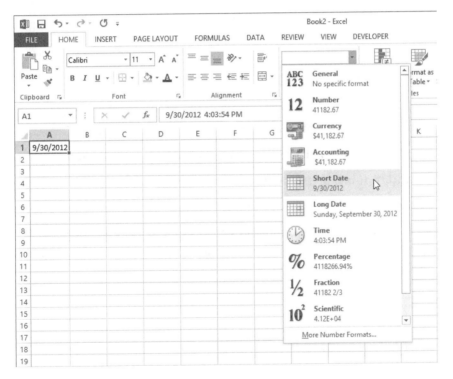

4   Press **Ctrl+1** to display the **Format Cells** dialog box.

5   Click the **Custom** category.

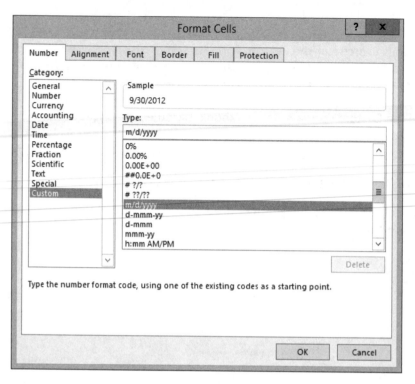

6   In the **Type** box, replace the selected formatting code **m/d/yyyy** as follows:

dddd mmmm dd, yyyy hh:mm:ss am/pm

7   Click **OK**.

The format now spells out months and days, and includes hours, minutes, and seconds. But if you were timing races or scientific experiments, you might need even more precision.

8   Press **Ctrl+1** again to display the **Format Cells** dialog box.

9   Make sure the **Custom** category is still active, and edit your custom formatting code, adding **.00** after the seconds, as follows:

dddd mmmm dd, yyyy hh:mm:ss.00 am/pm

10   Click **OK.**

Because the time component now includes fractional seconds, this moment in time actually occurred a few hundredths of a second earlier.

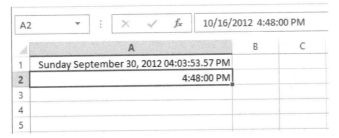

11   In cell **A2**, enter **41198.7**, and then press **Enter**.

12   Reselect cell **A2**, click the **Number** list on the **Home** tab, and then click **Time**. Cell **A2** displays only the time of day represented by the number you entered.

With cell A2 selected, look in the formula bar. The full date and time is displayed there, rather than the number that you entered. The underlying value is still there. This is an aspect of Excel formatting that's quite helpful. If you really need to view that serial value again, apply the General format from the Number Format list. (If you did this, press Ctrl+Z to undo before proceeding.)

13 Select cell **A3**, enter =A2-A1 and press **Enter**.

This simple formula returns a result that is formatted as a time value, similar to cell **A2**. (Excel adds formatting to an unformatted cell containing a formula that refers to formatted values.)

14 Reselect cell **A3**, click the **Number Format** list on the **Home** tab, and select **Long Date**.

Excel reveals the date Monday, January 16, 1900. This rather cryptically reveals the number of days that have elapsed between the two dates in the formula (16 days, given that 1/1/1900 is day 1). However, in this case, the desired outcome is to display elapsed *time*.

15 Press **Ctrl+1** to open the **Format Cells** dialog box.

16 Click the **Custom** category.

17 Replace the formatting code in the **Type** box with the following:

[hh]:mm:ss.000

18 Click **OK**. Now the elapsed time is 384 hours (16 days), 44 hours, and 6.432 seconds.

SEE ALSO For more information about using functions in Excel to calculate dates, see Chapter 19, "Manipulating numbers and text."

◢	A	B
1	Sunday September 30, 2012 04:03:53.57 PM	
2	4:48:00 PM	
3	384:44:06.432	
4		
5		

When you add brackets around the first component of a time format, Excel returns elapsed time. The brackets must be around the first component only; they will not work in any other position. However, you can change the code to show only elapsed minutes by deleting [hh]: and adding brackets around *mm* instead. Or, you can use the code [ss] to show only elapsed seconds. The code .000 appended to the seconds component of the format adds precision down to *milliseconds* (thousandths of a second), which is as precise as Excel will go. You can't add more than three zeros to the code.

⊗ CLEAN UP Save the Custom Formats.xlsx workbook and close it.

Following is a list with descriptions for several date formatting codes:

- **d (Day)** This code displays either numbers or text, depending on how many of them you include in the format. A single **d** displays the date as a number without leading zeros (1 or 16). A double **dd** displays the date as a number *with* leading zeros (01 or 16). Instead of displaying a date, using a triple **ddd** code displays the name of the day of the week, abbreviated (Sat). Similarly, using a quadruple **dddd** code displays the full name of the day of the week (Saturday). You can use both numeric dates and day names in formats. For example, a cell containing the date 12/6/2013 that is subsequently formatted using the code **dddd mmmm d** displays *Friday December 6*.

- **m (Month)** Like the day code, the month code displays either numbers or text, depending on how many you include in the format. A single **m** displays the month as a number without leading zeros (1 or 12). A double **mm** displays the month as a number *with* leading zeros (01 or 12). The triple **mmm** code displays an abbreviated month name (Dec). A quadruple **mmmm** code displays the full name of the month (December). (See also **mm (Minutes)**, later in this list.)

- **y (Year)** You can use the code **yy** to display just the last two digits of the year (13), or use **yyyy** to display the full year (2013).

- **h (Hour)** There are two ways to use the hour code: **h** displays the hour without leading zeros (2, 22), while the code **hh** displays the hour with leading zeros (02, 22). Note that Excel always uses a 24-hour clock unless you add the **am/pm** code.

- **mm (Minutes)** Obviously, minutes and months use the same code letter (**m**), so it's all about where you put them. In a date code, the **m** stands for months, in a time code (separated by colons), it's minutes. A single **m** displays minutes without leading zeros (5, 55), while the double **mm** displays minutes with leading zeros (05, 55).

- **s (Seconds)** A single **s** displays seconds without leading zeros (3, 33), and a double **ss** displays seconds with leading zeros (03, 33). Adding a period and one or two zeros to the end of a seconds code (**s.0**, **ss.0**, **s.00**, or **ss.00**) adds tenths or hundredths of a second to the display, respectively.

- **am/pm or a/p** Adding **am/pm** to the end of a date or time format code instructs Excel to display the time component based on a 12-hour clock. Case doesn't matter.

- **[ ] (Brackets)** Brackets around a time code tell Excel to return elapsed time rather than actual time. It is necessary to apply this format to formulas that calculate elapsed time, otherwise the results may not be what you expect. You can only use brackets with time codes, and only in the first section of the code, for example **[hh]:mm:ss** or **[mm]:ss**.

There are some code combinations that won't work. For example, you cannot use the am/pm format code with a bracketed elapsed-time code, which makes sense if you think about it. Mixing date codes and numeric format codes doesn't work, either. Feel free to experiment; Excel will let you know what doesn't work by displaying an error message if you try to create an unusable code.

TIP For more about date and time formatting codes, click the Help button in the upper-right corner of the Excel window, and enter *custom number format* into the search box. The topic *Create or Delete a Custom Number Format* contains all the options available.

Protecting worksheets

You and I might not think of protection as a format, but Excel does. You can use it like a format in the sense that you can apply it to some cells and not others. This allows you to lock all the cells in a worksheet to protect them from modification, or you can leave specific cells unlocked, allowing users of the workbook to enter data, and allowing you to specify exactly which areas in the worksheet you want to protect.

Excel assumes that you want to lock all the cells in a workbook if and when you activate protection, so all cells are formatted as *locked* by default.

In this exercise, you'll work with protection formatting by unlocking cells on a worksheet that you want to be able to edit after protection is turned on.

→ SET UP You need the Real-Estate-Transition_start.xlsx workbook located in the Chapter21 practice file folder to complete this exercise. Open the Real-Estate-Transition_start.xlsx workbook, and save it as Real-Estate-Transition.xlsx.

1 In the **Real-Estate-Transition.xlsx** workbook, click the arrow next to the **Name** box in the **Formula** bar, and select the name **Entries** to select all the user-input cells in column **B**.

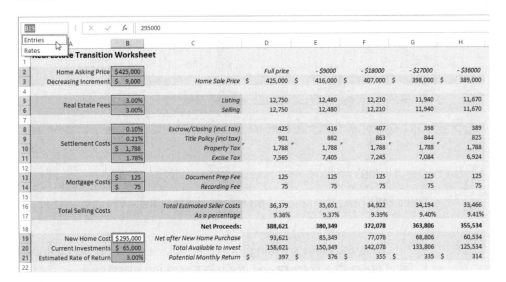

2 Click the **Format** button, on the **Home** tab, and take a look at the **Lock Cell** command.

The icon adjacent to the Lock Cell command is enclosed in a grey box, which indicates that it is currently active, or locked, as is the case with all cells in a worksheet unless you specify otherwise.

3   Click the **Lock Cell** command to unlock the selected cells.

4   Click the **Format** button again, and this time, click the **Protect Sheet** command to display a dialog box of the same name. You'll notice that the only allowed default settings involve selecting cells, unless you click additional options.

5   Click **OK** to turn on sheet protection without adding a password or selecting additional options.

6   Select cell **B3**.

7   Enter 8000 and then press **Enter**; Excel accepts the entry and **B4** becomes the active cell.

8   When you try to enter anything into a cell other than those you unlocked in column **B**, Excel prevents any entry and displays a warning message.

✖ CLEAN UP   Save the Real-Estate-Transition.xlsx workbook, and then close it.

You can protect formulas and data on worksheets that you need to share with others by using protection formatting. Or you can lock all cells on a sheet and optionally apply a password to prevent any changes from happening at all. Protection is applied per worksheet, so a workbook may contain both protected and unprotected sheets.

Protecting workbooks

Protection in Excel has many levels. You protected cells and sheets, so to display the various options for workbook protection, click the File tab to display the Backstage view, click Info, and then click the Protect Workbook button.

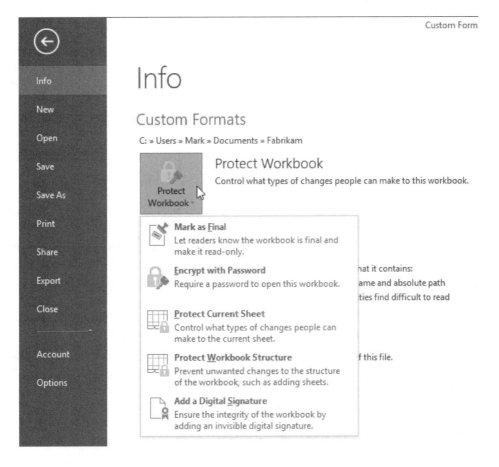

- **Mark as Final** Makes the workbook read-only

- **Encrypt with Password** Displays a dialog box allowing you to specify a password necessary to open the workbook

- **Protect Current Sheet** Prevents the editing of any locked cells on the current sheet and displays the same Protect Sheet dialog box shown earlier in this chapter, with which you specify allowable editing actions for the current sheet

- **Protect Workbook Structure** Allows you to open workbooks and edit worksheets, but not to rename tabs or move, hide, or unhide worksheets and windows

- **Add a Digital Signature** Allows you to apply authentication to a workbook by using a digital stamp, which you must purchase from an authorized digital certificate–issuing authority such as Verisign

Setting view options

When creating workbooks designed for presentation, you can control a variety of display settings by using commands on the View tab. The ribbon and controls of the Excel program and the workbook structure can be a distraction in themselves. Some of these settings are saved with the workbook, and thus can for all intents and purposes be considered among your formatting options. We'll start with the simplest worksheet imaginable to illustrate the remarkable amount of visual clutter you can eliminate if you want to.

In this exercise, you'll change the way your worksheet is displayed on screen.

 SET UP You need the FabrikamSummary2_start.xlsx workbook located in the Chapter21 practice file folder to complete this exercise. Open the FabrikamSummary2_start.xlsx workbook, and save it as FabrikamSummary2.xlsx.

1   With the **FabrikamSummary2.xlsx** workbook open, click the **View** tab.

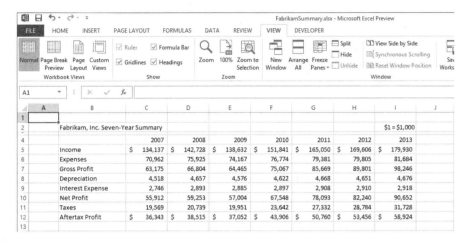

2   On the **View** tab, in the **Show** group, clear the **Gridlines**, **Headings**, and **Formula Bar** check boxes to deselect those options.

3   Double-click the **View** tab to collapse the ribbon and transform the tabs into a menu bar.

4   Click the **Ribbon Display Options** button, located in the upper-right corner of the screen, and click the **Auto-Hide Ribbon** command, which hides the ribbon and the status bar, maximizes the window and hides the **Quick Access Toolbar** and the tabs. (The formula bar and headings would be visible in this display mode if you hadn't already turned them off on the **View** tab.)

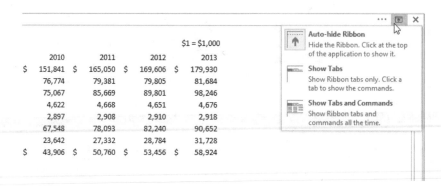

	2010		2011		2012		2013
				$1 = $1,000			
$	151,841	$	165,050	$	169,606	$	179,930
	76,774		79,381		79,805		81,684
	75,067		85,669		89,801		98,246
	4,622		4,668		4,651		4,676
	2,897		2,908		2,910		2,918
	67,548		78,093		82,240		90,652
	23,642		27,332		28,784		31,728
$	43,906	$	50,760	$	53,456	$	58,924

5   Click the ... (three dots) in the upper-right corner of the screen to temporarily display the ribbon.

6   Click the **Ribbon Display Options** button again and click **Show Tabs** to redisplay the tab names, the status bar, and the **Quick Access Toolbar**. The ribbon is still hidden.

7   Click the **View** tab to temporarily redisplay the ribbon. When you click a collapsed tab, it appears and stays visible until you click a command or click in the worksheet area.

8   Click anywhere in the worksheet area. The ribbon collapses again.

9   Double-click the **View** tab to redisplay the ribbon (or you can click **Ribbon Display Options**, and then click **Show Tabs and Commands**).

TIP You can double-click any ribbon tab to toggle the ribbon display on or off. If the ribbon is visible, double-clicking any tab hides it; if the ribbon is not visible, double-clicking any tab redisplays it.

You can create another view of a worksheet by using the New Window command on the View tab. This creates not another worksheet, but another window on the same worksheet, within which you can have an entirely different set of view options, regardless of whether the ribbon is collapsed.

10   Click the **New Window** command on the **View** tab; a new window appears entitled **FabrikamSummary2.xlsx:2**, displayed with the default **View** settings.

11   Click the **Zoom** button on the **View** tab, select **200%** and click **OK**.

12   Click the **Switch Windows** button and select the unchecked window (**FabrikamSummary2.xlsx:1**).

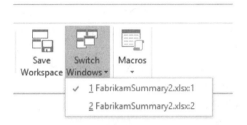

13   Click the **Zoom** button, select **75%** and click **OK**.

14   Click the **Arrange All** button, and accept the default **Tiled** option.

15   Click **OK**.

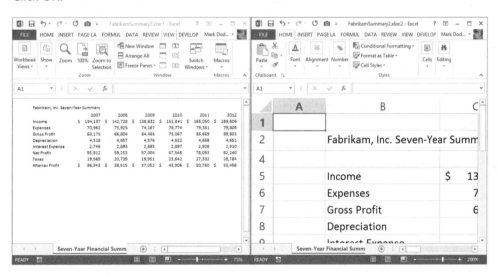

TIP You can click the View Side By Side button to do a row-by-row comparison of two workbooks or windows together onscreen. (If you have more than two workbooks or windows open, a dialog box appears allowing you to select one.) When you click the View Side By Side button, the Synchronous Scrolling button is engaged as well. If you want, click the Synchronous Scrolling button to turn it off, and scroll freely in either window.

Many of the settings you select on the View tab are saved with the workbook, including the display of gridlines, headings, and Zoom settings. When you save the workbook with any of these options changed, they persist the next time you open the workbook, including any additional windows created using the New Window command. However, you cannot save the layout of windows, such as the Tiled layout just discussed. But the windows are there, saved with the workbook; you'll just have to use the Arrange All command again to reset the layout. This is something you can't do in Excel 2013 that you used to be able to do. As a byproduct of the Single-Document Interface, the Save Workspace command had to be removed, because new windows are no longer contained within a workbook-specific workspace, but now are created in an entirely separate instance of Excel.

TIP You lose a lot of screen real estate with multiple windows open and a ribbon and Formula bar in each one. Click the Formula bar option on the View tab to hide it. Double-click any tab to collapse the ribbon (double-click the tab again to restore it).

Collapsing the ribbon and hiding the Formula bar are application settings that are not saved with workbooks. The configuration in place when you exit is displayed the next time you start Excel.

✕ CLEAN UP Close both windows of the FabrikamSummary2.xlxs workbook without saving.

Storing formats in templates

If you go to the trouble of creating beautiful and useful worksheets, chances are you would like to use them again, or at least repurpose parts of them. Custom formats you create only apply to the workbook in which you created them. But you can transfer them by copying custom-formatted cells and pasting them into other workbooks. So, you could create a boilerplate workbook to store your number formats created by using custom codes, as well as cell formats, tables, and so on. Or you can create a template. In addition, you can also store workbooks and formats in a location where you can easily retrieve a copy.

TIP You can save specific formatting options (fonts, colors, and effects) as themes, which can be easily used in other Excel workbooks as well as in other Office documents. See "Creating custom themes" earlier in this chapter.

If you have created and used templates in Office applications before, the procedure for saving and accessing templates works a bit differently in Office Professional 2013. Before you save your own templates, you need to first specify a Default Personal Templates Location. In order to do this properly, you need to create it first. So before you do anything else, open File Explorer and create a folder to store templates on your computer in a location of your choice. You can place a copy of a random Excel workbook in there too, if you want.

In this exercise, you'll save a workbook as a template.

 SET UP You don't need any practice files to complete this exercise. Start Excel, open a blank workbook, and follow the steps.

1 Click the **File** tab and then click **Options** to display the **Excel Options** dialog box.

2 Click the **Save** category.

3 In the **Default Personal Templates Location** box, enter the path to the folder you will use to store your templates (or for now, you can copy whatever is in the **Default Local File Location** box and edit it later).

4 Click **OK**.

5 Click the **File** tab, and then click **New**.

New

Search online templates

Suggested searches: Budget Invoice Calendars Expense List Loan Schedule

FEATURED PERSONAL

Custom Formats

On the New page, next to *Featured*, which previously stood alone, there is now a Personal category. When you click this category, any templates stored in your designated personal templates folder are displayed on the screen for you to open with a single click. (We added one for the purposes of this discussion; otherwise, the Personal category would not appear at all unless there was a subfolder in your Default Personal Templates folder.) As a matter of fact, any Excel workbooks stored in this folder will be presented as options in the Personal template category and will open as templates, whether or not you save them as such.

You can create as many templates as you choose, from workbooks containing only custom number formats to fully developed applications, and you can store them in your Default Personal Templates Location. When you open any workbook from the New page of the Backstage view, a copy is opened in Excel, using the original filename with an appended number. For example, a workbook or template named Custom Formats would open as Custom Formats1, which makes it harder to inadvertently overwrite the original file.

When you save a workbook created from a template, the Default Local File Location (specified in the Excel Options dialog box) is offered as the default folder, rather that the Default Personal Templates Location, which further protects the original file from being overwritten.

CLEAN UP Press Esc to close the Backstage view, and exit Excel without saving.

Key points

- Formatting helps transform raw numeric data into more accessible information.

- You can format cells, and you can format individual characters in cells.

- You can modify and create your own variations of Excel's built-in number formats.

- You can modify and create your own date formats, including special elapsed-time formats.

- Styles and themes are collections of formatting options that help you maintain consistency among documents.

- You can selectively apply protection formatting to lock and unlock individual cells, allowing you to ensure the integrity of formatting and critical formulas on the worksheet.

- You can open more than one window on the same workbook, and you can arrange all the open workbooks and windows onscreen for simultaneous viewing.

- You can store your formatting choices as templates, making them available for easy duplication.

21

Chapter at a glance

Freeze

Freeze worksheet panes so that you always know where you are, page 593

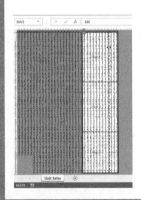

Print

Print specific rows and columns on every page of output, page 601

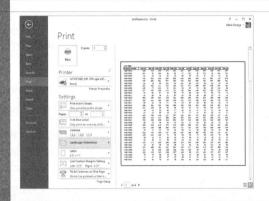

Break

Break your printed pages by dragging borders in Page Break Preview, page 604

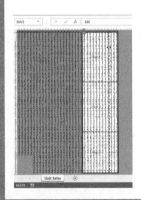

Drag

Drag worksheets between workbooks, page 612

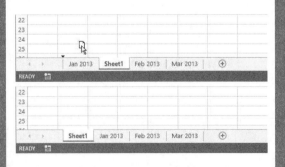

Manipulating workbooks and worksheets   22

IN THIS CHAPTER, YOU WILL LEARN HOW TO

- Use Excel's table features to insert and delete rows and columns.

- Keep row and column labels in view, in print and on screen.

- Adjust page breaks.

- Create and work with multisheet workbooks.

- Create multisheet formulas.

- Arrange workbooks and windows on screen.

Regardless of what you plan to put in them, it's important to know the basics of workbooks and worksheets. How do they actually work? Being able to to manipulate the structure of your workbooks may change your thinking about how to organize your data.

In this chapter, you'll learn how to insert and delete cells, rows, and columns; how to change display and print options; and how to use multiple sheets in a workbook.

PRACTICE FILES To complete the exercises in this chapter, you need the practice files contained in the Chapter22 practice file folder. For more information, see "Download the practice files" in this book's Introduction.

Inserting rows and columns

There are certain actions that accrue more usage in applications. Like copying and pasting in Microsoft Word, inserting and deleting rows and columns in Microsoft Excel is near the top of that list.

In this exercise, you'll insert some rows and add a column of totals with the help of Excel's table features. But first, you'll sort the existing worksheet.

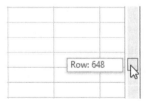 SET UP You need the FabrikamQ1_start.xlsx workbook located in the Chapter22 practice file folder to complete this exercise. Open the FabrikamQ1_start.xlsx workbook, save it as FabrikamQ1.xlsx, and then follow the steps.

1 With the **FabrikamQ1_start.xlsx** workbook open, make sure that cell **A2** is selected, and then click the **Data** tab.

2 Click the **Sort** button in the **Sort & Filter** group. Because the active cell is in a table, Excel automatically selects the entire table when the **Sort** dialog box appears.

3 In the **Sort by** list, select **Group**.

4 Click the **Add Level** button.

5 In the **Then by** list, select **Channel**.

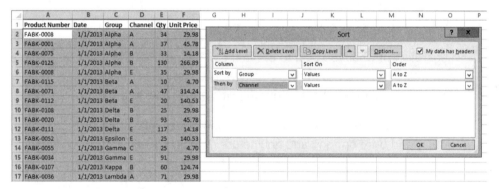

6 Click **OK** to sort the table.

7 Scroll down to row **648**, the first row of the **Omega** group listings. Notice the tiny ScreenTip near the scroll bar, for a live readout of the current row number as you drag the scroll box.

TIP Another way of navigating to a remote cell is to enter the cell address into the Name box on the left end of the formula bar. For this example, entering A648 would get you to row 648.

8   Select the entire row by clicking the **648** row heading number.

9   Click the **Omega A** worksheet tab at the bottom of the window.

10   Select row **2** by clicking the row heading number.

11   Hold the **Shift+Ctrl** keys and then press the **Down Arrow** key, which selects all the rows in the table.

12   Click the **Copy** button on the **Home** tab (or press **Ctrl+C**).

13   Click the **Q1-2013** worksheet tab at the bottom of the window.

14   Click the arrow below the **Insert** button, located in the **Cells** group on the **Home** tab of the ribbon.

15   On the **Insert** menu, click **Insert Copied Cells**. The new rows are inserted above the selected row. (Note that if you click the **Insert** button itself, rather than clicking the arrow button to display the **Insert** menu, **Insert Copied Cells** is still the default action.)

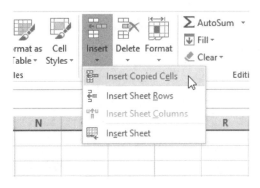

22

16   Click the **Find & Select** button in the **Editing** group on the **Home** tab, and then click **Go To**.

17   In the **Reference** box, enter E:E, and then press **Enter**. You'll notice that the entire column **E** is selected, just as if you had clicked the header. (You can use this same trick with rows; for example, entering 648:648 selects the entire row **648**.)

18   With column **E** selected, click the **Insert** button arrow, and then click **Insert Sheet Columns**. (Again, pressing the button arrow and pressing the button itself both yield the same result.)

19   Select cell **E1**, enter Sale, and press **Enter**. The next step is to add formulas to calculate totals. However, entering a formula into cell **E2** and then dragging the fill handle to copy the formula down the column, with 1043 rows of data, is a lot of dragging. There's an easier way.

20   With cell **E2** still selected, click the **Insert** tab, and then click the **Table** button in the **Tables** group.

21   In the **Create Table** dialog box, click **OK**.

22   Select cell **E2**.

23   Enter = (an equal sign), and then press the **Right Arrow** key once.

24   Enter * (an asterisk), and then press the **Right Arrow** key twice.

25   Press **Enter**, and watch as Excel automatically fills the rest of the column with equivalent formulas. The Excel table features made inserting these formulas very easy.

E2		✕ ✓ fx	=[@Qty]*[@[Unit Price]]			

	A	B	C	D	E	F	G	H
1	Product Number ▼	Date ▼	Group ▼	Channel ▼	Sale ▼	Qty ▼	Unit Price ▼	
2	FABK-0008	1/1/2013	Alpha	A	1019.32	34	29.98	
3	FABK-0001	1/1/2013	Alpha	A	1693.86	37	45.78	
4	FABK-0009	1/3/2013	Alpha	A	2289	50	45.78	
5	FABK-0009	1/4/2013	Alpha	A	2289	50	45.78	
6	FABK-0001	1/8/2013	Alpha	A	1693.86	37	45.78	
7	FABK-0001	1/11/2013	Alpha	A	4257.54	93	45.78	
8	FABK-0007	1/14/2013	Alpha	A	2709.08	44	61.57	
9	FABK-0008	1/15/2013	Alpha	A	1019.32	34	29.98	
10	FABK-0009	1/15/2013	Alpha	A	2609.46	57	45.78	
11	FABK-0007	1/18/2013	Alpha	A	2709.08	44	61.57	
12	FABK-0007	1/22/2013	Alpha	A	2709.08	44	61.57	
13	FABK-0006	1/22/2013	Alpha	A	9166.5	45	203.70	

TIP If you don't like the default table formatting, you can always choose another style. For example, you can switch back to the plain worksheet style used at the beginning of the exercise, by clicking the Table Tools Design tab (only available when the active cell is inside a table) and clicking the very first style in the Table Styles palette. You could also convert the table back to a regular cell range by clicking the Convert To Range button on the Table Tools Design tab. When you do so, the formulas are preserved, but they are converted from table reference formulas to regular Excel formulas.

✖ CLEAN UP Save the FabrikamQ1.xlsx workbook, and then close it.

Inserting and deleting cells

Believe it or not, inserted cells are among the most common worksheet problems. When you insert text in Word, for example, existing text shifts to accommodate it, because text processing is essentially linear.

Spreadsheets (and tables in Word) are modular. When you insert cells, you force existing cells, rows, or columns to move out of the way. Unlike with text insertion, you have options when inserting cells: you can push existing cells either to the right or down. Inserting rows and columns is fairly safe, because this usually keeps related data aligned properly. But inserting cells can easily misalign data.

In this exercise, you'll use the right approach to inserting and deleting cells, and you'll discover what happens when you do it the wrong way.

➔ SET UP You need the FabrikamQ1-B_start.xlsx workbook located in the Chapter22 practice file folder to complete this exercise. Open the FabrikamQ1-B_start.xlsx workbook, save it as FabrikamQ1-B.xlsx, and then follow the steps.

1. With the **FabrikamQ1-B.xlsx** workbook open, the **Omega A** tab active, and cell **B2** selected, click the arrow below the **Insert** button in the **Cells** group on the **Home** tab, and then click the **Insert Cells** command to display the **Insert** dialog box.

2. Make sure the **Shift cells down** option is selected. (Even though the **Entire row** option would be the appropriate choice in this case, leave the default option selected.)

3   Click **OK**. Notice that all the other cells in the same column have been pushed down, and in the process, all the data in column **B** is now misaligned with all the other data in the table.

4   Scroll down to row **41**, and notice that all the data in the column is now one cell lower, and all the sales records are now adjacent to incorrect dates.

▲	A	B	C	D	E	F	G
34	FABK-0062	3/4/2013	Omega	A	36	77.35	
35	FABK-0102	3/7/2013	Omega	A	-2	156.31	
36	FABK-0056	3/13/2013	Omega	A	24	138.96	
37	FABK-0125	3/13/2013	Omega	A	128	266.89	
38	FABK-0091	3/14/2013	Omega	A	55	140.53	
39	FABK-0059	3/19/2013	Omega	A	3	156.31	
40	FABK-0058	3/21/2013	Omega	A	33	124.74	
41	FABK-0044	3/21/2013	Omega	A	68	18.91	
42		3/22/2013					
43							

5   Press **Ctrl+Z** to undo.

6   Click the **Q1-2013** worksheet tab at the bottom of the screen; the worksheet contains an Excel table, and cell **E2** is selected.

7   Click the arrow below the **Insert** button in the **Cells** group on the **Home** tab, click **Insert Cells**, and then click **OK**; this time Excel inserted an entire row in the table instead of a single cell (and duplicated the **Sale** formula automatically), demonstrating how Excel's table features help ensure the integrity of your data.

▲	A	B	C	D	E	F	G
1	Product Number ▼	Date ▼	Group ▼	Channel ▼	Sale ▼	Qty ▼	Unit Price ▼
2					0		
3	FABK-0008	1/1/2013	Alpha	A	1019.32	34	29.98
4	FABK-0001	1/1/2013	Alpha	A	1693.86	37	45.78
5	FABK-0009	1/3/2013	Alpha	A	2289	50	45.78
6	FABK-0009	1/4/2013	Alpha	A	2289	50	45.78
7	FABK-0001	1/8/2013	Alpha	A	1693.86	37	45.78
8	FABK-0001	1/11/2013	Alpha	A	4257.54	93	45.78
9	FABK-0007	1/14/2013	Alpha	A	2709.08	44	61.57
10	FABK-0008	1/15/2013	Alpha	A	1019.32	34	29.98

8   Click the arrow below the **Delete** button in the **Cells** group on the **Home** tab, and notice that, when a table is selected, two additional commands appear for table rows and table columns. (The equivalent commands also appear on the **Insert** menu.)

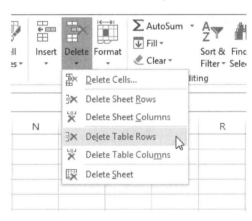

9   Click **Delete Table Rows**, which allows you to easily make modifications while leaving adjacent data on the worksheet undisturbed. Doing so removes only the selected rows in the table (in contrast, the **Delete Sheet Rows** command would remove selected rows all the way across the worksheet). Keep in mind, however, that inserting or deleting table rows or columns will still shift, and possibly misalign, adjacent cells.

TIP Consider the possibility of future modifications when building worksheets. If you'd like to put more than one table of data on a single worksheet, inserting and deleting rows in one table could affect tables to the right, and inserting and deleting columns could affect tables following it. Instead, consider putting additional tables on separate sheets in the same workbook. For more information, see "Creating a multisheet workbook" later in this chapter.

22

10   Click the **Seven-Year Financial Summary** worksheet tab at the bottom of the screen.

11   Select row **8** by clicking its heading number.

12   Click the **Delete** button on the **Home** tab, and notice the small triangles that now appear in the upper-left corner of each cell in rows **8** through **10**, indicating that there is a problem with the formulas in those cells.

13   Click cell **B8**, and then click the action menu that appears adjacent to the cell. There is not much the menu can offer that will help this time, other than **Edit in Formula Bar**, but there are a lot of cells to edit.

B8		×	✓	fx	=B6-B7-#REF!			
	A	B	C	D	E	F	G	H
1	Fabrikam, Inc. Seven-Year Summary							$1 = $1,000
3		2007	2008	2009	2010	2011	2012	2013
4	Income	$ 134,137	$ 142,728	$ 138,632	$ 151,841	$ 165,050	$ 169,606	$ 179,930
5	Expenses	70,962	75,925	74,167	76,774	79,381	79,805	81,684
6	Gross Profit	63,175	66,804	64,465	75,067	85,669	89,801	98,246
7	Depreciation	4,518	4,657	4,576	4,622	4,668	4,651	4,676
8	Net Profit	#REF!	#REF!	#REF!	#REF!	#REF!	#REF!	#REF!
9	Taxes	Invalid Cell Reference Error	#REF!	#REF!	#REF!	#REF!	#REF!	#REF!
10	Aftertax Profit		#REF!	#REF!	#REF!	#REF!	#REF!	#REF!
11		Help on this error						
12		Show Calculation Steps...						
13		Ignore Error						
14		Edit in Formula Bar						
15		Error Checking Options...						
16								
17								

14   Press the **Esc** key to dismiss the menu.

15   Press **Ctrl+Z** to undo the last action and restore the deleted cells. This is just a reminder that deleting cells can have consequences. In a large spreadsheet, you might not even be able to tell that something is wrong.

❌ CLEAN UP Save the FabrikamQ1-B.xlsx workbook, and then close it.

Removing stuff

You say *delete*, I say *erase*, she says *clear*. But let's be "clear" about what this means in Excel. What you remove, and how you do it, can make a huge difference to the integrity of your worksheet. Previously, you learned that removing cells, rows, or columns can adversely affect your worksheet structure. And of course, inadvertently removing formulas can have serious effects as well.

In Excel, removing cells completely is called *deleting*. The Delete commands on the Home tab (Delete Cells, Delete Sheet Rows, Delete Sheet Columns, and, if a table is selected, Delete Table Rows and Delete Table Columns) all change the worksheet structure by shifting remaining cells, rows, or columns up or to the left to fill the gap. Note that the Delete key on your keyboard does not "delete," in Excel terminology.

In Excel, deleting data in cells, but not the cells themselves, is called *clearing*. You can clear data by using one of the Clear commands on the Home tab (Clear All, Clear Formats, Clear Contents, Clear Comments, and Clear Hyperlinks). All of these commands remove specific cell contents, but do not alter the worksheet structure. Note that pressing the Delete key on your keyboard is equivalent to issuing the Clear command. The Backspace key also clears data in selected cells, unless you are editing text or a formula within a cell, in which case it just erases the character to the left.

SEE ALSO For more information, see "Moving and copying rows and columns" in Chapter 18, "Creating and editing worksheets."

22

Working with panes and page layout options

When you hear the words *page layout*, you probably think of printing, which used to be one of the top five issues reported by Microsoft product support. For Excel in 2013, printing has slipped down the list of issues considerably, perhaps because printing is easier than it used to be, or maybe because more people share data electronically or embedded in other documents like Microsoft PowerPoint presentations.

Of course, page layout is not just about printing, and especially in Excel, layout settings can actually affect not just printability, but the usability of a large worksheet.

In this exercise, you'll work with panes, hidden columns, margins, and the print area.

→ SET UP You need the UnitSales_start.xlsx workbook located in the Chapter22 practice file folder to complete this exercise. Open the UnitSales_start.xlsx workbook, save it as UnitSales.xlsx, and then follow the steps.

1   In the **UnitSales.xlsx** workbook, select cell **B3**.

2   Click the **View** tab.

3   Click the **Split** button in the **Window** group, and observe that Excel divides the worksheet into four segments, or *panes*, divided by gray bars. Each pane is more or less independent; the panes at the top will remain in place as you scroll down, and the panes at the left will stay in place as you scroll to the right. The **Split** button is a toggle; click it again to remove the split. If you needed only a single horizontal or vertical split, you could click and drag either gray bar off of the worksheet to remove it.

◢	A	B	C	D
1	Unit Sales			
2	Product Number	Group	Jan-07	Feb-07
3	FABK-0001	1	397	235
4	FABK-0002	1	144	125
5	FABK-0003	1	19	56
6	FABK-0004	2	413	654
7	FABK-0005	2	373	447
8	FABK-0006	1	88	34

4   Making sure that cell **B3** is still selected (and that the panes are still split), click the **Freeze Panes** button, and then click the **Freeze Panes** command in the menu that appears; the gray bars turn into thinner gray lines. Now the panes are locked; you can only scroll the lower-right pane. Rows **1** and **2** and column **A** all remain in place, which enables you to locate where you are in the worksheet at all times.

5   Scroll to the right and down. You can now navigate anywhere you want on the work-sheet, and you'll always be able to view the row and column headers. The following graphic illustrates this. Both cells **A1** and **CH129** are visible together onscreen.

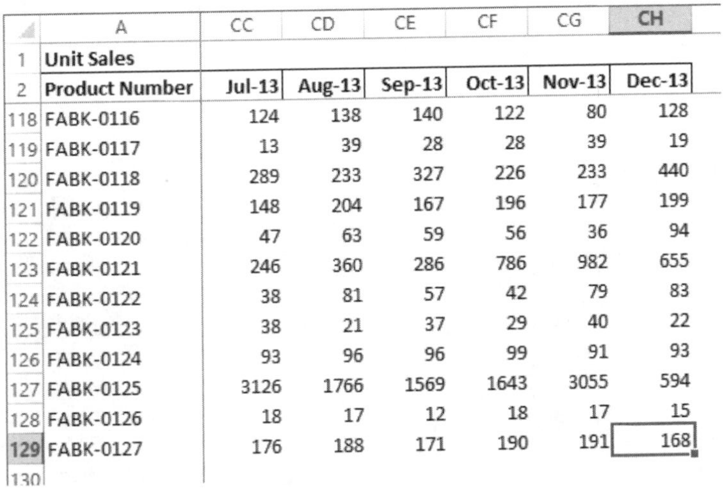

	A	CC	CD	CE	CF	CG	CH
1	Unit Sales						
2	Product Number	Jul-13	Aug-13	Sep-13	Oct-13	Nov-13	Dec-13
118	FABK-0116	124	138	140	122	80	128
119	FABK-0117	13	39	28	28	39	19
120	FABK-0118	289	233	327	226	233	440
121	FABK-0119	148	204	167	196	177	199
122	FABK-0120	47	63	59	56	36	94
123	FABK-0121	246	360	286	786	982	655
124	FABK-0122	38	81	57	42	79	83
125	FABK-0123	38	21	37	29	40	22
126	FABK-0124	93	96	96	99	91	93
127	FABK-0125	3126	1766	1569	1643	3055	594
128	FABK-0126	18	17	12	18	17	15
129	FABK-0127	176	188	171	190	191	168
130							

6   Press **Ctrl+Home** to return to the upper-left corner of the worksheet. Notice that, with **Freeze Panes** active, the upper-left cell in the active pane (**B3**) is selected rather than **A1**, which is normally the case.

7   Click the column letter **C** to select the entire column.

8   Scroll to the right until column **BV** (labeled **Dec-12**) is visible.

9   Hold down the **Shift** key and click the column letter **BV** to select all the columns ex-cept the 2013 totals.

10 Click the right mouse button anywhere in the selected column headers.

22

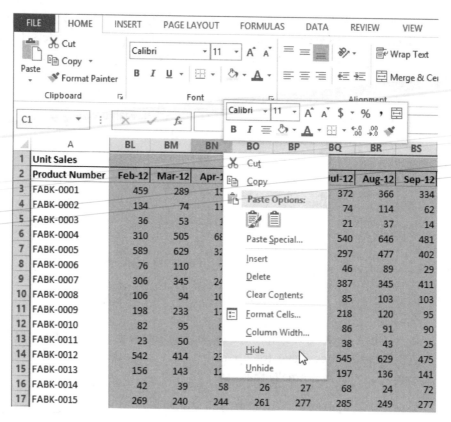

11   Click the **Hide** command to remove the selected columns from view, leaving only the 2013 columns visible. (The **Hide** command can also be found on the **Format** menu's **Hide and Unhide** submenu.) The relevant data on the worksheet is now easier to use, and the sheet is much easier to navigate. But you might want to print it, too.

12   Click the **File** menu, and then click **Print** to display the **Print Preview** window. Look at the preview image; not all the columns are visible; look at the bottom of the screen and notice that it will take six pages to print this sheet.

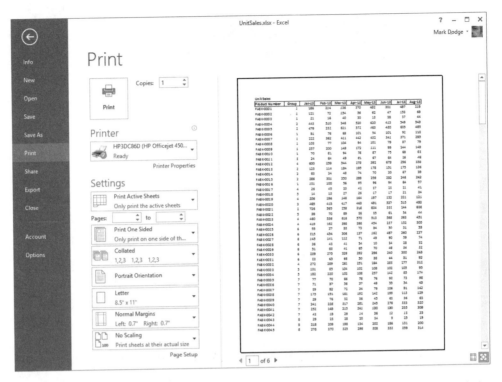

13   Click the **Margins** button (which currently displays **Normal Margins**), and then click **Custom Margins** to display the **Page Setup** dialog box.

14   Double-click each number in the **Top**, **Bottom**, **Left**, and **Right** boxes, and change them all to **.25**. Then select **Vertically** for the **Center on page** option. (Headers and footers are not used in this exercise, so don't worry about changing those numbers. Headers and footers wouldn't fit with such narrow margins, anyway.)

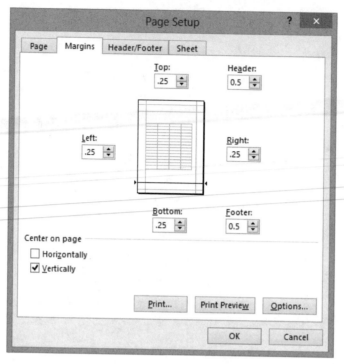

15   Click **OK**.

16   Click the **Scaling** button (which is currently set to **No Scaling**) and click **Fit All Columns on One Page**; notice that now, January through December are visible in the preview, and that this sheet will now require only three pages to print.

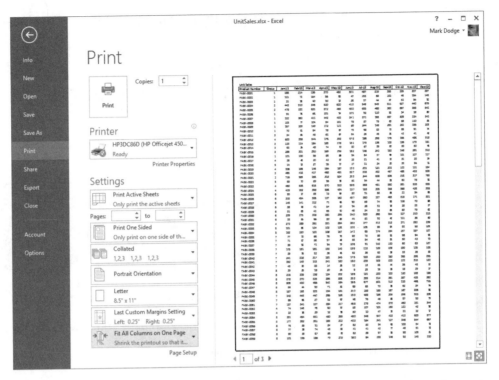

17   Press the **Esc** key to close the **Print Preview** window. These and any other print and page layout settings you make are preserved the next time you save, so that the sheet will print the same way the next time you open it.

18   Press **Ctrl+Home** to return to cell **B3**.

19   Drag through the **B** and **BW** column headers to select them.

20 On a selected column header, click the right mouse button, and then select the **Unhide** command.

	A	B	BW	BX	BY	BZ	CA	CB	CC
1	Unit Sales								
2	Product Number	Group	Jan-13	Feb-13	Mar-13	Apr-13	May-13	Jun-13	Jul-13
3	FABK-0001	1	186	214	136	370	482	301	497
4	FABK-0002	1	121	72	154	56	62	47	153
5	FABK-0003	1	21	16	40	30	13	38	37
6	FABK-0004	2	443	510	346	520	620	413	549

	A	B	C	D	E	F	G	H	I
1	Unit Sales								
2	Product Number	Group	Jan-07	Feb-07	Mar-07	Apr-07	May-07	Jun-07	Jul-07
3	FABK-0001	1	397	235	285	481	231	362	130
4	FABK-0002	1	144	125	139	136	65	83	80
5	FABK-0003	1	19	56	10	28	14	23	28
6	FABK-0004	2	413	654	502	330	651	604	442

21 Click the **View** tab, and then click the **Split** button to turn off the split/frozen panes.

22 Press **Ctrl+Home** and notice that this time, with panes unfrozen, cell **A1** is selected.

23 Press **Ctrl+G** to display the **Go To** dialog box.

24 Enter Z119 in the **Reference** box.

25 Hold down the **Shift** key and click **OK** to select the range **A1:Z119**.

26 Click the **Page Layout** tab, click the **Print Area** button, and then click **Set Print Area**.

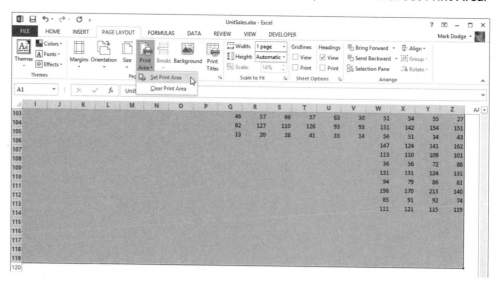

27   Click the **File** tab and click **Print** to display the **Print Preview** screen; notice that the sheet is still set up to include all the columns on one page.

28   Click the **Orientation** button (which currently shows **Portrait**), and then click **Landscape**.

> **TIP** The print area, along with other page setup settings, is saved with the worksheet. This is invaluable when you need to repeatedly print only a certain area of a worksheet.

✕ CLEAN UP Close the UnitSales.xlsx workbook without saving.

Printing row and column labels on every page

The Print Titles command, located on the Page Layout tab, allows you to specify rows and columns—typically containing labels identifying your detail data—to print on every page. This is similar to freezing panes, except that it only applies to printing, and you can specify any cell range on the worksheet, whether or not it happens to be adjacent to the labels.

In the previous exercise, you used the Hide command to conceal data that you didn't need to either display or print. In this exercise, you'll define the print area and print titles to customize your printed work.

→ SET UP You need either the UnitSales.xlsx workbook from the previous exercise or the UnitSales_start.xlsx workbook located in the Chapter22 practice file folder to complete this exercise. If you are using the UnitSales_start.xlsx workbook, open it and save it as UnitSales.xlsx. Then follow the steps.

1   Open the **UnitSales.xlsx** workbook, if it is not already open.

2   Click the **Name** box at the left end of the formula bar, and select the named range **thirteen**.

22

		B	C	D	E	F	G	H
A1					Unit Sales			
eight								
eleven								
nine	ber	Group	Jan-07	Feb-07	Mar-07	Apr-07	May-07	Jun-07
Print_Area		1	397	235	285	481	231	362
seven		1	144	125	139	136	65	83
ten		1	19	56	10	28	14	23
thirteen		2	413	654	502	330	651	604
twelve		2	373	447	330	381	515	362
8 FABK-0006		1	88	34	79	43	95	97
9 FABK-0007		1	388	377	266	230	320	240

3   Click the **Page Layout** tab.

4   Click the **Print Area** button, and then click **Set Print Area**.

5   Click the **Print Titles** button in the **Page Setup** group on the **Page Layout** tab to display the **Page Setup** dialog box with the **Sheet** tab active. Notice that the **Print Area** box already displays the reference **BW3:CH129**, the definition of the named range **thirteen**.

6   Click in the **Rows to repeat at top** box and then, on the worksheet, drag through row headings **1** and **2** to select the entire rows. Notice that when you click the worksheet, the dialog box collapses, revealing any cells that were hidden beneath. (You may need to scroll up a bit to view rows **1** and **2**.) This type of box enables you to navigate around the worksheet, and then select cells, rows, or columns, which serves to enter their references into the box.

7   Click in the **Columns to repeat at left** box, and then click the column **A** heading to select it. (Again, scroll to the left if necessary to make column **A** visible.)

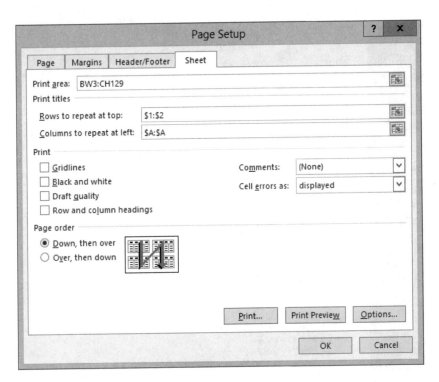

8   Click the **Print Preview** button in the **Page Setup** dialog box.

9   Click the **Orientation** button (which usually displays **Portrait Orientation**), and select **Landscape Orientation**.

22

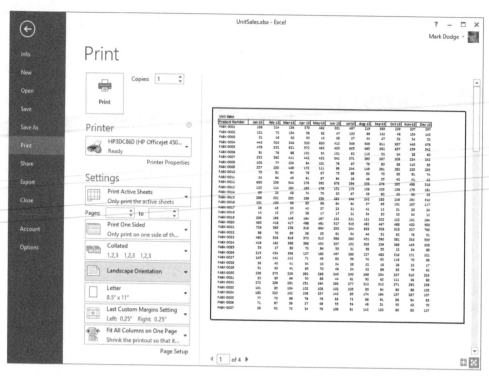

❌ CLEAN UP Save the UnitSales.xlsx workbook and close it.

Using the Print Titles command enables you to specify any range on the worksheet that you want to print, and includes the appropriate titles for you. This setting is saved with the worksheet. If you want to print another range, all you need to do is specify a different print area; you won't need to change the print titles again unless you add more rows or columns of information that you want to include.

Adjusting page breaks

When you're printing large Excel worksheets, the location of page breaks can be a real problem. If your table is a little bit too wide to fit on a sheet, for example, you may need to print a second page containing a single column, doubling the necessary size of the printout (for example, 10 pages become 20). Excel provides some help with this.

In this exercise, you'll control page breaks and page size by using Page Break Preview.

SET UP You need either the UnitSales.xlsx workbook from the previous exercise or the UnitSales2_start.xlsx workbook located in the Chapter22 practice file folder to complete this exercise. If you are using the UnitSales2_start.xlsx workbook, open it and save it as UnitSales.xlsx. Then follow the steps.

1   In the **UnitSales.xlsx** workbook, click the **Name** box at the left end of the formula bar and enter the cell address **BW3**.

2   Click the **View** tab, and then click the **Page Break Preview** button. This workbook already has a defined print area (as shown in the previous exercise): the white area visible in **Page Break Preview** mode.

Each printed page has a watermark number superimposed on it in this view. Don't worry, the numbers won't print.

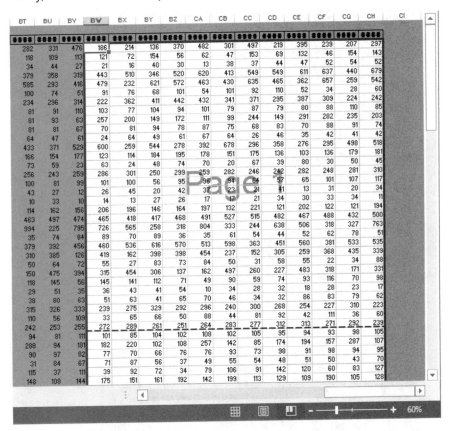

3   Click the **Zoom** button, in the **Zoom** group, on the **View** tab.

4   In the **Custom** box, enter 20, and press **Enter**. (Your screen size may differ, so feel free to scroll and adjust your zoom so that all of the white areas of the worksheet are visible in **Page Break Preview**.)

5   Click the **Page Layout** tab.

6   Click the **Orientation** button, and then click **Portrait**; the display adjusts and shows that you will now print six pages; the dotted blue lines indicate page breaks. You can drag the blue lines around in **Page Break Preview** mode. Page breaks will adjust accordingly, and the worksheet will be scaled to accommodate, if necessary.

7   Point to the vertical dotted line until the pointer turns into a double-headed arrow.

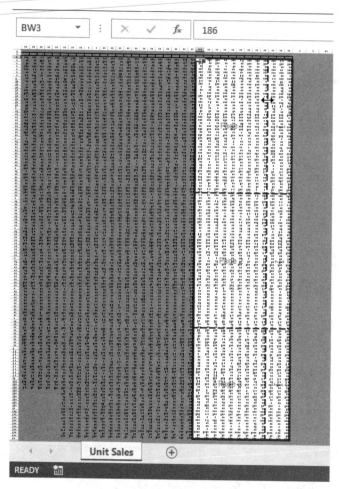

8   Click the vertical dotted blue line and drag it to the right, past the solid blue line. Take a look at the **Scale** percentage in the **Scale to Fit** area of the **Page Layout** tab; after you dragged the line, it changed to the percentage necessary to squeeze all the columns across one page for printing.

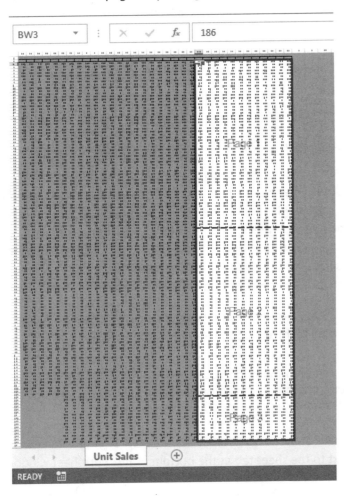

9   Click the **View** tab, and then click the **Normal** button to cancel **Page Break Preview** mode.

10   Press **Ctrl+Home** to display cell **A1**.

TIP Many View tab settings are saved with the workbook, including Page Break Preview. When you open a workbook, these settings as well as the active cell (or cell range) that was selected when you last saved are visible onscreen. You might want to change the view and select cell A1 or another cell in the main area of the worksheet before saving, especially if you share the workbook with others. In a multisheet workbook, the active sheet is also saved.

❌ CLEAN UP Save the UnitSales.xlsx workbook and close it.

Creating a multisheet workbook

Workbooks can contain as many worksheets as you can create, limited only by your good sense and your computer's memory. Putting multiple tables, data sets, presentation graphics, and similar items on a single sheet is not only unnecessary, it's probably unwise, as tempting as it may be to leverage a million rows and 16 thousand columns of sheet real estate. You can help maintain the integrity of your data and make it easier to work with by breaking free of the single-worksheet mindset. (For some good reasons not to put more than one table on a sheet, see "Inserting and deleting cells," earlier in this chapter.)

In this exercise, you'll create a multisheet workbook, format the sheets together, and then use selection and copying techniques to move data into them.

➡ SET UP You need the Q1-Transactions_start.xlsx workbook located in the Chapter22 practice file folder to complete this exercise. Open the Q1-Transactions_start.xlsx workbook, save it as Q1-Transactions.xlsx, and the follow the steps.

1   In the **Q1-Transactions.xlsx** workbook, click the **New Sheet** button *twice* (the plus-sign button next to the sheet tab at the bottom of the worksheet window) to add two new sheets to the workbook.

2   Double-click the **Q1-2013** tab, so that the name of the tab is highlighted.

3   Enter Jan 2013 and press **Enter**.

4   Double-click the **Sheet1** tab, enter Feb 2013, and press **Enter**.

5   Double-click the **Sheet2** tab, enter Mar 2013, and press **Enter**.

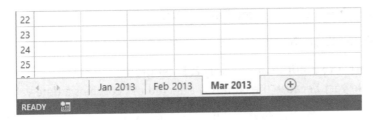

6   Click the **Jan 2013** sheet tab.

7   Select cells **A1:F1** (the column labels).

8   Press **Shift**, and then click the **Mar 2013** sheet tab to select all three sheets. Notice that **[Group]** now appears after the file name at the top of the Excel window.

9   Click the **Home** tab on the ribbon.

10   Click the **Fill** button in the **Editing** group, and then click **Across Worksheets**, a command that only appears when you have multiple worksheets selected.

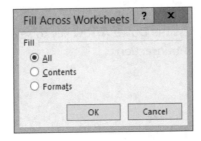

11   Make sure that **All** is selected in the **Fill Across Worksheets** dialog box, and then click **OK**. After this, you need to make sure that only one worksheet is selected, otherwise all the edits you make to the active sheet will be performed on the other selected sheets as well.

12   Click the **Feb 2013** sheet tab (which serves to deselect the group of sheets), then click the **Jan 2013** tab again.

13   Select cell **B2** (the first date in the **Date** column).

14   Click the **Data** tab on the ribbon.

15   Click the **Sort A to Z** button in the **Sort & Filter** group; the button is now labeled **Sort Oldest to Newest** because the currently selected cell contains a date value.

16   Press **Ctrl+F** to display the **Find and Replace** dialog box.

17   Enter 3/1/2013 into the **Find What** box and press **Enter**.

18   Click the **Close** button or press **Esc** to close the dialog box.

19   Press the **Left Arrow** key to select the cell in column **A** adjacent to the date.

20   Hold down the **Shift** and **Ctrl** keys, and then press the **Right Arrow** Key to select all the data in the row.

	A	B	C	D	E	F	G
738	FABK-0116	2/28/2013	Theta	B	31	138.96	
739	FABK-0119	2/28/2013	Theta	B	73	156.31	
740	FABK-0122	2/28/2013	Theta	B	42	472.19	
741	FABK-0124	2/28/2013	Theta	B	31	25.25	
742	FABK-0119	2/28/2013	Theta	C	72	156.31	
743	FABK-0098	2/28/2013	Theta	D	43	29.98	
744	FABK-0125	2/28/2013	Theta	E	138	266.89	
745	FABK-0075	3/1/2013	Alpha	A	36	14.18	
746	FABK-0001	3/1/2013	Alpha	B	40	45.78	
747	FABK-0008	3/1/2013	Alpha	B	33	29.98	

21   Press the **Shift** and **Ctrl** keys, and then press the **Down Arrow** key to select all the rows of the table below, containing March transactions.

22   Press **Ctrl+X** to cut the selected cells.

23   Click the **Mar 2013** sheet tab.

24   Select cell **A2**, and then press **Ctrl+V** to paste the cut cells.

25   Click the **Jan 2013** sheet tab, and then click any cell to deselect the empty range where you just removed cells. (If you don't do this, the next step won't work, because **Find** searches only the selected cells if more than one is selected.)

26   Press **Ctrl+F**, enter 2/1/2013, and press **Enter**.

27   Close the dialog box, and then press the **Left Arrow** key to select the adjacent cell in column **A**.

28 Hold down the **Shift** and **Ctrl** keys, and then press the **Right Arrow** key to select the row of data.

29 Press the **Shift** and **Ctrl** keys, and then press the **Down Arrow** key to select all the February transactions.

30 Press **Ctrl+X** to cut the selected cells.

31 Click the **Feb 2013** sheet tab.

32 Select cell **A2**, and then press **Ctrl+V** to paste the cut cells.

	A	B	C	D	E	F	G
1	Product N	Date	Group	Channel	Qty	Unit Price	
2	FABK-0075	2/1/2013	Alpha	A	43	14.18	
3	FABK-0125	2/1/2013	Alpha	A	139	266.89	
4	FABK-0001	2/1/2013	Alpha	C	45	45.78	
5	FABK-0008	2/1/2013	Alpha	E	43	29.98	
6	FABK-0115	2/1/2013	Beta	B	15	4.70	
7	FABK-0112	2/1/2013	Beta	C	25	140.53	
8	FABK-0072	2/1/2013	Beta	E	57	314.24	
9	FABK-0020	2/1/2013	Delta	A	102	45.78	
10	FABK-0108	2/1/2013	Delta	C	30	29.98	
11	FABK-0052	2/1/2013	Epsilon	A	30	140.53	
12	FABK-0107	2/1/2013	Kappa	E	67	124.74	
13	FABK-0036	2/1/2013	Lambda	A	81	29.98	
14	FABK-0049	2/1/2013	Lambda	B	89	14.18	
15	FABK-0038	2/1/2013	Lambda	D	51	156.31	
16	FABK-0059	2/1/2013	Omega	A	35	156.31	
17	FABK-0102	2/1/2013	Omega	B	38	156.31	
18	FABK-0090	2/1/2013	Theta	B	39	29.98	
19	FABK-0010	2/4/2013	Alpha	B	33	77.35	
20	FABK-0003	2/4/2013	Alpha	D	16	781.73	
21	FABK-0008	2/4/2013	Alpha	E	44	29.98	
22	FABK-0074	2/4/2013	Alpha	E	50	108.96	
23	FABK-0084	2/4/2013	Beta	A	29	123.15	
24	FABK-0071	2/4/2013	Beta	B	53	314.24	
25	FABK-0111	2/4/2013	Beta	D	65	9.43	

Jan 2013 | **Feb 2013** | Mar 2013 | ⊕

READY

22

❌ CLEAN UP Save the Q1-Transactions.xlsx workbook and keep it open for the next exercise.

Working with grouped sheets

When you select multiple sheets, [Group] appears next to the name of the workbook displayed at the top of the screen. If all the sheets in a workbook are selected (as in the previous exercise), just click any tab (other than the active sheet) to ungroup them.

However, if not all sheets in the workbook are selected, clicking another grouped tab activates the sheet, but does not release the group. Instead, click any non-grouped sheet to release the group. If you save a workbook with grouped sheets, the group will be there the next time you open it. Don't do it.

When sheets are grouped, anything you enter or edit in any one of them is duplicated in the others, including entering and formatting data, inserting graphics, changing column widths, and so on. This is a great feature when you need to create an assortment of similar worksheets. But be careful. Check that [Group] indicator and make sure it's gone before you start editing individual sheets.

Manipulating sheets

After you add sheets to a workbook, you can change their order; insert, delete, move, or copy sheets to other workbooks; or even create new workbooks from sheets.

In this exercise, you'll move, rename, and copy sheets in a workbook, and drag sheets between workbooks.

➡ SET UP You need either the Q1-Transactions.xlsx workbook from the previous exercise or the Q1-Transactions2_start.xlsx workbook located in the Chapter22 practice file folder to complete this exercise. If you are using the Q1-Transactions2_start.xlsx workbook, open it and save it as Q1-Transactions.xlsx. Then follow the steps.

1   In the **Q1-Transactions.xlsx** workbook, click the **Add Sheet** button (the plus sign) next to the sheet tabs at the bottom of the workbook window. **Sheet1** appears between the **Jan 2013** and **Feb 2013** tabs.

2   Click the **Sheet1** tab and drag it until the black arrow indicator is to the left of the **Jan 2013** tab.

3   Release the mouse button.

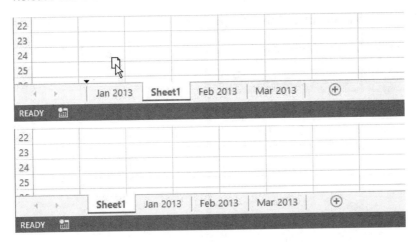

4   Double-click the **Sheet1** tab, enter Summary, and press **Enter**.

5   Right-click the **Jan 2013** tab to display the shortcut menu.

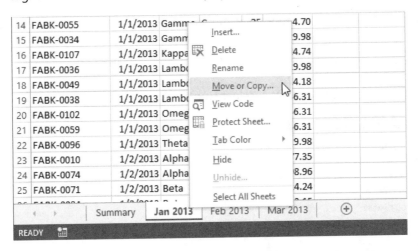

TIP Hiding a worksheet may be desirable if it contains information that others don't need to view but that may be vulnerable or unnecessarily confusing (such as formulas used to calculate values used elsewhere, or critical reference data that never changes). Hide the current worksheet by clicking the Format button on the Home tab and selecting Hide Sheet on the Hide & Unhide menu, or by right-clicking the tab of the sheet you want to hide and then clicking Hide. Once a sheet is hidden, you can unhide it with the Unhide command, which appears in the same locations as the Hide command, but only if a hidden sheet is present.

6   Click the **Move or Copy** command on the shortcut menu.

7   Click the **To Book** list and select **(new book)**.

8   Select the **Create a copy** check box.

9   Click **OK**, and Excel creates a new, unnamed workbook containing a copy of the **Jan 2013** worksheet.

10   Click the **View** tab.

11   Click the **Arrange All** button, select **Horizontal**, and then click **OK**.

12   Click the **Feb 2013** tab in the **Q1-Transactions.xlsx** workbook.

13   Hold down the **Ctrl** key and drag the **Feb 2013** tab to the other workbook; you'll notice that a small page icon with a plus sign in it appears next to the pointer, indicating a copy operation (if you didn't hold down **Ctrl**, you would move the sheet rather than copy it, and no plus sign would appear in the icon).

14   Release the mouse button and the **Ctrl** key.

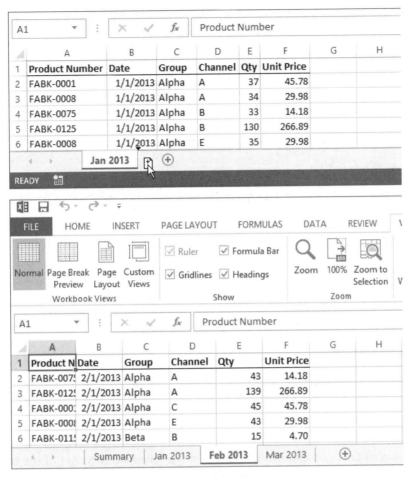

15   Close the unnamed workbook without saving.

❌ CLEAN UP Save the Q1-Transactions.xlsx workbook and close it.

Summarizing a multisheet workbook

Now that you've created a multisheet workbook, you need to be able to work with the data on those sheets. The sample workbook used in the following exercise is similar to the Q1-Transactions workbook used in the previous exercise, but formatting was added on the Summary sheet, and a column of totals was added to each detail sheet by using the technique described in "Inserting rows and columns," earlier in this chapter.

In this exercise, you'll use a basic summary sheet to summarize important data by using formulas that calculate data located on the detail sheets.

 SET UP You need the Q1-Summary_start.xlsx workbook located in the Chapter22 practice file folder to complete this exercise. Open the Q1-Summary_start.xlsx workbook, save it as Q1-Summary.xlsx, and then follow the steps.

1   On the **Summary** sheet of the **Q1-Summary.xlsx** workbook, select cell **C5**.

2   Enter =SUMIFS(

3   Click the **Jan 2013** sheet tab, and then click the **E** column header to select the entire column.

4   Press **F4** to change the reference to fixed (**$E:$E**).

5   Enter a comma.

6   Click the **C** column header to select the entire column.

7   Press **F4** to change the reference to fixed (**$C:$C**).

8   Enter a comma.

9   Click the **Summary** sheet tab, click cell **B5**, and then press **F4** three times to change the reference to mixed (**$B5**).

10   Press **Enter**.

11   Select cell **C5**, right-click the fill handle in the lower-right corner of the cell, and drag to the right to cell **E5**; a menu appears.

12   Click **Fill Without Formatting** to copy the formula without disturbing the border formats.

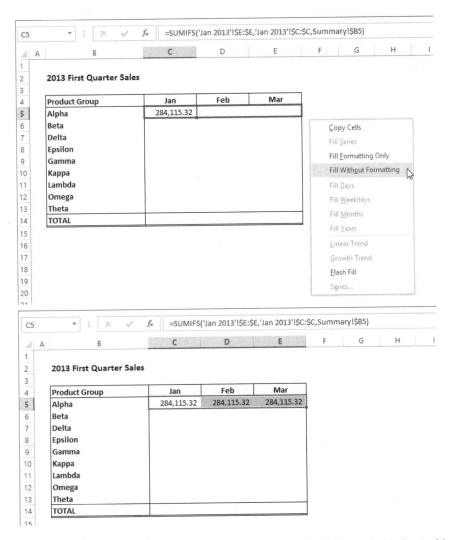

13   Select cell **D5**, double-click the formula bar to enable **Edit** mode (indicated in the status bar at the lower-left corner of the window), and change **Jan** to Feb in both references (being careful not to disturb adjacent spaces and apostrophes when deleting and typing.)

14 Press **Enter**.

15 Select cell **E5**, double-click the formula bar, and change **Jan** to **Mar** in both references.

16 Press **Enter**.

17 Select cells **C5:E5**.

18 To copy the formulas to the rest of the table, right-click the fill handle in the lower-right corner of cell **E5** and drag down to cell **E13**; a menu appears.

19 Click the **Fill Without Formatting** command to copy the formulas down the table without disturbing the border formats.

20 With all the formulas still selected, click the **Decrease Decimal** button in the **Number** group on the **Home** tab *twice*.

21 Select cells **C14:E14**.

22 Click the **AutoSum** button in the **Editing** group on the **Home** tab.

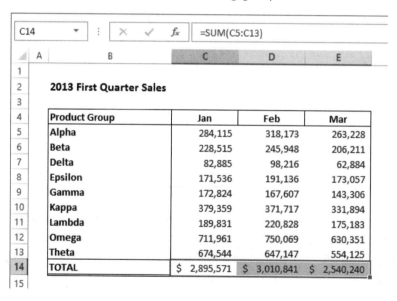

Product Group	Jan	Feb	Mar
Alpha	284,115	318,173	263,228
Beta	228,515	245,948	206,211
Delta	82,885	98,216	62,884
Epsilon	171,536	191,136	173,057
Gamma	172,824	167,607	143,306
Kappa	379,359	371,717	331,894
Lambda	189,831	220,828	175,183
Omega	711,961	750,069	630,351
Theta	674,544	647,147	554,125
TOTAL	$ 2,895,571	$ 3,010,841	$ 2,540,240

❌ CLEAN UP Save the Q1-Summary.xlsx workbook, but keep it open for the next discussion.

Working with sheet references

Let's take a closer look at one of the monthly Product Group formulas created in the previous exercise. The SUMIF function simply allows you to use criteria to select specific values to add, all of which reside on other worksheets in the example. Each of the three sections of this formula contains a *sheet reference*, characterized by the presence of an exclamation point separating the sheet name from the cell address.

Formula	=SUMIFS('Jan 2013'!$E:$E,'Jan 2013'!$C:$C,Summary!$B5)		
Function and arguments	SUMIFS(Sum_Range, Criteria_Range1, Criteria1, ...)		
	Sum_Range	Criteria_Range	Criteria
Sheet references	'Jan 2013'!$E:$E	'Jan 2013'!$C:$C	Summary!$B5
Description	Refers to the totals in the Sale column on the Jan 2013 sheet	Refers to the totals in the Group column on the Jan 2013 sheet	Refers to the names in the Product Group column on the Summary sheet

A cell reference such as *$B5* used in a formula always refers to a cell on the same sheet. But if you precede a cell reference with a sheet reference, such as *Summary!*, you can access values on the Summary sheet from any sheet in the workbook.

Just one criterion was used in these formulas (the Product Group name), but you can add up to 127 criteria, each with its own criteria range. Notice the difference between the references for Criteria Range and Criteria. The Criteria Range sheet name is enclosed in single quotation marks (apostrophes, if you prefer), but the Criteria reference is not. If a reference includes a space character, as in the sheet name Jan 2013, you must enclose it in single quotation marks.

If you have a set of identical sheets in a workbook (unlike the Q1-Summary workbook), you can use a *multisheet reference* to summarize values located in the same cell on each sheet. These are sometimes called "3-D references," since they escape the two-dimensional spreadsheet grid, drilling down into a stack of worksheets. For example, if a workbook contains a set of sales totals sheets for each month (named Jan, Feb, Mar, and so on) and cell B5 contains the equivalent value on each sheet, the following formula on the Summary sheet adds up the values in cell B5 on all the monthly sheets.

```
=SUM(Jan:Dec!B5)
```

22

The multi-sheet reference is similar to the sheet reference in the SUMIFS formula. Just take the names of the first and last sheets in the stack you want to summarize, and separate them with a colon to create a multisheet reference. And, of course, you need to surround the multisheet reference with single quotation marks if the sheet names include spaces.

```
=SUM('Jan 2013:Dec 2013'!B5)
```

Managing multiple workbooks

You can open as many workbooks at once as your computer's memory allows, and you can move among them by pressing Alt+Tab, the system shortcut for switching windows. This is relatively new behavior in Excel. Earlier versions embraced all open workbooks under one umbrella, so to speak; a single "instance" of Excel. Now, each workbook you open generates a new window—another instance of Excel—each with its own ribbon, sheet tabs, status bar, and so on. You may appreciate this behavior if you use multiple monitors.

In the previous chapter, we explored opening additional windows to view other areas of the same workbook, or to simultaneously view the same area in different ways. (For more information about view options, see "Setting view options" in Chapter 21, "Formatting worksheets.") Windows that you create this way look nearly identical to windows of other open workbooks, because they both create separate instances of Excel. One way to tell the difference is by looking at the workbook name displayed at the top of the screen. It is a window on a workbook if the name includes a colon followed by a number (indicating which window you're looking at, such as *Book1.xlsx:5*). Otherwise, the instance in question is a different workbook.

In this exercise, you'll create another workbook window and arrange workbooks and windows together on the screen.

 SET UP You need both the UnitSales_start.xlsx and FabrikamQ1_start.xlsx workbooks located in the Chapter22 practice file folder to complete this exercise. Open the Unit-Sales_start.xlsx workbook, and save it as UnitSales.xlsx. Open the FabrikamQ1_start.xlsx workbook, and save it as FabrikamQ1.xlsx. Then follow the steps.

1   Activate the **UnitSales.xlsx** workbook.

2   Click the **View** tab, and then click **New Window**.

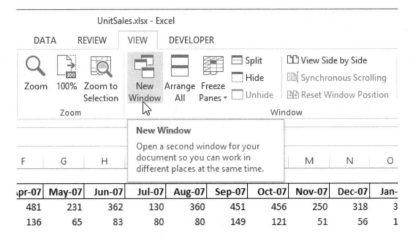

UnitSales.xlsx - Excel

F	G	H					M	N	O

.pr-07	May-07	Jun-07	Jul-07	Aug-07	Sep-07	Oct-07	Nov-07	Dec-07	Jan-
481	231	362	130	360	451	456	250	318	3
136	65	83	80	80	149	121	51	56	1

Notice that the workbook name displayed in the title bar becomes UnitSales.xlsx:2.

3   Click the **Arrange All** button in the **Window** group on the **View** tab, and then select the **Windows of active workbook** check box.

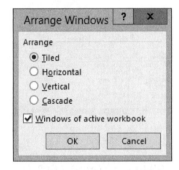

4   Click **OK**, and you'll notice that both active workbook windows are displayed side by side, ignoring the other open workbook. The title bars of the windows display the names **UnitSales.xlsx:1** and **UnitSales.xlsx:2**.

5   On the **View** menu of the **UnitSales.xlsx:2** window, click the **View Side by Side** button.

6   In the **Compare Side by Side** dialog box, select **UnitSales.xlsx:1** and click **OK**; the windows rearrange to horizontal tiling orientation. Notice that in the **Windows** group on the **View** tab, the **Synchronous Scrolling** button is highlighted automatically when you click the **View Side by Side** button.

7   Scroll up and down in the active window; the inactive window scrolls along with it.

8   Click the **View Side by Side** button again to turn it off; the windows rearrange to vertical tiling.

9   Click the **Arrange All** button again, select **Tiled**, and make sure that the **Windows of active workbook** check box is cleared.

10   Click **OK**, and another window appears, displaying the **FabrikamQ1.xlsx** workbook (as well any other workbooks that you may have open).

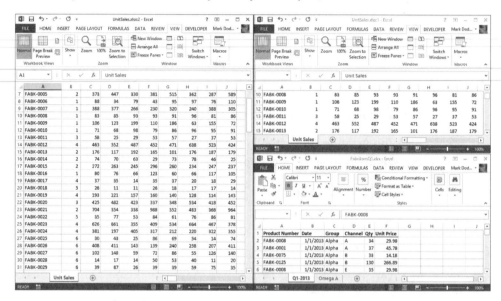

11   Click the **UnitSales.xlsx:1** window to activate it.

12   On the **View** tab, click the **Hide Window** button in the **Window** group, and the window disappears from the screen. Notice, however, that the remaining window still displays **UnitSales.xlsx:2** in its title bar.

13   Click the **Save** button at the top of the **Unit Sales** window.

14   Click the close window button (the **X**) in the upper-right corner of the **Unit Sales** window.

15   Click the **File** tab, click the **Open** command, and select the **Unit Sales** workbook you just closed (which should be near the top of the **Recent Workbooks** list). Notice that nothing seems to happen. Because the main window was hidden when you saved the **Unit Sales** workbook, it is open, but not visible.

16   On the **View** tab, click **Unhide**, which is only available if a hidden window is present. The **UnitSales.xlsx** filename is highlighted in the dialog box.

17   Click **OK** to unhide the workbook.

18   Click the **Save** button to save the workbook without the hidden window.

❌ CLEAN UP Save the UnitSales.xlsx workbook and close it.

Key points

- Excel's table features make it easier and safer to insert and delete rows and columns, as well as add rows or columns of formulas.

- You can convert tables back to regular cells by using the Convert To Range command.

- Use the Print Titles command to specify row and column labels to be printed on each page.

- Use the Freeze Panes command to keep row and column labels in view on screen.

- Page Break Preview allows you to adjust page breaks by dragging.

- To keep track of related data in the same workbook, click the New Sheet button to create additional sheets.

- You can summarize data in a multisheet workbook with formulas, by using sheet references.

- You can arrange all open workbooks and windows together on your screen by using the Arrange All button.

22

Chapter at a glance

Modify

Modify and change the style and color scheme of a selected chart, page 625

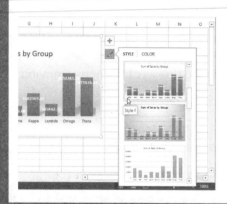

Filter

Filter data by using a slicer to focus on a specific category of data, page 634

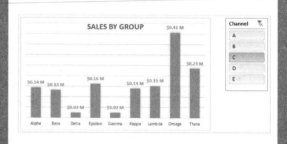

Specify

Specify periods of time by using a timeline, page 639

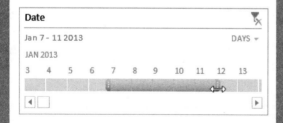

Arrange

Arrange and position objects by using the drawing alignment tools, page 644

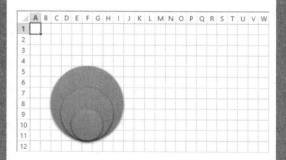

Creating charts and graphics

23

IN THIS CHAPTER, YOU WILL LEARN HOW TO

- Create and modify a chart.

- Add a slicer to a PivotChart.

- Add a timeline to a chart.

- Manipulate objects.

- Create and share graphics.

You may not think of Microsoft Excel as the program you go to when you need to create graphics (other than charts), but most of the graphical tools available in Microsoft PowerPoint and Word are also available in Excel. In this chapter, we'll show you how to create charts, slicers, and timelines, and we'll show you some tricks that have graphical consequences.

PRACTICE FILES To complete the exercises in this chapter, you need the practice files contained in the Chapter23 practice file folder. For more information, see "Download the practice files" in this book's Introduction.

Creating and modifying a chart

Not surprisingly, charts are the most often used graphics available in Excel, complementing Excel's number-crunching prowess. Charts can "wake up" dry numeric data, revealing underlying trends and unanticipated fluctuations that might otherwise be difficult to discern.

In this exercise, you'll explore a new feature in Excel 2013 called Recommended Charts that makes the process of adding a relevant graphic just a little bit easier. After you create it, you'll use some new chart-formatting controls to modify it.

SET UP You need the FabrikamSalesTable_start.xlsx workbook located in the Chapter23 practice file folder to complete this exercise. Open the FabrikamSalesTable_start.xlsx workbook, and save it as FabrikamSalesTable.xlsx.

1   In the **FabrikamSalesTable.xlsx** workbook, make sure that cell **A2** is selected (or any cell within the table).

2   Click the **Insert** tab, and then in the **Charts** group, click **Recommended Charts** to display the **Insert Chart** dialog box with the **Recommended Charts** tab selected.

3   Select the fourth thumbnail, **Clustered Column,** in which the chart title reads **Sum of Sales by Channel**. Excel automatically determined that a PivotTable can be used to analyze this data; six of the seven charts offered are PivotCharts, as indicated by the "pivot" icons displayed in the upper-right corner of each thumbnail.

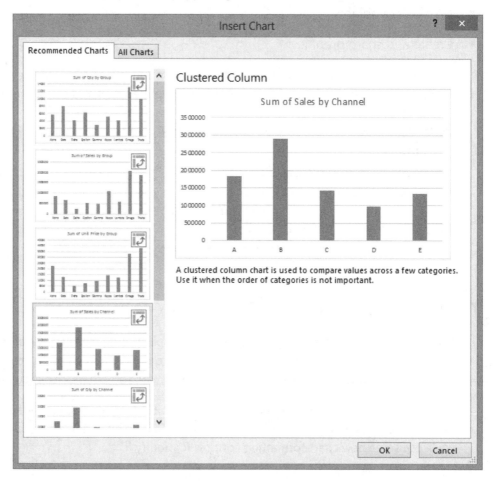

4   Click **OK**, and you'll notice that Excel creates a new worksheet, inserts a PivotChart and a PivotTable, displays the **PivotChart Fields** pane, and displays three **PivotChart Tools** tabs on the ribbon.

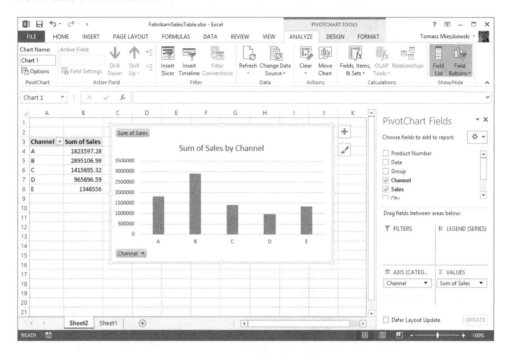

TIP If you click in the worksheet while a PivotChart is selected, the PivotChart Fields list and the PivotChart Tools tabs disappear. Click the chart to redisplay them.

5   In the **PivotChart Fields** pane, select the **Group** check box.

6   Clear the **Channel** check box. You'll notice that both the PivotTable and the PivotChart change accordingly, although the chart title is now incorrect.

7   Close the **PivotChart Fields** pane by clicking the close button (the **X** in the upper-right corner).

8   Click the chart title to select it.

TIP Don't double-click the chart title, or you'll display the Format Chart Title pane instead of selecting the title. This is a nice feature that you don't need right now, so if this happens, click the pane's close button (the X in the upper-right corner) to dismiss it.

23

9   Enter Sales by Group; the title does not appear to change, but the text appears in the formula bar as you enter it.

10 Press the **Enter** key, and the text in the title changes to match the text in the formula bar.

11 Click in the white area next to the chart title to deselect it.

12 Click the **Chart Styles** button to display the **Style** menu.

13 Move the pointer over any thumbnail to view a live preview of that style displayed on your PivotChart.

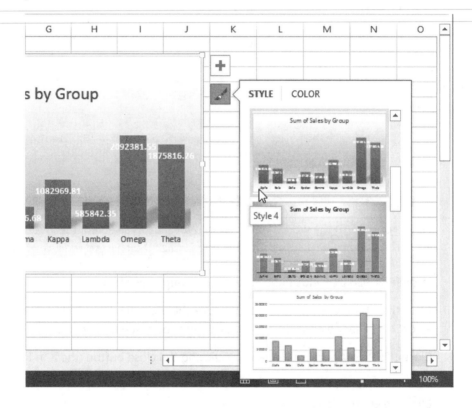

14 Click **Style 4**, a chart with 3-D shading, and then click the **Chart Styles** button again to dismiss the pane.

15 With the chart selected, click the **Chart Elements** button (the plus sign button above the **Chart Styles** button) to display its menu.

16 Clear the **Data Labels** check box; the sales totals disappear.

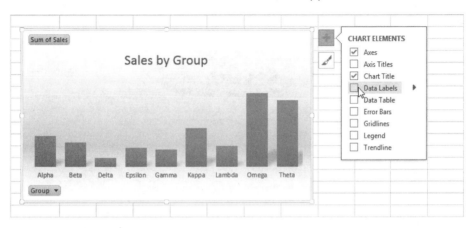

17 Click the chart to select it.

18 Click the **PivotChart Tools Analyze** tab.

19 Click the **Field Buttons** button in the **Show/Hide** group to hide the two grey buttons labeled **Sum of Sales** and **Group** that are displayed on the chart.

20 Click the **PivotChart Tools Design** tab.

21 Click the **Change Chart Type** button in the **Type** group.

22 Click **Pie** and then click the second pie type (**3-D Pie**) from the sketches displayed across the top of the **Change Chart Type** dialog box.

23

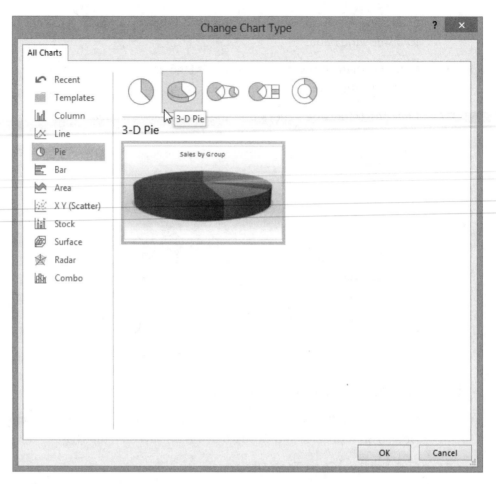

23 Click **OK**.

24 Click the **Chart Styles** button and select **Style 8**, a solid 3-D chart with rounded edges.

25 Click the **Chart Styles** button again to dismiss the menu.

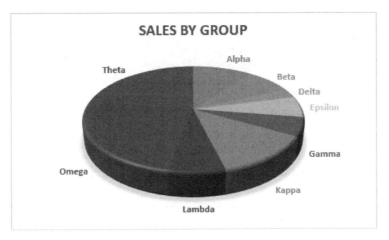

SALES BY GROUP

CLEAN UP Save the FabrikamSalesTable.xlsx workbook, and then close it.

TIP 3-D charts are great for presentations and publications, but when accurate representation of relative values is more important than cosmetics, use 2-D charts. The foreshortening that is applied to achieve the 3-D effect distorts the shape of the chart. Areas that appear "closer" seem proportionally larger.

Adding a slicer to a PivotChart

The cryptically named slicers feature was introduced in Excel 2010 for exclusive use with PivotTables, but new in Excel 2013, you can also use them with any kind of data table as well. Slicers are interactive filters that make it easy to determine both the cause and the result of changes in your worksheet, PivotTable, or PivotChart.

In this exercise, you'll add a simple slicer to a PivotChart.

23

SET UP You need the FabrikamSalesTable2_start.xlsx workbook located in the Chapter23 practice file folder to complete this exercise. Open the FabrikamSalesTable2_start.xlsx workbook, and save it as FabrikamSalesTable2.xlsx.

1   In the **FabrikamSalesTable2.xlsx** workbook, click the chart to activate all the context-sensitive tools and tabs.

2   Click the **PivotChart Tools Analyze** tab.

3   Click the **Insert Slicer** button in the **Filter** group; a dialog box of the same name appears.

4   Select the **Channel** check box.

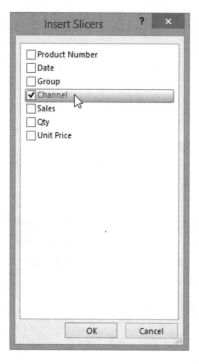

5   Click **OK** to dismiss the **Insert Slicers** dialog box.

6   Drag the **Slicer** box to the side, away from the chart. (We also resized the box a bit by dragging the square handles.)

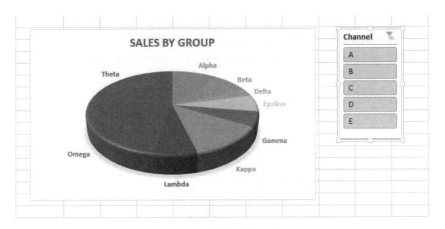

7   Click the **Slicer Tools Options** tab that appeared on the ribbon after you created the slicer.

8   Click the **More** button (the downward-pointing fast-forward button) in the lower-right corner of the **Slicer Styles** palette to open it.

9   In the **Slicer Styles** palette, click the thumbnail called **Slicer Style Other 2**.

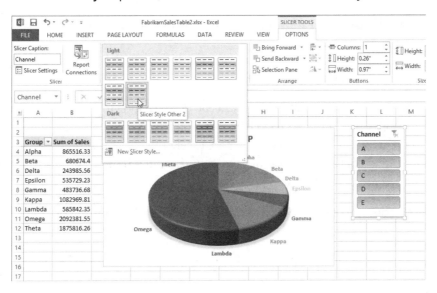

23

10 Click the **C** button in the slicer box to display the result in the chart. After you click, only the sales made through **Channel C** are represented, the **C** button is highlighted, and the **Clear Filter** button in the upper-right corner of the slicer box becomes active.

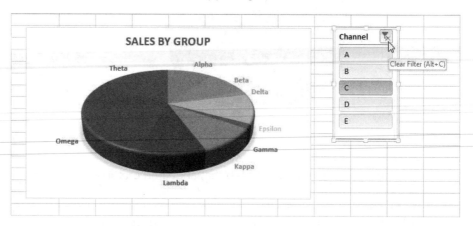

11 Click the other slicer buttons and notice the resulting changes made to the chart.

12 Click the **Clear Filter** button.

❌ CLEAN UP Save the FabrikamSalesTable2.xlsx workbook, and then close it.

Manipulating chart elements

After you create a chart, there is a lot you can do to change it. Sometimes it takes experimentation to arrive at the perfect chart that highlights salient information in a way that gets your point across. When a chart is selected, Excel provides many tools you can use to modify it, including context-sensitive tabs that appear on the ribbon, and the Chart Elements and Chart Styles buttons that appear adjacent to a selected chart.

In this exercise, you'll try using additional chart elements to look at your data in a different way.

1   In the **FabrikamSalesTable3.xlsx** workbook, click the chart to activate the context-sensitive chart tools and tabs.

2   Click the **PivotChart Tools Design** tab.

3   Click the **Change Chart Type** button in the **Type** group.

4   Click **Column**, and then click **OK**.

5   Click the **Chart Elements** button, point to **Data Labels**, and then click the small arrow that appears to the right of the option to display the submenu.

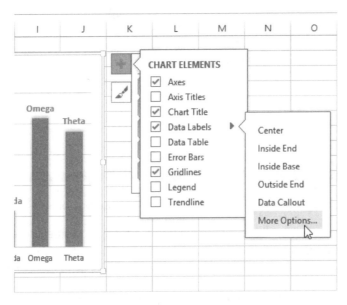

6   Click **More Options** to display the **Format Data Labels** pane.

7   In the **Label Options** section of the pane, select the **Value** check box, and clear the **Category Name** check box.

8   Dismiss the **Format Data Labels** pane by clicking its close button.

9   On the worksheet, select all the cells in column **B** containing values, cells **B4:B12**; you'll apply a format that scales them appropriately, so that they won't take up quite as much space on the screen—for example, using *$1.00 M* instead of *$1,000,000.00.*

10   Press **Ctrl+1** to display the **Format Cells** dialog box, and click the **Custom** category.

11   In the **Type** box, drag through the existing code to select it, and replace it by entering $0.00,," M"

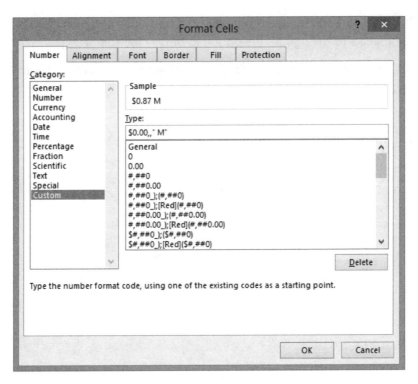

12   Click the **OK** button.

TIP In a custom number format code, putting a comma between digit placeholders tells Excel to include thousands separators. But if you put a comma following digit placeholders, Excel scales the number by a multiple of one thousand. Adding one comma scales the number to thousands, adding two commas scales the number to millions, and so on. For example, the format code 0.0,K would display the entry 12345 in thousands as 12.3K.

SEE ALSO For more information about number formatting codes, see Chapter 21, "Formatting worksheets."

13   Click in a blank area of the chart to activate it.

14   Click the **Chart Elements** button, point to **Chart Title**, and then click the small arrow that appears to the right of the option to display the submenu.

15   Click the **Centered Overlay** option, which allows the columns to sit a little taller in the chart.

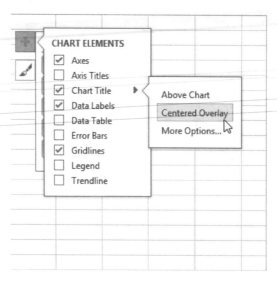

TIP Double-click any chart element to open a corresponding pane docked on the right side of the screen. For example, double-click the chart title to display the Format Chart Title pane.

16   With the **Chart Elements** menu still visible, point to **Axes**, and then click the small arrow that appears to the right of the option to display the submenu.

17   Clear the **Primary Vertical** check box.

18   Click the **Chart Elements** button to dismiss the menu.

19   Click cell **A1** on the worksheet to dismiss the chart controls and **PivotChart Tools** tabs.

20   Click the **View** tab on the ribbon and clear the **Gridlines** check box in the **Show** group.

21   Click the **C** button in the slicer box.

22   Click the other slicer buttons and notice the resulting changes made to the chart.

23   Click the **Clear Filter** button.

Especially when using slicers, this column chart works better than the original pie chart to visualize the sales of each product group and display the differences among channels.

❌ CLEAN UP Save the FabrikamSalesTable3.xlsx workbook, and then close it.

Adding a timeline to a chart

If your data includes dates, you can use Excel's new timeline feature to zero in on specific time periods, much like the slicer feature allows you to zero in on specific categories of data.

In this exercise, you'll add a timeline to your evolving chart.

➡ SET UP You need the FabrikamSalesTable4_start.xlsx workbook located in the Chapter23 practice file folder to complete this exercise. Open the Fabrikam-SalesTable4_start.xlsx workbook, and save it as FabrikamSalesTable4.xlsx.

1   Click the chart to activate the context-sensitive chart tools and tabs. (You may notice that the PivotTable is no longer visible on the worksheet. It was moved out of the way, to cells **X67:Y76**.)

2   Click the **A** button in the slicer box to display only sales through **Channel A**.

3   Click one of the borders of the chart to select it; three **PivotChart Tools** tabs—
     Analyze, **Design**, and **Format**—appear on the ribbon.

4   Click the **PivotChart Tools Analyze** tab.

5   Click the **Insert Timeline** button in the **Filter** group, and then click the **Date** option
     (the only option available in the dialog box) to select it.

     TIP You can also access the timeline feature by clicking the Timeline button on the
     Insert tab.

6   Click the **OK** button to create a timeline box; it will most likely appear on top of the
     chart.

7   Drag the timeline box to the side, out of the way.

8   Click in the worksheet to deselect the chart and timeline box.

9   Click the scroll bar at the bottom of the timeline box and drag it to the left so that
     JAN is visible.

10   Click the segment of the timeline bar below **FEB** to select it, and watch while the
     chart adjusts to display only February sales.

11   Drag the handle on the right side of the **FEB** timeline bar segment to expand the
     timeframe to include **MAR**. At this point, you have isolated the data displayed on
     the chart to include only those sales from **Channel A** that occurred in February and
     March.

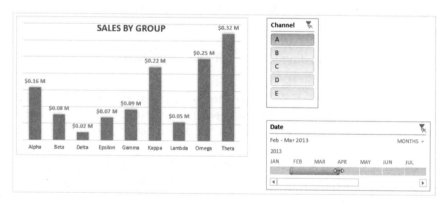

12   Click the **APR** timeline bar segment and notice that the chart goes blank, remind-
     ing you that data only exists for the first three months of the year in this particular
     workbook.

13   In the timeline box, click the small arrow adjacent to the word **Months** to display its menu, and click **Days**. Notice that the timeline bar now displays a separate bar segment for each day.

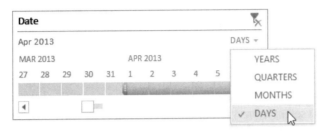

14   Scroll back to January and click the **Jan 7** segment on the timeline bar.

15   Click the handle on the right side of the selected timeline bar, and drag it to the right until January 7th through January 11th is selected. The chart changes to display only the selected data.

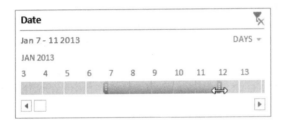

16   Make sure that the **Timeline Tools Options** tab on the ribbon is selected.

17   In the **Show** group, clear all four check boxes (**Header**, **Scrollbar**, **Selection Label**, and **Time Level**). These options are useful for cleaning up the layout and helping to limit user modifications.

18   In the **Show** group, select the **Header** check box (displaying the **Clear Filter** button).

19   Click the **Clear Filter** buttons in both the slicer box and the timeline box.

❌ CLEAN UP Save the FabrikamSalesTable4.xlsx workbook, and then close it.

Manipulating objects

So far in this chapter, you have created three objects: a PivotChart, a slicer box, and a timeline box. Essentially, anything that does not go into a cell is an object that "floats" above the worksheet. Most of the tools on the Insert tab create objects, including shapes, SmartArt, WordArt, text boxes, and pictures.

When you click an object to select it, the appropriate tabs appear on the ribbon containing tools you can use to format and manipulate the object. An additional Drawing Tools Format tab appears whenever you select more than one object (by holding down the Shift key and selecting multiple objects); this tab contains tools for grouping, stacking, and aligning objects.

In this exercise, you'll rearrange objects and do a little resizing and formatting, as well.

SET UP You need the FabrikamSalesTable5_start.xlsx workbook located in the Chapter23 practice file folder to complete this exercise. Open the Fabrikam-SalesTable5_start.xlsx workbook, and save it as FabrikamSalesTable5.xlsx.

1   In the **FabrikamSalesTable5.xlsx** workbook, click one of the borders of the chart to select it.

2   Hold down the **Shift** key and click the slicer box to add it to the selection; thick borders appear around both selected objects.

3   Click the **Drawing Tools Format** tab that appears on the ribbon.

4   Click the **Align Objects** button in the **Arrange** group and click the **Align Top** command. The tops of the two objects are now aligned. (The **Align Objects** button is labeled **Align** if your screen is wide enough to display it. But when you point to it, the ScreenTip says **Align Objects**.)

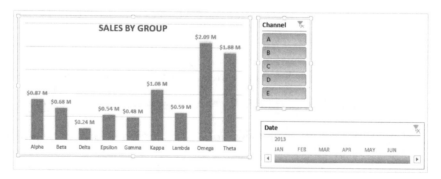

5   Click the timeline box, and then drag it below the chart.

6   Click the **Timeline Tools Options** tab on the ribbon.

7   Clear the **Header** check box in the **Show** group (which makes the timeline box narrower).

8   Press the **Shift** key and click the chart to add it to the selection; thick borders appear around both selected objects.

9   Click the **Drawing Tools Format** tab that appears on the ribbon.

10 Click the **Align Objects** button in the **Arrange** group, and then click the **Align Left** command. The left sides of the two objects are now aligned.

11 Click anywhere in the worksheet to deselect the two objects.

12 Click the timeline box.

13 Click the center square handle on the right side of the timeline box and drag it to the right to make it wider, until it is a little too wide; past the edge of the slicer box above it.

14 With the timeline box still selected, press **Shift** and click the slicer box to add it to the selection; thick borders appear around both selected objects.

15 Click the **Drawing Tools Format** tab that appears on the ribbon.

16 Click the **Align Objects** button in the **Arrange** group and then click the **Align Right** command; all the outside edges of the three objects should now be aligned.

17 Click anywhere in the worksheet to deselect the objects.

18   Click the slicer box to select it.

19   Click the lower-left square handle and drag it down and adjust until the bottom edge is lined up with the bottom edge of the chart.

20   Click the border of the chart to select it.

21   Click the **PivotChart Tools Format** tab that appears on the ribbon.

22   Click the **Shape Effects** button in the **Shape Styles** group, click **Shadow**, and then click the first option in the **Outer** section (**Offset Diagonal Bottom Right**).

23   Click in the worksheet to deselect the objects.

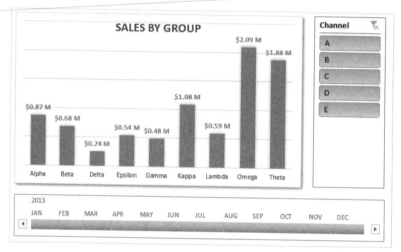

✖ CLEAN UP Save the FabrikamSalesTable5.xlsx workbook, and then close it.

Creating and sharing graphics

Excel probably doesn't immediately come to mind when you need to do some graphic design work, but why not? Excel has the same drawing tools that are available in other Microsoft Office applications, including Microsoft Word and Publisher. Excel workbooks can contain multiple sheets, which can be handy for filing graphic elements or sketches into categories. And of course, Excel doesn't only offer a drawing-grid feature; Excel is a grid that you can adjust.

Although no Office application will replace a dedicated graphics program, there's still a lot you can do with Excel, and you won't have to trek a steep learning curve to do it.

In this exercise, you'll take advantage of a few essential object-manipulation tricks as you create a simple logo.

SET UP You need the FabrikamLogo_start.xlsx workbook located in the Chapter23 practice file folder to complete this exercise. Open the FabrikamLogo_start.xlsx workbook, and save it as FabrikamLogo.xlsx.

1   In the **FabrikamLogo.xlsx** workbook, click the **Insert** tab on the ribbon.

2   In the **Illustrations** group, click the **Shapes** button, and then click **Oval** in the **Basic Shapes** group, and the pointer turns into a crosshair.

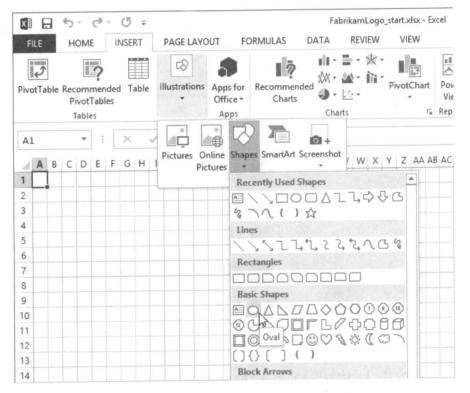

3   Position the crosshair pointer near the upper-left corner of cell **E7**.

4   Drag a shape while holding both the **Shift** and **Alt** keys, and draw a circle that is three cells wide (and of course, being a circle, is also three cells deep); **Shift** constrains the oval tool to create a perfect circle; **Alt** aligns ("snaps") the object to the cell gridlines.

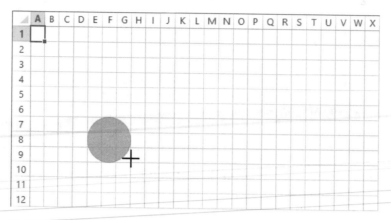

5　On the **Drawing Tools Format** tab that appears on the ribbon, click the **More** button (the downward-pointing fast-forward button) on the **Shape Styles** palette, and click **Intense Effect – Blue, Accent 1**.

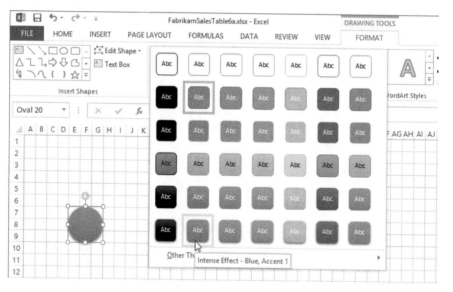

6　Click the **Insert** tab, and in the **Illustrations** group, click the **Shapes** button, and then click **Oval** in the **Basic Shapes** group.

7　Position the crosshair pointer near the upper-left corner of cell **D6**.

8   While holding both the **Shift** and **Alt** keys, click and drag to draw a concentric circle that is one cell wider (and one cell taller) than the first circle.

9   On the **Drawing Tools Format** tab, in the **Shape Styles** palette, click **Intense Effect – Blue, Accent 1**.

10   On the **Drawing Tools Format** tab, click the **Send Backward** button.

11   Click the **Insert** tab, and in the **Illustrations** group, click the **Shapes** button, and then click **Oval** in the **Basic Shapes** group.

12   Position the crosshair pointer near the upper-left corner of cell **C5**.

13   While holding both the **Shift** and **Alt** keys, draw a third concentric circle that is one cell wider than the second circle.

14   Click the **Drawing Tools Format** tab, and in the **Shape Styles** palette, click **Intense Effect – Blue, Accent 1**.

15   On the **Drawing Tools Format** tab, click the **Send Backward** button twice.

16   Press **Ctrl+A** to select all three objects.

17   Click the **Drawing Tools Format** tab, and in the **Arrange** group, click the **Align** button and then click **Align Bottom**.

18   Click any cell to deselect the objects.

23

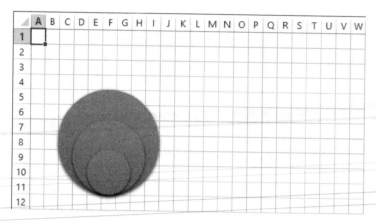

19   Click the **Insert** tab, and in the **Text** group, click **Text Box** and then click anywhere on the worksheet.

20   Enter fabrikam, inc.

21   Press **Ctrl+A** to select the text.

22   Make sure the **Home** tab is active, and then click the **Font** drop-down list and select your favorite display font (we used **Haettenschweiler**).

23   Click the **Font Size** drop-down list and select a large size (we chose **60** points).

24   Click the **Drawing Tools Format** tab, and in the **WordArt Styles** group, click the **Text Effects** button, click **Shadow**, and then click **Shadow Options** at the bottom of the menu.

25   In the **Format Shape** pane, set the color to white, set **Blur** to **0 pt**, set **Angle** to **50°**, and set **Distance** to **3 pt**; this will allow the black text to stand out against the blue circles.

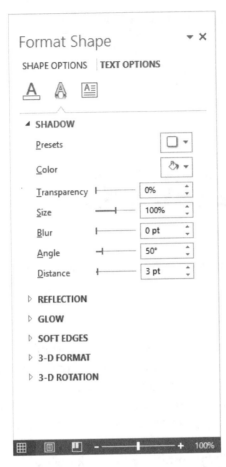

26   Click the dotted edge of the text box, and drag it so that the *f* is near the center of the circles.

27   Click anywhere in the worksheet to deselect the objects.

CLEAN UP Save the FabrikamLogo.xlsx workbook, and then close it.

Using graphics elsewhere

Over the years, Office applications have become increasingly interoperable, making it easy to leverage the output of an application like Excel for use in other applications like Word and PowerPoint. Today, Office programs share many of the same underlying technologies, such as graphics and charting features, AutoCorrect, fonts, styles, and more. But in terms of graphics, you can usually copy something you want to share, such as a chart, and then paste it where you need it. Doing so will usually work, but not always, especially if you want to scale it—that is, make it smaller (larger often doesn't work well), as with pictures and clip art.

In this exercise, you'll use techniques that will allow you to make a static, scalable graphic image from almost anything you can display on your computer. You'll create it in one workbook and copy it to another, but you can copy the image and use it anywhere.

SET UP You need the Logo_start.xlsx and the Report_start.xlsx workbooks located in the Chapter23 practice file folder to complete this exercise. Open the Logo_start.xlsx workbook, and save it as Logo.xlsx. Open the Report_start.xlsx workbook, and save it as Report.xlsx.

1 Activate the **Logo.xlsx** workbook; if it is not visible, press **Alt+Tab** to switch windows (hold down **Alt** and press **Tab** repeatedly to cycle through all the open windows).

2 Click any of the blue circles in the logo to select it.

3 Press **Ctrl+A** to select all the objects.

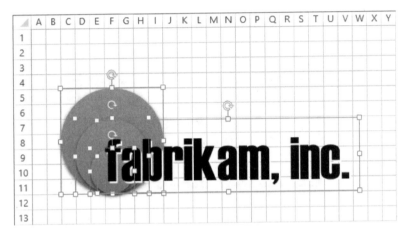

4 Click the **Drawing Tools Format** tab.

5 In the **Arrange** group, click the **Group Objects** button and then click **Group**.

6 Press **Ctrl+C** to copy the selected, grouped logo.

7 Press **Alt+Tab** (repeatedly, if necessary) and activate the **Report.xlsx** workbook.

23

8   Make sure cell **A1** is selected.

9   Press **Ctrl+V** to paste the copied logo at the location of the active cell, and you'll notice that it's just a bit too large.

10 Click the selection handle on the lower-right corner of the logo and, while pressing the **Shift** key, drag to the left to make it smaller. Although the circles seem to scale properly, the text does not. You can select the text in the pasted logo and change the font size directly, but that might not work in other situations, so we'll try a different approach.

11   With the logo selected, press the **Delete** key to remove the logo from the report.

12   Press **Alt+Tab** to return to the **Logo.xlsx** workbook.

13   Click the **View** tab on the ribbon.

14   In the **Show** group, clear the **Gridlines** check box.

15   Press **Alt+Tab** to return to the **Report.xlsx** workbook.

16   Click the **Insert** tab on the ribbon.

17   In the **Illustrations** group, click **Screenshot**. Notice that thumbnail images of open windows are represented in the **Available Windows** area of the menu that appears, including Excel workbooks and other open applications.

> **TIP** The only window from which you cannot take a screenshot is the current window—the window in which you clicked the Screenshot button. So, if you need to shoot the screen you're in, open another workbook and shoot from there. Then copy the resulting image anywhere you like.

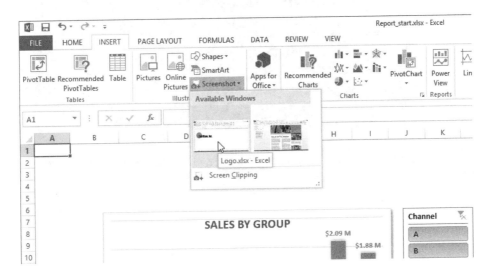

23

18   Click the **Logo.xlsx** thumbnail.

19   Click the **View** tab, click the **Zoom** button in the **Zoom** group, choose **50%**, and click **OK**, allowing you to view the entire pasted image on your screen.

20   Click the **Picture Tools Format** tab and click the **Crop** button in the **Size** group.

21   Drag the center black handles on each side of the image and adjust them to crop out the rest of the image around the logo.

22   When you're done cropping the image, click the **Crop** button in the **Size** group again to finalize your edits.

23   Click the **View** tab, click the **Zoom** button in the **Zoom** group, choose **100%**, and click **OK**.

24   Drag the cropped logo image to the upper-left corner of the worksheet.

25   Drag the selection handle in the lower-right corner of the logo image and make the logo smaller, so that it fits above the chart.

26   Click anywhere in the worksheet to deselect the object.

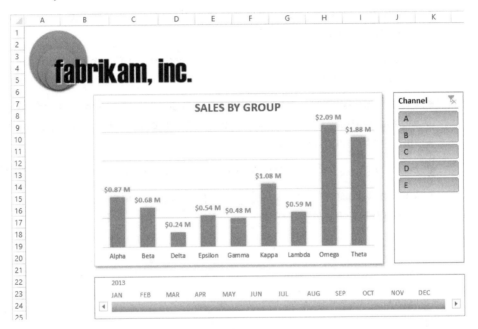

❌ CLEAN UP Save the Report.xlsx and Logo.xlsx workbooks, and then close them.

23

Key points

- The Recommended Chart feature makes intelligent assumptions about your data and suggests the most useful chart options.

- Slicers make it easy to filter underlying chart data with just one click.

- Timelines allow you to filter chart data by specifying specific date ranges to display.

- Charts and other objects in Excel can be scaled, sized, formatted, and otherwise manipulated just like any other type of graphic.

- Excel charts and graphics are compatible with other Office programs and can be copied and pasted directly.

- Holding down the Shift key while drawing an object constrains it; for example, pressing the Shift key while drawing with the Oval tool creates a circle; doing the same with the Rectangle tool creates a square.

- Holding down the Alt key while drawing an object forces it to align with the cell grid.

- You can take screen shots of Excel graphics (and worksheets) that you can easily crop, scale, and share with anyone.

Chapter at a glance

Configure

Configure a new email account,
page 659

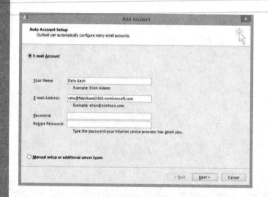

Navigate

Navigate the Outlook interface,
page 662

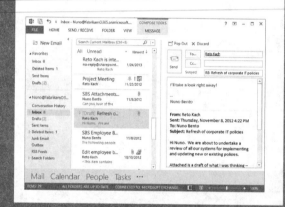

Discover

Discover what's new in Outlook 2013,
page 665

Getting comfortable in Outlook 2013

24

IN THIS CHAPTER, YOU WILL LEARN HOW TO

- Set up an email account.

- Navigate the Outlook interface.

- Discover new features of Outlook 2013.

  Microsoft Outlook 2013 organizes your email messages, calendars, contacts, tasks, and more—all in one place. It all starts with your email account. From there, you can start working with email messages, building your to-do list, scheduling appointments, and creating contacts for the people you frequently communicate with so you never have to remember an email address or phone number.

  In this chapter, you'll learn how to set up an email account. You'll also learn the important elements of the Outlook user interface and how to navigate around the folders in your account. Finally, you'll get introduced to some of the new features available in Outlook 2013.

Setting up an email account in Outlook

The first step is starting Outlook to set up your first email account. After that, you'll be ready to receive and send email, use the calendar, create contacts, and work with tasks. Note that this setup may not be necessary if you used a previous version of Outlook on the same computer. If you didn't, the Account Setup screen that runs the first time you start Outlook will step you through the process.

You typically start Outlook 2013 from the Start screen in Windows 8 or the Start menu in Windows 7. The first time you start Outlook, the welcome screen will appear.

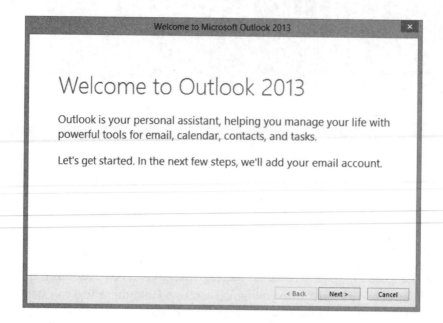

When you click the Next button, you'll be asked to add an email account.

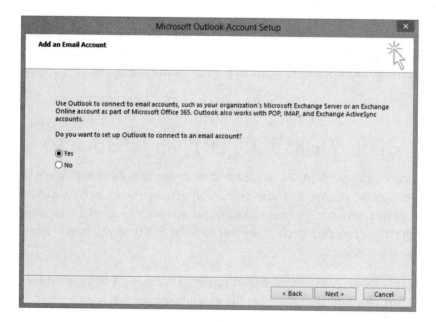

The Account Setup wizard will ask for your name, email address, and a password. That's usually enough, but if the automatic setup fails, Outlook will ask for a few more pieces of information, such as your mail server name.

If you don't have that information, your email provider or the person who manages your email account can give you the details.

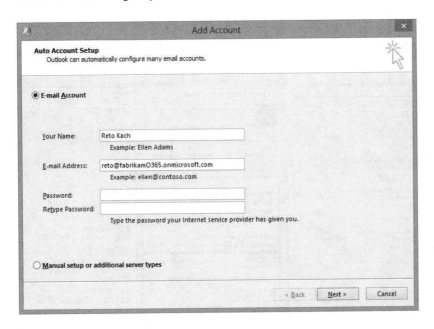

24

Navigating the Outlook interface

After your first account is configured, the main Outlook window is launched.

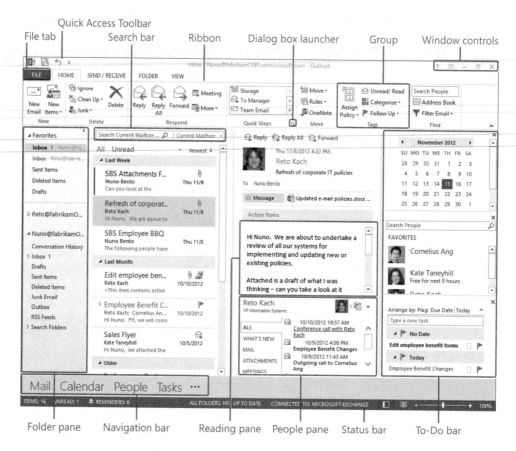

Quick Access Toolbar

File tab   Search bar   Ribbon   Dialog box launcher   Group   Window controls

Folder pane   Navigation bar   Reading pane   People pane   Status bar   To-Do bar

- **Ribbon** The ribbon is the main component of the Outlook interface and where is you'll find the primary commands for working with email messages and other types of items, browsing Outlook folders, searching for content, and managing various settings. It is made up of task-oriented tabs, and each tab has groups of related commands. For example, on the **Home** tab, the **Respond** group contains commands for replying to or forwarding email messages. Groups that have additional commands that aren't shown on the ribbon have a dialog box launcher. Clicking the dialog box launcher will display a task pane or dialog box with options that are related to the group. For example, if you click the dialog box launcher for the **Quick Steps** group, the **Manage Quick Steps** dialog box will be displayed, giving you more options for creating, editing, or deleting **Quick Steps**.

IMPORTANT

SEE ALSO For instructions on how to modify your display settings and adapt exercise instructions, see Chapter 1, "Getting comfortable in Office Professional 2013."

- **File tab** This is the first tab on the ribbon. Unlike other ribbon tabs, the **File** tab displays the **Backstage** view, where commands for adding accounts, changing account settings, and opening .pst files are located. The **Backstage** view is also where application options can be changed and where you can find information about your user account and your version of Microsoft Office.

- **Quick Access Toolbar** This toolbar holds your most frequently used commands. By default, **Send/Receive** and **Undo** have already been added.

  TIP To add other commands that you use the most to your Quick Access Toolbar, right-click the command you want and then click Add To Quick Access Toolbar. To remove a command from the Quick Access Toolbar, similar to adding a command, you right-click the command you wish to remove and then click Remove From Quick Access Toolbar.

- **Title bar** This bar appears at the top of the window and displays the name of the active folder and email account, along with the application name.

- **Window controls** These are displayed at the upper-right end of the title bar. Along with the standard **Minimize**, **Restore Down/Maximize**, and **Close** buttons, there are two additional buttons, **Help** and **Ribbon Display Options**, the latter of which is new in Outlook 2013.

24

- **Status bar** This bar appears at the bottom of the window and displays information about the current view, such as the number of items in the folder or whether a view filter is applied. It can also display information regarding the status of your folder synchronizations or server connection, depending on your account type. The far right end has view options for switching the display between normal and reading modes, along with a zoom slider to change the magnification of the **Reading** pane.

- **Folder pane** Docked to the left side, this pane displays shortcuts for your folder **Favorites** as well as the folders from all of your data files and email accounts.

- **To-Do bar** This panel on the right side can display any **Calendar Peeks**, **People Peeks**, or **Task Peeks** that you want to dock there.

- **Reading pane** When this is turned on, it can be visible at the bottom or to the right of the content selected in the folder.

- **Navigation bar** Displayed immediately above the status bar at the bottom, this bar shows text labels or icons for switching between various navigation modules, such as **Mail**, **Calendar**, **People**, or **Tasks**.

- **Search bar** The search bar is always found directly underneath the ribbon and can be used to search the current folder, subfolders, or even other mailboxes.

- **People pane** This is displayed underneath the **Reading** pane and lists related Outlook items or updates from connected social networks for the sender and email recipients of the selected message.

SEE ALSO For a more comprehensive list of ribbon and user interface elements, along with detailed instructions on how to customize your user interface, including the ribbon and Quick Access Toolbar, see Chapter 1, "Getting comfortable in Office Professional 2013."

Discovering what's new in Outlook 2013

This section introduces you to key application features for Outlook 2013 and provides screen shots, where applicable. The majority of the features included are discussed in detail, with step-by-step instructions, throughout this part of the book.

- **Inline replies** You can now draft your reply directly in the **Reading** pane without opening another window. For lengthier replies, you can pop your reply out of the **Reading** pane.

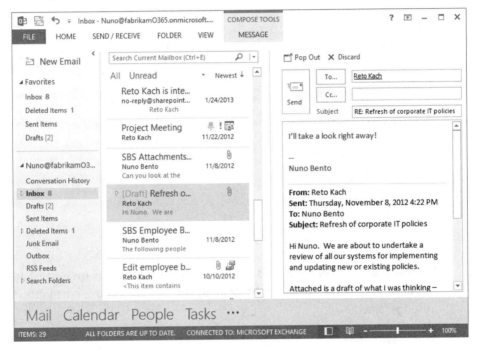

- **Draft email messages** Email messages you haven't sent are marked as **[Draft]** in the **Contents** pane. If you're replying inline in the **Reading** pane and you navigate away from your draft, the new draft indicator makes it easy for you to return to your pending email message.

- **Unread messages** Messages you haven't read are more clearly displayed in your **Contents** pane with a blue bar to the left and bold blue text. And you can now filter your email messages to unread messages only and return to all your messages by using the new **All** and **Unread** commands at the top of the pane.

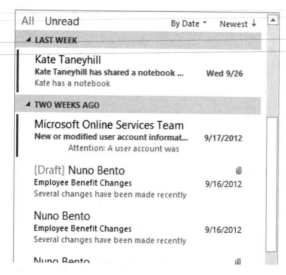

- **Delete button on messages** When you point to an email message, a new **Delete** button is displayed to the right, helping you quickly remove email messages you no longer need.

- **Navigation bar** The **Navigation** bar at the bottom of the window now uses text instead of images. And you can drag the navigation options to reorder them.

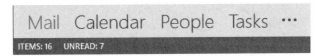

- **Peeks** When you point to a navigation option, peeks enable you to view details for that item. You can view your upcoming appointments, review contact availability, and display upcoming tasks without switching to a different view.

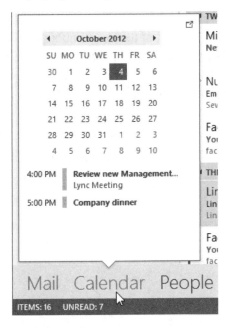

- **Weather bar** You can view your calendar and get a snapshot of the weather at the same time. The weather bar can help you plan activities and help you determine if you need to take your umbrella or sunglasses to a meeting away from your office.

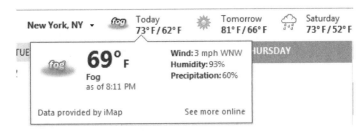

24

- **Custom folder sort** Now you can drag folders to a location of your choice in the folder list.

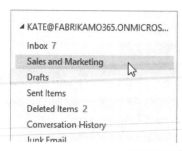

- **People cards** The new **People** card collects all of the details about your contacts. It merges information from multiple contacts and connected social networks in one view. The **People** card also displays availability, notes, organizational hierarchy, distribution list membership, and current social updates.

- **Attachment Reminder** Now Outlook can determine if an email message should contain an attachment and remind you to include it.

- **Improved search** Improvements to search help you find email messages, attachments, contacts, and appointments faster.

- **Exchange ActiveSync support** Now you can use Exchange ActiveSync for other email services, like Microsoft Live Hotmail, without the need for additional add-ins, and you can receive push-based updates.

Key points

- The Account Setup wizard will help you configure your first email account.

- Understanding the main Outlook interface will help you master the fundamentals for creating, reading, and managing your Outlook data.

- Outlook 2013 has many new features that help you work more efficiently.

24

Chapter at a glance

Create

Create and send messages,
page 672

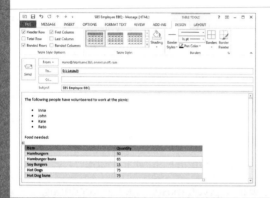

Attach

Attach files to messages,
page 686

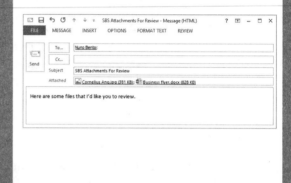

Respond

Respond to messages,
page 701

Using mail

IN THIS CHAPTER, YOU WILL LEARN HOW TO

- Create and send messages.

- Attach files to messages.

- View messages and message attachments.

- Configure Reading pane behavior.

- Respond to messages.

Microsoft Outlook 2013 is a personal information manager that offers business and personal email management tools for working with a wide variety of content, from calendars and scheduling to tasks and contacts. More importantly, Outlook is efficient and easy to use for handling the email workloads of busy users. Whether you use email for school, work, to communicate with family, or to manage your social life, Outlook is a capable tool. It has all of the collaborative features you expect for sending and responding to email messages, navigating through intuitive and flexible views of your messages, efficiently triaging your Inbox, and initiating interactive communications with people with whom you connect.

TIP In this chapter and throughout this book, email messages may be referred to as *messages*. For other types of Outlook items, we will use full descriptions such as *instant messages* or *text messages*.

Messages sent from Outlook do not have to be plain and boring. Apply rich formatting styles to your email text to draw attention to important sections or sentences. You can also use other powerful features to:

- Embed images, personalized signatures, and business information, such as Microsoft Excel charts and PowerPoint presentations.

- Mark your outgoing message as high priority, flag a copy of the sent message for follow-up, or include voting buttons to gather information from recipients.

- Request a read or delivery notification email message to be sent to you when recipients open your message or it's successfully delivered.

There are also many other new and enhanced features in Outlook 2013 focused on interactive communications. Deep integration into messaging software such as Microsoft Lync and Windows Live Messenger provide many ways to view the online status of people in your network, chat via text messages, and collaborate with people in your network via phone, video calls, or shared whiteboard sessions.

In conjunction with the People pane, the Social Connector built into Outlook pulls information from your social networks for keeping you better connected with your contacts. When this is coupled with informative and interactive Contact Cards, you have many options for staying informed and up to date with the people with whom you communicate the most.

In this chapter, you'll create, send, and view messages, with and without attachments. You'll view information about message participants, and then you'll reply to and forward messages.

PRACTICE FILES To complete the exercises in this chapter, you need the practice files contained in the Chapter25 practice file folder. For more information, see "Download the practice files" in this book's Introduction.

IMPORTANT

Creating and sending messages

Email messages are luckily very easy to create and send in Outlook. After you add recipients and provide a subject, your message is ready to be composed and delivered. A typical email message is made up of the following components:

- **To** This is the field where you enter the email addresses for all of the recipients. This is essential, because you can't send an email message without this information.

- **Subject** This is the title or topic of the email message. Be as descriptive as possible to summarize what the content is about, but try to keep it short.

- **Message Body** The full content of the message is contained in the message body. You can use basic or formatted text, as well as hyperlinks, tables, graphics, and other rich content.

Addressing messages

When you create a new message, a window is displayed that contains the main body where you compose your message, as well as a header section at the top which contains the address boxes for entering the email addresses of the recipients. The following address boxes are available:

- **To** This field is where you enter the email addresses for the primary recipients of the message who you expect to respond to your email. You must enter at least one address or the message has nowhere to go!

- **Cc** The "carbon copy" field is used for entering the email address of one or more secondary recipients. These are people who do not necessarily have to respond to your message, but by inference should be aware of what the message discussion or topic is about.

- **Bcc** The "blind carbon copy" field is also another location for entering one or more email addresses. However, this field has two very important distinctions from the other fields. The person or people listed in the **To** and **Cc** fields will not know that the **Bcc** recipients have also received the same message. In addition, replies to the message will not include the **Bcc** recipients. In a business setting, people usually include supervisors or managers as **Bcc** recipients who essentially need to monitor an email discussion silently without the primary recipients knowing that their conversations are being shared.

  TIP The Bcc field is not displayed by default in the header of email compose windows. To toggle the Bcc field on or off, click the Bcc button in the Show Fields group on the Options tab.

There are several ways to enter recipients into the address boxes:

- Enter the full email address—for example, *someone@example.com*.

- When you begin entering an email address, a drop-down list appears that contains addresses that begin with the characters you've entered. This **Auto-Complete** list is made up of email addresses that you've manually entered in the past.

- Enter the full name of the recipient if you have a **Contact** item with an email address for that person stored in any of your **Contact** folders.

- If you have a Microsoft Exchange mailbox configured in your Outlook profile, you need to enter only the alias (usually the first name) of the recipient.

- Click the **To**, **Cc**, or **Bcc** buttons to display the **Address Book** for selecting an existing email address.

25

When you manually enter a name or email address into one of the address boxes, Outlook will *validate* (or *resolve*) the address. This process cross-references the recipient's name or email address with entries in your address books. These address books are usually your Contact folders, but they can also include the Global Address List (for users on an Exchange network). All validated recipients' addresses will be displayed as fully underlined. This applies to names that you enter and for email addresses as well. For the latter, the display name of the recipient from its contact record will replace the email address after it is successfully resolved.

Email addresses can also appear as validated if there are no corresponding entries in any of your address books, provided that the format of the email address is correct; for example, *someone@example.com*. Note that validation does not check to confirm that the email address itself actually exists somewhere on the Internet. The format could be correct, but email messages with misspelled addresses can still be sent (and hopefully returned as undeliverable so you can check the email address and resend the message).

TROUBLESHOOTING When you enter a full name in any of the address boxes, Outlook will try to validate that name against the contents of only those Contact folders that are enabled as Outlook Address Books. So if you know for sure that you have a Contact item for the name you are entering, and it is not being validated, there's a chance that the Contact folder where the contact is stored may not be configured as an Outlook Address Book. You can enable or disable Contact folders as Outlook Address Books by right-clicking the selected folder in the Folder pane, clicking the Properties option, and selecting or clearing the Show This Folder As An Email Address Book check box on the Outlook Address Book page in the Properties dialog box.

Validation of the recipient's address can occur as you enter your message (if this feature isn't turned off). To validate addresses manually, click the Check Names button in the Names group on the Message tab.

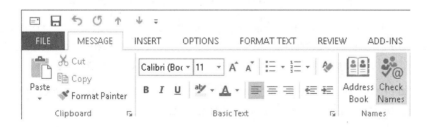

KEYBOARD SHORTCUT Press Ctrl+K to force Outlook to validate addresses.

When an address or name cannot be resolved, Outlook will display the Check Names dialog box.

With this dialog box, you can:

- Select from the suggested options.
- Click **Properties** to learn more about the selected option.
- Click **Show More Names** to display your address book.
- Click **New Contact** to create a new **Contact** entry in your default **Contacts** folder.

Saving and sending messages

Outlook has a built-in fail-safe mechanism that conveniently saves a copy of the message you are composing in the Drafts folder. You can also save a draft of the message whenever you want by clicking the Save button (represented by a floppy disk icon) on the Quick Access Toolbar. When you decide to resume composing your message at a later time, simply close your email (Outlook will prompt you to save the message if there are unsaved changes). You can later retrieve the draft of your message by locating it in the Drafts folder and double-clicking it to open it and pick up where you left off.

TIP You can change the settings for when and where draft email messages are saved on the Mail page of Outlook Options. You can choose a different folder other than the default Drafts folder to save a copy of your message, as well as adjust the minute interval for when messages are saved in the background.

25

When you are ready to send an email message, simply click the Send button or press Ctrl+Enter. The first time you use this keyboard shortcut, Outlook will prompt you to confirm whether you want to keep this as the shortcut for sending messages. Some people find this shortcut convenient, whereas others dislike it, because it can be easy to accidently trigger that shortcut and send the message before you've had a chance to finish it.

After the message has been sent (and even before it leaves the Outbox), Outlook will remove the copy if it exists in your Draft folder. By default, Outlook will also save a copy of the message in your Sent Items folder after it leaves your Outbox.

In this exercise, you'll compose an email message, save a work-in-progress copy of the message as a draft, and finally, send the message.

 SET UP You don't need any practice files to complete this exercise. Start Outlook, display your Inbox, and then follow the steps.

1   On the **Home** tab, in the **New** group, click the **New Email** button.

    A new message window opens.

    TIP By clicking the New Items button, you can choose to create any type of Outlook item such as an appointment, meeting, contact, or task. Other item types you can create from clicking this button include contact groups (formerly known as distribution lists), task requests, Internet faxes, and new Outlook data files.

2   In the **To** box, enter your own email address.

3   In the **Subject** box, enter SBS Employee BBQ.

> **IMPORTANT**

4   In the upper-right corner of the message window, click the **Close** button.

5   In the **Microsoft Outlook** message box, click **Yes**.

    The message window closes. In the Folder pane, the number in the unread message counter to the right of the Drafts folder increases by one.

6   In the **Folder** pane, click the **Drafts** folder. Your message and its current content are in this folder.

TROUBLESHOOTING By default, your Drafts folder should be listed in the Favorites section on the Folder pane. If the Folder pane or the Favorites section does not appear, you can turn either of them on by clicking the View tab in the main Outlook window and selecting Normal and/or Favorites from the drop-down list under the Folder pane button in the Layout group.

7   In the message list, double-click the message to open it for editing.

8   In the message body, enter this text: **The following people have volunteered to work at the picnic:** and press the **Enter** key twice. Then enter Inna, John, Kate and Reto, pressing **Enter** once after each of the first three names, and twice after the fourth name.

The list of names is currently unformatted.

9   Select the list of names. Then on the **Message** tab, in the **Basic Text** group, click the **Bullets** button (not the arrow on the side of the button).

> **TIP** The Bullets button and other paragraph formatting commands are also available in the Paragraph group on the Format Text tab. Many of the frequently used formatting commands are also available on the Mini Toolbar that appears above your cursor when you select text while editing.

10   With the bulleted list still selected, in the **Basic Text** group, click the **Bullets** arrow. The **Bullets** gallery expands.

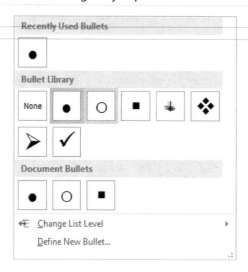

Notice the types of bullets available in the Bullet Library section of the gallery. You can change the list to use any of these bullets by clicking the bullet you want.

11   In the **Bullets** gallery, click **Change List Level.**

A multilevel list of bullets is displayed.

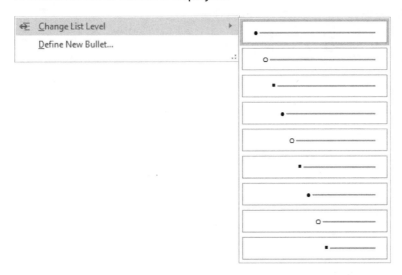

12 You can demote (or promote) a list item to any of nine levels, differentiated by the bullet character and indent level.

13 Press the **Esc** key twice to close the **Bullets** gallery without making changes.

14 Press **Ctrl+End** to move the cursor to the end of the message. Enter Food needed: and then press the **Enter** key twice.

15 On the **Insert** tab, in the **Tables** group, click the **Table** button.

The Table gallery expands.

16 In the **Table** gallery, point to the second cell in the sixth row.

A live preview of a two-column by six-row table appears at the cursor location.

25

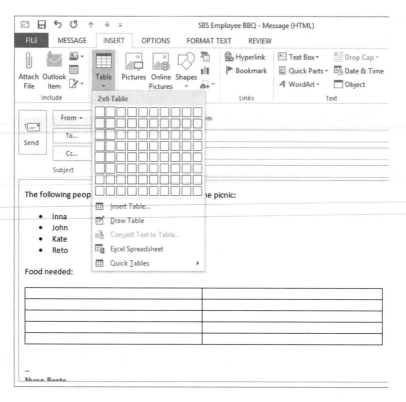

17 Click the selected cell to insert a two-column by six-row table in the message.

18 Enter the following information in the table, pressing the **Tab** key to move between table cells.

Item	Quantity
Hamburgers	50
Hamburger buns	65
Soy burgers	15
Hot dogs	75
Hot dog buns	75

The table and table content are currently unformatted.

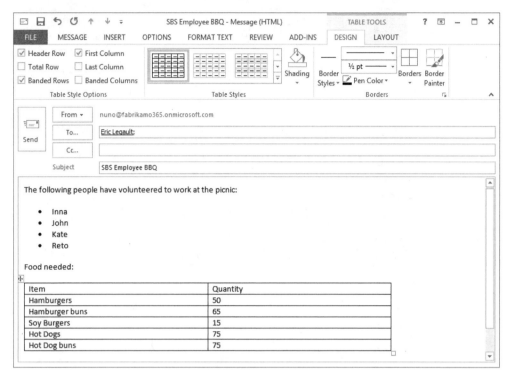

19   With the cursor still active in the lower-right table cell, click the **More** button in the
      Table Styles gallery on the **Table Tools Design** tool tab.

The Table Styles gallery expands. A box around the Table Grid thumbnail in the Plain
Tables section indicates the formatting of the active table.

25

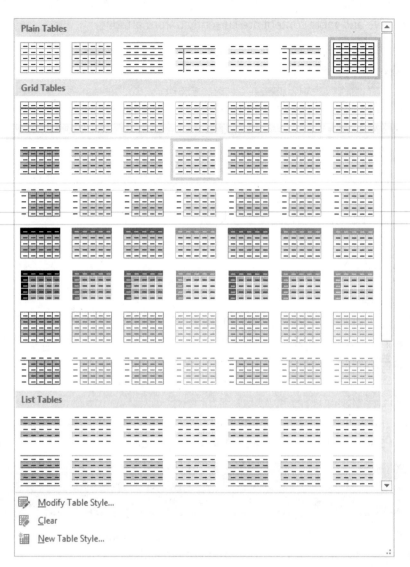

20   In the **Grid Tables** section of the **Table Styles** gallery, click the second thumbnail in the fourth row (the table with a blue header row, identified by the ScreenTip **Grid Table 4 - Accent 1**).

Outlook displays a preview when you point to the thumbnail, and then applies the selected table style.

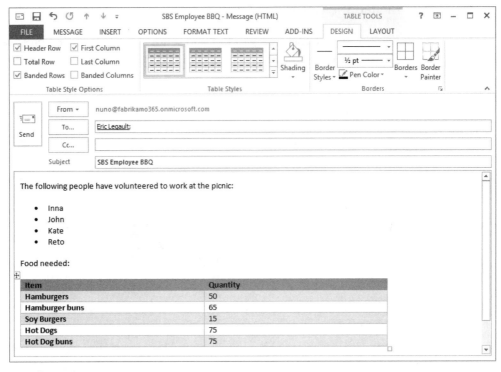

Notice that the default table style formats the text in the first column and the first row as bold.

21 On the **Design** tab, in the **Table Style Options** group, clear the **First Column** check box.

The text in the first column is now no longer bold, but the text in the header row remains bold.

22   In the message header, click the **Send** button. Make sure that you have addressed the message to yourself.

> **KEYBOARD SHORTCUT** Press Ctrl+Enter to send a message.

Outlook closes the message window and sends the message. The draft version of your message disappears from the Drafts folder.

23   In the **Folder** pane, click the **Inbox** folder.

The received message is in this folder.

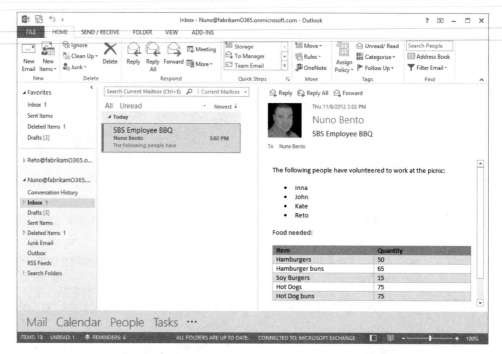

24   In the **Folder** pane, click the **Sent Items** folder.

The sent message is in this folder.

✕ CLEAN UP Display your Inbox. Retain the SBS Employee BBQ message in your Inbox and Sent Items folders for use in later exercises.

Managing multiple accounts

Outlook supports many different kinds of email accounts. POP accounts are commonly used by home users who access email via their local Internet service provider. Business and professional users typically use Microsoft Exchange accounts, and other account types such as IMAP or ActiveSync (for Outlook.com accounts) are supported as well. You can configure one or more of each of these account types to accommodate the supported accounts in your particular email configuration.

Regardless of what account types you have configured or how many of them you have, Outlook is smart enough to know which one to use at various times. For instance, if you receive an email message through your Exchange account, Outlook will default to sending an outgoing message from that same account when you reply to that message. Similarly, if you navigate to a folder for a different account, Outlook will send your message from that account.

If you have multiple accounts configured, you can change the sending account at any time when you are composing an email message. Simply choose from the available accounts in the list displayed by clicking the From button.

TIP You will not have the From button in the message header if Outlook is configured to connect to only one account. To display the From button, click From in the Show Fields group on the Options tab of the message composition window.

25

Attaching files to messages

Like most email clients, Outlook 2013 enables you to attach files to your outgoing messages. Your message can include a wide variety of files, from pictures, Microsoft Word documents, Excel workbooks, or others kinds of files. Before attaching your file, though, take a moment to consider whether you can reasonably expect the recipient to have the necessary software to open or view your attachment, and whether the file sizes are appropriate. Some Exchange networks even prevent email messages that exceed a certain size threshold from being sent *or* received. Similarly, POP accounts with most Internet service providers are known to reject the delivery of email messages that are received if they exceed 10 megabytes (MB) or even 5 MB in size. When in doubt, try to keep the total size of your attachments under 5 MB.

TIP The size of each file that you've attached is noted in brackets beside each file name in the Attached box in the message header—for example, *file1.txt (50 KB); file2.txt (2 MB)*. You can also view the total size of your outgoing message by first saving the message and then clicking the File tab and selecting the Info page on the left pane. The Properties section will display the total size of the email message.

Some files, however, such as application files (files that end with the .exe extension), databases, or other uncommon file types are not usually included as attachments. You don't have to worry about which files to avoid, because Outlook will warn you with a message asking you to confirm any potentially unsafe attachments before you send the message. You can then continue with the message delivery or cancel so that you can remove the attachments in question.

TIP You can also send an email message containing Microsoft Office files as attachments from within the Office program you're working in, by using commands in the Backstage view. For example, to send a Word document, open the document, click the File tab, click the Share page, and then click Email and Send As Attachment.

In this exercise, you'll send a Word document and an image file as attachments to an email address.

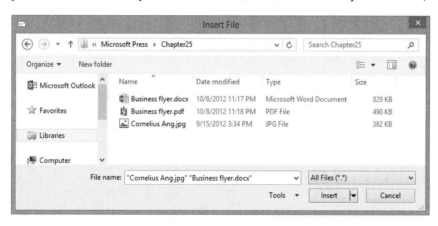

SET UP You need the Business flyer document and the Cornelius Ang photo located in the Chapter25 practice file folder to complete this exercise. Start Outlook, display your Inbox, and then follow the steps.

1. On the **Home** tab, in the **New** group, click **New Email**.

2. In the **To** box, enter your own email address.

   TIP If you completed the previous exercise, Outlook displays your email address in a list as you begin entering text. You can insert the address by clicking it or by pressing the Down Arrow key to select it (if necessary) and then pressing Enter.

3. In the **Subject** box, enter **SBS Attachments for Review**.

4. In the **Content** pane, enter **Here are some files that I'd like you to review**.

5. On the **Message** tab, in the **Include** group, click **Attach File**.

   TIP You can also drag a file selected in an open File Explorer window (or from your desktop) directly into the message body, and Outlook will attach the file for you.

   The Insert File dialog box is displayed and lists the contents of a folder (most likely your Documents library, but it could also be another recently used folder).

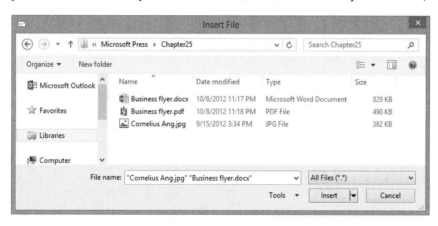

25

6   Navigate to your **Chapter25** practice file folder. In the **Chapter25** folder, click the
    Business flyer document, hold down the **Ctrl** key, click the **Cornelius Ang** photo, and
    then click **Insert**.

    The files appear in the Attached box.

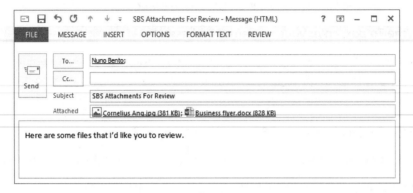

7   Click the **Send** button.

    TIP If you forget to attach a file, Outlook 2013 will conveniently warn you before you
    send the message. How does it know this? A simple search for relevant sequences
    of words in the subject message body—for example, *attached*, *attachment*, *attach-
    ing*, *enclosed*, *here is*, or *include*—is usually enough information to indicate that a file
    should be attached and to warn the user if there are no files attached. The context
    of these keywords is also crucial, and Outlook is smart enough to not trigger the re-
    minder if there is any ambiguity about the sender's intent.

❌ CLEAN UP When you receive the SBS Attachments for Review message in your
    Inbox, keep it for use in later exercises.

Viewing messages and message attachments

The main Outlook window may look a little daunting to some new users, but it's a well-designed layout for quickly viewing information at a glance. The relevant details of today's email messages or content in other mail folders are spread out over several areas within the interface. Knowing where to look is critical, and these are the key visual elements to focus on.

In the message list, look for:

- Icons that represent various item types—for example, email messages and meeting and task requests

- The name of the message sender

- The date/time you received the message

- Categorized or flagged messages

In the Reading pane, look for:

- Icons for actions taken on messages—for example, replied-to or forwarded messages with a date stamp for when the action occurred

- Message importance icons (high or low importance)

- Listings of other recipients in the **To** (and also maybe **Cc**) fields

- A thumbnail photo of the message sender

- The names of any attached files

- Icons for digitally signed or encrypted messages

25

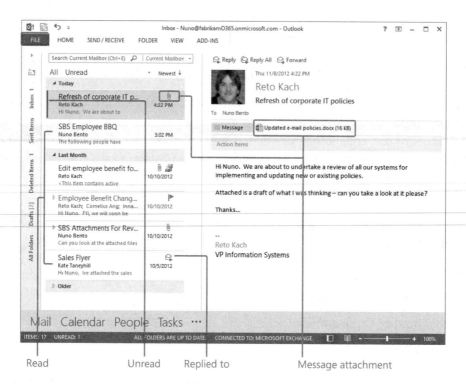

Read   Unread   Replied to   Message attachment

The message list has two primary views that you can switch between by accessing the view labels in the View bar at the top of the message list:

- **All** The default layout for viewing all messages in a folder

- **Unread** A convenient view that filters all messages in the folder so that only those messages that are unread are displayed

There are also various grouping methods that can be applied so messages are displayed in collapsible or expandable groups. Outlook shows messages grouped by date by default, but you can choose other groupings for the message list by clicking the arrow on the right end of the View bar:

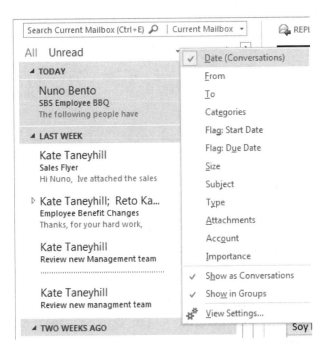

TIP Additional views (including custom ones that you can create) are available by clicking Change View in the Current View group on the View tab. The same view groupings from the View bar can also be accessed from the Groupings gallery in the Arrangement group on that same tab.

25

Unread email messages in the message list stand out rather noticeably. They are marked with a blue bar on the left and a bold subject line.

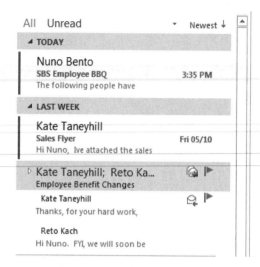

When you mark the message as read, the blue bar disappears and the subject line reverts to a non-bold font.

It can get distracting sometimes to review messages in the folder with all of the visual elements Outlook provides in the main window. When you want to focus on reading, there are a couple of ways to optimize your experience:

- Switch to **Reading Mode** by clicking the book icon near the right side of the bottom status bar (to the left of the zoom slider). The **Folder** pane collapses to the left, the **To-Do** bar disappears (if either are currently visible) along with any **Peeks** that are pinned to it, and the **Navigation** bar switches from a horizontal layout at the bottom to a compressed layout underneath the collapsed **Folder** pane. Switch back to **Normal Mode** by clicking the square icon to the left of the **Reading Mode** icon. The **Folder** pane and **To-Do** bar (if any of them were visible) will reappear, and the **Navigation** bar reverts to the horizontal layout.

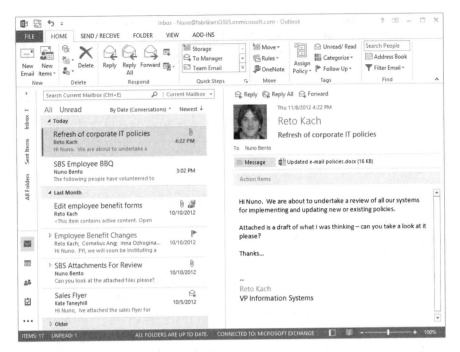

■ New to Outlook 2013 is the ability to auto-hide the ribbon and status bar, effectively maximizing the layout for a full screen mode (perfect for Outlook running on a tablet PC). This leaves much more room for displaying lists of email messages and for viewing content in the **Reading** pane. To turn this feature on, click **Ribbon Display Options** at the top right of the main Outlook window and select **Auto-hide Ribbon**.

- When the ribbon is hidden, all you need to do is point near the top of the Outlook window to display a thin bar with three tiny dots at the right. Clicking this bar will temporarily display the ribbon and status bar so that you can interact with it.

TIP Try combining both Reading Mode and the Auto-hide Ribbon mode. You'll get an even more optimized layout for your reading pleasure.

There are several ways that you can view the contents of the email messages:

- Open the message for viewing in a full window by double-clicking the message in the message list.

- Select the message and view the contents in the **Reading** pane.

- Show an excerpt of the beginning of the message directly in the message list. By default, Outlook displays a preview of the contents in a single line. However, you can change this to two or three lines (or turn message previews off), choosing the option you want by clicking **Message Preview** in the **Arrangement** group on the **View** tab. Keep in mind that three lines of preview text takes up more vertical space in the message list, which effectively reduces the number of messages you can view at once.

There are also several ways that you can view attachments in a message:

- Use the **Attachment Preview** feature. Click the attachment in the header of the **Reading** pane for the selected message (or in the message header for an item that's open in a full window). If the attachment is of a file type that is supported for previewing—for example, a Word document, Excel spreadsheet, PowerPoint presentation, or PDF file—then the message body will be replaced with the contents of the attachment.

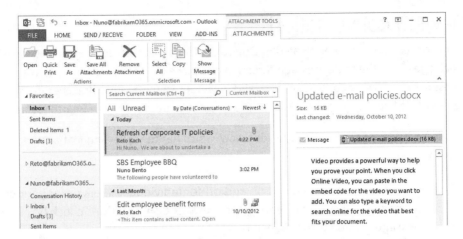

- Open the attachment directly by double-clicking it. The attachment will open in the default application for handling the file.

- Save the attachment to your hard drive and open it directly from there. Use this method if you are not sure whether you have anti-virus software that scans attachments in email messages, but you know you have virus protection in Windows. This way the anti-virus software can scan potentially dangerous attachments by opening the file from your hard drive.

TIP You can view the list of applications that can preview attachments by clicking Attachment And Document Previewers in the Attachment Handling area of the Trust Center dialog box in Outlook Options.

25

Viewing conversations

The Conversations view originated in Outlook 2007 as a convenient way of viewing email messages from the same message thread in one place. All of the responses to the original message can now be easily identified, and messages from separate branches (for example, a reply to a later reply, and not the original message) are decidedly easier to locate.

Outlook 2013 retains the Conversations view, which has the following features and capabilities:

- You can turn **Conversations** on and off for individual folders or for your entire mailbox by selecting or clearing the **Show as Conversations** check box in the **Message** group on the **View** tab.

- You can display messages from the same conversation that are stored in different folders—for example, your **Sent Items** folder or other locations.

- Switch between displaying the name of the message sender or the message subject in the conversation header.

- Conversation threads are collapsible and expandable. Conversations are collapsed by default:

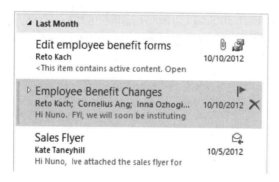

- The first click of the conversation message expands to show the most recent message at the top, followed by all other messages in the same folder.

- The second click fully expands the conversation to show messages from other folders (if the **Show Messages from Other Folders** option is selected through **Conversation Settings** in the **Messages** group on the **View** tab). If the **Always Expand Selected Conversation** option is active, then a second click to expand the conversation fully isn't required; it will expand completely with the first click.

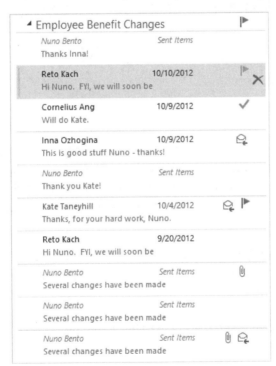

Except when discussing alternative views of messages, the graphics in this book depict messages arranged in Conversation view. A conversation of multiple messages is indicated by an arrow to the left of the conversation message header.

Configuring Reading pane behavior

The Reading pane is an indispensable tool for quickly reading messages without opening them. As simple as it is to use, it is also simple to configure. Aside from the two basic layouts, where the pane is shown on the right or at the bottom of the main Outlook window, there are other features that should be considered.

Viewing Reading pane content

The default size of content displayed in the Reading pane may be too small for some users, or even too large for others. Monitor sizes and various screen resolutions can make finding the right display setting tricky, but luckily there's a handy Zoom tool at your disposal. Easily accessible on the far right side of the bottom status bar, the Zoom controls enable you to easily change the size of the content in the Reading pane. To change the zoom level, drag the slider to the left or right or click the – or + icon to decrease or increase the magnification level.

Marking messages as read

Just as a torn envelope tells you at a glance that mail has been opened, an email message that's marked as read indicates that you have made some progress with managing your Inbox. Of course, the easiest way to mark email messages as read is to open the messages. However, opening dozens of messages just to have the messages marked as read is not always practical.

As you saw earlier, using the Reading pane is an effective way to read messages without opening the item fully. Reading messages in the main Outlook window with the Reading pane on also provides the following benefits:

- Messages can be marked as read after you have viewed the messages in the **Reading pane** for a defined number of seconds.

- Changing the selection from an unread message to another item can mark the selected message as read.

- To choose how you want the **Reading** pane to work, click **Options** in the **Reading** pane in the **Layout** group on the **View** tab.

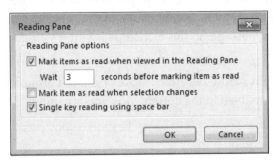

Single-key reading

One of the settings in the Reading pane controls whether single-key reading is enabled. This is activated by using the Single Key Reading Using Space Bar option. By turning this feature on, you can read messages very quickly by tapping the space bar. Pressing this key starts a sequence of events that generally happen in the following order:

- If a group or conversation is selected, pressing the **Spacebar** advances to the first message in the group or conversation.

- If a message is selected, pressing the **Spacebar** scrolls the contents in the **Reading** pane to the end of the message. If the message is lengthy, each tap of the **Spacebar** will advance the scroll bar one page at a time until the end of the message is reached

- After all pages of a message have been displayed by one or more presses of the **Spacebar**, tapping it again will advance to the next message in the group or conversation.

- If there are no more messages in the group or conversation, pressing the **Spacebar** will select the header of the next group or conversation in the message list.

KEYBOART SHORTCUT Use the Shift+Space bar keyboard shortcut to page up through the text in the Reading pane for a multi-page message.

25

The Spacebar is not the only key you can use. You can also quickly go through your list of messages by using the scroll keys on your keyboard (the Up Arrow, Down Arrow, Left Arrow, and Right Arrow keys) in the following ways:

- Use the **Up Arrow** and **Down Arrow** keys to change the selection to the previous or next message in the list. Note that you won't be able to view all of the pages in the **Reading** pane for a lengthy message, so this technique is better suited for skimming rather than reading.

- Use the **Left Arrow** and **Right Arrow** keys to collapse or expand grouped messages or conversations (if either are enabled in the current view you are using).

KEYBOARD SHORTCUT Use the Page Down and Page Up keyboard shortcuts to go to the item at the bottom or top of the screen.

The People pane

Powered by the Social Connector add-in, the People pane is an interactive window that complements the Reading pane and displays information from your contact's social networks as well as relevant Outlook items. The People pane can display the following items:

- Status updates from social networks

- Messages and attachments that you have received from that person

- Upcoming meetings with a contact

To display the People pane, select any message to facilitate the following actions:

1 On the **View** tab, in the **People** group, click **People pane** and select **Normal** in the drop-down menu.

2 Click any of the tabs on the left of the **People** pane to switch between various views of their social updates (**All, What's New, Mail, Attachments**, and **Meetings**).

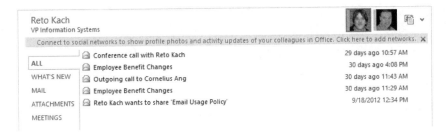

SEE ALSO For more information about the Social Connector, see Chapter 28, "Managing contacts and people."

Responding to messages

Outlook provides many methods for responding to messages and other Outlook items. Depending on which approach you prefer, you can initiate actions on messages by:

- Clicking the action buttons at the top of the message header in the **Preview** pane

- Clicking buttons in the **Respond** group

- Clicking commands that you've added to the **Quick Access Toolbar**

- Right-clicking an item in the message list and choosing a menu command. (Note that not all message actions listed in this section are available in this menu.)

Inline replies

New in Outlook 2013 is the ability to reply to an email message without even opening it. By default, the basic message response actions no longer open up a separate window for your response. You can now reply directly in the Reading pane.

25

1 In the message list, select a message.

2 In the **Reading** pane, click an option: **Reply**, **Reply All**, or **Forward**.

3 Enter your response and click **Send**. If you choose to forward the message, you must also enter an email address for the recipient.

4 If you'd rather display your reply in a separate window, click **Pop Out** at the top of the message header. You can also turn off inline replies completely in the **Mail Options** dialog box if you always prefer to compose your message in a separate window.

TIP If Outlook saves a draft of your inline reply (or you save your in-progress message manually), you will find the draft in your Inbox and not the Drafts folder. The message will be bundled with the original message you are replying to and will be noticeably prefixed with [Draft] in the subject line.

Regardless of how you prefer to respond to messages, you can initiate a reply in three different ways:

- **Reply** This action is the most commonly used. It creates a new email message already addressed to the original message sender and copies the text from the message body of the received message to the message body of the response message. The subject line is also copied and prefixed with **Re:**.

- **Reply All** Same as the **Reply** action, but also copies all of the main recipients as well as the **Cc** recipients from the original message to the reply message. The main recipients will be populated in the **To** address box, and the **Cc** recipients will go in the **Cc** address box.

TIP Be careful when using Reply All. You don't want to inadvertently send a response to a lot of people when you only meant for the original sender to view your message. Similarly, some messages may be addressed to dozens or even hundreds of recipients (especially if any of the recipients are distribution lists that can contain a large number of members). You may need to trim the recipient list if your reply is not relevant to all of them.

- **Reply with Meeting** Creates a meeting invitation addressed to all main and **Cc** recipients copied from the original message. As with replies, the message text and subject (without the *Re:* prefix) from the original message are also copied. Note also that you cannot use this reply type inline in the **Reading** pane.

With all of these methods, you will have space at the top of the message body to enter your response. You will also have the option of adding or removing recipients from the address boxes that were populated for you. However, if the original message had attachments, those will not be included with any email or meeting responses.

Forwarding messages is similar to replying to messages but is usually used for sending to different people. Types of forwarding include:

- **Forward** As with replies, the original message text is included in the newly created message. However, you are responsible for adding recipients, since recipients from your source message are not copied.

- **Forward As Attachment** A new email message is created containing the original message attached as a .msg file with the same name as the original message's subject line text. The subject line is copied over with a *FW:* prefix, but the original message content is not included in the message body (it already exists in the attachment!).

KEYBOARD SHORTCUT There are many keyboard shortcuts available to facilitate responding to messages: Reply (Crl+R), Reply All (Ctrl+Shift+R), Reply With Meeting (Ctrl+Alt+R), Forward (Ctrl+F) and Forward As Attachment (Ctrl+Alt+F).

25

If you reply to or forward a received message from an open item window, the original message will remain open after you send your response. If you prefer to have the original message window close after you send your message, you can change this option on the Mail page of the Outlook Options dialog box by selecting the Close Original Message Window When Replying Or Forwarding in the Replies And Forwards option, and then clicking OK.

If you have instant messaging software such as Microsoft Lync or Windows Live Messenger installed, you may also have these actions available:

- **Reply with IM** Starts an instant message conversation with the message sender.

- **Reply All with IM** Starts an instant message conversation with the message sender and all of the other recipients.

- **Call** Uses telephony calling functionality to place Voice Over IP (VOIP) calls over the Internet from your computer to the telephone number of the original message sender.

- **Call All** Uses telephony calling functionality to place VOIP calls over the Internet from your computer to the telephone numbers of all the message recipients.

Other Outlook items have different response options, such as:

- **Meeting Invitations** Includes options to accept, decline, or tentatively accept the meeting request.

- **Task Assignments** Recipients can accept or decline the task.

- **Voting Messages** Senders may sometimes add voting options to an outgoing email message and will collect the results to aid in making some kind of important decision (like what kind of coffee to purchase for the staff break room). You can identify these messages by the informational icon in the message header that also contains text on how to vote (by either choosing your response from the drop-down in the **Reading** pane or the **Vote** option in the **Respond** group on the **Message** tab for an open message).

Key points

- The Auto-Complete list is a convenient way to quickly choose from frequently entered email addresses and names when you are composing a message.

- Email messages don't have to be boring. Use powerful layout options, colorful fonts and themes, and other rich content to create memorable or professional messages.

- There are many ways to preview message content through various view settings and with the Reading pane.

- Single-key reading, judicious use of keyboard shortcuts, and replying in the Reading pane are effective ways for reading email messages and managing your Inbox.

25

Chapter at a glance

Schedule

Schedule and change appointments and meetings, page 707

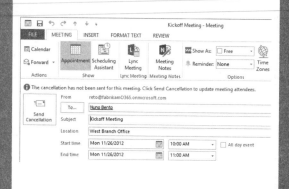

Respond

Respond to meeting requests, page 722

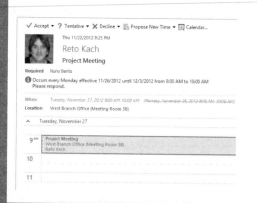

Display

Display different views of a calendar, page 723

Staying on schedule

26

IN THIS CHAPTER, YOU WILL LEARN HOW TO

- Schedule and change appointments.

- Schedule and change meetings.

- Respond to meeting requests.

- Display different views of a calendar.

- Use the Date Navigator.

The traditional paper calendar hanging on a wall, plastered with penciled annotations and colorful stickers, just can't compete in the age of collaboration software. You can't share it easily, you can't track meeting invitations, nor is it particularly mobile. Microsoft Outlook 2013 has deep calendaring features and much more to help busy people manage their schedules effectively in a digital world.

In this chapter, you'll create and update appointments and meeting requests. You'll respond to meeting requests you receive, and use the Data Navigator and Calendar views to change the display of your Calendar.

PRACTICE FILES You don't need any practice files to complete the exercises in this chapter.

Scheduling and changing appointments

One of the main advantages of calendaring in Outlook is the ability to view your bookings and availability at a glance when looking at a Month view of your calendar. This can also be an ideal layout for quickly creating new appointments or adding notes to existing ones, while staying mindful of other bookings that month.

With Quick Entry mode, you can rapidly add or edit entries in your calendar without having to open a new appointment window every time you want to manage your schedule.

In this exercise, you'll add and edit appointments by using Quick Entry mode.

 SET UP You don't need any practice files to complete this exercise. Start Outlook and display your calendar, and then follow the steps.

1   On the **Home** tab, in the **Arrange** group, click **Month**.

2   Click any day in the calendar where you want to create an appointment.

3   Click again to access **Quick Entry** mode, or simply start entering **Boss' Birthday** and press the **Enter** key.

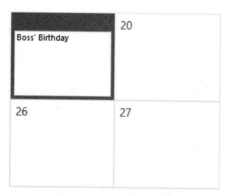

TROUBLESHOOTING If a new appointment window opens, you may have made your second click too fast instead of entering into Quick Entry mode. Just close the window without saving and try again, allowing a second or two to elapse between the first click that selects the day and the second click that accesses Quick Entry mode. Then you can enter your appointment title directly inside the day square in the calendar.

An all-day event (an appointment without a specific start and end time) is now visible in the day you selected. Editing an appointment is just as easy.

4   Click the **Boss' Birthday** appointment entry in the calendar.

5   Click it again to enter **Quick Entry** mode.

6   Append to the subject line by entering a single space followed by **(buy gift)**, and press **Enter**.

The edited subject is immediately applied to the appointment item for your boss'
birthday.

✖ CLEAN UP Delete the Boss' Birthday appointment so you don't get a reminder for
this event.

Using Quick Entry mode to create date-specific events

Although using Quick Entry in the Month view of your calendar can be useful for managing
your schedule as you plan appointments around existing ones for the current month, creating Quick Entry items in this mode limits you to quickly creating all-day events. If you wish
to create appointments with specific start or end times, you can use Quick Entry mode in
the Day, Work Week, Week, and Schedule views as well.

In this exercise, you'll add an appointment for a specific time by using Quick Entry mode.

➜ SET UP You don't need any practice files to complete this exercise. Display your
calendar, and then follow the steps.

1   On the **Home** tab, in the **Arrange** group, click **Week**.

2   On the **View** tab, in the **Arrangement** group, choose **60 Minutes - Least Space for
    Details** from the **Time Scale** drop-down list.

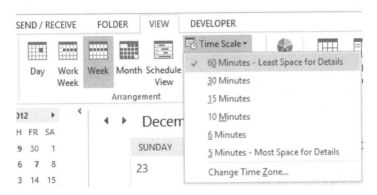

26

3   Click in the **12 PM** row in any day of the week where you want to create an
    appointment.

4   Enter Take boss out to lunch and press **Enter**.

An appointment starting at 12:00 P.M. and ending at 1:00 P.M. is created in the day
you selected.

	SUNDAY	MONDAY	TUESDAY	WEDNESDAY	THURSDAY	FRIDAY	SATURDAY
	16	17	18	19	20	21	22
12 AM							
1							
2							
3							
4							
5							
6							
7							
8							
9							
10							
11							
12 PM			Take boss out to lunc				
1							
2							
3							
4							

TIP You can use the Zoom slider at the bottom right of the status bar to decrease or increase the Time Scale values in all calendar views except Month view.

⊗ CLEAN UP Delete the Take Boss Out To Lunch appointment so you don't get a reminder for this event.

Creating recurring appointments and using appointment features

Although Quick Entry is useful for efficiently creating many appointments, some details and functions can only be set by creating an appointment using the New Appointment window. Here you can set or edit many different values such as:

- Appointment subject
- Location
- Start and end dates and times
- Whether the appointment is an all-day event
- Reminder time
- Availability status (Free, Working Elsewhere, Tentative, Busy, or Out of Office)
- Appointment recurrences
- A different time zone for the appointment

In this exercise, you'll create a recurring appointment that encompasses many of these features.

 SET UP You don't need any practice files to complete this exercise. Display your calendar, and then follow the steps.

1 On the **Home** tab, in the **New** group, click the **New Appointment** button (or press **Ctrl+N**).

2 In the **New Appointment** window that opens, enter Bi-weekly Project Review in the **Subject** line.

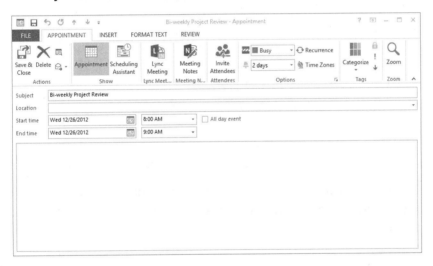

3 Enter West Branch Office in the **Location** line.

4 Click the calendar icon in the **Start time** field and choose **Friday** of the following week.

5 Select **10:00 AM** from the drop-down list to the right of the **Start time** field.

6 Select **11:00 AM** from the drop-down list to the right of the **End time** field.

7 On the **Appointment** tab, in the **Options** group, choose **Out of Office** from the **Show As** box.

26

8   On the **Appointment** tab, in the **Options** group, choose **1 day** from the **Reminder** box.

9   On the **Appointment** tab, in the **Options** group, click the **Recurrence** button.

10   In the **Recurrence pattern** area, ensure that **Weekly** is chosen and **Friday** is selected. Enter **2** in the **Recur every** box.

11   In the **Range of recurrence** area, select **End after** and enter **5** in the **occurrences** box.

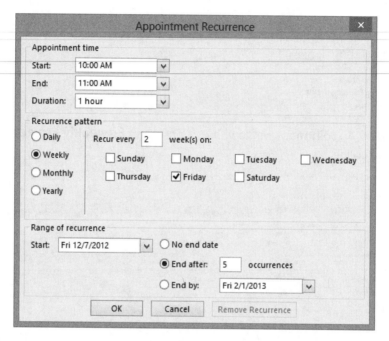

12   Click **OK**. The **Recurrence** button in the **Options** group should now be selected, and a **Recurrence** label is added underneath the **Location** box showing the details of the recurrence pattern.

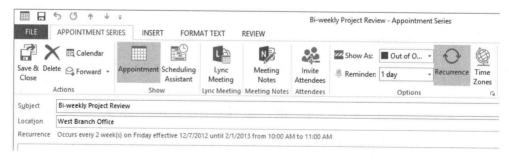

13   On the **Appointment Series** tab, in the **Actions** group, click **Save & Close**.

14   On the **Home** tab, in the **Arrange** group, click the **Month** button.

Note that entries labeled *10:00am Bi-weekly Project Review; West Branch Office* are now visible in every second Friday of the visible weeks in the calendar. You can advance the Calendar view to the following month to verify that the calendar contains the other two recurring appointment entries.

CLEAN UP Select any of the Bi-weekly Project Review entries in your calendar and press the Delete key. Choose Delete The Series in the Confirm Delete dialog box that opens, to remove all recurrences of this appointment from your calendar.

Creating appointments from messages

An email message can frequently spawn related appointments by the nature of its content, such as event descriptions in the subject line or detailed event information in the body of a message. However, copying and pasting this information to and from the appointment and email message can become a cumbersome chore. Luckily, there are a few ways to automate this task.

In this exercise, you'll create an appointment that will use the subject and message body from an existing email message.

SET UP You don't need any practice files to complete this exercise. Display your Inbox, and then follow the steps.

1   Select any message in your Inbox.

2   Drag the message to the **Calendar** label in the **Navigation** bar (or the **Calendar** icon, if your **Navigation** bar is set to **Compact** mode) until the pointer changes to a selection rectangle with a superimposed plus (+) icon.

| Nuno Bento | |
| Project recap | 10/7/2012 |

Calendar   People   Tasks   ...

REMINDERS: 11

26

3   Release the mouse button.

A new appointment window opens, with the subject of the appointment copied from the subject of the email message, and the message body of the appointment copied from the content of the message. The appointment date will be today's date, with a start time of the next hour or half-hour block (whichever is closest to the current time) and a length of 30 minutes.

You can also use another approach that displays additional options for creating an appointment from a message, as the following steps demonstrate.

4   Select another message in your Inbox.

5   Right-click and drag the message to the **Calendar** label or icon.

6   Select **Copy Here as Appointment with Attachment** from the shortcut menu that appears.

Copy Here as Appointment with <u>T</u>ext
Copy Here as Appointment with <u>S</u>hortcut
<u>C</u>opy Here as Appointment with Attachment
<u>M</u>ove Here as Appointment with Attachment
Copy Here as Meeting <u>R</u>equest
C<u>a</u>ncel

A new appointment window opens, with the subject of the appointment copied from the subject line of the email message, and the message body of the appointment containing the source email message as an embedded attachment. The appointment date will be today's date with a start time of the next hour or half-hour block (which-ever is closest to the current time) and a length of 30 minutes.

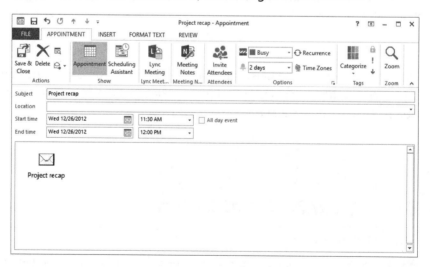

CLEAN UP Close any open appointment windows created in the last three exercises and click No to discard your changes.

Configuring a Quick Step to create an appointment from an email message

Quick Steps are very useful tools for automating actions in Outlook that may take several steps to complete, essentially compressing them into a single step. Some of a Quick Step's functions can be used for creating items like email messages, tasks, and appointments.

In this exercise, you'll configure a Quick Step to create an appointment from an email message.

➡ SET UP You don't need any practice files to complete this exercise. Display your Inbox, and then follow the steps.

1 On the **Home** tab, in the **Quick Steps** group, click **Create New**.

2 In the **Edit Quick Step** dialog box, select **Create an appointment with text of message** from the **Appointment** area in the **Actions** box.

3 Select **Ctrl+Shift+1** from the **Shortcut key** list box.

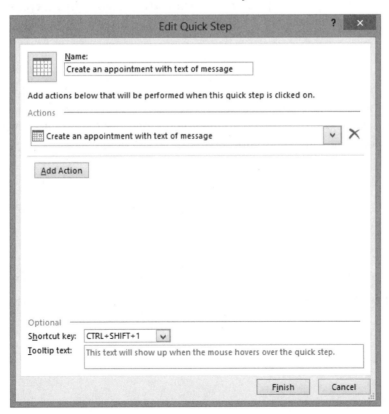

4   Click **Finish**.

5   Select a message in your Inbox.

6   Press **Ctrl+Shift +1**.

A new appointment window opens, with the subject of the appointment copied from the subject of the email message, and the message body of the appointment copied from the content of the email message. The appointment date will be today's date with a start time of the next hour or half-hour block (whichever is closest to the current time) and a length of 30 minutes.

TIP If you prefer the convenience of using keyboard shortcuts to trigger a Quick Step, but also prefer to create appointments from a message that include the full original message as an attachment, you can create a second Quick Step. Simply select the Quick Step created in the previous steps in the Manage Quick Steps dialog box, click Duplicate, and change the Action to Create An Appointment With Attachment. Don't forget to give the Quick Step a different name and keyboard shortcut assignment.

❌ CLEAN UP Close any open appointment windows created in this exercise and click No to discard your changes.

Scheduling and changing meetings

Meeting items are very similar to appointment items, because they are also events on your calendar. However, meeting items have the following key differences:

- Meeting organizers invite one or more attendees.

- Meeting requests are special versions of appointment items that can be sent by email to the invited attendees.

- Meeting requests can require that users reply with a response.

- Meeting attendees can suggest an alternate date and time for the event.

Like appointments, meetings are easy to create, but they require a few different steps.

In this exercise, you'll create and schedule a new meeting.

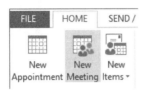 **SET UP** You don't need any practice files to complete this exercise. Display your Calendar, and then follow the steps.

1   On the **Home** tab, in the **New** group, click the **New Meeting** button (or press **Ctrl+N**).

2   In the new meeting window that opens, enter your email address in the **To** box.

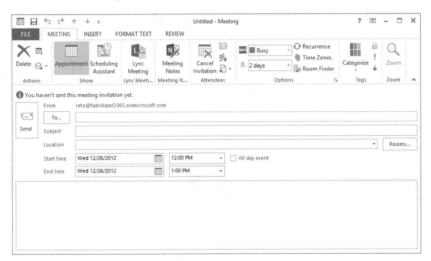

3   Enter Kickoff Meeting in the **Subject** line.

4   Enter West Branch Office in the **Location** line.

5   Click the calendar icon in the **Start time** field and choose **Monday** of the following week.

6   Select **9:00 AM** from the drop-down list to the right of the **Start time** field.

26

7   Select **10:00 AM** from the drop-down list to the right of the **End time** field.

8   On the **Meeting** tab, in the **Attendees** group, click **Request Responses** from the **Response Options** button to clear that option.

9   Click the **Send** button.

10   Navigate to your Inbox and select the meeting request when it is delivered.

The meeting request lists the date, time, and location of the event exactly as you had entered it. The message body also displays a convenient Calendar Preview showing a three-hour block of time beginning at the meeting start time so you can easily determine if you have any existing appointments that may interfere.

Because you are also the meeting organizer, you do not have any options to respond to the request, so the info bar at the top of the Reading pane merely indicates that no response is required.

CLEAN UP Keep the Kickoff Meeting appointment available for further exercises in this chapter.

Advanced scheduling features

A primary difficulty when scheduling a meeting is finding a time that works for all the people who need to attend it. Outlook can access and display the availability of attendees that you have added to a meeting request if they are part of your organization or have published their schedules on the Internet. You can then easily locate a time slot available to everyone or have Outlook find a convenient time for you.

The Scheduling Assistant (or Scheduling) page is accessed through the Show group on the Meeting (or Appointment) tab. Here, you have more control over the attendees you are inviting. You can mark an attendee as required or optional, or add rooms or equipment (like projectors) as attendees if you are using Microsoft Exchange or Microsoft Office 365.

This page displays your desired meeting time as a blue vertical bar spanning the chosen start and end times. If free/busy information is available for individual attendees, any bookings they have during the chosen timeframe will be displayed as a horizontal bar under the time slot they are booked. The color of this bar notes their status as per the displayed color legend (for example, Busy or Tentative).

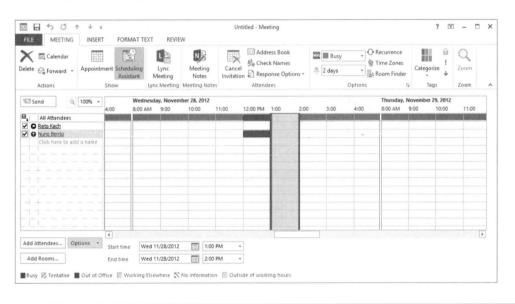

26

Updating and canceling meetings

You might find it necessary to change the date and time of a meeting, change the location, add and remove attendees, or even cancel the meeting entirely.

In this exercise, you'll update an existing meeting and send an update to its attendees. Then you'll cancel the meeting and notify meeting attendees of the cancellation.

 SET UP You don't need any practice files to complete this exercise. Display your Calendar, and then follow the steps.

1   Locate the **Kickoff Meeting** appointment in your calendar and double-click it to open it.

2   Select **10:00 AM** from the drop-down list to the right of the **Start time** field.

3   Edit the **Location** field to read West Branch Office (Meeting Room 3B).

4   Click **Send Update**.

5   Select the updated meeting request when it arrives in your Inbox.

The changes you made to the meeting time and location are noted in the When and Location areas. There's no need for meeting attendees to manually edit their calendar when meeting organizers make changes, because Outlook updates the entry as soon as the update notification is received.

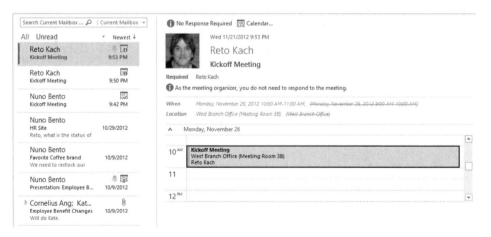

When you need to cancel a meeting, you can create and send a meeting update email message to inform meeting attendees of the cancellation, so they can remove the appointment from their calendar.

6   Select the **Kickoff Meeting** appointment in your calendar.

7   On the **Meeting** tab, in the **Actions** group, click the **Cancel Meeting** button.

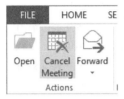

8   In the meeting window that opens, click **Send Cancellation**. You can optionally enter text into the body of the message before sending to explain why the meeting was cancelled.

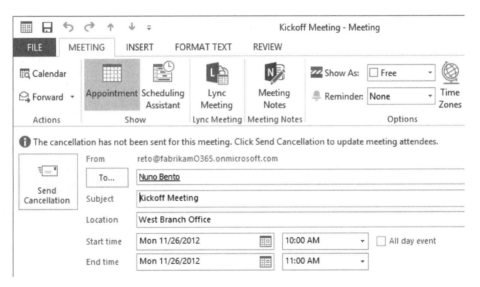

26

Responding to meeting requests

When someone adds you as an attendee to a meeting that they are scheduling, you will receive a Meeting Request email message with various response options. The event will automatically be added to your calendar as a tentative appointment. However, you can still either accept the invitation, tentatively confirm or decline the request, or tentatively confirm or decline the request with a proposed new time for the meeting (the latter options will only be visible if the meeting organizer has enabled allowing new time proposals for the event). You can also open your calendar to show the planned date and verify that you don't have any conflicts. All of these options are available in the Reading pane when you select the Meeting Request or in the Respond group when you open the item.

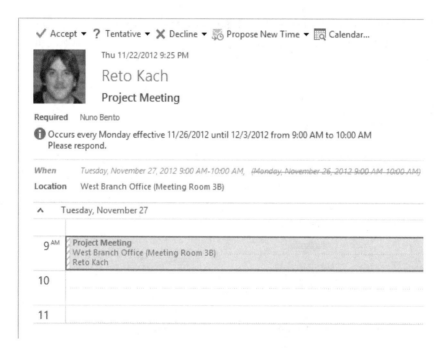

All response options have additional options for editing the response before sending it so that you can add a message to the organizer. You also have the option to not send a response at all. Although your own calendar will show your response status, consider that the meeting organizer will not be able to accurately tally meeting attendance given the absence of your response. Otherwise, when you choose Send The Response Now, the meeting request will be deleted. If you choose to accept, the tentative entry on your calendar will be updated. If you decline, the entry will be deleted.

If your default email account is based in Microsoft Exchange Server or Office 365, Outlook also has special automatic processing features for accepting or declining meeting requests. From the File tab, click Options, then click the Calendar page and scroll down to the Automatic Accept Or Decline Area and click the Auto Accept/Decline button.

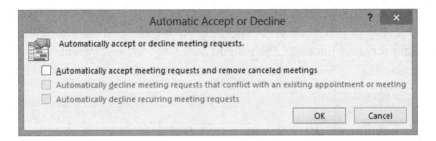

Displaying different views of a calendar

You can select from many different views and arrangements for the display of your calendar. Each has a specific purpose or particular strength for helping you to make sense of your schedule in whatever way you prefer or find more efficient.

Views

The Calendar module offers four distinct views of content, which are available from the Change View button in the Current View group on the View tab.

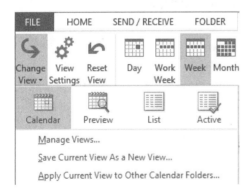

26

These views are:

- **Calendar** This is the standard view in which you display your Outlook calendar. Also known as the **Day/Week/Month** view, it is ideal for viewing events in a set block of time or arrangement (see the next section, "Arrangements"). Entries in this view appear as shaded rectangles containing the time and subject, and optionally the location and meeting organizer as well (depending on the view and the available space, some details may be truncated). The colored bar on the left end indicates the organizer's availability.

- **Preview** This view is identical to the **Calendar** view but also displays the **Reading** pane to show a compressed view of the full **Appointment** item when you select an entry.

- **List** This table-based view displays a grid-style listing of events, similar to how you typically view email messages. It is ideal for sorting and grouping appointments by multiple fields, such as **Start Date** or **Categories**.

- **Active** Similar to the **List** view, this view applies a filter to the list so that only events that occur on or after today's date are visible in the grid.

TIP Add the Change View command in the Current view group on the View tab to the Quick Access Toolbar so you can easily switch between these views.

Arrangements

Using the Calendar view exposes different arrangements for changing the layout of your calendar. You can choose your preferred arrangement and access other features via the buttons in either the Arrange group on the Home tab or the Arrangement group on the View tab:

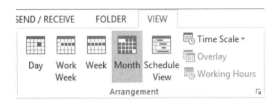

- **Day** This view is made up of hour rows for listing calendar entries at the lowest possible time level compared to the other arrangements. You can choose from various time detail levels via the **Time Scale** button or use the **Zoom** slider in the **Status bar** to increase or decrease the current time detail level. Shaded rows indicate time that's outside of your defined working day. You can change your work hours by clicking the dialog box launcher in the **Arrangement** group and changing the values in the **Start time** and **End time** drop-down list boxes in the **Work time** area in the **Outlook Options** dialog box. Each side of the grid has two button tabs labeled **Previous Appointment** and **Next Appointment**, so you can quickly skip to viewing the full day for the next, past, or future event. If you are looking at today's date, a thin blue horizontal line intersects the hour for the current time, so you can easily differentiate between any earlier and future appointments in your day.

- **Week** This view also lists calendar entries in hour rows and has the same features as the **Day** arrangement, but displays events in vertical columns for each of the seven days of the week. If you are looking at the current week's list of events, the column header for the current day will be shaded. The first column will be for the day you define as the beginning of your work week. The default is **Sunday**, but you can change this setting by clicking the dialog box launcher in the **Arrangement** group and selecting the week day from the **First day of week** box in the **Work time** area in the **Outlook Options** dialog box.

26

- **Work Week** This view is identical to the **Week** arrangement, but limits the displayed day columns to what you define as your working week. You can change these settings by clicking the dialog box launcher in the **Arrangement** group and selecting or clearing the check boxes for each weekday in the **Work time** area in the **Outlook Options** dialog box.

- **Month** This view displays one calendar month at a time, including the adjacent weeks for a total view of six weeks.

- **Schedule View** This view has an inverse layout compared to the other arrangements. It displays hours as vertical columns, while all events for the period selected in your calendar (up to two weeks) are displayed horizontally. **Schedule** view is ideal for comparing multiple calendars.

TIP You can view multiple calendars side by side by selecting two or more calendars in the bottom area of the Folder pane. If you prefer to view the entries from multiple calendars consolidated into a single arrangement, on the View tab, in the Arrangement group, click the Overlay button. You can also change each calendar's display color through the Color button in the Color group next to the Arrangement group.

IMPORTANT

Using the Date Navigator

You can use the Date Navigator to change the day or range of days shown in the Calendar pane. It displays up to six weeks at a time for each of the two-month blocks stacked vertically at the top of the Folder pane. The current date is highlighted by a blue square, and dates containing events will be shown in bold. The weeks currently visible in the Calendar pane will be shaded in the Date Navigator.

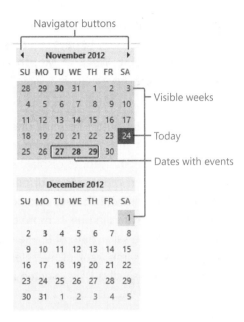

Navigator buttons

Visible weeks

Today

Dates with events

You can display a specific day, week, or range in the Calendar pane by selecting it in the Date Navigator. Use these techniques to work with the Date Navigator:

- To display a day, click that day. If you're displaying the calendar in **Month** view, the display changes to **Day** view. If you're displaying the calendar in **Day** or **Schedule** view, the display updates to the selected day. If you're displaying the calendar in **Work Week** or **Week** view, the display updates to the week containing the selected day if it differs from the current week.

- To display a week, click the margin to the left of that week. In any calendar view, selecting a week in the **Date Navigator** changes the display to **Week** view.

26

- To display a range of days, click the start day of the range and drag until the pointer is over the last day of the range. A maximum of seven weeks or 42 days can be selected. The length of the range determines whether the **Day**, **Week**, or **Month** view is selected. If you want to select a range for the **Schedule** view, that view must be selected.

- To change the displayed month, click the **Previous** or **Next** button to scroll one month back or forward, or click one of the month names and hold down the mouse button to display a range of months, point to the month you want to display, and then release the mouse button. To scroll beyond the seven-month range displayed by default, point to the top or bottom of the month list. In **Month** view, scrolling the month displays the entire month (and possibly some days in one or more of the adjacent months); in **Day** or **Schedule** view, it displays the same date of the selected month, and in **Week** or **Work Week** view, it displays the same week of the selected month. If you have a date range selected, the same range will still be selected in the month that you scroll to.

Calendar item peeks

Although not technically a view, Calendar Item Peeks have been introduced in Outlook 2013 so you can quickly view the full details of an appointment. In any view except Schedule view, simply point to any entry in a calendar, and the details will "peek" out in a pop-up pane.

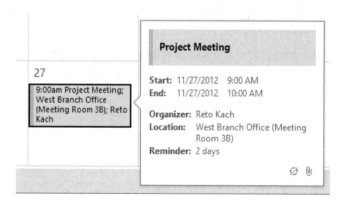

The Calendar Item Peek displays additional information about appointments that is not visible in the Calendar pane, such as the end time, reminder time, whether the event is recurring, or if it has an attachment. You cannot edit the event details in the pop-up pane.

Key points

- You can create and manage appointments and all-day events in your calendar.

- You can use Outlook to set up meetings, invite participants, and track their responses.

- You can use the Scheduling Assistant features to quickly identify meeting times of a specific duration during which your planned attendees are available.

- You have your choice of many different views and arrangements that are possible in a calendar.

- You can change the dates and date ranges displayed in the Calendar pane by using the Date Navigator, by using navigational buttons within the Calendar pane, or by using commands on the ribbon.

- Calendar overlays or the Scheduling view are ideal for viewing multiple calendars at once.

- There are many ways to create an appointment from an email message.

26

Chapter at a glance

Create

Create and update tasks,
page 732

Remove

Remove tasks and items from task lists,
page 740

Assign

Assign tasks to other people,
page 742

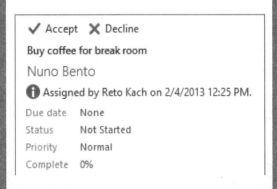

Manage

Manage task assignments,
page 742

Working with tasks

27

IN THIS CHAPTER, YOU WILL LEARN HOW TO

- Create tasks.

- Update tasks.

- Remove tasks and items from task lists.

- Manage task assignments.

To-do lists are omnipresent in the routines of organized and busy people. Whether they take the form of ad-hoc additions to a scrap of paper stuck to your refrigerator door, careful entries in a daily planner, or the behavior of neurons to facilitate working memory, effective task management is an important part of everyone's lives.

Microsoft Outlook 2013 is another useful tool for storing and managing tasks, and it is much more efficient than relying on fragile pieces of paper or overworked brains. Outlook's To-Do List, Tasks peeks, and task folders are optimum for this purpose. You can create tasks, assign due dates, receive reminder notifications, and mark tasks as complete when you finish them. You can delegate tasks to other people, monitor their status, and even receive progress reports as certain milestones are reached.

In this chapter, you'll create tasks, delegate tasks to other people, and manage your own tasks, as well as task assignments. You'll also learn different ways of how tasks can be viewed and organized.

PRACTICE FILES You don't need any practice files to complete the exercises in this chapter.

Creating tasks from scratch

You can create a task item from scratch by using any of the following methods from within the Tasks module:

- While in any tasks folder or the **To-Do List**, click **New Task** on the **Home** tab, enter the task details in the task window that opens, and then save and close the task.

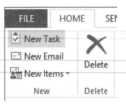

- If the **To-Do List** view is active, enter the task description in the **Type a new task** box at the top of the list, and then press the **Enter** key to create a task with the default settings.

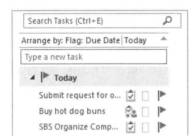

- In any tasks folder, depending on the active view, enter the task description in the **Click here to add a new Task** box in the new item row, press the **Tab** key to move to subsequent fields, fill in other information, and then press **Enter**.

TROUBLESHOOTING If you the Click Here To Add A New Task box is not displayed, you may have a non-table view active in the current folder, or a view that is configured differently. Click the View Settings button in the Current View group on the View tab, then click the Other Settings button. Ensure that both the Allow In-Cell Editing check box and Show 'New Item' Row check box are selected in the Other Settings dialog box.

You can also create tasks outside the Tasks module when you are working in non-task folders:

- Click the **New Items** button, in the **New** group on the **Home** tab, and select **Task** from the menu.

- When the **To-Do** bar is displayed with a **Tasks** peek showing, enter the task description in the **Type a new task** box and press **Enter**.

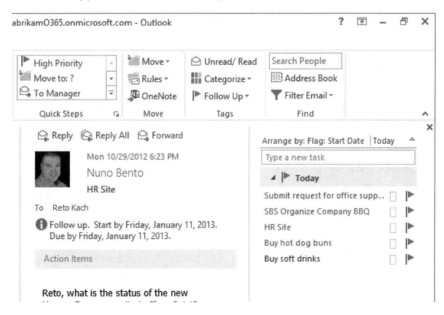

In any task folder or task view, you can assign one or more categories to a task, change the due date, add a reminder, mark the task as complete, or delete the task. The commands for these actions are available on the menu that's displayed by right-clicking the task title, category, or flag in the task list.

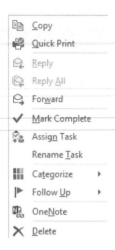

TIP Tasks do not have reminders set on them by default as appointments in your calendar do. You can turn on reminders from the Outlook Options dialog box by selecting the Tasks page and selecting the Set Reminders On Tasks With Due Dates check box.

In this exercise, you'll create a task in the new task item window.

 SET UP You don't need any practice files to complete this exercise. Open Outlook, click the Mail icon in the Navigation bar, and select your Inbox.

1 Click the **New Items** button in the **New** group on the **Home** tab, and select **Task** from the menu.

2 In the **Subject** box of the task item window that opens, enter SBS Organize Company BBQ.

3 Click the calendar icon in the **Start date** box, and then on the calendar, click **Today**.

   The information bar at the top of the task header updates to show Due Today.

4   Click the **Status** box, and then in the list, click **In Progress**.

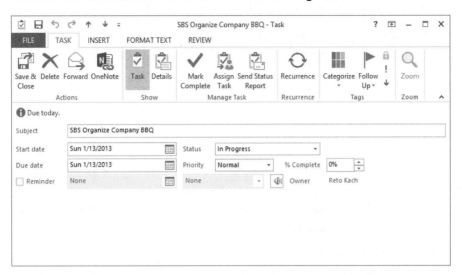

5   Click **Save & Close** in the **Actions** group on the **Task** tab.

6   Display your Inbox, if it is not already current. If the **Tasks** peek isn't visible on the **To-Do** bar, click the **To-Do bar** button on the **View** tab, in the **Layout** group, and select **Tasks**.

In the Tasks peek, the SBS Organize Company BBQ task is listed under the Today heading.

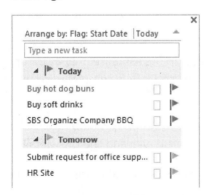

✖ CLEAN UP Retain the SBS Organize Company BBQ task for use in later exercises.

27

Setting task options

Tasks are very easy to create and only require an entry in the Subject field. You can also set other properties to make it easier to identify and manage your tasks:

- **Start date and due date** Most tasks views focus on showing either the start date or due date. When tasks haven't been completed by their due date, they are displayed with red text.

- **Status** The status field stores information about the progress of the task. States include **Not Started**, **In Progress**, **Completed**, **Waiting on someone else**, and **Deferred**. You can also set a percentage value for how much of the task is complete. Setting this to a non-zero value will change the status to **In Progress**, while setting it to **100%** will set the status to **Complete**.

- **Priority** Tasks are created with a **Normal** priority assignment by default. Setting the priority to **High** will also display a red exclamation point icon in any task views that show the **Priority** column, while a **Low** priority displays a blue down-arrow icon. You can sort and filter tasks based on their priority.

- **Recurrence** Recurring tasks recreate themselves on a defined schedule after they are marked as completed. Recurrence patterns that are available are similar to those used with recurring appointments; for example, every week on Tuesday, the 10th of every second month, and so on.

- **Category** As with all other Outlook items, you can assign one or more categories to any task.

- **Reminder** You can set reminders on tasks in the same manner as for appointments. The reminder will persist with the task until the task is completed or the reminder is cleared or dismissed.

- **Privacy** Tasks that are marked as private prevent people who have been granted delegate permissions on your **Tasks** folder from viewing the task details.

Although only the Subject field is mandatory, many of the other task properties are extremely useful when you need to sort, filter, or prioritize your tasks.

Creating tasks from Outlook items

Many items in Outlook become actionable, whereby they may contain content that is suitable for creating a task based on that information. The long way to create these task items would be to copy and paste the subject line and message body from the source item to the new task. However, there are quicker and more efficient ways to create tasks from existing items. Depending on the method that you use, you can either create a new task from an existing item or simply transfer the existing item to your task list by flagging it.

To create a new task from an existing email message, contact, appointment, or note:

- Drag the item to the **Tasks** label on the **Navigation** bar and release the mouse button.

- Right-click the item, hold down the mouse button, drag it to the **Tasks** label on the **Navigation** bar, and release the mouse button. This will display a menu with three choices: **Copy Here as Task with Text**, **Copy Here as Task with Attachment**, and **Move Here as Task with Attachment**. Choose the method that you prefer.

- Any of those methods opens a task window with the subject line populated from the subject line of the source item, and the message body containing either the text of the original item's message body or an attachment copy of the original item. You can then change any of the other task properties, add an additional attachment, assign the task to someone else, and so on.

Instead of creating tasks, you can use the To-Do List to keep track of email messages that require follow-up:

- Click the flag icon that appears to the right of the message when you select it or point to it. This flags the email message as a to-do item, which copies the email subject into the new to-do item entry. These entries will only appear in the **Task** peek on any **To-Do** bar or in the **To-Do List** folder in the **Tasks** module. Note that these to-do items will default to a start date and due date of the current date.

- Right-click the flag icon that appears to the right of the message when you select it or point to it. This will display a menu with additional flag options where you can specify a due date: **Today**, **Tomorrow**, **This Week**, **No Date**, or **Custom** (to set specific start and end dates). You can also add a reminder for a specific time and date, mark previously flagged email messages as complete, or clear the flag. There is also a **Set Quick Click** option, where you can choose the default action when you click the flag icon: **Today**, **Tomorrow**, **This Week**, **Next Week**, **No Date**, or **Complete**.

27

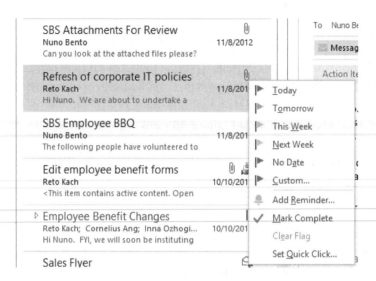

- Drag the message to the **Tasks** peek on the **To-Do** bar and drop it inside any visible group header until a red line with start and end arrows appear, and then release the mouse button. The **Tasks** peek must be arranged by **Categories**, **Start Date**, **Due Date**, or **Importance** for this to work (the **Folder** and **Type** arrangement will not work). The current arrangement type and the values of existing to-do items will dictate which value you can auto-assign with this method. For example, a to-do list arranged by **Start Date** may display items grouped only by **Today** and **Tomorrow**, so you can drag an email message into the **Today** header to create a to-do item entry with a **Start Date** value of **Today**. You would not be able to set the **Start Date** to **Next Week**, for example, because there are no items in the list with a flag set for the following week, and thus no **Next Week** header is visible.

Updating tasks

As actionable items, tasks often require changes to their details as you make progress on them. You may need to change the start or due dates, modify the task status or priority, or update the completion value. For the purposes of this next exercise, assume that you are waiting for the results of an employee survey that is asking for food preferences. You want to update the task to reflect your progress, change the task due date, and remind yourself to follow up if you do not receive the survey results by the end of the day.

In this exercise you'll update the status, completion percentage, and due date of a task in your task list.

 SET UP You need the SBS Organize Company BBQ task you created earlier in this chapter to complete this exercise. If you didn't create that task, you can do so now, or you can substitute any task in your default task list. Display your To-Do List in the Tasks module, and then follow the steps.

1   In the tasks list, double-click the **SBS Organize Company BBQ** task.

2   Click the **Status** box, and then in the list, click **Waiting on someone else**.

3   In the **% Complete** box, enter or select (by clicking the arrows) 25%.

4   In the item body, enter the following on a new line:

     Awaiting results of food preference survey.

5   Click the **Due date** box, and then on the calendar, click the next day.

     The information bar at the top of the task header changes to reflect the new due date.

6   Select the **Reminder** check box. Click the calendar icon in the adjacent box, and then on the calendar, click the due date.

27

7 Click the arrow on the next box adjacent to the **Reminder** calendar icon, and then in the list, click **4:30 PM**.

8 On the **Task** tab, in the **Actions** group, click **Save & Close**.

In the To-Do List, the SBS Organize Company BBQ task moves under the Tomorrow heading.

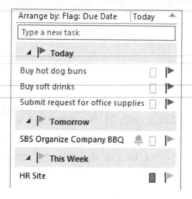

TROUBLESHOOTING If your Tasks peek isn't showing the arrangement as described, right-click the Arrange By header and select Due Date.

✖ CLEAN UP No cleanup is required, although you can delete the SBS Organize Company BBQ task if you want.

Removing tasks and items from task lists

Several actions affect how tasks or to-do items are included or displayed on task lists: marking tasks or flags as complete, removing flags from to-do items, or deleting the item entirely.

Although deleting a task list entry removes the item completely, marking it as complete still retains a record of the item but hides it from certain task list views. To mark a task or to-do item as complete:

- In the **Tasks** module, click a task folder or the **To-Do List**, select an entry, and then on the **Home** tab, in the **Manage Task** group, click **Mark Complete**.

- If the current view in a task list includes a check box column (for the **Complete** field), select the entry and then select the check box.

- If the current view in a task list includes a flag column, select the entry and then click the flag icon.

- In any view, right-click an entry, and then click **Mark Complete**.

- Open a task, change the value in the **Status** box to **Completed** or the **% Complete** value to **100%**, and save your changes.

Depending on the current view, when a task or to-do item is marked as complete, the entry's text will be crossed through, the Complete check box will be selected, or the flag icon will change to a check mark. If you open a completed task, the Status box will show Completed and the % Complete box will show 100%. In some views (such as the Active and Overdue views), the entry won't be listed at all if the view has a filter applied that hides completed items.

When to-do items are marked as completed, the source message or contact that was flagged as a to-do item remains in its original location.

Another way to remove a task or item from a task list is to remove its flag:

- In any task list view, select an entry and click **Remove from List** in the **Manage Task** group on the **Home** tab.

- Select an entry in a **Tasks** peek on the **To-Do** bar and click **Remove from List** in the **Manage Task** group on the **Task List** tool tab

- Right-click any entry in any task list and click **Follow Up**, then click **Clear Flag** if this menu item is present (this action is only available for task list entries that originate from a flagged email message).

To delete a task or flagged item:

- In a tasks folder, select the task and click **Delete** in the **Delete** group on the **Home** tab.

- In any view, right-click the task, and then click **Delete**.

27

Managing task assignments

Most tasks that you create by using the default settings are actionable items meant to remind you to do something. If you need to collaborate on a task or delegate it to other people, you can also assign that task to someone else. When other people accept these tasks, you have the option of keeping a copy of it in your task list so that you can monitor their progress and receive status reports when they are completed. Copies of assigned tasks may appear (depending on the current task list view) with a clipboard icon coupled with a blue arrow and a person graphic. You can view the status of tasks you have assigned to other people by using the Assigned view in the To-Do List folder.

Assigned tasks work regardless of whether the recipient is on your Microsoft Exchange server network or not (such as if you use a POP or IMAP email account with an Internet service provider), or even if they use an email client other than Outlook.

- Recipients in your Exchange server network will receive a special **Task Request** item instead of an email message. These items appear in their Inbox with a **Reading Pane** header showing **Accept** and **Decline** buttons, as well as detailed information about the task, such as the due date, status, and priority.

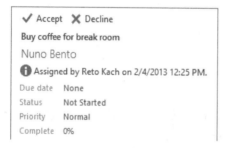

- Recipients using non-Outlook email clients receive a standard email version of a **Task Request**. However, these messages still show the full details of the task, and the recipient can reply to the email message and manually indicate whether he or she accepts the task or not.

When tasks are accepted, you can no longer update your copy of the task if you chose to retain one. The assignee then becomes the task owner, and you become the task organizer.

Existing tasks that you have created for yourself can be assigned to other people.

In this exercise, you'll delegate a task to another Outlook user.

→ SET UP You don't need any practice files to complete this exercise. Open Outlook, click the Tasks label on the Navigation bar, click the To-Do List, and then follow the steps.

1   Double-click any task in your list that hasn't been assigned to someone else.

2   In the task item window that opens, click **Assign Task** in the **Manage Task** group on the **Task** tab.

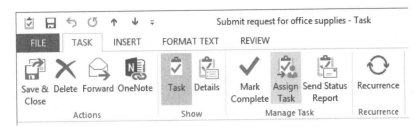

3   In the **To** box that appears in the task header, enter the email address of the person you want to assign the task to.

Note that the Keep An Updated Copy Of This Task On My Task List and Send Me A Status Report When This Task Is Complete check boxes are selected by default.

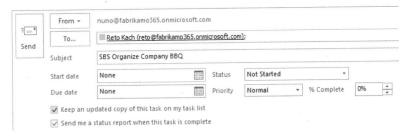

4   In the task header, click the **Send** button. If a message box notifies you that the task reminder has been turned off, click **OK**.

Outlook sends the task request and notifies you when the assignee accepts or declines the task.

✖ CLEAN UP No cleanup is necessary.

27

Reclaiming an assigned task

If a task assignee declines a task assignment for a task and you have kept a copy in your task list, you have the option of reclaiming that task for yourself or reassigning it to another person.

To reclaim or reassign a declined task:

1 Open the declined task assignment message in your Inbox, or open the copy of the assigned task from your **To-Do List** or **Task** folder

2 In the **Manage Task** group, click **Return To Task List** to reclaim the task, or click **Assign Task** to reassign it.

Dealing with tasks other people assign to you

When someone using Outlook assigns a task to you, you will receive a task assignment request in your Inbox. To accept or decline the assignment, select the task request and click either the Accept or Decline button at the top of the Reading Pane. You will have an option to edit your response before sending the reply.

Other task request actions are available by double-clicking the task request message to open it:

- Click **Reply** in the **Respond** group to respond to the task assignor without accepting or declining the task request.

- Click **Forward** in the **Respond** group to forward the task request to another person without reassigning it.

- Click **Assign Task** in the **Manage Task** group to reassign the task to someone else.

After you have accepted an assigned task, you can send the task assignor updates as you make progress on the task. To send these updates:

- Locate and open the task.

- Click **Send Status Report** in the **Manage Task** group. Outlook creates a new email message containing the details of the task.

- Address the message to people you want to send the report to and then send the message.

Key points

- You can create tasks for yourself and assign tasks to other people.

- You can organize tasks by assigning categories to them and grouping them by category in Tasks peeks or folder views.

- Outlook displays tasks in the Tasks module, in Tasks peeks on the To-Do bar, and in the Daily Task List in some Calendar views.

- When you assign tasks, Outlook sends a task request to the assignee, who can accept or decline the task. If you keep a copy of the task on your task list, it is updated when the assignee updates his or her copy.

- You can set a reminder on a task to receive a notification before its due date.

- You can update tasks assigned to you and send status reports to the task assignor.

- The status of a task can be set to Not Started, In Progress, Completed, Waiting On Someone Else, or Deferred.

- After you mark a task as completed, you can remove it from your task list or delete it.

- You can create one-time tasks or recurring tasks that regenerate themselves after you complete the current occurrence.

27

Chapter at a glance

View

View contact details in various ways, page 747

Manage

Manage and update contacts, page 755

Connect

Connect with friends and colleagues on social networks, page 758

Managing contacts and people

28

IN THIS CHAPTER, YOU WILL LEARN HOW TO

- Work with different views of contacts.

- Add and update contact items.

- Connect to social networks and view social updates.

Staying in touch with people can be a daunting challenge given busy workloads. Add a wide range of communication methods and social integration to the mix, and keeping track of contact data and activities can become quite cumbersome. With Microsoft Outlook 2013, it is now easier than ever to maintain a clutter-free collection of contact details from multiple sources.

In this chapter, you'll create and update contacts. You'll use different ways to view contacts, and connect to social networks to view social updates.

PRACTICE FILES You don't need any practice files to complete the exercises in this chapter.

Viewing contacts

Outlook doesn't just display boring, flat lists of your contacts. It excels at presenting your data in a variety of appealing ways, depending on what method you are most comfortable with or find more functional for specific tasks. You can view contacts in aggregated views like the new People Hub in Outlook 2013, display Contact Cards to show a mix of contact data and social updates, use the People peek to search for or store your favorite contacts, or use traditional table and card-based folder views to list your contacts.

747

Using the People Hub

New in Outlook 2013 is the People Hub. This new default view for your contact folders serves as a central dashboard for viewing contacts from your Outlook profile or connected social networks.

In the People Hub, you can:

- View a person's contact information from multiple contacts or sources in an aggregated view on their **Contact Card**.

- View a contact's social network updates from any social networks you've added. Discover if they are friends with you on that network, or if they have public social network updates.

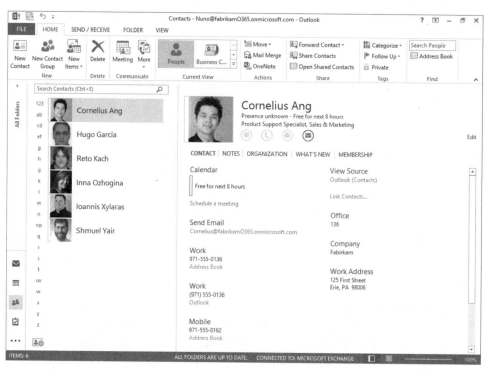

Viewing Contact Cards

Detailed information about the people you are connected with in Outlook is visible within Contacts Cards. To view the full Contact Card or a Contact Card preview for someone, you can point to, click, or double-click a contact name anywhere in Outlook.

You can also display a full Contact Card by:

- Double-clicking the name of the sender, which is located alongside the photo box in the message header of a selected or open email message.

- Double-clicking any name in any of the address fields in the message header.

- Right-clicking a name in the message header and selecting **Open Contact Card.**

- Pointing to an entry in the **People** peek and clicking the down arrow in the lower-right corner of the **Contact Card** preview.

- Selecting a contact in a **Contacts** folder with the **People** view active.

TIP Click the pushpin icon in the upper-right corner of a fully expanded Contact Card to pin the card open. You can drag it around your screen to keep it open as a reference and even view it outside of the main Outlook window. Pin several cards open at once to keep the details of people you frequently communicate with visible at a glance.

28

Basic information for the person is listed in both the preview and full Contact Card modes:

- The contact's full name.
- A description of that person's present state or online status.
- The person's title and position.

A row of action buttons is displayed under the basic contact information. You can use these buttons to initiate instant messaging discussions or phone or video calls, or quickly create an email message.

When you fully expand a Contact Card, a row of tabs appears, displaying information that is even more detailed.

- **Contact** Displays links to initiate various actions
- **Organization** Displays information about the contact's manager and direct reports (Microsoft Exchange accounts only)
- **What's New** Displays information from that contact's social networks
- **Membership** Displays information about the distribution lists that a contact is a member of (Exchange accounts only)

Using contact views

Every Contacts folder has a standard list of views for displaying contacts in a variety of layouts. You can choose from the available views by:

- Selecting a view from the gallery in the **Current View** group on the **Home** tab.

- Selecting a view from the **Change View** button in the **Current View** group on the **View** tab.

Each default view displays information about your contacts either as cards or in a list:

- **People** The new default view for Outlook 2013 displays a simple list of contacts with photo thumbnails and a detailed **Contact Card** for a selected contact.

- **Business Card** This view shows a summary of the contact's information in a view that's similar to the display of data on a business card. You can edit the business card layout for individual contacts without affecting the appearance of other contacts.

- **Card** This view is similar to the **Business Card** view, but it's not as graphical, and it's constrained to a list of narrow columns, so the information in the cards may be truncated.

- **Phone** This view displays a table layout that lists each contact's name, company, and phone numbers.

- **List** This view is similar to the **Phone** view, but with slightly different columns and with contact records grouped by **Company**.

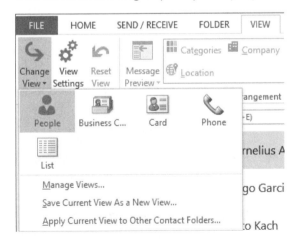

28

Using the People peek

You will undoubtedly have a number of people that you communicate with on a frequent basis. What better way to keep these important contacts front and center then by adding them to a list of favorites? That's exactly what you can do now with the People peek.

You can interact with the People peek in these ways:

- With your mouse, point to the **People** icon located in the **Navigation** bar.

- Pin the **People** peek to the **To-Do** bar so that it's always visible.

The People peek contains a search capability that lets you search for people. The system helps you find people from all of your contacts. In the search results, you can preview a person's Contact Card or right-click the entry to add that person to your list of favorites, if you wish.

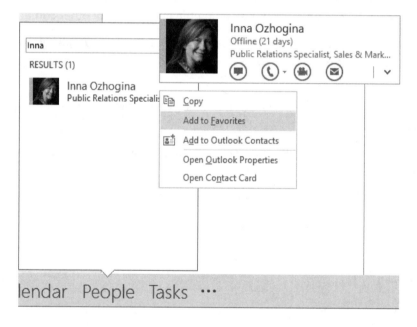

TIP As with the Calendar peek and Tasks peek, the People peek can be docked in other Navigation modules, such as Calendar and Tasks. Keep in mind that if you dock or undock a peek from a module type, that change is global to all folders for that type and isn't persisted for individual folder types. For example, if you have a second calendar called Personal, you cannot have the People peek docked only in your Personal calendar but not your default calendar.

Creating contacts

The contact information for people and companies that you communicate with is stored in contact items within any Contacts folder in Outlook. Contacts can store many types of information, including:

- Name, company name, and job title
- Business, home, and alternate addresses
- Business, home, mobile, pager, and other telephone numbers
- Webpage URLs, instant messaging (IM) account names, and up to three email addresses
- A contact photo
- Free-form notes or rich content (such as clip art, charts, and tables) in the contact message body
- Business-related information (such as department, office location, and names of managers and assistants)
- Personal information (such as nickname, spouse, birthday, and anniversary)

In this exercise, you'll create a new contact item in your default Contacts folder.

 **SET UP** You don't need any practice files to complete this exercise. Open Outlook, click the People icon or label on the Navigation bar, select a contacts folder, and follow the steps.

1. On the **Home** tab, in the **New** group, click **New Contact**.

   A new contact item window opens.

2. In the **Full Name** box, enter Cornelius Ang.

3. In the **Company** box, enter Fabrikam.

4. In the **Job Title** box, enter Product Support Specialist.

5. In the **E-mail** box, enter Cornelius@fabrikamO365.onmicrosoft.com.

   A second or third email address can be entered by choosing E-Mail 2 or E-Mail 3 from the drop-down list box beside the E-Mail box.

6. In the **Phone numbers** area, enter 9715550136 in the **Business** box and 9715550162 in the **Mobile** box.

28

7   In the **Addresses** area, click in the box to the right of the **Business** box, enter 125
     First Street, press the **Enter** key, and then enter Erie, PA 98006.

     Additional addresses can be entered by choosing the address type from the drop-
     down list box beside the Business box.

8   In the **Actions** group, click **Save & Close**.

     The contact window closes. The Contacts folder now includes the new contact item
     for Cornelius Ang.

✖ CLEAN UP No cleanup is required. Retain the Cornelius Ang contact item for use in
later exercises or as a reference.

TIP The default display name format for email addresses when displayed in email headers
is *First Name (email@domain.com)*. If you want to change the way email addresses for a
contact are displayed in email headers (to something much shorter, for example, perhaps
without an email address), you can simply edit the value in the Display As box in that
person's contact item.

Using inline editing

New in Outlook 2013 is the ability to use inline editing with contacts. If you actively manage your contacts to keep their information up to date, you no longer have to open the entire contact window every time you want to make changes. This feature makes it easier than ever to update a contact with additional email addresses or phone numbers. To use inline editing:

- Display the **People** view in any **Contacts** folder.

- Select a **Contact** and click the **Edit** button on the **Contact Card.**

- Make your changes and click **Save.**

28

Managing linked contacts

Managing contacts can be difficult when there are many sources that contain your contact information. For example, you may have a folder for work-related contacts and another for personal contacts. If you have configured social networks for use with the People pane, Outlook will also store contact data for those people as well. With all of these different contact records, it's unlikely that the information in every item would be identical.

Outlook 2013 now aggregates the information about the same person from multiple contacts into a single view on that person's Contact Card. The View Source section lists the source(s) of the contact data (Outlook, LinkedIn, Facebook, and SharePoint) for that person. You can click the Link Contacts label to display a dialog box where you can:

- Delete linked contacts

- Enter a name into the search box to search for other contacts that you want to link with the current contact

Configuring a social network account

The People pane (also known as the Social Connector) brings social views of your colleagues and friends from multiple social networks right to your email and contacts list. With Outlook 2013, you can monitor and grow your network by creating connections to Facebook, LinkedIn, and SharePoint. Microsoft is planning to release more social providers in the near future.

In this exercise, you'll create a social network connection for either Facebook, LinkedIn, or SharePoint.

➡ SET UP You don't need any practice files to complete this exercise. You will need an active account for Facebook, LinkedIn, or SharePoint. Open Outlook, and follow the steps.

1   Click the **File** tab, select the **Info** page, click **Account Settings,** and choose **Social Network Accounts**.

2   Select the check box next to the social network where you already have an account set up.

3   Enter your user name in the **User Name** box and password in the **Password** box (or the URL for your SharePoint site in the **URL Address** box).

    If you want this social network to be the default source of contact photos and social updates, select the By Default, Show Photos And Information From This Network When Available check box.

28

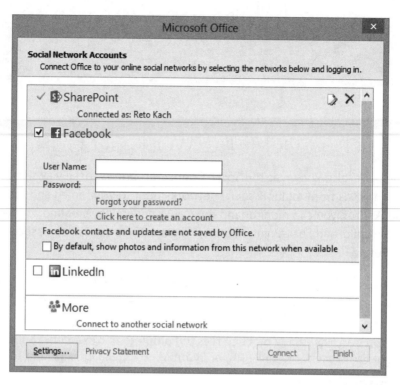

4   Click **Connect**, then click **Finish** after the connection confirmation.

5   Click **Close** after the **Microsoft Office** dialog box opens and displays a congratulations message.

CLEAN UP No cleanup is required.

Viewing social network updates

After a social network is configured, Outlook gathers the relevant data and social content for your contacts. This information is displayed in certain locations, of which the primary mechanism is the People Pane. To display the People Pane and view social updates for a contact:

- On the **View** tab, in the **People Pane** group, click **People Pane,** and then select **Normal.**

- Select or open an email message, or open a full **Contact** item window (not a **Contact Card**) from a **Contacts** folder.

- Click any of the tabs on the left side of the **People Pane** to switch between various views: **All, What's New, Mail, Attachments**, and **Meetings** (the first two will contain social network updates).

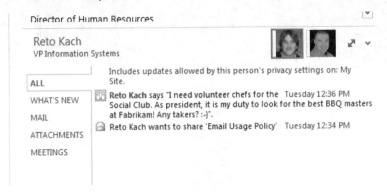

Key points

- The People Hub is a convenient dashboard for viewing aggregated information about contacts in a single location.

- Edits to Contact Cards from the People view update the information in all linked contacts.

- The People peek is a convenient tool for quickly searching contacts or managing your favorites.

- Viewing social network updates lets you keep up to date with the activities of friends and colleagues.

28

Chapter at a glance

Organize

Categorize and flag email messages, page 764

Plan

View and schedule your appointments, page 767

Search

Find messages from related conversations or senders, page 773

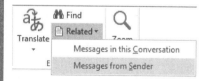

Create

Quickly create email messages, appointments, tasks, and contacts, page 779

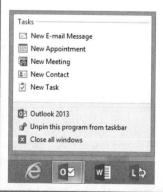

Saving time with Outlook

29

IN THIS CHAPTER, YOU WILL LEARN HOW TO

- Flag and categorize messages.

- Plan your schedule.

- Organize your mail.

- Search for content.

- Quickly create Outlook items.

Microsoft Outlook is very much the center of focus for many people when they are working on their computers, and it's often the first application that is opened at the start of the work day and the last one to be used at the end of the day. It is invaluable as a communication tool, organizer, and repository for important information. As such, people rely on it to get their work done as quickly as possible. Learning how to efficiently use key features in Outlook will help you maximize your productivity.

Keeping your Inbox organized so you can read and access important mail more efficiently can be a daunting challenge! Though it can be tricky to prioritize what you need to work on in Outlook, a number of features can make this process easier to master.

In this chapter, you'll flag and review important messages, plan your schedule, organize your mail, and quickly search for and create Outlook content.

PRACTICE FILES You don't need any practice files to complete the exercises in this chapter.

Flagging and reviewing important messages

There are many ways to prioritize and organize your email messages so that you can better manage the conversations that require action. Although it would be nice if email senders would stamp their important message as high priority so you didn't have to, only the recipient (you) truly knows which messages are really important.

Though you can easily create rules to auto-prioritize incoming email messages in various ways (such as by assigning flags or categories to messages with specific subject lines or from specific people), there is a simple technique that you can use in most situations that will satisfy many users.

The ability to flag email messages in Outlook is a much-used feature. Categorizing email messages is also a frequent task. When you combine the two approaches, you have a very simple, flexible, and efficient technique for prioritizing your Inbox. First, let's start with the basics for each approach.

Applying a message flag

Attaching flags to email messages is one of the easiest ways to make a message stand out in your folder. Flags are excellent indicators that tell you that a message requires an action or that it is important to you. All flagged messages in a folder will display a red flag icon in the flag column.

In this exercise, you'll apply a flag to an email message.

 **SET UP** Start Outlook, and follow the steps.

1   In the message list, point to a message. Icons for available message actions will appear.

2   Click the flag icon to apply a flag.

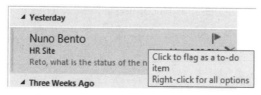

CLEAN UP No cleanup is required.

TIP Right-click the flag icon to view more options.

Categorizing a message

Assigning one or more categories to an email message is another way to make a message stand out. Similar to flagged messages, email messages that have been categorized will have one or more colored boxes displayed in the Categories column.

In this exercise, you'll apply a category to a message.

➡ **SET UP** Start Outlook, and follow the steps.

1   Select a message in your Inbox.

2   Right-click the message, and then select one or more categories from the **Categorize** menu.

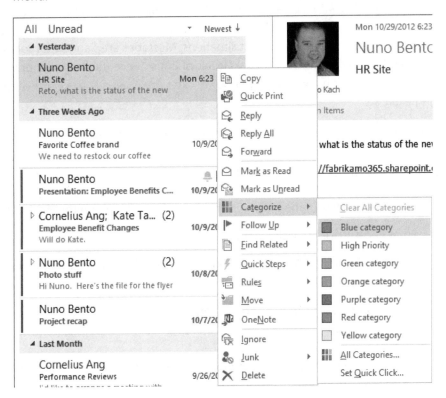

TIP A quicker way to categorize a selected email message is to use the Quick Click feature by clicking in the Categories column to apply a default category. However, to use this feature, you must have the Reading Pane set to the bottom view, or you can expand the message list if the Reading Pane is on the right, until the Categories column appears. Choose the Set Quick Click option from the bottom of the Categorize menu to change your default category.

 CLEAN UP No cleanup is required.

Creating a high-priority Quick Step

A powerful technique for classifying and eventually triaging important messages is achieved by combining a flag with a category. By creating a Quick Step, you can efficiently process and later view high-priority email messages with minimal effort. This approach uses simple assumptions that should work in most situations. Messages are flagged for follow-up tomorrow and are assigned to one of two levels of importance (high priority or urgent). For simplicity of illustration, only the high priority category is used in the Quick Step in the following exercise.

In this exercise, you'll create a Quick Step to apply a flag and category to an email message.

 SET UP Start Outlook, and follow the steps.

1   Click **Create New** in the gallery in the **Quick Steps** group on the **Home** tab.

2   Enter High Priority in the **Name** box.

3   Click the **Choose an Action** box, and select **Flag Message** in the **Categories, Tasks and Flags** group.

4   Select **Tomorrow** from the **Choose flag** box.

5   Click **Add Action**.

6   Click the new **Choose an Action** box, and select **Categorize message** in the **Categories, Tasks and Flags** group.

7   Select **All Categories** from the **Choose category** box.

8   Click **New** in the **Color Categories** dialog box and enter High Priority in the **Name** box. Select a color from the **Color** drop-down list, click **OK** in the **Add New Category** dialog box, and finally, click **OK** in the **Color Categories** dialog box.

9   Optional: In the **Edit Quick Step** dialog box, choose a keyboard shortcut key from the **Choose a shortcut** box and enter any descriptive text you like in the **Tooltip text** box.

10   Click **Finish.**

To use your new Quick Step, simply select a message and choose one of the following options:

- Choose **High Priority** from the gallery in the **Quick Steps** group on the **Home** tab.

- Right-click the message and select **High Priority** from the **Quick Steps** menu.

- Enter the keyboard shortcut for the Quick Step if you assigned one.

✖ CLEAN UP No cleanup is required.

Reviewing high-priority messages

After you've classified one or more messages by using the High Priority Quick Step, it's a simple matter to differentiate them within your mailbox.

In this exercise, you'll change the view of your Inbox to group email messages by flags or categories.

SET UP Start Outlook, display your Inbox, and follow the steps.

1   Click the drop-down menu in the view bar at the top of the message list.

2   Select **Flag: Start Date** or **Categories.**

Outlook will reorder the messages in the view by grouping them according to the flag date (or items with no flags) or category (or items with no categories).

CLEAN UP No cleanup is required.

Using the Calendar peek to plan your schedule

The Calendar folder may not always be active, or you may not have the To-Do bar visible. Yet your calendar can be instantly visible regardless of your configuration, when you simply show the Calendar peek.

In this exercise, you'll display and use the Calendar peek to view appointments.

SET UP Start Outlook, and follow the steps.

1. Point to **Calendar** at the bottom of your **Navigation Bar**. A pop-up window appears showing a list of today's appointments.

2. Click any date to view the appointments for that day.

3. Double-click any appointment to open that item in its own window.

4. Click the arrowed rectangle in the upper-right corner to dock that peek to the **To-Do Bar.**

   TIP You can view your calendar in other navigation modules (like People or Tasks) by docking the Calendar peek to the To-Do Bar in those folders as well.

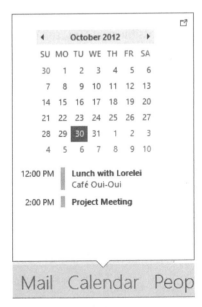

CLEAN UP No cleanup is required.

Planning ahead with the Weather bar

When you need to travel to an appointment, staying aware of inclement weather is a practical strategy for ensuring you arrive at your destination on time. You can now view the weather forecast for the next three days above your calendar in the Calendar module or any calendar folder.

The default city may not be your current location, but you can easily add a location and switch between two or more locations.

In this exercise, you'll display and customize the Weather bar.

 SET UP **Start Outlook, and follow the steps.**

1   Click the name of the current location and select **Add Location** from the drop-down list.

2   Enter the name of a city and press the **Enter** key. The **Weather** bar will be updated to reflect the weather for the newly added location.

3   If your search for a location displays multiple possible matches, select the correct one from the list.

4   To view weather in multiple locations, click the name of the current displayed location and then select another location from the list.

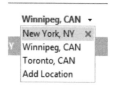

TIP You can delete a location from the list by clicking the X next to the city.

5   For more detailed weather information, point to one of the days in the three-day forecast.

6   Click **See more online** to open a webpage with full weather details.

7   To configure advanced options for the **Weather** bar, display the **Outlook Options** dialog box in the **Backstage** view by clicking the **File** tab, then clicking **Options**, **Calendar**, **Weather**. Here you can toggle the **Weather** bar on or off, as well as switch the temperature display between Celsius and Fahrenheit.

❌ CLEAN UP No cleanup is required.

Organizing your mail with Folder Favorites

The Folder Pane (formerly called the Navigation pane) is the sole tool for viewing all of the folders available in the current Outlook profile. Without it, you would have no way of browsing to find a particular folder. Even then, if you had hundreds of folders arranged in varying degrees of hierarchy depth, finding folders that you frequently use could quickly become a challenge. However, Folder Favorites is the perfect method for pinning your often-accessed folders to a convenient and easily accessible list.

In this exercise, you'll add favorite folders to the Folder Pane.

SET UP Start Outlook, and follow the steps.

1   Ensure that both **Normal** and **Favorites** are checked in the drop-down menu of the **Folder Pane** button in the **Layout** group on the **View** tab.

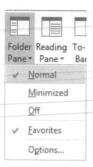

2   Right-click a folder in the folder list at the bottom of the **Folder Pane** below the **Favorites** section, and select **Show in Favorites**.

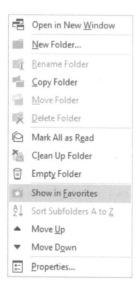

TIP To remove a folder from your list of favorites, right-click any folder in the Favorites section (or the same folder that you want to remove from the folder list at the bottom of the Folder Pane) and select Remove from Favorites.

3   The folder is added to the list of favorites in the **Folder Pane**.

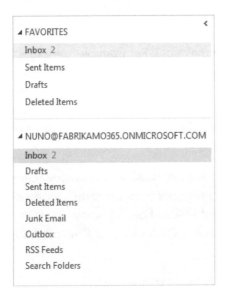

Rearranging key folders

All of the folders that you add to the Favorites section are simply added to the end of the list. You can arrange them in your preferred order of importance by dragging the folders up and down within the list.

New to Outlook 2013 is the ability to arrange folders in any of the folder hierarchies inside the main folder list on the Folder Pane. Simply drag the folder (or right-click and choose Move Up or Move Down) until it is in the desired location.

TIP If you rearrange the folders while in the Folders module, the arrangement will carry over to the Folder Pane as well (and vice-versa).

Searching for related messages

Navigating through voluminous folder hierarchies or even clicking folders in your Favorites list is not an ideal method for finding email messages. For example, messages from a conversation or from a specific person that are filed in one or more folders can be difficult to track down. When you select an email message and you need to display related messages at a glance, switching back and forth between folders (assuming you know the locations of these messages) is definitely not ideal. A far better approach is to utilize existing search functionality built into Outlook.

Email messages that share the same subject line are classified in Outlook terms as a conversation. Outlook can display a filtered list of messages from the same conversation (as long as they are stored in the same mailbox or .pst file). Although you can easily search for email messages by subject with a custom search query, Outlook has built-in methods that can do this kind of search for you automatically.

There are two ways to view related messages in a conversation.

- Right-click an email message that may have related messages in the conversation, and choose **Find Related, Messages in this Conversation.**

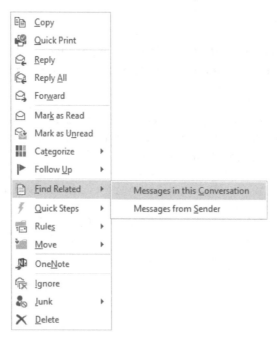

- Open an email message and choose **Messages in this Conversation** from the **Related** drop-down list in the **Editing** group on the **Message** tab.

TIP If the results of your search do not appear to include the content you expected, click the More link at the bottom of the message list underneath the Showing Recent Results label. By default, Outlook only shows recent items in the search results to improve search performance.

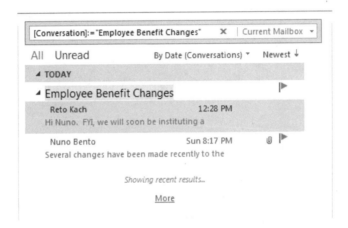

Finding messages from a specific sender

Similar to finding related messages, Outlook can display a list of email messages sent from a specific sender. Though you can easily use a custom search query to search for email messages from someone, methods are already built in that can do this kind of search for you automatically.

In this exercise, you'll search for email messages from a specific person.

SET UP Start Outlook, display any mail folder, and follow the steps.

1 Right-click an email message and choose **Find Related, Messages from Sender**.

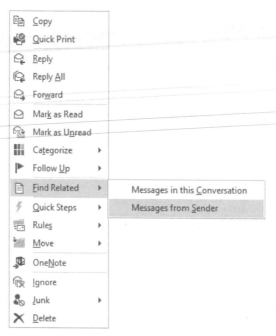

2 Open an email message and choose **Messages from Sender** in the **Related** drop-down list in the **Editing** group on the **Message** tab.

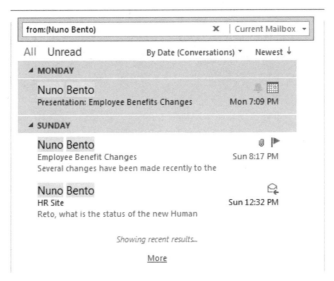

CLEAN UP No cleanup is required.

Conducting quick searches

You can waste a lot of time trying to find that one piece of information that you need at a moment's notice. When you need to find an email message in a hurry, the Instant Search feature is the easiest way. Outlook continuously builds an up-to-date index of your data by using Windows Search so that it can quickly show relevant results before you have even finished typing a keyword.

Click in the Search box (or press Ctrl+E) and begin typing a search term. As you enter text, the message list is filtered to show email messages containing your search term. Continue typing to filter the list to show content containing more letters of your search term, whole words, or even an entire phrase.

You can change the scope of the search by expanding or narrowing the folder locations. Click the drop-down list in the Search box and choose from Current Folder, Subfolders, Current Mailbox, or All Outlook Items.

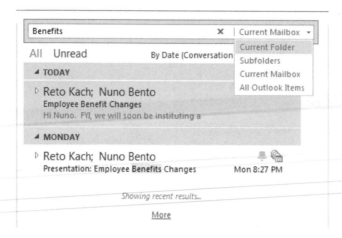

TIP If you don't like the way Instant Search behaves, there are many advanced options to configure. Click File, Options, Search and configure your preferences by using the available settings.

Using Search Folders to view today's mail

Search Folders are special folders in Outlook that aggregate email messages from multiple folder locations into a single view. You can specify search criteria that narrow the result set of the search so that only messages that match the conditions of the search are included in the list of email messages within the folder.

For example, you can use Search Folders to view mail that has been flagged and mail from and to specific people. Although there are no default Search Folders that you can jump in and start using, they are very easy to create. You can choose from a selection of common search criteria types or build a completely custom Search Folder.

IMPORTANT

In this exercise, you'll create a Search Folder to display all email messages that have been received, sent, or filed to another folder today.

1   In the main Outlook window, click the **Folder** tab and click the **New Search Folder** button in the **New Ribbon** group.

2   Scroll down the list in the **New Search Folder** dialog box and select **Create a custom Search Folder** in the **Custom** area.

3   Click **Choose** and enter Today's Mail in the **Name** box in the **Custom Search Folder** dialog box.

4   Click **Criteria**.

5   On the **Messages** page of the **Search Folder Criteria** dialog box, select **received** in the **Time** box and **Today** in the box beside it.

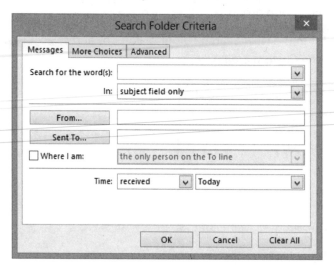

6   Click **OK**, and then click **OK** again in the **Custom Search Folder** dialog box, and click **OK** again in the **New Search Folder** dialog box.

❌ CLEAN UP No cleanup is required.

TIP If you later want to exclude email messages from specific folders (such as the Deleted Items or Drafts folders) from the Today's Mail Search Folder, you can always edit the folder criteria. To do so, right-click the Search Folder in the Folder Pane and select Customize This Search Folder. Then click the Browse button to display a list of folders with check boxes that can be selected or cleared to match your specific search terms.

Outlook will automatically navigate to the Search Folder after it is created and will display only email messages that have been sent or received on today's date.

Creating items quickly

For a long time, Outlook has provided many convenient shortcuts for quickly creating new items. Some of the following methods may already be familiar to experienced users, but re-gardless of your level of expertise, these are essential timesaving ways for creating content.

29

- Click the first button in the **New** group on the **Home** tab or press **Ctrl+N**. Regard-less of the module that you are in (for example, **Mail**, **Calendar**, or **People**), this is the quickest way to create a new email message, new appointment, and so on.

- If you need to create an item that has a different type then the currently active mod-ule, select the item type that you wish to create from the **New Items** drop-down list in the **New** group on the **Home** tab.

- You can also right-click the Outlook icon in the Windows taskbar and create a new item from the available options.

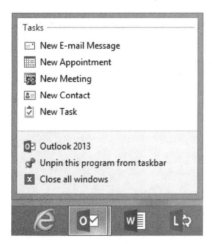

Creating contextual appointments, contacts, and tasks from email messages

Creating new items from scratch is not an efficient approach when there is contextual information that should be included in the item. If you receive an email message that contains relevant content, don't waste time by copying text from the message and pasting it (or painstakingly typing it!) into the new item.

In this exercise, you'll create contextual items from an email message.

➡ SET UP **Start Outlook, display any mail folder, and follow the steps.**

1   Drag an email message to the **Calendar** button on the **Navigation Bar** to create a new appointment.

2   Drag the email message to the **People** button on the **Navigation Bar** to create a new contact.

3   Drag the email message to the **Tasks** button on the **Navigation Bar** to create a new task.

The new items will also contain the following items:

- The subject of the original email message in the subject line of the new appointment or task.

- The sender's name and email address of the original email message as the full name and default email address of the new contact.

✖ CLEAN UP **No cleanup is required.**

Key points

- Search Folders and Instant Search can help you quickly find the content you need.

- Flags and categories are helpful tools to classify your content.

- Peeks are convenient ways to show today's appointments.

- It's easy to manage and arrange your folders the way you want.

Chapter at a glance

View

View the normal view of OneNote,
page 785

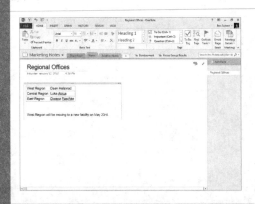

Dock

Use OneNote in Docked To Desktop view,
page 786

Capture

Capture ideas with a OneNote Quick Note,
page 789

Getting comfortable in OneNote 2013

30

IN THIS CHAPTER, YOU WILL LEARN HOW TO

- Get started with OneNote 2013.

- Explore the OneNote 2013 user interface.

- Modify the way OneNote looks.

- Identify new and improved features in OneNote 2013.

Microsoft OneNote 2013 is a free-form note-taking, collaboration, and research tool. It's a powerful place to capture all of your notes in the classroom or in business meetings, or even just random ideas that come into your head. You can share your notes with co-workers, family members, or anybody else you'd like to. You can also synchronize your notes across a wide variety of devices from desktops to laptops, tablets, and even your smartphone.

In this chapter, you'll explore the OneNote 2013 interface and learn about new and improved features.

Getting started with OneNote 2013

You typically start OneNote 2013 from the Start screen in Windows 8 or the Start menu in Windows 7. The very first time you start OneNote, it will walk you through a quick process to create your first notebook. Every time you start OneNote after that, the new OneNote main screen will appear.

From the main screen, you can access your opened notebooks, create new notes, or open other notebooks.

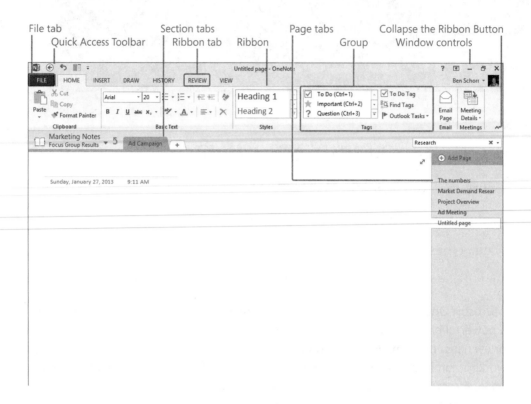

File tab   Quick Access Toolbar   Section tabs   Ribbon tab   Ribbon   Page tabs   Group   Collapse the Ribbon Button   Window controls

■ **Ribbon** The main component of the OneNote interface and where you'll find the primary commands for working with the content of your notes. The ribbon is made up of task-oriented tabs, and each tab has groups of related commands. For example, on the **Home** tab, the **Clipboard** group contains commands for copying and pasting information in your OneNote notebooks.

IMPORTANT

SEE ALSO For instructions on how to modify your display settings and adapt exercise instructions, see Chapter 1, "Getting comfortable in Office Professional 2013."

■ **File tab** The first tab on the ribbon. Unlike other ribbon tabs, the **File** tab displays the **Backstage** view, where commands for working with the entire contents of a note-book, such as **New**, **Print**, **Share**, and **Export**, are located. The **Backstage** view is also where application options are located, and where you can find information about your user account and your version of Microsoft Office.

- **Quick Access Toolbar** Holds your most frequently used commands. By default, **Back**, **Undo**, and **Dock to Desktop** have already been added.

  TIP To add other commands you use the most to your Quick Access Toolbar, right-click the command you want on the ribbon, and then click Add To Quick Access Toolbar. To remove a command from the Quick Access Toolbar, similar to adding a command, you right-click the command you wish to remove and then click Remove From Quick Access Toolbar.

- **Title bar** Appears at the top of the window and displays the name of the active page along with the application name.

- **Notebook pane** Appears at the left side of the screen and provides access to your open notebooks and sections.

- **Section tabs** Appear across the top of the page and provide another means of access to your sections and section groups.

- **Page tabs** Appear at the right side of the screen and give you access to your individual pages.

SEE ALSO For a more comprehensive list of ribbon and user interface elements, along with detailed instructions on how to customize your user interface, including the ribbon and Quick Access Toolbar, see Chapter 1, "Getting comfortable in Office Professional 2013."

Exploring the OneNote interface

OneNote 2013 has a few options that let you control how it looks, which can significantly change your experience with the product. Most of these options can be found on the View tab of the ribbon in OneNote.

- **Normal view** A bit self-explanatory; this is the view you'll normally use in OneNote with the ribbon, **Notebook** pane, section, and page tabs all accessible.

- **Full Page view** Pushes all of the tools off the screen so that you have the maximum amount of room for notes. This is most often used on small screens or tablets, or if you just really want to minimize distractions and like to work on a "clean canvas." To exit **Full Page** view, click the **Normal View** button that appears as a double-headed arrow in the upper-right corner of the screen.

- **Dock to Desktop** A handy view when you want to work on other things but keep your notes visible to the side of the screen. **Dock to Desktop** will appear as a column on the right side of your screen (by default) where you can read, edit, and create your notes while leaving the rest of the screen free for other applications. To return to **Normal** view, click the **Normal View** button, which appears as a double-headed arrow at the upper-right of the window.

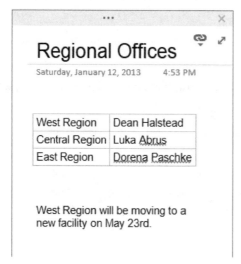

TIP A common approach is to have a OneNote page docked to the desktop, as a "scratch pad" of sorts to take notes on random phone calls, articles you want to remember for later, and so on. You can use it as something of a daily work journal, creating a new page each day.

TIP The docked window is on the right side of the screen by default, but you can move it to the top, bottom, or left side of the screen by simply grabbing the title bar at the top of the window and dragging it to where you want it.

- **Page Color** Enables you to choose different background colors for your pages. The colors you can choose from are very subtle but can be handy for differentiating different types of pages in your section. These colors apply only to the "paper" of your page, not to the page tab.

- **Rule Lines** This button lets you turn on or off line guides on the background of your page; this is essentially turning your clean sheet of blank paper into a college-ruled page or graph paper. They are mostly helpful if you're using ink to take notes and want the guides to align your writing or sketching. For typed notes, they're often a hindrance, because it's difficult to align your typing with the lines.

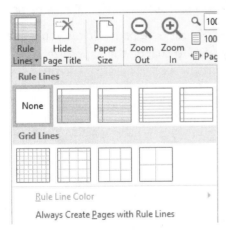

TIP The rule lines are light blue by default; you can change the color of them by selecting the Rule Line Color option in the Rule Lines gallery.

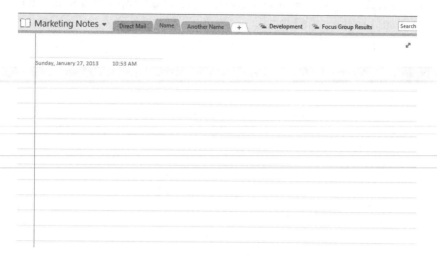

- **Hide Page Title** A surprisingly dangerous option. In fact, it should more properly be called "Remove Page Title," because it doesn't just hide the title. It actually removes the title, not only from the top of the note page, but from the page tab as well. If you use this option, your page will take on the name of whatever the first thing you've written on the page is. If you attempt to rename the page from the page tab, the page title area that you previously hid will reappear with that new name.

- **Paper Size** Lets you specify the size of your note page. Unless you're planning to print your notes, there is rarely any need to change the paper size.

- **Zoom group** The options in this group let you display your notes larger or smaller so that you can read them more easily or display more of them on the screen at a time.

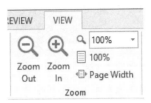

- **New Window** Opens an additional OneNote window. By default, the new window will have the same note page that you're currently looking at, and you would typically then navigate in that new window to a different page so that you could have multiple OneNote pages open at the same time. You can use **New Window** to open as many windows as your computer has resources to display.

- **New Docked Window** Opens an additional OneNote window as a docked window that sits along the side of your screen, so you can have another application visible on the rest of the screen. Unlike the **Dock to Desktop** button we talked about earlier, this one opens an additional OneNote window instead of changing the view of your existing OneNote window.

- **Send to OneNote Tool** Perhaps this seems a little out of place on the **View** tab, since the dialog box it launches doesn't immediately appear to have much to do with viewing OneNote. Look all the way to the right side of the dialog box, however, and you'll find the **New Quick Note** command. That opens a small window similar to a sticky note on the screen, where you can quickly capture notes or ideas much as you might scribble on a scrap of paper.

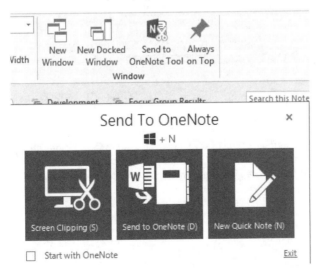

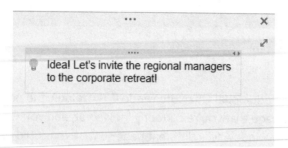

- **Always on Top** Pins the current note page so that it always appears on top of any other applications you have running. Obviously, this works best when OneNote is running in a window, rather than full screen, so that you can still view and work with other applications while OneNote is in the foreground on part of the screen.

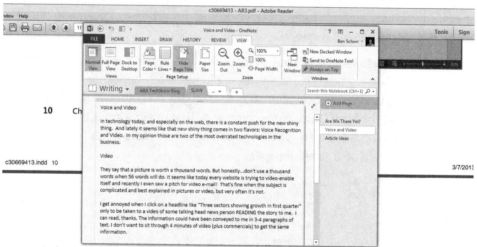

Identifying new and improved features in OneNote 2013

This section introduces you to key application features for OneNote 2013 and includes screen shots where applicable. The majority of the features included are discussed in detail along with step-by-step instructions throughout this part of the book.

Identifying new and improved features in OneNote 2013

This section introduces you to key application features for OneNote 2013 and includes screen shots where applicable. The majority of the features included are discussed in detail along with step-by-step instructions throughout this part of the book.

- **Full Screen Mode** In **Full Screen Mode**, OneNote tucks almost all of the user interface out of the way.

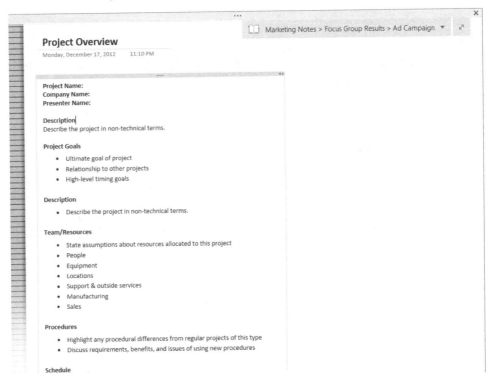

- **Tighter Microsoft SkyDrive Integration** When you create a new notebook, OneNote now defaults to offering to store it on your SkyDrive, where it can be easily shared with your other devices, colleagues, or family.

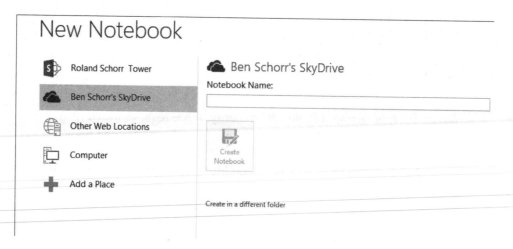

- **Enhanced Export** OneNote can export your notes into a variety of formats, including PDF and .docx (Microsoft Word).

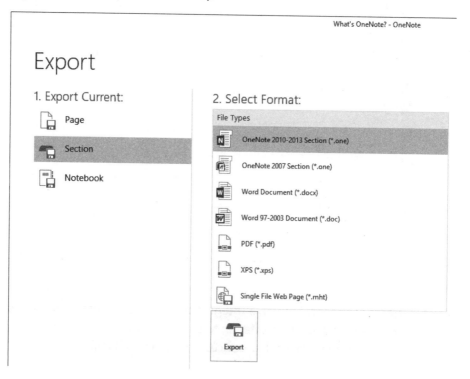

- **Embedded Content** OneNote 2013 has the ability to embed Microsoft Excel or Visio content. That content is dynamic, meaning that as it changes in the original file, the changes will be reflected in OneNote. The files can't be directly edited in OneNote, but a handy **Edit** button will open the file in Excel or Visio where it can be easily updated.

The numbers

Wednesday, October 17, 2012   9:18 PM

The numbers - Spreadsheet

January	10
February	20
March	15
April	25
May	27
June	30
July	32
August	35
September	31
October	36
November	40
December	44

Key points

- OneNote 2013 is a free-form note-taking and research software product. You can use it to capture notes, ideas, or web content; record audio or video; annotate images; and draw with ink or shapes—everything you can do with a paper note pad and more.

- There are a number of new features in OneNote 2013, including increased integration with SkyDrive for improved sharing and synchronizing; new views like Full Screen Mode; and improved integration with Excel and Visio for integrating dynamic content.

Chapter at a glance

Organize

Organize notebooks and sections,
page 797

Insert

Insert images and work with ink,
page 802

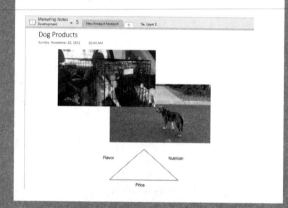

Recover

Recover deleted sections or pages,
page 810

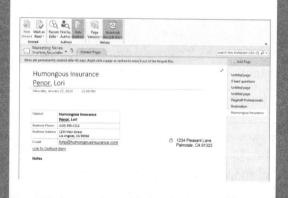

Working with notebooks, sections, and pages

31

IN THIS CHAPTER, YOU WILL LEARN HOW TO

- Create and organize notebooks.

- Create, organize, and manage sections and section groups.

- Create and organize pages and subpages.

- Add and organize notes.

- Insert images and work with ink and shapes.

- Recover deleted sections or pages.

Microsoft OneNote is built around the metaphor of a spiral-bound notebook—though of course you can have multiple notebooks in OneNote if you like. Each notebook is divided into sections, and each section contains the pages where your notes are located.

Before you can get started capturing ideas and research with OneNote, you need to get your notebooks, sections, and pages set up. Adding notebooks is easy. You need to decide where you want to store them and what you want to call them, but after that, you're ready to go. You can have as many notebooks as you have storage space for. Notebooks must have at least one section, but they don't have to have more than one. Likewise, each section has to have at least one page, but can have only one. It's not likely you'll want to have a notebook that has only a single section and single page in it, but you can.

In this chapter, you'll learn how to create and organize notebooks, sections. and pages—the basic building blocks of OneNote.

PRACTICE FILES You don't need any practice files to complete the exercise in this chapter.

Creating a notebook

Creating a notebook is quite simple to do. Simply click the File tab to go to the Backstage view and then choose New. The New Notebook page appears, and it's time to make your first important choice—where to put your new notebook.

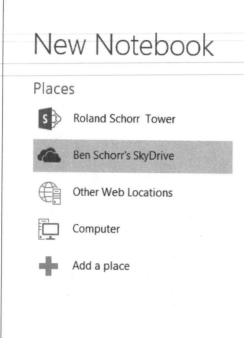

OneNote shows you the list of places it recognizes and gives you the option to add a place that it doesn't. It's worth noting that the Add A Place option only offers choices of places in the cloud. You won't get local or network locations there. The default location in OneNote 2013, as in many programs of the Microsoft Office Professional 2013 suite, is on your Microsoft SkyDrive. On the list shown just previously, you may notice from the icon that the first place listed is a Microsoft SharePoint site.

When you are choosing a location to store your new notebook, there are a few things you should know:

- If you plan to share this notebook with mobile devices, only the Windows Phone version of OneNote mobile can access notebooks stored on SharePoint. If you're an iPhone, iPad, or Android user, you'll need to store the notebook on SkyDrive.

- If you plan to share this notebook with other PCs, you can select any network location those PCs also have access to. A network file share, network storage device, SharePoint, or SkyDrive will all work fine as long as all of the PCs involved can access that location.

- After you've selected your location, give your notebook a name. Choose a name that makes sense to you, but try not to make it too long. *Marketing* and *Clients* are great names. *Collection of notes about my trips throughout North Carolina, California, Canada, and much of Southern Mississippi* is a poor name.

- With your location chosen and notebook named, click **Create Notebook**. Your new notebook is created and opened in OneNote with a single section and a single page within that section.

Creating and organizing sections

OneNote helpfully creates the first section for you, and it's a safe bet that you don't really want that section to be named *New Section 1*. To rename the section, right-click the section tab and select Rename from the menu that appears (or just double-click the name on the section tab).

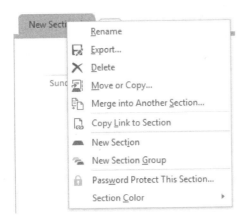

The same naming guidelines you followed for the notebooks apply to sections, as well. The names should be descriptive but not ridiculously long or detailed.

TIP Try to avoid using too much punctuation in notebook or section names. Notebooks are stored as folders and sections as files; too much punctuation can cause problems with synchronization and file storage.

Creating a new section is as simple as clicking the + tab. When you do so, OneNote creates a new section and names it *New Section x*. Rename it to whatever you'd like, as described previously.

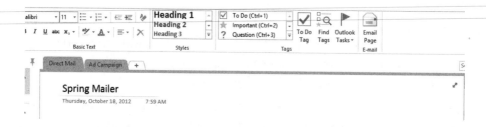

If you'd like to rearrange the order of your sections, just click a tab and drag it left or right along the tab row above your page or drag a section up or down on the Navigation pane at the left.

SEE ALSO If you need a refresher on section tabs or the Navigation pane, see Chapter 30, "Getting comfortable in OneNote 2013."

Section groups

Now that we've looked at notebooks and sections, you're probably wondering what section groups are. Section groups are merely an organizational construct that let you group your sections together in a logical fashion (hence the name).

- To create a section group, right-click any of the section tabs or the empty space to the right of the section tabs and select **New Section Group**.

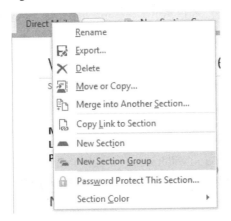

- A group called **New Section Group** will be created, which you can right-click and rename.

- Click the section group to go into it, and click the green swirly arrow at the left side of the section tabs to go back up to the previous level.

TIP You can create just about as many layers of section groups as you want, but don't get too crazy about it. Nine layers of section groups could be rather difficult to easily navigate.

To add a section to a section group, click in that section group and create a new section. To move existing sections into a section group, drag them onto the section group.

Creating and organizing pages

The real work in OneNote gets done on pages. All the rest (notebooks, sections, section groups) are just a framework to help organize those pages. Everything we talk about when it comes to typing notes or inserting images or ink happens on pages.

Creating a page is quite simple:

- At the top of the page list on the right side of the screen, click **Add Page**. A new page is created.

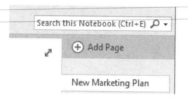

As with sections and section groups, your page will have a default name; for example, *Untitled Page*, which you are encouraged to change. There are several ways to rename your page:

- Right-click the page tab and select **Rename**

- Click in the page title area of the page (above the horizontal line) and enter a name for your page.

- Enter some text on the page. In the absence of a formal name, OneNote will use whatever the first line of text is for the title of the page.

TIP You can create as many pages as you like in a particular section.

After you've created your page, you can change the order by dragging it up or down in the page list on the right side of the window.

TIP A popular feature request is the ability to sort pages alphabetically. OneNote 2013 doesn't include that feature, but there have been PowerToys available for download in the past that could do it.

After the page is created, click anywhere on the page to begin adding notes and content.

Creating subpages

A subpage is a regular page that is indented a bit in the page list in order to show that it is a subpage of the page above it. Do you have to use subpages? No, but you might want to, because an organizational construct will separate related data onto multiple pages.

To create a subpage, follow these steps:

1   Create a new page, as described previously, below the page where you want the subpage to appear.

2   Right-click the tab of that new page and select **Make Subpage**, or drag the subpage tab to the right.

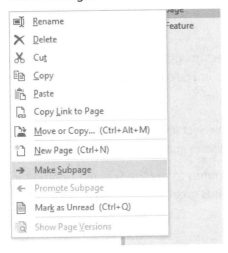

Adding and organizing notes

Adding notes to a page in OneNote is as simple as clicking where you'd like the note to appear and adding your content. Most often, that content tends to be typed notes, but it can also be ink, images, web content, and more.

To add typed text, click where you want the text to appear and begin entering text. Don't be too concerned if you decide to change the layout later. You can move your notes around on the page whenever you want.

To format your text, select the text you want to format and use the formatting tools on the Home tab of the ribbon or on the Mini Toolbar that appears just above the selected text. You can apply various font colors, font sizes or types, effects like Bold or Underline, and also highlights to your text.

OneNote makes a basic set of Styles that you can use to format your notes. To apply a style, select the text you want to apply the style to, and then select the style you want to apply from the Styles gallery on the ribbon.

TIP The styles in OneNote 2013 can't be customized, and you can't create your own style. You're limited to the predefined styles that are included with the product.

Inserting images

There are a number of ways you can insert images into your notes in OneNote 2013. First, select the note page where you want the image to appear. Then use one of the following techniques to insert your image:

- On the **Insert** tab, click **Pictures** to select an image from your hard drive or **Online Pictures** to search online sources for an image or piece of clip art to insert.

- On the **Insert** tab, click **Screen Clipping** to use the **Screen Clipping** tool to select and insert a portion of your screen. This is great for inserting images of error messages or other on-screen content.

- If you have a scanner connected to your computer or device, you can click **Scanned Image** on the **Insert** tab to insert an image from your scanner.

- In some cases, you can drag images from other applications right into your notes.

- You can press the **Windows logo key+N** to open the **Send to OneNote** tool, then press **N** again to start a screen clipping action. Select a section of the screen you want to clip, and then paste it into your notes.

SEE ALSO We'll talk more about screen clipping in Chapter 35, "Saving time with OneNote."

- After you've inserted an image into OneNote, you can move it to wherever you would like it to appear on the page. Just drag the image to place it. You can also resize the image by dragging one of the image's handles that appear at the sides and corners of the image when you select it.

Working with ink and shapes

OneNote was originally created to be the "killer app" on the original tablet PCs. Back in the early 2000s, Microsoft got on board to promote a variant of the laptop computer that had a touch screen. Some were laptops where the screen could lie flat; these were called *convertibles*. Others had screens that detached entirely from the keyboard, much like early, primitive, iPads. These were called *slates*. The devices ran a version of Windows that was designed specifically for tablets, and OneNote (then OneNote 2003) was a powerful tool for those early efforts at tablet computing. Though those tablets never really took off, OneNote has endured and thrived, and the ink capability of those early devices has continued in OneNote.

In this exercise, you'll explore the inking capabilities of OneNote.

SET UP You don't need any practice files to complete this exercise. Just open OneNote and open a blank page that you can practice drawing on.

1   Click the **Draw** tab.

2   On the **Draw** tab, in the **Tools** group, you'll find a selection of pen colors and thicknesses. Click one of the pens from the pen gallery to select it, or click the **More** button on the right edge of the gallery to expand it and show more pen choices.

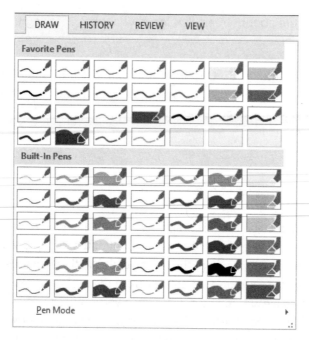

3   After you've selected a pen, click in the page area. Then draw, write, or annotate with that pen, using your mouse or a stylus.

4   To change back to entering text, click the **Type** button at the left end of the **Draw** tab.

❌ CLEAN UP Delete the practice drawing page if you want to.

Custom pens

If you can't find the pen you want, you can create a custom pen by clicking the Color & Thickness button in the middle of the Draw tab.

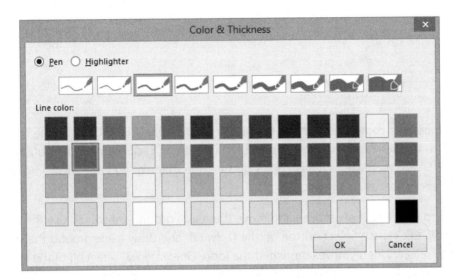

Shapes

Next to the Color & Thickness button you'll find the Shapes gallery. These shapes may look like the kind of shapes you're used to in other applications, but actually, they're just pre-defined ink strokes. That's important to understand, because you use the pens gallery to select the color and thickness of the lines in your shape.

To create a shape, select the pen you want to use from the pens gallery, and then select the shape you want to draw from the shapes gallery. Use your mouse or stylus to drag the shape onto the page where you want it to appear.

Didn't get it exactly the right size or precisely where you want it? Just drag and drop the shape where you want it or grab one of the resizing handles and make the shape larger or smaller.

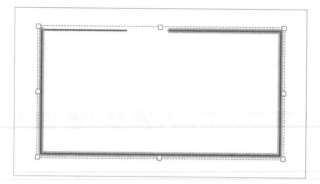

If you want multiple copies of the same shape, select your shape, click Copy on the ribbon (or press Ctrl+C), then move to another part of the page and click Paste on the ribbon (or press Ctrl+V). You can make as many copies of the same shape as you like, then drag those shapes to various places on the page.

If you want to select multiple shapes and move them as a group, you should use the Lasso Select option. Click Lasso Select button on the Draw tab and draw a line around the shapes you want to select. When you've completed the loop, OneNote will select all of the items within that Lasso. Then you can drag the shapes or delete the group as you choose.

If the shape isn't aligned the way you'd like, you can rotate it to the right or left. Select your item and click Rotate on the Draw tab (or right-click the shape and select Rotate from the shortcut menu) to display more choices for how you can rotate the shape.

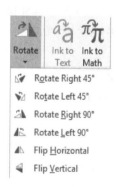

Erasing ink or shapes

If you don't like what you've drawn, you can use a couple of methods provided by OneNote to erase it. The first way, if it's something you just drew, is to simply use Undo (press Ctrl+Z). You can undo several steps in case you wish to go back further than one step. Just continue pressing the key combination until you've removed the steps you don't want.

If you accidentally undo one too many steps, you can use Redo (press Ctrl+Y) to advance one step.

If you want to do a somewhat more determined sculpting of your ink, you can use the Eraser tool on the Draw tab. When you click the Eraser tool, the pointer turns into an eraser that you can use to erase ink or shapes (or parts of them) from your page.

31

TIP The eraser can be used to erase parts of drawings but not of inserted images.

You have four different types of erasers to choose from. To select one, click the arrow below the Eraser button to view the menu.

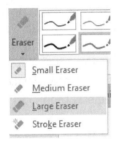

The types of erasers are described in the following list.

- **Small Eraser** An eraser with a small head for very fine work.

- **Medium Eraser** An eraser that is a bit bigger than the small eraser; used for faster erasing.

- **Large Eraser** A rather large eraser head; used for wiping large swathes of the page in quick strokes.

- **Stroke Eraser** A special eraser that removes entire ink strokes with a single click. This eraser is useful for quickly removing a specific ink stroke without disturbing other ink around it.

Inserting space

Sometimes you'll want to move items down the page so that you can insert other items above them. The Insert Space tool helps you do that. Just point above the items you want to move down, click the Insert Space button on the Draw tab, and drag down to move all of the items below that point down.

Insert space

You can also insert space horizontally with the Insert Space tool. Simply point to the side of the page; the Insert Space line will change from a horizontal line to a vertical line. Then you can drag left or right to move everything over.

The Insert Space button can also be used to remove space. If you have some blank space in your page and you want to move everything below that space up, point above the items you want to move up, click Insert Space, and drag up to remove the excess space.

To illustrate how this works, enter some text on the page. Then enter some text in a different note container that appears somewhat lower on the page. Next, click Insert Space on the Draw tab, and point to the space between those two note containers. Then drag down to insert more space between them.

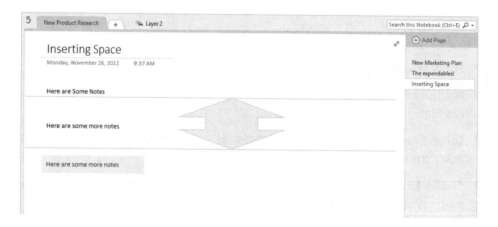

Arranging shapes

Shapes don't only exist in two dimensions in OneNote. You can also layer them front to back, and for that you use the Arrange tool.

To place a shape in front of another shape, select that shape, click the Arrange tool on the Draw tab, and select Bring To Front.

After you've brought the shape to the front, drag it on top of the shape you want it to be in front of. In the following graphic, you can see that the Arrange tool has been used to bring the photo of the dog in the crate to the front of the image, and send the other dog photo to the back. Then the front photo was moved so that it overlaps the back photo.

If you play around with the Arrange features, you'll find that you can create some complex layers of shapes.

Recovering deleted sections or pages

If you've deleted a page or section and want to get it back, then the Notebook Recycle Bin is your friend.

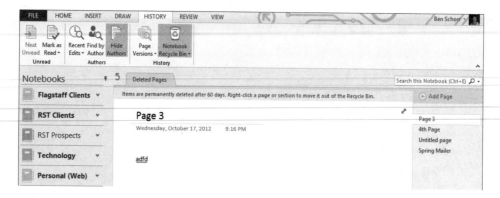

Following are the steps for restoring deleted sections or pages.

1. On the **History** tab, click the **Notebook Recycle Bin** button , and then select **Notebook Recycle Bin** from the menu that appears. OneNote displays deleted pages or sections it still has from the current notebook.

2. To restore a section or page, right-click the tab for the section or page, choose **Move or Copy**, and move it back to where you'd like it in the notebook.

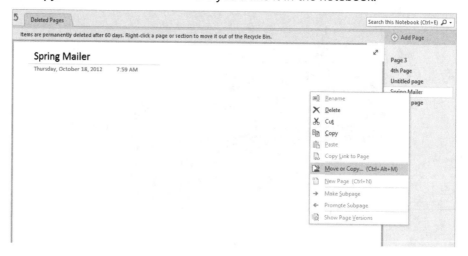

TIP You can also drag to move deleted pages from the Notebook Recycle Bin back to the regular notebooks.

3   If you're sure that you don't need anything in the **Recycle Bin**, you can empty it to save a little bit of space. Just click **Notebook Recycle Bin** on the **History** tab. Then select **Empty Recycle Bin** from the menu.

Key points

31

- OneNote 2013 uses notebooks, sections, and pages to help you organize your notes. You can have as many notebooks as you like, each containing one or many sections. Each section can contain one or many pages.

- You can move pages and sections between notebooks.

- On a page, you can take notes with text, images, ink, shapes, or other kinds of content.

- Ink and shapes are drawn with pens, which can have many different colors or thicknesses.

- Ink and shapes can be moved, resized, or rotated as needed.

- OneNote's eraser provides several options for cleaning up any mistakes.

- If you accidentally delete a section or page, it can be recovered from OneNote's Notebook Recycle Bin.

Chapter at a glance

Apply

Apply tags to notes in OneNote,
page 814

Connect

Connect an Outlook meeting to a
OneNote page, page 819

Organize

Organize data in tables,
page 830

Using organizational tools

32

IN THIS CHAPTER, YOU WILL LEARN HOW TO

- Tag your notes to make them easier to find and understand.

- Use styles to do basic formatting of your notes.

- Connect OneNote to Outlook for a power-integrated experience.

- Use hyperlinks to tie your notes together.

- Create and organize tables.

- Search your notes to find information fast.

In Chapter 31, "Working with notebooks, sections, and pages," you learned how to create notes. In this chapter, you'll examine some of the tools Microsoft OneNote 2013 gives you to organize your notes more effectively. Data capture is only half of the note-taking process. If you can't find those notes later, they aren't really very effective. Fortunately, OneNote provides a number of tools to make it easy to organize and locate those notes once you've taken them.

PRACTICE FILES You don't need any practice files to complete the exercises in this chapter.

Using tags

One of the powerful organizational features of OneNote is the ability to flag your notes with tags. Tags let you categorize and even prioritize your notes in certain ways. OneNote 2013 comes with a couple of dozen predefined tags, plus the ability to create as many of your own custom tags as you'd like. You can apply a tag that indicates that a particular note is a question, or a to-do item, or perhaps an action item that has been delegated to somebody else. You can tag items as contact information or a book to read. You can use tags to indicate that a particular item is important, or even critical.

You'll find the tags for OneNote on the Home tab of the ribbon, in the Tags gallery.

More button

In this exercise, you'll use tags to categorize some notes.

 SET UP You don't need any practice files to complete this exercise. Start OneNote and use existing notes or enter some practice notes on your own. Then follow the steps.

1   Navigate to the page where you want to tag some notes.

2   Click a note you'd like to tag.

3   Make sure you're on the **Home** tab of the ribbon, and click the **More** button to expand the **Tags** gallery.

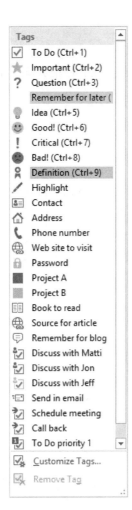

4   Click the tag you would like to apply to the selected note.

You can apply several tags to the same note if you'd like. To remove a tag, right-click it and select Remove Tag.

✕ CLEAN UP There's no cleanup required unless you wish to undo the changes you made to your tags. You'll have to do it manually though, because there's no option to reset a tag.

Creating and customizing tags

You can customize any of the built-in tags, or you can create entirely new tags of your own.

In this exercise, you'll customize one of the built-in OneNote tags.

➡ SET UP You don't need any practice files to complete this exercise. Start OneNote and follow the steps.

1   Make sure you're on the **Home** tab of the ribbon. Click the **More** button to expand the **Tags** gallery.

2   Click **Customize Tags**.

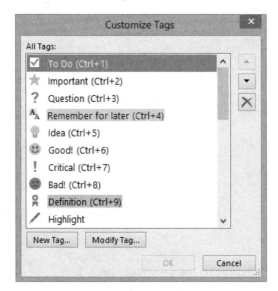

3   Select the **Remember for Later** tag to modify, and click it.

4   Click **Modify Tag**.

5   Click the **Symbol** button.

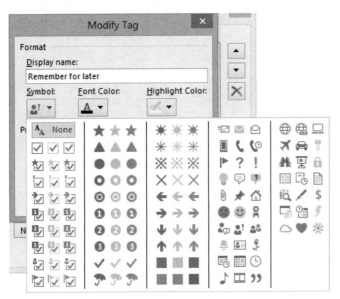

6   Select an alternate symbol for that tag and click it.

7   Click **OK** twice to get back to your notes page.

❌ CLEAN UP   No cleanup is necessary after this exercise.

32

It's just that easy to modify any existing tags that you like. Note that any modifications you make will not affect any notes that have already been tagged with that tag.

Creating your own custom tags is essentially the same procedure as the previous one. The only difference is that in Step 4 you would click New Tag instead of Modify Tag, and you would need to type a name in the Display Name field in the dialog box.

Using styles to format your notes

Though styles have been an important feature in Microsoft Word for years, OneNote 2010 introduced the concept of styles to OneNote. The feature has not changed much in OneNote 2013, but it remains a useful way to apply consistent formatting to your notes.

To use a style, select a piece of text that you would like to format with that style, then select the style you want to apply from the Styles gallery on the Home tab of the ribbon.

Styles in OneNote are especially useful for headings, quotes, and code samples. They help them stand out from the rest of your notes.

TIP The styles in OneNote can't really be customized natively, and there's no facility for adding custom styles to the list. The exception to this is the Normal style, which can be customized, in a manner of speaking, by accessing the menu bar and clicking File, Options, General and then changing the default font. There are third-party utilities, such as OneTastic, that offer some facility for customizing styles.

TIP If you really need to create a custom style, you can get part of the way there by creating a custom tag instead. The elements of a tag include font color and font highlighting. So although you can't set the font typeface or size, you could at least create a style, of sorts, that changes the color and highlighting of your selected text. Revisit the previous section for instructions about how to use and create custom tags.

Connecting OneNote to Outlook

One of the things that makes OneNote a powerful tool for task and project management is its ability to tie into another member of the Microsoft Office Professional 2013 suite—Microsoft Outlook.

There are really two kinds of integration that are important for you to know: integrating Outlook to OneNote, and integrating OneNote to Outlook.

There are a number of items in Outlook that you can connect to OneNote. The first and surprisingly least useful of these types of items is the email message.

Sending email messages to OneNote

You can easily send email messages to OneNote, which leads some people to try to use OneNote as some sort of massive archive system for email messages. Unfortunately, that's a task for which OneNote is not really well suited. It's better if you use Outlook itself to archive your messages. Its search capabilities are better, and the messages are more useful in their native format.

That said, it can be useful to send an email message to OneNote in order to add it to an archive of research or a project plan.

To send an email message to OneNote, you can select the message in the message list (or open the email message) and click the Send To OneNote button on the Home tab of the ribbon.

OneNote will display a dialog box that asks where you'd like to put that email message. If you select an existing page, OneNote will append the contents of that email message to that existing page. If you select a section, then OneNote will create a new page in that section, populated with the contents of the email message.

OneNote will insert your email message content into the selected location and even preface it with a header that indicates the subject, whom the message was from, to whom it was sent, and when it was sent.

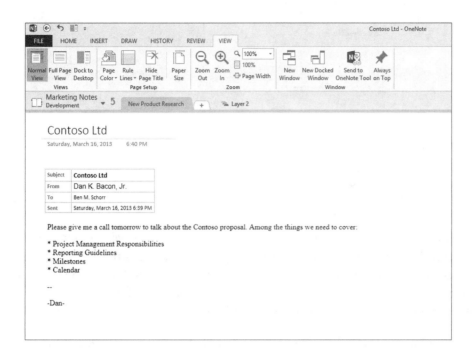

Connecting appointments to OneNote

Far more useful than email messages are appointments or meeting items from the Outlook calendar. By sending these to OneNote, you create a workspace where you can take (and share) detailed notes about the meeting while retaining a two-way link between the OneNote page and the Outlook appointment item.

Sending an appointment or meeting item to OneNote is done almost exactly the same way as sending an email message (see the previous section). You select or open the item in Outlook and click the Meeting Notes button on the ribbon.

When you click Meeting Notes, a dialog box is displayed that asks if you'd like to share your notes with the meeting, or if you're going to take notes on your own.

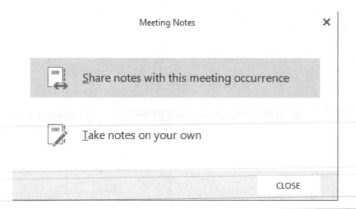

If you select Share Notes With This Meeting Occurrence, OneNote will prompt you for a notebook and section to locate these shared notes. You may notice that not all of your notebooks are listed as possible choices. The reason is that shared notes can only be located in notebooks that are stored in shared locations, such as SkyDrive or Microsoft SharePoint. Notebooks you have on your local hard drive won't be listed as options here.

If you choose Take Notes On Your Own, OneNote will offer you any notebook you have, because sharing is not a consideration.

With either choice, subject to the aforementioned limits, as with the email messages, OneNote will ask where you'd like to send the appointment item and append it to an existing page or create a new page for you, whichever you choose.

The appointment page in OneNote will include a header that tells when the meeting was scheduled for, a link back to the original Outlook item, and a list of participants (hyperlinked so that clicking on a name will initiate an email message to an individual), followed by a large area for taking extensive notes.

TIP In Chapter 35, "Saving time with OneNote," recording audio in your notes is mentioned. You can use that to capture an even richer version of the meeting, but first you should make sure you have permission from the other participants before you start the recording.

Annotating contacts

Perhaps what you'd like to take notes on is not a what or a when but rather a who. You can send an Outlook contact item to OneNote in order to create a rich set of notes on that contact.

To send the contact item to OneNote, simply select or open the contact item in Outlook and click the Linked Contact Notes button on the ribbon.

As with the other types of items, OneNote will ask you where in OneNote you'd like to place this contact item. If you select an existing page, OneNote will append the contact to that page. If you select a section, OneNote will create a new page for you, in that section, with the contact information.

32

Humongous Insurance
Penor, Lori
Saturday, January 12, 2013   11:39 PM

Contact	Humongous Insurance Penor, Lori
Business Phone	(310) 555-1212
Business Address	1234 Main Street Los Angeles, CA 90068
E-mail	lorip@humongousinsurance.com

Link to Outlook item

Notes

The page title will include the company name (if any) and the person's name (if any). Below that, a table repeats the name information, displays the phone and address information, and then displays the hyperlinked email address.

TIP Obviously, the information that can be displayed is limited by the information that's available. If you don't have the contact's email address, it won't magically appear here.

Finally, below the contact information you'll have an extensive area to take notes.

TIP This can be a good place to insert photos or images of the person, satellite photos, maps of their office location, or captured content from the contact's website.

Connecting OneNote tasks to Outlook

In past versions of OneNote, there were several different kinds of content that it would attempt to connect to Outlook, especially addresses and contact information. None of that worked especially well, so in OneNote 2013, there is just one piece that integrates to Outlook.

If you have an action item in OneNote, you can flag it with an Outlook task flag and the item will automatically appear on the Outlook Tasks list. Better still is that the connection is a two-way sync, which means that if you mark the task as complete in either OneNote or Outlook, it will be marked as complete in the other program, too.

Let's try flagging a task for follow-up. In this exercise, you'll flag a task for follow-up.

 SET UP You don't need any practice files to complete this exercise. Start Outlook 2013 and start OneNote. Then follow the steps.

1   In OneNote, navigate to or create a page you can use for practice.

2   Enter a note that is a sample action item, such as **Call Bob**.

3   Click the **Outlook Tasks** button on the **Home** tab of the ribbon.

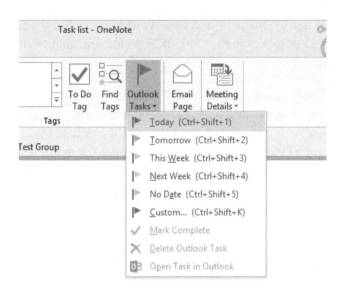

4   Click **Today** to flag the item for follow-up today. Outlook will place a red follow-up flag in front of your item. Even more important is that a corresponding item will be automatically added to your **Tasks** list in Outlook.

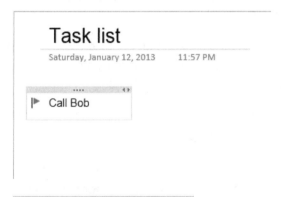

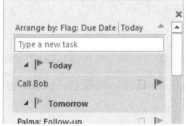

CLEAN UP You probably will want to delete that test item from your Outlook tasks list.

You can take notes on the task in OneNote, and when you've completed the task, simply left-click the flag in either OneNote or in the Outlook Tasks list. The item will be marked as complete in both products.

TIP The text that appears in the Outlook Task list is the exact text you flagged in OneNote. There isn't any context to it. That means that if you have multiple identical tasks on multiple pages (for example, "Follow Up"), you will find it difficult to differentiate those items in the Outlook tasks list. Try being a little more verbose in those cases. For example, use "Follow up: Tailspin Toys Project;" "Follow up: Contoso Marketing;" or "Follow up: Wingtip Toys proposal," and so on.

Using hyperlinks to tie your notes together

The concept of hyperlinks in information access goes back nearly 50 years, and almost nobody who uses the Internet today can remember a time when the Internet didn't use hyperlinks to navigate from place to place. OneNote 2003 supported hyperlinks to outside content and websites, but it was OneNote 2007 that introduced the concept of internal hyperlinks—links between notes in OneNote.

Internal hyperlinks let you create a link on any page that will take you to any note, page, section, or notebook you have. There are a couple of different ways to create internal hyperlinks. Let's take a look at the traditional way to do it first.

In this exercise, you'll create hyperlinks that take you from one location in your notes to a different location in your notes.

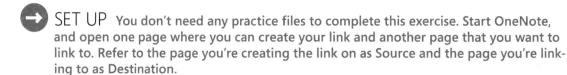 **SET UP** You don't need any practice files to complete this exercise. Start OneNote, and open one page where you can create your link and another page that you want to link to. Refer to the page you're creating the link on as Source and the page you're linking to as Destination.

1 Locate the page you want to link to (**Destination**, in this example) in your page tabs.

2 Right-click the page tab of the **Destination** page and click **Copy Link to Page**.

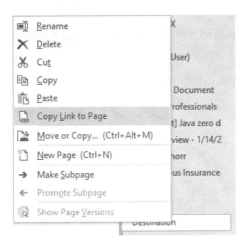

3   Navigate to or create a page referred to as **Source**.

4   Click the **Source** page and click **Paste** on the **Home** tab of the ribbon. OneNote will paste the link you just copied.

5   Click the link you just created (**Destination**) to make sure the hyperlink takes you directly to the **Destination** page.

In this manner, you can easily create links from any page to any page. Some people use these techniques to build a Table of Contents page that simply contains links to the pages they use most often, even if those pages are located in totally different notebooks. It's a quick and simple way to navigate if you have an extensive set of notebooks.

If you right-click on any section or notebook in the Notebook pane at the left, you'll find a Copy Link To item on the shortcut menu. That lets you use the same technique you just learned to create links to notebooks or sections.

TIP Right-click the note handle to the immediate left of any note paragraph in OneNote. You'll find Copy Link To Paragraph listed there. Click it, then paste that link into your Source page. Yes, you've just created a hyperlink directly to a specific paragraph of notes.

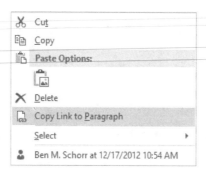

 CLEAN UP No cleanup is required.

Creating custom hyperlinks to other pages

One thing you'll notice in what you've done with hyperlinking so far is that the link you're creating has the same text as the name of what you're linking to. But what if you want to have a completely different piece of text that is a link to the page?

In this exercise, you'll create hyperlinks with custom text that take you from one place in your notes to another page in your notes.

SET UP You don't need any practice files to complete this exercise. Start OneNote and use the same Source and Destination pages that were created in the previous exercise.

1 Right-click the **Destination** page and click **Copy Link to Page**.

2 Navigate to the **Source** page.

3 Enter Where we want to go anywhere on the page.

4   Select the text you just entered.

5   Click the **Insert** tab on the ribbon, and then click **Link** or press **Ctrl+K** to open the **Link** dialog box.

6   Click in the **Address** field and paste in the link you copied to the **Destination** page by right-clicking and selecting **Paste** or pressing **Ctrl+V**.

7   Click **OK.**

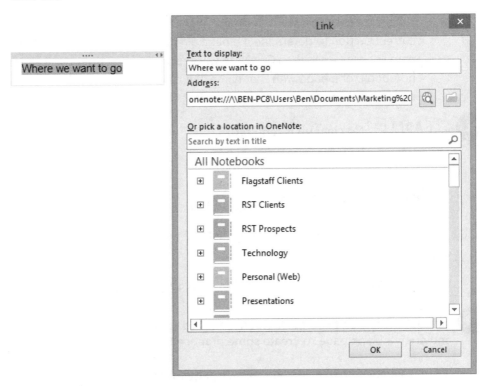

8   Click the **Where we want to go** link to confirm that it takes you to the **Destination** page.

The power of this technique may not be immediately obvious, but what it means is that by using the Link dialog box (via clicking Insert and then clicking Link, or pressing Ctrl+K), you can attach hyperlinks to any item in OneNote. That can be a word within a sentence or an item in a table—even a picture or piece of clip art on a page can have a hyperlink attached to it; it will take you to another notebook, section, page, or paragraph whenever you click it.

OneNote 2010 introduced a new way to create hyperlinks between pages. Capitalizing on the popular concept of a *wiki*, OneNote now supports what are called *wiki-style links*. A wiki link is traditionally created by enclosing the text you want to be the source of the link in double square brackets ([[text]]).

TIP Try this: On your Source page, enter *Let's go to the [[Destination]]*. When you press the spacebar after that last square bracket, OneNote should automatically convert the word *Destination* to a link to your Destination page.

When you enclose a word or phrase in double square brackets, OneNote looks in the current section to determine if a page already exists with that name. If a page by that name doesn't exist, then OneNote will check all of the other sections in the current notebook for a page with that name. If it can't find one, OneNote will automatically create a new, blank page in the current section with the enclosed text as its name.

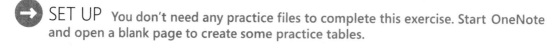 CLEAN UP No cleanup is required.

Creating and organizing tables

Tables are a useful organizational construct in OneNote. They allow you to arrange and organize data within a familiar structure.

Creating a basic table is quite easy. In this exercise, you'll create a basic table.

➜ SET UP You don't need any practice files to complete this exercise. Start OneNote and open a blank page to create some practice tables.

1   Navigate to or create your practice page for tables.

2   Click anywhere on the page and enter a piece of text.

3   Press the **Tab** key and enter some more text.

4   Press **Tab** again and enter some more text.

5   Press **Enter**.

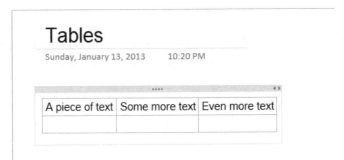

Each time you press Tab on that first line, you'll add another column onto your table. When you press Enter, you'll create a new row. From then on, your table will have just that many columns (three in this exercise), and pressing Tab will simply move you across those three columns and then on to the next row.

⊗ CLEAN UP You may want to keep the practice tables page you just created for the next exercise. If you don't plan to do the next exercise, you can delete the practice tables page.

Using the Insert Table feature

Another way to create a table, if you already know the size of the table you want, is to use the Insert Table feature.

In this exercise, you'll use the Insert Table feature to create a new table.

➜ SET UP You don't need any practice files to complete this exercise. Start OneNote. If you deleted the page you created in the previous exercise, create a blank new page to use in this exercise.

1 Locate your practice tables page.

2 Click at the location on the page where you'd like to insert the table.

3 Click the **Insert** tab on the ribbon.

4   Click the **Table** button.

5   On the table tool that drops down, select a table up to a maximum of 10 columns wide by 8 columns long. Using your mouse pointer, select a table that fits your needs, and click it.

In the following example graphic, a table has been selected that is 7 columns wide by 6 columns long. A blank table is inserted into your notes that's the size you specified.

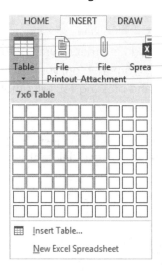

TIP If you want to create a table larger than the 10 x 8 maximum that the Insert Table tool allows, click Insert Table at the bottom of the Insert Table gallery instead. In the dialog box that appears, you can create a table with up to 99 columns and 99 rows.

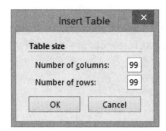

If you need to add (or delete) columns or rows from your table after it's been created, just click in your table, click Table Tools, and then click the Layout tab that appears on the ribbon.

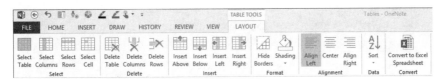

Here you'll find tools for selecting particular cells, rows, or columns; deleting rows or columns (or the entire table); or inserting rows or columns. You can also hide the borders of your table, add shading, or change the alignment of your text within the cells.

Another useful setting lets you sort your data in the table according to the currently selected column, either ascending or descending.

Finally, if your table has a lot of data in it, and you'd like to do some analysis or calculations on that data, you can convert it to an Excel spreadsheet.

✖ CLEAN UP You can delete the table practice page if you want.

Searching your notes to find information quickly

Having great notes is only half the battle. Being able to find those notes later is every bit as important. The search function in OneNote makes it easy for you to quickly find notes across pages, sections, or notebooks.

Above the page list on the right side of your notebook, you'll find the search box. You can click there to enter a query or you can press Ctrl+E on your keyboard.

When you're in the search box, enter your search term, and OneNote will search the selected scope (by default it's All Notebooks) for the term.

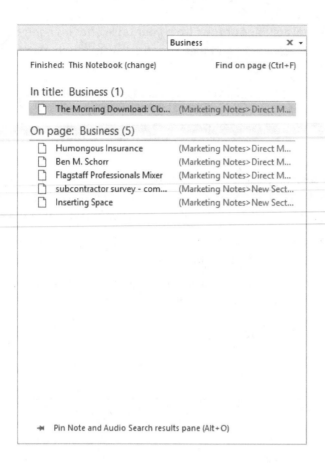

If you click any of the results, OneNote will display the page on the left side with the search term highlighted. Click any other search result and that page will be displayed in a similar manner. Note that once you click away from the search results pane, it will disappear, and you'll have to click the search box again and re-enter your search phrase before the results will be displayed again.

TIP It's not just text that OneNote is going to search. You can search for audio recordings, the audio portion of video recordings, text recognized in pictures you've inserted, and any handwritten notes in OneNote.

Changing your search scope

Perhaps you want to narrow (or broaden) the search scope. When you click in the search box, the search results pane opens, and at the upper left OneNote indicates what your current search scope is. If you'd like to search more (or less) of your content, you can change that scope. Click that link, and OneNote will allow you to change the scope to one of the following:

- This Section
- This Section Group
- This Notebook
- All Notebooks

In this exercise, you'll change the scope of your search to search across a larger (or smaller) selection of your notes.

SET UP You don't need any practice files to complete this exercise. Start OneNote, and then follow the steps.

1   Click in the search box at the upper right of the screen.

2   Click **This Notebook (change)**.

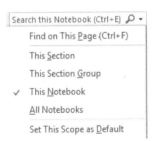

3   Select the scope you want to search. OneNote will perform your search across that scope.

> **TIP** If you want that scope to be the default from now on, click the scope link at the upper-left corner of the search results pane again, and click Set This Scope As Default at the bottom of the list.

TIP Instead of clicking the search box and changing the scope each time you only want to search the current page, press Ctrl+F on your keyboard and enter your search term.

❌ CLEAN UP No cleanup is necessary for this exercise.

TIP To find an exact phrase in OneNote, enclose your phrase in quotation marks like this: "Key products in the eastern region." To limit your search results to a page that contains multiple words (not necessarily together), use AND in your query like this: *Sales AND Bicycles.*

OneNote will find variations of words if you don't use the quotation marks. For example, a search for *serving* will also find *serves*.

If you want to do a more leisurely examination of your search results without the search results pane constantly closing, click the Pin Note And Audio Search Results Pane link at the bottom of the search results pane. That will cause the pane to open as a task pane along the right side of the screen and stay open until you close it.

Key points

- Tags let you categorize, highlight, and even prioritize notes.

- Styles help you apply consistent formatting to your notes.

- Integration between OneNote and Outlook makes both products better at supporting your productivity.

- Hyperlinks let you connect notes with each other as well as the outside world.

- Tables give you a structure for organizing certain kinds of information.

- A powerful search capability makes it easy to find your notes.

32

Chapter at a glance

Share

Share your OneNote notes via SkyDrive,
page 842

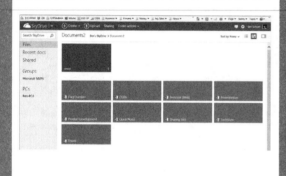

Collaborate

Connect to teammates by storing notebooks
on a common network drive, page 844

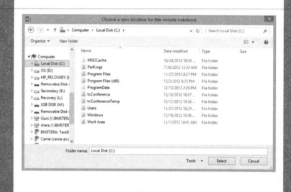

Communicate

Use OneNote and Outlook together to send
your notes to anybody, page 854

Sharing notes with others

33

IN THIS CHAPTER, YOU WILL LEARN HOW TO

- Share notes by using SkyDrive.

- Make notes available to your team on a network drive.

- Use SharePoint to share notes with your entire department.

- Send notes via email.

- Export your notes to other formats.

In Chapter 31, "Working with notebooks, sections, and pages," you learned how to create notes. In this chapter, you'll examine some of the tools OneNote gives you to share those notes with others. Data capture is made even more powerful by collaborating on those notes with others.

PRACTICE FILES You don't need any practice files to complete the exercises in this chapter.

Creating a new notebook on SkyDrive

In Chapter 31, "Working with notebooks, sections, and pages," you learned that the preferred storage location for OneNote files is Microsoft SkyDrive. When you store notebooks on SkyDrive, you can synchronize them with other computers and devices you own (described in Chapter 34, "Using OneNote everywhere"), and you can also share them with other people.

In this exercise, you'll create a new notebook located on SkyDrive.

SET UP You don't need any practice files to complete this exercise. Log into your Microsoft account, and then start OneNote. If you don't already have a Microsoft account, go to *http://www.live.com* and sign up for one (it's free).

1   In OneNote, click the **File** tab, and then click **New**.

2   Make sure your SkyDrive is selected as the storage location.

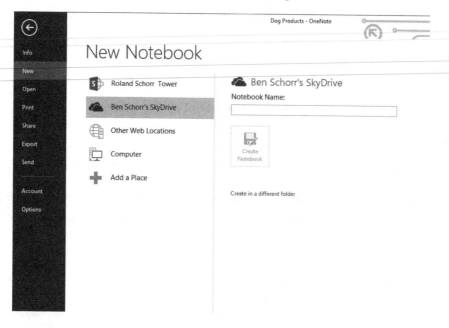

3   Give the notebook a name, and click **Create Notebook**.

4   OneNote will ask if you want to invite other people to share the notebook. Click **Invite people**.

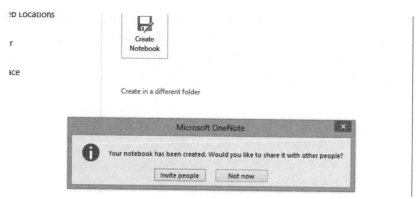

5   OneNote will open the **Share Notebook** page and give you some options for inviting people.

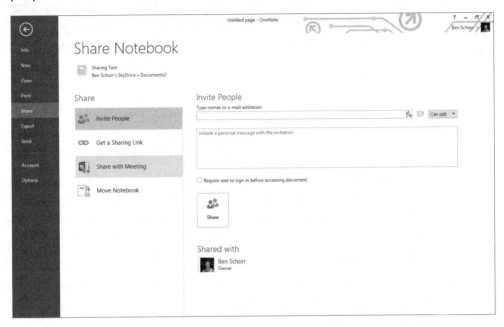

6   In the **Type names or email addresses** field, enter the names or email addresses of people you'd like to share this notebook with. If there are multiple names, you can separate them with semicolons (;).

7   Enter a personal message in the box provided, with a quick explanation of what the notebook is that you're sharing.

8   Click **Share** to send the invitations.

CLEAN UP You may want to delete the practice notebook you just created; otherwise, no cleanup is required.

You do have some control over the permissions these users will have.

To the right of the field where you list he people to share with, you'll find a control that lets you specify if those people can edit the notebook or if they are to have Read-Only access. If you need to give some people Edit permissions and others Read-Only, then invite them in two separate steps. Invite the editors first, then click the File tab on the ribbon, click Share, and repeat steps 6-8 with the permissions field set to Can View.

TIP If you're paranoid about security, you can check the Require User To Sign In Before Accessing Document check box to make it more difficult for a passerby to open your notebook from the intended user's computer by using cached credentials.

After the other users start using your notebook, if they have Can Edit permissions, any changes they might make will be seamlessly synchronized to your notebook, and your changes will be seamlessly synchronized to theirs. Under ideal circumstances, these changes may appear in nearly real time. Under most circumstances, due to Internet performance and other factors, the appearance of changes may be delayed by a matter of minutes.

If you've got an existing notebook that is already on SkyDrive that you would like to share, you can simply click the File tab on the ribbon, then click Share and go through steps 6-8 as described previously.

Moving a notebook to SkyDrive

If you have an existing notebook that is not on SkyDrive that you would like to share via SkyDrive, clicking the File tab and then Share will cause OneNote to prompt you to move the notebook to SkyDrive.

In this exercise, you'll move an existing notebook to SkyDrive.

➡ SET UP You don't need any practice files to complete this exercise. Start OneNote, open a local notebook, and then follow the steps.

1 Select the notebook you want to share.

2 Click the **File** tab, and then click **Share.**

3 Make sure your SkyDrive account is selected as the destination location. Click it once if you need to select it.

4　You may change the notebook's name if you want to.

5　Click **Move Notebook**.

6　OneNote will notify you that the notebook is now syncing to the new location.
　Click **OK**.

7　OneNote will return you to the **Share Notebook** page and ask if you want to invite
　other people to share the notebook. If so, click **Invite people**.

　OneNote will open the Share Notebook page and give you some options for inviting
　people.

8　In the **Type names or email addresses** field, enter the names or email addresses of
　people you'd like to share this notebook with. If there are multiple names, you can
　separate them with semicolons (;).

9　Enter a personal message in the box provided with a quick explanation of what the
　notebook is that you're sharing.

10   Click **Share** to send the invitations.

OneNote will give you the same options to control what kind of sharing you'd like to offer: Can Edit or Can View.

⊗ CLEAN UP   No cleanup is required unless you want to remove the notebook you just created.

Stopping sharing in SkyDrive

If you'd later like to remove permissions for one or more users who share the notebook, click File, then click Share. A list of users that the notebook is shared with is displayed near the bottom of the screen. Right-click the name of the person whose permissions you'd like to change, and you'll have the option to change their permissions to Can View (or Can Edit if they were already Can View people), or you can remove their access entirely.

Using a file server to share notes

Many companies have a network file server (or many file servers) where it's common for users to store and share documents, spreadsheets, and other files with others in the company. This can be an excellent place to store OneNote notes for several reasons:

- It's central and presumably accessible to all members of your team.

- It's always on, which means there's no need to worry if turning your computer off at the end of the day will disrupt others' access to the notebooks.

- It's presumably secure, within the corporate firewall and thus not easily accessible to the outside world. If the information in your notes is sensitive, you may be reluctant to store those notes on a server outside the company walls (like SkyDrive).

- Your information technology (IT) department should be making sure it's regularly backed up to protect against data loss.

There are also a few disadvantages to storing your notes on the company file server:

- It's more difficult to share the notes with people outside the company.

- Unless you have a facility in place for remote access, your user may not be able to synchronize changes when they're outside of the office.

- You can't synchronize the notebooks to any mobile devices like iPads or Android phones, because those (currently) require SkyDrive for sharing.

- Sharing your notebooks via the company server is more or less like sharing any other kind of file via the company server. You'll need a folder on the company server that everybody you want to share with has the proper permissions to (read, or read/write).

  TIP This will be easier if you map a drive letter on your local computer to the share where the destination folder exists. You can do that in File Explorer by clicking Map Network Drive, entering the destination share, and selecting an available drive letter.

In this exercise, you'll create a notebook on a network file share.

SET UP You don't need any practice files to complete this exercise. Start OneNote.

1   Click the **File** tab, then click **New**.

2   Select **Computer** as the destination location.

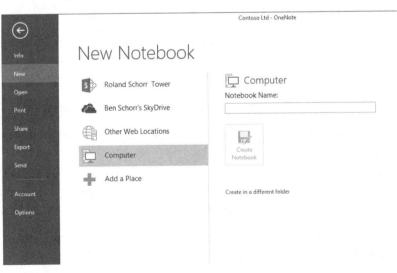

3   Click **Create in a different folder**.

     OneNote will open the browser dialog box to let you select a different location.

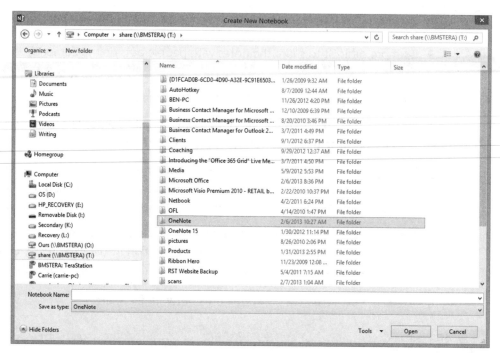

4   In the **Places** pane on the left, expand **Computer** and find the drive letter that you mapped to the destination share. If you didn't map a drive letter to it, expand the **Network** group instead, find the server where the notebook is to be hosted, expand that device, and select the share where the folder is located.

5   In the **Folders** pane on the right, navigate to and select the folder where you want the notebook to be hosted. Remember, because you intend to share this notebook, you'll have to choose a folder that the people you intend to share with can access.

6   Enter a notebook name into the field at the bottom of the dialog box.

7   Click **Create**. OneNote will create the notebook with the initial section and page.

8   Click **File**, then click **Share**.

9   Click **Email Others About the Notebook**. OneNote will create an Outlook email message with a link to the new notebook already in the body of the message.

10   Address the message to the people you want to share with, enter any explanatory text you want, and then click **Send**.

Any changes you make to the notebook will be automatically and immediately synchronized to any of the other users who have that notebook open in their OneNote at the time. Synchronizing changes to a corporate server over a local network can be extremely fast, sometimes approaching real-time speeds.

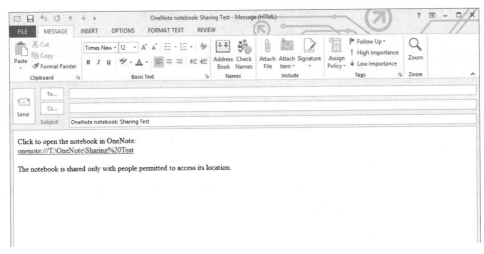

CLEAN UP If you didn't intend to keep the notebook you just created, you can close it from OneNote and delete it from the folder where it was created. If you actually invited others to share it in step 10, you may want to let them know it was just practice.

Stopping sharing on a file server

There are a couple of ways to stop sharing via a file server. First, you can revoke the access permissions to the file or folder where the notebook exists.

Second, you can relocate the notebook from the server to a different location that others don't have permission to, like your local hard drive.

In this exercise, you'll move a notebook from its location on the network file share to a different location.

SET UP You don't need any practice files to complete this exercise. Start OneNote, and open a notebook that is being shared on your network server that you want to stop sharing.

1   Right-click the notebook that you want to relocate in the **Notebook** pane at the left.

2   Select **Properties**.

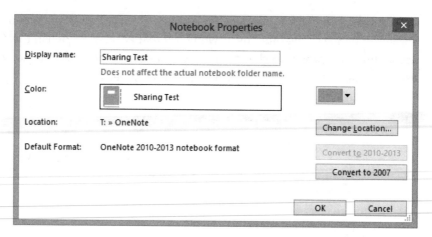

3   Click **Change Location**.

4   OneNote will prompt you to navigate to the new location for the notebook. Select a folder to move the notebook to.

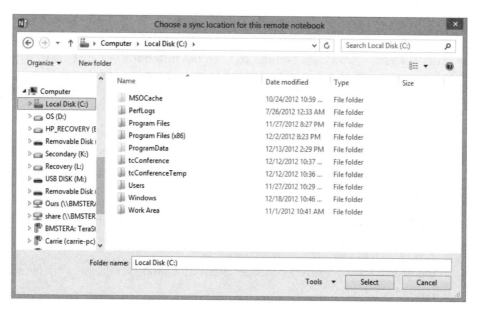

5   OneNote will acknowledge your success. Click **OK**.

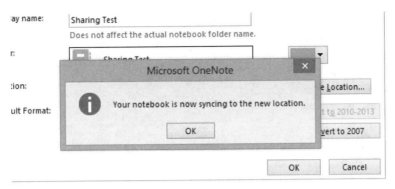

Sharing notes via SharePoint

Sharing your notebooks via Microsoft SharePoint gives you some of the advantages of sharing via SkyDrive, along with some of the advantages of sharing via your local network. SharePoint is more likely to be remotely accessible than your local network drive is, and companies may feel that they have more control over SharePoint from a security standpoint (especially if your SharePoint server is hosted on premises). If you're using a Windows Phone and Windows tablets, you'll be able to sync your SharePoint-hosted notebooks to your mobile devices, but (currently) if you're using Android or iOS, you can't.

The first step in sharing a notebook via SharePoint is to select or create a document library on the SharePoint site where your OneNote notebooks will be hosted. For this example, a dedicated document library just for OneNote notebook was created, named *OneNote*.

If your SharePoint site is an Office 365 or SharePoint Online site, then you've got an easy path ahead of you. When you click File and then New your Office 365 or SharePoint account is listed as one of the options. Select that option, and OneNote will display a list of recent folders that you can choose from. If the folder you want to use is not visible, click Browse, select the OneNote document library you created (or any other document library you want), name your notebook, and click Create. Job done.

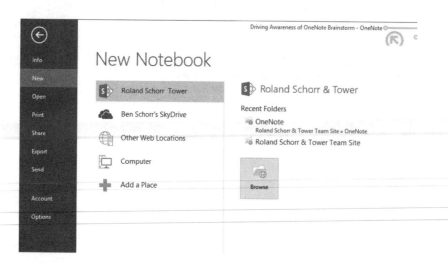

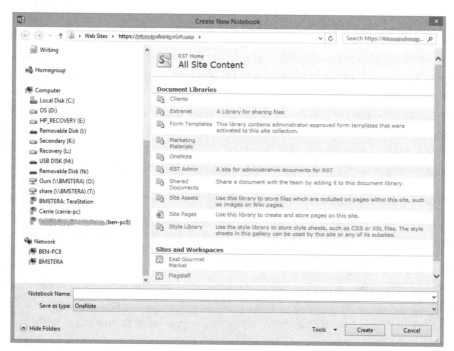

TIP If you have an Office 365 or SharePoint Online account, but the account isn't listed, you may have to add it. Click File, then Account, and add the service.

If you don't have an Office 365 or SharePoint Online account, then your route to hosted SharePoint notebooks may be slightly more primitive, but it's still not difficult to do.

In this exercise, you'll create a new notebook and move it to a corporate SharePoint server.

SET UP You don't need any practice files to complete this exercise. Start OneNote. Log into your SharePoint account if you aren't already logged in. Remember, this exercise is for people who are using corporate SharePoint. If you have SharePoint Online or Office 365 SharePoint, you can create new notebooks in essentially the same way SkyDrive users do.

1 Click the **File** tab, then click **New**.

2 Select **Computer** for your location.

3 Enter a name in the **Notebook Name** field, and then click **Create Notebook**.

4 In the OneNote **Notebook** pane, right-click your notebook and select **Properties**. Be sure to remember the notebook's location.

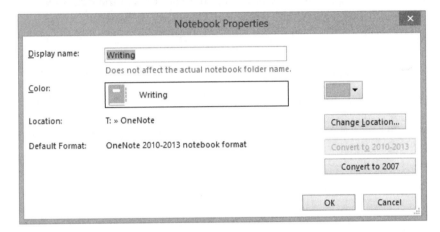

5 Click **Cancel**.

6 Right-click your new notebook again and choose **Close this notebook**.

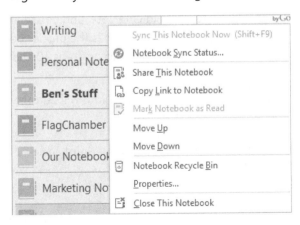

7   Open your SharePoint site in Windows Internet Explorer.

8   Navigate to the document library where you want your OneNote notebook to be. You'll probably find your list of libraries along the left side of the window.

9   Upload your notebook to the document library.

TIP If you don't want that notebook to stay in your SharePoint library, you can delete it from SharePoint.

TIP It is often easiest to upload your notebook to the document library by clicking the Library tab in SharePoint and selecting Open With Explorer. Then you can just drag the OneNote folder to the document library.

10   Confirm that your OneNote notebook now appears in the document library, and then click the down arrow to the right of the OneNote notebook's name.

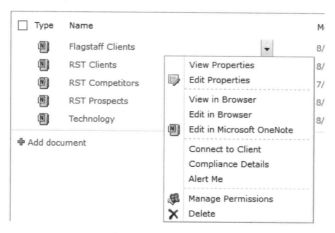

11   Select **Edit in Microsoft OneNote**.

At this point, your new notebook will re-open in OneNote, and you're all set for sharing. Make sure anybody else you want to share it with has the proper permissions in SharePoint to access the notebook. They'll only need to do steps 10 and 11 in order to open it for themselves.

Now that your notebook is shared via SharePoint, OneNote will automatically sync any time you have a connection to that SharePoint server.

❌ **CLEAN UP** You can delete that notebook from your SharePoint server if you want to.

Sharing notes with others during a meeting

One of the new features of OneNote 2013 is the ability to easily share notes with others in a meeting. When you create, or accept, a meeting item in Outlook 2013, you can click the Meeting Notes button to create a OneNote page that will serve as a place to take notes during the meeting. That's not new; OneNote has done that for years. What's new is that now when you do that, OneNote will ask you if you want to take notes on your own or share notes with others in the meeting.

Select Share Notes With The Meeting and OneNote will prompt you to select a section (and page, if desired) from among your shared notebooks. If you select an existing page, that page will be attached to the meeting invitation in Outlook and shared with the other attendees. If you merely select a section, a new page will be created (and shared with those attending the meeting).

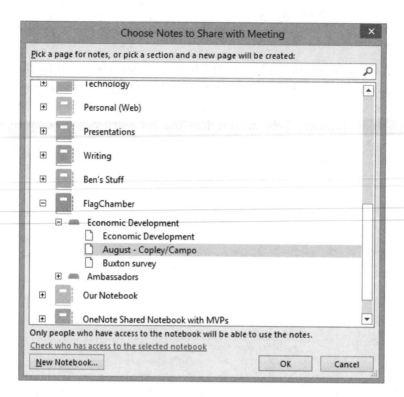

TIP In order to share meeting notes, the notebook containing the shared page has to be in a location that the other attendees can access. If the other attendees are all within your own company, then you can probably use a notebook shared on the company SharePoint server or a Windows file server. If some of the attendees don't have access to that resource, then you're better off using a notebook stored on SkyDrive.

During the meeting, you and the other attendees can take notes in the shared page, and you'll all be able to view each other's notes, almost like a shared whiteboard.

Sending notes via email

If you don't want to share a live notebook, another option is to send your notes via email. OneNote makes that very easy to do. Simply go to the page you want to share and click the Email Page button on the Home tab of the ribbon. OneNote will launch Outlook and create a new email message with the note page in the body of the message. All you need to do is address the message and click send. The recipient does not need to have OneNote in order to read the notes.

Email Page

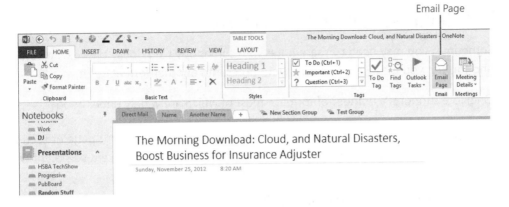

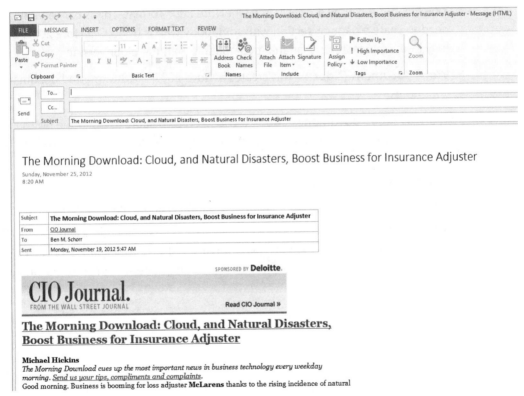

TIP OneNote can optionally include a .one file containing the page you're emailing as an attachment to the email item. If that attachment doesn't appear when you create a new email message, then you need to enable that option. In OneNote, click the File tab, click Options, and then click Advanced, and in the Email Sent From OneNote section, make sure that the Attach A Copy Of The Original Notes As A OneNote File check box is selected.

Exporting to other formats

Sometimes you may need to share notes with somebody who doesn't have OneNote at all, and for that you may want to export your notes into another format.

OneNote supports a number of formats, most of which are widely understood.

- **OneNote 2010-2013 section (*.one)** This exports the current page or section as a .one file in the OneNote 2010-2013 format. Anybody with a recent version of OneNote will be able to open it, except those who have OneNote 2007.

- **OneNote 2007 section (*.one)** This also exports the current page or section as a .one file, but this time it does it in a OneNote 2007 format. This is convenient if you need to share a page or section with somebody who is using OneNote 2007, but you may lose a few features that aren't compatible with the older version.

- **Word document (*.docx)** This creates a Word 2007-2013 formatted document from your notes.

- **Word 97-2003 document (*.doc)** If you need to be able to open the notes in an older version of Word, you can export your page or section into the venerable .doc format.

- **PDF (*.pdf)** With this option, you can export your selected page, section, or notebook into the widely accepted PDF format. This format is essentially read-only.

- **XPS (*.xps)** You can also export your selected page, section, or notebook into XML Paper Specification (XPS) format. This format is not very widely used, however, so don't be surprised if the person you send it to isn't quite sure what to do with it.

- **Single file webpage (*.mht)** This option exports your selected page or section as an HTML document that can be viewed in most common web browsers.

- **OneNote package (*.onepkg)** Exports your selected notebook into a special *package* file that can be unpacked by OneNote 2007, OneNote 2010, or OneNote 2013. This is a great option for archiving a OneNote notebook, or if you need to ship an entire notebook to a user who has OneNote but doesn't want to use SkyDrive or SharePoint to share the file.

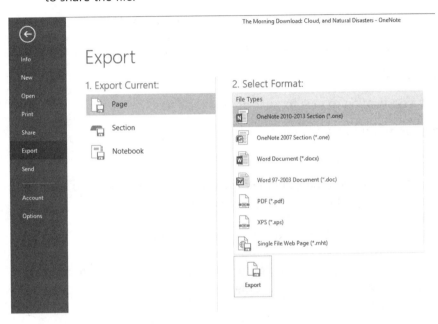

Exporting your notes into one of these formats is easy.

In this exercise, you'll export notes into another format.

SET UP You don't need any practice files to complete this exercise. Start OneNote and open a notebook, section, or page that you can practice exporting.

1 Select the page, section, or notebook you want to export.

2 Click **File**.

3 Click **Export**.

4 Select the scope of your export (page, section, or notebook).

5 Select the format you want to export to (see the bulleted list before this exercise).

6 Click **Export**.

7 Select a destination to save to (such as your local hard drive).

8 Give your exported file a name.

9 Click **Save**.

After that is done, you can send the exported file to the person you want via email, flash drive, or any other file sharing mechanism you choose.

CLEAN UP You can delete the exported file you created.

TIP Though you can export to a variety of formats, you can really only import from the .one or .onepkg formats. You can insert content from the other formats, but it's not the same as re-creating native OneNote content.

Key points

- OneNote 2013 makes it easy to share your notes with other people.

- You can store notebooks on a commonly accessible location such as SkyDrive, SharePoint, or a Windows file share and invite others to open those notebooks in their copy of OneNote.

- When you share notebooks from a common storage location, everyone's edits and changes will be synchronized to all of the other participants for a truly collaborative experience.

- You can email notes to people who don't have OneNote, and they'll be able to read your notes in their email client.

- You can export your notes into a wide variety of compatible formats, such as .docx or PDF, and send those files to others.

33

Chapter at a glance

Synchronize

Synchronize notebooks to multiple computers, page 861

Edit

Edit your notes in any web browser with OneNote Web App, page 864

Access

Access OneNote with OneNote Mobile on Windows Phone 8, page 872

Using OneNote everywhere

34

IN THIS CHAPTER, YOU WILL LEARN HOW TO

- Sync your notes among multiple computers.

- Access your notes in a web browser.

- Use OneNote on your phone or tablet.

In Chapter 33, "Sharing notes with others," you learned to use your notes to collaborate with others. In this chapter, you'll share notes with yourself. These days it's common for people to have multiple devices that they use on a regular basis, and your notes are more powerful and useful if you can have them with you no matter what device you're using.

The most important thing to sort out, when you're going to sync your notes among multiple computers, is the platform you're going to use to host the notes. Will you use Microsoft SkyDrive, SharePoint, a USB flash drive, or some sort of network-attached storage?

After you've figured that part out, then keeping your notes synchronized is fairly easy. With Microsoft OneNote 2013, the most common platform to use for syncing notes is going to be SkyDrive, because Microsoft Office Professional 2013 makes it so easy to locate your notebooks there.

PRACTICE FILES You don't need any practice files to complete the exercises in this chapter.

Syncing your notes by using SkyDrive

So let's try creating a notebook that we'll use on multiple computers. One of the natural ways to want to do that is by using the Microsoft SkyDrive cloud storage service.

In this exercise, you'll create a notebook in SkyDrive and then synchronize it to a second computer.

1   Open OneNote and click the **File** tab, then click **New**.

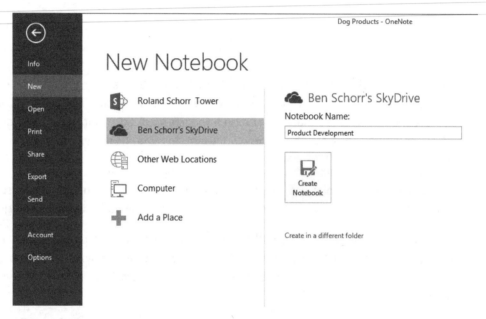

2   Make sure that your SkyDrive account is selected in the first column of the **New Notebook** page.

3   Give your notebook a name, and click **Create Notebook**.

4   OneNote will ask if you want to share the notebook with other people. If you want to invite other people, click **Invite People** and invite them to the notebook. As you may recall, this process was discussed in Chapter 33, "Sharing notes with others." If you're only going to share the notebook with yourself on other devices, then click **Not Now**.

5 Go to the other computer you want to synchronize this notebook with.

6 Open OneNote.

7 Click **File**, then click **Open**.

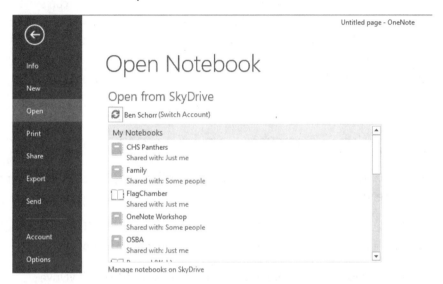

8 A list of notebooks that you can open on SkyDrive is displayed. Find the notebook you just created, and click that notebook. It will open in OneNote.

Just like that, you've now got a notebook open on both devices.

TIP Click the default first page created in the new notebook and enter some text. Then look at the same notebook on the other device. Assuming that both devices are connected to the Internet, the text should be displayed within a matter of seconds or a couple of minutes.

TIP Go to SkyDrive in Internet Explorer and find a SkyDrive-hosted notebook that isn't open in your OneNote desktop yet. Right-click the notebook and click Open In OneNote to add it to your OneNote desktop.

SEE ALSO To review the procedures for creating notebooks, read the material in Chapter 31, "Working with notebooks, sections, and pages."

This same process works for other locations as well. You can store your notebooks on a network drive, as long as all of your PCs can access that network drive. Then they'll be able to sync. You can also store your notebooks on Microsoft SharePoint and sync them that way. Just remember that as of this writing, only PCs can sync notebooks located on a network drive, and only PCs or a Windows Phone can sync notebooks located on SharePoint.

 CLEAN UP No particular cleanup is necessary.

Accessing your notes in a web browser

There's another good reason to store your notebooks on SkyDrive (or SharePoint). It's known as OneNote Web App.

Any notebooks you store on SkyDrive can be opened and edited in the web browser, even on computers and devices that don't have OneNote installed.

In this exercise, you'll open a notebook in OneNote Web App on SkyDrive.

→ SET UP You don't need any practice files to complete this exercise. You'll need to have created at least one notebook in SkyDrive to complete this exercise. Refer to the previous exercise for a refresher.

1 Open your web browser and navigate to **https://skydrive.live.com**.

2 Log in, if prompted.

3 Find your notebooks. They should be easy to locate, because they'll be displayed in a purple color and they'll have the OneNote icon. By default, they should be located in the **Documents** folder, though you could have chosen a different folder when you created them.

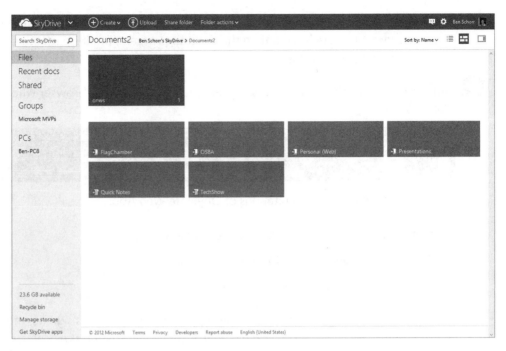

4   Select the notebook you'd like to open, and click it.

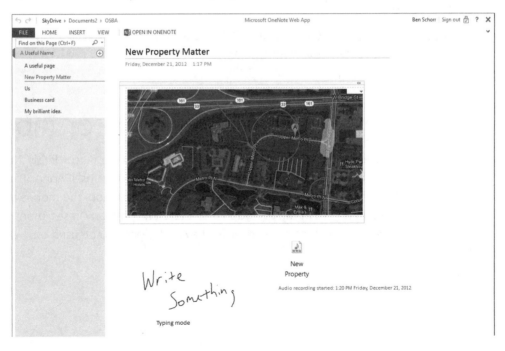

At this point, the notebook you select will open in the browser. OneNote Web App is considerably more limited than the desktop program, but it's perfectly sufficient to let you read or edit notes.

⊗ CLEAN UP No cleanup is necessary. Simply close your web browser when you're finished.

There are a couple of other limitations of OneNote Web App:

- It will display inked notes but can't create any.
- There is support for tags but no customized tags.
- It doesn't support audio or video recording.

You can easily add pages in OneNote Web App by clicking the plus sign next to the section title in the upper-left of the browser window. After you've created the new page, enter a title in the title area at the top of the page, and you can then click anywhere on the page and start typing notes.

Any pages and notes you create will automatically sync to any devices you have that are connected to your SkyDrive with OneNote.

Using OneNote on your phone or tablet

The best notes are the ones that go with you wherever you are. Accordingly, Microsoft has created OneNote Mobile apps for a number of different platforms: iPhone, iPad, Android, and Windows Phone, just to name a few. Like OneNote Web App, the mobile apps are considerably more limited than the desktop OneNote is and, in many cases, more limited than a web app due to the nature of the devices they're designed to be used on.

Any notes you create in the mobile apps can be synchronized to your desktop version of OneNote or even shared with other users. Previously, you learned how to synchronize your notes among multiple computers. In Chapter 33, "Sharing notes with others," you learned how to use your notes to collaborate with others.

These apps are slightly different from each other and evolve so quickly that it's likely that most of them will have changed by the time you read this book. With that recognition, this section offers information on how to use each application without being so specific that this content will be outdated before the ink dries.

Using OneNote on an iPhone or iPad

OneNote Mobile for the iPhone or iPad (they are two separate apps) can be found in the iTunes App store. Currently, it's free for up to 500 pages of notes, which is actually quite a few. If you need to exceed that number of pages, then the upgrade is just a one-time charge of $4.99 currently.

Both versions of OneNote Mobile for iOS have the following key features:

- Support for multiple notebooks
- Support for viewing tables
- The ability to create bulleted lists or checklists
- The ability to insert photos in notes
- Support for OneNote tags
- The ability to search for notes

34

Both versions of OneNote Mobile for iOS have the following key limitations:

- Synchronization requires a (free) Windows account with SkyDrive.
- They do not currently support inked notes.
- Creating new notebooks or renaming sections has to be done in the desktop or Web App; they will then sync to the Mobile app.
- They do not support password-protected sections.
- They are not available in all countries.
- They require iOS 4.3 or later.

To be honest, the only real difference between the two versions is that the iPad version is optimized for the larger screen of the iPad.

In this exercise, you'll install OneNote Mobile for iOS on your iPhone or iPad.

SET UP You don't need any practice files to complete this exercise. You need an iPhone or iPad with at least iOS 4.3 and an active Internet connection to complete this exercise.

1   To get OneNote for iOS, turn on your iPhone or iPad.

2   Navigate to the **App Store**.

3   Search for **OneNote**.

4   Locate the official OneNote Mobile for iOS app.

5   Click the app to download and install it.

> **TIP** Be sure to select the correct app. The OneNote Mobile for iPhone app won't look right on the larger screen of the iPad, and the OneNote Mobile for iPad app won't run on the iPhone.

CLEAN UP No cleanup is required.

When you've installed OneNote Mobile for iOS and you run it for the first time, it will ask you to sign into your Microsoft account (SkyDrive). If you don't have one, you can sign up for the account, for free, by going to *www.live.com* or clicking the link the OneNote Mobile app will offer you.

After you've signed into your Live account, you'll find that the OneNote Mobile app already has one notebook created. It's called *Personal (Web)*, and it's required for OneNote Mobile to store unfiled notes. You can't create additional notebooks in the Mobile app; however, you can create additional notebooks in the SkyDrive OneNote Web App or on your desktop OneNote (make sure they're stored on SkyDrive), and those notebooks will synchronize to the OneNote Mobile app.

TIP Do you own an iPhone and an iPad? You can install OneNote Mobile on both devices, and the notes you take on one will automatically sync to the other!

Creating new notes is easy. Navigate to the notebook and section where you want to locate the page, and click the New Page button at the bottom of the app. You can enter in any notes you like, and when you're finished, just go back to the page list in the section.

To create bulleted lists or checklists in your notes, tap the appropriate button (just above the keyboard) and then start typing your list. Each time you tap the return button, a new list item will be created.

If you want to insert a photo into your notes, just tap the location in your notes where you want the picture to appear. Then tap the camera button that appears just above the keyboard.

To find notes on your iPhone or iPad, click the Search button in the lower-left corner of the screen, and then enter your search term or phrase into the search box that appears at the top of the screen.

TIP You can save a lot of time by using the Recents feature. Click the Recents button at the bottom of the screen to view a list of recently used pages. If you have one (or more) that you plan to refer to often, you can even pin them to the top of the Recents list by clicking the pushpin icon to the right of the page name on the Recents list.

Using OneNote Mobile for Android

OneNote Mobile for Android can be found in the Google Play store. Unlike the iOS version, there is just one version of the Android app, which works on both Android phones and Android tablets. Currently, it's free for up to 500 pages of notes, which is actually quite a few. If you need to exceed that number of pages, the upgrade is just a one-time charge of $4.99 currently.

OneNote Mobile for Android has the following key features:

- Support for multiple notebooks
- Support for tables
- Support for hyperlinks to external sites (but not internal hyperlinks, yet)
- Spell check
- The ability to insert photos into notes

OneNote Mobile for Android has the following key limitations:

- Synchronization requires a (free) Windows account with SkyDrive.
- It does not currently support inked notes.
- Creating new notebooks has to be done in the desktop or Web App; they will then sync to the Mobile app.
- It is not available in all countries.
- It requires Android 2.3 or later.

In this exercise, you'll install OneNote Mobile for Android on your Android device.

SET UP You don't need any practice files to complete this exercise. You need an Android phone or tablet with at least Android version 2.3 installed and an active Internet connection to complete this exercise.

1 To get OneNote for Android, turn on your Android device.

2 Navigate to the **Google Play Store**.

3 Search for **OneNote**.

4 Locate the official OneNote Mobile for Android app and click the app to install.

CLEAN UP No cleanup is required.

When you've installed OneNote Mobile for Android and you run it for the first time, it will ask you to sign into your Microsoft account (SkyDrive). If you don't have one, you can sign up for the account, for free, by going to *http://live.com*.

After you've signed into your Live account, you'll find that the OneNote Mobile app already created a notebook for you called *Personal (Web)*. It's required for OneNote Mobile to store unfiled notes. You can't create additional notebooks in the Mobile app; however, you can create additional notebooks in the SkyDrive OneNote Web App or on your desktop OneNote (make sure they're stored on SkyDrive), and those notebooks will synchronize to the OneNote Mobile app.

There are two ways to create new pages in OneNote Mobile for Android, and the difference tends to confuse new users a bit. The New Page button at the top of the screen is actually a New Quick Note button. Any notes you create with that button will be stored in the Unfiled Notes section just like Quick Notes you create with OneNote 2013. If you want to create a new page in the current section, however, click the menu button and select New Page from the menu that appears.

To create a bulleted or numbered list or a checklist, tap the appropriate button from the menu at the top of the screen when you're editing a note. Then start typing your list items. Each time you tap the return key, a new line appears for your next list item.

To insert a photo into your notes, tap where you'd like the image to appear, then tap the camera button on the left end of the menu at the top of the screen.

TIP You can save a lot of time navigating around by using the Recents feature. Click the Recents button (it looks like a clock) at the top of the screen. and a list of your recently used pages will appear.

34

Using OneNote Mobile on a Windows Phone

OneNote Mobile comes preinstalled on Windows Phone 7.x and 8.x. Currently, it's free for as many notes as your device can store. Not surprisingly, OneNote Mobile for Windows Phone is the most capable of the Windows Mobile versions.

OneNote Mobile for Windows Phone has the following key features:

- Support for multiple notebooks
- Support for tables
- Support for SkyDrive and SharePoint synchronization
- Support for inserting photos and audio recordings in your notes
- The ability to create bulleted or numbered lists or checklists
- The ability to display inked notes
- Support for searching within the app

OneNote Mobile for Windows Phone has the following key limitation:

- Creating new notebooks has to be done in the desktop or Web App. In turn, they will sync to the Mobile app.

The first time you run OneNote for Windows Phone, it will give you the option to open any notebooks you have stored in your OneNote folder. If you're a SharePoint user, especially via Microsoft Office 365, you'll also have the option to sign into that service and open any notebooks you have stored there.

As with the other OneNote Mobile apps, the Windows Phone version always has one notebook created called *Personal (Web)*, and it's required for OneNote Mobile to store unfiled notes. You can't create additional notebooks in the Mobile app. However, you can create additional notebooks in the SkyDrive OneNote Web App or on your desktop OneNote (make sure they're stored on SkyDrive), and those notebooks will synchronize to the OneNote Mobile app.

To create pages on OneNote Mobile for Windows Phone, click the New Page button that looks like a plus sign (+) at the bottom of the screen. Then you can enter your notes on the page that appears.

To insert a photo into your notes, tap where you'd like the photo to appear, and then tap the camera button at the bottom of the screen.

To insert an audio recording, tap where you'd like the recording to be placed in your notes, tap the microphone button at the bottom of the screen, and then start speaking.

TIP You can add a new note in Windows Phone 8 at any time. Just long-press and release the Windows button at the bottom of the phone. When the phone displays *Listening* say "Note," then speak the text of the note you'd like to take.

Using OneNote with a Windows 8 tablet

Windows 8 tablets are a bit of an anomaly. They are capable of running the full version of Office Professional 2013, but they also come with a special version of OneNote that is optimized for the touch interface.

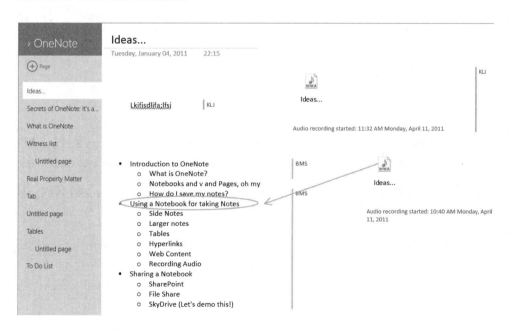

The touch-enabled version of OneNote is in the Windows 8 store on any Windows 8 device (not just tablets). Though it does have some innovative features (like the radial user interface, as shown following this text), it also has significant limitations in the current version. For example:

- Only SkyDrive-shared notebooks are easily accessed.

- Audio or video recording is not supported.

- There is a limited set of note tags and no customization.

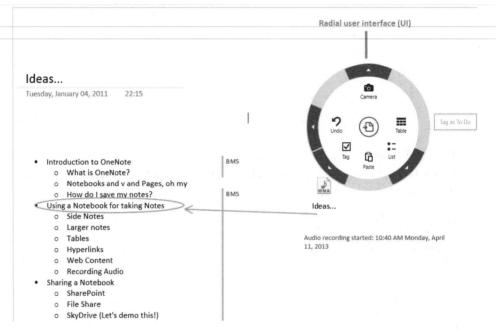

Like most of the Windows Store (formerly called *Metro*) apps in Windows 8, the special Windows 8 OneNote app is fairly limited compared to the full-fledged desktop version.

You can find the OneNote Windows Store app in the Windows Store on any Windows 8 computer.

TIP Windows RT is different from Windows 8. The version of OneNote that comes bundled with Windows RT is substantially the same as OneNote 2013.

Key points

- OneNote gives you a lot of opportunities to use your notes wherever you are.

- Using SkyDrive, SharePoint, a network drive, or even a simple USB flash drive, you can share notes between multiple devices.

- If your notes are stored in SkyDrive or SharePoint, you can access them from any computer with a web browser via OneNote Web App.

- OneNote Mobile lets you access your notes on the go on your iPhone, iPad, Android, Windows tablet, or Windows Phone devices.

34

Chapter at a glance

Find

Find tags in your notes with the Tags
Summary pane, page 877

Record

Record audio in your notebook,
page 881

Capture

Capture ideas quickly and easily with
Quick Notes, page 882

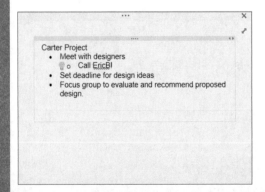

Saving time with OneNote

35

IN THIS CHAPTER, YOU WILL LEARN HOW TO

- Find tags.

- Record audio.

- Capture ideas and information with Quick Notes.

- Insert screen clippings into your notes.

- Create linked notes that connect to documents, presentations, webpages, or other notes.

- Create templates on which to build your notes.

Microsoft OneNote 2013 is a surprisingly powerful tool for collecting and organizing ideas and research, and getting your projects moving in the right direction. In this chapter, you will learn about tools that you may not have even realized OneNote 2013 has.

OneNote is for unstructured data, so it's appropriate for this chapter to introduce you to these tools in no particular order.

PRACTICE FILES To complete the exercises in this chapter, you need the practice files contained in the Chapter35 practice file folder. For more information, see "Download the practice files" in this book's Introduction.

Finding tags

In Chapter 33, "Sharing notes with others," you learned about adding tags to notes. You can tag a note as a phone number, as *Important*, as a to-do item, or even as a question. There's a tags gallery right there on the Home tab of the ribbon that offers you many tags, as well as the ability to create your own custom tags.

Did you know there's a powerful tool in OneNote for finding those tags after you've used them? Immediately to the right of the Tags gallery, you'll find Find Tags, and if you click it, the Tags Summary pane on the right side of the screen shows you all the tags you've used. You have a few options for what you can do with that tool.

At the bottom of the pane, you can use the Search option to set the scope that the Tags Summary is going to apply to. Click the arrow on the right end of the field to display a drop-down list of choices.

Following are several useful options:

- All notebooks
- This notebook
- This section
- This page group (which is as close to *this page* as you can get)
- Today's notes

The Tags Summary pane is a static pane. That means that if you add, change, or remove a tag from the notes, the Tags Summary results don't automatically change. To update the pane, click the Refresh Results button located below the Search field.

In this exercise, you'll use the Find Tags feature to quickly locate tags that you've assigned to your notes.

 SET UP **Start OneNote and open a OneNote page with a few sample notes.**

1   Click a paragraph in your notes.

2   Assign a tag to that paragraph from the **Tags** gallery on the **Home** tab of the ribbon.

3   Repeat steps 1 and 2 as desired.

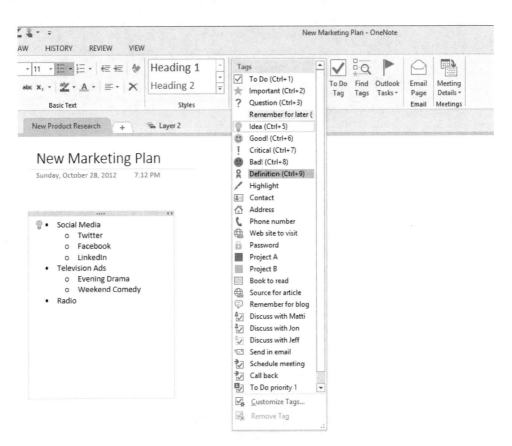

4   Click **Find Tags** on the **Home** tab of the ribbon.

5   The **Tags Summary** pane appears on the right side of the screen, showing all tagged
    items within the selected scope (**Page**, **Section**, **Notebook**, **This Week**, and so on).

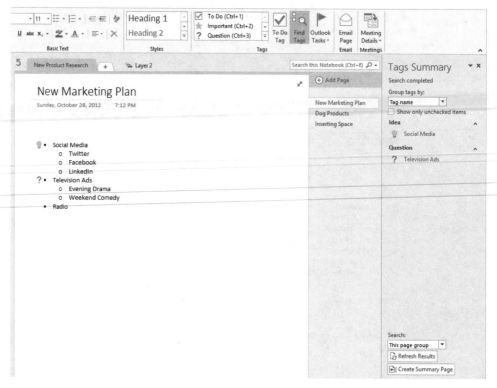

6   Select a tag and click it. OneNote will immediately take you to the page and paragraph where that tag is located.

⊗ CLEAN UP You'll probably want to reuse your page of sample notes for other exercises, so you don't need to do anything with them at this point.

Tags are great organizational tools when you're browsing your notes, because they help you quickly identify what you've written. They're even more powerful when you can find them later.

TIP The next time you're in a meeting, take notes with OneNote. When you have questions, flag them with the Question tag. When you get to the part of the meeting where it's time to ask questions, use the Find Tags feature to gather all of your questions into one pane so you can quickly refer to them.

Recording audio

While you're attending those meetings, there's another powerful feature available that gives you the ability to record audio. The audio recording appears right on your note page, so it's readily available when you want to play it back later.

TIP Be sure you have permission to record the audio in your meeting. In some cases, it's required by law, but in all cases, it's just good manners to let folks know they're being recorded.

To start recording audio, click the Insert tab on the ribbon, and then click Record Audio. Be warned that the recording will start as soon as you click the button. Therefore, don't click Record Audio until you're ready to start recording.

While the audio is recording, continue taking notes normally. When you're ready to stop recording, click the Stop button on the ribbon (it looks like a square). It's as easy as that. OneNote will insert your audio recording into your notes as an icon along with a portion of text that details when the audio was recorded.

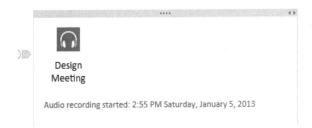

To play your audio back later, just double-click the icon that OneNote inserts into the notes.

Later, when you're playing the audio, OneNote highlights the notes you were taking while the audio was being recorded. As a bonus, you can take notes while listening to the audio playback, and OneNote will synchronize those notes to the recording as well.

TIP If you plan to do a lot of audio recording, you should invest in a decent microphone. The ones built into most laptops are good enough to record your voice, but they aren't likely to produce excellent quality audio in a large meeting.

TIP The next time you're on a technical support phone call, put the support person on speakerphone and use the OneNote recording feature to record the call as he or she helps you. Any notes you take during the call will be synchronized to the audio. This enables you to save the instructions for future use. Just make sure it's legal to record phone calls where you are.

Using Quick Notes

Have you ever been sitting at your desk when some brilliant idea that's unrelated to what you're working on hits you? When that happens, just press the Windows key+N and then another N; OneNote will open a Quick Note window for you that looks like a small sticky note on the screen. This enables you to write down the thoughts you had for future reference.

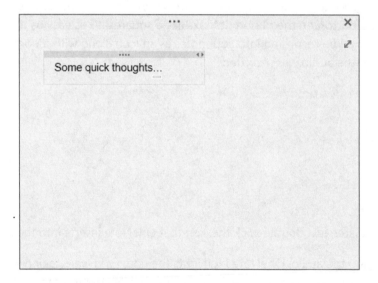

You can have as many Quick Notes open at a time as you want, and you can easily file them, print them, share them, or delete them if they turn out to not be so brilliant.

To access the ribbon commands in a Quick Note, click the three dots on the bar at the top of the Quick Note window.

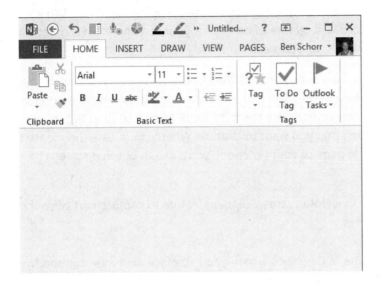

If you close a Quick Note without filing it, OneNote will automatically put it in the Quick Notes section at the bottom of the OneNote Notebook pane on the left.

To access Quick Notes, press Windows key+N and then press N again when the Send To OneNote window appears.

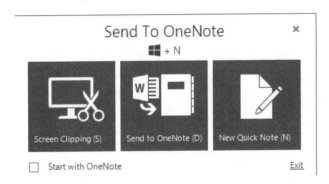

Quick Notes are a great way to take notes during phone calls or when you just want to capture random ideas that occur during the day, rather than scribbling them on the back of pieces of paper.

Using screen clipping

OneNote has always had a very good integrated screen clipping capability. What's screen clipping? It's the ability to take a picture of an area of your screen, which is great for capturing error messages, images, or other content.

To use the screen clipping capability, press the Windows key+S (OneNote doesn't even have to be open at the time). Your screen will dim somewhat, and your mouse pointer will turn into a crosshair pointer, and you can use the left mouse button to drag the mouse pointer across an area of the screen that you want to capture. When you release the mouse button, OneNote will ask you what page of your notebook you'd like to put that screen clipping on. It's as simple as that.

In this exercise, you'll use OneNote's screen clipping feature to capture part of your screen and insert it into your notes.

➡ SET UP You need a page in OneNote where you can place an image clipped from your screens to complete this exercise.

1   Check to make sure that the **Send to OneNote tool** is on your system tray (where the clock is; usually in the lower-right corner of your screen). It should be there by default, but if it isn't, start OneNote, click the **File** tab, click **Options**, and then click **Display**. Then ensure that the **Place OneNote icon in the notification area of the taskbar** check box is selected.

Send to
OneNote tool

2   Press **Windows key+S**.

3   When the screen dims, move your mouse pointer to the upper-left corner of the area of the screen you would like to clip.

4   Press and hold the left mouse button while dragging down and right across the area of the screen you want to capture.

5   When you've selected the area you want, release the left mouse button.

6   OneNote will ask you what page you would like to place the clipping on. Select a page, and click **OK**.

✖ CLEAN UP You can delete the page where you sent your practice screen clippings, if you want.

Screen clippings are a powerful way to capture things happening on your screen (like a portion of a webpage or an error message) in your notes.

Using linked notes

OneNote 2010 introduced the ability to take linked notes. What that means is that while you're working on a Microsoft Word document, a Microsoft PowerPoint presentation, or even when you're browsing websites in Windows Internet Explorer, you can have OneNote docked to the side of the screen where you can take notes. As you take notes, OneNote stores a link with the notes to the document or websites you were working with when you took those notes, so that you can easily return to them.

To use linked notes, open the document, presentation, or website you want to take notes on, open or create the OneNote page where you want to take the linked notes, and then click the Dock To Desktop button on the View tab in OneNote.

When you're done taking notes, you can click the Normal View button on the View tab of the OneNote ribbon or just close the docked page.

In this exercise, you'll use OneNote to take notes that are linked to a Word document.

➜ SET UP Start OneNote.

1   Start Word.

2   Open a document in Word that you want to take notes about.

3 In OneNote, navigate to the page where you want to take those notes.

4 Click the **View** tab on the ribbon.

5 Click the **Dock to Desktop** button. OneNote will dock itself to the right side of the screen, by default. The Word document should now occupy the rest of the screen.

6 Take notes in the OneNote page while navigating up or down in the Word document. Your notes will be linked to the Word document.

7 To exit docked view, click the **Normal View** button, which looks like a two-headed arrow at the upper-right corner of the docked window.

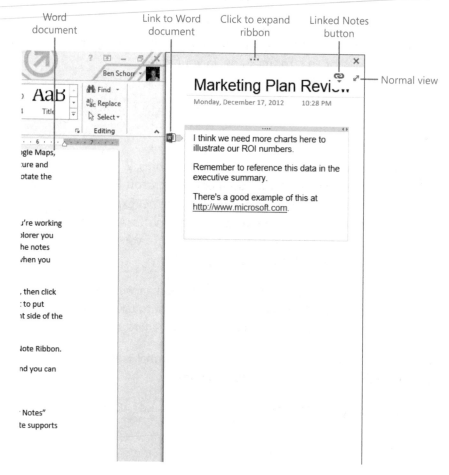

Word document | Link to Word document | Click to expand ribbon | Linked Notes button

Normal view

Marketing Plan Revi...

Monday, December 17, 2012   10:28 PM

I think we need more charts here to illustrate our ROI numbers.

Remember to reference this data in the executive summary.

There's a good example of this at http://www.microsoft.com.

x

TIP Your Word document must be saved and named at least once for the linking to work. If you want to create linked notes on a brand new document, you'll need to save it first.

CLEAN UP No cleanup is required.

To use those linked notes later, navigate to the page where you took those notes, and you can click the provided links to jump back to the document or website you were working with.

Searching your images

In Chapter 31, "Working with notebooks, sections, and pages," you learned how to insert a photo image or document into OneNote. You can use the screen clipping feature, print from the original application to OneNote, or go to the Insert tab in OneNote and select Pictures, Online Pictures, Screen Clipping, or even Scanned Image.

Did you know that OneNote can automatically try to recognize any text that appears in those images? That process is called *OCR* or *Optical Character Recognition*.

Naturally, the results will vary by the quality of the picture and the legibility of the text. However, a photo of handwritten text on a whiteboard could be successfully recognized, if the photo is clear and the handwriting is fairly easy to read. A photo of a printed stop sign will very likely be recognized.

In this exercise, you'll insert an image into a page of notes.

SET UP You need the 35 Practice image 1.jpg image located in the Chapter35 practice file folder to complete this exercise. Create a practice OneNote page that you can insert an image into.

1   Navigate to the OneNote page you want to insert the image on.

2   Click the location on the page where you want to place the image.

3   Click the **Insert** tab on the ribbon.

4   Click the **Pictures** button.

5   Navigate to and insert the **35 Practice image 1.jpg** file

6   Next, confirm that the page will be indexed. Right-click the image you just inserted and select **Make Text in Image Searchable**.

7   Set the language you want to use.

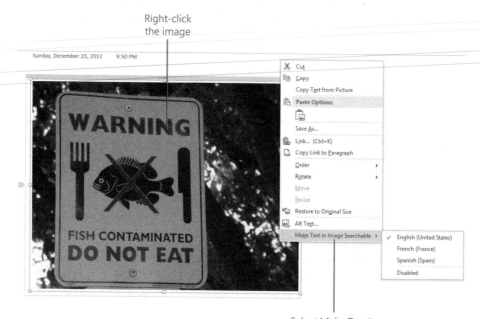

Right-click the image

Select Make Text in Image Searchable

OneNote will attempt to index the text in the image in the background, and that text will subsequently appear in your search results if you look for that string (or part of it).

✖ CLEAN UP You can delete the practice images page you created in this exercise.

TIP The next time you get a long PDF report, print it to OneNote instead of to paper. As long as Make Text In Image Searchable is enabled, OneNote will index the text of the PDF, which will make it easy to find specific items even in long PDF files.

Inserting a spreadsheet

One of the features folks have been asking for in OneNote since the very beginning has been the ability to embed content from other file types in a OneNote document other than just being able to print it there. OneNote 2013 has some of that capability with the Insert Spreadsheet feature.

In this exercise, you'll embed a Microsoft Excel spreadsheet on a OneNote page.

SET UP You need the 35 PracticeSpreadsheet.xlsx workbook located in the Chapter35 practice file folder to complete this exercise.

1 Open OneNote.

2 Navigate to a page where you want to insert the sample spreadsheet.

3 On the **Insert** tab, click **Insert Spreadsheet**.

4 OneNote will ask if you want to insert a new spreadsheet or an existing spreadsheet.

5 Select **Existing Excel Spreadsheet**.

6 Navigate to the folder containing the **35 Practice Spreadsheet** and select it.

7 Click **Insert**.

8 OneNote will ask if you want to **Attach File**, **Insert Spreadsheet**, or **Insert a Chart or Table**.

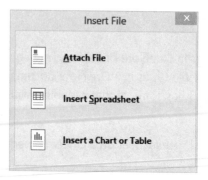

9   Choose **Insert Spreadsheet**. OneNote will insert the spreadsheet you selected onto
the note page.

> **TIP** If your workbook has multiple sheets and you only want to insert one sheet of
> the workbook, right-click the spreadsheet in OneNote and click Select What To Dis-
> play from the shortcut menu. OneNote will display a list of the sheets in the work-
> book, and you can select the one you want.

✕ CLEAN UP There are no specific clean-up tasks.

Any changes that were made to the sheet will automatically be updated in OneNote. However, you can't edit the sheet in OneNote. To do that, you would have to click the Edit button in the upper-left corner of the window, which will open Excel. Then you can make and
save your changes, which will appear in OneNote.

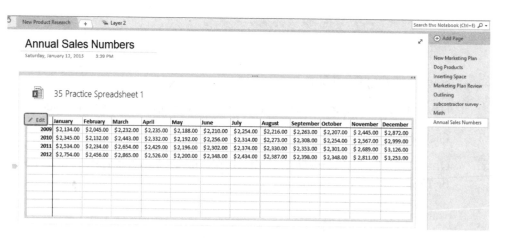

Using the Napkin Math feature

If you asked 100 OneNote users what Napkin Math was. about 98 respondents wouldn't know the answer. Napkin Math is the name given to the feature in OneNote where you can enter a mathematical equation and OneNote will solve it for you.

For example: enter 2+2= then press Enter, and OneNote will insert the 4 for you. Napkin Math understands a surprising number of mathematical operators. In addition to addition, subtraction, multiplication, and division, it can also do exponents (squared, cubed, x5, and so forth), square roots, percentages, and more. You can use the currency symbol ($) to have it treat the result as currency, and you can even enter some fairly long formulas.

$5*4=$20.00

Napkin Math cannot calculate with variables or references like Excel does. It won't let you create a calculated cell in a table, for example. In that instance, you would do better to use the inserted spreadsheet tool discussed in the previous section.

35

Formatting with templates

If the plain white sheets of electronic paper are just a little too plain for you, then you can dip into the OneNote collection of templates. Templates are pre-created pages that already contain specific elements such as formatting, tables, graphics, or instructions.

In this exercise, you'll use a template to create a new page in OneNote.

➡ SET UP **Start OneNote.**

1   Click the **Insert** tab on the ribbon.

2   Click the **Page Templates** button.

3   From the **Recently Used** list, select a template you use often (if any), or click the **Page Templates** item at the bottom of the menu to open the **Templates** pane on the right side of the screen.

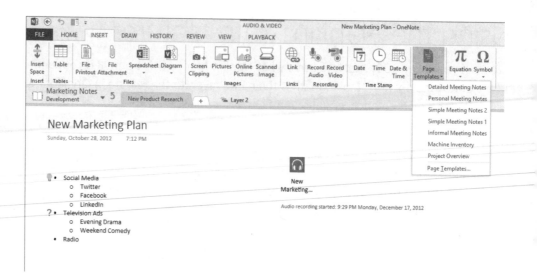

4   Select a template from the **Templates** pane by expanding the category (such as **Academic** or **Business**) and clicking the template you like. If you don't like the template you selected, simply repeat step 3 and select a different template. After you enter notes onto the page, you won't be able to change the underlying template and keep your notes. You'll have to create a new page with the new template and move your notes to it.

On the Templates task pane, you can select from among a couple dozen pre-created templates, including special types of notes pages, planners, and more. Or, you can create your own.

TIP To create your own template, create a page that is exactly the way you want it—page title, paper color, any tables or content you want inside—and then click the Templates pane. Click the Save Current Page As A Template link at the bottom of the Templates pane. OneNote will ask you to give your template a name. Then you can save it in the My Templates section at the top of the Templates pane.

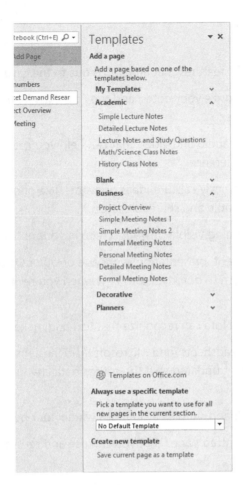

CLEAN UP You can delete any practice pages you created during this exercise.

Page templates are a unique way to create pages that have pre-existing formatting so they are ready for you to enter notes without having to create new formatting parameters each time.

Key points

- OneNote 2013 has some powerful features that aren't obvious to the casual observer.

- Tags help you organize and categorize your notes, and the Find Tags feature makes it easy to find your tagged items later.

- OneNote has the ability to record audio and video that can help you more accurately capture notes in a meeting or conference.

- Quick Notes make it possible to quickly capture ideas or events (like phone calls) as they occur and make them searchable and shareable later.

- Screen clippings let you save anything visible on your screen in your notes.

- If you're taking notes on a document, presentation, webpage or other OneNote page, you can link your notes to that item to quickly return to it when you review the notes later.

- If there is text in your picture, OneNote can recognize that text and make it searchable.

- OneNote 2013 lets you insert spreadsheets (and Microsoft Visio files) into your notes and keeps the inserted spreadsheet updated so if the source data changes, the table in your notes changes too.

- Napkin Math lets you make quick and simple calculations within your notes.

- Templates let you create pre-formatted pages that you can use and re-use in your notes.

Chapter at a glance

Start

Start Access from the Windows Start screen, page 898

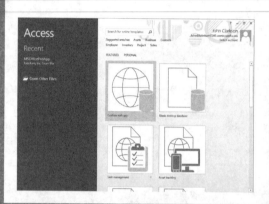

Navigate

Navigate the Web App design interface, page 901

Explore

Explore a Web App in a browser, page 903

Investigate

Drill down for related information, page 905

Getting comfortable in Access 2013

36

IN THIS CHAPTER, YOU WILL LEARN HOW TO

- Start Access 2013.

- Look at the desktop database window.

- Explore the Web App window.

- Use the browser.

- Discover what's new in Access 2013.

Microsoft Access 2013 is firstly a relational database that can be used to structure your data in a form that ensures the consistency and integrity of the data, while flexibly enabling you to evolve the database design over time to keep meeting the needs of your business. In addition to simply storing your data, the product enables you to construct a rich user interface, where you can easily search, filter, and present data held in the underlying database tables.

If you are developing a desktop database (one that is stored on your computer), you'll appreciate the ease with which Access creates queries, which bring the data in your tables together. Then you can add forms that provide a sophisticated interface for maintaining the data, and reports for creating presentations more suited for printing.

Access 2013 now offers a new feature for creating a Web App that makes the data available by using Microsoft Office 365 in a browser to enable users at remote locations to share data. Yet it still manages to offer you the same productivity and familiar desktop experience that you get when developing a traditional desktop database solution.

Because many of you will want to understand how a desktop database can be created and explore the great features Access provides for this, Chapters 37–39 focus on these features. For those of you who want to dive into the new fantastic features of delivering a database experience in a web browser, those topics are introduced in Chapter 40, "Creating and sharing a Web App."

In this chapter, you'll discover the different design interfaces used for desktop and Web App development experiences, along with some of the great new features in Access 2013 for developing Web Apps.

Starting Access 2013

You typically start Access 2013 from the Windows Start screen in Windows 8 or the Start menu in Windows 7. You can also start Access 2013 by opening a desktop database from an email attachment or by double-clicking a desktop database from a place such as your Windows desktop, or you can open an existing Web App from an Office 365 Team Site.

If you are upgrading from Microsoft Office 2003 to Office Professional 2013, then you will notice a big difference in the user interface. Introduced in Office 2007, the ribbon provides a tabbed interface for working in the product. Depending on what you are doing, the ribbon will display additional tool tabs to assist you in a particular task. The database window of Access 2003 has been replaced with a more powerful searchable Navigation pane on the left side of the interface that enables you to filter objects of one or more types.

If you are already familiar with Access 2010, then you will find that the desktop database has improved productivity, but the major revision in the product has been the introduction of the new Web App.

When you start Access without opening a file, the new Access Start screen is displayed.

IMPORTANT

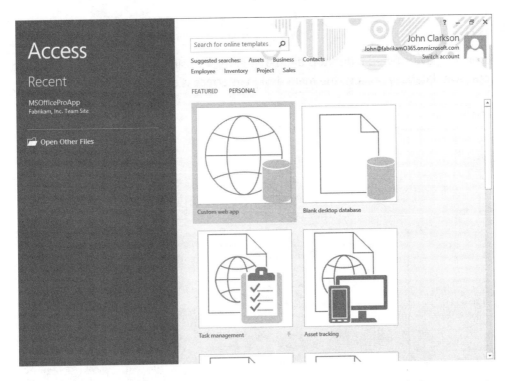

From the Start screen, you can open a recently used database or Web App, or create a new one from either a template or as a blank design into which you can add, import, or create new data tables. Access 2013 enables you to create two significantly different types of database. The first is called a desktop database and is held on your computer. The second type is called a Web App and is held either in Office 365 or on your on-premise Microsoft SharePoint 2013 server.

36

Looking at the desktop database window

After you have created a desktop database, either by using a template or after setting up your own database objects, the main design interface is displayed.

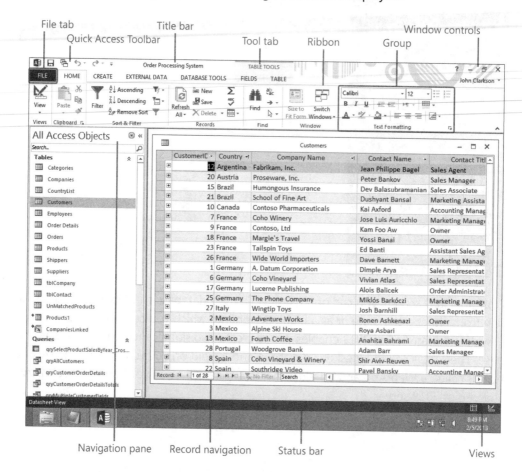

File tab
Quick Access Toolbar
Title bar
Tool tab
Ribbon
Group
Window controls

Navigation pane
Record navigation
Status bar
Views

- **Ribbon** The main component of the Access interface and where you'll find the primary commands for working with the content of your database. The ribbon is made up of task-oriented tabs, and each tab has groups of related commands. For example, on the **Home** tab, the **Clipboard** group contains commands for copying and pasting information in your database. Groups that have additional commands that aren't shown on the ribbon have a dialog box launcher or drop-down set of choices to perform further operations.

- **File tab** The first tab on the ribbon. Unlike other ribbon tabs, the **File** tab displays the Backstage view, where commands for working with the entire contents of a database are located. The **Backstage** view is also where application options are located and where you can find information about your user account and your version of Microsoft Office.

- **Quick Access Toolbar** Holds your most frequently used commands. By default, **Save**, **Undo**, and **Redo** have already been added.

  SEE ALSO In Chapter 37, "Understanding Access 2013 databases," you'll configure the Quick Access Toolbar to improve your productivity.

- **Title bar** Appears at the top of the window and displays the application title.

- **Window controls** Displayed on the right edge of the title bar, along with the standard **Minimize**, **Restore Down/Maximize**, **Close**, and **Help** buttons.

- **Status bar** Appears at the bottom of the window and displays status information, such as the optional description of a field in a table, when you have the cursor in that field.

- **Navigation pane** Enables you to locate and filter objects in your database.

- **Record navigation** Enables you to efficiently move between data records in a table.

- **Views** Enables you to quickly switch between different views of an Access object (for example, when working with a table, query, report, or form).

36

Exploring the Web App window

After you have created a Web App, either by using a template or after setting up your own database objects, the main design interface is displayed.

SEE ALSO In Chapter 40, "Creating and sharing a Web App," you'll learn about developing a Web App.

The Web App is designed to be displayed in a browser window. The design interface can then be launched to display your final work in a browser. A unique feature of Access 2013 is that it endeavors to provide you with a similar design experience to that of a desktop database, preserving many of the desktop database features.

The design interface consists of the following key elements:

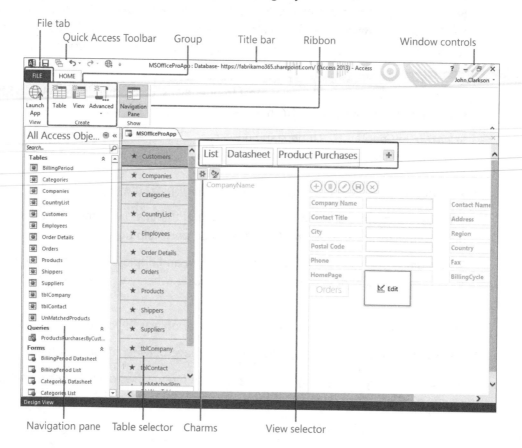

File tab
Quick Access Toolbar   Group   Title bar   Ribbon   Window controls

Navigation pane   Table selector   Charms   View selector

- **Ribbon** The main component of the Access interface and where you'll find the primary commands for working with the content of your Web App design.

- **File tab** The first tab on the ribbon, displaying the **Backstage** view.

- **Quick Access Toolbar** Holds your most frequently used commands. By default, **Save**, **Undo**, and **Redo** have already been added.

- **Title bar** Appears at the top of the window and displays the application location.

- **Window controls** Displayed on the right edge of the title bar, along with the standard **Minimize**, **Restore Down/Maximize**, **Close**, and **Help** buttons.

- **Navigation pane** Enables you to locate and filter objects in your Web App. This is only visible in the design interface.

- **Table selector** Displays a list of the tables in your application. These table captions can be hidden and renamed, and can also display different icons, without affecting the underlying details of the table. This is the primary browser navigation interface.

- **Charms** Enable you to display a drop-down list of choices in some ways similar to the options available from a right-click on the desktop interface.

- **View selector** Enables you to create new views of the data in a table. Users can select different views of the information to be displayed in a browser window.

TIP Notice that in the very center of the screen is a large Edit button. This button is used to edit the selected view and not the design of the table. It is very important not to get confused by some of the subtle changes in the Web App design interface.

Displaying results in a browser

36

The Access desktop experience is very similar when designing a database and using the resulting design, but with a Web App, the experience is significantly different because the resulting design is displayed in a browser.

The following example has not been designed by a developer, but was automatically created by Access. That's the power of Access. It saves you from doing the hard work when developing a basic interface to the data.

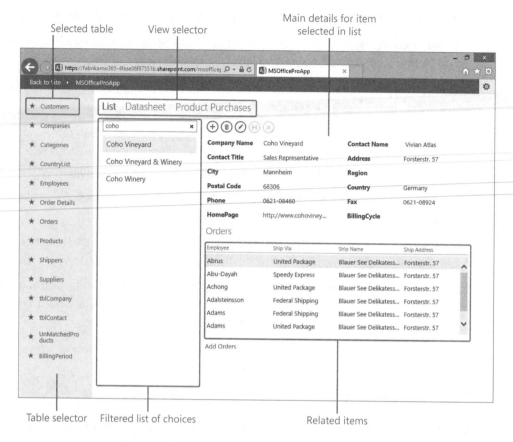

Selected table · View selector · Main details for item selected in list

Table selector · Filtered list of choices · Related items

The following list describes the main areas of the browser interface:

- **Table selector** This works like the main menu for users.

- **Selected table** When a user selects a table, the **View** selector for the table is displayed, and it's the first view shown on the screen.

- **List** The **List** view has a panel that can be filtered to display a list of selected choices.

- **View selector** This enables the user to select a view of the data.

- **Main details** After the user makes a choice from the list of choices, the main details are then displayed.

- **Related items** Because Access knows how tables are related to each other, it can automatically create a related list of items. If you then click any item, it will drill down to display further information on a detailed record.

Discovering what's new in Access 2013

This section introduces you to key application features for an Access 2013 Web App and includes screen shots, where applicable. The majority of the features included are discussed in detail, along with step-by-step instructions, in Chapter 40, "Creating and sharing a Web App."

- **Table templates** Add common tables to your Web App from available templates, such as **Orders**, **Contacts**, **Customers**, **Clients**, and more.

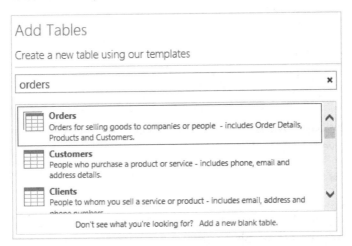

- **Automatic views** When you create a new table, new views, such as a **List** and **Datasheet** view, are automatically created.

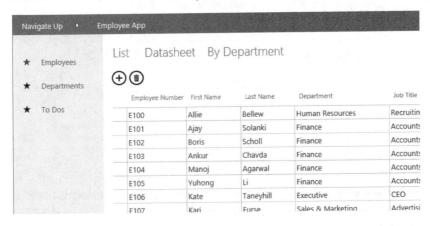

- **Autocomplete control** This feature offers a list of suggestions for completion when you begin typing in a field.

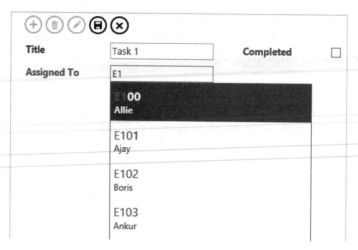

- **Action Bar** This bar provides new controls for record commands such as **New**, **Delete**, **Edit**, **Save**, and **Cancel**.

- **Charms** When you select an object, a charm will display a pop-up pane with options to enable you to modify the object's properties.

- **Summary view** Groups records on a common field or performs basic calculations, such as **Sum** or **Average**. You define the field used for grouping the data and the details to be displayed when each group is selected. The view is then automatically created.

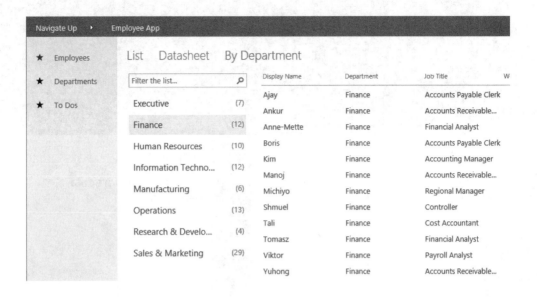

Key points

- You typically start Access 2013 from the Windows Start screen in Windows 8 or the Start menu in Windows 7.

- Access 2013 supports the creation of desktop databases held on your computer or network.

- Access 2013 supports the creation of Web App databases running in an Office 365 plan including Access or an on-premises installation of SharePoint 2013 with Access Services.

- A Web App is designed by using a design interface in Access 2013 on your computer. The interface is similar to the design interface used for developing a desktop database, but the final application is viewed in a browser.

- The design interface for a desktop database uses the Navigation pane to enable you to locate your design objects. The Web App design interface also uses the Navigation pane, but it includes a table selector that provides the navigation interface when viewed through a browser.

- A Web App includes a number of new controls that are specially designed for using an application in a browser interface.

Chapter at a glance

Create

Create a desktop database,
page 911

Import

Import and export data,
page 915

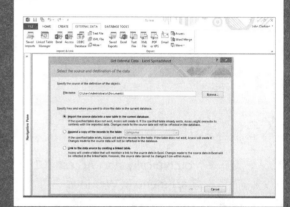

Work

Work with data in a datasheet,
page 924

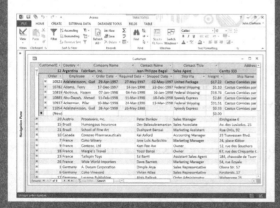

Link

Link Access to external data,
page 936

Understanding Access 2013 databases

37

IN THIS CHAPTER, YOU WILL LEARN HOW TO

- Create a desktop database.

- Import and export data.

- Navigate the user interface.

- Work with data in a datasheet.

- Configure Access options.

- Link Access to external data.

- Compact, repair, and encrypt a database.

Microsoft Access allows you to structure and store your information in a set of database tables and can efficiently manage and share large amounts of data. In addition to quickly locating information, the database ensures consistency in the information by linking together the data in different tables. The product allows you to present the data through both professional-looking forms and reports.

If you are moving from Microsoft Office 2003 to Office Professional 2013, then you will notice a big difference in the user interface. Introduced in Office 2007, the ribbon provides a tabbed interface for working in the product. Depending on what you are doing, the ribbon will display additional tool tabs to assist you in a particular task. The database window of Access 2003 has been replaced with a searchable Navigation pane on the left side of the interface that allows you to filter objects of one or more types.

If you are already familiar with Access 2010, then you will find that the desktop database has improved productivity, but the major revision in the product has been the introduction of the Web App.

Access 2013 enables you to create two distinct but related types of databases. The first is a desktop database; this is a database where the components are held in one or more files on your computer or network. The second type of database is called a Web App; this is a new feature in Access and means that the database is stored in Office 365, and the user interface is displayed in a browser window. When developing a Web App, you use a design interface on your computer that is similar to the familiar desktop database interface.

We will leave a discussion of Web App databases until Chapter 40, "Creating and sharing a Web App." In this chapter, we provide detailed steps so that you can perform activities and at the same time familiarize yourself with how to productively work with the Access desktop database interface.

PRACTICE FILES To complete the exercises in this chapter, you need the practice files contained in the Chapter37 practice file folder. For more information, see "Download the practice files" in this book's Introduction. Note that the MSOfficeProBlank.accdb practice file is created in this chapter, so it is not included in the practice files.

An Access desktop database contains different types of objects:

- **Tables** Your data is held in a number of tables. The data in most of the tables will be linked to data in other tables. Using this approach of linking or relating data between tables is a key feature of the database and reduces the need to duplicate information.

- **Queries** These bring together the data from one or more tables and present the data either through a datasheet, form, or report. Note that a datasheet is not a separate object, but the interface when displaying data from either a table or query.

- **Forms** These allow more flexibility in presenting data than that allowed in a datasheet. They are the most popular method for viewing and managing data. Of particular note are parent/child forms and subforms, where the subforms display related data from other tables.

- **Reports** Allow you to create a paper-based presentation of your data for printing or previewing on the screen. One unique presentation feature of reports is the ability to have multiple layers of grouping when presenting data.

- **Macros** This is a programming feature for automating operations. Macros can be found in several places in the database; a discussion of macros is beyond the scope of this chapter.

- **Modules** These are used for advanced programming, using the Microsoft Visual Basic for Applications (VBA) programming language common to the other Office products. This topic is also beyond the scope of this chapter.

Creating a desktop database

Your Access desktop database consists of a single file, which you will create and save on your computer. There are two different methods to get started with a database. You can either choose to create a database by using a predefined template database, or you can start by creating an empty database.

In this exercise, you'll create a desktop database.

 SET UP You don't need any practice files to complete this exercise, but the MSOffice-ProBlank.accdb database you create here will be used in further exercises in this chapter. Start Access from the Start screen (Windows 8), or from the Start menu (Windows 7) that is displayed when you click at the left end of the Windows taskbar.

1   Click **Blank desktop database**.

2   Enter the file name MSOfficeProBlank.

3   Click **Create**.

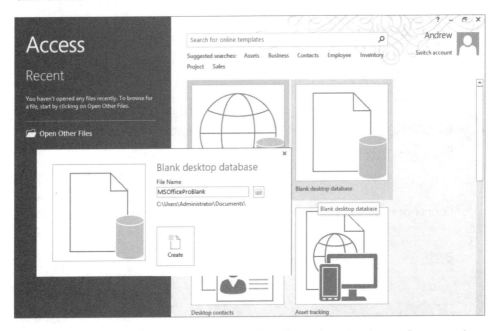

TIP When starting Access, you will notice a list of template databases; for example, Asset tracking (Web App) and the templates prefixed with the name *Desktop*. Desktop asset tracking will create a desktop database. It is worth taking the time to look at a few of these to get some ideas for creating your own applications.

Your database will look similar to the following.

When you create a blank database, Access will open to display a new table called *Table1*. This feature allows you to start using one of several techniques for creating blank tables, which we will look at in the next chapter.

4   Click on the **X** to close the **Table1** object.

The main ribbon will be displayed without any design objects in the database. The Navigation pane displaying All Access Objects is empty.

Ribbon tab   Navigation pane   Ribbon icon   Ribbon group

❌ CLEAN UP Close the MSOfficeProBlank database. This will close Access.

Managing trust locations and macro security

Sooner or later, you will come across the following when opening a database.

Because we live in a world where some people will try and hack or subvert systems, and because Office files can be sent by email from unknown sources, Microsoft, by default, switches off features, and it is up to you to decide what to enable.

If you click the Enable Content button, then the next time that you open the database, you will not need to again answer this question, because you previously enabled content in the file. However, if you use the file system to copy the file, rename the file, or move the file to a different location, then you will again be challenged to enable the content.

There are two aspects of trust that you can manage. The first is the location of a file. Trust locations allow you to establish folders where you can place files that will be trusted. This means that you will not need to enable content for files placed in these folders (this feature can also be switched off, allowing files to be opened from any location). The second aspect of trust is whether the application should be allowed to execute certain macro commands or VBA programming code. Although we will not cover these topics in this book, you should be aware of this capability.

If you are working with your own databases or databases from a trusted source, then managing the trust locations and macro security should not pose a problem. But if you are downloading content from the Internet and macro security is fully enabled and trusted locations disabled, then it is possible that when you open a database, malicious code could be executed without any warning. The final decision is your responsibility, but in this section, we will show you how to enable macros and how you can manage your trusted locations.

In this exercise, you'll set security parameters for a database.

 SET UP You need the MSOfficeProBlank.accdb database from the previous exercise to complete this exercise. If you have not already closed the MSOfficeProBlank.accdb database, then close the database and reopen to display the security warning shown at the beginning of this section. If the security warning does not appear, then continue to follow through the exercise, and you should find that your trust settings have already been altered.

1   From the **File** tab, select **Options** at the bottom of the page.

2   Select the **Trust Center** option.

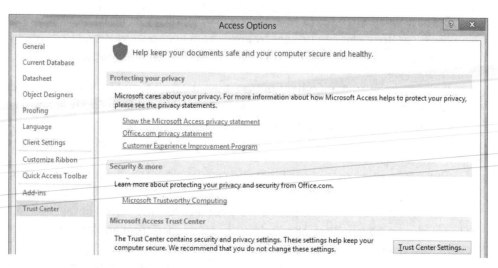

3   Click **Trust Center Settings**.

4   Select **Macro Settings** and **Enable all Macros**.

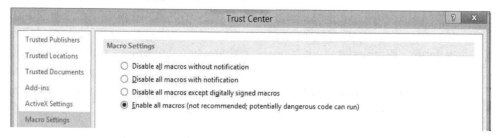

5   Click **Trust Locations**.

The next choice is a bit more complicated, because you can either decide to add specific folders where you will trust files, or you can disable the trust locations; trusting files on any location. To enable content at all locations, proceed as follows:

6   Click the check box to **Disable All trust Locations**, or add specific folders to be trusted. Then click **OK**.

❌ CLEAN UP Leave the MSOfficeProCompleted database open for use in later exercises.

Importing and exporting data

Access has wizards to guide you through specific operations; these are particularly useful when it comes to importing or exporting data. When you import data, you are making a copy of the original data and storing that data in your database file.

In this exercise, you'll import data into a database.

➡ SET UP You need the MSOfficeProBlank.accdb database from the previous exercise, and the MSOfficeProData.accdb database and CompanyNames.xlsx spreadsheet located in the Chapter37 practice file folder to complete this exercise. Open the MSOfficePro-Blank.accdb database if it is not already open. The CompanyNames.xlsx sample spreadsheet contains a list of company names and URLs. You will import this list into your database.

1   Click the **External Data** tab.

2   Click **Excel** in the **Import & Export** group.

3   Browse in the **File Name** box to locate the **CompanyNames.xlsx** spreadsheet.

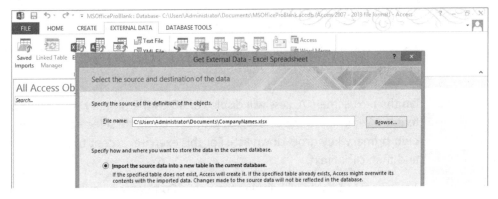

4   Ensure that the first button to **Import data** is selected, and press **OK**. The **Import Spreadsheet Wizard** will now be displayed.

5   Select the **First Row Contains Column Headings** check box, and notice how the display changes to remove the column headings from the data records. Click **Next**.

6 Click the second **URL** column, and use the drop-down **Data Type** to change the data type to a **Hyperlink**, and then click **Next**.

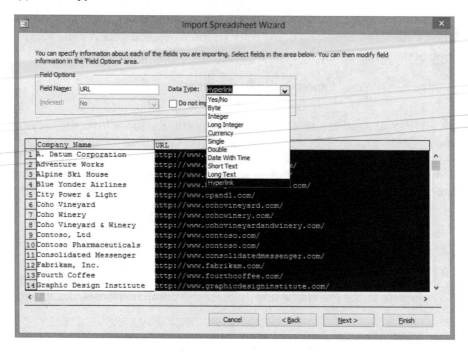

TIP This stage in the wizard allows you to select an appropriate data type for the column that will be created to hold the data.

7 On the next screen, Access will display an **ID** as the primary key (if you wanted a different column to be the primary key, then it could be selected from the **Choose my own primary key** drop-down list). For this exercise, accept the default choice of **ID**, and then click **Next**.

8 The **Import to Table** will display the name **Companies**. You can change the name of the new table at this point. Click **Finish**.

9 The very last screen allows you to save these steps if you will need to repeat them. Click **Close** (you do not need to save the steps).

10 Double-click the table now shown in the **Navigation** pane to display your data.

TIP Click the X next to field list to close this window. This allows for more space to display the data contained in your table.

CLEAN UP Close the Companies table and retain the MSOfficeProBlank database for use in later exercises.

Importing from another Access database

When you import data from another Access database, you can choose to import any of the available design objects. The MSOfficeProData.accdb database contains data that you will need in the following exercise. You will import some of the items in this database into your blank database.

In this exercise, you'll import data from another Access database.

SET UP You need the MSOfficeProBlank.accdb database from the previous exercise and the MSOfficeProData.accdb database from the Chapter37 practice file folder to complete this exercise. Open the MSOfficeProBlank.accdb database, if it is not already open.

1   Click the **External Data** tab.

2   Click **Access** in the **Import & Export** group.

3   Locate the **MSOfficeProData.accdb** file in the **File Name** box.

4   Leave the default selection of **Import tables, queries, forms** active, and click **OK**.

You will then have the option to import different Access objects from the database.

5   On the **Tables** tab, click **Select All** to highlight all the tables.

6   Click the **Forms** tab and click to highlight the **frmCustomers** form. Then click **OK** to import all the tables and the selected form.

7   Click **Close** when prompted to save the import steps (you do not need to save a record of these steps, because you will not repeat this operation).

TIP If you import several tables that have relationships, then the relationships will also be imported by default into the new database.

❌ CLEAN UP Retain the MSOfficeProBlank database for use in later exercises.

Exporting data from an Access database

Access supports the export of data from both tables and queries (which we will discuss in the next chapter). To export data, select the table or query in the Navigation pane and then either use the right-click option to select an export format, or use the appropriate icon on the ribbon.

In this exercise, you'll export data from an Access database.

➡ SET UP You need the MSOfficeProBlank.accdb database from the previous exercise to complete this exercise. Open the database, if it is not already open.

1   In the **Navigation** pane, click the **Customers** table.

2   Click the **External Data** tab, and click the **Text File** icon in the **Export** group.

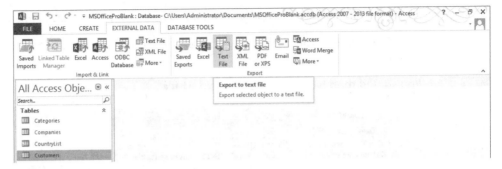

This will then display the Text File Export wizard.

3 Use the **File name** text box to browse to a location to save your exported data.

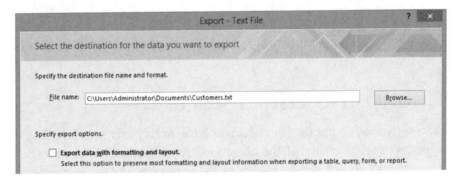

4 Do not make any further selections, but click **OK** to proceed.

TIP Choosing to export the data with formatting will result in a format that is not easily imported into other programs, but it does result in a simple text layout that could be printed.

It is recommended that you follow through and accept the default selections. More details will be revealed regarding important choices as we proceed through the steps. This wizard, which is similar to the Import Text Wizard, has a number of advanced choices.

5 On the next wizard page, you can choose between **Delimited** or **Fixed Width**, **Delimited**; which is the default for a more standard choice. An **Advanced** option (bottom left) allows you very detailed control of how each column is exported. Click **Next** to proceed.

6 The next wizard page allows you to change the delimiters used for the export, and you can optionally include field names. Click the box to **Include Field Names on First Row**.

7   Change the **Export to file name** setting, if required, and then click **Finish**.

8   Click **Close** when prompted to save the export steps (you do not need to save the steps).

You should then have produced an export file.

❌ CLEAN UP Leave the MSOfficeProBlank database open for use in later exercises.

Navigating the user interface

There are two key components in navigating the Access user interface. The first is the Navigation pane, which lists all the objects in your database. This can also be changed to display either all your objects or objects of a specific type. The key to productivity with this part of the interface is the search bar, which allows you to quickly locate an object and then click to change or activate the object.

There are several useful features in the Navigation pane.

- **Search** When you enter words in a partial pattern, the **Navigation** pane will filter results.

- **All Access Objects** This drop-down list allows you to quickly change what is ordered in the pane.

- **Shutter bar open/close option** This allows you to minimize the **Navigation** pane to the left.

- **Navigation options** These options permit much finer control of the behavior of the navigation bar.

All Access Objects

Right-click the title of the Navigation pane
to see the Navigation options.

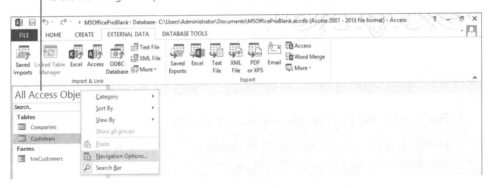

Search bar   Shutter bar

Working with the tabs

The second and complementary approach to navigating the Access interface is to use the ribbon. Although you will quickly become familiar with the options on the ribbon to create new objects, after an object has been opened, the ribbon Home tab allows you to quickly change the design of an object.

The File tab is often called the Backstage view—a behind-the-scenes set of choices for configuring Access and performing general operations, such as opening a database or saving a database in a different format. One of the most important menu choices in the Backstage view is the Options choice, because this choice contains a very large number of settings that can be used to control the behavior of the database.

One of the great strengths of Access is that you can do the same thing in more than one way. At first, this may appear confusing, but as you gain familiarity with the product, it is a very useful feature. Access is a powerful development tool. You may find that when you decide to make certain changes in the environment, some paths to features are no longer available. As a simple example, you could choose to hide or fully customize the ribbon, in which case you would then be relying on a right-click to provide you with features that would otherwise associate with the ribbon.

Access has five key ribbon tabs, although, as you open different objects, additional tabs will become available, depending on the context. Following is a list of the tabs and their usage.

- **File** The File tab provides general options and settings for working in the product.

- **Home** This tab is used principally for formatting, filtering, and selecting data while you view the data.

- **Create** This tab is used to create new objects.

- **External Data** This tab is used to import, export, and link to external data.

- **Database Tools** This tab is associated with general operations in maintaining your database.

The File tab has the following features:

- **Info** Allows you to compact and repair your database and encrypt the database with a password.
- **New** Allows you to create a new database.
- **Open** Provides a path to opening recently accessed databases.
- **Save** If you have a design object open, this will save any changes.
- **Save As** This has two functions. If you have an object open, you can save any changes to the object, but more importantly, it allows you to save the database in an alternative format.
- **Print** Allows you to print an object that is open and active.
- **Close** Closes the database.
- **Account** Displays helpful information for connecting to online services.
- **Options** The Access options have been described earlier in this chapter, and are used to configure both the Access installation and database-specific options.

In this exercise, you'll use the Navigation pane to open an object and then switch to Design View.

 SET UP You need the MSOfficeProBlank.accdb database from the previous exercise to complete this exercise. Open the database, if it is not already open.

1 Double-click the **Companies** table in the **Navigation** pane.

This will then display the two tool tabs, Fields and Table. The Fields tool tab will allow you to add or alter the design of the table, and the Table tool tab allows more advanced macro programming for the table. Notice the View drop-down list on the left, which allows you to quickly switch between the Datasheet View and the Design View for changing the design of a table.

2   In the **Navigation** pane, double-click the form **frmCustomers**. Then, on ribbon, click the **View** arrow and select **Design View**.

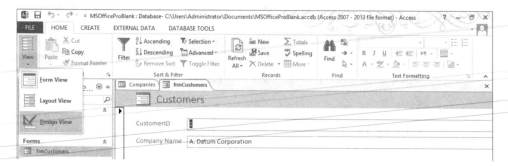

The tabs now change as shown below. The **Form Design Tools** have three tabs for assisting in the layout of a form:

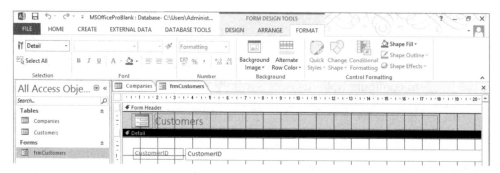

TIP If you right-click the ribbon, you can choose to unpin the ribbon. This means that the ribbon will float and drop down when required.

✖ CLEAN UP Close the Companies table and form frmCustomers, and retain the MSOfficeProBlank database for use in later exercises.

Working with data in a datasheet

Each table of data in a database has an associated datasheet. The datasheet allows you to present and interact with the data in the database. It has a series of columns across the top and a series of rows containing the data records. You can adjust these presentations by hiding, freezing, and ordering the columns without changing the underlying design of the table.

Datasheets are limited in controlling how a user can interact with the data (when compared to using a form), but they are also a key feature to understand, because you can further exploit the power of a datasheet through a form. A form can be used to present data as a datasheet and make use of a number of more sophisticated features to extend the datasheet with capabilities only available through the form's Datasheet View.

In this exercise, you'll work with datasheets.

SET UP You need the MSOfficeProBlank.accdb database from the previous exercise. Open the database, if it is not already open.

1   At the lower left of a datasheet are navigation buttons for moving to the first, next, previous, and last records. In the **Navigation** pane, double-click the **Customers** table to open the datasheet.

2   Click **New (blank) record** in the set of navigation controls located in the lower-left corner of the screen (the icon has a >* symbol). This will take you to a new record.

3   Move to the **Company Name** column and enter the words: Adventure Works 2. The **Record Selector** will change from a star (new record) to a pencil (editing record symbol).

4   Click the next row, or press **Shift+Enter** to save your changes to the record. The **Record Selector** will no longer show the pencil symbol.

5   Click the **Record Selector** to highlight the row, and then press the **Delete** key. Access will prompt you to confirm deleting the record. Click **Yes** to delete the record.

   TIP To edit data, move to the appropriate row/column and begin entering text. You can undo changes by pressing the Esc key or using the Undo icons on the Quick Access Toolbar.

CLEAN UP Close the Customers table and retain the MSOfficeProBlank database for use in later exercises.

Sorting a datasheet

Sorting data in a datasheet means that you can very quickly locate and display a subset of data without the need to use more sophisticated methods such as queries.

In order to sort by multiple columns, you need to use drag and drop to order the sorted columns from left to right (this is the order in which columns are sorted). Individual or selected groups of columns can be sorted either in an ascending or descending sort.

In this exercise, you'll sort data in a datasheet.

SET UP You need the MSOfficeProBlank.accdb database from the previous exercise to complete this exercise. Open the database, if it is not already open.

1 In the **Navigation** pane, double-click the **Customers** table to open the datasheet.

2 Click the **Country** heading (scroll right to locate the column), and drag this column to the left of **Company Name**.

3 Click the **Country** heading, and holding down the **Shift** key, click **Company** (so that both columns are highlighted).

4 On the **Home** tab of the ribbon, in the **Sort & Filter** group, click **Ascending**. This will sort by **Country**. Then, sub-sort those results by **Company Name**.

5 Click the **X** in the upper-right corner to close the datasheet. You will be prompted to save the design changes made to the table. Click **Yes** (the next time you open the table, the **Column** order and **Sorting** will be remembered).

CLEAN UP Retain the MSOfficeProBlank database for use in later exercises.

Filtering a datasheet

Access supports several techniques for filtering the data in a datasheet. If you click a column heading, then you can filter by specific data values. Alternatively, right-click in a field and then filter the data by a variety of matching options on the shortcut menu. This section will demonstrate these two techniques.

In this exercise, you'll filter data.

➡ SET UP You need the MSOfficeProBlank.accdb database from the previous exercise to complete this exercise. Open the database, if it is not already open.

1 In the **Navigation** pane, double-click the **Customers** table to open the datasheet.

2 On the column heading for **Country**, click the right drop-down arrow in the **Column Heading**. Clear the **(Select All)** option, and select the single country **France** and click **OK**.

3 Click in the **Contact Title** column containing **Owner** in the row where the **CustomerID** has the value **9**.

4 Right-click and select **Equals "Owner."** This will then further filter the results.

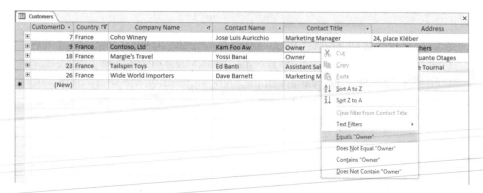

5   Close the **Customers** datasheet and then answer **No** when prompted to save the changes to the design.

> **TIP** You will notice when filtering data that on left side of the navigation buttons is a symbol indicating that the data is filtered. Click this button to unfilter all the results.

CLEAN UP Retain the MSOfficeProBlank database for use in later exercises.

Adjusting the presentation of a datasheet

The height of rows, width of columns, and general look and feel of a datasheet can be defined for each individual datasheet. Columns can also be hidden or frozen (allowing you to scroll to the right while keeping some information in view).

In this exercise, you'll define the look and feel of the data presented in a datasheet.

SET UP You need the MSOfficeProBlank.accdb database from the previous exercise to complete this exercise. Open the database, if it is not already open.

1   In the **Navigation** pane, double-click the **Customers** table to open the datasheet.

2   To adjust the row height, point to the **Record Selector** (the pointer will change to a selection arrow), then move the pointer down to the horizontal grid line (still pointing at the **Record Selector**; the pointer will change its shape to a horizontal bar). Click, hold, and drag down to adjust the row height.

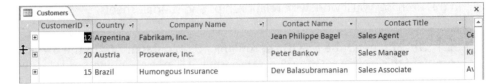

3   On the **Home** tab, in the **Text Formatting** group, at the lower right is a very small di-
    agonal arrow. Click the arrow to display the **Datasheet Formatting** window.

4   Select an **Alternate Background Color** and click **OK**.

Datasheet Formatting

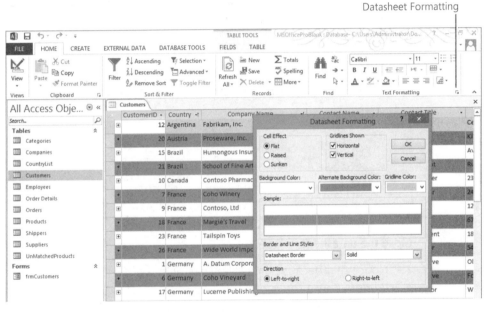

5   Close the datasheet without saving any design changes.

✖ CLEAN UP Retain the MSOfficeProBlank database for use in later exercises.

Working with a subdatasheet

By default, every table has an automatic feature where, by using the relationships, it can expand related data in other tables. This enables you to explore the relationship between data
in your tables with a minimum of effort.

In this exercise, you'll work with relationships and subdatasheets.

→ SET UP You need the MSOfficeProBlank.accdb database from the previous exercise to complete this exercise. Open the database, if it is not already open.

1   In the **Navigation** pane, double-click the **Customers** table to open the datasheet.

2   Click the + symbol next to **Company.** This will expand the relationship, showing the **Orders** for the **Company.**

3   Click the + symbol for any **Order.** This expands the relationship between each **Order** and the **Order Details.**

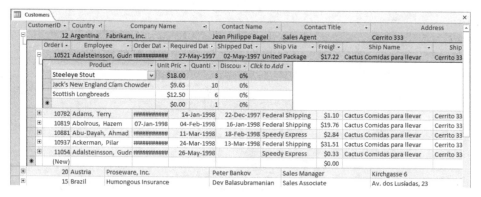

4   Close the datasheet.

TIP Notice that because the Order Date field is not wide enough to show the available information, a series of # symbols are displayed. To avoid this, you can grab the right edge of the column header and drag it to the right, increasing the column width.

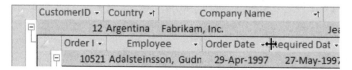

✖ CLEAN UP Retain the MSOfficeProBlank database for use in later exercises.

Copying and pasting from a datasheet

Access provides great support for the Microsoft Office Clipboard operations. Copy and paste can be used to make copies of tables (with or without data) and copies of forms and reports by using the Navigation pane to select objects, highlight the object, and use Ctrl+C and Ctrl+V to make copies of and paste the objects.

This functionality has some special applicability when you are working in the design tools; for example, with a query, you can copy columns on the query grid, or with a form or report, you can copy sets of controls.

It is also possible to copy rows of data between tables (subject to the tables having an identical structure), or within a table.

In this exercise, you'll copy data to the Clipboard to paste into other applications.

SET UP You need the MSOfficeProBlank.accdb database from the previous exercise to complete this exercise. Open the database, if it is not already open.

1   In the **Navigation** pane, double-click the **Customers** table to open the datasheet.

2   Open a copy of Microsoft Excel to view the results of the copy and paste operations.

3   Click the upper-left corner of the datasheet. This will select the entire datasheet, which will darken to indicate everything is selected.

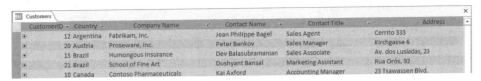

4   Press **Ctrl+C**, switch to a new sheet in Excel, click in an empty cell, and then press **Ctrl+V** to copy the data.

5   Returning to Access, click a column heading to select the column.

6   Press **Ctrl+C**, switch to a new sheet in Excel, click in an empty cell, and then press **Ctrl+V** to copy the column of data.

37

7   Returning to Access, in the datasheet, click in a cell under the column **Company Name**. Move the pointer towards the upper-left corner of the cell as the pointer shape changes to a large + symbol. Click and drag the pointer down and over associated cells.

CustomerID ▾	Country ▾	Company Name ▾	Contact Name ▾	Contact Title ▾
12	Argentina	Fabrikam, Inc.	Jean Philippe Bagel	Sales Agent
20	Austria	Proseware, Inc.	Peter Bankov	Sales Manager
15	Brazil	Humongous Insurance	Dev Balasubramanian	Sales Associate
21	Brazil	School of Fine Art	Dushyant Bansal	Marketing Assistant
10	Canada	Contoso Pharmaceuticals	Kai Axford	Accounting Manager
7	France	Coho Winery	Jose Luis Auricchio	Marketing Manager
9	France	Contoso, Ltd	Kam Foo Aw	Owner
18	France	Margie's Travel	Yossi Banai	Owner
23	France	Tailspin Toys	Ed Banti	Assistant Sales Agent
26	France	Wide World Importers	Dave Barnett	Marketing Manager
1	Germany	A. Datum Corporation	Dimple Arya	Sales Representative

CustomerID ▾	Country ▾	Company Name ▾	Contact Name ▾	Contact Title ▾
12	Argentina	Fabrikam, Inc.	Jean Philippe Bagel	Sales Agent
20	Austria	Proseware, Inc.	Peter Bankov	Sales Manager
15	Brazil	Humongous Insurance	Dev Balasubramanian	Sales Associate
21	Brazil	School of Fine Art	Dushyant Bansal	Marketing Assistant
10	Canada	Contoso Pharmaceuticals	Kai Axford	Accounting Manager
7	France	Coho Winery	Jose Luis Auricchio	Marketing Manager
9	France	Contoso, Ltd	Kam Foo Aw	Owner
18	France	Margie's Travel	Yossi Banai	Owner
23	France	Tailspin Toys	Ed Banti	Assistant Sales Agent
26	France	Wide World Importers	Dave Barnett	Marketing Manager
1	Germany	A. Datum Corporation	Dimple Arya	Sales Representative

8   Press **Ctrl+C**, switch to a new sheet in Excel, click an empty cell, and then press **Ctrl+V** to copy the data.

> **TIP** An interior area of cells can also be selected by clicking into the first cell, then holding down the Shift key and clicking into the bottom right cell.

❌ CLEAN UP Retain the MSOfficeProBlank database for use in later exercises, and close it.

Changing between tab pages and overlapping windows

Surprisingly, deciding if you want to change between tab pages and overlapping windows is probably one of the most important decisions you can make with a database. It is key for determining what you want to get out of Access, and how you envision using the product.

The first question you should ask is, "Do I intend to use Access as a tool for others to use?" If others will use what you construct in Access, then ask: "To what extent do I want to allow others to use the underlying product, and do I want to allow them to make changes to what I've created?"

Often, people who use Access for themselves don't really care much about the fine detail of the interface, because they just make changes according to the tasks they want to accomplish. Basically, their goal is more flexibility and productivity with important tasks.

However, when you build something for other people to use, you must think a great deal about whom they are, what they're trying to achieve, and what you'll allow them to do.

Access supports two basic user interface (UI) presentations, and this is set as an option for the database. You can choose a tabbed interface, which is what we have seen so far in this chapter, where each object opens in a separate tab. The second option is to use overlapping windows. The tabbed interface can be used when designing something for your own use, but it's often more desirable to use overlapping windows if you want to construct something for others to use. One reason is you can start to create windows which pop up on top of other windows.

In this exercise, you'll work with tabbed interfaces and overlapping windows.

SET UP You need the MSOfficeProBlank.accdb database located in the Chapter37 practice file folder to complete this exercise. Open the MSOfficeProBlank.accdb database.

1   From the **File** tab, choose **Options**.

2   Select the **Current Database** option on the left.

3   Change the **Document Window Options** to **Overlapping Windows**.

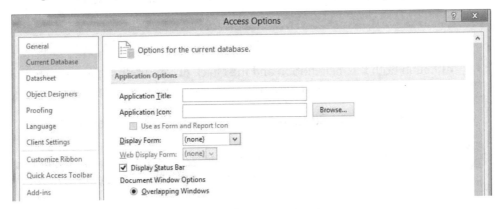

4   Click **OK**, and **OK** again to close the database prompt.

5   Close and re-open your database.

6   In the **Navigation** pane, double-click any table and notice how the table opens in a separate window.

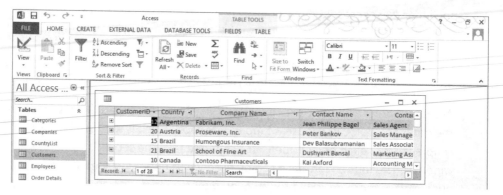

> **TIP** Notice that you can still maximize the window by clicking the second square from the far right in the table window.

❌ CLEAN UP **Retain the MSOfficeProBlank database for use in later exercises.**

Configuring Access options

In addition to the context-sensitive ribbon used to interact with Access, above the ribbon in the upper-left corner is the Quick Access Toolbar. The Quick Access Toolbar can be customized to display icons that help you work more efficiently with Access.

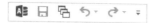

Although both the main ribbon and the Quick Access Toolbar can be customized, it is more common to customize the Quick Access Toolbar by adding features.

In this exercise, you'll add features to customize the Quick Access Toolbar.

➡ SET UP **You need the MSOfficeProBlank.accdb database from earlier in this chapter to complete this exercise. Open the database, if it is not already open.**

> **TIP** Access also supports extensive features for replacing the built-in ribbon with very powerful custom ribbons; this requires the use of more advanced VBA programming.

1   Right-click the **Quick Access Toolbar** and select **Customize Quick Access Toolbar.** Make sure your pointer is positioned to the right of the main Access icon in the very top-left corner. This will then display the **Access Options** screen.

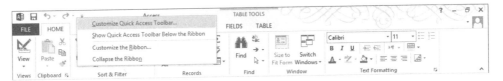

2   Use the **Choose commands from** drop-down list to select **Commands Not in the Ribbon**.

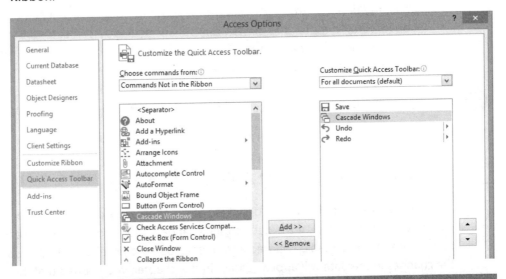

37

IMPORTANT

3   Click **Cascade Windows**, then click **Add**. Click **OK** to save your changes.

4   Open both the **Companies** and **Customers** datasheets by double-clicking each table in the **Navigation** pane.

5   Click the new **Cascade Windows** icon on the **Quick Access Toolbar** to cascade the windows.

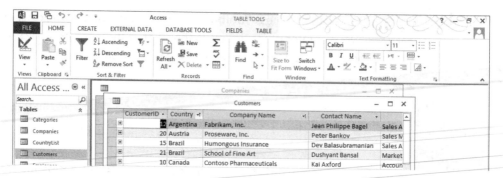

TIP Both for the main ribbon and for the Quick Access Toolbar, there is an option to unpin the ribbon with a right-click. If you chose this option, it will minimize the ribbon (providing more area in the desktop) and then you can extend the ribbon to show choices that float on top of your desktop when you point to the ribbon. This option applies more obviously to the main ribbon than to the Quick Access Toolbar.

❌ CLEAN UP Retain the MSOfficeProBlank database for use in later exercises.

Linking Access to external data

Access has a great set of features for linking to data that is held in other systems. When a database is linked to data, if the data is then changed outside of the database for another system and the linked table is closed and then re-opened or refreshed by pressing Shift+F9, the changes in the data will appear. Earlier in this chapter, you learned that importing data makes a copy of the data. With linking, you dynamically view the data in another system or in an external file.

A link to data in another system will appear in the Navigation pane with a different icon than the standard local Access Table Icon. When you open a linked table in a number of situations, (depending on the type of data you are linked to), you can directly edit the data in the linked table. This changes the data stored in the originating file or system.

In organizations where data is held in IBM mainframes, on a Microsoft SQL Server server, on Excel spreadsheets, on Microsoft SharePoint, and in other sources, Access is a very powerful tool for both importing and linking to data. You can also use Access to produce management reports for data held in other systems.

In this exercise, you'll link to a table of data in another Access database.

SET UP You need the MSOfficeProBlank.accdb database created in earlier exercises and the MSOfficeProData.accdb database located in the Chapter37 practice file folder to complete this exercise. Open the MSOfficeProBlank.accdb database, if it is not already open.

TIP When you link from one Access database to another Access database, if you want to change the design of the table, then you need to do that in the other database. You cannot change the design by using the linked table. Although this may seem like a restriction, this is also a very clever feature, which is not shared by data when linked to anything other than Access. If you change the design of the linked table in the other Access database, then the linked table will automatically know that the design has been changed. Then it will show those changes (normally when you do this linking to data in other systems, you need to refresh the linked table with the Linked Table manger to view the changes).

1   Click the **External Data** tab.

2   Click **Access** in the **Import & Export** group.

3   Locate the **MSOfficeProData.accdb** database file in the **File Name** box.

4   Change the default selection to **Link to the data source** and click **OK**.

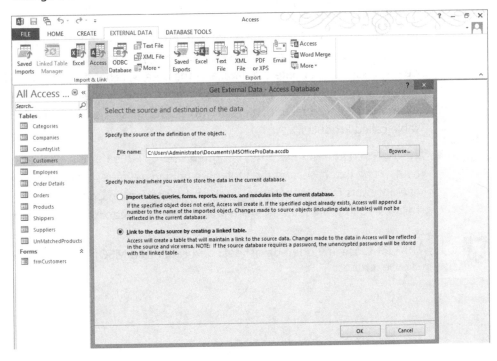

5   Select the **Products** table, and click **OK**.

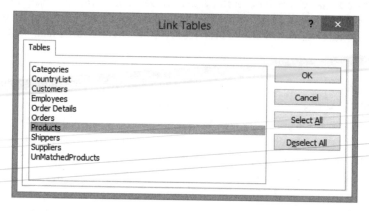

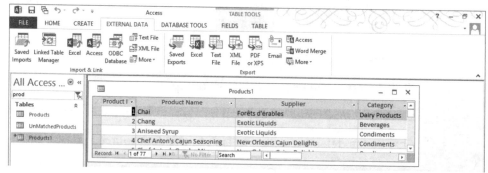

Notice that the icon for the linked table to products is slightly different than the one for a table held inside your Access database. If you open this table, you can edit, delete, insert, and update the data, and the data will change in the linked database. This is a very clever feature that allows Access to update the original data. Also in this example, the linked table name is shown as Products1, because you already have a table called Products.

TIP Access databases are often designed where all the items except the tables are held in one database, and the tables are held in a different database. This method enables users to have their own copy of the application on their local hard drive but to link to and share the data from another Access database on the network.

✖ CLEAN UP Close any open datasheets and retain the MSOfficeProBlank database for use in later exercises.

Linking to data in Excel

Linking Access together with Excel means that you can share data between Office applications and take advantage of the strengths of each product. For example, you could have data in Excel, which you need to combine with data in Access, and rather than repeatedly importing a copy of the data from Excel, linking means that Access can work with a dynamic link to the Excel data. Therefore, when the data in Excel is updated, Access will always have the latest changes in the data.

In this exercise, you'll link data in Excel.

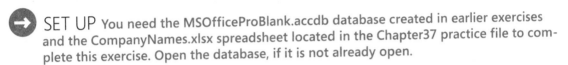 SET UP You need the MSOfficeProBlank.accdb database created in earlier exercises and the CompanyNames.xlsx spreadsheet located in the Chapter37 practice file to complete this exercise. Open the database, if it is not already open.

1 Click the **External Data** tab.

2 Click **Excel** in the **Import & Export** group.

3 Locate the **CompanyNames.xlsx** file in the **File Name** dialog box.

4 Change the default selection to **Link to the data source** and click **OK**.

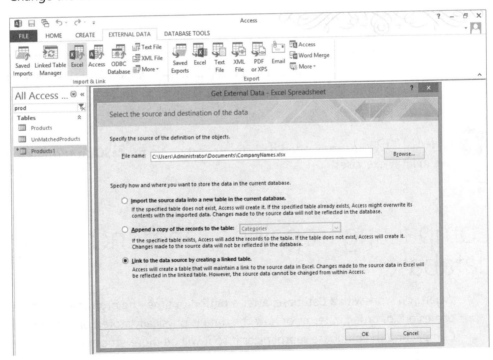

This will then launch the Link Spreadsheet Wizard.

5   Click **First row contains column headers**. Then click **Next**.

6   Because the sample database has already imported this table, change the default linked **Table Name** to CompaniesLinked. Click **Finish**.

7   Click **OK**. The table has now been linked.

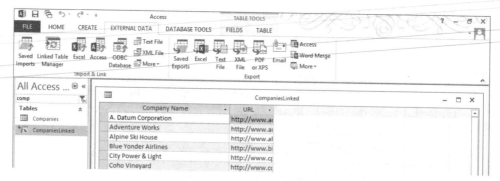

A very subtle difference between this and a linked Access table in which you can change the data, is that with a linked Excel table, you cannot change the data. So, what you link to can determine the available features when you are working with the linked data.

TIP After you link to tables from other sources, you may need to refresh the links to allow for changes in the design of tables in the other systems (for example, when using ODBC) or to allow for file paths that have changed. The Link Table Manager in the External Data Tab – Import & Link Group can guide you through the process of changing the links.

❌ CLEAN UP Close any open datasheets and retain the MSOfficeProBlank database for use in later exercises.

Compacting, repairing, and encrypting a database

When you work with a database, after a period of time, the organization of the data becomes out of order, in terms of how the data is physically stored on the storage medium. Compacting the database reorganizes it so it will be more efficient to work with the data in the database.

If the database is shared by more than one user, then you need to ensure that no one else is using the database before you compact it. How often you need to compact a database depends on how often the database is used, and how many changes are made to the data. As an example, an individual's Accounts database might only get compacted maybe once a year, but at the other extreme, a shared database with forty users could need compacting every couple of days.

With the idea of compacting and repairing a database, the repair function fixes something that has gone wrong with the structure of the files. Because Access is a shared file database, and certain parts of the database (notably indexes) get copied into a local computer's memory, and users can switch off their computers, inconsistencies in the database indexing can occur. The repair operation fixes these inconsistencies. Again, deciding when to perform a repair operation depends upon how much data is changed and how many shared users are working in the database.

In this exercise, you'll perform a repair operation in a database.

SET UP You need the MSOfficeProBlank.accdb database created in earlier exercises to complete this exercise. Open the database, if it is not already open.

IMPORTANT

1   Click **File**, **Info**, and then **Compact & Repair Database**. The database will then be compacted, repaired, and re-opened.

37

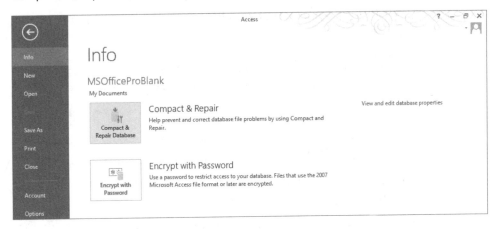

TIP If you have a database that contains a large amount of data, and/or is used by a number of users on a regular basis, and you need to compact and repair the database every couple of days, then this is a good indication that you should consider converting the data storage to a SQL Server solution. You can still keep Access as a front-end, but moving the data to a SQL Server solution will then require less maintenance.

 CLEAN UP Retain the MSOfficeProBlank database for use in later exercises.

Encrypting with a password

If you need to protect your database, then Access offers an option that will both encrypt the data and secure the database with a password. The level of security you will obtain here is excellent, but it would not necessarily protect your data against a determined hacker. You should plan for using additional techniques to secure the data as appropriate to your security needs. This level of security will certainly prevent casual file browsers from opening or deciphering your data.

Database passwords and encryption are an excellent offering to provide an additional level of protection for certain files to augment network security.

In this exercise, you'll encrypt a database with a password.

 **SET UP** You need the MSOfficeProBlank.accdb database created in earlier exercises to complete this exercise. Open the database, if it is not already open.

1   Click **File**, **Info**, then **Encrypt with Password**. The following warning will then most likely appear:

In order to apply or remove a password or encryption from a database, you need to open the database using a very specific technique.

2   Click **OK** to close the message. Use the **Open** page to browse to or otherwise locate your database.

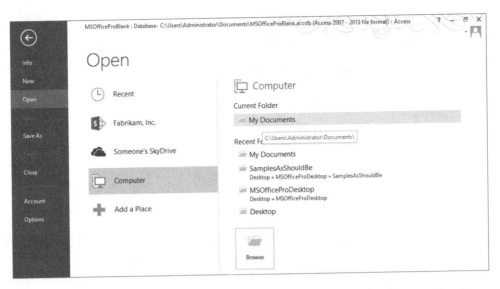

3   When prompted to select your database, ensure that you use the **Open** option to **Open Exclusive**.

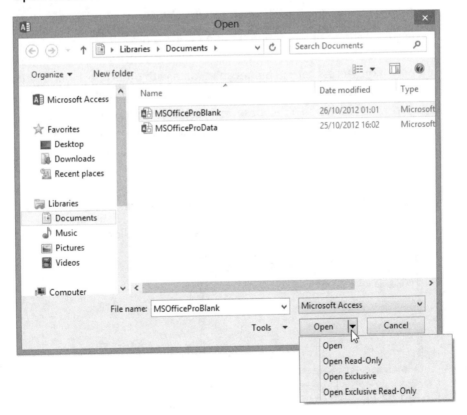

4 Click **File**, **Info**, then **Encrypt with Password**. You will then be able to create a password and encrypt your database. Enter and verify your password. Click **OK**.

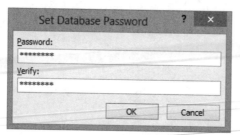

5 You will also receive the following warning when you choose this option. Click **OK**.

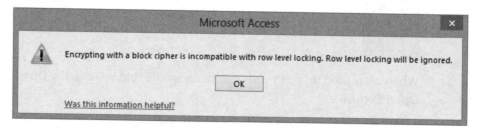

TIP This warning means that although Access is designed to allow multiple users to share data, because you have chosen to further constrain the sharing of data with encryption, Access can no longer share data with other users with the normal flexibility of locking individual rows, because it will lock pages of data. This is not normally a serious limitation in a database with just a few users. However, for a database that is shared with a larger number of users, you would probably not want to impose encryption. Encryption reduces performance and offers less flexibility in the method for locking data.

6 Return to the **Info** page, and click **Decrypt Database**.

7 Enter your password to decrypt the database, then click **OK**.

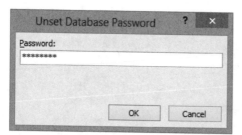

✖ CLEAN UP Close the MSOfficeProBlank database and save the file.

Key points

- Access can create two distinct types of databases. The first is a desktop database. You can either create a blank desktop database or use one of a number of template desktop databases. The second type of database is a Web App, which is discussed in Chapter 40, "Creating and sharing a Web App."

- Data can be imported from a wide variety of Office files and other databases. Data can be exported from both tables and queries (discussed in the next chapter).

- Navigating the user interface effectively involves understanding how to use both the Navigation pane and ribbon. The Quick Access Toolbar provides a useful tool for customizing how you work with Access.

- There are a large number of configurable settings in a database, and these are set by using the Backstage view database options.

- Access allows you to link to data held in other database systems or files. When Link Tables is used, the data is held outside of Access and will appear to change as data is modified in the source application. This makes Access a fantastic tool for gathering and reporting on data held in other systems.

37

Chapter at a glance

Create

Create tables for your data,
page 948

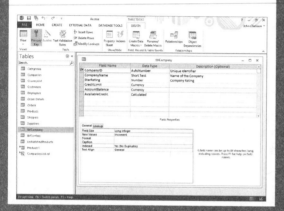

Link

Link tables together with relationships,
page 963

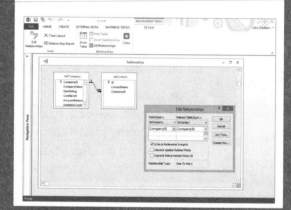

Create

Create a select query,
page 971

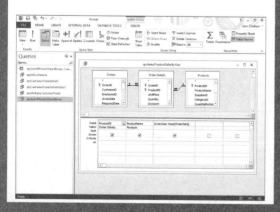

Add

Add calculations and parameters to queries,
page 983

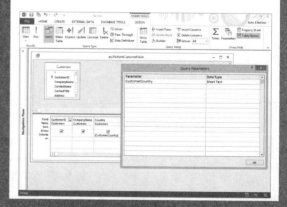

Creating basic tables and queries

38

IN THIS CHAPTER, YOU WILL LEARN HOW TO

- Create tables for your data.

- Add validation and calculated fields to your tables.

- Link tables together with relationships.

- Create a select query.

- Work with query criteria.

- Add parameters to queries.

- Work with totals and crosstab queries.

Inside every Microsoft Access database is a design or layout of data. The data is normally split into more than one table, and the design combines the data in various tables by using relationships. If you are used to only working with spreadsheets, then think of this as spreadsheets that are very tightly linked together.

Databases need to evolve quickly to meet both a changing business environment and your own changing skill level as you learn more about different design techniques when creating your databases. Access is a perfect tool for trying out your ideas and quickly changing your design. You will, however, find that as your system expands it will become a more complex task when you want to make fundamental changes. That's why starting from a well-informed viewpoint will help you later when you're developing your design.

As your design splits your data into a set of tables, it makes the database more flexible to work with, but you need a method to bring the data back together. Select queries allow you to create a new datasheet that brings data together from several tables. These queries can then be used to construct other queries, forms, and reports.

In this chapter, you will learn how to create tables to hold your data, link the tables together by using relationships, and use queries to display data from the tables.

PRACTICE FILES To complete the exercises in this chapter, you need either the MSOfficeProBlank.accdb practice file that was created in Chapter 37 or the practice file contained in the Chapter38 practice file folder. For more information, see "Download the practice files" in this book's introduction.

Creating tables for your data

Access provides three distinct approaches to creating tables that hold the data in your database.

- You can use one of the predefined templates to start with a solution that contains tables, forms, reports, and other components that you may need.

- If you already have data in a spreadsheet or other data source, you can import the data into new tables.

- If you are starting from scratch and you cannot find a suitable template to start from, you can create a new set of tables.

In practice, you may want to utilize a combination of these.

If you are creating a table for the first time or importing data to create a table, and you allow Access to create a primary key, the new key field will be called *ID*. You may wonder why it is always called *ID* and why you need a primary key.

Without getting into a deep discussion of the theory behind relational databases, in brief, each table needs a way of uniquely distinguishing each record in the table from other records in the table. One of the simplest ways to do this is to allocate a unique number for each row of data in the table; any field or combination of fields can be designated as the primary key, as long as the data or combination of data values are unique for each row in the table.

It is recommended that you always have a primary key (PK) on a table, in particular, when a database will be shared with more than one user. The database needs to keep track of when data is changed, and a PK is an efficient way to do this.

If the key is automatically added by the database, it is named *ID*, because Microsoft has made this choice to avoid any difficulties in naming a key that could be language specific. If you had a table called *Contacts*, then renaming the automatically added *ID* field to have a specific meaning such as *ContactID* would be a sensible choice to help distinguish the *ID* from other primary keys also called *ID* in the database.

A relational database relates data between tables. To do this, you need a unique reference to a row in another table, which is exactly what a PK provides. When you have this linking field to a PK in a different table, it is called a Foreign Key (FK). Making the names of the PK and all FKs the same is a good decision. It means that when you link tables together, it is easy to identify which fields to join together (you will join an FK to a PK).

If you allowed all tables to have a primary key called *ID*, and all foreign keys to have a similar name, you would have a problem when a table had one or more foreign keys. You would then need to rename the foreign keys, because field names in a table must be unique. If, as described previously, you had renamed the primary key *ID* in a table called *Contacts* to *ContactID*, then when it is used in a related table as a foreign key, it could also be named *ContactID*. By using this naming convention, the problem of conflicting names for the foreign keys in a table is avoided.

TIP Later, if you choose to look at converting your desktop data to a Web App, then it is worth noting that a Web App only supports a numeric ID for primary keys on tables.

In this exercise, you'll create a table in Design view.

➡ SET UP You need the MSOfficeProBlank.accdb database created in the previous chapter, or the practice file of the same name located in the Chapter38 practice file folder, to complete this exercise. Open the database, if it is not already open.

1   Click the **Create** tab, and then click **Table Design** in the **Tables** group. This will open a blank table called **Table1** in **Design** view.

2   In the first row, enter CompanyID for the **Field Name**, select **AutoNumber** for the **Data Type**, and enter the optional **Description** property as Unique Identifier.

3　In the second row, enter CompanyName for the **Field Name**, select **Short Text** for the **Data Type**, and enter the optional **Description** property as Name of the company.

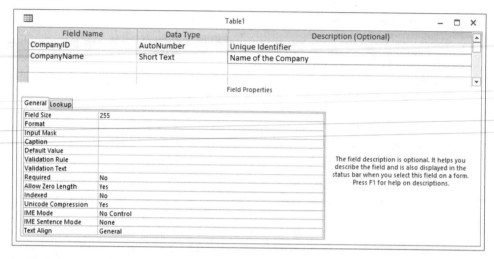

In Design view, when you click in each field name in the list, you will notice that the Field Properties tabs (General and Lookup) will change depending on the data type for the selected row. All fields have a Caption property, which can be used to display an alternative Caption or title for the Field (this is the fourth item in the Field Properties on the tab named General).

4　Click the **Caption** property on the **General** tab for the **CompanyName** field, and enter the text Company Name.

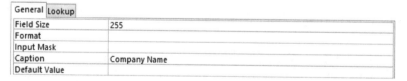

TIP When naming objects such as a field, it is common to name the field with no spaces in the name and then re-title the Caption with spaces. Also, avoid using special characters such as % in a field name (use the word *percentage* rather than the symbol). Avoiding spaces and special characters can simplify later work when referring to objects in SQL, forms, and reports.

5   Click the **CompanyID** field, and then click the **Primary Key** button. This action will display a small key icon on the row selector for the field.

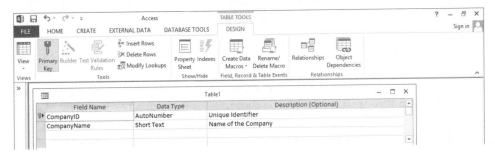

6   Click **Save** on the **Quick Access Toolbar** (top left on the screen).

7   Enter the name **tblCompany** when saving your table, and then click **OK**.

8   Close the **Design** view for this new table.

9   From the **Navigation** pane, double-click your new **tblCompany** table to open the datasheet and enter sample data (add at least two rows).

Notice that the field called CompanyName is displayed with the caption *Company Name*, and the Description field property is displayed in the lower-left corner of the screen in the status bar.

❌ CLEAN UP Close the tblCompany datasheet. Retain the MSOfficeProBlank database for use in later exercises.

38

Creating a table in Datasheet view

You will now create a second table using an alternative technique; this method allows you to add fields while also viewing data in the table.

In this exercise, you'll create a table in Datasheet view.

 SET UP You need the MSOfficeProBlank.accdb database from the previous exercise to complete this exercise. Open the database, if it is not already open.

1   Click the **Create** tab, and then click **Table** in the **Tables** group. This will open a blank table called **Table1** in **Datasheet** view.

2   Click the **Click to Add** drop-down list and select **Short Text**.

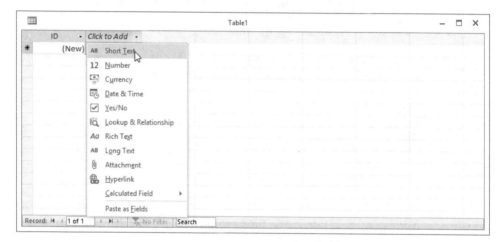

3   Enter text over the default field name **Field1**, which will be highlighted with the name for your **ContactName** field.

4   Click in the blank row in the **ContactName** field. This will save your change to the field name. Then enter the contact name **Kim Abercrombie**.

5   Click the **Name & Caption** icon in the **Properties** group.

6   Change the **Caption** for the field to **Contact Name**. Then Click **OK**.

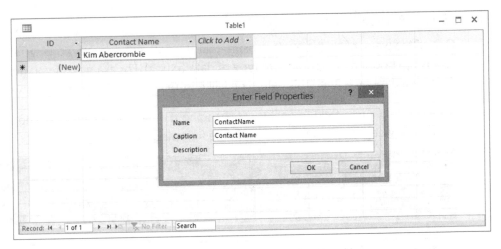

7   Click **Save** on the **Quick Access Toolbar**. This will display a **Save As** window.

8   Enter the table name **tblContact**, and click **OK** to save the table.

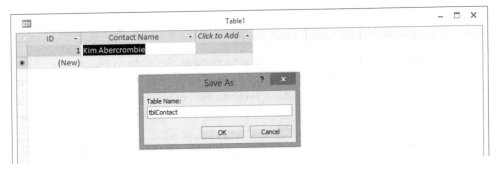

TIP The two techniques for changing the design of a table in Design view or in Data-sheet view are complementary, and you can switch between both when working on your existing tables. When a table is open, click the Table Tools and select the Fields tab, which will display the design options for Datasheet view. Alternatively, right-click a table in the Navigation pane and choose Design view.

❌ CLEAN UP Close the tblContact table. Retain the MSOfficeProBlank database for use in later exercises.

Choosing a field data type

One of the ways in which you can ensure that the data entered into your system is correct is by choosing an appropriate type of data to hold. For example, if you hold dates in a DateTime data type, then this data type will ensure that you can only hold a valid date/time.

When adding a new field to a table, or changing the data type for an existing field, you can choose between the data types listed in the following table.

IMPORTANT

Data type	Description
Short Text	Can hold up to 255 characters of text. This was called Text in earlier versions of Access.
Long Text	Large amounts of text. This was called a Memo field in earlier versions of Access. These fields can also be used on forms and reports to support Rich Text Formatting.
Number	Whole number that has no decimal places (Long Integer), floating-point number (Double), and fixed-point number (for example, decimal (28,6), 6 decimal places).
	Also supported are Byte and Integer for smaller whole numbers, Single for less precise floating point numbers, and for backwards compatibility, a Replication ID (older data type).
Date/Time	Date and time.
Currency	Money.
Autonumber	Automatic number, default long integer, which is added as you start entering text in a new record.
Yes/No	True, False (default is False).
OLE Object	Older field type for storing an image or document.
Hyperlink	Stores hyperlinks to local or Internet documents and data.
Attachment	Can hold multiple copies of other documents such as spreadsheets and PDF files for each record.
Calculated	A calculation combining fields together. For example, adding or multiplying values from other fields.
Lookup	Creates a foreign key lookup to data in another table.

TIP To simplify options when choosing a number, consider using a long integer for whole numbers and a double for numbers with decimal places. For images and documents, consider using an Attachment rather than the older OLE Object data type.

Adding validation and calculated fields to your tables

A field validation rule is a method of ensuring that when data is recorded that it meets certain criteria. For example, a person's age is between an upper and lower limit, or an event priority is in a set of choices such as low, medium or high priority. Each field is allowed to have a single validation rule, which will check that the data entered meets the specified criteria before saving any changes to the record.

For example, when entering a customer rating from 1 to 4, you could define a validation rule as the value being *between 1 and 4.*

In this exercise, you'll add validation to a field.

 SET UP You need the MSOfficeProBlank.accdb database from the previous exercise to complete this exercise. Open the database, if it is not already open.

1   From the **Navigation** pane, right-click **tblCompany** and select **Design** view.

2   Add a new field called StarRating with the **Number** data type.

	Field Name	Data Type	Description (Optional)
⑧	CompanyID	AutoNumber	Unique Identifier
	CompanyName	Short Text	Name of the Company
	StarRating	Number	Company Rating

3   In the field properties, check that there is no default value for the new field.

4   In the **Validation Rule** property, enter Between 1 and 4.

5   In the **Validation Text** property, enter the words Enter a Star Rating from 1 to 4.

General	Lookup
Field Size	Long Integer
Format	
Decimal Places	Auto
Input Mask	
Caption	
Default Value	
Validation Rule	Between 1 And 4
Validation Text	Enter a Star Rating from 1 to 4
Required	No
Indexed	No
Text Align	General

38

6   Click **Save** to save your design. When prompted to test existing data for the new validation rule, click **No**. Note that you will only be prompted to do this if the table contains data.

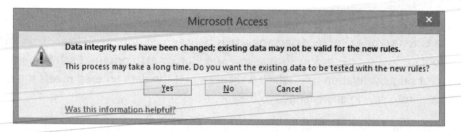

TIP Other useful field properties to set in connection with validation are to provide a default value for a field, setting the Required field property to ensure that a value is entered, and also to use the Input Mask property to provide a template mask when entering data such as a telephone number.

7   Click the **View** icon on the **Home** tab to display the table in **Datasheet** view.

8   Enter a value of 9 for the **Star Rating** field on any record and click to move the cursor to a new row. This will then display a warning that the data value must be between 1 and 4. Click **OK** to close the warning.

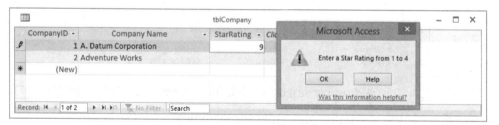

9   Change the value to 2, and click to move the cursor to a new row. The value for the star rating should now be accepted.

❌ CLEAN UP Close the tblCompany datasheet. Retain the MSOfficeProBlank database for use in later exercises.

Adding a table validation rule

Field validation rules are not permitted to refer to values in other fields. You are allowed one Table Validation rule per table, and this rule can compare the values between fields. For example, you could check that a field named [CreditBalance] was less than or equal to [CreditLimit].

In this exercise, you'll use the Expression Builder to assist when creating a Table Validation rule.

 SET UP You need the MSOfficeProBlank.accdb database from the previous exercise to complete this exercise. Open the database, if it is not already open.

1 From the **Navigation** pane, right-click **tblCompany** and select **Design** view.

2 On the **Design** tab, in the **Show/Hide** group, click the **Property Sheet** icon. This will display the table properties.

3 Add a new field called CreditLimit with the data type **Currency**.

4 Add a new field called AccountBalance with the data type **Currency**.

5 Click **Save** to save the design of the table.

IMPORTANT

6 On the **Design** tab, in the **Show/Hide** group, click **Property Sheet** (if the property sheet is not already displayed).

7 On the right, in the table properties area, click in the **Validation Rule** box, then click the ellipse **...** build button. This will then display the **Expression Builder**.

8   Use the list of fields (a field is selected by double-clicking the name in **Expression Categories**) combined with entering text to create the expression [AccountBalance] <= [CreditLimit].

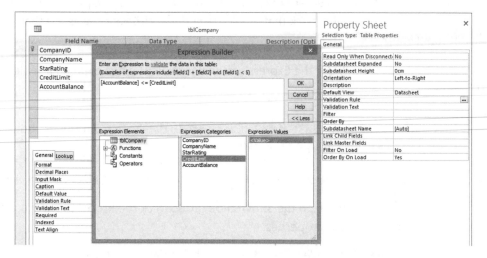

9   Click **OK** to close the **Expression Builder**, and then click **Save** to save the design of your table.

10   If you already have data in the table, then you will be prompted to test the validation rule. Answer **No** to the prompt.

11   Click the **View** icon on the **Home** tab to display the datasheet for the table.

12   Enter the numeral 100 for the **CreditLimit** field and 200 for the **AccountBalance** field in any of the rows you have added to the table. Then click in a blank row. The validation rule will prevent you from saving the data.

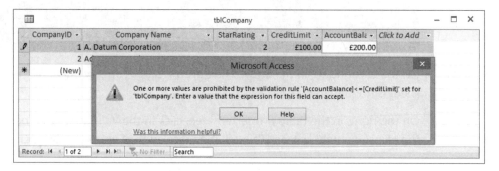

13 Click **OK** to close the warning. Change the **Account Balance** to 50, and then click in a blank row. The validation rule will then accept your change.

> **TIP** If you do not enter a value for the CreditLimit, but only enter a value for the AccountBalance, this is allowed. The reason for this is that the CreditLimit then has no value (or Null Value). This could be prevented by making both fields required (so they must have values) and ensuring that for any existing records that values are provided for the fields. Also notice that when you add a new field with a default, the default only applies when entering new records and does not change any empty values in existing records.

❌ CLEAN UP Close the tblCompany datasheet. Retain the MSOfficeProBlank database for use in later exercises.

Adding a calculated field

If you have a calculation that you'll use in many parts of an application, rather than adding this to each query, report, or form, you can build the calculation into the structure of the table by adding a calculated field to the table design. An example of a suitable calculation would be comparing an account balance that was maintained for a customer with a credit limit to display available credit. Another example could be calculating the volume of a container from fields that recorded the length, height, and width.

In this exercise, you'll add a calculated field to a table.

➡ SET UP You need the MSOfficeProBlank.accdb database from the previous exercise to complete this exercise. Open the database, if it is not already open.

1 From the **Navigation** pane, right-click **tblCompany** and select **Design** view.

2 Add a new field called AvailableCredit with a data type of **Calculated**.

3 In the **Expression Builder**, use the list of fields (a field is selected by double-clicking the name) combined with entering text to create the expression [CreditLimit] - [AccountBalance].

38

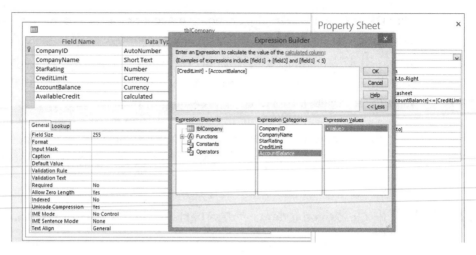

4　　Click **OK** to close the **Expression Builder**.

5　　In the **AvailableCredit** field's **Format** property, select **Currency**.

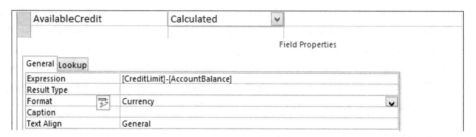

6　　Save the design of your table.

7　　Click the **View** icon on the **Home** tab to display the table in **Datasheet** view.

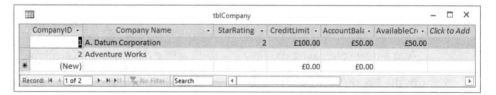

As you make changes in the CreditLimit or AccountBalance fields and then move to another field, the AvailableCredit calculation will be updated to reflect your changes.

TIP Use the build button (the ellipsis, ...) on the calculated field's expression to view an existing calculation in the Expression Builder and browse the available built-in functions that you can use. You cannot use functions such as Now or Date, because these functions can have changing values. So although the calculated field feature is flexible, for some calculations you will need to use queries that do not have the same restrictions on the use of certain functions.

✖ CLEAN UP Close the tblCompany datasheet. Retain the MSOfficeProBlank database for use in later exercises.

Indexing a table

If you have tables with only a few hundred or a thousand records, then you could skip this topic. But, if you have tables with tens of thousands of rows, then indexing becomes more important. It's only when you have larger amounts of data that it becomes more efficient for the database to search by using an index (on small tables any indexes may be ignored), and because the database has to maintain indexes, there is a cost in having them, so you don't want to build indexes that may not be used.

It's a good idea when choosing a field to index that you select a field that is commonly searched and contains lots of different values (the index is selective). Fields that have only a few values will not spilt the data into enough groups to make having the index worthwhile. As a rough guide, having maybe five to ten indexes on a large table would be acceptable. Over-indexing will create additional overhead in the database. Normally, you add an index when a search or report is slow, and then check to verify that it makes the operation faster.

To understand how an index works, consider if you were to look for a book in a bookshop. You would appreciate the ordering of books into topic sections, such as education, cooking, science, and so forth, since this speeds up locating a book. The topic sections act like an index to quickly locate a book. If you knew the author but not the topic, then you could search through a list (index) of authors, which would make it easier for you to find the location of the book.

38

Indexes make the retrieval of data faster, yet at a slight cost of maintenance. When data gets changed, the index needs to be updated. When you have relationships, the FK (foreign key) is automatically indexed to improve performance

In this exercise, you'll index a field in a table.

 SET UP You need the MSOfficeProBlank.accdb database from the previous exercise to complete this exercise. Open the database, if it is not already open.

1   From the **Navigation** pane, right-click **tblCompany** and select **Design** view.

2   In the **CompanyName** field, click the drop-down list on the **Indexed** property.

3   Select **Yes (No Duplicates)**.

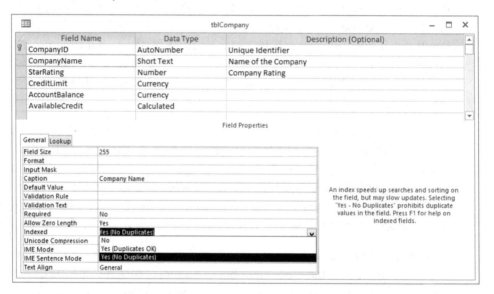

4   Click **Save** to save the changes to your table.

5   Click the **View** icon on the **Home** tab.

6   In a new blank row, enter a duplicate value for the Company Name field, and then click in a blank row to try and save the change. The index will prevent the duplicate value from being saved.

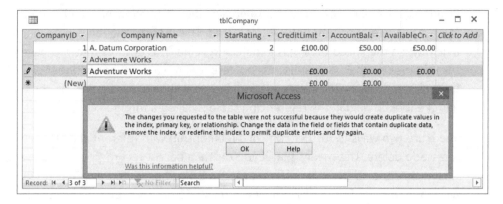

7   Click **OK** to close the warning, and then press the **Esc** key to undo the change to the record you were adding.

> **TIP** The database index offers two options: one that allows duplicated values and the other to prevent duplicate values. If you create an index that allows duplicate values, then you're indexing to only improve the speed of searching and retrieving data. However, if you index to prevent duplicate values, then in addition to improving speed, you're adding a rule to ensure that values in the index are unique.

✖ CLEAN UP Close the tblCompany datasheet. Retain the MSOfficeProBlank database for use in later exercises.

Linking tables together with relationships

At the heart of a database is the idea of a relationship—relationships ensure that your data is consistent. For example, you can't have an order for a product that no longer exists in the database. Access has a fantastic feature called the Lookup Wizard, which will assist you in creating these relationships between tables. The database also has a graphical interface that can be used when you need to establish relationships without adding additional fields.

38

Relationships enable you to support two activities. A relationship can be a rule, and in this form, it has referential integrity (RI) enforced. This means that you can only enter a value in a field when the linked table has a matching value. This ensures that you have integrity in the database so that you cannot have references to values that no longer exist. The data will be consistent. The field that you are looking up will be a primary key on the related table, and the lookup field in the referencing table is called a foreign key.

There are two ways to further control a relationship with referential integrity. The first is a cascade delete. This means that if you delete a parent record (for example, a customer), then a child record (for example, an order) will also be deleted. The second option is to have a cascade update. This works mainly when you do not use numerical values for primary keys on a table. For example, if you had a Customer table with a lookup to a Country table, and you tried to change the name of a country that was in use, referential integrity would prevent this. However, if you had enabled a cascade update, it would allow this and cascade the change back to all the related records.

The second use of relationships is to provide guidance for when you want to join tables in queries. This feature is not often used on its own in Access, because you can always override the relationship settings in a query. It gets a little more complex here, because the use of specifying a join in a relationship can be independent of defining a relationship.

The join, by default, shows only those matched records between both tables, but it can be set to include all parent records, including those without child records, or any child records with unmatched parent records (a less popular choice). Consider adding a Customer table and related Country table to a query in order to display additional country information for the customer (queries are discussed later in this chapter). The default join would not show any customers who did not have a value for the joining Country field. You could have defined the default join in the relationship to always include all customers, so that when building queries, all customer records are always shown by default.

To recap, if you define a relationship between two tables with or without enforcing RI, and you change the default join property, then when you add those tables to the query grid, they will inherit the settings in the join that you defined for that relationship.

In this exercise, you'll use the Lookup Wizard to create a relationship between two tables. This is the easiest method for creating relationships in new tables, when you do not already have the foreign key fields that will be used to support the relationship.

SET UP You need the MSOfficeProBlank.accdb database from the previous exercise to complete this exercise. Open the database, if it is not already open. Ensure that you do not have tblCompany open in Design view before proceeding.

1   From the **Navigation** pane, right-click **tblContact** and select **Design** view.

2   On a new line, enter the words CompanyID in the **Field Name**, and in the **Data Type,** select **Lookup Wizard**. This will start the **Lookup Wizard**.

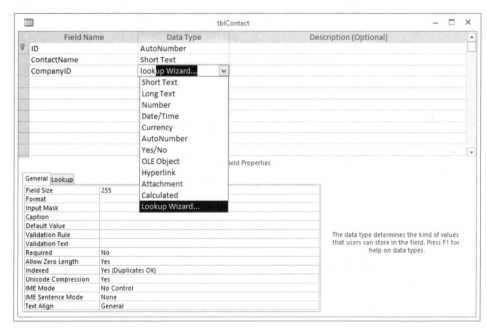

3   Leave the default choice set to **I want the lookup field to get the values from an-other table or query** and click **Next**.

4   Click to highlight **Table: tblCompany** in the list of tables and queries, and click **Next**.

5   Select the two fields **CompanyID** and **CompanyName** by using the arrow buttons, and click **Next**.

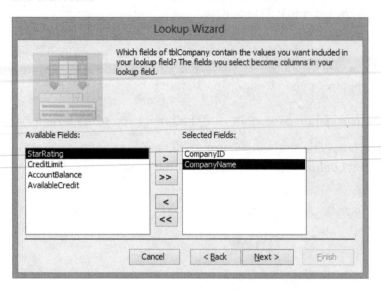

6   In the fields to sort, select **CompanyName** and click **Next**.

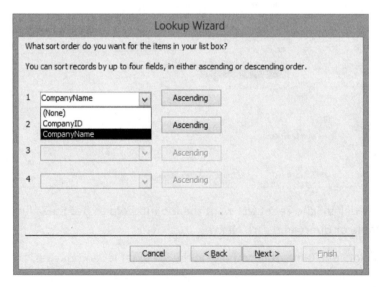

7   On the next screen, leave the check box selected to hide the key column (this is the default) and click **Next**.

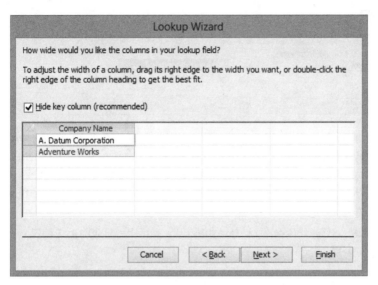

8   On the final screen, leave the default label name **CompanyID**, and then select the **Enable Data Integrity** check box and ensure that **Restrict Delete** is selected. Click **Finish**. When prompted, click **Yes** to save the table.

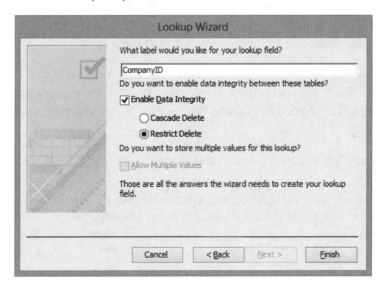

38

9   Click the **View** button on the far left and select **Datasheet** view. You can now use the drop-down list to assign a company to a contact.

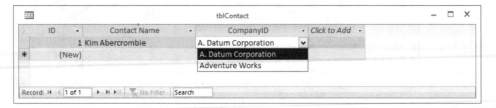

TIP On the screen where you selected the check box to enable data integrity, there was a Cascade Delete option. If you had selected that option, then when you deleted a company, all the child contact records would also be deleted. In the relationship diagram discussed next, you could change your relationship to have this feature.

✖ CLEAN UP Close the tblContact datasheet. Retain the MSOfficeProBlank database for use in later exercises.

Creating a manual relationship

When viewing relationships, it's important to understand two distinct features of the design interface. First, it's a picture and a very powerful tool for showing different parts of your design. For example, you can delete a table from the diagram, and this will not actually delete the table from your database. It simply removes it from the picture.

It is also a tool for maintaining relationships. When you click a relationship and press the Delete key, it will delete the relationship. After having deleted the relationship, if you then say No to saving any changes when closing the diagram, then the relationship would still have been deleted.

In this exercise, you'll delete a relationship and then manually re-create the relationship.

➡ SET UP You need the MSOfficeProBlank.accdb database from the previous exercise to complete this exercise. Open the database, if it is not already open.

1   Close any open tables.

2   Click the **DatabaseTools** tab, and then click **Relationships** in the **Relationships** group.

3   Click **All Relationships** in the **Relationships** group (this will add the new relationship to the diagram between the **tblCompany** and **tblContact** table).

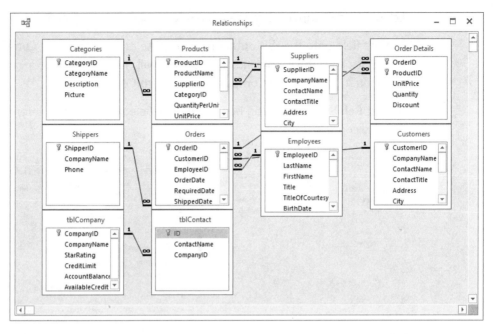

4   Click the relationship line between the two tables: **tblContact** and **tblCompany**. The line will become slightly thicker to indicate the relationship is selected.

5   Press the **Delete** key and click **Yes** to delete the relationship.

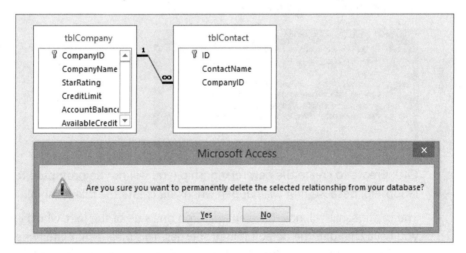

Having deleted the relationship, you will now manually create the same relationship. Note that when you deleted the relationship, it did *not* delete the lookup; this is independent of the relationship.

6   Click the field **CompanyID** in the table **tblCompany** to highlight the field.

7   Drag the field onto the **tblContact** table as close as you can to the **CompanyID** field at the bottom of the list of fields. The pointer will change from a stop sign to a plus sign when it points to the **CompanyID** field in **tblContact**.

8   The **Edit Relationships** dialog box will appear. Select the **Enforce Referential Integrity** check box.

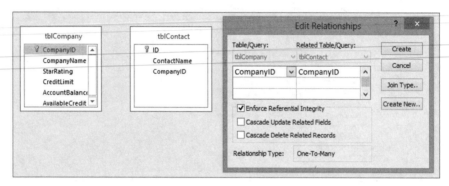

9   Click the **Join Type** button.

10 In the **Join Properties** dialog box, select the **Include ALL Records from 'tblCompany' and only those records from 'tblContact' where the joined fields are equal** option. Click **OK** to close the **Join Properties** dialog box.

11 Click **Create** to create the new relationship (you will not be prompted to save the relationship, because that will happen when you create the relationship).

The relationship will now have an arrow on one side of the join, which indicates that you have changed the default join properties. This means that later when you create queries and add these tables, by default, the query join property will be set to match what is defined in the relationship view.

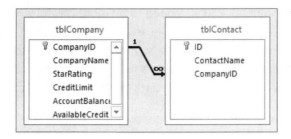

12 Click **Close** to close the diagram. Click **OK** to save changes to the diagram.

Note that when you were prompted to save changes to the diagram that you were just saving the picture and not the relationship. That was saved earlier when you created the relationship.

TIP On very complex diagrams, you can delete all the tables from the diagram and then add just one table of interest to the diagram (by using the Show Table option). Then if you click Direct Relationships, it will add to the diagram only those tables that are directly related to the originally selected table. This makes the tool very useful for navigating through a complex design and focuses on one particular table.

✖ CLEAN UP Retain the MSOfficeProBlank database for use in later exercises.

Creating a select query

A select query allows you to bring together data from a number of tables and present the data in a single view. Another feature of a query is that you can layer one query on top of another. This means that when you are presented with the most challenging problems, you can break each problem into a set of simpler problems on individual queries, which can then be combined. Breaking down a problem into a set of simpler steps also means that you can base several problems on a common set of initial steps, so you can reuse parts of your design.

When adding a table or query to another query, you can select all fields from a table/query by using a * for selection (as we will describe in this exercise). This has the advantage that when a new field is added to an underlying table, it will automatically be included in the query. The only disadvantage of this technique is that you will not get the best performance if you ask to display all the fields, but then use only some of the available fields, as opposed to just selecting the fields that you need. You also need to be more careful when applying filtering against a field, because you need to make an additional selection of the fields against which you will be applying the filter criteria, also making sure not to select the box to show those fields (which is the default when adding a field). Otherwise, it gets confusing when you later create forms or reports based on the data that contains duplicate fields.

In this exercise, you'll create a query that includes all fields from a table.

 SET UP You need the MSOfficeProBlank.accdb database from the previous exercise to complete this exercise. Open the database, if it is not already open.

1   Click the **Create** tab, and then click **Query Design** in the **Queries** group.

2   In the **Show Table** dialog box, click to highlight the **Customers** table, and click **Add**.

3   Click **Close** to close the **Show Table** dialog box.

   TIP You can double-click the table name to add it to the diagram, rather than clicking the Add button.

4   Either double-click the * (asterisk) above the list of field names or drag the * onto the query grid. This adds **Customers.*** to the query grid.

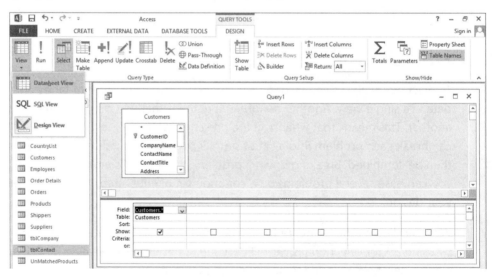

5　On the **Design** tab, click **Datasheet View** in the **View** drop-down list to display your results.

6　After viewing the results, click **Design View** on the **View** list to return to the query grid.

7　Click **Save** to save your query with the name qry**AllCustomers**.

8　Click **OK**.

TIP You can quickly switch a query between the three views: to view data in Datasheet, view or the Design view, or to view the SQL code (SQL is the underlying language in which queries are stored). There are also three buttons on the lower-right of the design area to switch between the Datasheet, SQL, and Design views.

 **CLEAN UP** Retain the MSOfficeProBlank database for use in later exercises.

Creating a query by selecting specific fields

When you create a query by selecting only the fields of interest, this has the advantage of improving the speed of the query and makes it easier to maintain the information being displayed without including a number of fields that are not of interest. Access supports several techniques for adding individual fields and groups of fields to a query.

In this exercise, you'll create a query that only selects individual fields from a table.

SET UP You need the MSOfficeProBlank.accdb database from the previous exercise to complete this exercise. Open the database, if it is not already open.

1　Click the **Create** tab, and then click **Query Design** in the **Queries** group.

2　In the **Show Table** dialog box, click to highlight the **Customers** table and click **Add**.

3　Click **Close** to close the **Show Table** dialog box.

4　Double-click the field **Customer ID** and then **CompanyName**. This will add the two fields to the query grid.

38

5 Display the results by clicking **Datasheet View** in the **View** drop-down list, and then return to **Design** view by clicking **Design View** in the **View** drop-down list.

TIP You can also use the Shift key to highlight several fields, then drag the multiple selected fields onto the Query Grid.

6 Click **Save**, and save your query as **qryMultipleCustomerFields**.

7 Click **OK**.

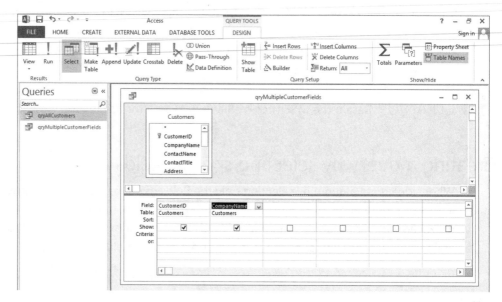

8 Close the query.

 CLEAN UP Retain the MSOfficeProBlank database for use in later exercises.

Joining multiple tables in a query

When your data is split into multiple tables, queries allow you to add more than one table onto the grid to bring the data back together in a single view.

When adding multiple tables to the query grid, the database will use your relationships to join the tables together. It will use the join function as defined in the relationship to include all records on either side of the relationship (if the default join was changed in the relationship diagram).

In this exercise, you'll create a query that selects fields from more than one table.

SET UP You need the MSOfficeProBlank.accdb database from the previous exercise to complete this exercise. Open the database, if it is not already open.

1   Click the **Create** tab, and then click **Query Design** in the **Queries** group.

2   In the **Show Table** dialog box, double-click each of the three tables: **Customers**, **Orders**, and **Order Details**, to add each table to the query grid. Then close the **Show Table** dialog box.

3   Double-click the following fields to add them to the query grid: **CompanyName (Customers)**, **OrderDate (Orders)**, **ProductID**, **UnitPrice**, **Quantity**, and **Discount** (all from **Order Details**).

4   On the **Design** tab, click **View** and select **Datasheet View** to inspect the results.

5   Click the **Design** tab view and select **Design View** to return to the design interface.

> **TIP** If a query does not seem to be showing all the records you expect, sometimes this can occur because of the join properties. In Design view, if you double-click in a relationship line, it will display choices for forcing all records from one side of a relationship to be displayed. (We saw this displayed earlier when manually creating a relationship.)

6   Click **Save**, and enter the name **qryCustomerOrderDetails**.

7   Click **OK**.

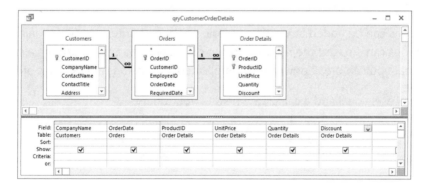

8   Close the query.

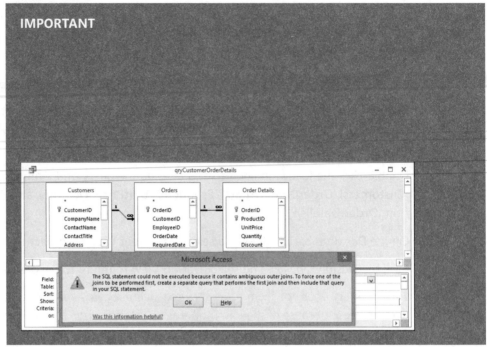

CLEAN UP Retain the MSOfficeProBlank database for use in later exercises.

Working with query criteria

Calculations can be added to create new columns and as criteria to filter against columns. Calculations can also use the results of other calculations to create further calculations. This means that you can break down very complicated calculations into a series of simpler steps.

In this exercise, you'll add a calculated field to your query.

SET UP You need the MSOfficeProBlank.accdb database from the previous exercise to complete this exercise. Open the database, if it is not already open.

1   From the **Navigation** pane, right-click the query **qryCustomerOrderDetails** and select **Design** view.

2   On the query grid, in a column with a blank field name, right-click and select **Build**.

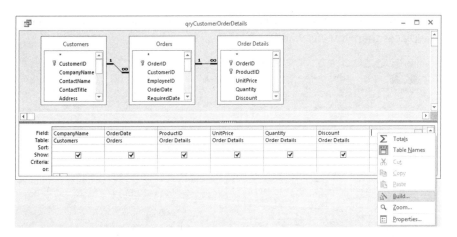

3 Use the **Expression Builder** to create the following calculation: LinePrice: [UnitPrice] * [Quantity] *(1 - [Discount]), by either entering the text in the dialog box or by selecting the fields from the available expression.

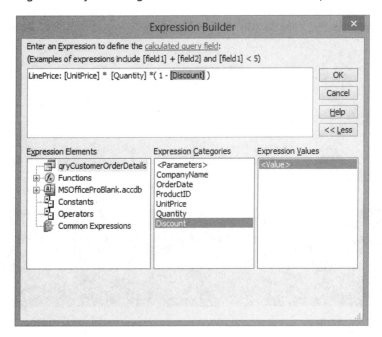

4 Click **OK** to close the **Expression Builder**.

5 If the **Property Sheet** is not already displayed, then click the new **LinePrice** field and select **Properties**.

6 Change the **Format** to **Currency** (otherwise the calculation will display more decimal places than you will want).

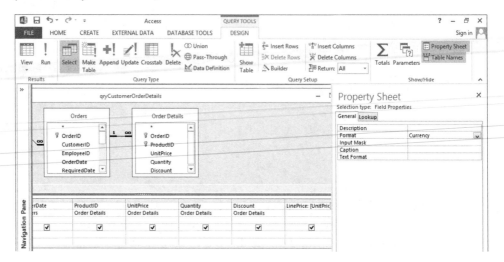

7 Click **Save**, click the **View** button on the **Design** tab, and then select **Datasheet View**.

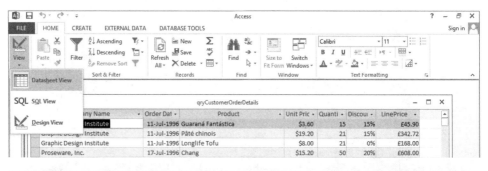

IMPORTANT

8 Close the query.

❌ CLEAN UP Retain the MSOfficeProBlank database for use in later exercises.

Filtering and sorting a field

Applying criteria to filter the data in a query is extremely flexible. You can filter the data in one table based on the data in other tables, or you can construct expressions to filter the data.

In this exercise, you'll take an existing query designed earlier in this chapter and add both sorting and filtering to the query grid.

➡ SET UP You need the MSOfficeProBlank.accdb database from the previous exercise to complete this exercise. Open the database, if it is not already open.

1   From the **Navigation** pane, right-click the query **qryAllCustomers** and select **Design view**.

2   Double-click the two fields: **Country** and **CompanyName** (you will need to scroll down the table to display both fields). Add both fields to the query grid.

3   In both fields, clear the **Show** check box.

4   In both fields, select the **Sort** row and select an **Ascending** sort.

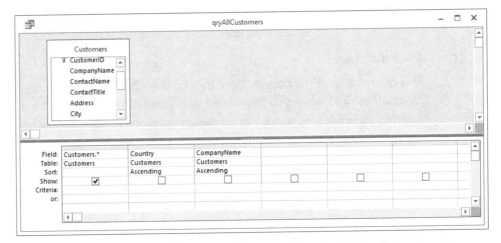

IMPORTANT

5   In the **Criteria** row below the **Country** column, enter the word france and click any other area of the screen. Access will add quotes around your text.

6   In the **Criteria** row below the **CompanyName** column, enter co* (the * means ignore any remaining letters, and all company names beginning with the letters *co* are selected). Click any other area of the screen. Access will change the syntax to **like** "co* ".

7   Click **Save** to save your query, and use the **View** icon on the **Design** tab to select **Datasheet View** to display the results.

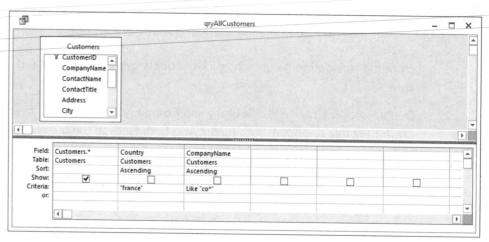

8   Close the query.

This query will sort the data by Country and then by CompanyName (data is sorted from left to right when you have more than one field to sort on). The data will be filtered to show records with an exact match to France in the Country field, and a partial match to any CompanyName beginning with the letters *co*.

TIP If you have used other database products, you may be familiar with using a % symbol for a wildcard match on text in a query. Here we use the * for a wildcard text match. You may also have used single quote marks in text criteria. These can also be used, but double quotes are more common. The following table shows examples of query criteria.

Symbol	Example	Description
*	*John John* *John*	Wildcard searching in text fields.
#	#01/10/2012#	Matches a date. You do not need to use the # symbol.
BETWEEN	BETWEEN 1 and 4 BETWEEN #01/10/2012# AND #05/10/2012#	Number or date range comparison.
IN	IN(1,22,44,55) IN("France","USA")	Set of data values.
<>, >, <, <=, >=,!=	> 25 <> " France "	General and arithmetic comparison. The <> and != symbols both mean "not equal to."
[?]	Fr[?] Would match Fra, FrB, frC ...	Character pattern matching, match any character.
[#]	000[#] Would match 0001, 0002...	Character pattern match (0-9) for a single character.
[A-Z]	DNA[A-Z] Would match DNAA,dnaB...	Character pattern match (A-Z) for a single character.

 CLEAN UP Retain the MSOfficeProBlank database for use in later exercises.

Adding multiple criteria to a query

Each line in the query grid represents a set of conditions that work together. You read the filter on different fields as *criteria1 AND criteria2 AND criteria3...*, where the criteria is applied against individual fields. When you enter text in a second line, you are creating an alternative set of criteria that can be measured against a different set of columns, such as *criteria4 AND criteria5...* The query then processes the results based on the combination of both sets of criteria *(criteria1 AND criteria2 AND criteria3...) OR (criteria4 AND criteria5...)*.

In this exercise, you'll add multiple criteria to a query.

38

1   From the **Navigation** pane, right-click the query **qryAllCustomers** and select **Design** view.

2   Below the **Country** field criteria line containing the text **"france"**, enter the word germany. The database will add quotation marks around the text criteria.

3   Below this line and on the right side under **CompanyName**, enter a*. The database will change this to like "a* ".

4   Click **Save** to save your query, and use the **View** icon on the **Design** tab to select **Datasheet View** to display the results.

Field:	Customers.*	Country	CompanyName			
Table:	Customers	Customers	Customers			
Sort:		Ascending	Ascending			
Show:	☑	☐	☐	☐	☐	☐
Criteria:		"france"	Like "co*"			
or:		"germany"				
			Like "a*"			

5   Close the query.

This query now has three sets of independent criteria: customers in France with names beginning with *co*, customers in Germany, and customers in any country with a name beginning with the letter *a*. Note that duplicate values are not shown if a record meets more than one set of the criteria.

TIP In Access, SQL is not case sensitive, so searching for *France* is the same as searching for *france* or *FRANCE*. Performing a case-sensitive search is more complicated and would require using matches against ASCII character codes.

✕ CLEAN UP Retain the MSOfficeProBlank database for use in later exercises.

Adding parameters to queries

Another technique for filtering uses parameterizing a query, which means that you can prompt a user to enter a choice for a parameter, and this choice will be used to filter the presented data.

Using parameters can mean that rather than having several queries to produce similar presentations but with different choices, you can reduce this to having one query handle an unlimited number of choices supplied through one or more parameters.

In this exercise, you'll add parameters to a query.

 SET UP You need the MSOfficeProBlank.accdb database from the previous exercise to complete this exercise. Open the database, if it is not already open.

1   From the **Navigation** pane, right-click the query called **qryMultipleCustomerFields** and select **Design** view.

2   On the **Design** tab, click the **Parameters** button in the **Show/Hide** group.

3   Enter a new parameter named CustomerCountry, and select the **Short Text** data type.

4   Click **OK** to close the **Query Parameters** dialog box.

IMPORTANT

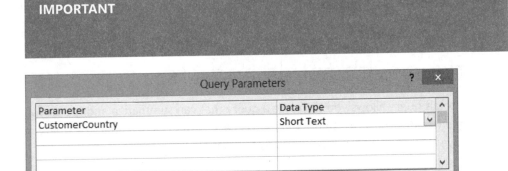

5   Double-click the field called **Country** (you will need to scroll down the **Customers** list of fields to find this).

6   In the **Criteria** row below the **Country** column, enter [CustomerCountry]. As you begin to enter text, the IntelliSense helper will assist you in completing the parameter name.

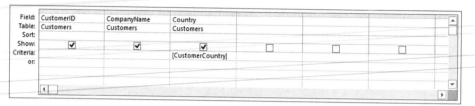

7   Click **Save** to save the changes to the query.

8   Click the **View** button on the **Design** tab and select **Datasheet View** to display the data. When prompted, enter France for the country and click **OK**.

9   Press **Shift+F9**, and you will again be prompted to enter text. This time, enter Germany for the country and click **OK**.

10   Close the query.

> **TIP** To create a wildcard pattern match for the country name, you could change the Criteria to like "*" & [CustomerCountry] & "*".

⊗ CLEAN UP Retain the MSOfficeProBlank database for use in later exercises.

Working with totals and crosstab queries

A totals query allows you to create a query that can summarize and group your data. These queries add a new row to the query grid called Total. Each field in the query now needs to have a value for this new property as follows:

- **Group By** This means that the calculations will be summarized over the field, grouping the results.

- **Where** This means the field is used only for filtering the records that go into the calculation.

- **Expression** This allows you to have a calculation on a summary operation.

- **Sum, Avg...** These are the aggregate or summary operations. For example, Sum means add up the values and Avg means average the values, and so on.

In this exercise, you'll create a totals query.

➡ SET UP You need the MSOfficeProBlank.accdb database from the previous exercise to complete this exercise. Open the database, if it is not already open.

1. In the **Navigation** pane, click the query **qryCustomerOrderDetails**, then press **Ctrl+C** followed by **Ctrl+V** to copy and paste the query.

2. In the **Paste as** dialog box, enter **qryCustomerOrderDetailsTotals** for the query name and click **OK**.

    TIP Copy and paste can be used in the Navigation pane to make a copy of any Access object.

3. Right-click the new query **qryCustomerOrderDetailsTotals** and select **Design** view.

4. Click in the **OrderDate** column and then click **Delete Columns** on the **Design** tab in the **Query Setup** group to remove the column.

    TIP It is faster to click in the Column Heading Bar (just above the column name). The column will change to a black background color, and pressing the Delete key will delete the column. This can also be used with copy and paste to make a copy of a column, which is useful when creating complex calculations.

5. Repeat step 4 to delete **ProductID**, **Quantity**, **UnitPrice**, and **Discount**. This then leaves two columns remaining: **CompanyName** and **LinePrice**.

6. Add the column **Country** from the **Customer** table to the query grid (you will need to scroll down the **Customer** table to display this field and double-click in the field).

7. Click the **Totals** icon on the **Design** tab in the **Show/Hide** group.

8. In the line **Total:** below the **Country** field is a drop-down list of choices. Choose **Where** from the list of values.

38

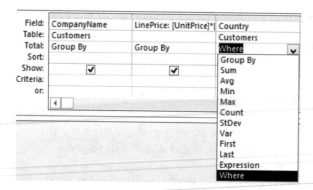

9   Enter the value france in the criteria for the **Country** column. The design tool will add the double quotes for text criteria.

10   In the **Total:** for the **LinePrice**, select **Sum**.

11   Click **Save** to save your design work.

12   Use the **Datasheet** view selected from the **View** button on the **Design** tab to display the results.

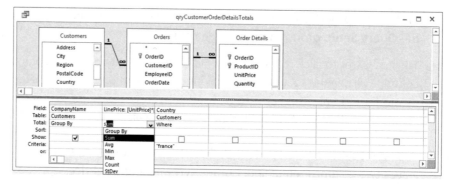

After saving your query, if you re-open it in Design view, the LinePrice column has changed slightly, the Total will read as Expression, and the calculation will include Sum in the following: *LinePrice: Sum([UnitPrice]*[Quantity]*(1-[Discount]))*. This is because Access does not save a graphical picture, but instead saves the SQL code, and it uses a set of internal rules to standardize how the SQL code is saved.

TIP When we added the Where selection, we could have left the default Group By and added the criteria *france*. However, this then has a slightly different meaning. It would mean "calculate the sum of LinePrice for all customers in all countries and then display the value for customers in France." Changing the Group By to a Where statement means "find only those records in France and then calculate the sum for each company." This is more efficient, because the calculation is performed for fewer records.

❌ CLEAN UP **Retain the MSOfficeProBlank database for use in later exercises.**

Crosstabulating data

Crosstab queries are a bit more difficult to create unless you are designing them on a regular basis. So, this is a good opportunity to create a query using the Query Wizard, which will build the basic crosstab query that you can change if required using the standard design tools.

A crosstabulation is similar to an Excel Pivot (only not quite so powerful), but it is very well suited to creating a data presentation that can be used as a basis for a form or report. The crosstab takes data in a column and generates a set of column headers based on that data. It then allows you to select other fields for grouping and creating a single summary of the data.

In this exercise, because crosstabs are often constructed by using queries, you will start by designing a suitable query to get the data you need for the crosstab.

➡️ SET UP **You need the MSOfficeProBlank.accdb database from the previous exercise to complete this exercise. Open the database, if it is not already open.**

1   Select the **Create** tab and click **Query Design**.

2   Double-click the **Orders**, **OrderDetails**, and **Products** tables. Then close the **Show Table** dialog box.

3   Double-click the fields **ProductID (OrderDetails)**, **ProductName (Products)**, and **OrderDate (Orders)**.

4   Edit the field **OrderDate**, changing it to the calculation OrderYear :
     Year([OrderDate]).

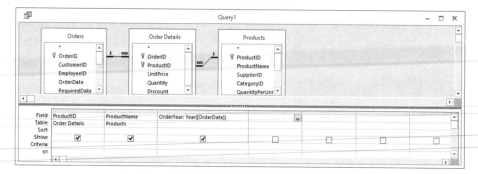

5   Click **Save**, and save the query as qrySelectProductSalesByYear. Click **OK**.

6   Close the query. You have now prepared the data that you will use for the crosstab.

7   Select the **Create** tab, and click **Query Wizard** in the **Queries** group.

8   Select **Crosstab Query Wizard** and click **OK**.

9   Click **Queries**.

10   Highlight the query **Query:qrySelectProductSalesByYear** and click **Next**.

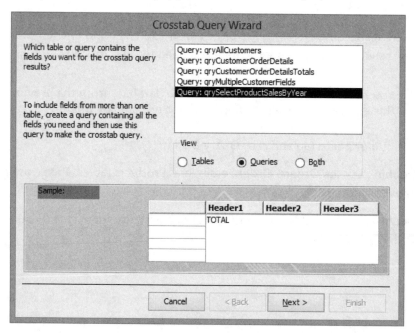

11   Select the **OrderYear** as the row heading. Then click **Next**.

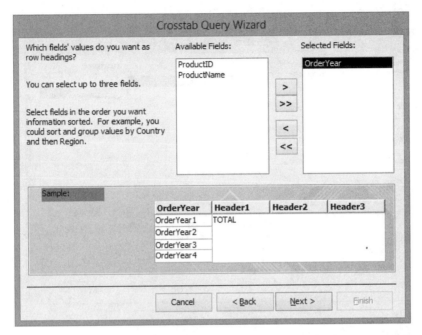

12   Select the **ProductName** for the column heading, and then click **Next**.

38

13 Select the **ProductID** field. In the **Functions** list , highlight **Count**, and then click **Next**.

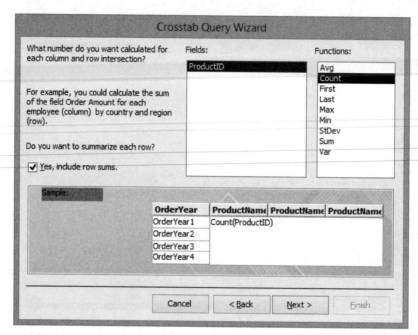

14 Click **Next**, and then click **Finish**. The crosstabulation of the data will be displayed.

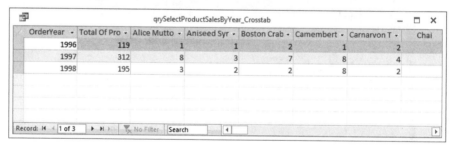

CLEAN UP Save the MSOfficeProBlank database for use in later exercises.

Key points

- When you are creating tables, it's important to define a primary key, which guarantees the uniqueness of each row in a table. When this key is then referenced in another table, it is called a foreign key in the referencing table, and the tables can then be joined by a relationship.

- Adding field validation to your tables means that you can check the data entered in each field. You can also add one table validation rule, which can compare values from different fields.

- The Lookup Wizard is an invaluable tool for creating relationships between tables.

- Select queries allow you to bring together data from several tables and create sophisticated filters involving multiple criteria.

- Adding parameters to a query allows you to enter filter criteria when running the query.

- Queries can include the totaling of values and can present data as a crosstabulation.

38

Chapter at a glance

Create

Create a continuous form,
page 995

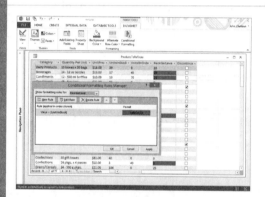

Tie

Tie your forms together with a navigation
form, page 1009

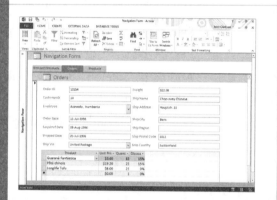

Create

Create a tabular report with grouping,
page 1015

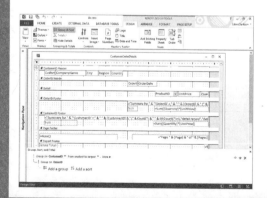

Create

Create a parent/child report,
page 1023

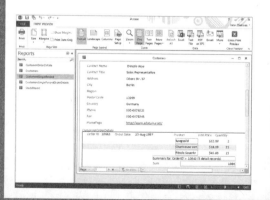

Designing forms and reports

39

IN THIS CHAPTER, YOU WILL LEARN HOW TO

- Create a continuous form.
- Create a single record form.
- Create a parent/child form.
- Tie your forms together with a navigation form.
- Create a single record report.
- Create a tabular report with grouping.
- Create a parent/child report.

Although a Microsoft Access datasheet is very good for interacting with a tabulation of data, using a form or report provides a rich variety of presentations to enhance the user experience.

A form can present data by using one of three layout: a datasheet, a continuous form (which is also a tabulation of the data), and a single-form layout. A form can also be embedded on another form to create a parent/child presentation of the data, and this supports combinations of the three layouts.

A form has a default view property that can be set as follows:

- **Single form** Displays a single record on each page
- **Continuous form** Shows tabulation like a datasheet but is more flexible
- **Datasheet** Displays as a datasheet, but can use features such as conditional formatting
- **Split form** Displays both as a datasheet and as a single form.

When you are working with a form, it can be switched between three views:

- **Form view** Displays the form with its default view
- **Layout view** Allows data to be viewed and the layout adjusted
- **Design view** Changes the design layout of the form

A special type of form called a *navigation form* allows you to create a form that links together other forms, allowing users to easily work with data in the different presentations.

Reports provide a presentation of data which is easily printed or saved; for example, in a PDF format. Like forms, reports can support either a tabulation of records or a single-record layout. A report can also be embedded on another report to create a parent/child presentation; the embedded report is called a *subreport*.

A report can be displayed by using one of four views:

- **Report view** Displays a continuous unpaginated report
- **Print preview** Displays the data with pagination as it will appear when printed
- **Layout view** Allows the data to be viewed and the layout adjusted
- **Design view** Allows the report design to be changed

In this chapter, you'll learn how to create forms and reports, which allow greater control over layouts than simple datasheets. They support the use of different presentation controls and enable programming logic by using either macros or Microsoft Visual Basic for Applications (VBA) to provide further enhancement to the objects.

PRACTICE FILES To complete the exercises in this chapter, you need either the MSOfficePro-Blank.accdb practice file that was used in Chapter 38 or the practice file contained in the Chapter39 practice file folder. For more information, see "Download the practice files" in this book's Introduction.

Creating a continuous form

A continuous form will display records in tabulation similar to a datasheet, but the form has five sections.

- **Page header** Header information is shown only if a form is to be printed.

- **Form header** This section can contain controls and other information.

- **Detail** The detail section contains the main data fields.

- **Form footer** This section is used for summary information.

- **Page footer** Footer information is shown only if a form is to be printed.

A continuous form can be created by using the Form wizard, which gives you a greater degree of control on the final layout but requires you to make more choices and complete more steps (you will find examples of this later).

In this exercise, you'll discover the simplest method for creating a continuous form that will use the More Forms: Multiple Items template. This method will create a form based on the table or query that is highlighted in the Navigation pane.

 SET UP You need the MSOfficeProBlank.accdb database used in the previous chapter, or the practice file of the same name located in the Chapter39 practice file folder, to complete this exercise. Open the database, if it is not already open.

1   In the **Navigation** pane, click to select the **Products** table.

2   Click the **Create** tab.

3   Click the **More Forms** button in the **Forms** group and select **Multiple Items** from the drop-down list.

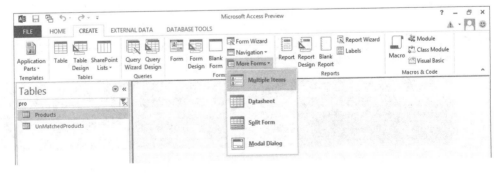

The form will be displayed in Layout view, which allows you to make adjustments to the layout.

4   Point to the bottom edge of a row until the pointer changes shape, and then drag the bottom of the row up to reduce the row height (this will reduce the height for all rows of data).

5   Click the **Save** button, and save the form with the name **frmListOfProducts**.

> **TIP** You can change your form design in both Layout view and Design view. Each view has its own strengths; if you are unable to create your presentation as you would like it in Layout view, then you can switch to Design view.

✖ CLEAN UP Retain the MSOfficeProBlank database for use in later exercises.

Working with a form in Layout view

The control layout for a form can either be stacked, tabular, or removed. Whether or not the control layout is active depends upon how a form has been created. When a control layout is active, you cannot freely move the controls and labels to any position on the form. However, you can have the controls aligned with labels, or aligned with other controls (depending on the type of layout). If you find that the control layout is too restrictive, then it can be removed.

In this exercise, you'll continue with the form from the last exercise, which is already in Layout view. You can then make further adjustments to the layout by using the form layout tools.

➔ SET UP You need the MSOfficeProBlank.accdb database from the previous exercise to complete this exercise. Open the database, if it is not already open.

IMPORTANT

1. Ensure that the form is in **Layout view**. (If you closed the form created in the previous exercise, right-click the form in the **Navigation** pane and select **Layout** view.) Click the **Arrange** tab on the **Form Layout Tools** tool tab.

2. Click in the **Supplier** column.

3. Click the **Select the Column** button in the **Rows & Columns** group.

4. Drag the **Supplier** column to the right of the **Category** column and release the mouse button to move the column.

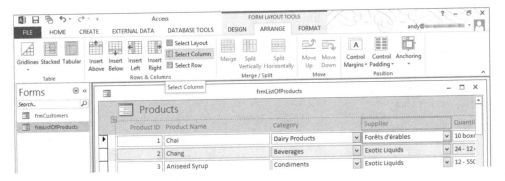

5. Click **Save** to save your changes, and close the form.

TIP If you display the form in Design view and examine the form's properties, you will notice that the Default view is set to Continuous Forms. This setting provides the tabulation of the data in the form. If you change this setting to Datasheet, save the design change, and close the form. The next time you open the form, the layout will look the same as it would in a datasheet.

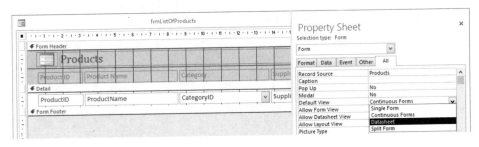

❌ CLEAN UP Retain the MSOfficeProBlank database for use in later exercises.

Creating a datasheet with conditional formatting

In this exercise, you'll create a form that is displayed in Datasheet view and take advantage of conditional formatting, which is a feature not normally available on a datasheet.

→ SET UP You need the MSOfficeProBlank.accdb database from the previous exercise to complete this exercise. Open the database, if it is not already open.

1   In the **Navigation** pane, click to highlight the **Products** table.

2   Click the **Create** tab.

3   Click the **More Forms** icon in the **Forms** group and select **Datasheet** from the drop-down list of choices. This will then display the form as a datasheet.

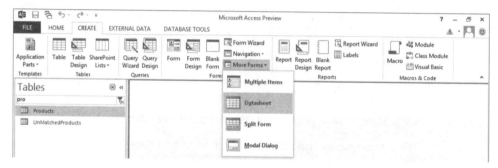

4   Click **Save** and save the form as ProductsToReOrder.

5   Scroll to the right and click in the **ReorderLevel** column.

6   Click the **Conditional Formatting** button, which will display the **Conditional Formatting Rules Manager**.

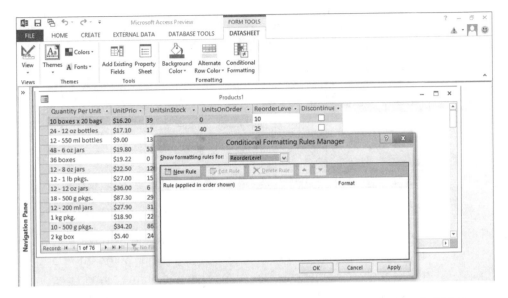

7   The **Show Formatting Rules for** box should be displaying **ReorderLevel**. Click the **New Rule** button.

8   Below the text, in the **Format cells only where the** area, leave the first selection, **Field Value Is**, and in the second drop-down, list select **greater than**.

9   Next to the third text box, click the **Build** button.

10   In the **Expression Categories** section of the Expression Builder dialog box, select **UnitsInStock**, (you will need to scroll down to view this), and then double-click **<Value>** in the **Expression Values** list.

39

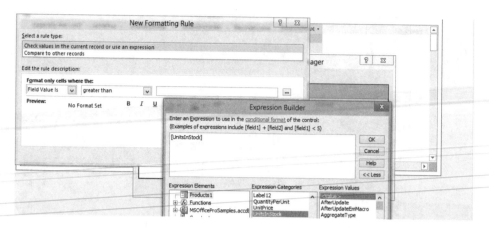

TIP The Expression Builder shows all the labels and field controls on the form, although this form looks like a datasheet (later you can go into Design view to view this). Labels and other controls can be changed on the form in Design view, and this makes a form in Datasheet view more flexible than a simple datasheet.

11 Click **OK** to close the **Expression Builder**.

12 Change the background color of the field in the ruler to **Red**.

13 Click **OK** to save the **New Formatting Rule**.

14 Click **OK** to close the **Conditional Formatting Rules Manager**.

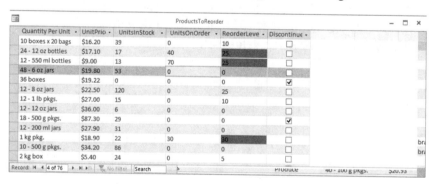

15 Close the form, and click **Yes** to save the changes.

❌ CLEAN UP Retain the MSOfficeProBlank database for use in later exercises.

Creating a single record form

A single record form displays one record at a time and is also different from a continuous form in that field labels are placed in the detail section and attached to the controls.

In this exercise, you'll use the Form wizard to create a single record form.

SET UP You need the MSOfficeProBlank.accdb database from the previous exercise to complete this exercise. Open the database, if it is not already open.

1　On the **Create** tab, in the **Forms** group, click the **Form Wizard** button.

2　In the **Table/Queries** drop-down list, select the **Products** table.

3　Click the double arrow >> to select all the available fields for the table.

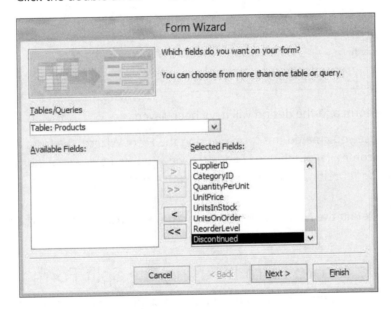

4　Click **Next**.

5　On the next screen, leave the default **Layout** set to **Columnar**, and click **Next**.

6　On the next screen, leave the default **Title**, and leave the default selection set to **open the form to view or enter information**, and click **Finish**.

39

7   The form will then be displayed in **Form** view.

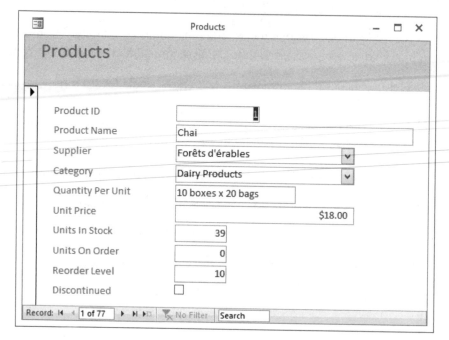

8   Close the form and the design will have been saved.

> **TIP** Because you created this form by using the Form Wizard, the form does not have an active control layout. If you change the view to Layout view, the individual controls can be repositioned to any location on the form.

❌ CLEAN UP   Retain the MSOfficeProBlank database for use in later exercises.

Creating a single record form by using the Split Form template

The Split Form template creates a form that displays a single record form layout in the upper part of the form, and in the lower part it displays a Datasheet view that is tabulating the set of records.

This has the advantage of providing a Datasheet view where you can vertically scroll through the rows and display the row that the cursor is displaying, which is also shown as a single record form (avoiding the need to also scroll the datasheet left and right to view other fields).

In this exercise, you'll create a single record form by using the Split Form template.

→ SET UP You need the MSOfficeProBlank.accdb database from the previous exercise to complete this exercise. Open the database, if it is not already open.

1   In the **Navigation** pane, click to select the **Employees** table.

2   Click the **Create** tab.

3   Click the **More Forms** button in the **Forms** group, and then select **Split Form**.

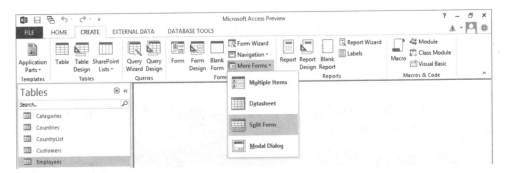

TIP In a split form, the datasheet and single record are synchronized. As you move to different records in the Datasheet view, the same record is also displayed in the single record portion of the form.

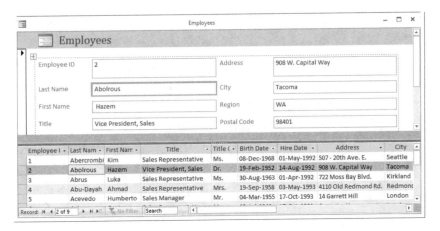

4   Close the form and save it with the default supplied name **Employees**.

✖ CLEAN UP Retain the MSOfficeProBlank database for use in later exercises.

39

Creating a parent/child form

A parent/child form can be created by using the Form wizard, but because you have relationships between your tables, you can take advantage of the relationships to assist in creating a parent/child layout. (This relationship feature is controlled by the subdatasheet property in the table.) These forms are also sometimes called *form/subform* or *master/detail forms*.

In this exercise, you'll create a parent/child form.

SET UP You need the MSOfficeProBlank.accdb database from the previous exercise to complete this exercise. Open the database, if it is not already open.

1   In the **Navigation** pane, click to select the **Orders** table.

2   Click the **Create** tab, and in the **Forms** group, click the **Form** button. The form will open in **Layout** view.

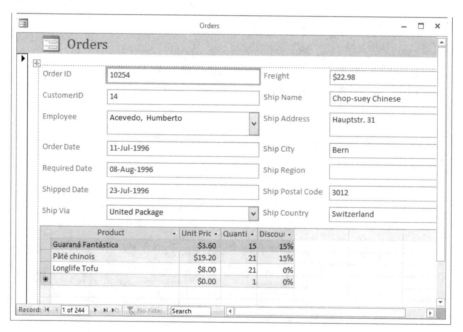

3   Click **Save**, and save the form with the name Orders. When you are viewing the form, as you page through the **Orders** records, the **Order Details** records shown in the bottom area of the form will change; the parent record is linked by a relationship to the child records.

4   Close the form.

> **TIP** If you open the Form Orders in Design view, the area listing the Order Details in the lower part of the screen uses a subform control, which is set to display the Table Order Details. If you look at the control's properties, you will notice that both the Link Master fields and Link Child fields are set to OrderID, which is the common field that relates data between the two tables. A subform control can display data from another form, or directly from a table or query by using the Source Object property of the subform control.

❎ CLEAN UP   Retain the MSOfficeProBlank database for use in later exercises.

Creating a parent/child pop-up form by using the Form Wizard

In the previous exercise, you discovered how relationships in Access can be used to create a parent/child form. It is also possible to create parent/child forms by using the Form Wizard to get better control of the resulting presentation. When using the Form Wizard, you have the option of displaying the child records either as a subform on the same page with the parent record or in a separate pop-up form.

In this exercise, you'll make the child records open in another form.

➡ SET UP   You need the MSOfficeProBlank.accdb database from the previous exercise to complete this exercise. Open the database, if it is not already open.

39

1   Click the **Create** tab, and in the **Forms** group, click the **Form Wizard** button.

2   In the **Tables/Queries** drop-down list, select **Table: Categories**.

3   Select all the available fields, using the double arrow >>.

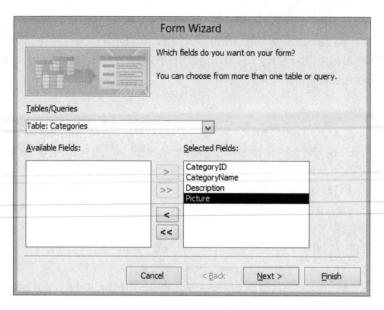

4   Staying on this page, in the **Tables/Queries** drop-down list, select **Table: Products**.

5   Select the **ProductID** and **ProductName** fields.

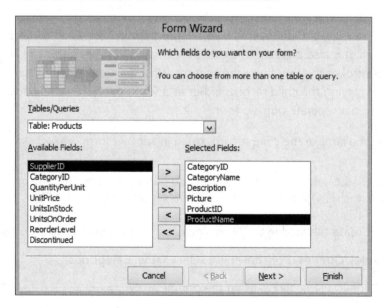

TIP When you continue choosing different related tables, Access builds a list of the fields you want across several tables. This is a very clever feature of the Form Wizard. In the next wizard screen, you'll choose how you want to view your data. This step asks you to select the table that will act as the parent record.

6   Click **Next**.

7   Select **Linked forms** in the lower-right area of the screen.

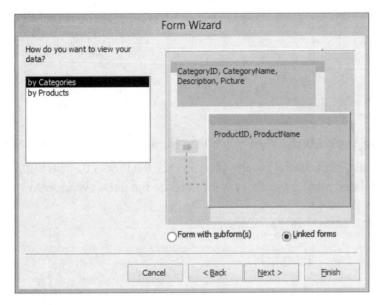

8   Click **Next**.

9   On the next screen, name the first form Categories and the second form ProductDetails, and leave the default selection set to **open the form to view or enter information**.

10   Click **Finish**.

11   Click the **View** button on the **Home** tab and select **Design View**.

12   Right-click **Categories** and select **Send to Back**. You can also reposition the button if you want. The issue here is that the wizard builds the form so that the label obscures the button and thus stops the button from working. Sending the label behind the button solves the problem.

39

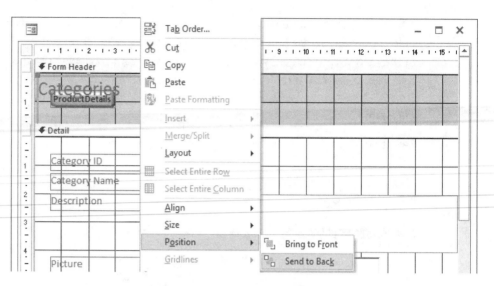

13   Click **Save**, then click the **View** icon on the **Home** tab, and select **Form View**.

When displaying a master record, you can click the ProductDetails button to display a list of related records (you may want to resize the details window to show more records).

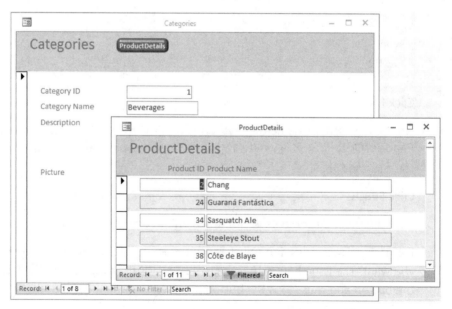

TIP If you resize the pop-up window showing the product details, either to show more records or to widen the window to show more columns, and then click Save, the settings will be remembered and used when you redisplay the window.

14   Close all open forms.

❌ CLEAN UP Retain the MSOfficeProBlank database for use in later exercises.

Tying your forms together with a navigation form

A navigation form allows you to create a special user interface form that helps users display other forms. It can be the starting point in creating a fuller application. This feature allows you to interactively link several forms together into a structure, but you don't need a programming background to make it work.

In this exercise, you'll create a navigation form linking together other forms created in earlier exercises.

➡ SET UP You need the MSOfficeProBlank.accdb database from the previous exercise to complete this exercise. Open the database, if it is not already open.

1   On the **Create** tab, in the **Forms** group, click the **Navigation** button (you don't need to select a table before doing this).

2   Select the first option to create a form with **Horizontal Tabs**.

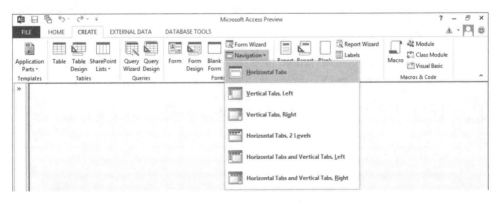

3   Use the **Shutter** bar to fully display the contents of the **Navigation** pane (if it is not already open, click the **>>** symbol on the top right of the **Navigation** pane) so that the **Navigation** pane is displayed next to the form (the new form is in **Layout** view).

4   Drag the three forms **frmListOfProducts**, **Orders**, and then **Products** onto the tab at the top of the **Navigation** form (drop them at the position where it says **(Add New)**).

5   Click **Save**, and save the form with the name Navigation Form.

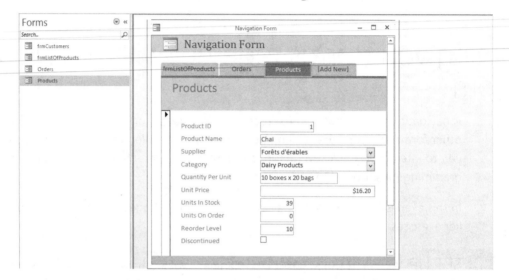

TIP Access has great support for dragging objects in Layout or Design view. You can drag forms onto other forms to create subforms, or you can drag a report onto another report to create a subreport. The navigation form is a special case where dragging an object produces a navigation button.

6   You can now click any of the new tabs to view the appropriate form displayed.

7   Close the form.

You have now created an interface for your application, so when you display the form called Navigation Form, you can click the tabs to display data in other forms.

✖ CLEAN UP   Retain the MSOfficeProBlank database for use in later exercises.

Creating a single record report

A single record report allows you to display one record of data. The advantage of this report is that it gives you flexibility for placing fields in both a vertical and horizontal position on the page.

In this exercise, you'll create a single record report by using the Report Wizard.

SET UP You need the MSOfficeProBlank.accdb database from the previous exercise to complete this exercise. Open the database, if it is not already open.

1   On the **Create** tab, in the **Reports** group, click **Report Wizard** (you don't need to select a table before doing this).

2   In the **Tables/Queries** drop-down list, select the table named **Table: Customers**.

3   Click the double arrow >> to select all fields, and then click **Next**.

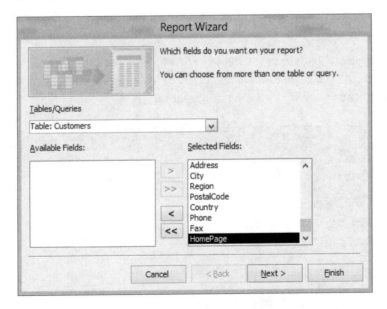

4   On the next page, for groupings, make no selection and click **Next**.

5   On the next page, select **CompanyName** from the drop-down list to sort by a single field.

39

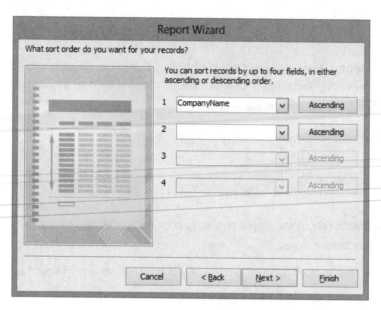

6   In the next screen, change the report layout to **Columnar**, leave **Orientation** set to **Portrait**, and click **Next**.

TIP A very useful feature of the Report Wizard is the option to adjust the field width so all fields fit on a page (this is selected by default). This is particularly useful when you are adjusting the layout for a tabular report.

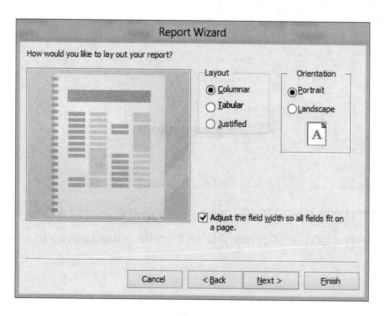

7   On the final page, do not make any changes to the default selections, and then click
    Finish.

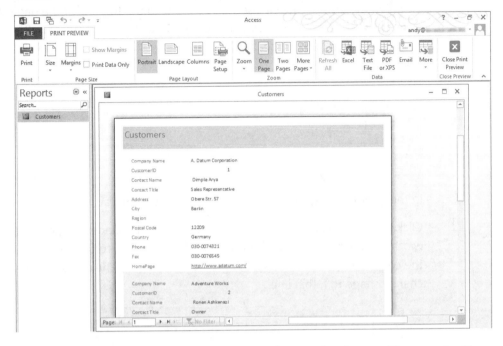

8   After previewing the report, click the **Close Print Preview** button. The report will
    then be displayed in Design view.

    The report contains the following sections:

    - **Report header** Displayed at the beginning of the report, often used for a front
      cover page

    - **Page header** Displayed with each page; allows a banner to be added on each
      page

    - **Detail section** Displays the fields and is often surrounded by additional levels
      of groups

    - **Page footer** Used to display pagination counts and date/time at the bottom
      of each page

    - **Report footer** Displayed at the end of a report; often used to show summary
      totals for the report

39

9   To add a page break after each **Customer** record, in Design view, scroll down until the page footer appears. Drag the footer down to create a small gap between it and the last control, **HomePage**. As you point to the top line of the page footer, the pointer will change shape. You can then grab the line and drag it further down the page to create additional space.

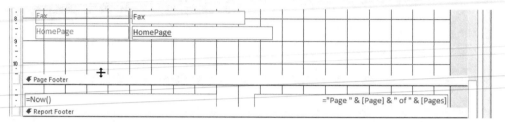

10   In the **Report Design Tools** tool tabs, click the **Design** tab.

11   Click the **Controls** button to access a list of controls. (Depending on your screen width, the controls may be displayed without the need to drop-down through the control list.) Click the **Insert Page Break** selection. The mouse pointer will now change shape to a thin line.

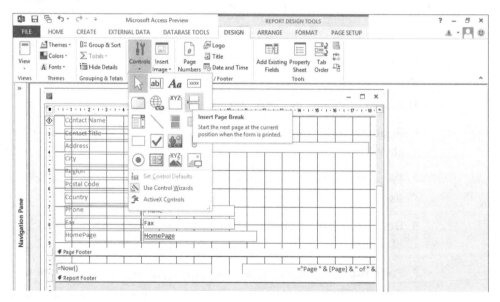

12   Click in the **Detail** section, on the left just above the page footer and below the last control (**HomePage**), to add the page break.

13   Click **Save** to save the report.

14   Click the **View** button and select **Print Preview** to display each record on a separate page.

15   Click **Close Print Preview**, and then close the report.

IMPORTANT

○

✖ CLEAN UP **Retain the MSOfficeProBlank database for use in later exercises.**

Creating a tabular report with grouping

A report can display data in a row presentation similar to a datasheet, but with grouping. This is where fields that would otherwise show repeating values can be moved into header sections above the main tabulation of the data.

In this exercise, you'll create a tabular report with grouping by using the Report Wizard.

➡ SET UP **You need the MSOfficeProBlank.accdb database from the previous exercise to complete this exercise. Open the database, if it is not already open.**

1   On the **Create** tab, in the **Reports** grouping, click **Report Wizard**. (You don't need to select a table before doing this, but if you have selected a table in the **Navigation** pane, then the wizard will assist you further by displaying the selected table name in the **Table/Queries** selection.)

2   In **Table/Queries**, select the table **Table: Customers**.

3   Add only the five fields **CustomerID**, **CompanyName**, **City**, **Region**, and **Country**.

39

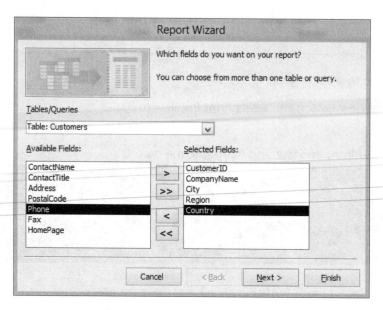

4   Staying on this page, in **Tables/Queries**, select the table **Table: Orders**, then add the two fields **OrderID** and **OrderDate**.

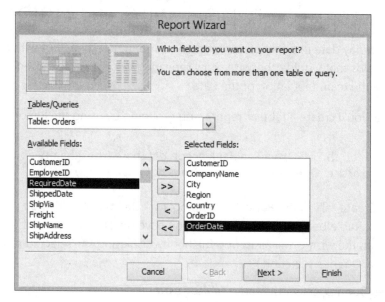

5   Staying on this page, in **Tables/Queries**, select the table **Table: Order Details**, and then add the four fields: **ProductID**, **UnitPrice**, **Quantity**, and **Discount**.

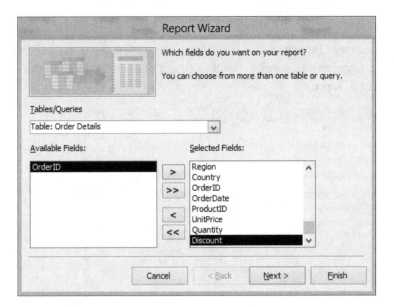

6   Click **Next**.

7   In this screen, you can choose from different available groupings. Accept the default grouping **By Customers**, and then click **Next**.

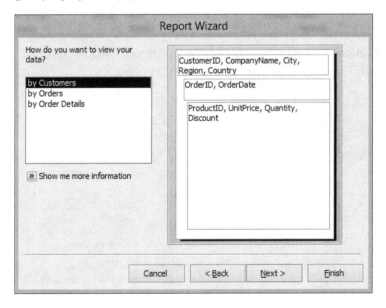

8   The next page allows you to add a further level of groupings, but for now, make no selection, and click **Next**.

9   On the next page, click the **Summary Options** button.

10   In the **Summary Options** dialog box, click to select **Sum** for the **Quantity** row (you will later change this to a more useful calculation), click **OK** to close the dialog box, and then click **Next**.

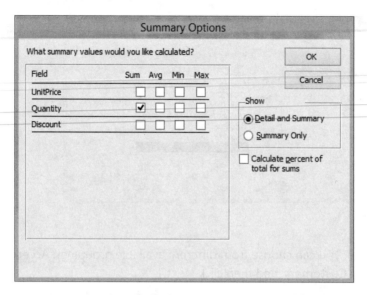

11   In the next screen, which can be used to adjust the layout, click **Next**.

12   On the final page, change the **Title** of the report to CustomerOrderDetails and click **Finish**. The report will then open in **Print Preview**.

13   Close the **Print Preview**.

This is a more complex report, and although it contains all the required information from three tables in the system, it will need minor changes to improve the layout. You will need to close the Print Preview to make changes in the report. The main adjustments involve moving the labels around to the positions shown in the following graphic (widening the fields where required to remove any # symbols indicating that a field is too narrow to display all the data), and changing the expression for the *SUM* calculation to use the expression *SUM([Quantity]*[UnitPrice])*. This occurs in two places on the report (to do this, you would display and change the control source property for the calculation).

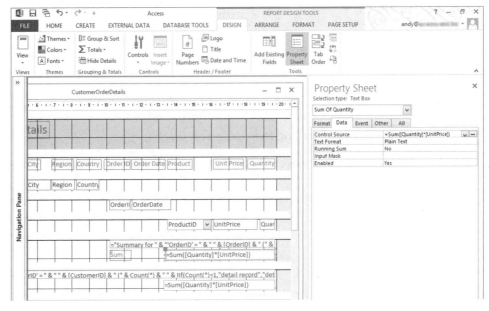

14   After making these changes, click the **View** button and select **Print Preview** to display the report.

39

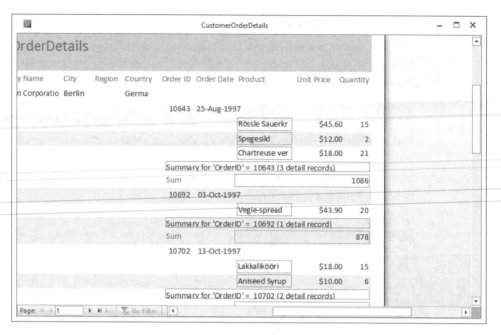

15   Close **Print Preview**, and then close and save the report.

> **TIP** Although we have been talking about a single record report and a tabular re-
> port, in a report, this distinction is not reflected in any report property. It just makes
> it easier to describe what we are doing. A tabular report can be turned into a single
> record report by moving the controls to different positions. Note that this is not the
> same as for a form, where you have the Default view property that controls how the
> form is displayed.

❌ CLEAN UP   Retain the MSOfficeProBlank database for use in later exercises.

Creating a continuous report with conditional formatting

In this exercise, you'll create a continuous report based on a query, and then add data bar
conditional formatting, which compares values with other records and displays the result as
a data bar.

SET UP You need the MSOfficeProBlank.accdb database from the previous exercise to complete this exercise. Open the database, if it is not already open.

1   On the **Create** tab, click **Query Design** in the **Queries** group.

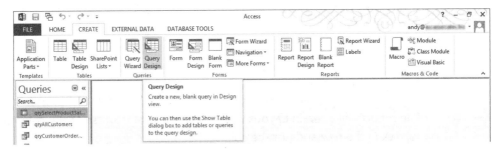

2   Double-click the **Products** table in the **Show Table** dialog box, and then click **Close** to close the **Show Table** dialog box.

3   Double-click the **CategoryID** and **UnitsInStock** fields in the **Products** table to add them to the query grid.

4   Click the **Totals** button, on the **Design** tab in the **Show/Hide** group.

5   Change the **Total** expression for the **UnitsInStock** field from **Group By** to SUM.

6   Click **Save**, and save the query as **qryStock**.

7   Close the query by clicking the **X** in the upper-right area of the window.

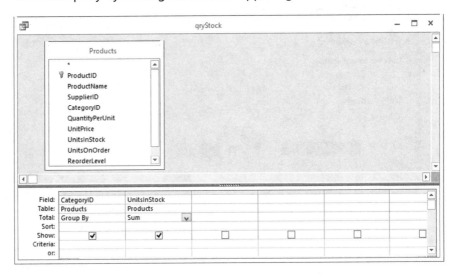

8 In the **Navigation** pane, select the **qryStock** query.

9 Click the **Create** tab, and click the **Report** button in the **Reports** group.

10 The report will open in **Layout** view; click the **SumOfUnitsInStock** column (make sure to click in the row and not the column heading).

11 In the **Report Layout Tools** tool tabs, click the **Format** tab, then click the **Conditional Formatting** button.

12 Click the **New Rule** button.

13 Change the rule type to **Compare to other records**.

14 Change the **Shortest Bar** type to **Number** and enter 1 in the **Value** field, and change the **Longest Bar** type to **Number** and enter 1000 in the **Value** field.

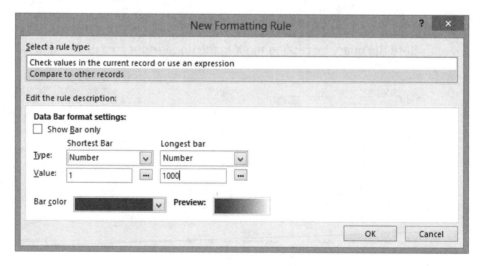

15   Click **OK** to save the rule, then click **OK** to close the **Conditional Formatting Rule Manager**.

16   Click **Save** and save the report with the name StockReport.

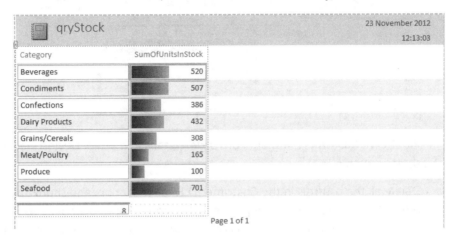

17   Close the report.

❌ CLEAN UP   Retain the MSOfficeProBlank database for use in later exercises.

Creating a parent/child report

A parent/child report is a great layout when you need to display a main record and related child records. These reports are sometimes called *master/detail* or *report/subreport reports*.

In this exercise, you'll create a parent/child report.

➡ SET UP   You need the MSOfficeProBlank.accdb database from the previous exercise to complete this exercise. Open the database, if it is not already open.

39

1   In the **Navigation** pane, select the report **Customers**, right-click and select **Copy**, right-click and select **Paste**, and name it CustomersSingleRecord.

2   Select the **CustomerOrderDetails** report, right-click and select **Copy**, right-click and select **Paste**, and name it CustomersSingleRecordOrderDetails.

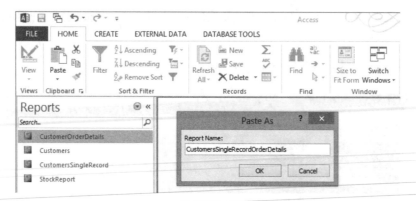

3 Right-click **CustomersSingleRecordOrderDetails** and select **Design** view from the shortcut menu.

4 Delete all the controls in the **CustomerID Header** section, and shrink the area to remove any white space. (The pointer will change shape to a bar as you point just above the **OrderID** header. Then click to select the line and drag upward to shrink the **CustomerID Header** section.)

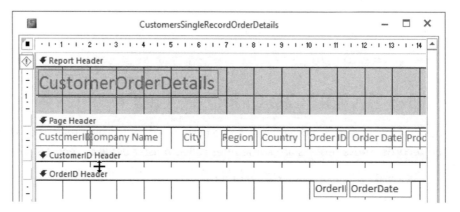

5 Delete the title **CustomerOrderDetails** label in the **Report Header** section and shrink the area to remove any white space.

6 Delete any controls in the **Page Footer** section, and shrink the area to remove any white space.

7 Delete any controls in the **Report Footer** section, and shrink the area to remove any white space.

8 Drag the labels **OrderID**, **Order Date**, **Product**, and **Unit Price** from the **Page Header** section to new positions in the **OrderID Header** section (reposition the **OrderID** and **OrderDate** text boxes).

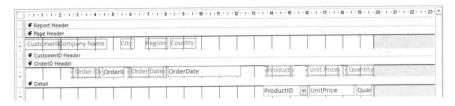

9　Delete any other controls in the **Page Header** section and shrink the section to re-move any white space.

10　Click **Save**.

11　Close the report window by clicking the **X** in the upper-right corner of the window (this is very important, in preparation for the next step).

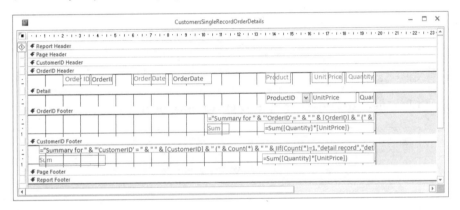

12　In the **Navigation** pane, click to highlight the **CustomersSingleRecord** report, then right-click and select **Design View**.

13　Remove the **Page Break Control** (click the control and press the **Delete** key) added in an earlier exercise, and drag the **Page Footer** section down to create more space.

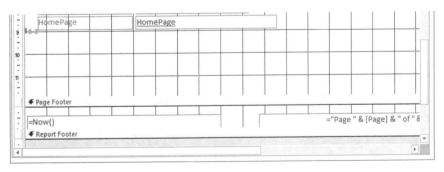

39

14 Ensure that the **Navigation** pane is displayed, and drag the report called **Customers-SingleRecordOrderDetails** onto the **CustomersSingleRecord** report just above the **Page Footer** in the area of white space that you have created. This will create a subreport.

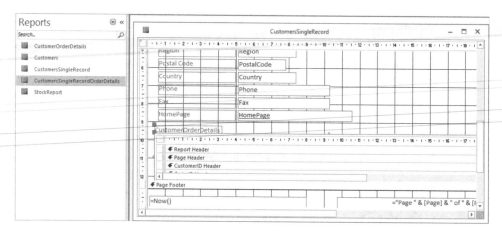

15 Click **Save**.

16 Click **View** and select **Print Preview** to view the report.

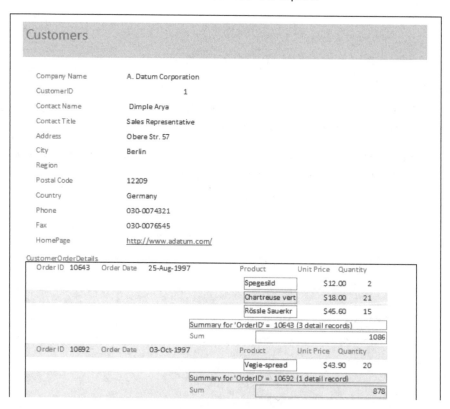

Your report will not look identical to the one we have shown here, because with a subreport, you need to make further adjustments to the layout to get it to fit exactly as you require on the page. The adjustments required depend on where you positioned the subreport control on the main report, the width of the subreport control, and the actual width of the subreport itself. Following are some guidelines for improving the layout of your report. The first problem you are likely to find is that the main report spills over onto two pages. This is because when you added the subreport, it increased the width of the main report.

17   Close the **Print Preview**.

18   Make sure that your subreport control is as far to the left as you can position it.

19   Reduce the size of the subreport control.

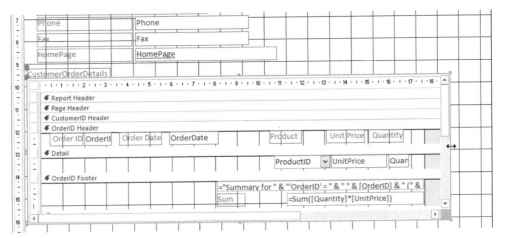

20   Reduce the width of the main report, because this may have increased when you added the subreport control.

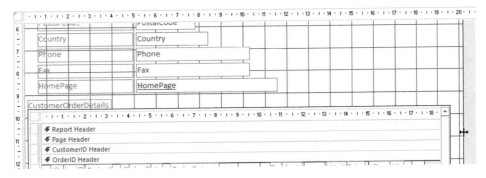

39

21   Click the **Save** button.

22   Click the **View** button and select **Print Preview**. At this point, a warning message box could appear, indicating that the subreport could not display all the information.

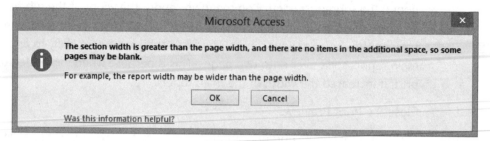

23   Close **Print Preview** and then close the parent report.

24   Open the **CustomersSingleRecordOrderDetails** report in **Design view** (right-click the report and select **Design View** from the **Navigation** pane).

25   Adjust the position of controls so that the overall width of the report can be reduced to allow it to fit within the available width of the subreport control on the parent report.

26   Click **Save** and close the report.

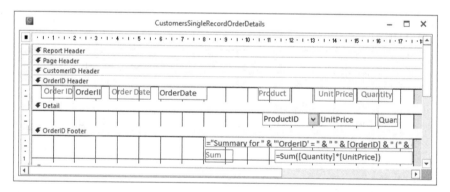

TIP If you are creating a report linking a parent record to a single set of related child records, then you can either create a parent/child report as described in this section, or you can create a continuous report and use groupings as described in the previous section; these are equivalent techniques. If, however, you need to show several sets of child records, then the grouping approach cannot be used. For example, to add a list of employees for each customer record, you could add an additional subreport to your parent/child report.

✕ CLEAN UP Close the database.

Key points

- Forms can be created to show data as a continuous list of records, a datasheet, a single record, or a combination of a single record with a datasheet in a split form presentation.

- Having relationships in your design means that you can take advantage of Access's automatically creating a single record layout, which also displays related records in a subform by using the related table's datasheet.

- Forms can be created that use the Datasheet view to provide a tabulation of data similar to a datasheet, but allowing more sophisticated presentation features such as conditional formatting.

- Parent/child forms can be created, which either display related records in a subform control or display related records in another form.

- A navigation form allows you to create a tabbed interface for linking to and displaying other forms.

- Reports allow you to format data for printing. They can be constructed by both summarizing the data by grouping and by using a parent/child subreport structure.

- Like forms, reports can use conditional formatting to add color to your presentations.

- Both forms and reports can display data from a set of tables or queries.

39

Chapter at a glance

Manage

Manage applications with Team Site,
page 1044

Interact

Interact with data by using views,
page 1049

Investigate

Drill down into information,
page 1049

Create

Create template tables,
page 1051

Creating and sharing a Web App

IN THIS CHAPTER, YOU WILL LEARN HOW TO

- Create a blank Web App.

- Import data.

- Navigate and launch a Web App.

- Work with views.

- Add a new blank table and lookup.

- Create a query and summary view.

- Create a Web App from a template.

A Microsoft Access 2013 Web App enables you to save the data and design of your database in the Microsoft Office 365 Cloud, which means that you can share the data with other workers at different geographical locations.

Web App tables can be created by importing the data from an existing Access database or other data sources, by using one of a number of built-in templates, or by creating blank data tables.

Tables are automatically provided with two web browser views of the data: the List Details view, which displays the data in a list with related data and a drill-down list that displays detailed records, and the Datasheet view, which provides a tabulated datasheet. You can manually create additional views, including summary views containing summary calculations.

The Web App also supports queries and a table selector to tie your tables together. (A table selector is a vertical list of tables, in which the captions shown for each table can be changed.) Although browser-based reports are not currently supported, you can create a separate desktop database for reporting. This reporting database links to the shared data in the cloud that enables you to combine features from both the desktop and the cloud to create stunning new applications.

When creating a new Web App, you can either:

- Create a blank Web App that is empty.

- Use one of a number of predefined templates that will create a Web App that already contains a number of tables and views.

Whichever method you use to create the application, you can then add more content by:

- Creating new tables

- Importing existing data, which creates new tables

- Selecting new tables to add from a list of template tables

After you have created content for your Web App, you can then navigate in design view by using either the new table selector or the familiar Access Navigation pane. Users will interact with your application in a browser by using the table selector. To view the finished interface, launch the Web App, which will then be displayed in a browser window.

Everything that you do when working on the design of the Web App is automatically saved in the cloud; this means that on another device you could use Office 365 to open an existing Web App to continue working on the design in Access.

Users who need to work with your shared application can do so without needing to have Access installed on their computers. Because the Web App interface is browser based, you only need a local installation of Access to make changes in the Web App design.

In an Access desktop database, the idea of a relationship and a lookup are independent, but in a Web App, the features of a relationship are part of the lookup; there is no feature to directly display relationships.

In an Access desktop database, the datasheets support subdatasheets, which are based on the relationships and enable you to quickly display related information. Although a Web App does not have subdatasheets, the lookup feature in a Web App is a very important part of creating an effective user experience. It enables users to drill down through views of the data and display associated details.

Before you can get started developing a Web App, you will need a Microsoft Office 365 Business Plan (which includes Office Professional 2013) or in your own organization's Microsoft SharePoint 2013 Server running Access Services.

In this chapter, you'll learn how to create Web Apps.

Signing in to Office 365

If you are not already signed in to Office 365, then you will find that signing in before following any of the later steps will make creating a Web App a simpler process to follow.

In this exercise, you'll sign in to Office 365.

→ SET UP You don't need any practice files to complete this exercise. Start Access from the Start screen (Windows 8) or from the Start menu (Windows 7) that is displayed when you click at the left end of the Windows taskbar.

1   Click **Sign in to get the most out of Office**.

2   Type the email address of the account you would like to use with Office, and click **Next**.

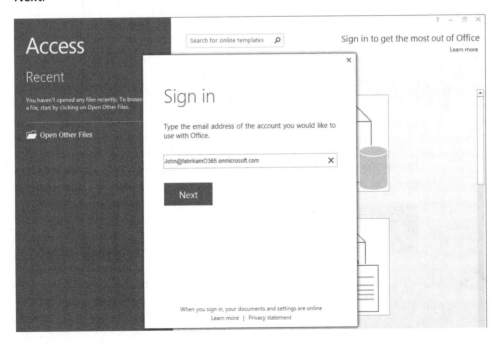

3   Enter your user ID and password, and select the **Keep me signed in** check box (to avoid needing to repeatedly enter this information in later steps).

4   Click **Sign in**.

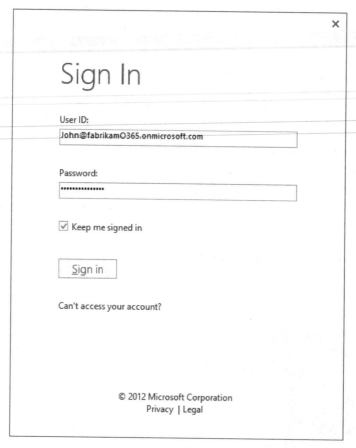

After you have successfully signed in to your account, there is a Switch Account link located in the upper-right area of the screen, which enables you to work with a different account.

CLEAN UP Leave Access open for use in later exercises.

Creating a blank Web App

In this exercise, you will start by creating a blank Web App. This will not initially have any content, but you will start to build upon this in subsequent exercises by importing data from Excel and a desktop Access database. As a result of importing data, Access will automatically build views of the data to create an application.

This Web App created in this exercise will be used in other exercises.

In this exercise, you'll create a blank Web App.

➡ SET UP You don't need any practice files to complete this exercise. Start Access, if it is not already open, and then follow the steps.

1 Select **Custom web app**.

2 Enter the name MSOfficeProApp.

3 If you are signed in, you can choose from two available locations—one for personal use and the other for shared use (**Team Site**). Select **Team Site** and click **Create**. (When you make a selection from these two choices, a detailed URL is shown in the **Web Location** box; for example, *https://fabrikamo365.sharepoint.com/*. This can also be directly edited.)

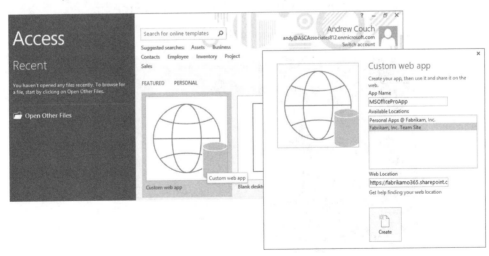

40

You now have a new, blank application named MSOfficeProApp.

 CLEAN UP Close Access.

Opening an existing Web App

Access provides a combined list of the most recent desktop databases and Web Apps that you have been working on. This allows you to quickly return to work on your Web App.

In this exercise, you'll learn how to open an existing Web App.

→ SET UP You need to have created the MSOfficeProApp Web App in the previous exercise to complete this exercise. Start Access, if it is not already open, and then follow the steps.

1 From the **Recent** list of files, search for **MSOfficeProApp**.

2 Click **MSOfficeProApp** to open the Web App.

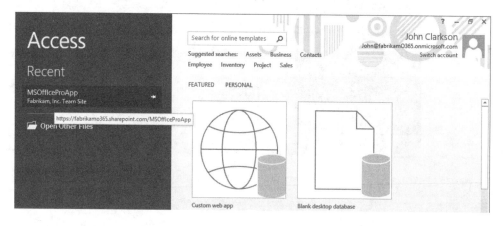

TIP If your application does not appear on the Recent list of files, then follow the instructions in the "Opening a database in Access from Team Site" section later in this chapter.

❌ CLEAN UP Leave Access and the MSOfficeProApp Web App open for use in later exercises.

Importing data from a spreadsheet

A Web App can import data from a number of different sources. In this exercise, you will import data from an Excel spreadsheet.

➡ SET UP You need to have created the MSOfficeProApp Web App earlier in this chapter, and you need the CompanyNames.xlsx spreadsheet located in the Chapter40 practice file folder, to complete this exercise. Start Access, if it is not already open, and then follow the steps.

1 If it is not already open, open the **MSOfficeProApp** Web App as described in earlier sections.

2 On the **Home** tab, in the **Table** page, at the bottom of the page, click **Excel**.

3 Browse to locate the sample spreadsheet **CompanyNames.xlsx**.

4 Click **OK**; this will launch the **Spreadsheet Import** wizard.

5 On the first wizard page, select the option **First Row Contains Column Headings**, and then click **Next**.

6 On the second wizard page, click to highlight the **URL** column and, using the **Data Type** drop-down list box, change the data type to **HyperLink**, then click **Next**.

40

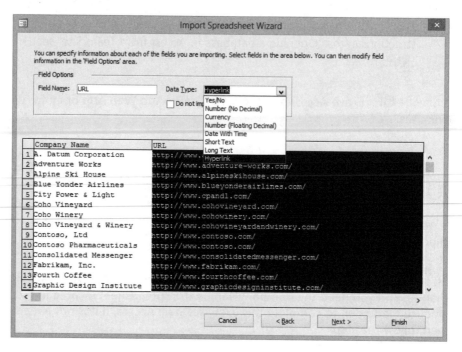

7 On the next screen, leave the default name **Companies** for the table and click **Finish**.

8 Click **Close** on the screen that confirms that all objects were imported successfully.

TIP If you need to convince yourself that the data as well as the structure has been imported, then click the Launch App button to display the data in a view.

❌ CLEAN UP Leave Access with the MSOfficeProApp Web App open for use in later exercises.

Importing data from an Access desktop database

When you are importing data from an existing Access database, the import process will also import relationships from existing tables. It will also, where possible, convert data types to the supported Web App data types. If a data type is not supported, then it will not be imported.

In this exercise, you'll import tables and data from an existing Access desktop database. This also has the advantage of converting existing relationships to provide lookups that tie data together from different tables.

→ **SET UP** You need to have created the MSOfficeProApp Web App earlier in this chapter, and you need the MSOfficeProData desktop database located in the Chapter40 practice file folder, to complete this exercise. Start Access, if it is not already open, and then follow the steps.

1   If it is not already open, open the **MSOfficeProApp** Web App as described in earlier sections.

2   On the **Home** tab, click **Table** to return to the screen with options for creating and importing data.

3   In the lower area of the page, click **Access** to import data from an existing Access desktop database.

4   Browse to locate the **MSOfficeProData.accdb** sample database.

5   Click **OK** to display the **Import Objects** window.

6   Click **Options** to display the import options, which will not be changed for this exercise.

40

7   Click **Select All** to import all available tables.

8   Click **OK** to import the tables. You may have to wait while the processing is completed.

9   After the import is completed, a message will appear, warning that OLE Object data types have not been imported for the field **Picture** in the **Categories** table (this is an example of an unsupported data type which cannot be imported). Click **Close**.

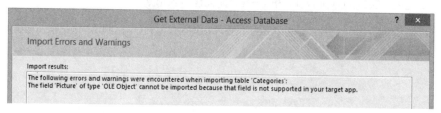

TIP Both OLE Objects and Attachment Data Types in an Access desktop database do not have a matching data type in a Web App, and will be excluded from the import. This is simply a limitation when importing existing data into a Web App.

❌ CLEAN UP   Leave Access with the MSOfficeProApp Web App open for use in later exercises.

Navigating a Web App with the table selector

When tables are created, a Web App will automatically create at least two views per table, which can be used to work with the data in each table. The views are listed in the horizontal view selector. The list of table names down the left side of the window is called the table selector, which users will use to navigate between tables in your Web App. The caption for each table defaults to the table name, but the captions can be changed, reordered, or hidden from view.

In this exercise, you'll navigate a Web App with the table selector.

→ **SET UP** You need to have created the MSOfficeProApp Web App earlier in this chapter to complete this exercise. Start Access, if it is not already open, and then follow the steps.

1   If it is not already open, open the **MSOfficeProApp** Web App as described in earlier sections.

2   Click the **Customers** table.

3   Drag the table to the top of the list, at the top of the table selector.

4   Click the **Settings/Actions** charm to display options for working with the table, including the option to hide a table.

5   Click the **X** to close the **Settings/Actions** charm.

> **TIP** When you are designing an interface for your application, the primary list of choices will be the tables caption names in the table selector. However, associated with each table is a list of views that are tabulated horizontally in the view selector to the right of the table name. Note the two views marked List and Datasheet.

❌ CLEAN UP Leave Access with the MSOfficeProApp Web App open for use in later exercises.

Navigating a Web App with the Navigation pane

In addition to providing the table selector to enable users to work with a table, a Web App in design can display a Navigation pane similar to that found in a desktop database.

In this exercise, you'll navigate a Web App with the Navigation pane.

➡ SET UP You need to have created the MSOfficeProApp Web App earlier in this chapter to complete this exercise. Start Access, if it is not already open, and then follow the steps.

1   If it is not already open, open the **MSOfficeProApp** Web App as described in earlier sections.

2   On the **Home** tab, click **Navigation Pane.**

3   Right-click the **Customers** table.

4   Select **Open** to display the **Customers** table data.

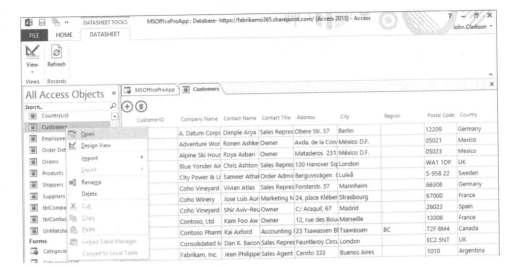

5   To hide the **Navigation pane**, click the **Home** tab, and then click the **Navigation Pane** button on the ribbon again.

TIP When you open a table to display data as shown above, it is called a Preview Datasheet, and is different from the Datasheet view, which can only be displayed in a browser and will be discussed later.

✖ CLEAN UP Leave Access with the MSOfficeProApp Web App open for use in later exercises.

Launching a Web App

To work with the data in your Web App and to view the browser-based user interface, you need to display the application in a browser window by launching the application.

In this exercise, you'll display the results of your design in a browser-based user interface.

40

SET UP You need to have created the MSOfficeProApp Web App earlier in this chapter to complete this exercise. Start Access, if it is not already open, and then follow the steps.

1   If it is not already open, open the **MSOfficeProApp** Web App as described in earlier sections.

2   Click **Launch App** on the **Home** tab.

3   Log on to Office 365, if prompted.

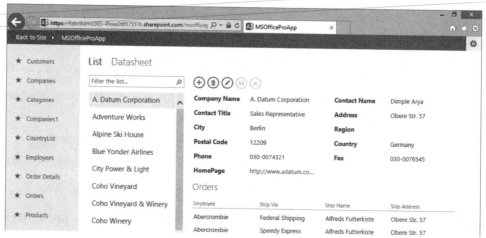

CLEAN UP Close Access.

Opening a database in Access from Team Site

Users who need to work with your Web App do not need Access installed on their computers, because the Web App interface is a web browser. Also, if you do have Access installed on a computer or cannot easily locate your Web App on the Recent files list (for example, when going to a new computer), then you can use Team Site to locate the Web App and then customize the app in your local copy of Access to make design changes.

In this exercise, you'll open an existing Web App in Access.

1 Log on to your Office 365 portal.

2 Click the **Sites** menu.

3 Click **Team Site**.

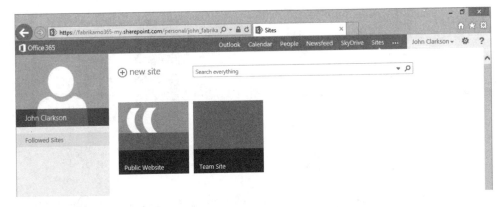

4 From the **Team Site** screen, click **Site Contents** (lower left).

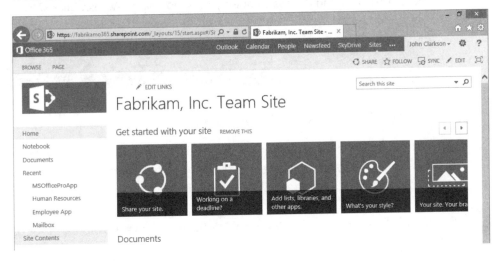

40

5 Click the **MSOfficeProApp** Web App.

TIP This is the method that a user would use to interact with your Web App through the Team Site.

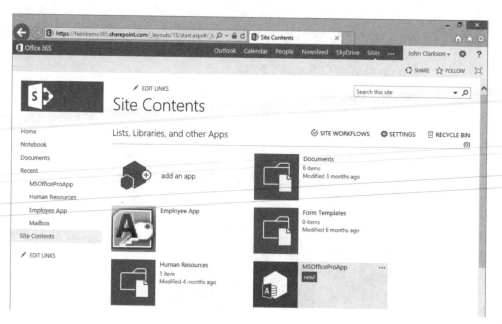

6   When displaying the Web App, click the **Settings** charm (upper right).

7   Click **Customize in Access** to open your Web App in Access. Click **Open** to confirm
    opening the file.

TIP If you have launched your application as described in the previous section, a
Back To Site option will appear in the upper-left area of the screen; this will take
you directly to your applications on Team Site.

✖ CLEAN UP Leave Access with the MSOfficeProApp Web App open for use in later
exercises.

Working with views

Each table in the Navigation pane has a set of views through which you can interact with the data. Each table, by default, has a List Details view and Datasheet view. You can also provide additional views for each table.

The user interface in a browser operates vertically, first by selecting an appropriate table in the table selector on the left side of the page, and then, for the table, selecting a view from the horizontal list of views in the view selector.

The lookups in your Web App provide additional navigation features for displaying related information and allowing pop-up windows to display further details on the data.

Working with a Datasheet view

The Datasheet view is similar to the datasheet found in a desktop database.

In this exercise, you'll insert and then delete a record.

 SET UP You need to have created the MSOfficeProApp Web App earlier in this chapter to complete this exercise. Start Access, if it is not already open, and then follow the steps.

1   If it is not already open, open **MSOfficeProApp** in Access and launch the app as described in an earlier section.

2   Click the **Customers** table in the table selector.

3   Click **Datasheet** in the view selector.

4   Click the + icon to add a new record.

40

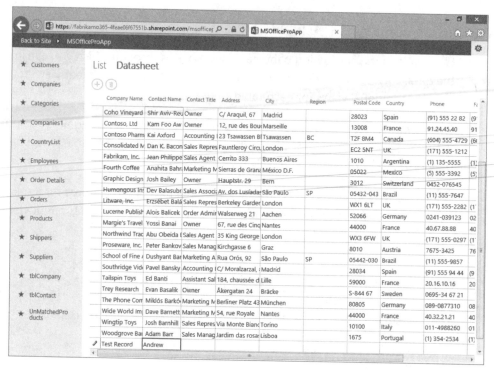

5   Enter a company name and contact name. Notice that the pencil appears in the record selector on the left of each row, indicating that you are editing the record.

6   Click in any other row to save the changes to the new record.

7   Click back into any part of the record that you have entered, and click **Delete** (the bin icon) shown in the upper-left area below the **List Details** view.

8   Click **Yes** to confirm that you wish to delete the record, when prompted to confirm the delete operation.

> **TIP** Click any column header to display a drop-down list of choices for sorting and filtering the data by the selected column.

❌ CLEAN UP   Leave Access with the MSOfficeProApp Web App open for use in later exercises.

Working with a List Details view

A List Details view provides a more sophisticated interface for working with data. The screen consists of two areas. The first area, on the left of the screen, lists the records and allows data to be quickly filtered to locate particular sets of records. The second area, on the right of the screen, displays both the record details and a set of related records.

On the view selector, the List Details view is abbreviated to display only the word List, but these two terms have the same meaning.

In this exercise, you'll work with a List Details view.

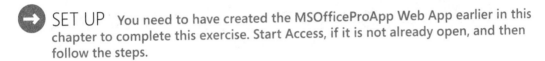 SET UP   You need to have created the MSOfficeProApp Web App earlier in this chapter to complete this exercise. Start Access, if it is not already open, and then follow the steps.

1   If it is not already open, open **MSOfficeProApp** in Access and launch the app as described in an earlier section.

2   With the **Customer** table selected in the table selector, click **List** in the view selector.

3   In the search box, enter Coho, then press **Enter** to filter the results.

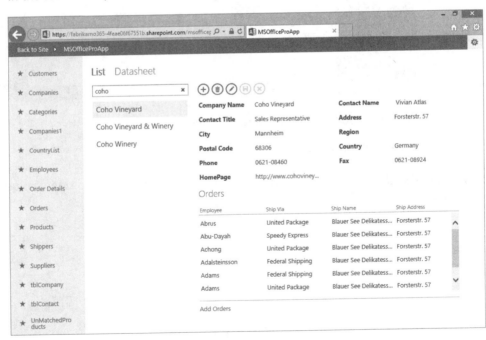

TIP Above the main record shown on the right are a set of icons for editing the main details. The screen can also display related information below the main details.

4   Click on an order, and one of the records in the related information area appears. The order is displayed, along with a list of order details records.

5   Click the text **Add Order Details** at the bottom of the screen. This will display a pop-up window enabling a new item to be added to the order details.

6   In the pop-up window, enter **chef** in the **Product** text box; this filters and locates a matching lookup value by using a process called Autocomplete.

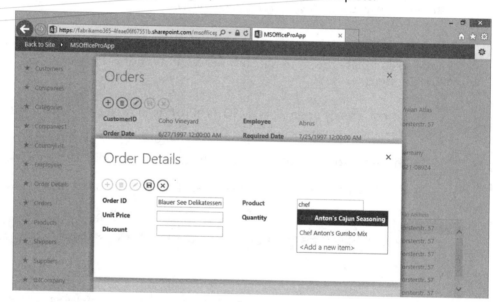

7   Fill in the additional details and click **Save**.

8   Close the pop-up window.

⊗ CLEAN UP   Leave Access with the MSOfficeProApp Web App open for use in later exercises.

Adding a new blank table

Although a Web App can create tables from a list of built-in template tables, you may prefer to create a new blank table, which does not have any fields, and then add only the fields that you require. You can also relate one table to another by adding lookup fields, which can then be displayed to a user with an Autocomplete control.

In this exercise, you'll create a new blank table, which will then be used as a lookup in the next section.

SET UP You need to have created the MSOfficeProApp Web App earlier in this chapter to complete this exercise. Start Access, if it is not already open, and then follow the steps.

1 If it is not already open, open **MSOfficeProApp** in Access as described in earlier sections.

2 Click the **Table** button on the **Home** tab.

3 Click the **add a new blank table** hyperlink located within the text in the lower-right corner of the screen.

add a new blank table

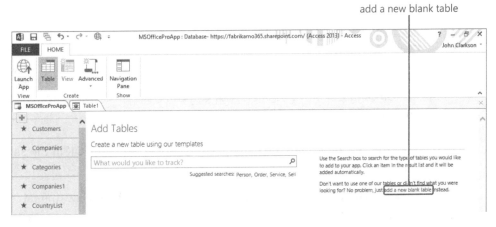

TIP You can also add new tables from a list of template tables by typing into the box that asks, What Would You Like To Track?

40

4   Change the **Field Name** of the **ID** field to BillingID.

5   On the next blank line, enter BillingPeriod for the **Field Name**, then use the drop-down **Data Type** list to select **Short Text**.

6   While your cursor is in the new field, **Field Properties** are displayed in the lower part of the screen. Change the **Character Limit** to 40.

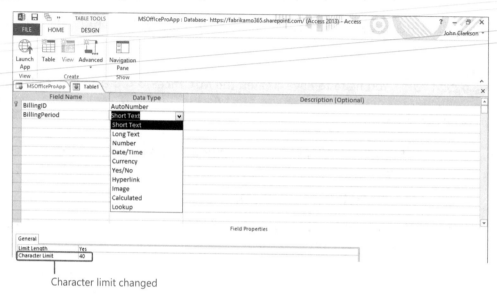

Character limit changed

7   Click **Save** (upper left).

TIP When creating a new table, Access automatically adds a primary key field called ID. You cannot remove this field, but you can change the name from ID to a more informative name.

8   Save the new table with the name BillingPeriod, and click **OK** in the **Save As** window.

9   Click the **Design** tab, click **View**, and then click **Datasheet** view (the table in the **Datasheet Preview** is displayed, which enables you to enter new data without opening a browser window).

10   Enter two new rows with the values **Monthly** and **Weekly** for **BillingPeriod.**

11   Click the **X** on the **BillingPeriod** tab to close the **Datasheet** view.

⊗ CLEAN UP   Leave Access with the MSOfficeProApp Web App open for use in later exercises.

Creating a lookup

In this section, you'll learn how to create a lookup query from the Customers table and have it applied to the BillingPeriod table created in the last section. It is important to notice that in a desktop database, a lookup will appear as a drop-down list of choices, but in a Web App, it appears as an Autocomplete field.

A lookup ensures that a user makes choices from an available set of values (often selected from another table); it can also ensure good accuracy in the database by preventing records being deleted that are related to records in other tables. But probably the biggest bonus of a lookup is that it informs a Web App as to how to display related data and enables a drill-down into related records. This is an important part of helping a user navigate through your design.

40

In this exercise, you'll create a lookup.

SET UP You need to have created the MSOfficeProApp Web App earlier in this chapter to complete this exercise. Start Access, if it is not already open, and then follow the steps.

1 If it is not already open, open the **MSOfficeProApp** Web App in Access as described in earlier sections.

2 Click the **Customers** table in the table selector.

3 Right-click and select **Edit Table**.

4 Scroll down through the table to locate a blank row, enter BillingCycle for the **Field Name**, then click **Lookup** from the **Data Type** drop-down list. This will start the **Lookup** wizard.

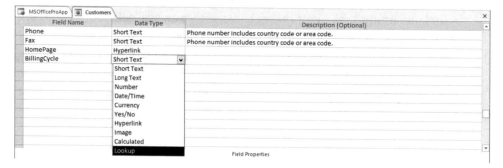

5 On the first page, click **I want the Lookup field to get the values from another table or query.**

6 In the list of tables, click **BillingPeriod**.

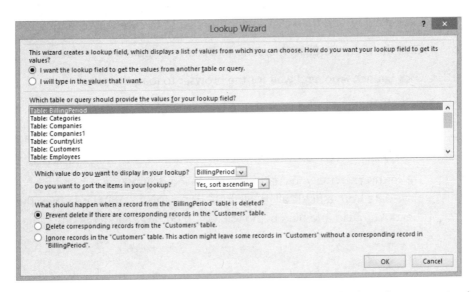

TIP When deciding which table you want to provide the lookup data, you can also choose the fields to display and how to sort the choices. The lower part of the screen provides options for choosing from a set of available rules to relate the data between the tables.

7   Click **OK**.

8   Click **Save** (upper left of the screen).

9   Click **View** on the **Design** tab, and then click **Datasheet** view. This displays your table in the **Datasheet Preview**.

10   Scroll to the right to display the new **BillingCycle** Autocomplete field.

11   Enter **W** into the **BillingCycle** field; the Autocomplete control will then search and display matching choices.

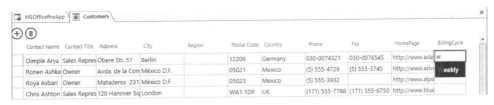

40

12 Click **Weekly**, and then click in another record to save your changes.

13 Click the **X** on the **Customers** tab to close your table.

14 Click **Launch App**, and wait for the browser to load the page.

15 Click the **BillingPeriod** table in the table selector.

16 Click **Weekly** in the list of data values; this displays all customers with a value of **Weekly** in the **BillingCycle** field.

TIP In this exercise, you created a field called BillingCycle, which looks up and displays data from a field called BillingPeriod in the BillingPeriod table. The names of the lookup field and field being looked up do not need to be the same.

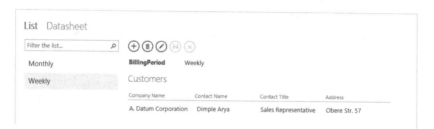

⊗ CLEAN UP Close the browser window, but leave Access with the MSOfficeProApp Web App open for use in later exercises.

A Web App enables you to create queries that can bring data together from several tables. In this exercise, you'll create a query that displays the total number of product purchases made by each customer, for each product.

➜ SET UP You need to have created the MSOfficeProApp Web App earlier in this chapter to complete this exercise. Start Access, if it is not already open, and then follow the steps.

1 If it is not already open, open the MSOfficeProApp Web App in Access as described in earlier sections.

2 Click **Advanced** on the **Home** tab.

3 Click **Query**.

4   Add the tables **Customers**, **Orders** and **Order Details** to the query, and then double-click each table name in the list to add the table to the query grid.

5   Click **Close** to close the **Show Table** dialog box.

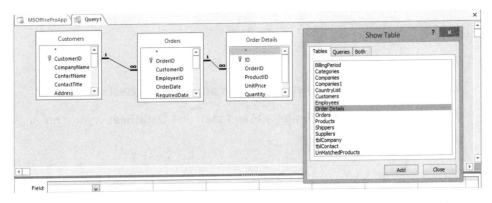

6   Double-click the **CompanyName** field in the **Customers** table. This adds the field to the query grid.

7   Double-click the **ProductID** field in the **Order Details** table.

8   Double-click the **ID** field in the **Order Details** table.

9   Click **Totals** on the **Design** tab. This adds a new row called **Totals** to the query grid.

10   Below the **ID** field, in the **Totals** row, click **Count** from the drop-down list of choices. (This creates a query that counts the number of times each customer has ordered a specific product.)

40

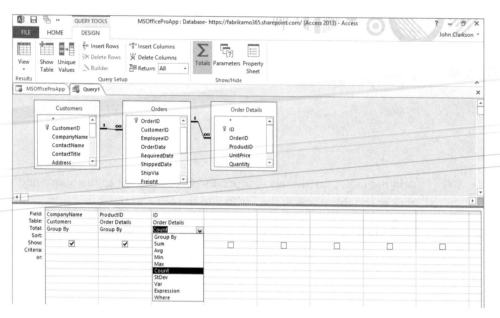

11   Click **Save and** save the query as ProductsPurchasesByCustomer.

12   Click **View** on the **Design** tab, and then click **Datasheet** view to preview the results.

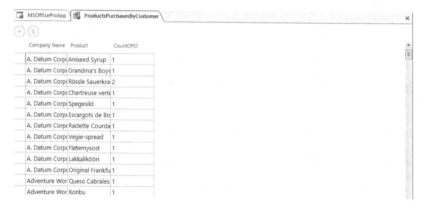

13   Click **X** on the **ProductsPurchasesByCustomer** tab to close the **Datasheet** view.

SEE ALSO For more information on creating queries and working with totals, see Chapter 38, "Creating basic tables and queries."

CLEAN UP Leave Access with the MSOfficeProApp Web App open for use in later exercises.

Creating a summary view

A summary view has special features to summarize the data and displays totals by using built-in summary functions; for example, to calculate a sum over one field grouped by another field.

In this exercise, you'll take the totals query created in the previous exercise and create a summary view that can display both totals of product purchases for each customer and a breakdown of those totals for each product.

 SET UP   You need to have created the MSOfficeProApp Web App earlier in this chapter to complete this exercise. Start Access, if it is not already open, and then follow the steps.

1   If it is not already open, open the **MSOfficeProApp** Web App in Access as described in an earlier section.

2   Click the table selector to highlight the **Customers** table.

3   Click the + icon next to the **Datasheet** view.

4   Enter the name **Product Purchases** for the view.

5   Select **Summary** for the **View Type**.

6   Select **ProductsPurchasesByCustomer** for the **Record Source** (the available choices will include the **Customers** table and any queries using the **Customers** table).

7   Click the **Add New View** button.

This will add a new view, Product Purchases, to the Customers table view selector.

8   Click **Edit** in the center of the screen.

9   Click to highlight the box on the left containing the **Company Name** field.

10   Click the **Data** charm next to the box. This will open the **Data** window.

11   Enter Total Purchases for the **Calculation Header**.

12   Choose **CountOfID** for the **Calculation Field**.

13   Choose **Sum** for the **Calculation Type**.

14   Click the **X** to close the **Data** window (the first box will be used to display a list of all customers and show the total number of times that each customer purchased products).

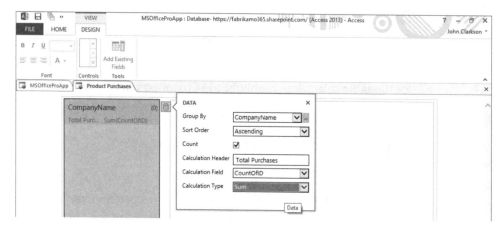

15   Click to highlight the second empty box on the right.

16   Click the **Data** charm next to the box on the right; the **First Field** box displays **ProductID**.

17   Enter Product in the **First Caption** field.

18   In the **Second Field** box, click **CountOfID**; this displays a caption field for the **Second Field**.

19   Enter Purchases in the **Second Caption** field.

20   In the **Third Field** box, select **No data source**.

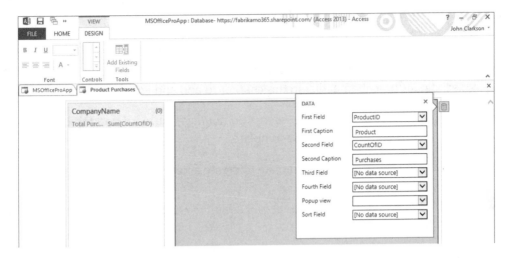

21   Click **X** to close the **Data** pop-up window.

TIP Notice that although you have made selections for the second box, when the Data pop-up window is closed, no information is shown in this box. The information is shown only when displaying the Data window.

22   Click **Save,** then close the view window. Next, click the **X** on the **Product Purchases** tab.

23   Click **Launch App**.

24   Click **Customers,** and click the **Product Purchases** view.

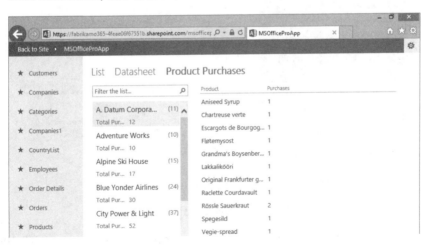

CLEAN UP   Close the browser window, and close the Access database.

Creating a Web App from a template

Template databases are available to help get you started and create a set of tables and views that you can further adapt to meet your specific needs. You can then use the other techniques described earlier in this chapter to add and link other tables of data together.

The templates available in Access that do not have the word desktop before their names will create a Web App from the template.

In this exercise, you'll use a template to create a new Web App.

SET UP You don't need any practice files to complete this exercise. Start Access, and then follow the steps.

1   Click the **Project management** Web App template.

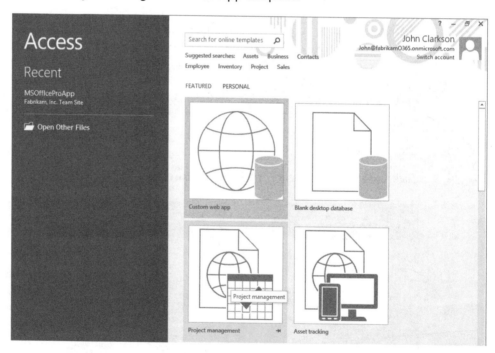

2   Enter ProjectManager for the **App Name**.

3   Select **Team Site** from the **Available Locations**.

4   Click **Create** to create the template application. You need to wait while the template is downloaded and the site is prepared.

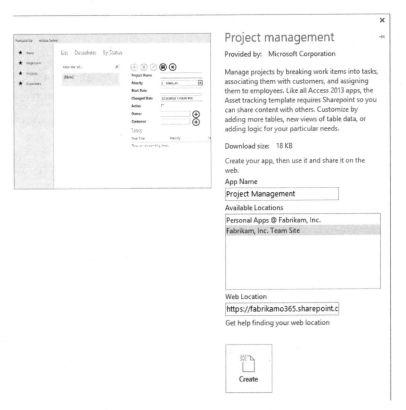

This will create your template application that you can customize and adapt.

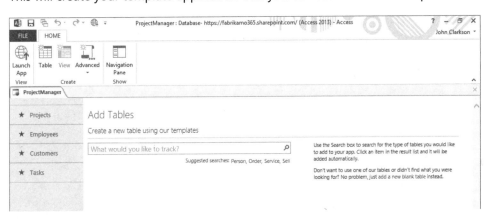

TIP If you receive a warning message that the app is being created but is not yet available, follow the instructions described earlier to go to the Team Site and download the application when it becomes available.

✖ CLEAN UP Close Access.

Key points

- A Web App enables you to share data so that users can collaborate through a browser interface, without the need to have Access installed on local computers or devices.

- A familiar desktop interface is used to design the Web App, and all changes are automatically saved to the app stored in the cloud.

- Tables can be imported from other data sources, created by using templates, or created from scratch.

- Tables are organized in a vertical list called the table selector. The table caption name is displayed, which can be changed, hidden, or reordered in the list.

- Users interact with your application by using List Details, Datasheet, or Summary views, organized in the horizontal view selector displayed for each table.

- Everything is stored in the cloud, which means you can change an existing Web App from any computer or device that has Access installed.

- Tables in the application are tied together by using lookups, which allow users to drill down into related areas of data.

Chapter at a glance

Launch

Launch Publisher 2013,
page 1068

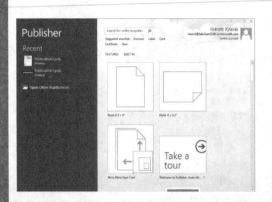

Work

Work with any of the featured or built-in
templates, page 1070

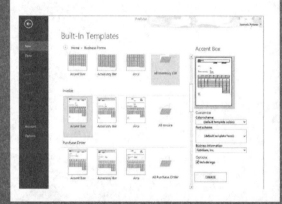

Learn

Learn how to use the ribbon-based user
interface, page 1071

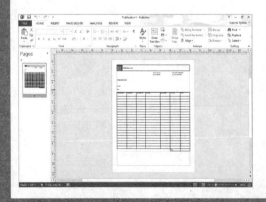

Explore

Explore the key new features in
Publisher 2013, page 1074

Getting comfortable in Publisher 2013

41

IN THIS CHAPTER, YOU WILL LEARN HOW TO

- Launch Publisher 2013 and open existing publications.

- Use existing templates for creating publications.

- Navigate the new user interface.

- Explore the new and improved features in Publisher 2013.

Microsoft Publisher 2013 is a desktop publishing application that is similar in some ways to Microsoft Word 2013. Although Word is all about creating documents from the simple to the more complex, Publisher 2013 is best used when you need to create publications with an emphasis on visual communication and design rather than text composition.

With Publisher 2013, you can create visual publications such as greeting cards, calendars, certificates, newsletters, posters, banners, and graphically rich catalogs. It comes with a wide variety of templates that can be used to quick-start your publication work.

If you work in marketing, public relations, branding, or organizing events, a tool like Publisher 2013 can prove to be very valuable in your communication work.

In this chapter, you'll learn the basics: how to launch the application, its main interface elements, how to find the templates available for it, and which are the key features introduced in this version.

Exploring the Publisher 2013 user interface

You typically start Publisher 2013 from its shortcut on the Start screen in Windows 8 or the Start menu in Windows 7.

— The Publisher 2013 icon and shortcut

You can also start Publisher 2013 and open a file at the same time by opening a publication from an email attachment or by double-clicking one from a place like your Windows desktop or File Explorer.

When you start Publisher without opening a file, the new Publisher Start screen appears.

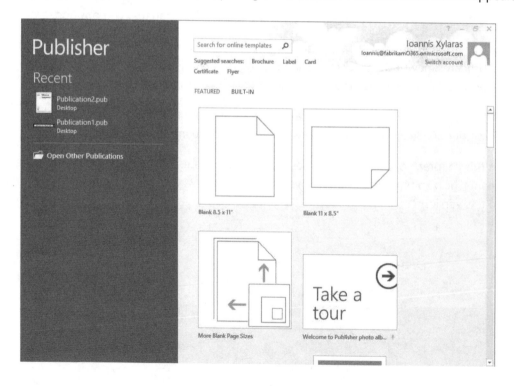

TIP When you open a file directly, the Publisher Start screen is not shown.

From the Start screen you can open a recently used publication, open an existing publication, or create a new one from a featured or built-in template.

Featured templates are available online through the Microsoft Office templates database. When you click a template, a preview window is shown to give you an idea of what the template looks like and provide a brief description of it that includes its download size and the rating given by others who have used it. When you click Create, the template is downloaded and then opened.

To navigate through the available templates, you can use the back and forward arrows, shown on the left and right of the preview window.

Next template

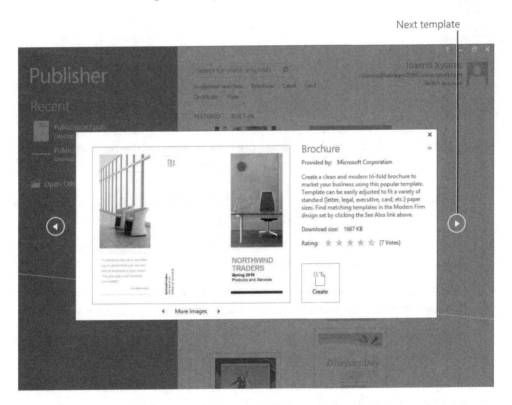

Unlike the templates for most of the other Office applications, the built-in templates for Publisher are installed together with Publisher 2013 and are available locally, without an active Internet connection being required.

41

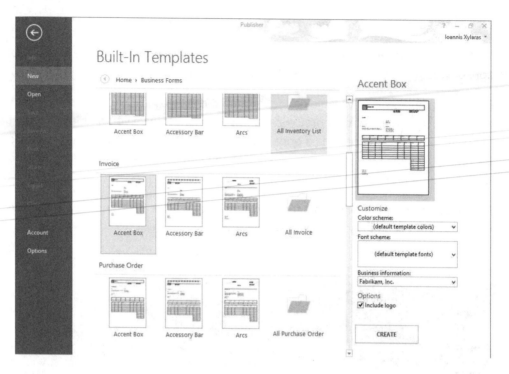

When you click a built-in template, a small preview appears on the right side of your screen. You can also customize aspects such as the following:

- **Color scheme** When you click this drop-down list box, it displays several template color schemes. Pick the one you prefer for your publication.

- **Font scheme** This drop-down list box displays a list of default fonts available for the selected template and a preview of how they look.

- **Business information** Select any predefined business information available for completion or create new information that will be used to populate your publication.

- **Page size** Select the size you want from the options available. The size can vary depending on the template you choose.

Depending on which built-in template you choose, you might have additional options that can be set prior to creating the publication. The ones just listed are common to most templates. When you click Create, a draft publication is created using your settings.

After you create or open a publication, the main window will be displayed.

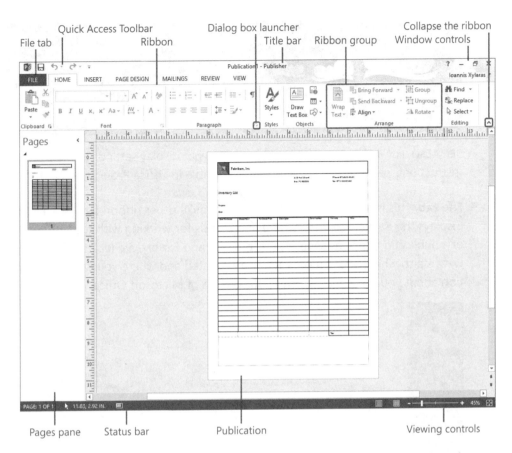

Let's take a look at each major interface element and learn about its purpose and how useful it is when creating publications:

- **Ribbon** The ribbon is the main component of the Publisher interface and where you'll find the primary commands for working with the content of your publications. The ribbon is made up of task-oriented tabs and each tab has groups of related commands. For example, on the **Home** tab, the **Clipboard** group contains commands for copying and pasting information in your publications. Groups that have additional commands that aren't shown on the ribbon have a dialog box launcher. Clicking the dialog box launcher will display a pane or dialog box with options that are related to the group. For example, if you click the dialog box launcher for the **Paragraph** group, the **Paragraph** dialog box will be displayed, giving you more choices on how paragraphs are aligned, how much space is used between lines, and so on.

41

SEE ALSO For instructions on how to modify your display settings and adapt exercise instructions, see Chapter 1, "Getting comfortable in Office Professional 2013."

- **File tab** This is the first tab on the ribbon. Unlike other ribbon tabs, the **File** tab displays the **Backstage** view, where commands for working with the entire contents of a publication, such as **Save As**, **Print**, **Share**, and **Export**, are located. The **Backstage** view is also where application options are located and where you can find information about your user account and your version of Microsoft Office.

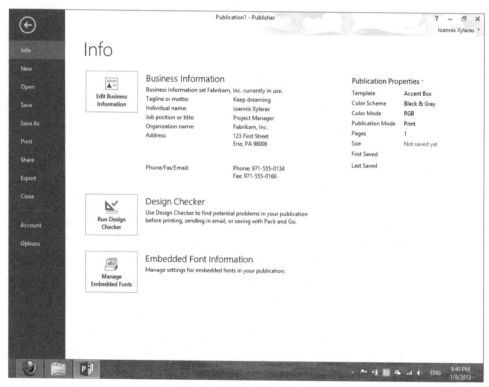

- **Quick Access Toolbar** This toolbar holds your most frequently used commands. By default, **Save**, **Undo**, and **Redo** have already been added.

   TIP To add other commands you use the most to your Quick Access Toolbar, right-click the command you want and then click Add To Quick Access Toolbar. To remove a command from the Quick Access Toolbar, similar to adding a command, right-click the command you wish to remove and then click Remove From Quick Access Toolbar.

- **Title bar** The title bar appears at the top of the window and displays the name of the active publication along with the application name. If you're working with a publication that hasn't been saved, the title bar will include a name such as *Publication1 – Microsoft Publisher*. After the file has been saved, the title bar will reflect the name of the saved publication.

- **Window controls** These are displayed on the right end of the title bar. Along with the standard **Minimize**, **Restore Down/Maximize**, and **Close** buttons, there are two additional buttons, **Help** and **Ribbon Display Options**. The latter is new in Publisher 2013.

- **Collapse the ribbon** This can be used to collapse or minimize the ribbon. When it is clicked, the ribbon is minimized, and the button turns into **Pin the Ribbon** which, when clicked, maximizes the ribbon. The collapsing or pinning of the ribbon can be accomplished also when you double-click any of its tabs or press **Ctrl+F1**.

- **Status bar** The status bar appears at the bottom of the window and displays information about the current publication, such as the current page number, object position, and size. The right end has view controls for switching your publication from a one-page spread to a two-page spread, along with a zoom slider to change the magnification of your active publication.

- **Pages pane** This pane appears on the left side of the window and displays a preview of the pages that are part of the publication you are working on. It can be used to scroll between pages and enables you to select the one you want to work on.

- **Publication** The publication you are working on is always displayed in the middle of the Publisher window, depending on your viewing settings. This is the place where you select items, arrange them, and edit them to look the way you want them to look.

SEE ALSO For a more comprehensive list of ribbon and user interface elements, along with detailed instructions on how to customize your user interface, including the ribbon and the Quick Access Toolbar, see Chapter 1, "Getting comfortable in Office Professional 2013."

41

Discovering what's new in Publisher 2013

There are quite a few new key features in Publisher 2013. In this section, you'll discover some of the most visible improvements in Publisher 2013, and you'll learn how to use some of them in the exercises included in the next two chapters of this book.

- **Picture background** Turn any picture in your publication into a full-page or tiled background image.

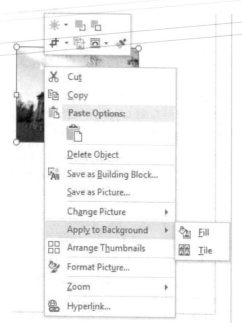

- **Photo center printing** Export each page of your publication as an image file, such as a JPEG or TIFF. Take or send the results to your favorite photo center and get printed photos of your publication.

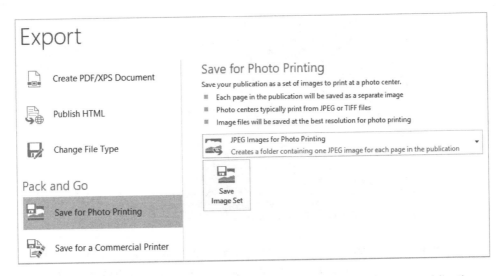

Export

Create PDF/XPS Document

Publish HTML

Change File Type

Pack and Go

Save for Photo Printing

Save for a Commercial Printer

Save for Photo Printing

Save your publication as a set of images to print at a photo center.

- Each page in the publication will be saved as a separate image
- Photo centers typically print from JPEG or TIFF files
- Image files will be saved at the best resolution for photo printing

JPEG Images for Photo Printing
Creates a folder containing one JPEG image for each page in the publication

Save Image Set

- **Insert multiple pictures** Select multiple pictures for insertion in your publication, and they'll be added to the scratch area next to your publication for quick insertion.

- **Drag-and-drop picture swapping** Use drag and drop to swap pictures in your publications. Swapped pictures retain previously applied formatting and size, making it easy to decide which image fits your content the best.

- **Picture effects and formatting options** Now you can add reflections, glow, soft edges, bevel, and three-dimensional rotation effects to your images. Select your effects from preset galleries or use the new **Format Shape** dialog box to fine tune and create custom effects.

- **Text effects** Similar to picture effects, you can now add shadows, reflections, glows, and bevels to your text. Choose from preset galleries or add custom text effects.

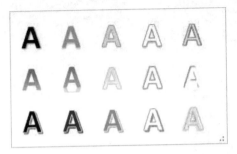

Key points

- Publisher is best used to create publications that have an emphasis on design and visual communication.

- Publisher is able to export your publications in a wide variety of formats, including images for printing or commercial printing.

- The application includes a large number of built-in templates that can be used as a start for your publishing work, as well as featured templates available online.

- Publisher 2013 includes several enhancements and new features that are convenient when working with multiple pictures and picture and text effects.

41

Chapter at a glance

Use

Use templates to create publications,
page 1080

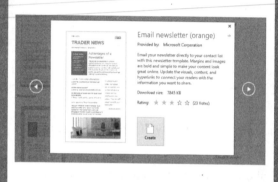

Add

Add business information to publications,
page 1087

Work

Work with WordArt, text effects, and stylistic
sets, page 1099

Import

Import pictures in your publications,
page 1106

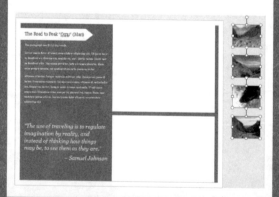

Creating publications

42

- Use templates to create publications.

- Add business information to publications.

- Customize the page design of a publication.

- Format the text in your publications.

- Work with pictures in your publications.

- Use rulers, guides, baselines, and other tools.

- Import Word documents into Publisher.

Microsoft Publisher 2013 is a complex tool that enables some advanced publication editing. You will come to appreciate its features and will find it more useful the longer you work with it.

To get you started quickly, Publisher offers a wide gallery of templates you can use. Don't hesitate to spend some time browsing through its galleries. You'll discover useful and good-looking templates.

When it comes to editing tools, Publisher offers what you would expect for manipulating all kinds of objects from text boxes to pictures. It also has useful rulers, guides, baselines, and other tools that make it easy for you to align objects, insert them in the right place, and so on.

In this chapter, you'll learn all the important basics about working with Publisher 2013: how to use templates to create publications, add all kinds of elements and objects, add business information quickly to any of your publications, customize the page design of a publication, customize text, work with WordArt and text effects, work with pictures and picture placeholders, and format and align pictures. Last but not least, you'll learn how to import Word documents into Publisher.

Using templates to create publications

As mentioned in the previous chapter, Publisher 2013 offers featured online templates as well as built-in templates. Both template galleries are useful when creating publications, to speed up the creation process. You simply pick a template that best fits your needs, create a publication using it, add your own customization, save it, and then use it in your work.

If you are interested in creating a blank publication, you can use the first three templates displayed in the Featured gallery: Blank 8.5x11" (sometimes named Blank A4 (Portrait)), Blank 11x8.5" (sometimes named Blank A4 (Landscape)), or More Blank Page Sizes.

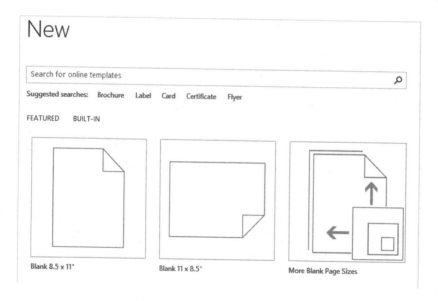

If the first two sizes don't meet your needs, click More Blank Page Sizes to display a long list of sizes to choose from.

In this exercise, you'll browse through the available featured and built-in templates, search for templates, and create a new publication based on an existing template.

SET UP You don't need any practice files to complete this exercise. Start Publisher 2013, and follow the steps.

1   On the Publisher **Start** screen, look for the featured template named **Yearly photo calendar** and click it. A preview of the template is displayed.

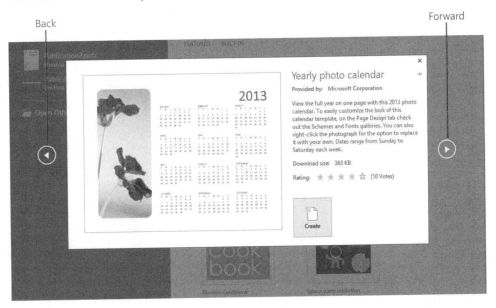

TIP Depending on your screen resolution, you might have to scroll down a bit to find this template. However, on high-resolution displays, it will be easy to spot without the need for scrolling. If you still can't find it, you can search for it by using the search box.

2   Click the **Forward** arrow once to view the next available featured template.

3   Click the **Back** arrow once to return to the **Yearly photo calendar** template.

4   Close the template by clicking the small **X** in the upper-right corner of the preview window. You are back to the Publisher **Start** screen.

5   Click the **Built-In** section of templates. A list is displayed with all the available template types.

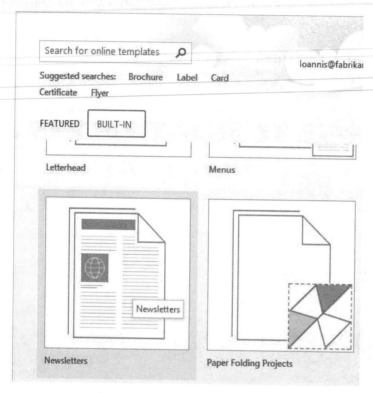

6   Scroll down and look for **Newsletters** and click the button with the same name. A list with all built-in newsletter templates is shown.

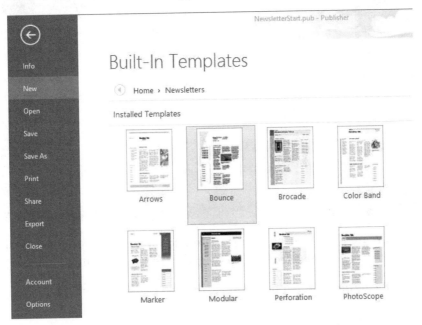

7   Click the **Back** arrow in the **Backstage** view (upper left) to get back to the Publisher **Start** screen.

8   In the search box at the top of the **Start** screen, enter the word newsletter and press **Enter**. A list is displayed with all the newsletter templates available in the online template gallery.

9   Click the template named **Email newsletter (orange)** (the fourth result in the list, which includes the picture of a green desktop, on the bottom) and a preview will be displayed.

42

10   Click **Create** to create a new publication using this template. Publisher takes some time to download this template and creates a new publication based on it.

11   Save the newly created publication and name it **NewsletterStart**.

❌ CLEAN UP Close Publisher 2013.

Adding elements into your publications

When creating a publication, you can insert all kinds of elements and objects. Because covering all of them in separate step-by-step exercises would require many more pages than there is room for in this book, you'll learn about each group of buttons found on the Insert tab. This will give you a good idea about what you can or cannot add to your publications.

The first group on the Insert tab is Pages. Here you have the following options:

- **Page** This option allows you to insert a new blank page, a duplicate of the currently selected page, or a new page before and after a specified page.

- **Catalog Pages** These pages let you merge multiple records from a data source, such as a Microsoft Excel worksheet, Access database, or Word table into your publication. For example, you can insert a product catalog that lists your company's products and use it in your presentations.

Let's take a look at the other groups and buttons on the Insert tab:

- The **Tables** group includes only the **Table** button and enables quick creation of tables with a given number of rows and columns, just like in Word.

- The **Illustrations** group includes plenty of buttons for elements that can be added. First, you can add pictures from your computer or from the web (by using the **Online Pictures** button). Then you can add shapes of all kinds, by using the **Shapes** gallery. Last but not least, you can insert only placeholders for your pictures and add the pictures later, when they are available.

- Publisher also enables you to insert many kinds of premade blocks, by using the galleries in the **Building Blocks** group. The **Page Parts** button opens a gallery that includes different premade headings, pull quotes, and sidebars.

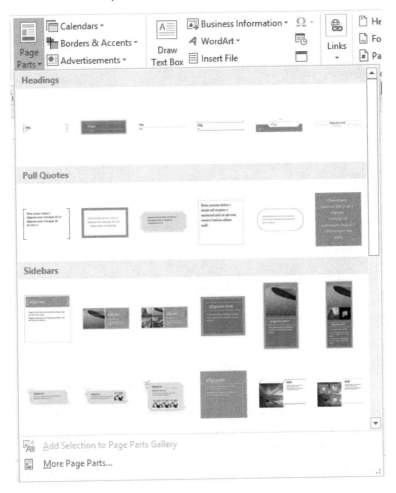

42

- The **Calendars** button opens a gallery with premade calendars that can quickly be added to your publication.

- You can add different types of borders and accents by clicking **Borders & Accents** and selecting one of the available elements.

- The **Advertisements** button opens a gallery with ad blocks that can be quickly customized and used in print or other publications.

- The **Text** group includes plenty of buttons. The **Draw Text Box** button enables you to draw and add a text box to your publication. The **Business Information** button enables you to add different business information fields. You can learn more about it in the next section of this chapter.

- The **WordArt** button shows a gallery with all kinds of WordArt styles that can be added to your publication.

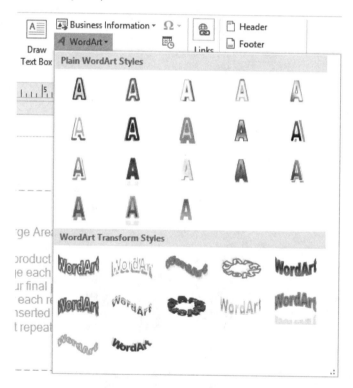

- The **Insert File** button is for adding files to your publications, as attachments. The **Symbol** button can be used to add different kinds of symbols to the text used in your publications. The **Date & Time** button is used for adding date and time information to text boxes or tables. The **Object** button is similar to **Insert File**, in the sense that it enables you to add files of all kinds to your publications. However, unlike **Insert File**, it enables you to add more different types of files. These files can be embedded into your publications.

- The **Links** group enables you to add hyperlinks to visual and text elements as well as bookmarks. Bookmarks are links to a given location in your publication, whereas hyperlinks are links to files, webpages, or email addresses.

- The **Header & Footer** group includes buttons for adding headers, footers, and page numbers to your publication. You can also set the position of the page numbers and format them to look as you wish.

Now that you know the different kinds of elements and objects that can be added to your publications, let's take some of the more important elements and learn how to use them in more detail.

Adding business information to publications

Many templates like brochures, business forms, or business cards also include detailed business information. Instead of adding it manually in every publication, you can store one or more business information sets in Publisher 2013.

Business information sets store information like individual names, job positions or titles, organization names, addresses, contact details, taglines or mottos, and company logos.

When you create a new publication, you can then select one of the existing business information sets and it gets automatically applied to the publication. The business information sets are applied from the right side panel, shown when selecting a template for preview. You can also create more information sets and apply the one you want for each publication.

After a business information set is created, you can update any publication during the editing process and insert just portions of a set. Go to the Insert tab on the ribbon and look for the Text group. Click Business Information and then the field you want to add. The selected field is added to the publication. Repeat the same procedure for adding other fields until you are done.

In this exercise, you'll create a business card and a business information set to add to the business card you created.

→ SET UP You don't need any practice files to complete this exercise. Start Publisher 2013. On the Start screen, click the Built-In Templates gallery. Then follow the steps.

1   Find the **Business Cards** category of templates and click it. A list with templates for business cards is shown.

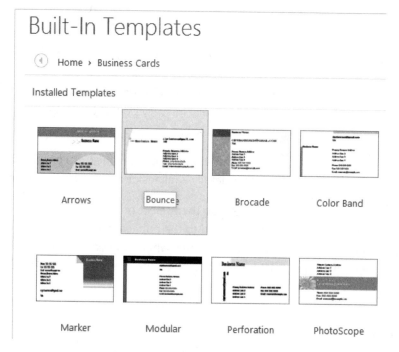

2   Select the **Bounce** template (the second in the list) and make sure that the default color and font schemes are selected.

3   Click **Create** in the **Preview** panel on the right, and the business card is created.

4   On the **Insert** tab, in the **Text** group, click the **Business Information** button.

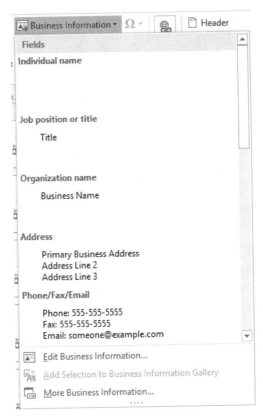

5   Click **Edit Business Information** located at the bottom of the **Business Information** gallery. The **Create New Business Information Set** dialog box opens.

   TROUBLESHOOTING If you have at least one business information set already created, the Business Information window is opened instead of Create New Business Information Set. To create a new set, click the New button in the Business Information window, and follow the remaining steps.

6   Complete all the appropriate fields with the business information you want to add, such as individual name, job title, organization name, address, and so on.

7   Enter a name for the set in the **Business Information set name** field.

8   Click **Add Logo** to open the **Insert Picture** dialog box.

42

9   Select your company's logo and click **Open**.

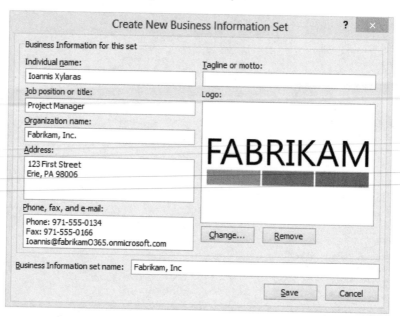

10 When you have finished entering all the information, click **Save**. The **Business Information** dialog box opens, showing a preview of the data you just entered.

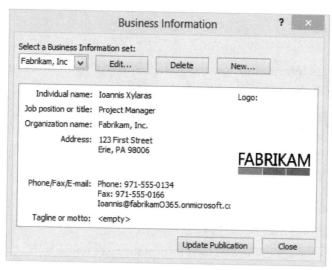

11 Click **Update Publication** and notice how your business card is automatically populated with the data you entered.

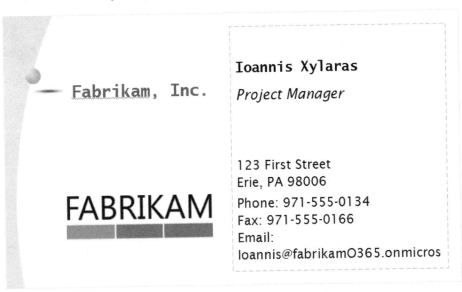

❌ CLEAN UP Save your business card and close Publisher.

Customizing the page design of a publication

When creating a publication, you can control almost every aspect of the design. You can change page orientation, size, margins, the color scheme applied to each page, fonts, and the background.

In this exercise, you'll use basic page design elements, such as page orientation, color scheme, fonts, and background.

42

 SET UP You need the Fabrikam Employee Newsletter A.pub file located in the Chapter42 practice file folder to complete this exercise. Start Publisher, open the Publisher file, and then follow the steps.

1   Select pages **2** and **3** that are shown as a two-page spread, in the **Pages** panel.

2   On the **Page Design** tab, in the **Page Setup** group, click the **Orientation** button and choose **Landscape**.

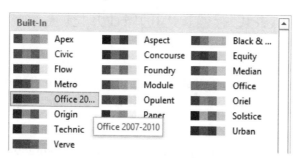

3   Notice how the orientation of the publication changes. Then, click the **Orientation** button again and choose **Portrait**.

4   In the **Schemes** group, click the **More** button to open a palette of color schemes that can be applied to the publication.

5   Select the **Office 2007-2010** scheme, and notice how the color scheme used for the publication changes.

6   Click the **Fonts** button in the same group and select **Civic Georgia**. Notice how the font changes in your publication.

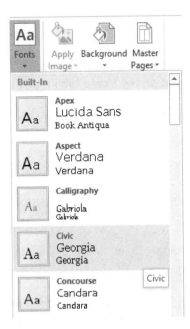

7   In the **Page Background** group, click the **Background** button to view a gallery of backgrounds that can be applied to your publication.

8   Select the first solid background, **10% tint of Accent 1**. Notice how the background color of your publication has changed.

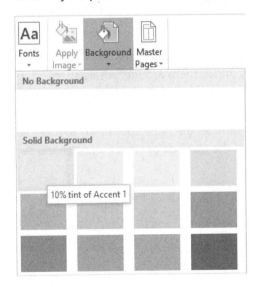

❌ CLEAN UP Close Publisher without saving the changes.

42

Customizing text font, color, and style

Publisher 2013 offers quite a few tools that you can use to format the way text is displayed in your publications. The most basic tools are found on the Home tab in the ribbon.

The Font group enables you to pick the font you want applied for your text selection, and its size.

You can also set it to be bold, italic, or underlined by clicking the appropriate buttons. When you click the small arrow near the Font Color button, a palette with scheme colors is displayed. You can pick any of the available choices, or create your own custom colors, tints, or fill effects.

In the Paragraph group, tools are available for creating bullet point lists, for aligning text, and for changing the line and paragraph spacing.

The Styles button gives you access to a gallery of styles you can apply to any text selection, just like in Word. You can also create your own custom styles if the default choices don't meet your needs.

SEE ALSO For more information on styles, see Chapter 8, "Formatting documents."

The Arrange group enables you to group elements in your publications; wrap the selected text as you wish; and bring forward, send backward, or rotate different elements, including text.

Working with text boxes in Publisher is very similar to working with text boxes in Microsoft PowerPoint. You can resize text boxes, move them around, rotate them, and so on. Unlike in PowerPoint, when you enter text in a text box in Publisher and there is no room left to display everything you type, you are warned in a very visual way. The text box has red selection handles as well as a series of dots on the right side. This is to make sure you notice the problem and modify the size of the text box or what is entered inside it.

In this exercise, you'll zoom a publication to its full size, select text, and change its font, color, and style.

SET UP You need the NewsletterStart.pub publication you created in an earlier exercise to complete this exercise. If you did not create this publication, you can use the NewsletterStart.pub publication located in the Chapter42 practice file folder. Open the publication, and then follow the steps.

1   On the **View** tab, in the **Zoom** group, click the **100%** button to view the publication at its original size.

2   Select the text box with the date, in the upper-left corner of the publication, which says **May 6, 2016**.

3   Select the text inside and enter October Edition, Volume 36.

     You will notice that 36 is not displayed, and that the text box has red selection handles.

4   Move your mouse pointer to the lower-right corner until the mouse pointer changes to a sizing pointer.

5   Drag the pointer to the right, until **36** has enough room in the text box to be displayed.

6   Select the **TRADER NEWS** text inside the next text box.

7   Replace it by entering EMPLOYEE NEWS in its place.

42

8   With the text still selected, on the **Home** tab, in the **Font** group, click the **Font** gallery to view a list of available fonts.

9   Scroll down until you find the **Calibri Light** font, then click to select it.

10 With the text still selected, click the arrow near the **Font Color** button, in the **Font** group.

11 Below the **Scheme Colors** palette, click **More Colors**. The **Colors** dialog box opens.

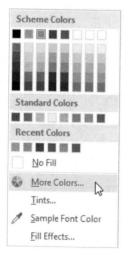

12   Click the **Custom** tab and enter the following values: 51 for **Red**, 91 for **Green**, and 116 for **Blue**. Notice how each color changes according to the values you entered.

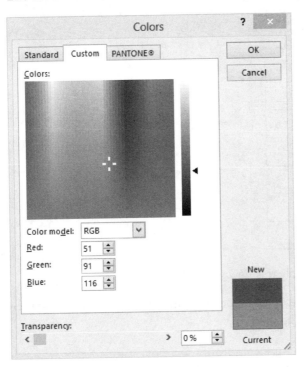

13   Click **OK** and you are back to your publication.

14   Click somewhere in the empty space near the publication, and notice how the text color and font have changed.

15   Select the text, **Advantages of a Newsletter**.

16   Then, on the **Home** tab, in the **Styles** group, click **Styles** to view the **Styles** gallery.

42

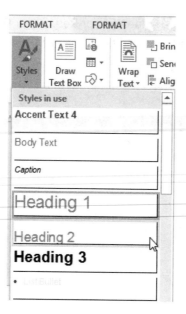

17   Click **Heading 2** to apply this new formatting.

18   Click somewhere in the empty space near the publication and notice how the size of the selected text has changed.

❌ CLEAN UP Save the publication. You can compare the end result you obtained with the practice file NewsletterEnd, which is included in the Chapter42 practice file folder.

Working with WordArt, text effects, and stylistic sets

Publisher 2013 includes a few advanced text-formatting tools, like WordArt styles and text effects. Depending on the text you have selected, you have access to a dynamic list of WordArt styles that can be applied. These styles can add shadows, reflections, different fills, and so on. Using the Text Effects drop-down list, you can also add different types of shadows, reflections, glows, and bevel effects.

If you are creating publications on a regular basis, you surely know about OpenType, and you are using OpenType fonts from time to time. This font format was developed jointly by Microsoft and Adobe and provides larger glyph limits than traditional fonts, cross-platform support, and support for advanced typographic features useful to professionals; for example, true small caps, different styles of figures, and extensive sets of ligatures and alternates, as well as complete sets of accented characters and diacritical marks.

Publisher 2013 bundles the following OpenType fonts: Calibri, Cambria, Cambria Math, Candara, Consolas, Constantia, Corbel, Gabriola, Palatino Linotype and Sylfaen. Also, it provides support for some or all of the advanced typographic features you would expect when working with such fonts. For example, when text is selected, you are given access to additional stylistic sets you can apply to modify how the text looks in your publication. Following are the available stylistic sets when using the Gabriola OpenType font, bundled with Publisher 2013.

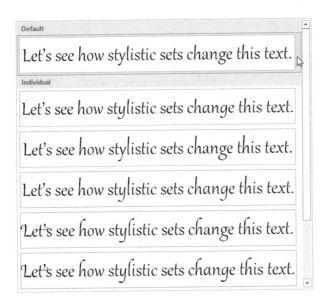

42

TIP If you're not using an OpenType font for your text, then the stylistic sets are not available. Even for some OpenType fonts like Corbel, stylistic sets are not available. Advanced typography features are available only for fonts that support them, and most fonts do not provide such support.

In this exercise, you'll apply different WordArt styles to your text. Then, you'll add text effects and apply a different stylistic set when using an OpenType font.

 SET UP You need the FabrikamA.pub file located in the Chapter42 practice file folder to complete this exercise. Start Publisher, and open the FabrikamA.pub file. Then follow the steps.

1   On the **View** tab, in the **Zoom** group, click the **100%** button to view the publication at its original size.

2   Select the text **TRADER NEWS** (the title of the publication).

3   On the **Format** tab found beneath **Text Box Tools**, in the **WordArt Styles** group, click the **More** button to open the **Styles** gallery.

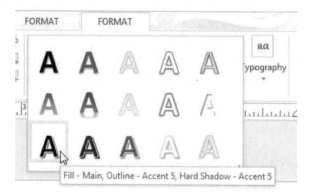

4   Click the **Fill – Main, Outline – Accent 5, Hard Shadow – Accent 5** style.

5   Click somewhere in the empty space near the publication and notice how the text has changed.

6   Select the text **Advantages of a Newsletter**.

7   On the **Format** tab beneath **Text Box Tools**, in the **WordArt Styles** group, click **Text Effects**.

8   Click **Glow** and then **Accent 3, 5 pt glow** (the third on the list).

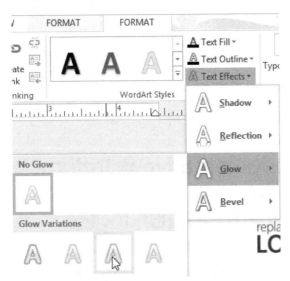

9   Click somewhere in the empty space near the publication and notice how the text has changed.

10   Select the text **Tips for Producing a Newsletter**.

11   On the **Format** tab beneath **Text Box Tools**, click the **Typography** button.

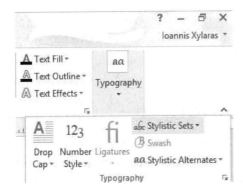

TIP If you have a computer display with a high resolution (1920x1080), the Typography button won't appear. Instead, you will have a Typography group. If that is the case, in step 12, click the Stylistic Sets button and follow the remaining instructions.

42

12   Click **Stylistic Sets**. This opens a gallery of stylistic sets you can apply to the selected text.

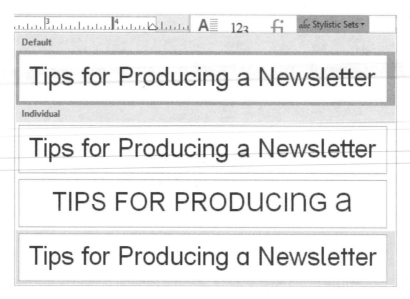

13   In the **Individual** section, select the third and last from the list.

14   Click somewhere in the empty space near the publication and notice how the text has changed.

✖ CLEAN UP Save the publication. You can compare the end result you obtained with the practice file FabrikamAEnd included in the Chapter42 practice files folder.

Using picture placeholders and captions

When you have to create a publication, and you don't yet have all the images available for use, Publisher 2013 enables you to do the maximum amount of work possible until they are available. Instead of inserting actual pictures, you can add picture placeholders and manipulate them as if they were pictures. Then, when the pictures you need are available, you can quickly add them and finalize your publication. Picture placeholders are found on the **Insert** tab, in the **Illustrations** group.

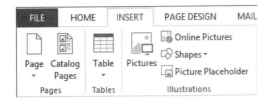

The placeholder is a white box with a picture thumbnail in the center. It can be resized and dragged as if it was a real image.

TIP When you resize the picture placeholder (or an actual picture), if you resize it by using the handles on its corners, it changes its size while maintaining its proportions. When you resize it using the handles in the middle of each side, it changes its size and its proportions.

You can even add captions, corrections, and picture effects to it, just like you would with a picture. When you add the picture, all the customizations you made to the placeholder are applied to the picture. Also, if the picture does not exactly fit the placeholder, it is automatically cropped to fit into the dimensions you have set.

In this exercise, you'll add a picture placeholder, change its size and position, add a picture to it, and then add a caption to the picture.

SET UP You need the Travel.pub file and the PictureA.JPG image file, both located in the Chapter42 practice file folder, to complete this exercise. Start Publisher, open the Travel.pub file, and if needed, use the Zoom slider in the lower-right corner of the Publisher window to adjust the way you view the publication, so it fits into the publication window. Then follow the steps.

1   Select page **1**.

2   On the **Insert** tab, in the **Illustrations** group, click the **Picture Placeholder** button. Publisher adds a small placeholder box to the middle of page **1**.

3   Select the picture placeholder and drag it to the lower-right corner of the white box found on page **1**.

42

4   Drag its margins to fill the available white space, and so that it is aligned with the top green margin of the page.

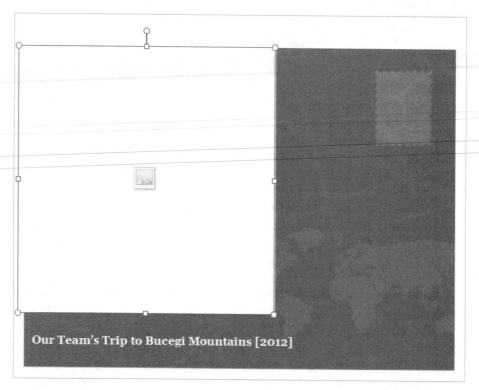

Our Team's Trip to Bucegi Mountains [2012]

5   Click the picture thumbnail found in the middle of the placeholder. The **Insert Pictures** dialog box opens.

6   Click **Browse** to open the **Insert Picture** dialog box.

7   Browse to the location where you stored the practice files required for this exercise, and select **PictureA.JPG**.

8   Click **Insert**. The picture has now been added to the placeholder and it's been automatically cropped to the size of the placeholder.

9   Click somewhere in the empty space of page **1** to apply the crop.

10   Select the image that was just added by clicking it.

11   On the **Format** tab, in the **Picture Styles** group, click **Caption**. This opens the **Captions** gallery.

Picture Styles

12   In the **Captions** gallery, go to the **Overlay** section and select **Box, Reversed – Layout 4**, so that it is added to the image.

Overlay

Box, Reversed - Layout 4

42

13   Double-click the text found in the caption box to select it.

14   On the **Home** tab, in the **Font** group, select the font size **22** to make the text more visible.

15   With the text still selected, enter Breathtaking visuals ahead.

16   Notice how the text has changed and how it looks with your changes applied.

CLEAN UP Save the publication. You can compare the end result you obtained with the practice file TravelA.pub included in the Chapter42 practice file folder.

Importing, swapping, and formatting pictures

Working with pictures in Publisher is rather similar to working with them in PowerPoint. However, there are a few important differences that make working with images easier. For example, in Publisher, you can add as many pictures as you need at one time. They are all displayed on the scratch area (on the right side of the publication window), and you can drag them to the page where you need to add them. This is new in Publisher 2013.

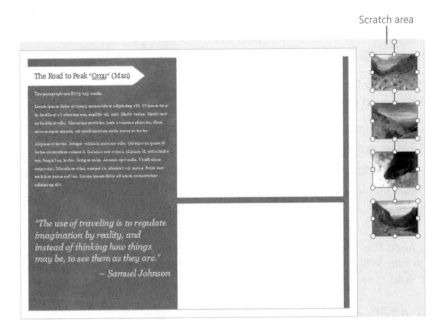

Another useful feature is the ability to swap between pictures in your publications. Swapped pictures retain previously applied formatting and size, making it easy to see which image fits your content the best. It won't cause any alignment issues as you would encounter in other Microsoft Office applications. This makes the process of creating visual publications in Publisher much faster.

For formatting pictures, Publisher gives you access to the same standard tools available in other Office applications:

- **Picture Corrections** Select between different presets for brightness and contrast to improve the way the picture looks.

- **Picture Color Options** Different coloring options are available through the **Recolor** button. You can select between color variations like grayscale, sepia, cyanotype, and so on.

- **Picture Styles** Use this option to add various types of frames to your images, so that they integrate better with the visuals of your publication.

- **Picture Border** You can add borders of different patterns, weights, and colors.

42

- **Picture Effects** This option enables you to add different types of effects to your pictures, such as shadows, reflections, glows, and more.

- **Caption** If you want to add caption text to an image, you can choose between different presets.

- **Wrap Text** Just like in Word, you can set the way text wraps around images.

- **Bring Forward & Send Backward** Like other objects, pictures can be set so that they are displayed on top or behind other objects.

- **Align** You can align pictures with other objects in your publications, so that they are displayed in an orderly fashion.

In this exercise, you'll add multiple pictures to your publication. Then, you'll use the swap feature, you'll align pictures, and you'll add picture effects and styles. Last but not least, you will apply a picture as a background to a page in your publication.

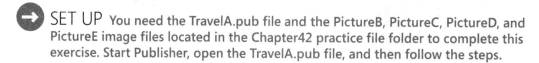 SET UP You need the TravelA.pub file and the PictureB, PictureC, PictureD, and PictureE image files located in the Chapter42 practice file folder to complete this exercise. Start Publisher, open the TravelA.pub file, and then follow the steps.

1   Go to page **2** of the publication.

2   On the **Insert** tab, in the **Illustrations** group, click **Pictures**. The **Insert Picture** dialog box opens.

3   Select the pictures **PictureB** to **PictureE** (using **Ctrl+click** to select each image), and click **Insert**. The selected picture files are added to the scratch area of page **2**.

4   Click somewhere on the empty space in the publication window to deselect all pictures.

5   Select the first picture in the scratch area (the one on the top) and drag it to the upper-left margin of the first empty text box on page **2**.

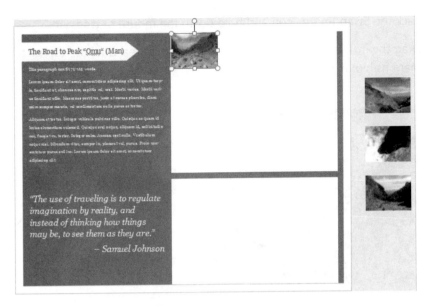

6   Drag the margins of the picture until it fills the empty space around it.

7   Point to the middle of the picture for a few seconds, until a **Swap Image** icon is displayed.

8   Click the **Swap Image** icon and hold down the mouse button.

9   Drag the image to the top picture in the scratch area, until the top picture has its margins highlighted in pink.

10   When the margins of the picture in the scratch area are highlighted in pink (and only then), release the mouse. Notice how the pictures have been swapped.

11   Select the top picture in the scratch area (which is the same one you added in step 6) and drag it to the upper-left corner of the second empty text box on page **2**.

12   Resize it to fill the available empty space around it.

13   Select both images on page **2** (**Ctrl+click** on each image).

14   On the **Format** tab, in the **Arrange** group, click **Align,** and then **Align Left**, so that both pictures are aligned appropriately.

15   Click somewhere in the empty space in the publication window to deselect both pictures. Then, select only the top picture on page **2**.

16   On the **Format** tab, in the **Picture Styles** group, click **Picture Effects** to open a gallery with effects.

17   Click **Glow** and then, in **Glow Variations**, select **Accent 2, 5pt glow**. The glow effect is applied to the first picture.

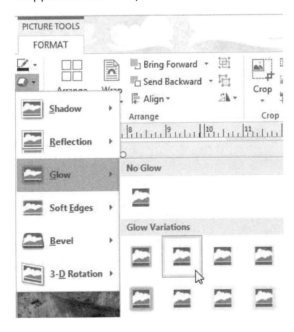

42

18   Select the second picture on page **2**.

19   On the **Format** tab, in the **Picture Styles** group, click the **More** button. This opens a
      gallery with styles that you can apply.

20   Select the fourth style in the list (**Drop Shadow Rectangle**). Notice how the image
      has changed.

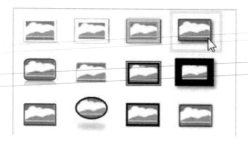

21   On page **3**, right-click the top image in the scratch area (the one with the dog).

22   In the shortcut menu, select **Apply to Background** and then **Fill**.

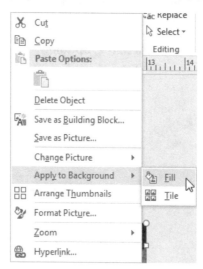

23   Notice how the image has been applied as a background to page **3**.

❌ CLEAN UP Save the publication. You can compare the end result you obtained with
the practice file TravelB.pub included in the Chapter42 practice file folder.

Working with rulers, guides, baselines, and other tools

If you have completed the previous exercises in this chapter, you probably have already noticed that Publisher offers several tools to help you align objects in your publications, including rulers, guides, and others. To view the features that are enabled, on the View tab on the ribbon, look in the Show group. The enabled tools are marked with a check mark.

By default, Publisher has enabled the following tools:

- **Guides** These adjustable drawing guides are shown when you are aligning objects in your publication. You can also add your own custom guides.

- **Fields** Publisher shows which items in your publication are data fields (for example, **Business Information** fields like **Organization name** or **Address**).

- **Rulers** Publisher shows rulers next to your publication that allow you to measure distances, alignments, and so on.

- **Page Navigation** This displays the **Pages** pane on the left, which displays a thumbnail of each page in the publication.

- **Scratch Area** This area shows the objects or portions of objects that are located outside of the page boundaries.

- Additionally, you can enable the following tools:

- **Boundaries** Displays the boundaries for shapes, text boxes, and pictures.

- **Graphics Manager** Enables a **Graphics Manager** pane on the right side of the **Publisher** window, to review and manage the images added to your publication.

- **Baselines** Shows baselines to help you align objects to the baselines of text in the publication.

42

In this exercise, you'll create your own custom guides, in addition to those existing by default.

SET UP You don't need any practice files to complete this exercise. Start Publisher 2013 and create a blank 8.5x11" publication. Then follow the steps.

1   Go to the ruler on the left and position the mouse pointer on its margin until the pointer changes and a ScreenTip is displayed that says **Create Vertical Guide**.

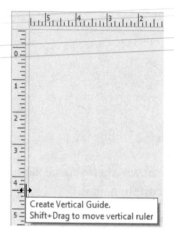

2   Drag the pointer to the middle of the page to create a vertical guide.

3   Go to the top ruler and position the pointer on its margin, until the pointer changes and a ScreenTip is shown that says **Create Horizontal Guide**.

4   Drag the pointer to the middle of the page to create a horizontal guide. The end result should look similar to the following image.

TIP When positioning the mouse pointer on the margin of a ruler, if you press Shift on your keyboard and then drag the pointer, you can move the whole ruler and change its position in the publication window.

✖ CLEAN UP Quit Publisher without saving the changes you made to the publication.

Importing Word documents into Publisher

If you need to move data from a Word document to Publisher, you might be tempted to simply use the old copy and paste functionality. Even if this works, the end result is a mess that takes a lot of time to correct. Luckily, there is an Import Word Document feature in Publisher that, although a bit cumbersome to work with, does a good job of importing many elements from your documents.

Publisher is able to import the following from Word: text; inline objects such as pictures, tables, and Office Art objects; and text formatting (bold, italic, and underline).

This feature will not import page orientation, page size, margin settings, objects that float on a page, WordArt objects, custom styles and style names, complex page structures such as tables of contents and indexes, the contents of text boxes, or changes in section and column formatting.

Even though Publisher can import many elements, it doesn't mean that an imported document will look great as soon as you import it. For example, you can end up with some lines of text that seem unintelligible.

Fabrikam's First Community Kitchen

Annual Employee Recognition Excursion

Page 2

Don't worry; your text is not lost. It's just that its font and size information did not get migrated correctly to Publisher. Select the text, change its font and size, and you'll be able to read it and use it in Publisher.

After the import is done, Publisher shows an Extra Content panel on the right. It will display the types of items that were imported, highlighted with a check mark. Those objects that could not be imported, or that didn't fit into the publication, are not selected.

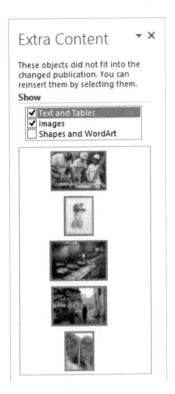

You can select those objects to determine if they were imported correctly. You can also deselect some objects that you don't want imported, and they won't be included in your publication.

In this exercise, you'll import a Word document into Publisher.

42

SET UP You need the Fabrikam Employee Newsletter_no video.docx file located in the Chapter42 practice file folder to complete this exercise. Start Publisher 2013, and open Fabrikam Employee Newsletter_no video.docx. Then follow the steps.

1 On the Publisher **Start** screen, click the **Built-in** section of templates.

2 Scroll until you find the **Import Word Documents** button, and click it. It is located after **Greeting Cards**. You are asked to select an installed template to apply to the imported document.

3 Select the **Axis** template, and customize the color scheme to **Apex** and the font scheme to **Verdana**.

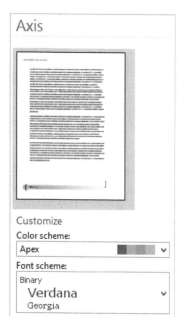

4 Click **Create**. This opens the **Import Word Document** dialog box, where you need to select the **Fabrikam Employee Newsletter_no video.docx** practice file.

5 After you have selected the file, click **OK**. Publisher now takes some time to convert the selected document.

6 After the document is imported, start customizing your publication.

CLEAN UP Save the publication for future reference and exit Publisher.

Key points

- Publisher 2013 provides a large list of templates you can use to quick-start the publication process.

- You can store one or more Business Information sets in Publisher 2013 and use them to add business information to your publications, without manually entering it each time.

- Publisher 2013 provides support for OpenType fonts and, for some, you are given access to additional stylistic sets you can apply to modify how text looks in your publication.

- Instead of inserting actual pictures, you can add picture placeholders and manipulate them as if they were pictures. The actual pictures can be added later and all your formatting gets automatically applied.

- Publisher offers a quick way to add multiple images to a publication and it makes it easy to swap between them.

- Publisher is able to import Word documents and successfully handle elements like text; inline objects such as pictures, tables, and Office Art objects; and text formatting (bold, italic, and underline).

42

Chapter at a glance

Save

Save your publications,
page 1122

Share

Share publications via email,
page 1123

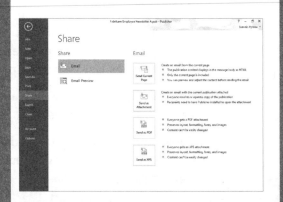

Print

Print publications,
page 1124

Export

Export publications as PDF or XPS files,
page 1129

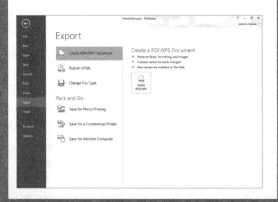

Saving, sharing, and exporting publications

43

IN THIS CHAPTER, YOU WILL LEARN HOW TO

- Save your publications.

- Share publications via email.

- Print publications.

- Prepare publications for commercial printing.

- Export publications as PDF or XPS files.

Just like other Microsoft Office Professional 2013 applications, Microsoft Publisher 2013 also includes cloud integration. You can easily save your publications to cloud locations such as Microsoft SkyDrive or SharePoint Online and work with them as if they were saved locally on your computer.

In this chapter, you'll learn all the important basics of saving, storing, sharing, printing, and exporting your publications. You will learn how to save a publication in different formats and how to export publications as PDF or XPS files.

PRACTICE FILES To complete the exercises in this chapter, you need the practice files contained in the Chapter43 practice file folder. For more information, see "Download the practice files" in this book's Introduction.

Saving your publications

Saving publications in Publisher 2013 works as in all other Office applications. Click the File tab to access the Backstage view, and then click the Save As tab. Options are displayed for saving your publications:

- If you have signed in with your Microsoft account or your SharePoint account, the first options listed will be about saving to the cloud. As a reminder, if you save your publication to a cloud location, you can access it from almost any device that has an Internet connection.

- You can save files on your computer by clicking **Computer** and then browsing to the location where you want the publication to be saved. In the **Computer** list, Publisher displays the current folder and your recent folders. Clicking **Browse** enables you to select a different location on your computer.

You can save a publication in a wide variety of formats, from .pub files (specific to Publisher 2013) to Word documents or images (for example, .png or .jpeg). If you want to save your publication so that it can be used on other computers with an older version of Publisher installed, you should select the Publisher 98 Files (*.pub) or Publisher 2000 Files (*.pub) format, depending on the exact version installed. However, if you have installed Microsoft Publisher 2007 or 2010 on the other computers you are working on, there is no need to change the format. Publisher 2013 files will work just as well.

Sharing publications via email

In the Backstage view in Publisher 2013, you can find the Share page. It offers options for sharing your publications via email:

- **Send Current Page** This option opens Microsoft Outlook (or your default email client) and sends only the current page as an HTML message.

- **Send as Attachment** This opens Outlook (or your default email client) and sends your entire publications as a .pub file, attached to the email message.

- **Send as PDF** This option converts your publication to the PDF format and sends it as an attachment.

- **Send as XPS** This converts your publication to the XPS format and sends it as an attachment.

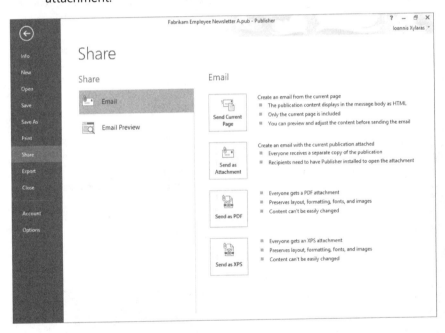

The Email Preview button opens your publication in the default browser and displays it as an HTML email message.

Printing your publications

Printing is not very different in Publisher than in other Office applications. You have the usual options: selecting the printer, changing its properties, choosing which pages to print and in what paper size, choosing whether to print on one side or both, and choosing to print your publication as a color or grayscale publication.

When choosing the paper size for printing your publication, Publisher scales the output, and if the printed results do not look correct, you probably don't have paper with the size you selected. If you are based in North America, the most common paper size is Letter 8.5"x11". If you are based in Europe, the most common paper size is A4. Before printing, make sure you select the actual paper size you have available in your printer.

What's different, though, is that when you print a publication using a specific group of settings, you can select a box that says Save Settings With Publication, at the bottom of the Print page.

This setting enables you to save your print settings with the publication file and have them applied automatically the next time you print it.

In this exercise, you'll print specific pages in your publication and save your printing settings.

 SET UP You need the FabrikamAEnd.pub file located in the Chapter43 practice file folder to complete this exercise. Open the file and turn on your printer.

1   Click the **File** tab to display the **Backstage** view.

2   Click **Print** to access the printing options.

3   Select the printer where you want to print the document.

4   In the **Settings** section, go to the **Pages** text box and enter 1-3, instead of the entire publication. Publisher will spend some time generating a preview of the pages you specified.

5   Click the **Paper Source** button (the third in the **Settings** section) to open a list of usable paper sizes, and select **Letter 8.5"x11" 22x28cm**.

6   Click the **Composite RGB** button and select **Composite Grayscale**.

7   Make sure the **Save settings with publication** check box is selected.

8   Click **Print** and wait for your publication to get printed.

⊗ CLEAN UP   Close Publisher 2013 and view your printed publication.

If you use the same publication file again, even on another computer, the print settings you have chosen will be applied automatically when you print it. Obviously, you can change the print settings at any time and your changes will be saved if the Save Settings With Publication option is selected.

Saving for photo printing or commercial printing

Because Publisher is a tool that can be used for creating commercial publications, it offers a few special export features that are useful in this line of work:

- **Save for Photo Printing** This option creates a folder where each page in your publication is saved as a separate image. The images are saved at the best resolution available for photo printing, and they can be stored in two formats: .jpeg and .tiff.

- **Save for a Commercial Printer** Publisher provides a few presets for commercial printing: commercial press, high quality printing, standard, and minimum size. Depending on what you choose, the file quality and file size will vary. Obviously, for any kind of commercial printing, you should choose **Commercial Press** as the preset. For each preset you can choose options for Publisher 2013 to create a PDF and a Publisher copy of the publication, only a PDF file, or only a Publisher file.

- **Save for Another Computer** This enables you to pack your publication into a compressed file that includes the publication itself and the images you added as separate files. Also, the fonts you have used are embedded so that they can be viewed correctly on other computers. Then you can burn the publication on a disc and use it on other computers.

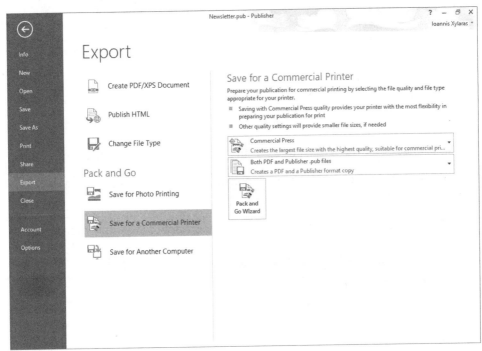

To help you become familiar with how to save a publication for commercial printing, in this exercise, you'll save a file and learn how it works.

SET UP You need the Newsletter.pub file located in the Chapter43 practice file folder to complete this exercise. Open the file, and follow the steps.

1 Click the **File** tab to display the **Backstage** view.

2 Click **Export** to access a list with all the export options available.

3 In the **Pack and Go** section, click **Save for a Commercial Printer**.

4   Make sure **Commercial Press** is selected.

5   Click **Both PDF and Publisher .pub files** and select **Publisher .pub file**.

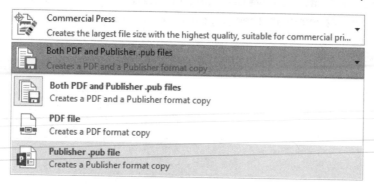

6   Click **Pack and Go Wizard** to open the wizard of the same name.

7   When asked to select where you would like to pack your publication to, select **Other location**.

8   Click **Browse** and select the folder where you want to store the publication.

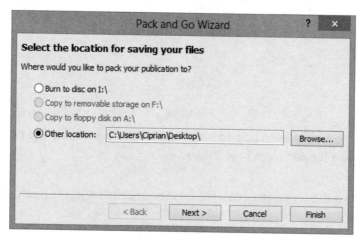

9   Click **Next** and wait for the publication to be packed. You are informed when the process is complete.

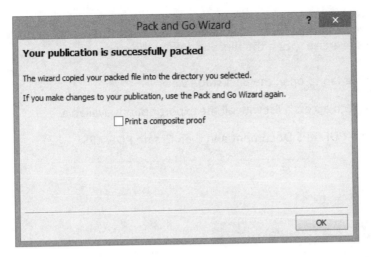

10   Clear the **Print a composite proof** check box.

11   Click **OK**.

✖ CLEAN UP Close Publisher 2013.

The publication is now archived in a compressed file at the location you specified.

Exporting publications to PDF or XPS format

Exporting publications in the PDF or XPS formats has the following advantages:

- It preserves your fonts, formatting, and images. Therefore, the publication will be viewed correctly on any computer or device.

- The person receiving the publication doesn't require a copy of Publisher in order to view the publication you created.

In this exercise, you'll save a publication as a PDF file.

SET UP You need the Newsletter.pub file located in the Chapter43 practice file folder to complete this exercise. Open the file, and follow the steps.

1   Click the **File** tab to open the **Backstage** view.

2   Click **Export** to access a list with all the export options available.

3   Click **Create PDF/XPS Document** and then **Create PDF/XPS**.

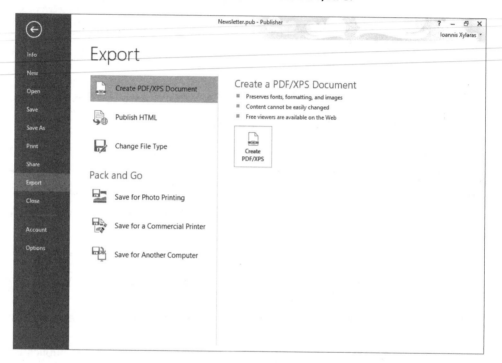

4   In the **Publish as PDF or XPS** window, browse to the location where you want to save the PDF file.

5   Enter the file name you want to use and, in the **Save as type** list, select **PDF (*.pdf)**.

6   Click **Publish** and wait for the publication to be converted to the PDF format. The file is then opened with the default PDF viewing application.

SEE ALSO In Windows 8, the default app for viewing PDF and XPS files is Reader. If you want to learn more about this app and Windows 8 in general, don't hesitate to read *Windows 8 Step by Step* by Ciprian Rusen and Joli Ballew (Microsoft Press, 2012). It serves as a great manual for Windows 8 users.

CLEAN UP After viewing the publication in the PDF format, close the application in which you have viewed it. Then close Publisher.

Saving publications using the XPS format is done the same way. The only difference is that at step 5, you select XPS Document (*.xps) as the file type.

Key points

- You can save your publications locally on your computer, or in the cloud, on your SkyDrive or your company's SharePoint site.

- Publications can be easily shared via email, either as attachments or as HTML email messages.

- When printing a publication, you can save your print settings together with the publication, so that they automatically get applied anytime you want to print it.

- Publisher 2013 is the only Office application that has features for commercial printing at very high resolutions and quality settings.

- Exporting publications as PDF or XPS files allows others to view them without having Publisher installed on their computer or device.

Index

Symbols

A

P

Z

About the authors

Andrew Couch has been working with Microsoft Access since 1992 as a developer, trainer, and consultant. He is a joint founder of the UK Access User Group and has been a Microsoft Access Most Valuable Professional (MVP) for the past six years. Other publications with Microsoft Press include *Microsoft Access 2013 Plain & Simple* (2013) and *Microsoft Access 2010 VBA Programming Inside Out* (2011). Andrew also provides free technical articles for Access at *www.upsizing.co.uk/TechLibrary.aspx*.

Mark Dodge has been working with and writing about Microsoft software since 1989, and is co-author of the Microsoft Press titles *Microsoft Office Excel 2013 Inside Out* (2013) and the *MOS 2013 Study Guide for Excel Expert* (2013). As a senior writer in the Office group at Microsoft, he created print, online, and multimedia documentation for all Microsoft Office software, and continues to work as a contract technical writer and editor, most recently in emergency management planning at FEMA. Mark is a lifelong jazz and rock musician, in addition to being an award-winning fine art photographer.

Eric Legault has spent most of the past 17 years working independently and with various Microsoft Certified Partners and ISVs as a developer and consultant for solutions based on the Microsoft Messaging & Collaboration platform (Microsoft Outlook, Exchange, Office, and SharePoint). Since becoming an Outlook MVP in 2003, he has developed dozens of custom Outlook solutions for companies around the world and has juggled many roles, such as speaker, author, community leader, marketer, business strategist, and technical evangelist. His current passion project is planning, developing, marketing, and supporting an innovative line of Outlook add-ins as a Product Manager for *www.OutlookAppins.com*. He lives with his wife and kids in Winnipeg and spends his spare time cheering on the Winnipeg Jets, working out, studying to be an amateur astronomer/alien ambassador, listening to heavy metal, shredding on his guitar, and wondering if it's not too late to be a rock star.

Beth Melton, Office MVP since 2000 and Microsoft Office Specialist Master Instructor, has been teaching others how to use Office applications more efficiently and developing custom Office solutions for almost 20 years. She co-authored *Microsoft Word 2007 Inside Out* (Microsoft Press) and is is a regular contributor to several websites, including Microsoft Office Online.

Beth spends her leisure time with her three children and enjoys finding different ways to give back to her community by integrating her love of technology, newly developed culinary skills, and passion for healthy eating.

Ciprian Adrian Rusen loves technology and loves writing. You can find more of his "how to" guides at 7 Tutorials, where he helps Windows and Windows phone users get the best possible computing experience from their computers and devices. He also co-authored *Windows 8 Step by Step* (Microsoft Press, 2012), a great guide for all who want to try Windows 8 and learn what this operating system has to offer.

Ben M. Schorr is a technologist and Chief Executive Officer for Roland Schorr & Tower, a professional consulting firm headquartered in Honolulu, Hawaii with offices in Los Angeles and Arizona. He is also the author of several books and articles on technology, including *The Lawyer's Guide to Microsoft Outlook* (American Bar Association, 2013), *The Lawyer's Guide to Microsoft Word* (American Bar Association, 2012), and *OneNote in One Hour* (American Bar Association, 2013). He's been a Microsoft MVP for more than 15 years and involved with management and technology for more than 20. In his free time, he's an Ironman triathlete and a high school football coach. He currently lives in Flagstaff, Arizona with his wife, Carrie.

Echo Swinford began her PowerPoint career in 1997, and has been a Microsoft PowerPoint MVP since 2000. She holds a Master's degree in New Media from the Indiana University-Purdue University at the Indianapolis School of Informatics. Echo is the owner of Echosvoice, a PowerPoint consulting firm specializing in custom template development, presentation creation, makeovers and cleanup, and PowerPoint training for large and small corporate clients. Echo has written and co-written three PowerPoint books and has a string of tech editing credits to her name. Visit her website at *www.echosvoice.com*.